Sydney

timeout.com/Sydney

Published by Time Out Guides Ltd, a wholly owned subsidiary of Time Out Group Ltd.
Time Out and the Time Out logo are trademarks of Time Out Group Ltd.

© **Time Out Group Ltd 2008**
Previous editions 1997, 2000, 2001, 2004, 2006.

10 9 8 7 6 5 4 3 2 1

This edition first published in Great Britain in 2008 by Ebury Publishing
A Random House Group Company
20 Vauxhall Bridge Road, London SW1V 2SA

Random House Australia Pty Limited 20 Alfred Street, Milsons Point, Sydney, New South Wales 2061, Australia
Random House New Zealand Limited 18 Poland Road, Glenfield, Auckland 10, New Zealand
Random House South Africa (Pty) Limited Isle of Houghton, Corner Boundary
Road & Carse O'Gowrie, Houghton 2198, South Africa

Random House UK Limited Reg. No. 954009

Distributed in USA by Publishers Group West
1700 Fourth Street, Berkeley, California 94710

Distributed in Canada by Publishers Group Canada
250A Carlton Street, Toronto, Ontario M5A 2L1

For further distribution details, see www.timeout.com

ISBN: 978-1-84670-060-6

A CIP catalogue record for this book is available from the British Library

Printed and bound by Firmengruppe APPL, aprinta druck, Wemding, Germany

The Random House Group Limited supports The Forest Stewardship Council (FSC), the leading international forest
certification organisation. All our titles that are printed on Greenpeace approved FSC certified paper carry the FSC
logo. Our paper procurement policy can be found at http://www.rbooks.co.uk/environment

Time Out carbon-offsets all its flights with Trees for Cities (www.treesforcities.org).

Time Out Guides Limited
Universal House
251 Tottenham Court Road
London W1T 7AB
Tel + 44 (0)20 7813 3000
Fax + 44 (0)20 7813 6001
Email guides@timeout.com
www.timeout.com

Editorial

Editors Juliet Rieden and Katie Ekberg
Deputy Editor Edoardo Albert
Listings Editor Georgia Toomey
Proofreader Cathy Limb
Indexer Ismay Atkins

Managing Director Peter Fiennes
Financial Director Gareth Garner
Editorial Director Ruth Jarvis
Deputy Series Editor Dominic Earle
Editorial Manager Holly Pick
Assistant Management Accountant Ija Krasnikova

Design

Art Director Scott Moore
Art Editor Pinelope Kourmouzoglou
Senior Designer Henry Elphick
Graphic Designers Gemma Doyle, Kei Ishimaru
Digital Imaging Simon Foster
Advertising Designer Jodi Sher

Picture Desk

Picture Editor Jael Marschner
Deputy Picture Editor Katie Morris
Picture Researcher Gemma Walters
Picture Desk Assistant Marzena Zoladz

Advertising

Commercial Director Mark Phillips
International Advertising Manager Kasimir Berger
International Sales Executive Charlie Sokol
Advertising Sales (Sydney) Ad Pack Australia
(colin.m@adpacau.com)
Advertising Assistant Kate Staddon

Marketing

Marketing Manager Yvonne Poon
Head of Marketing Catherine Demajo
Sales & Marketing Director, North America Lisa Levinson
Marketing Designers Anthony Huggins, Nicola Wilson

Production

Group Production Director Mark Lamond
Production Manager Brendan McKeown
Production Controller Caroline Bradford
Production Coordinator Julie Pallot

Time Out Group

Chairman Tony Elliott
Financial Director Richard Waterlow
Group General Manager/Director Nichola Coulthard
Time Out Magazine Ltd MD Richard Waterlow
Time Out Communications Ltd MD David Pepper
Time Out International MD Cathy Runciman
Group IT Director Simon Chappell

Contributors

Introduction Juliet Rieden. **History** Juliet Rieden (*The other history* Miranda Herron, Juliet Rieden). **The Future's Green** Ben Cubby. **Sydney Today** Ed Gibbs (*The tide is turning* Katie Ekberg). **Where to Stay** Katie Ekberg. **Sightseeing** Katie Ekberg, Ed Gibbs, Louise Goldsbury, Juliet Rieden, Prue Rushton. **Restaurants, Cafés, Bars & Pubs** Katie Ekberg, Juliet Rieden, Myffy Rigby. **Shops & Services** Katie Ekberg, Hannah Rand (*From rags to riches* Hannah Rand, Juliet Rieden; *Where I Shop* Juliet Rieden). **Festivals & Events** Katie Ekberg (*Free seats for NYE fireworks* Juliet Rieden). **Children** Lisa Doust, Katie Ekberg. **Clubs** Ed Gibbs (*The pleasure principle* Juliet Rieden). **Film** Katie Ekberg (*All that Baz, Destination Sydney* Ed Gibbs). **Galleries** Juliet Rieden. **Gay & Lesbian** Cara Davis. **Music** Annette Dasey. **Sport & Fitness** Katie Ekberg (*Coming to a beach near you* Juliet Rieden). **Theatre & Dance** Juliet Rieden. **Short Trips** Louise Goldsbury. **Directory** Katie Ekberg, Juliet Rieden (*Average climate* Georgia Toomey).

Maps john@jsgraphics.co.uk. **Map on p335** reproduced with kind permission of Sydney Ferries Corporation.
Map on p336 reproduced with kind permission of CityRail.

Photography Michelle Grant; except page 25 Adam McLean/Fairfaxphotos.com; page 28 Rex Features; pages 106, 247, 261 Getty Images; page 215 Steve Coburn; page 254 Keith Saunders; page 267 Steve Lunam; page 271 Jason Capobianco; page 272 AFP/Getty Images; page 275 (top) Blue Mountains Tourism Ltd; pages 273, 275 (bottom) Photolibrary.com; page 279 CEPHAS/Jeff Drewitz; page 284 Tourism New South Wales; page 290 National Portrait Gallery Canberra.

The following images were provided by the featured establishments/artists: pages 21, 22, 202, 225, 228, 262.

The Editor would like to thank *Time Out Sydney* magazine, Deni Hines and all contributors to previous editions of *Time Out Sydney*, whose work forms the basis for parts of this book.

Contents

Introduction

As part of the Australia Day celebrations in January 2008, New South Wales Premier Morris Iemma named female surfing champ Layne Beachley, New Zealand-born actor Russell Crowe and businessman Peter Holmes à Court as Sydney's ambassadorial triumvirate. Iemma's choice of a female from the traditionally male sport of surfing, an oscar-winning actor with a home in the heart of the capital and a former theatre producer from one of Australia's wealthiest families gives a telling insight into what locals consider to be Sydney's unique strengths and how they are shifting.

Beachley's achievements in a male-dominated world are no one-off and today you're as likely to find women patrolling the waves as surf lifesavers, and riding them as avid surfers. Crowe is a fearless actor, arguably Australia's finest male talent, and his global success has done plenty to counteract the ill-informed 'lack of culture' tag that the Emerald City constantly shakes its fist at. Holmes à Court, meanwhile, fled Australia and his family as a young rebellious buck to make his own path and seek 'something better', and then boomeranged back in the millennium after 16 years away to share what he had learned overseas and reclaim the splendour of his home shores.

'Sydney is the best place to live and work,' he said famously, choosing it over Melbourne, Perth, New York, Los Angeles and London.

Of course, this vote of confidence comes as no surprise to Sydneysiders, who already know they live in one of the best cities on the planet. The mild climate, with most days seeing seven hours of sunshine, means the outdoor life – swimming, sailing, drinking and eating alfresco in world-class restaurants – is a huge pull. But increasingly it's also the city's cultural life that's attracting the crowds – the flamboyance of its Gay & Lesbian Mardi Gras, the eclectic wonder of the Sydney Festival, the burgeoning theatre culture (given a huge injection by the return of Cate Blanchett to run the Sydney Theatre Company with her playwright husband), and the numerous food and music festivals.

And tourists seem to agree with Holmes à Court's sentiments too with a steady annual increase in visitor numbers, although in late 2007 the statistics showed a marked change in emphasis. Brits may still make up the largest proportion but the numbers are on the decline, with more and more Thai, Chinese, Indian, Malaysian and New Zealand tourists flying in instead. Proof, if proof were needed, that colonials no longer rule this multicultural paradise.

ABOUT TIME OUT CITY GUIDES

This is the sixth edition of *Time Out Sydney*, one of an expanding series of more than 50 guides produced by the people behind the successful listings magazines in London, New York, Chicago, Sydney and many more cities around the world. Our guides are all written and updated by resident experts who have striven to provide you with all the most up-to-date information you'll need to explore Sydney, whether you're a local or a first-time visitor.

ESSENTIAL INFORMATION

For all the practical information you might need for visiting the city, including customs and immigration information, disabled access, emergency telephone numbers, the lowdown on the local transport network and a list of useful websites, turn to the Directory section at the back of this guide. It starts on page 292.

THE LOWDOWN ON THE LISTINGS

We've tried to make this book as useful as possible. Addresses, telephone numbers, websites, transport information, opening times, admission prices and credit card details have all been included in the listings, as have details of other selected services and facilities. However, owners and managers can change their arrangements at any time. Before you go out of your way, we strongly advise you to call and check opening times and other particulars. While every effort has been made to ensure the accuracy of the information contained in this guide, the publishers cannot accept responsibility for any errors it may contain.

PRICES AND PAYMENT

Our listings detail which of the four major credit cards – American Express (AmEx), Diners Club (DC), MasterCard (MC) and Visa (V) – are accepted by individual venues. Many businesses will also accept other cards.

The prices we've supplied should be treated as guidelines, not gospel. Fluctuating exchange rates and inflation can cause charges, particularly in shops and restaurants, to change rapidly. If prices vary wildly from those we've quoted, ask whether there's a good reason, then please email to let us know. We aim to give the best and most up-to-date advice, and we always want to know if you've been badly treated or overcharged.

THE LIE OF THE LAND
Sydney is a sprawling mass of suburbs clustered around a compact city centre, and at first the sheer number of suburbs can be baffling. The central area, however, is much easier to fathom, and small enough to explore on foot. To make both book and city easier to navigate, we've divided Sydney into areas. They are: Central Sydney; Eastern Suburbs; Inner West; North Shore; Northern Beaches; Parramatta & the West; The South; and Sydney's Best Beaches.

MAPS
The map section at the back of the guide – which starts on page 320 – includes orientation and overview maps of New South Wales and the Sydney metropolitan area. Detailed street maps to the centre of Sydney are on pages 326-333, with maps of the suburbs of Bondi, Manly and Newtown on page 334.

The street maps now pinpoint specific locations of hotels (❶), restaurants (❶), cafés (❶) and bars and pubs (❶). We've also marked key beaches (❶). Map references in the guide indicate the page number and, where appropriate, the grid square on those maps. There's also a street index, starting on page 316. On page 335 you'll find Sydney Ferries routes, and on page 336 the CityRail train network in suburban Sydney.

TELEPHONE NUMBERS
The international dialling code for Australia is 61, and the code for Sydney is 02 (drop the zero if calling from overseas). Standard Sydney phone numbers have eight digits. The 02 area encompasses the whole of New South Wales, and if you're calling from within NSW you don't need to use the area code (so we haven't included it in the listings). Call rates depend on distance – the further away you're phoning, the more it will cost. 1800 numbers are free when dialled within Australia, but are not necessarily accessible countrywide, and cannot be dialled from abroad. 13 and 1300 numbers are charged at a 25c flat fee.

For more on phones, including information on free and premium-rate numbers, see p305.

LET US KNOW WHAT YOU THINK
We hope you enjoy *Time Out Sydney* and we'd like to know what you think of it. We welcome tips for places that you consider we should include in future editions, and take notice of your criticism of our choices. You can email us at guides@timeout.com.

There is an online version of this guide, along with guides to more than 50 other international cities, at **www.timeout.com**.

In Context

Features

History

Reconciling the past.

People have inhabited the area now known as Sydney for tens of thousands of years. When Captain James Cook turned up in 1770 with orders that he should 'with the consent of the natives take possession of convenient situations in the name of the king', he noted that those natives 'appear to be the most wretched people on earth. But in reality they are far happier than we Europeans'. Not surprisingly, the first words the Europeans ever heard from the Aboriginal inhabitants of the Sydney area were 'Warra! Warra!' – meaning 'Go away!'

On 29 April 1770 Cook landed at Botany Bay, which he named after discovering scores of plants hitherto unknown to science. Turning northwards, he passed an entrance to a harbour where there appeared to be safe anchorage. Cook called it Port Jackson after the Secretary to the Admiralty, George Jackson.

Back in Britain, King George III was convinced that the east coast of the island, which had been claimed for him and named New South Wales, would make a good colony.

For one thing it would help reduce Britain's overflowing prison population. For another, a settlement in the region would be convenient both as a base for trading in the Far East and in case of a war with the French or Dutch.

STEPS TO SETTLEMENT

On 13 May 1787 Captain Arthur Phillip's ship, *Sirius*, along with three provisions ships, two warships and six vessels of convicts, set sail from Portsmouth. On board were some 300 merchant seamen, their wives, children and servants, and nearly 800 convicts. Thirty-six weeks later, on 18 January 1788, after stops in Tenerife, Rio de Janeiro and the Cape of Good Hope, the *Sirius* arrived at Botany Bay. The rest of the First Fleet arrived a couple of days later. Fewer than 50 passengers had perished en route – not a bad rate for the period.

At that time of year, Botany Bay turned out to be a grim site for the new colony: there was little fresh water and it was exposed to strong winds and swell. One plus was that the naked 'Indians' seen running up and down the beach 'shouting and making many uncouth signs and gestures' turned out to be relatively friendly. Eager to make a good impression, Phillip and a small party of frock coats took a rowing boat to meet their new subjects. The meeting went well: the British exchanged a looking glass and beads for a wooden club.

Probably relieved that his first contact with the locals had not gone awry – when William Jansz of the Dutch East India Company had met Aboriginal people in 1606 he reported back that they 'killed on sight' – Phillip decided to search for Port Jackson. He returned with glowing reports: it was 'one of the finest harbours in the world, in which a thousand sail of the line might ride in perfect security'. This is one of the earliest descriptions of Sydney Harbour.

That same day, Phillip's men caught the improbable sight of two ships approaching from the sea. These were the French frigates *La Boussole* and *L'Astrolabe*, commanded by Jean-François de Galaup, Count de la Pérouse, who was on a voyage of discovery through the southern hemisphere. Surprised by the old enemy, Phillip decided to up-anchor the whole fleet the following morning and lead it to Sydney Cove – named after Viscount Sydney, the minister responsible for the colony.

"The epidemics fuelled a belief among white settlers that the Aboriginal peoples were doomed to extinction."

The First Fleeters set to as soon as they arrived. Trees were felled, marquees erected, convict shacks constructed from cabbage palms, garden plots dug and a blacksmith's forge set up. On 7 February the settlers gathered to hear Phillip declared the first governor of the state of New South Wales and its dependencies. It wasn't long, though, before convicts started to disappear. Several were found clubbed or speared to death, probably in revenge for attacks on the locals. Food ran dangerously low, scurvy took hold and the settlers' small herd of cattle began to diminish.

During the next few weeks the animosity between the settlers and the indigenous people came to a head, and the disappearance of several more convicts and a marine provoked Governor Phillip to try to capture some natives in a bid to force talks. Two boats were sent to Manly (named after the 'manly' nature of the undaunted Aborigines seen there). Following courteous overtures, the settlers suddenly grabbed an Aboriginal man, called Arabanoo, and rushed him to a boat under a hail of stones and spears. Arabanoo's hair was cut, his beard shaved and he was bathed and dressed in European clothes. But despite attempts by the settlers to persuade him to tell his compatriots that they meant no harm, no ground was gained on the path to friendship.

In those early days, capturing Aborigines to turn them into honorary white men was all the rage. Two such captives, Bennelong and Colbee, were rough-and-ready types, scarred from warfare and smallpox. Colbee soon bolted, but Bennelong stayed for five months and eventually, dressed in top hat and tails, travelled to London to have tea with the royal family. He gave his name to the point of land where a hut was built for him – and on which the Sydney Opera House now stands.

Early in 1789 the local Aborigines began to succumb to smallpox contracted from the British or from sailors on the French vessels that had put in at Botany Bay. Hundreds were soon dead, among them Arabanoo. The epidemics fuelled a belief among white settlers, then and later, that the Aboriginal peoples were doomed to extinction.

RISE OF THE RUM CORPS

If conditions were bad for the settlers at first, they worsened as the seasons progressed. Two years and two months after the First Fleet had sailed, Britain sent its first relief to Sydney. Carrying a small stock of provisions, the *Lady Juliana* arrived in 1790 with more than 200 convicts on board. Most were women, and almost all were too weak to work. This Second Fleet also brought a regiment known as the New South Wales Corps (NSWC), which had been formed to replace the marines. They found the settlement short of clothes, while rations had become so meagre that it was feared that everyone might starve to death.

Both soldiers and convicts were so frail through lack of food that the working day had to be shortened. Thefts became commonplace, and penalties for stealing increased. Meanwhile, the Aboriginal peoples were prospering on the food that grew, leaped or swam all around them, but the first settlers were so bound by the diet of the mother country that they would rather have starved than 'eaten native'.

By the end of June 1790, four more ships had sailed into Port Jackson, carrying with them a stock of convicts transported in abominable conditions. Some 267 people had died en route, and of the 759 who landed, 488 suffered from scurvy, dysentery or fever. Between 1791 and 1792, the death rate matched London's at the height of the Great Plague. Those remaining alive were forced to struggle on. Men faced a lashing from the cat-o'-nine-tails if they

didn't work hard. The women had it little easier and were forced into long hours of domestic work or kept busy weaving in sweatshop conditions.

Finally, though, the arrival of yet more transports from England, bringing with them convicts, free settlers and supplies, meant that life in the colony began to pick up. In October 1792 Phillip reported that nearly 5,000 bushels of maize had been harvested and around 1,700 acres were under cultivation. In December that year, Phillip returned to England convinced the settlement would last.

It was almost three years before another governor arrived to take Phillip's place. The commanders of the NSWC used this interim period to their own advantage by granting officers rights to work the land and employ convicts to do it for them. Thanks to a shortage of money, rum rapidly became common currency, and as the NSWC ruled the rum trade it became known as the Rum Corps.

Things progressed slowly until 1808, when Governor William Bligh (of *Mutiny on the Bounty* fame) was deposed in a military coup. Bligh's evil temper and his attempts to deal with the corruption of the NSWC, which had bullied his predecessors through their control of the colony's rum, led to his downfall. The Rum Corps arrested the governor and imprisoned him for a year – the only time in Australian history when an established government has been overthrown by force.

The Corps ruled until Bligh was sent back to England and a new governor, Lachlan Macquarie, arrived. Macquarie later wrote that on his arrival he found the colony 'barely emerging from a state of infantile imbecility,

The other history

It's estimated that the first people arrived in Australia 50,000 to 70,000 years ago, travelling by foot from the north across land bridges and later by boat. Australian Aboriginals have one of the oldest continuous cultures in the world, but there was never a unified nation: instead, people grouped into an estimated 500 clans or tribes, speaking some 250 languages and living a mainly nomadic life.

One of the most difficult things for the individualist, capitalist Europeans to understand when they colonised Australia was the indivisible interrelationship of land, spirituality and culture to Aboriginal people. According to traditional indigenous laws, no individual can own, sell or give away land. Land belongs to all members of the community, and they in turn belong to the land. Ownership of a particular region was established during the Dreaming or Dreamtime – the time of creation. The thread of creation stories tells of spiritual ancestors who came from the sky or earth, creating the world, giving life to animals and people, and establishing laws.

The settlers saw the indigenous Australians as backward because they did not grow crops, use metal or make pottery. What they could not grasp was the complex and environmentally sensitive way Aboriginal people had adapted to the vagaries of the climate: travelling light with portable tools and weapons to the best hunting and gathering grounds; managing grassland with fire to promote plant growth, thereby attracting animals; and harvesting the abundant seafood found in the country's coastal areas.

As the settlement of Sydney staggered through its first years, the local indigenous population was almost wiped out by diseases such as smallpox. Those who survived were then caught in a cycle of dispossession, violence and armed resistance. The founding of the Commonwealth of Australia in 1901 ignored Aboriginal people, excluding them from the national census. This was not an oversight: from the early days of settlement it was widely assumed that Aboriginal people were doomed as a race. By the 1930s, however, it became impossible to ignore that they were vigorously resisting extinction.

In 1939, assimilation became federal government policy. Indigenous people were expected to abandon their own culture and fit into white society. The most heartbreaking and controversial aspect of this brutal policy was the forcible removal of children – now known as the 'stolen generations' – from their parents. These children were placed in institutions or fostered out to white homes as part of what has since been described as 'a policy of cultural genocide'. It is thought that 100,000 people were affected from 1910 to the 1970s, when the policy was officially halted.

The 20th century was marked by the growth of political activism, which led in turn to a slow process of reconciliation. In 1967, more than 90 per cent of Australians voted ▶

BABYLON
SAUNA AND SPA
巴 比 倫 桑 拿 殿

BABYLON

Recover, relax and refresh at Babylon Sauna and Spa. Start with a sauna or steam, soak in a relaxing spa then revitalise and soothe the soul with anyone of Babylon's Massages.

Choose from a traditional Chinese Massage, Korean style, Aromatherapy, Body Scrub or a good old fashioned head and foot massage. With over 50 masseurs available every day, we will have a style to suit your needs.

They have separate area for men and women, with luxurious lound areas to relax. So when you're visiting Sydney, don't forget to take time out to recover, relax and refresh with a massage at Babylon Sauna and Spa.

Level 2, Market City Shopping Centre, Haymarket, Chinatown, Sydney, 2000
Open 11am - 3am   7days   phone: 9281 8886

and suffering from various privations and disabilities: the country impenetrable beyond 40 miles from Sydney'. A great planner, Macquarie oversaw the building of new streets and the widening of others. He named three of the largest streets: George Street, after the king, Pitt Street, after the prime minister, and the grandest of all he named Macquarie Street, after himself. With the help of convict architect Francis Greenway, he set about building a city to be proud of, with a hospital, several churches, a sandstone barracks and Macquarie Lighthouse (still on South Head) to guide ships into the harbour.

TAKING ROOT

With the discovery of the fertile hinterland beyond the Blue Mountains in 1813, the colony advanced in earnest. The flow of migrants

increased after the end of the Napoleonic Wars in 1815, and soon farms and settlements dotted the regions around Sydney and Parramatta. In 1822 Macquarie was forced from the colony by powerful landowners; he returned to Scotland and died in London in 1824.

There still remained the issue of defence: Sydney was seen as prey to any passing foe. The city's vulnerability and its isolation from the distant motherland was confirmed in 1830 when its citizens woke to find that, in the night, four American frigates had passed through the Heads and sailed up to Sydney Cove without anyone noticing. Since that day, Australia has been paranoid about attack, whether from the Russians during the Crimean War, Yankee privateers or the Spanish. Fear of an invasion from Asia has been a constant undertone of government policy in more recent times.

▶ ## The other history (continued)

in a national referendum to empower the federal government to make legislation in the interests of indigenous people and to count them as citizens in the census.

On top of this, the Mabo and subsequent Wik court cases in the 1990s sent shock waves through Australian society. The British had claimed Australia without treaty or payment because they categorised it as *terra nullius* – land belonging to nobody. The court rulings recognised that indigenous Australians were in fact the original inhabitants of the land, and that British settlement did not necessarily extinguish their native title. Fear and uncertainty about potential land claims grew until ultimately the Howard government stepped in and watered down the ownership rights, tying potential claims cases up in courts for years to come.

In 1997 an enquiry into the stolen generations produced a controversial report that shamed white Australians, but Prime Minister Howard refused to apologise (instead, he issued a statement of 'regret'). Nevertheless, a wave of reconciliatory activity ensued. In 2000 the People's Walk for Reconciliation saw an unprecedented 300,000 march across Sydney Harbour Bridge. In February 2008 Prime Minister Kevin Rudd delivered a formal official apology to Aborigines for 'past injustices', stating that the aim was 'to build a bridge of respect with indigenous Australia'. At the time of going to press a Senate enquiry was considering potential government-funded compensation.

It's a start, but the battle's not yet won. Aboriginal people on average live 20 to 25 years less than the rest of the population. They suffer persistent problems of economic disadvantage, substance abuse, domestic violence and discrimination, exacerbated by limited access to employment, education and health facilities in the remote areas where so many live. In 2007 a new report also uncovered incidences of child sex abuse within Aboriginal communities, prompting the government to move in authorities once again.

Within the indigenous community there are contradictory views on the way ahead. Passively accepting government handouts is seen by some as perpetuating the problems. The emphasis now is on targeting money and finding innovative long-term social solutions while involving the indigenous community fully in the decision-making process.

At last it seems that the status of Aboriginal people – for so long the invisible underclass – is improving. It's now usual to preface public events with an acknowledgement of the 'traditional owners' of the area; the red, black and yellow Aboriginal flag is flown on public buildings; important sites, such as Uluru, have been handed back to Aboriginal ownership; and more and more indigenous people are appearing in various sectors from the arts and sports to public services, law and politics.

None of this can make up for the lost centuries of repression, but it's a giant leap forward on the path towards a social harmony that has so long eluded this fractured nation.

Finding transportation ruinously expensive, the British government sought to have the infant colony subsidise the cost. Convict labour was increasingly used to generate income. As in all slave societies, the workforce was inefficient, and the colony soon became the dumping ground for England's unemployed working classes rather than her criminals. Most of these free immigrants were bonded to their colonial employers, their passage paid for by the sale of land. In 1840 transportation of convicts to New South Wales was abolished. A total of 111,500 convicts – of whom just 16,000 were women – had arrived in NSW and Tasmania.

By 1849 the population of convicts was outnumbered by free settlers. A new type of vessel, the clipper ship, had cut the sailing time from England to Australia by 49 days, to just 91. In the 1850s gold was discovered in New South Wales and Victoria, and prospectors rushed to Australia from all over the world. During the 1880s more than 370,000 arrived, mostly of British or Irish descent. Rich British businessmen poured money into the country and mine owners and farmers profited.

> "After the war, Australia once again needed to boost the size of its population. The slogan 'populate or perish' was coined."

Governor Phillip had ensured as far back as 1790 that some physical distance was maintained between the government precinct to the east of what is now known as Circular Quay, and the barracks and convict quarters to the west. Built into the steep sandstone cliffs, this no man's land – now known as the Rocks – quickly became as degenerate as the worst of London's slums. Tiers of narrow streets and sandstone stairs crammed with makeshift shacks led up from waterfront pubs and cheap lodging houses to comfortable terraced houses inhabited by sea captains and stevedores. The massive influx of immigrants in the mid 1800s meant that housing was scarce, a problem exacerbated by many inner-city homes being converted into storehouses and offices.

By the late 19th century, the Rocks was known as Sydney's worst den of iniquity. Prostitution, drunkenness, theft and street gangs were rife. Sailors ashore after months at sea were robbed of everything they owned or press-ganged straight on to another vessel.

The increasingly squalid goings-on and the build-up of rubbish, silt and sewage made conditions in the Rocks perfect for rats and the bubonic plague carried by their fleas. In the first nine months of 1900 the plague killed 103 people. Crowds stormed the Board of Health's offices demanding a share of the colony's meagre supply of anti-plague medicine. The Rocks and Darling Harbour were quarantined and in 1902 the Sydney Harbour Trust was set up to clean up the harbour: it later announced that it had pulled from the water 2,524 rats, 1,068 cats, 283 bags of meat, 305 bags of fish, 1,467 fowl, 25 parrots, 23 sheep, 14 pigs, one bullock, nine calves and nine goats.

CIVILISING MISSIONS

In the 1880s Sydney's remaining Aboriginal inhabitants were rounded up into a camp at Circular Quay and given government rations in a bid to keep them off the streets. In 1895 an Aboriginal reserve was set up at La Perouse, near Botany Bay – far from the centre of the city. By the end of the 19th century most of the area's indigenous inhabitants were restricted to reserves or in missions, where they were introduced to the supposed benefits of Christianity and European civilisation.

By this time it was apparent that, though the Aboriginal population was in decline, the mixed-descent population was increasing. The fact that the latter group had some European blood meant that there was a place for them – albeit a lowly one – in society. Many children of mixed race were forcibly separated from their parents and placed in segregated 'training' institutions before being sent out to work. Girls were sent to be domestic servants to satisfy the nation's demand for cheap labour. It was also held that long hours and exhausting work would curb their supposed promiscuity.

The Commonwealth of Australia came into existence on 1 January 1901. The country had 3.8 million inhabitants, and more than half a million of them crowded on to the streets of Sydney to celebrate the inauguration of the nation. The Aboriginal peoples weren't recorded in the first census, however. They had to wait until 1967, when 90 per cent of the public voted to make new laws relating to Aboriginal people. This led the way for them to be recognised as Australian citizens, and to be included in the census of 1971.

POPULATE OR PERISH

After a lull following the 1890s depression, migration revived. In the years leading up to 1914, 300,000 mainly British migrants arrived, half of whom came on an assisted-passage scheme. In 1908 a Royal Commission set up to advise on the improvement of Sydney concluded that workers should be moved out of the slums to the suburbs. Six years later, however, World War I broke out. Around 10,000 volunteers in

Kaleemera Australia! Greek immigrants arrive in the Great Southern Land.

Sydney queued to go on the 'big adventure'. Most were sent to Gallipoli – a campaign that became synonymous in the Australian collective memory with British arrogance, callousness and incompetence. By the time the Allied forces were withdrawn in January 1916, the combination of lacklustre Allied leadership and stiff Turkish resistance meant that casualties were well above 50 per cent, with little to show for thousands of lost lives. After the disaster of Gallipoli, Australia was not going to return to a subservient colonial role: the nation had come of age.

With the end of World War I it was reasoned that to defend Australia properly the country needed more people. A further 300,000 migrants arrived in the 1920s, mostly from England and Scotland, a product of the policy known as 'White Australia'. The origins of the policy can be traced to the mid 19th century, when white miners' resentment towards Chinese diggers boiled over in violence. The 1901 Immigration Restriction Act placed 'certain restrictions on immigration' and provided 'for the removal from the Commonwealth of prohibited immigrants'. For example, applicants were required to pass a written test in a specific, usually European, language – with which they were not necessarily familiar. It was not until 1974 that Australia eliminated such official racial discrimination from its immigration policy.

Australia's vulnerability to attack came back to haunt it during World War II. On 31 May

1942, three Japanese midget submarines powered through the Heads and into Sydney Harbour. The first got tangled in a net across the harbour mouth, but the others slipped past. The third midget was spotted and attacked, but the second took the chance to fire two torpedoes at the US cruiser *Chicago*. Both missed, but one sank the depot ship HMAS *Kuttabul*, killing 19 Australian and two British naval ratings asleep on board. Except for Aborigines and settlers killed in early skirmishes, these 21 men have been the only victims of enemy action on home ground in Sydney's history.

After the war, Australia once again decided it needed to boost the size of its population. The slogan 'populate or perish' was coined, and a new immigration scheme organised. In 1948, 70,000 migrants arrived from Britain and Europe. By the late 1950s most migrants were coming from Italy, Yugoslavia and Greece.

In 1951 the concept of assimilation was officially adopted as national policy, with the goal 'that all persons of Aboriginal descent will choose to attain a similar manner and standard of living to other Australians'. Eradication of Aboriginal culture was stepped up during the 1950s and '60s, when even greater numbers of Aboriginal children were removed from their families. Many Aboriginal babies were adopted at birth and later told that their true parents had died. The removal of children from their parents was halted in the 1970s, but the scars remain. The 'stolen generations' became the subject of fierce debate in Australia. Expat director Phillip Noyce's 2002 film *Rabbit-Proof Fence* – the story of three stolen children who run away from a camp and attempt to walk home over 1,000 miles of inhospitable country – brought the story to the world.

In 1964 Australian troops joined their US counterparts in action in Vietnam. As in the States, anti-Vietnam War sentiment became a hot issue, and tens of thousands of Australians blockaded the streets of the major cities. A new Labor government, led by Gough Whitlam, came to power in 1972 after promising a fairer society and an end to Australia's involvement in the war. Within months the troops were brought home. Not long afterwards 'Advance Australia Fair' replaced 'God Save the Queen' as the national anthem, the Queen's portrait was removed from post office walls and her insignia on mailboxes painted out. Land rights were granted to some Aboriginal groups, and in 1974 the government finally put an end to the White Australia policy that had largely restricted black and Asian immigration since 1901. Two years later the official cord to Britain was cut when the Australian Constitution was separated from that of its motherland.

Ties with Britain loosened further in 1975 during a messy political wrangle, when the Conservative opposition moved to block the government's supply of money in the upper house. Without a budget, Gough Whitlam's government was unable to govern, so the Queen's representative, Governor-General John Kerr, sacked it and made opposition leader Malcolm Fraser prime minister. There was fury that an Australian-elected government could be dismissed by the monarch's appointee, and resentment towards Britain flared.

A THIRD CENTURY BEGINS

Immigration continued throughout the 1980s and '90s, but now there were quite a few new faces among the crowds hoping for a better life in the 'lucky country'. Hundreds of thousands of migrants began arriving from Asia. Today, on average, around 90,000 people emigrate to Australia each year, from more than 150 countries. Of settlers arriving in 2002/3, the biggest groups were those born in the UK (13.3 per cent), New Zealand (13.1 per cent), China (7.1 per cent), India (6.1 per cent), South Africa (4.9 per cent), the Philippines (3.4 per cent) and Indonesia (3 per cent). With such a multicultural mix you'd think it was time to reconsider the 'self-governing republic' option – but you'd be wrong. In a close-run national referendum in 1999, 55 per cent of the electorate voted to keep the Queen as head of state; of Australia's six states, only Victoria wanted a republic.

Cathy Freeman.

Some 460,000 Aborigines and the ethnically distinct people from the Torres Strait Islands off northern Queensland live in Australia today, but a rift still exists between them and the rest of the population. Aboriginal life expectancy is 20 years lower than that of other Australians; the infant mortality rate is higher; the ratio of Aboriginal people to other Australians in prisons is disproportionately high, and many are still restricted to the fringe of society.

In 1992 the 'Mabo decision' marked a breakthrough in Aboriginal affairs: the High Court declared that Australia was not *terra nullius* ('empty land') as it had been termed since the British 'invasion'. This decision resulted in the 1993 Native Title Act, which allowed Aboriginal groups and Torres Strait Islanders to claim government-owned land if they could prove continual association with it since 1788. Later, the Wik decision determined that Aboriginal people everywhere could make claims on government land that was leased to agriculturists. But Prime Minister John Howard's Liberal coalition government, under pressure from farming and mining interests, curtailed these rights.

In response, Aboriginal groups threatened (but did not mount) major demonstrations during the 2000 Sydney Olympics. The Olympic opening ceremony paid tribute to the country's

Aboriginal origins, and the flame was lit by Aboriginal runner Cathy Freeman. To outsiders it seemed that Australia was embracing its past rather than marginalising it, but indigenous Australians themselves were less impressed. John Howard, in particular, has come in for harsh criticism for his refusal to apologise for the actions of past generations.

IN HOWARD'S ASYLUM

With the reconciliation issue bubbling in the background, Howard's government turned its attentions to stemming the influx of refugees. In the late 1990s asylum seekers from Iraq and Afghanistan landed in Australia only to face a grim, prison-like existence in detention centres in the middle of the South Australian desert – most notoriously, at Woomera (now closed). Processing their cases has taken years, and many are still in virtual incarceration, with their future prospects unresolved.

"Prime Minister Rudd wasted no time in righting what many consider to be Howard's grave errors."

In 1999 when victims of war-ravaged Kosovo came knocking, the Australian government was slow to respond. Eventually, local and international pressure forced Howard's hand and the refugees were admitted, but only for a short respite on newly created 'safe haven' (ie temporary) visas. In August 2001 Howard played tough guy once again, turning away a Norwegian cargo ship carrying 400 Afghan and Iraqi asylum seekers, whom the captain had rescued from a leaky ferry. As the ship neared Australian shores, Howard – with one eye firmly on the voters – steeled himself for a showdown. 'I believe it is in Australia's national interests that we draw a line on what is increasingly becoming an uncontrollable number of illegal arrivals in this country,' he asserted.

Much unseemly to-ing and fro-ing followed. At one point, the government claimed that the refugees were blackmailing the Australian navy into rescuing them by throwing their children overboard. Later – after Howard had won the 2001 election – it was revealed that the pictures that had been flashed across the news had been taken a day later and were actually shots showing the bona fide rescue of the asylum seekers after their boat had sunk. Ultimately, the refugees weren't allowed to set foot on Australian soil: most ended up on the tiny Pacific island of Nauru.

Although heavily criticised internationally, Howard's strong-arm – and, say many, racist –

policies proved popular at the ballot box and he won a third term in office in 2001, sending the opposition Labor party into free fall. Howard's government was returned once more in 2003, although NSW has remained a Labor stronghold under Bob Carr, who lasted ten years as premier before retiring in 2005, to be replaced by Morris Iemma.

Australia may be geographically removed from the centres of world affairs, but it is increasingly involved in some of the 21st century's key military issues. Australian troops led the UN peacekeeping force in East Timor in 1999, and in 2006 led a force to put down rebellion in the Solomon Islands. More controversially, the Australian army has been heavily involved backing up US adventures in both Afghanistan and Iraq.

The nation has suffered for it: the 2002 Bali nightclub bombings killed 88 Australians (out of a death toll of 202), while another attack in Bali in 2005 killed four Australians. The Australian embassy in Jakarta, Indonesia, was also bombed in 2004, though none of the 11 dead was Australian. Jemaah Islamiah, a militant South-east Asian Muslim group, has been blamed for all three attacks. Perhaps to calm that perennial sense of national vulnerability, in 2004 the Howard government announced a cruise missile programme to give Australia the region's 'most lethal' air combat capacity.

Antagonism towards Australia's Muslim communities grew after the bombings, and fears of more violence were raised when 15 people were arrested in November 2005 for allegedly planning bomb attacks in Sydney and Melbourne. All this may or may not have helped stoke up race riots in Cronulla and other oceanside suburbs a month later.

The climate has been hotting up too: the worst bush fires for more than 20 years killed nine people in South Australia in 2005, and 1 January 2006 was Sydney's hottest day since 1939, with a high of 44.3°C (111°F).

RUDD'S BRAVE NEW NATION

At the end of 2007, Australia entered what promises to be a new and exciting political era with the landslide victory of the Labor party that delivered the youthful, Mandarin-speaking Kevin Rudd to the leadership. Prime Minister Rudd wasted no time in righting what many consider to be Howard's grave errors, joining a host of other nations in ratification of the Kyoto Protocol for climate change and delivering a formal apology to the Aboriginal people for the historic injustices that go right back to the First Fleet. Much is expected of the new PM, although whether he and his party can deliver remains to be seen.

Key events

40,000BC The Aboriginal Dharug tribal group occupy the area that is now Sydney.
29 April 1770 James Cook and Joseph Banks sail the Endeavour into Botany Bay.
26 January 1788 Settlement of the First Fleet at Sydney Cove.
1789 Smallpox epidemic among local Aboriginal people.
1808 NSWC officers, known as the Rum Corps, overthrow Governor William Bligh.
1810-21 Governor Macquarie instils order.
1813 WC Wentworth, George Blaxland and William Lawson are the first Europeans to cross the Blue Mountains.
1840 The transportation of convicts to NSW is outlawed by the British government.
1842 The city of Sydney is officially incorporated; the first councillors are elected.
1851 A gold rush begins and Sydney's population rises to 96,000 by 1861.
1855 The colony's first steam railway, the Sydney to Parramatta line, is completed.
1858 Men are granted the vote in NSW.
1878 Seamen begin a six-week strike over the use of Chinese labour, setting in motion a movement that would lead to the White Australia policy.
1901 Ceremony of united Commonwealth of Australia as an independent monarchy in the British Commonwealth, in Centennial Park. Edmund Barton is sworn in as prime minister.
1902 Women get the vote in NSW state elections.
1906 The world's first surf lifesaving club is founded at Bondi. Laws banning daylight beach bathing are scrapped.
1908 Canberra becomes Australia's capital.
1914-18 Of the 330,000 Australians sent to fight in World War I, 60,000 perish.
1922-30 The Empire Settlement Scheme moves thousands of working-class families from the industrial towns of the UK to Sydney.
1932 Sydney Harbour Bridge is opened.
1942 Three Japanese subs steal into Sydney Harbour and torpedo a ferry with Allied naval officers on board, killing 19.
1960-67 Aboriginal peoples are granted the vote and included in census figures.
1965-72 Australian troops sent to Vietnam.
1972 The Australian Labor Party gains power.
1973 Sydney Opera House is opened by the Queen and declared a wonder of the world.
1975 Governor-General Sir John Kerr, the Queen's representative, sacks the country's

Labor government. The seeds of a serious Australian republican movement are sown.
1978 Hundreds of thousands of Vietnamese refugees enter the country; the first arrivals are illegal, stealing into Darwin by boat.
The first gay and lesbian Mardi Gras ends in violence after police attack 1,000 marchers.
1985-6 A gang war for control of Sydney's prostitution, gambling and drug rackets rages. A web of business connections between the underworld and the police is exposed.
1988 One million celebrate bicentennial at Sydney Harbour. Aboriginal peoples protest.
1992 Sydney Harbour Tunnel opens. The Mabo case inserts the legal doctrine of native title into Australian law, allowing Aborigines to claim traditional rights to land.
1996 Liberal coalition government under John Howard wins power, ousting Labor Party.
1998 John Howard's coalition government narrowly wins a second term.
1999 Australian troops lead a peacekeeping force in East Timor. Referendum proposals to make Australia a republic are defeated.
2000 The Olympic Games, held at Sydney's Homebush Bay, are deemed the 'best ever'.
2001 A Norwegian ship carrying rescued refugees is refused entry to Australia and sent to a remote Pacific island. John Howard is elected prime minister for a third term.
2002 Bombs in Bali nightclubs kill 202, including 88 Australians. Australian troops join UN peacekeeping forces in Afghanistan.
2003 NSW Premier Bob Carr's Labor government is re-elected for a third term. Australian troops sent to the war in Iraq.
2004 Riots in Redfern follow the death of an Aboriginal teenager. Parliamentary committee clears government of lying about Iraqi weapons of mass destruction. Fatal bomb attacks outside Australian embassy in Jakarta. John Howard wins fourth term.
2005 Bob Carr retires; Morris Iemma takes over as NSW premier. Riots in Cronulla involving white and Lebanese youths.
2007 The Labor Party, under Kevin Rudd, sweeps to power with a landslide victory over John Howard, who loses his Sydney seat of Bennelong to TV journalist Maxine McKew.
2007 Prime Minister Rudd signs documents ratifying Kyoto Protocol on climate change, reversing the previous government's policy.
2008 Kevin Rudd says 'sorry' to the Aboriginal people for 'past injustices'.

Wharf Building, **Sydney Theatre Company**. *See p23.*

The Future's Green

Turning off and tuning in to a sustainable future.

With the harbour glittering in the background, breakers crashing on the beaches and a cool breeze rolling in off the Pacific, it's hard not to be content in Sydney.

But in a place this relaxed and comfortable, it is perhaps a little too easy to become complacent. The citizens of Australia's biggest and richest city have been forced to face up to some tough questions in the last year. When it comes to climate change, Sydneysiders – all four million of them – have been among the world's worst offenders.

If the Pacific breeze doesn't turn up, just flick a switch and start the air conditioner, because nine out of ten homes now have one – or more than one. If the trains are unreliable, as they sadly often are, then jump in the car – the average home now has two. And why bother recycling your rubbish when this giant continent has so much empty space that it actually imports waste from more geographically-challenged neighbours?

Unsettling thoughts like these have been percolating through the public consciousness for years, to little apparent effect. But the shift, when it finally came, was sudden.

In November's federal election, Sydneysiders rounded on a government they had firmly backed for over a decade in favour of an opposition that made climate change the centre of its election strategy. A new national government, whose first act was signing the Kyoto Protocol on climate change, brought the leadership in line with the grassroots. Overnight, green thinking became cool – if a little nerdy.

Sydneysider Tim Flannery, an ecologist and historian who spent much of his tenure as 2007 'Australian of the Year' campaigning against global warming, believes public opinion was at breaking point.

'The debate had been won midway through 2007,' he says. 'People wanted change, they desperately wanted to see something done. Now, hopefully, they're getting it.'

COMETH THE EARTH HOUR

What began as a modest initiative involving a handful of businesses and the non-profit World Wildlife Fund ended up taking Sydney by storm in 2007. More than half the city's population took part in Earth Hour, during which lights were turned off for an hour in March as a symbol of the need for action on climate change and energy efficiency.

The event was, as intended, symbolic – the act saved the equivalent in greenhouse gas emissions of taking a mere six cars off the road for a year, a statistic tirelessly recycled in sceptical newspaper columns. And the energy grid, the majority of which is still fed by coal-burning power stations, did not decrease production at all.

> ## 'Overnight, green thinking became cool – if nerdy.'

But it was all great fun for those who took part. Restaurants served dinners by candlelight, couples wedded in moonlit parks and the night became a 'where were you?' talking point.

The real impact of Earth Hour, however, was felt at a local level. The event inspired thousands of individuals and groups to take some form of action to reduce energy use. In the southern suburb of Hurstville, an Anglican priest re-branded his place of worship an 'eco-church' and led the charge to get solar panels fitted on local buildings, while another group on Sydney's northern beaches pledged that they would not buy any non-recyclable goods for a year – a promise they look very likely to keep.

It has become a point of honour – and financial prudence in an eco-friendly

marketplace – for bigger businesses to play their part. Owners of the main office towers in the central city, North Sydney and Parramatta all signed up to Earth Hour. Even McDonald's, which switched off most of its energy-hungry golden arches for the inaugural event, will carry energy-saving tips on its food trays, timed to coincide with the next big switch-off.

Images of Sydney's usually-luminous skyline falling dark flashed around the world in 2007, and they left a lasting impression. When the event takes place again this year it will be far bigger – and this time Sydneysiders won't be alone in the dark. At least fourteen other cities, including Chicago, Toronto, Tel Aviv, Manilla and Copenhagen, have signed up to take part.

THE WEIGHT OF WATER

Placed precariously on the edge of the world's driest continent, Sydney has always had to keep a careful eye on its water supply. With a drought that has entered the record books in parts of NSW as the longest and driest since

60

EARTH HOUR

7.30 pm Saturday March 31, 2007
See your world in a whole new light
www.earthhour.org

WWF

The Sydney Morning Hera

Cleaning up their act

Carbon emissions will take centre stage this year at the Sydney Theatre Company (*see p270* **The Cate factor**), thanks to plans hatched by artistic directors Cate Blanchett and her partner Andrew Upton to make the iconic waterfront venue more eco-friendly.

The pair announced in July 2007 that the theatre, housed in a converted wharf in Sydney's Walsh Bay, would be fitted with solar panels, rainwater tanks and a host of other energy-saving devices, with an ultimate aim of taking the building off the national grid. Bicycles have also been provided for staff to travel to and from work.

The modifications will be funded by public and private money, as well as donations from clear-conscience show-goers, but there would be no 'green levy' on tickets according to Upton – although exact details have yet to be revealed and developmental red tape could still prove a stumbling block.

Many major Australian theatres have taken similar steps. Sydney's biggest arthouse theatre, the Belvoir Street Theatre (*see p268*), has a recycling programme for its theatre sets along with all glass and paper. Melbourne's Malthouse Theatre, meanwhile, has placed a 50 cent surcharge on tickets in an effort to raise $50,000 to pay for carbon offsets, following an audit which found that the organisation generates an average of 600 tons of carbon each year – the equivalent of about 2,000 standard cars. The neighbouring Melbourne Theatre Company has reduced its water consumption by 74 per cent. And this year's Adelaide Festival of the Arts aims to go carbon neutral by asking, in concert programmes, for donations from festival goers to buy offsets.

Nor are Blanchett and Upton failing to practice what they preach. The couple last year renovated their $10 million mansion in the waterside suburb of Hunters Hill to incorporate green features such as a 20,000-litre water tank, high-tech solar panelling, low-energy lighting and grey water recycling.

white settlement, grim water restrictions have been in place for several years, and every conversation about the rain seems to contain a reference to falls in the dam catchment areas.

The NSW government is pushing ahead with a desalination plant at Kurnell on the southern fringe of the city, controversial because of the environmental damage wrought by its construction and the hefty $1.4 billion price tag. Scientists have also pointed out that the huge underwater vaccum cleaners sucking in seawater and pumping out brine are unlikely to have a positive effect on surrounding marine life sanctuaries. When eventually completed, the plant could provide up to a third of the city's drinking water – 500 megalitres – but would push up household water bills by 100 per cent if the government honours its promise to offset greenhouse gases generated by the energy-intensive plant.

The answer to the city's water woes, many feel, is to use it more intelligently. The government, perhaps in an attempt to shake off some of the heat it attracted over desalination, announced plans in January to make its Parliament House self sufficient in terms of water consumption, utilising rooftop tanks and a nearby underground aquifer.

But such efforts invite scrutiny, and it emerged in the same month that the air keeping parliamentarians cool while they debate is chilled by a leaky air conditioning system in the building's basement – one that uses refrigerant gases with the same potential for global warming as 4,500 four-wheel drive vehicles.

In July, the government announced rebates for rainwater tanks on city homes, with $500 per tank and an extra $1000 to connect the tank to toilets and washing machines. So far, residents have taken to the plan on a modest scale, with about 700 applications received in the first six months. It's not much, but it's enough to save the main dams from supplying water for 620,000 loads of dirty washing, Sydney's main dam at Warragamba reached 60 per cent of its capacity late in 2007, but the rise was timed with an outbreak of toxic algae, which forced the city's Catchment Authority to extract water from pipes deep below the surface.

Demand for water has actually decreased as each local council examines ways of recycling water that would otherwise run off into the harbour or the ocean. In Waverley, the local authority that governs a large slice of eastern Sydney including Bondi Beach, huge underground storage tanks have been harnessed for just this purpose, allowing many of the council's own activities to run independently of the mains supply – a pattern that is now being reflected around the city.

But the zealous guarding of water supplies has coined a new term, 'water rage', and led to many a divisive stand-off over suburban hosepipes, plus one sickening tragedy. In November 2007, Ken Proctor was watering his lawn outside the restricted time in the southern suburb of Sylvania when he was set upon by another man and died of heart failure.

PLAYING WITH POWER

In a trend-setting move, the owners of many of Sydney's most iconic skyscrapers voluntarily signed up to strict codes of energy efficiency in December 2007. The plan, to be monitored by non-profit group the Total Environment Centre, will see about one-eighth of Australia's office space committed to the 'five star' green ratings now required of all new government buildings.

The retrofit changes, most of them simply a matter of replacing old lights and air conditioning units while installing better insulation and tinted windows, will save an estimated 50,000 tonnes of carbon dioxide per year. New offices must meet or exceed the same standards to gain construction approval.

A sudden rash of solar panels has also sprung up across many residential areas in the past year, fuelled by both the power-saving benefits and the chance to use Sydney's sunny climate to sell excess power back to the main grid. Many local councils now have the stated aim of generating all their power from renewable sources, though few will achieve this by 2015. In Blacktown, a sprawling, working-class municipality in Sydney's west, the city's biggest solar farm was opened in February, generating 100 kilowatts from 650 panels.

Major changes are also afoot in the average Sydney household, as an obsession with personal carbon footprints takes hold. The federal government has moved to ban incandescent light bulbs in homes, and Sydneysiders have taken to far more efficient fluorescent lights with gusto. On current evidence, incandescent bulbs will have all but vanished when the ban takes effect in 2010.

In March this year, the NSW government will recommence a scheme to buy back old fridges across the city. The ageing white goods have been identified as a major source of leaking greenhouse gases and big energy consumers. Two thousand people are already on the list to have their fridge picked up in return for a cash payment. In December, the government also committed to fit each household in the city with so-called 'smart meters', which allow residents to monitor and compute their energy use, and take advantage of off-peak energy use times to turn on the dishwasher.

Around the state, the number of people willing to add extra costs to their monthly energy bills for using renewable power more than tripled last year. Nearly eight per cent of Australians now choose to pay more for their energy to be sourced from solar and wind farms, and that number is expected to reach a quarter of the population by 2010. The hit on the wallet ranges from an extra $50 a year for ten per cent green power to $400 for 100 per cent. The nation's biggest wind farm, to be built near Broken Hill in the west of the state, will eventually supply up to five per cent of the state's power needs.

But the city's addiction to fossil fuels will be hard to break, with abundant coal reserves and an immensely powerful mining lobby. A vast new coal mine, to be dug at Anvil Hill about 150 kilometres (93 miles) north of Sydney, was approved by the state government in 2007, and will add to Australia's greenhouse gas emissions by 12.6 million tonnes.

In the southern coalfields, on the city's southwest outskirts, longwall mining continues apace, causing subsidence which has ruined some native waterways and forced mining companies to buy up dozens of houses in the village of Appin that have disintegrated as coal has been tunnelled out from beneath them.

A GREENER CITY

Like many global cities, Sydney is getting greener from the grassroots up, as pressure from citizens forces elected leaders to act. The evidence is now being seen in legislation and on the streets, where tree-planting programmes have taken off in every local government area.

This is not to say there haven't been setbacks. Sydney's plan to turn the congested eyesore of William Street into a leafy boulevard went astray when vehicle pollution and shallow planting killed most of the trees off. The huge Sydney conurbation remains chronically addicted to the internal combustion engine, and bike riders have made little headway into the automotive culture despite the emergence of a network of cycleways around the inner city.

But the overall picture is one of halting progress. More land, especially on the city's sprawling western edge, is now allocated to parks than ever, including the Western Sydney Regional Park, which at more than 540 hectares is twice the size of London's Hampstead Heath. In December 2007 the state government completed a four-year 'stocktake' of native wildlife in and around the city, and found most species in healthy numbers, while the planned network of natural bush corridors will allow the various wallaby, potoroo and koala colonies to move from place to place without needing to ever scent a house or road.

All of which means that, while the war is far from over, the battle may yet be won.

Sydney Today

Traffic problems, spiralling rents – can Rudd rescue the city?

A glistening, jaw-dropping harbour that cries romance and boasts iconic venues, a buzz that no other Australian city can lay claim to, a plethora of nightlife options that outweighs its medium-sized population: Sydney is the single gateway to Australia and its one true global city. And it's come a long way fast.

The Sydney of today couldn't be more different from the city that showed itself off to the world with the 'best ever' Olympics back in 2000. Since that pivotal moment in its short history, Sydney has experienced unprecedented growth (with up to 1,000 new residents reportedly flocking in every week), faced a raft of related crises with housing (chronic shortages, booming property values) and suffered a crumbling infrastructure and skills deficit, as well as headline-grabbing issues relating to race, drugs and crime.

The jewel in Australia's crown – boasting an enviable lifestyle for its four million inhabitants and with some of the finest dining on the planet – Sydney has also seen its global status comfortably confirmed with an ever-booming influx of the rich and famous, who gleefully

endure the long-haul flight to play in the five-star surrounds once reserved for eastern suburbs high-rollers. Yet behind the apparently beautiful façade (its rival Melbournites refer to Sydney as 'the tart' and to their own Victorian capital as 'the lady') lies a murky underbelly of so-called crises and epidemics, from the aforementioned crime, housing and racial tensions to the on-going gridlock that commuters face on a daily basis.

As the decade draws to a close, Sydney finds itself at a crossroads. Will the newly elected Labor federal government have the ability to force the so-far ineffectual NSW state government to act on the dilemmas now facing Australia's unofficial global capital? Only time will tell. But for the moment, progress on key issues remains painfully slow.

THE RENT SQUEEZE

For those relocating to the Harbour City, the reality of the 'rental drought' was all too clear in 2007. The Real Estate Institute of New South Wales reported vacancy rates were at a record low of 0.9 per cent, and that rents would be

Turning the tide

With a 100-year history, the voluntary Surf Life Saving Clubs (SLSC) that patrol Sydney's beaches not only represent all that is great about Australia's volunteer culture, but show how the city has changed politically and socially. Until 1980, the clubs were a bastion of Anglo Saxon male dominance, teeming with square-shouldered, bronzed embodiments of top-to-toe fitness launching themselves fearlessly into the waves, while their women folk sat on the beach clutching towels.

But then a quiet revolution began to swell, achieving success when women were finally permitted to take their place alongside men, training for their bronze medallion so that they too could become full and active SLSC members and patrol the beaches as equals. The response was astonishing, and today women make up 41 per cent of members, while in the under-14s Nippers Clubs (which train kids from as young as five to brave the waves safely) girls make up an impressive 49 per cent of members.

Nor is it just the male/female ratio that has been addressed; in recent years the clubs have actively recruited members from differing ethnic and cultural backgrounds, aiming to produce a team of volunteers that truly represents Australia's multicultural society. In the wake of the racially motivated Cronulla Beach riots in 2005, a special outreach programme called 'On the Same Wave' was set up to attract ethnic minorities to the nation's most iconic volunteer group.

Under the programme, 22 Lebanese, Palestinian, Syrian, Egyptian and Libyan men and women aged 14 to 40 signed up. One Muslim girl, Mecca Laalaa from Cronulla, hit the international press when she embraced her new weekend job in what became known

as a 'burquini'. This revolutionary piece of swimwear – created for the SLSC by a local fashion designer – is a two-piece lycra suit that covers all, with a natty hood for the hair. Mecca was delighted. 'They don't think Muslim women swim,' she said.

The suit has since taken off, with Muslim girls all over Australia joining up. And just to prove the inclusion doesn't stop there, gay SLSC members marched in last year's Mardi Gras. If you want to know what Sydney is about, it's all happening at the SLSC.

bumped up by an average of $30 a week. For those looking to find a place to live, a sea of 50 or more prospective tenants greeted them at every stop, all elbowing their way to complete application forms. And while 1,800 new apartments were planned for 2008 in Sydney – and the media's reporting of the 'crisis' was deemed overly dramatic, with vested interests from real estate powerbrokers seemingly to blame – there were no signs of relief. What, then, does the state government plan to do about it? No one is quite sure, although new powers for the rental tribunal will allow landlords to evict tenants faster if they fall behind with their rent,

and the state government remains under pressure to cut land tax for investors and red tape for building approvals.

Nor is the long-held Aussie dream of buying one's home getting any easier. While the 'first home buyers grant' of $7,000 helps, the average three-bedroom house easily tops $1 million. The auction-crazy years may have passed, but the expected downturn hasn't occurred. The upshot is that many continue to rent well into their thirties, and often only buy with their ageing parents' help. Investors may be smiling at the squeeze – predicted by analysts to last beyond the end of the decade – but renters are not.

HORSING AROUND

Sydneysiders love a flutter on the horses, and no one could have foreseen one of the nation's favourite pastime being threatened by anything but an act of god. But that's exactly what happened in August 2007, when an outbreak of the horse-targeting EI virus spread through the state at a rate of knots. Nearly 400 race meets had to be called off in the lead-up to the Melbourne Cup, with a reported $500 million of betting turnover slashed from the state's fourth largest revenue earner. Although the big day in Victoria did go ahead, the future for the industry looks bleak, with many predicting a full recovery to take years. Glebe's Harold Park Raceway even introduced camel racing to fill the void left by the lack of its horse carriage races, a tongue-in-cheek measure that lasted into 2008. When the accounts are finalised, that venue alone predicts that the outbreak is likely to have resulted in a $2 million loss, even with the camels.

SECURITY LOCKDOWN

As if being denied their favourite social pastime wasn't bad enough, Sydneysiders have also had to deal with being locked out of their own city. In the wake of the London bombings and US government-fuelled terrorism jitters, Sydneysiders discovered the realities of living in a global city partaking in the War on Terror when world leaders descended for the Asia-Pacific Economic Cooperation (APEC) summit in September 2007. With the biggest security operation ever seen in Australia – at a whopping cost of $330 million to taxpayers – Sydneysiders found themselves locked out of the CBD. High fencing resembling a giant cage was erected to keep troublemakers and the curious away, and a plethora of 'clear ways' were set up as George W Bush and 20 other world leaders arrived to meet and discuss economic strategies. Over 1,800 security guards and police were ready, but the reality was a mere inconvenience – and a huge anticlimax. Just 17 arrests were reported, the most infamous being members of the comedy skit series *The Chaser* sailing through checkpoints. Ironically, then, while some bemoan the loss of Australian values under former Prime Minister John Howard's 11-year regime in Canberra, such global security measures also served to show that the Aussie larrikin was in fact alive and well – and more timely than ever. *The Chaser*'s skit – in which the show's team were dressed as Muslims led by an Osama Bin Laden lookalike – even made the CNN news.

THE ICE AGE

On top of the ravages of the War on Terror, Sydneysiders are also having to deal with a powerful new drug that's sweeping the city's streets. The use of 'ice' – a popular term for crystal methamphetamine – reached epidemic proportions in 2006, when over 50,000 addicts nationally were reported to be in the throes of the most dangerous addiction yet seen in Australia. The drug's effects – bringing out psychotic and violent behaviour in less stable users – became all-too obvious as crime ballooned, with an increase of over 50 per cent in firearm robberies in inner Sydney in the year that followed, and with police pointing the finger of blame squarely at the prevalence and popularity of ice. The social effects of the drug on the wider community spread to events like dance music festival Parklife, although no specific figures have been published.

GRIDLOCKED

The one common grievance facing commuters in Sydney remains just that: getting to and from work. The creaking train system carries up to a million passengers every day, but services are invariably late, cancelled or – at best – unpredictable. A plethora of bus routes all descend centrally on Railway Square, at the top of the bustling George Street central precinct. But because 75 per cent of commuters drive their cars to work, the mix makes for a traffic-choked nightmare. A congestion tax was mooted by Lord Mayor Clover Moore, but with the state government's focus on building roads and tunnels – all funded by increasingly unpopular tolls – the solution remains a thorny issue between the City of Sydney council and the state government. Moore wants an integrated public transport system with a light rail network servicing the CBD to help ease the strain and cope with the expected 20 per cent rise in population in inner Sydney by 2021. Morris Iemma's state government – re-elected in March 2007 despite a wealth of headline-making controversy and a general air of ineffectiveness – wants more buses. At the time of writing, the issue remains frustratingly unresolved. And the traffic just gets slower and slower – driving from the regenerated suburbs of Alexandria and Waterloo to the CBD, for example, can take up to 45 minutes during peak times.

A NEW PM: A BETTER SYDNEY?

Australia's federal election at the close of 2007 saw a UK-style turnaround, with 11 long years of John Howard's conservative Liberal reign coming to an almighty end. In its place came new-style Labor under the leadership of Mandarin-speaking Kevin Rudd. Perceived by some as a Tony Blair for Oz, what precisely this man means for the Harbour City remains unclear, but as soon as the election was over in

November, the city – in true Aussie style – went into 'silly season' party mode in the lead up to the Christmas/summer break, a holiday split between a feeling of jubilation in the 'Kevin 07' brigade and regret in Liberal supporters. Not that it was an open-and-shut case: former ABC TV journo turned politico Maxine McKew historically nabbed Howard's seat of Bennelong – the first time a sitting PM had lost his seat – but Liberal stalwart Malcolm Turnbull surprisingly held his Wentworth contingent in the eastern suburbs.

John Howard's hugely unpopular Industrial Relation laws, which helped unseat him, are due to be redesigned by 2010, and Rudd insists he will ease the housing crisis as a priority during his term in office. In the meantime, Rudd has stated that the secondary home the PM enjoys – the grand and perfectly placed Kirribilli House (*see p112*) on Sydney Harbour's North Shore – will now only be used for weekend events and for hosting dignitaries, with the far less ornately furnished lodge in Canberra being his primary residence. (Howard famously used Kirribilli House as his main digs, much to the outrage of opposition politicians and Canberrans.) Will this signify a shift in the perception of Sydney as the nation's 'other capital'? In global terms, it's unlikely. But nationally, it's an indication that Rudd is keen to redraw the public perception of the PM as a man of the people who will live where his people expect him to, and where he is most accessible for parliament. Sydney, meanwhile, will most likely remain Australia's showpony.

HOW THE OTHER HALF LIVE

If world leaders descending on the city weren't proof enough of Sydney's global stature in 2007, the ever-increasing influx of celebrities flocking to Aussie shores – usually opting for five-star spots such as the Park Hyatt Hotel in The Rocks – was affirmation that Sydney had indeed become the new hot spot for musicians, sportsmen, actors and the like. Tabloid-style rag the *Daily Telegraph* salivates with gleeful gossip about the latest rumoured arrival in its Confidential section – and with good reason. Among the long list of names who have recently appeared on Sydney's shores are Justin Timberlake, Christina Aguilera, David Beckham, Elton John, Sir David Attenborough, Kate Bosworth and Jerry Seinfeld. All are brought out to promote their wares, of course, be it a new movie, playing shows, plugging memoirs or, in the case of Beckham, playing with LA Galaxy in front of an adoring capacity crowd at Sydney Olympic Park's ANZ Stadium. Such is the fervour when stars like Becks or Timberlake arrive in town that the local news carries typically excitable reports on their whereabouts and – most importantly – whether or not they behaved. In a scene reminiscent of the days when UK stars such as The Who and Joe Cocker were berated for their surly behaviour (Cocker was actually booted out), the media relentlessly hounded Timberlake, angered at his refusal to play the game (the Aussie media expects its visitors to be cheerful, polite and gushing about travelling Down Under). Tragically, the late Heath Ledger was famously so exasperated by an increasingly headline-hungry, celebrity-obsessed Sydney media on his return from Hollywood that he packed up and left his Bronte beachside digs for the US, where he died alone in a Manhattan apartment in 2008.

But while the excitement about US visitors in particular may seem parochial, it's also a clear indication that Sydney (and Australia in general) has few of its own to hold up. The likes of Geoffrey Rush and Cate Blanchett still call Australia home, but a large number of aspiring musicians and actors – and even sportsmen – flee for the US and UK to build their careers. It's unlikely that this migration will ever cease: Australians – celebrity or otherwise – are known for their wanderlust. But as Sydney grows, it's likely that many will eventually return. And with this city as their home, why wouldn't they?

Paris Hilton on Bondi Beach.

Where to Stay

Where to Stay 30

Features

Medusa Hotel. *See p40*.

Where to Stay

Sleeping bags or silk sheets, there's a bed for every head in Sydney.

Park Hyatt Sydney. *See p32.*

As Sydney grows as an international hub, the hotel industry is growing with it. The range of hotels, serviced apartments, backpacker hangouts and boutique havens can be quite dazzling, but at least it means there's something for everyone. Prices at the top end compete with those you'll find in any top world city. The secret is to peek behind the glass palaces, look outside the city centre and seek out the many unusual, independently-run establishments. On prices, the key is to work the internet. Booking online can save you hundreds of dollars, with prices often as low as half the rack rate. Standards are pretty high, wherever you go: Sydneysiders are used to their spaces being spick and span and this is reflected in their hotels. Additionally, in recent years a designer-led, contemporary chic has rippled through the industry with rooms looking more and more Philippe Starck-inspired and less chintz and scary carpet. Many places nowadays

❶ Green numbers given in this chapter correspond to the location of each hotel as marked on the street maps. *See pp326-334.*

opt for an Eastern/Zen feel, and there's a lot of glass and steel around too.

In the centre, by and large you'll find the five- and six-star establishments in prime positions, many with fantastic harbour views. The four-star-plus hotels are strung around the central sightseeing areas: the Rocks, Circular Quay, George Street, Hyde Park and Darling Harbour. Meanwhile, a swag of backpacker joints congregate around Kings Cross, nearby Potts Point and Darlinghurst, and Elizabeth Bay. Staying in these areas means you'll have access to plenty of restaurants and bars, but if you want to see the tourist sights you'll need to catch a CityRail train back into town.

The inner-west suburbs, such as Newtown and Glebe, are likewise a short train or bus ride from the city centre, but have the advantage of good pubs and a student atmosphere, if that's more your scene. Newtown's bustling King Street can be noisy and traffic-polluted, but that's just part of its charm.

If you fancy staying near the beach, you can't go wrong with Bondi, Coogee or Manly. The bus journey from Bondi and Coogee into the city can be a pain, but the beach atmosphere is fabulous. If you stay in Manly (a popular option with British visitors), you're limited by the ferry service from the city, which stops around midnight. For the full seaside experience, head for the northern beaches, such as Newport, Collaroy or the stunning but pricey Palm Beach.

In the end, though, where you stay may depend on when you come. The busiest tourist times are between November and May. The beach areas are packed from mid December to late January, when the school holidays are in full swing. If you want a room during Mardi Gras (February/March) or a harbour view at New Year, you'll have to book well in advance.

There are two new hotels opening in late 2008: the Accor-run Pullman **Sydney Olympic Park** (www.pullmanhotels.com), a 212-room tower that is perfectly placed for concerts at Homebush, and the Barclay (www.thebarclay.com.au) in Kings Cross, a 41-room renovation of an exisiting hotel that promises to bring more jet set glamour to the already sparkling Bayswater Road in the heart of Sydney's red light district.

Serviced apartments, listed at the end of this chapter, are often a good option for long stays.

KEEP IN MIND

● Room prices vary greatly, but in general Sydney is less expensive than many European cities, and you should be able to get a decent double room in the city for under $200 a night.
● In Australia pubs are also called 'hotels'. Many pubs do have rooms at reasonable prices, but standards are mixed, so ask to see the accommodation first. Also check that there is adequate soundproofing.
● Despite increased government intervention, there are still a number of illegal backpacker hostels operating all over Australia. Their flyers are pasted on lamp-posts or pinned to backpacker bulletin boards. While the prices may be tempting, these places can be cramped fire traps that flout accommodation laws. For an up-to-date list of recommended legal hostels, see www.hostelaustralia.com, www.visitnsw.com.au or www.yha.com.au.

ABOUT THE LISTINGS

Most hotels are air-conditioned, but not all – check first if this is an important requirement. Rates quoted below are 'rack' rates, standard prices that are often higher than what you'll pay. It's always worth asking for standby prices, weekly rates or special deals – you may well get them, even in the peak season. Top hotels also often offer discounts at weekends, when business people with a life are sleeping in their own beds. A ten per cent Goods & Services Tax (GST) applies to all

hotels and hostels (as well as tours, internal air fares and restaurant meals), and by law it has to be part of the advertised price.

Note that 1800 telephone numbers are toll-free, and 1300 numbers are always charged at a local rate – but these only work within Australia, not if you're dialling from abroad.

The CBD & the Rocks

Deluxe

Four Seasons Hotel Sydney

199 George Street, at Essex Street, CBD, NSW 2000 (1800 142 163/9238 0000/www.fourseasons.com). CityRail/ferry Circular Quay. **Rates** $275-$555 double. **Rooms** 531. **Credit** AmEx, DC, MC, V. **Map** p327 F4 ❶

The former Regent Hotel (some taxi drivers still know it by that name) was bought by Canadian chain Four Seasons in the early 1990s and since then has been quietly delivering an extremely high level of service within very plush surroundings indeed, as evidenced by the fact that it was the official Olympic headquarters in 2000 and Olympic officials certainly don't sleep rough. The decor is expensive looking in a modern way, with a pared-down opulence. All the rooms are spacious and have marble

The best Hotels

For beach chic
Enjoy cool beachside lodgings at Coogee's **Dive Hotel** (see p47), Bondi's **Ravesi's** (see p47), Whale Beach's **Jonah's** (see p49) or **Manly Pacific Sydney** (see p50).

For designer touches
Sleep in style-mag splendour at **Blacket** (see p33), **Blue, Woolloomooloo Bay** (see p41), **Establishment** (see p35), **Medusa** (see p40) or **Sebel Pier One** (see p35).

For families on a budget
Save money for ice-creams at **Hotel Altamont** (see p41), **Newport Arms Hotel** (see p50) or **Y Hotel City South** (see p49).

For five-star glamour
Spot a celeb at **Park Hyatt Sydney** (see p32), **Shangri-La Hotel** (see p33) or **Sheraton on the Park** (see p33).

For old-fashioned charm
Step back in time at **Hughenden Hotel** (see p44), **Lord Nelson Brewery Hotel** (see p36), **Observatory Hotel** (see p32) or **Simpsons of Potts Point** (see p43).

bathrooms; some overlook Walsh Bay, the Harbour Bridge and the Opera House, while the rest have city views. The 32nd-floor Executive Club caters to high-flying business types with its corporate concierge, separate check-in and added goodies such as meetings facilities and complimentary refreshments.
Bar. Business centre. Concierge. Disabled-adapted rooms. Gym. Internet (high-speed/wireless pay terminal). No-smoking floors. Parking ($33). Pool (outdoor). Restaurants (2). Room service. Spa. TV (cable).

Hilton Sydney

488 George Street, between Park & Market Streets, CBD, NSW 2000 (9266 2000/reservations 9265 6045/www.hiltonsydney.com.au). CityRail Town Hall. **Rates** $365-$590 double. **Rooms** 577. **Credit** AmEx, DC, MC, V. **Map** p327 F6 **2**
Since its refurbishment three years ago, the Hilton has reinstated itself as one of the city's premier five-star hotels – quite an achievement as it's done that despite being without the otherwise obligatory harbour view. From the light-filled, four-storey-high lobby with its spiralling aluminium sculpture to the 31 'relaxation' rooms and suites, it is an undeniably classy experience. The design throughout is impeccable, with limestone flooring, plush fabrics, mood lighting and (in the suites) open-plan spa bathrooms. Eating and drinking spots include Luke Mangan's Glass brasserie (*see p145*) and wine bar, the Zeta cocktail bar (*see p180*) and the historic Marble Bar (established 1893) in the basement, left untouched during the refurbishment. There are also extensive conference and business facilities, and a top-end health club with gym, indoor pool, saunas and steam rooms. Great views, too, from the higher floors over nearby Sydney Tower.
Bars (3). Business centre. Concierge. Disabled-adapted rooms. Gym. Internet (high-speed/wireless). No smoking. Parking ($40). Pool (indoor). Restaurant. Room service. Spa. TV (cable/DVD).

InterContinental Sydney

Corner of Bridge & Phillip Streets, CBD, NSW 2000 (1800 221 335/9253 9000/www.sydney. intercontinental.com). CityRail/ferry Circular Quay. **Rates** $470-$830 double. **Rooms** 509. **Credit** AmEx, MC, V. **Map** p327 G4 **3**
Set in a building that dates all the way from 1851, the InterContinental now features such modern extras as high-speed internet access and digital TV in all rooms, plus two TV broadcast and video conferencing studios. Rooms have a classic-contemporary feel and come with either harbour or city views. Sleek restaurant/lounge bar Mint Bar & Dining serves contemporary cuisine, the sandstone-arcaded Cortile café dispenses traditional high tea, and Café Opera offers a seafood buffet. The luxurious rooftop lounge, with its uninterrupted harbour views, is only accessible to Club InterContinental members, who pay extra for such privileges as a personal concierge service. The vistas from the top over Sydney Harbour are spectacular, and available to all guests from the indoor swimming pool on the 31st floor.

Bars (2). Business centre. Concierge. Disabled-adapted rooms. Gym. Internet (high-speed). No-smoking floors. Parking ($30). Pool (indoor). Restaurants (2). Room service. Spa. TV (cable/pay movies).

Observatory Hotel

89-113 Kent Street, between Argyle & High Streets, Millers Point, NSW 2000 (9256 2222/www. observatoryhotel.com.au). CityRail/ferry Circular Quay. **Rates** $369-$825 double. **Rooms** 100. **Credit** AmEx, DC, MC, V. **Map** p327 E4 **4**
A consistent favourite among the more well-heeled visitors to the city, the service-oriented Observatory has the feel, and indeed some of the looks, of a typical European grand hotel. Tones are hushed as the army of staff attend to every need and desire of the guest. The furniture is mainly rich mahogany with a mass of antiques and lush drapes, and there is almost a gentleman's club feel to some of the public rooms. The hotel is owned by Orient-Express and its refined elegance has garnered a mass of awards. Rooms boast original artworks, plus marble bathrooms, CD players hidden away in antique armoires and high-speed internet points. Most rooms have views of Walsh Bay or Observatory Hill. The Observatory's renowned spa, which comes with an indoor pool complete with a sparkling night-sky ceiling, is quite something; it offfers deluxe treatments by Payot and La Prairie.
Bar. Business centre. Concierge. Disabled-adapted rooms. Gym. Internet (high-speed). No-smoking floors. Parking ($40). Pool (indoor). Restaurant. Room service. Spa. TV (cable/pay movies/DVD).

Park Hyatt Sydney

7 Hickson Road, The Rocks, NSW 2000 (9241 1234/www.sydney.park.hyatt.com). CityRail/ferry Circular Quay. **Rates** $675-$1,025 double. **Rooms** 158. **Credit** AmEx, DC, MC, V. **Map** p327 F3 **5**
Since opening in 1990, the Park Hyatt has played host to a steady stream of celebrities, heads of state and international jet-setters with money to burn. The jaw-dropping, close-up vista of both the Opera House and the Harbour Bridge is a major selling point, but you get what you pay (a lot) for – the cheaper rooms offer just glimpses of what the more expensive suites have framed through their windows. A recent refurbishment has transformed the top-end suites into über-minimalist apartment-style hangouts. Extras include a rooftop swimming pool, deluxe spa and much-vaunted 24-hour butler service. There are also LCD TVs, CD/DVD players, high-speed internet connections and marble bathrooms. The chic harbourkitchen&bar restaurant provides yet more amazing views (through floor-to-ceiling glass doors) and excellent food, while the harbourbar offers cocktails and tapas. The Club Bar caters to whisky fans, but anti-smoking laws mean that it's no longer a cigar haven. **Photo** p30.
Bars (2). Business centre. Concierge. Gym. Internet (high-speed/wireless). No smoking. Parking ($26). Pool (outdoor). Restaurant. Room service. Spa. TV (cable/DVD/pay movies/satellite).

Blocking the light from **Blacket**.

Shangri-La Hotel

176 Cumberland Street, between Essex & Argyle Streets, The Rocks, NSW 2000 (9250 6000/www. shangri-la.com). CityRail/ferry Circular Quay. **Rates** $349-$522 double. **Rooms** 563. **Credit** AmEx, DC, MC, V. **Map** p327 E4 ⑥

Ideally located between the Opera House and the Harbour Bridge, this is another five-star spot with undeniably breathtaking views. And, what's more, the views are there from every room, which is one reason for it's popularity. Rooms here are some of the largest in the city and service remains a major priority, with lots of extra touches designed to maintain a loyal base of regulars. The Horizon Club executive lounge on the 30th floor, with its towering 18m (60ft) glass atrium, comes at a premium but with complimentary breakfast and snacks and business facilities it's well worth it. The swanky Blu Horizon cocktail bar is popular with city boys, while Altitude restaurant on the 36th floor offers unbeatable picture-postcard views of the the harbour, the bridge and the Opera House. Decor is a mix of modern eastern with classic hotel chic, but really you don't look at the furniture with views like these. There's also a gym and indoor swimming pool.
Bar. Business centre. Concierge. Disabled-adapted rooms. Gym. Internet (high-speed). No-smoking floors. Pool (indoor). Restaurants (2). Room service. Spa. TV (cable/DVD).

Sheraton on the Park

161 Elizabeth Street, between Market & Park Streets, CBD, NSW 2000 (1800 073 535/9286 6000/www. sheraton.com). CityRail St James. **Rates** $280-$590 double. **Rooms** 557. **Credit** AmEx, DC, MC, V. **Map** p327 F6 ⑦

Overlooking bucolic Hyde Park, this huge award-winning hotel occupies a prime location in the central business and shopping district. The grand lobby screams luxury with its massive black marble pillars and curved staircase, and the rooms have a refined, modern and quasi-nautical design theme (all stripes and circles), and feature black marble bathrooms. There's a spacious pool and fitness centre on level 22, the Conservatory Bar on level one and a tea lounge off the lobby, which offers 'contemporary' high tea served by stylish black-clad waiters.
Bar. Business centre. Concierge. Disabled-adapted rooms. Gym. Internet (high-speed). No-smoking floors. Parking ($40). Pool (indoor). Restaurant. Room service. Spa. TV (cable).

Westin Sydney

1 Martin Place, between Pitt & George Streets, CBD, NSW 2000 (1800 656 535/8223 1111/www. westin.com). CityRail Martin Place. **Rates** $625-$745 double. **Rooms** 416. **Credit** AmEx, DC, MC, V. **Map** p327 F5 ⑧

Here you get the best of both worlds – a sense of history married to some very contemporary design and deluxe service. Located in pedestrianised Martin Place, smack-dab in the middle of the CBD, the Westin is partly housed in what used to be the General Post Office, built in 1887. Rooms in the heritage-listed building feature high ceilings and period details, while tower rooms have floor-to-ceiling city views and a more contemporary look (think stainless steel and pale wood). There is a renowned spa and a spectacular atrium as well as a selection of restaurants and bars in the GPO building. Exercise addicts take note: the 'Workout Rooms' come with treadmill, weights, a yoga mat and other fitness paraphernalia.
Bar. Business centre. Concierge. Disabled-adapted rooms. Gym. No-smoking floors. Internet (high-speed). Parking ($35). Pool (indoor). Restaurant. Room service. Spa. TV (cable/pay movies).

Expensive

Blacket

70 King Street, at George Street, CBD, NSW 2000 (9279 3030/www.theblacket.com). CityRail Martin Place or Wynyard. **Rates** $210-$230 double. **Rooms** 41. **Credit** AmEx, DC, MC, V. **Map** p327 E6 ⑨

A boutique hotel, with a typically boutique aesthetic to match: muted colours, running the gamut from charcoal to beige, complement the clean lines and minimalist furniture. Opened in 2001, the Blacket is housed in a 19th-century bank building designed by architect Edmund Blacket, so there are a few period flourishes here and there. But the hotel's restaurant, Level Three, is very 21st-century – all glass, chrome

and white leather booths – while the Privilege Bar in the basement draws a predominantly young urban crowd with its drink specials and DJs.

Bars (2). Concierge. No smoking. Parking ($30). Restaurant. Room service. TV.

Establishment

5 Bridge Lane, at George Street, CBD, NSW 2000 (9240 3100/www.establishmenthotel.com). CityRail Circular Quay or Wynyard/ferry Circular Quay. **Rates** $450 double. **Rooms** 31. **Credit** AmEx, DC, MC, V. **Map** p327 F5 ⑩

Although it only has 31 rooms, including two penthouse suites, the Establishment's cool clout far outweighs its capacity. Exceedingly stylish, this place would be perfectly at home in the smarter districts of London or New York. Catering to celebrities, fashionistas and those with deep pockets, the complex incorporates two critically acclaimed restaurants, Sushi e and est., three bars including Hemmesphere and a popular nightclub, Tank. As for the guest rooms, half are all sharp angles, minimalist Japanese elements and flashes of bright colour, while the others are more subdued – choose what suits your mood. Expect luxurious touches at every turn (Philippe Starck taps, Bulgari toiletries, Bose stereo systems).

Bars (3). Business centre. Concierge. Gym. Internet (high-speed). No-smoking floors. Restaurants (2). Room service. TV (cable/DVD).

Four Points by Sheraton Darling Harbour

161 Sussex Street, at Market Street, CBD, NSW 2000 (1800 074 545/9290 4000/www.fourpoints. com). CityRail Town Hall/ferry Darling Harbour/ Monorail Darling Park. **Rates** $468-$2,268 double. **Rooms** 630. **Credit** AmEx, DC, MC, V. **Map** p327 E6 ⑪

With 630 rooms including 45 suites, this place caters to large tour groups, executives and the international conference crowd: the Sydney Convention & Exhibition Centre is a stone's throw away, and the hotel is within walking distance of several museums as well as Chinatown and the central business and shopping districts. All mod cons are provided, such as high-speed wireless internet, large work desks and cable TV. Some rooms have balconies overlooking Darling Harbour. There are high-tech conferencing facilities, a fitness centre and a sprawling shopping centre with a food court. The glassed-in Corn Exchange restaurant offers an elaborate seafood buffet, the historic Dundee Arms pub specialises in barbecued pub grub, and locally brewed beer and cocktails are served in the Lobby Lounge.

Bars (2). Business centre. Concierge. Disabled-adapted rooms. Gym. Internet (wireless). No-smoking floors. Parking ($35). Restaurant. Room service. TV (cable/pay movies).

Grace Hotel

77 York Street, at King Street, CBD, NSW 2000 (9272 6888/www.gracehotel.com.au). CityRail Martin Place or Wynyard. **Rates** $560-$610 double. **Rooms** 382. **Credit** AmEx, DC, MC, V. **Map** p327 E6 ⑫

This charming hotel is housed in an 11-storey corner block – a loose copy of the Tribune Tower in Chicago – that began life in 1930 as the headquarters of department store giant Grace Brothers. During World War II General MacArthur directed South Pacific operations from here. A total refurbishment was completed in 2005, but many of the original features, such as the lifts, stairwells, marble floors and ornate ironwork, have been retained and restored to great effect. Rooms, however, are modern, large and comfortable, and all have bathtubs. The indoor heated lap pool is small, but there's also a sauna and a steam room, plus a sun-filled fitness centre and rooftop terrace. While the rack rate here seems high, there are usually much more reasonable internet offers to be had. Bar77Grace serves cocktails and innovative bar food.

Bars (2). Concierge. Disabled-adapted rooms. Gym. Internet (high-speed). No smoking. Parking ($30). Pool (indoor). Restaurant. Room service. Spa. TV (cable/pay movies).

Rydges World Square

389 Pitt Street, at Liverpool Street, CBD, NSW 2000 (1800 838 830/8268 1888/www.rydges.com). CityRail Central or Town Hall/Monorail World Square/LightRail Central. **Rates** $460-$580 double. **Rooms** 443. **Credit** AmEx, DC, MC, V. **Map** p329 F8 ⑬

Located in the new shopping and entertainment precinct known as World Square, the Rydges (which was converted from the previous Avillion hotel) was still a work in progress at the time of writing. The restaurant had just completed its refurbishment and the bar was waiting for an upgrade; the guest rooms, meanwhile, had been completed to a comfortable (albeit rather blandly furnished) standard. Since it is within easy walking distance of Darling Harbour, Chinatown and the Queen Victoria Building, this hotel is popular with business people and those seeking cheaper (relatively speaking), good-quality rooms. There's also a large fitness centre and a retail plaza that connects to the lower lobby.

Bar. Business centre. Concierge. Disabled-adapted rooms. Gym. Internet (high-speed). No-smoking floors. Parking ($35). Restaurant. Room service. TV (cable/pay movies/satellite).

Sebel Pier One

11 Hickson Road, on Dawes Point, Walsh Bay, NSW 2000 (1800 780 485/8298 9999/www.sebelpierone. com.au). CityRail/ferry Circular Quay then 15min walk. **Rates** $225-$405 double. **Rooms** 160. **Credit** AmEx, DC, MC, V. **Map** p327 F2 ⑭

Another successful marriage of historic architecture and contemporary design, this sleek, chic boutique hotel has water views in the most unexpected places, including beneath your feet: the glass floor in the lobby is quite the showpiece. Located in a converted warehouse at the quiet end of the Rocks, the rooms feature much of the original timber and ironwork. Some rooms have telescopes, some have Walsh Bay or partial Bridge views, and all have wireless internet connection and slick modern furnishings. The Front restaurant and wine bar offers alfresco dining and cocktails on the water, while the private pontoon is convenient for those travelling by water taxi or private yacht.

Bar. Business centre. Concierge. Disabled-adapted rooms. Gym. Internet (high-speed). No smoking. Parking ($25). Restaurant. Room service. TV (cable/pay movies).

Moderate

Central Park Hotel

185 Castlereagh Street, at Park Street, CBD, NSW 2000 (9283 5000/www.centralpark.com.au). CityRail Town Hall/Monorail Galeries Victoria. **Rates** $150-$210 double. **Rooms** 35. **Credit** AmEx, DC, MC, V. **Map** p329 F7 ⑮

With its motto 'hip on a budget', the less-expensive little sister of Blacket's (*see p33*) is perfect for those who love to be in the heart of the action. Located on a busy city corner, this compact urban hotel has standard en-suite rooms, 'studios' with an additional double sofa bed and a spa bath, and seven airy, two-storey loft apartments that can sleep up to four people. Some rooms overlook Hyde Park. Perched above a busy bar, restaurant and gaming room complex, the noise is kept to a minimum with efficient soundproofing and window seals.

Concierge. Disabled-adapted rooms. Internet (dataport). No smoking. Parking ($40). TV (cable/DVD).

Lord Nelson Brewery Hotel

19 Kent Street, at Argyle Street, Millers Point, NSW 2000 (9251 4044/www.lordnelson.com.au). CityRail/ferry Circular Quay. **Rates** $130-$190 double. **Rooms** 9. **Credit** AmEx, DC, MC, V. **Map** p327 E3 ⑯

Time marches on, but you wouldn't know it at the Lord Nelson, whose motto is 'You've been praying, the Lord has delivered'. The clean and relatively spacious Victorian-style rooms with plantation shutters are air-conditioned, but the look and feel of the place

Blingpackers

Pensione.

They wear designer shades, customised Birkenstocks and smart jeans, and they wouldn't be seen dead with a koala hanging off their backpack: meet the blingpackers, a growing tribe of urban travellers who are shaping the future of the budget hotel industry in the Emerald City. The 'BPs', as they're known to the hostels and boutique hotels who are falling over themselves to win their custom, are an eclectic group. More than just your average gap-year backpacker, BPs are twenty- and thirty-somethings taking a career sabbatical, couples with children who want to put a 'travelling' spin on the school hols, new partners cementing their relationship with a few months on the road… the list goes on.

And in response to this new breed of tourist comes a more enloved species of low-rent accommodation. Exit bed bugs, rickety towering bunks, swirly carpets and bobbly blankets; enter a new era of slick, spotless hostels jostling for design kudos with contemporary furniture, up-to-the-minute bathrooms, kitchens, plush pillows, freshly ground coffee and perfectly mixed cocktails. To name a few names, you might want to swap peeling wallpaper for textbook *Wallpaper** at: **Legend Has It… Westend** (*see p37*), **Pensione** (*see p37*), **Railway Square YHA** (*see p37*), **Wake up!** (*see p39*), **Hotel Altamont** (*see p41*) and **Y Hotel City South** (*see p49*).

is pure 19th-century colonial – the pub opened in 1841 and claims to be the oldest in the city. There are only nine guest rooms, all with original bare sandstone walls, and, despite the antique feel, most come with en suite bathrooms. The laid-back downstairs brasserie hewn from the convict quarried sandstone serves contemporary Australian cuisine, while the bar, serving ploughmans' lunches, and the microbrewery (see p180) draw a lively crowd.
Bar. No smoking. Internet (dataport). Restaurant. TV.

Palisade Hotel

35 Bettington Street, at Argyle Street, Millers Point, NSW 2000 (9247 2272/www.palisadehotel.com). CityRail/ferry Circular Quay. **Rates** $123-$128 double. **Rooms** 8. **Credit** AmEx, DC, MC, V. **Map** p326 D3 ⓱
Things are pretty basic at the Palisade – there's no air-conditioning, lift or private bathrooms so think carefully about booking in high summer – but if you're looking for views and old-time charm at very affordable prices, this is a good choice. Another historic Rocks property, the hotel was built in 1916, and behind its imposing brown brick façade are a popular pub, with crackling log fires in winter, and a seriously good restaurant (see p146) that attracts the pre-theatre crowd. Tip: for the best harbour views, request one of the rooms on an upper floor.
Bar. No smoking. Restaurant.

Russell

143A George Street, at Globe Street, The Rocks, NSW 2000 (9241 3543/www.therussell.com.au). CityRail/ferry Circular Quay. **Rates** $150-$290 double. **Rooms** 29. **Credit** AmEx, DC, MC, V. **Map** p327 F4 ⓲
With a great location in the middle of the Rocks, just a stroll away from the hustle and bustle of Circular Quay, the Russell still somehow manages to feel more like a cosy country B&B than a city-centre hotel. Housed in a turreted 1887 building, rooms feature such period flourishes as ornate fireplaces, antique brass beds, marble washbasins, pine dressers and floral bedspreads and wallpapers. Some rooms are en suite, and some have portable air-conditioners and TVs. There's also the pleasant Acacia breakfast room on the ground floor, the historic Fortune of War pub and a tiny rooftop garden.
Bar. Internet (shared terminal). No smoking. Parking ($30). Restaurant. TV.

Budget

Legend Has It... Westend

412 Pitt Street, between Goulburn & Campbell Streets, CBD, NSW 2000 (1800 013 186/9211 4588/www.legendhasitwestend.com.au). CityRail Central or Museum/LightRail Central. **Rates** $30 dorm; $80 double. **Rooms** 90. **Credit** MC, V. **Map** p329 F8 ⓳
Who says backpackers have it rough? Located just around the corner from Central Station, this clean

and modern hotel is rightly popular with anyone on a budget, including families. There are laundry facilities, a commercial-grade kitchen, a café, plus extras geared toward working holidaymakers, such as an in-house travel agency and jobs board. There's always something going on here, making it the perfect option for travellers on their own – at the time of writing Friday is wine and cheese night and Saturday is barbie night. Rooms (most do come with air-conditioning) are either en suite or have a private bathroom adjacent. The reception is open 24 hours daily, breakfast is astonishingly good value at just two dollars and airport transfers are offered to guests staying for three or more nights.
Disabled-adapted room. Internet (high-speed pay terminal). No smoking. TV (TV room).

Pensione

631-635 George Street, between Goulburn & Campbell Streets, CBD, NSW 2000 (1800 885 886/9265 8888/www.pensione.com.au). CityRail Central/Monorail World Square. **Rates** $115 double. **Rooms** 72. **Credit** AmEx, DC, MC, V. **Map** p329 E8 ⓴
The Pensione is part of the Eight Hotels group of affordable, stylish hotels in central Sydney. On the edge of Chinatown opposite World Square, budget accommodation really doesn't come much better than this (although, as a result, you should choose your rooms wisely as it can get noisy). Yes, some rooms are very small, but they're all kitted out with a mini fridge, TV, air-con and phone, and feature modern tiled bathrooms that wouldn't look out of place in a glossy homes mag. There are around 15 family rooms, the largest sleeping up to six, so it's a good option for young families who want something urban and edgy. Other facilities include internet kiosks and wireless internet in the guest lounge, a kitchenette and a coin-operated laundry.
Bar. Disabled-adapted rooms. No smoking. Internet (wireless in guest lounge). Parking ($23). Restaurant. TV (cable).

Railway Square YHA

8-10 Lee Street, at Railway Square, Haymarket, NSW 2000 (9281 9666/www.yha.com.au). City Rail/LightRail Central. **Rates** $29.50-$33 dorm; $86-$107 double. **Rooms** 65. **Credit** MC, V. **Map** p329 E9 ㉑
This YHA hostel, built in a former parcels shed, is very near its Central counterpart (see p39). The design incorporates a real disused railway platform, with some dorms housed in replicas of train carriages (very Harry Potter); bathrooms in the main building adjacent. Most dorms have between four and eight beds, and there are a couple of en-suite double rooms. It's clean and bright, with a large open-plan communal area dotted with sofas, a sizeable kitchen, laundry facilities and an internet café. Mod cons include a fun small spa pool and air-conditioning. It's very popular, so book ahead.
Disabled-adapted rooms. Internet (high-speed pay terminals). No smoking. Pool (outdoor). Restaurant. TV (DVD/TV room).

Rooftop pool - Sydney Central YHA

Railway Square YHA

Sydney Central YHA

Scubar - Sydney Central YHA

Spa pool - Railway Square YHA

Carriage dorm - Railway Square YHA

Glebe Point YHA

Bondi Beachouse YHA

Sydney Beachouse YHA, Collaroy

Cronulla Beach YHA

BACKPACK SYDNEY
STAY WITH YHA

Whatever you want to see and do in Sydney, YHA has a hostel for you. From the city to the beach, 5 star luxury to working holiday accommodation, there are 6 YHA's to choose from.

Save 10% off as a YHA / Hostelling International member!

Sydney Central YHA	+61 2 9218 9000
Railway Square YHA	+61 2 9281 9666
Glebe Point YHA	+61 2 9692 8418
Bondi Beachouse YHA	+61 2 9365 2088
Sydney Beachouse YHA, Collaroy	+61 2 9981 1177
Cronulla Beach YHA	+61 2 9527 7772

AT LEAST
10% off
ACCOMMODATION
for all
YHA members

JOIN NOW

jump onboard, jump online > yha.com.au

HOSTELLING INTERNATIONAL

Sydney Central YHA

*11 Rawson Place, at Pitt Street, CBD, NSW 2000
(9218 9000/www.yha.com.au). CityRail/LightRail
Central.* **Rates** $35-$41.50 dorm; $100-$123
double/twin. **Rooms** 155. **Credit** MC, V.
Map p329 E9 ㉒

The largest of the YHA properties in Sydney, this
place has it all. Deep breath: kitchen, laundry, separate games, dining and TV rooms, high-speed internet terminals, mini supermarket, café, underground
bar and a rooftop pool, sauna and barbecue area
with panoramic city views. Popular activities
include pub crawls, big-screen movie nights and
walking tours. All of this is housed in an imposing,
heritage-listed building opposite Central Station.
There are around 50 twin rooms, some en suite, and
dorms that sleep up to eight.

*Bar. Disabled-adapted rooms. Internet (high-speed
pay terminals). No smoking. Parking ($14). Pool
(indoor). Restaurant. TV (TV rooms).*

Wake up!

*509 Pitt Street, at George Street, Haymarket,
NSW 2000 (1800 800 945/9288 7888/www.
wakeup.com.au). CityRail/LightRail Central.*
Rates $28-$36 dorm; $98-$108 double; $115 triple.
Rooms 500 beds. **Credit** MC, V. **Map** p329 E9 ㉓

Located opposite Central Station, this award-winning hostel is part of that new breed – big, clean, effi-
ciently run and with very proactive security, despite
the party atmosphere. A major refurbishment in
2006 has made it better than ever. The common
areas are like a twentysomething's dream, with circular sofas, a funky TV lounge, endless banks of
computers for internet use, a street café, kitchen,
laundry, ATMs and a travel agent to organise your
trips and help with finding work locally. The air-
conditioned dorms sleep four, six, eight or ten, and
some are women-only. There are also double and
twin rooms, some with private showers. Bedlinen is
provided and check-in is 24 hours.

*Bar. Disabled-adapted rooms. Internet (high-speed
pay terminals). No smoking. Restaurant. TV
(DVD/TV room).*

Y Hotel Hyde Park

*5-11 Wentworth Avenue, at Liverpool Street,
CBD, NSW 2010 (1800 994 994/9264 2451/www.
yhotel.com.au). CityRail Museum.* **Rates** $35 dorm;
$92-$142 double/twin. **Rooms** 121. **Credit** AmEx,
MC, DC, V. **Map** p329 G8 ㉔

Run by the venerable old YWCA, this spot attracts
all kinds (and both sexes), from budget-conscious
business travellers to families and young singles.
Deluxe rooms, corporate and studio rooms are all en
suite and come with TV, fridge and high-speed internet connection. Family rooms have three beds, while
backpacker rooms sleep four. All are clean and contemporary and have basic furniture. Rates include
continental or light breakfast; laundry facilities, a
café and a kitchen round off the services. The location, just south of Hyde Park, is fantastic.

*Business centre. Internet (wireless). No smoking.
Parking ($17.50). TV.*

Darling Harbour & Pyrmont

Deluxe

Star City Hotel & Serviced Apartments

*80 Pyrmont Street, between Jones Bay Road & Union
Street, Pyrmont, NSW 2000 (1800 700 700/9657
8393/www.starcity.com.au). LightRail Star City/
Monorail Harbourside/bus 443, 449.* **Rates** $390-
$525 double. **Rooms** 482. **Credit** AmEx, DC, MC, V.
Map p326 C6 ㉕

Gambling is big business in Australia. And nowhere
is it bigger than at this little slice of Las Vegas, Oz-
style. The numbers are dizzying: 306 standard
rooms, 43 suites with 24-hour butler service, two
penthouses, 131 fully serviced apartments (rates
from $550), 11 restaurants and bars, two theatres
and – of course – a casino that's open 24 hours a day.
Facilities include a spa and health club and an
indoor-outdoor pool with panoramic views of the
city. The Astral bar on the 17th floor has a large outdoor terrace with fantastic views.

*Bars (6). Business centre. Concierge. Disabled-
adapted rooms. Gym. Internet (high-speed). No-
smoking floors. Parking ($26). Pool (outdoor).
Restaurants (11). Room service. Spa. TV (cable/
pay movies/satellite).*

Expensive

Novotel Sydney on Darling Harbour

*100 Murray Street, at Allen Street, Darling
Harbour, NSW 2000 (1300 656 565/9934 0000/
www.novoteldarlingharbour.com.au). CityRail Town
Hall/Monorail/LightRail Convention.* **Rates** $372-
$458 double. **Rooms** 525. **Credit** AmEx, DC, MC, V.
Map p328 D7 ㉖

Next door to the Sydney Convention & Exhibition
Centre, the Novotel is aimed mainly at business travellers. As a result, all the rooms come stuffed with
communication gizmos such as LCD TVs, broadband and wireless internet access, and mobile
phone- and laptop-charging stations. The panoramic harbour and city views are lovely, and there's also
a swimming pool, tennis court, gym and sauna. The
hotel is home to Liquid – an average cocktail bar
with a good outdoor terrace – and a restaurant, Dish.

*Bar. Business centre. Concierge. Disabled-adapted
rooms. Gym. Internet (high-speed/wireless). No-
smoking floors. Parking ($30). Pool (outdoor).
Restaurant. Room service. TV (cable/pay movies).*

Moderate

Hotel Ibis Darling Harbour

*70 Murray Street, at Allen Street, Darling
Harbour, NSW 2000 (1300 656 565/9563
0888/www.accorhotels.com.au). CityRail Town
Hall/Monorail/LightRail Convention.* **Rates** $189-
$400 double. **Rooms** 256. **Credit** AmEx, DC, MC, V.
Map p326 D6 ㉗

Medusa.

This is a no-frills, get-what-you-pay-for option in a good location. The rooms are on the small side, but were refurbished with a cool new look in late 2007. For location alone it's still good value for your money, especially if you manage to get a cheap internet rate. Some rooms have views of Darling Harbour and the city, while others look over Pyrmont. The Ibistro bar and restaurant has an outdoor terrace. *Bar. Disabled-adapted rooms. Internet (high-speed). No-smoking floors. Parking ($25). Restaurant. TV (cable).*

Darlinghurst & Surry Hills

Expensive

Medusa

267 Darlinghurst Road, between Liverpool & William Streets, Darlinghurst, NSW 2010 (9331 1000/www. medusa.com.au). CityRail Kings Cross. **Rates** $310-$420 double. **Rooms** 18. **Credit** AmEx, DC, MC, V. **Map** p329 H8 ㉓

What's not to love about a heritage-listed Victorian mansion that's been painted pink? Embodying a very Darlinghurst sense of urban chic, the Medusa is an ode to colour and design, all interesting angles and bright flourishes of imagination. The lobby is pink, too, with bulging floral mouldings and an oversized paper chandelier. All rooms have luxe touch-

es like Aveda toiletries and fluffy bathrobes, plus a kitchenette and CD player. The expansive Grand Rooms feature period fireplaces, groovy chaises longues and a sitting area. The recently added business suite, including generous desk space and wireless internet, can be rented hourly, while rooms around the diminutive courtyard are pet friendly. *Business centre. Internet (wireless). No smoking. Room service. TV (cable/DVD).*

Moderate

Crown Hotel

589 Crown Street, at Cleveland Street, Surry Hills, NSW 2010 (9699 3460/www.crownhotel.com.au). Bus 352, 372, 393, 395. **Rates** $160-$200 double. **Rooms** 8. **Credit** MC, V. **Map** 329 G11 ㉙

This very hip yet thoroughly unpretentious complex opened in 2005, and there's nothing quite like it in Surry Hills, land of fab restaurants but very few hotels. On the ground floor is Players, an airy pub converted from an 1880s hotel, plus an upscale wine shop. Level two features Dome, a sexy cocktail bar complete with chandeliers, a glass bar and a huge mural based on François Boucher's baroque painting *Girl Reclining*. Last but not least are the hotel rooms, equally stylish and featuring deluxe extras such as L'Occitane bath products, Egyptian cotton bedlinen and wall-mounted 42-inch plasma screen TVs.

Bars (3). Disabled-adapted rooms. Internet (high-speed). No smoking. TV (cable/DVD).

Kirketon
229 Darlinghurst Road, between Farrell & Tewkesbury Avenues, Darlinghurst (1800 332 920/ 9332 2011/www.kirketon.com.au). CityRail Kings Cross. **Rates** $220-$365 double. **Rooms** 40. **Credit** AmEx, DC, MC, V. **Map** p330 H8 ③⓪
Originally built in the late 1930s and now one of the Eight Hotels group, owner of various budget boutique operations in Sydney, the Kirketon had a major refurbishment in 2007. Rooms today come with nice touches such as chocolates and Kevin Murphy toiletries, and the overall design is contemporary minimalist, with rich colours and slick bathrooms with showers. The dining room and bar – where chef Eric Tan serves ultra-modern international cuisine – remain popular with locals.
Bar. Concierge. Internet (wireless). No smoking. Parking ($25). Restaurant. TV (cable/DVD/VCR).

Budget

Hotel Altamont
207 Darlinghurst Road, between Liverpool & William Streets, Darlinghurst, NSW 2010 (1800 991 110/ 9360 6000/www.altamont.com.au). CityRail Kings Cross. **Rates** $109-$129 double. **Rooms** 15. **Credit** AmEx, MC, V. **Map** p330 H8 ③①

This is the hotel equivalent of Stella McCartney designing a collection for H&M – luxury on a sensible budget. The Altamont (part of the Eight Hotels stable) is housed in a colonial Georgian mansion that has been given an elegant, thoroughly contemporary makeover. There are skylights throughout the hotel, a glass-fronted, light-filled lobby and lounge, heavy custom-built wooden beds and dressers in the very spacious bedrooms, and a lovely, ornate Tuscan roof terrace. The loft suite was once the VIP room of the famous Cauldron nightclub, frequented by the likes of Mick Jagger and accessed by a stairway hidden away from the lenses of roving paparazzi. Rooms range from the said airy suite with its soaring ceilings and walk-in wardrobe to family rooms suitable for six with a combination of bunk beds and king or queen beds. Unsurprisingly, it's hugely popular, so it's best to book well in advance.
Bar. Internet (wireless high-speed). No smoking. Parking ($15). TV (cable/DVD).

Kings Cross, Potts Point & Woolloomooloo

Deluxe

Blue, Woolloomooloo Bay
Woolloomooloo Wharf, 6 Cowper Wharf Road, opposite Forbes Street, Woolloomooloo, NSW 2011 (9331 9000/www.tajhotels.com). CityRail Kings Cross then 10 min walk or bus 311. **Rates** $415-$875 double. **Rooms** 100. **Credit** AmEx, DC, MC, V. **Map** p330 H6 ③②
The former W hotel in the historic Woolloomooloo Wharf is now owned by Taj, India's luxury hotel and resort chain. While the edge may have been blunted a little, it's still a funky, alternative hotel with lots to offer those who like something a bit different from their five-star hangout. The plush rooms feature original elements from the old wharf building, and there's a fitness centre, indoor pool and the very popular Water Bar (*see p184*). The hotel has no restaurant, but there's an array of high-class, high-priced eateries along the marina edge of the wharf (rooms on this side have the best views). The hotel occupies only part of the swanky wharf development; there's also a complex of exclusive apartments and the deluxe Spa Chakra, which is pricey but divine.
Bar. Business centre. Concierge. Disabled-adapted room. Gym. Internet (high-speed). No-smoking floors. Parking ($40). Pool (indoor). Room service. Spa. TV (cable/DVD/pay movies).

Expensive

Diamant Hotel
14 Kings Cross Road, at Penny's Lane, Potts Point, NSW 2011 (1800 816 168/9295 8888/8899/ www.diamant.com.au). CityRail Kings Cross. **Rates** $400-$600 double. **Rooms** 76. **Credit** AmEx, DC, MC, V. **Map** p330 J7 ③③

This new boutique hotel features the best accommodation in the area. It's part of the Eight Hotels group (which also owns the Altamont and Kirkton in Darlinghurst and the Pensione in the CBD) and is undoubtedly the swishest addition to the set. A major feature is that all rooms have opening windows – this may not sound revolutionary, but in a city of air-conditioned high-rise towers, it's quite a boast. Bells and whistles include 42-inch plasma-screen TVs, iPod docks and DVD and CD players. Some rooms have private courtyards with comfy furniture, while the Harbour View Room has just that, with the bridge bang centre. The Penny's Lane restaurant (see p158) is already a local favourite. *Bar. Business centre. Concierge. Internet (high-speed wireless). Parking ($35). Restaurant. Room service. TV.*

Moderate

Simpsons of Potts Point

8 Challis Avenue, at Victoria Street, Potts Point, NSW 2011 (9356 2199/www.simpsonshotel.com). CityRail Kings Cross. **Rates** $235-$325 double. **Rooms** 12. **Credit** AmEx, DC, MC, V. **Map** p330 J6 ㉞

A very elegant and charming place, combining the stylishness and comforts of a boutique hotel with the informal sociability of a B&B. Located at the quieter end of a tree-lined street, the lovingly restored mansion was built in 1892 and still retains many of its original Arts and Crafts details. The high-ceilinged guest rooms are old-fashioned, but elegantly so, and by no means dowdy. This is the life: sipping a free port and sherry by an open hearth in winter (OK, the fires are gas-powered imitations), tucking into a continental breakfast in the conservatory, thumbing through the hardbacks in the library… Book well in advance as Simpsons gets a lot of repeat business, and note that it doesn't have a licence to sell alcohol. *Internet (wireless). No smoking. Parking (free). TV.*

Victoria Court Hotel

122 Victoria Street, between Orwell & Hughes Streets, Potts Point, NSW 2011 (1800 630 505/ 9357 3200/www.victoriacourt.com.au). CityRail Kings Cross. **Rates** $88-$250 double. **Rooms** 22. **Credit** AmEx, DC, MC, V. **Map** p330 J6 ㉟

Leafy Victoria Street is an interesting mix of posh restaurants, ramshackle youth hostels and converted Victorian mansions – all just around the corner from the strip clubs and general sleaze of Kings Cross. This small hotel, formed from two 1881 terraced houses, is a celebration of Victorian extravagance, from the four-poster beds to the floral-printed everything (carpeting, curtains, wallpaper). All rooms are air-conditioned and have private bathrooms; some have marble fireplaces and wrought-iron balconies. Breakfast is served in the gorgeous plant-filled courtyard around a bubbling fountain. *Internet (dataport/high-speed pay terminal). No smoking. Parking ($11). TV.*

Budget

Eva's Backpackers

6-8 Orwell Street, at Victoria Street, Kings Cross, NSW 2011 (1800 802 517/9358 2185/www. evasbackpackers.com.au). CityRail Kings Cross. **Rates** $30 dorm; $80 double. **Rooms** 28. **Credit** MC, V. **Map** p330 J6 ㊱

With its friendly, laid-back atmosphere and reputation for being very clean and quiet (rare for a backpackers' hostel in this neighbourhood), Eva's has rightfully gained a following. There are twin, double and dorm rooms, some en suite, some with air-conditioning. Extras include free breakfast, a kitchen, a laundry room with free washing powder, wake-up calls, luggage storage facilities, broadband internet access and a rooftop terrace and barbecue area with fabulous views over Sydney. Located at the (less dodgy) Potts Point end of Kings Cross, it's on a quiet street, but close to everything. *Internet (shared terminal). No smoking. TV (DVD/TV room).*

Hotel Formule 1 Kings Cross

191-201 William Street, between Forbes Street & Kirketon Road, Kings Cross, NSW 2011 (9326 0300/www.formule1.com.au). CityRail Kings Cross. **Rates** $89 double. **Rooms** 115. **Credit** AmEx, DC, MC, V. **Map** p330 H7 ㊲

The Accor Group budget hotel with a chequered flag logo – the idea is you're having a pitstop, get it? – is basic, but clean and very functional with bunk, twin or double beds, en suite bathroom and in-room TVs. Set on the busy part of William Street, it can feel like you're on a race track at times, and don't expect any special comforts, but everything you need is here. There's no restaurant, but with Kings Cross and Darlinghurst on your doorstep you won't starve. *Disabled-adapted rooms. No smoking. Internet (shared terminal). Parking ($20). TV (pay movies).*

O'Malley's Hotel

228 William Street, at Brougham Street, Kings Cross, NSW 2011 (9357 2211/www.omalleyshotel. com.au). CityRail Kings Cross. **Rates** $79 double. **Rooms** 15. **Credit** MC, V. **Map** p330 H7 ㊳

It may be attached to a popular Irish pub and live music venue, and, yes, it's dangerously close to everything that's wrong with Kings Cross, but don't write off O'Malley's. The 1907 building's rooms are all en suite and feature lovely period touches along with old-fashioned charm. The location is quite convenient, too: just two minutes from the rail station. The Harbour View suite has a kitchen. *Bar. No smoking. TV.*

Original Backpackers Lodge

160-162 Victoria Street, between Darlinghurst Road & Orwell Street, Kings Cross, NSW 2011 (9356 3232/www.originalbackpackers.com.au). CityRail Kings Cross. **Rates** $30 dorm; $75-$95 double/twin. **Rooms** 35. **Credit** MC, V. **Map** p330 J7 ㊴

Established in 1980, this sprawling hostel in a Victorian mansion may look a little on the lived-in

side, but it has plenty of character – not to mention lots of extras such as a lovely spacious courtyard, free bedlinen and towels, 24-hour check-in and complimentary airport pick-up (very welcome after spending a day on an aeroplane). There are single, double and family rooms as well as ten-person dorms, some of which are women-only. All rooms have televisions and fridges, and some have balconies, although most bathroom facilities are shared. There's usually something going on in the courtyard, whether it's karaoke or an Aussie barbie. The kitchen is big and modern, with food lockers, and there are laundry facilities available as well.
Internet (high-speed, pay terminals). No smoking. TV (cable/DVD/TV room).

Paddington, Woollahra & Double Bay

Deluxe

Stamford Plaza Double Bay
33 Cross Street, between Bay Street & New South Head Road, Double Bay, NSW 2028 (1300 301 391/9362 4455/www.stamford.com.au). Ferry Double Bay/bus 323, 324, 325, 326, 327. **Rates** $500-$550 double. **Rooms** 140. **Credit** AmEx, DC, MC, V. **Map** p331 N7 ⓵
There's a distinctly old-money vibe to the Stamford Plaza, whose guest list has included everyone from American presidents to European and Hollywood royalty (so the brochure proudly claims). Rooms feature traditional furniture, 18th-century paintings and balconies overlooking the courtyard or the yachts in Double Bay. On the top floor is an impressive presidential suite with its own marble foyer entrance, four balconies looking over the harbour and a dining room for private parties. There's a rooftop (heated) pool and terrace accessible to all guests, and high tea in the antiques-filled lobby lounge is a very chic affair. The Bay Grill restaurant offers smart dining, while Winston's Lounge, with its chandeliers and grand piano, has the aura of an old-fashioned private club but serves casual food including Singaporean dishes and pizza.
Bar. Business centre. Concierge. Disabled-adapted rooms. Gym. Internet (high-speed). No-smoking floors. Parking ($20). Pool (outdoor). Restaurant. Room service. TV (cable/pay movies).

Moderate

Hughenden Hotel
14 Queen Street, at Oxford Street, Woollahra, NSW 2025 (9363 4863/1800 642 432/www.hughenden hotel.com.au). Bus 333, 352, 378, 380. **Rates** $158-$268 double. **Rooms** 36. **Credit** AmEx, DC, MC, V. **Map** p332 L11 ⓵
This four-star boutique hotel was thought to be a lost cause when sisters Elizabeth and Susanne Gervay bought it back in 1992. But instead they set about transforming the crumbling, grand 1870s mansion into what it is today: an award-winning hotel offering sophisticated modern accommodation in comfortable old-world surroundings. All rooms are en suite, and there's also an attached four-bed terraced house that can be rented in its entirety. Elizabeth is an artist and Susanne an author, so literary events and art exhibitions take place regularly. There's a cosy lounge, an old-fashioned bar with a baby grand piano (played once a month by talented night porter Victor) and a sun terrace. Quaife's restaurant is named after the original owner, founder of the colony's medical association, and serves bistro-style dishes in generous portions. Three rooms are designated as pet friendly.
Bar. Disabled-adapted rooms. Internet (wireless). No smoking. Parking (free). Restaurant. Room service. TV.

Sullivans Hotel
21 Oxford Street, between Greens Road & Verona Street, Paddington, NSW 2021 (9361 0211/www. sullivans.com.au). Bus 352, 378, 380, L82. **Rates** $165-$180 double. **Rooms** 64. **Credit** AmEx, DC, MC, V. **Map** p332 H9 ⓵
This exceedingly friendly, family-run hotel has a great location in Paddington, with fabulous independent cinemas and bookshops virtually outside the door. The central business and shopping districts, as well as the eastern suburbs' beaches, are also just a short bus ride away. All rooms have private bathrooms, and there are some interconnecting family rooms available as well. You can make the most of the weather with the solar-heated pool and garden courtyard, or just relax in the ground-floor breakfast room overlooking busy Oxford Street. The hotel's owners also rent out their alpine chalet (three beds, two baths) in the Blue Mountains.
Disabled-adapted rooms. Gym. Internet (high-speed wireless). No smoking. Parking (free). Pool (outdoor). TV.

Vibe Rushcutters
100 Bayswater Road, next to Rushcutters Bay Park, Rushcutters Bay, NSW 2011 (13 8423/8353 8988/ www.vibehotels.com.au). CityRail Edgecliff or Kings Cross. **Rates** $310-$330 double. **Rooms** 245. **Credit** AmEx, DC, MC, V. **Map** p330 K7 ⓵
The Vibe hotel chain tries to be many things at once – stylish, affordable, young – and, by and large, it succeeds in achieving these goals. Rooms may be on the small side but they get lots of light, and facilities here include a spacious fitness centre with steam room. While the rooftop pool is a little exposed on windy days, its panoramic vista of Rushcutters Bay Park (great for jogging), the water and the city is superb. There's a cocktail bar, and a restaurant with a pleasant covered terrace. There are two other Vibes in town: one in North Sydney and one on Goulburn Street in the city.
Bar. Business Centre. Concierge. Disabled-adapted rooms. Gym. Internet (high-speed/wireless). No-smoking floors. Parking ($16.50). Pool (outdoor). Restaurant. Room service. TV (cable/pay movies).

Budget

Golden Sheaf Hotel

429 New South Head Road, at Knox Street, Double Bay, NSW 2023 (9327 5877/www.goldensheaf. com.au). Ferry Double Bay/bus 323, 324, 325, 326, 327. **Rates** *$90 double.* **Rooms** *9.* **Credit** *AmEx, MC, V.* **Map** *p331 N8* 44

This art deco pub (a long-time meeting spot for posh young eastern-suburbs types) has always been known for its lovely, leafy beer garden. But a refurbishment a few years ago saw the creation of nine handsome and large en suite rooms, all pared down and modern in design, though some original details were allowed to remain. Such cheap accommodation is a rare find in fancy Double Bay, but be warned: don't expect much peace and quiet, especially in summer – the pub hosts DJs and live music performances nearly every night of the week.

Bars (5). No smoking. Parking (free). Restaurant. TV (cable).

Bondi & Coogee Beaches

Expensive

Swiss-Grand Resort & Spa

180-186 Campbell Parade, Bondi Beach, NSW 2026 (1800 655 252/9365 5666/www.swissgrand.com.au). CityRail Bondi Junction then bus 333, 380, 381, 382/bus 333, 380. **Rates** *$215-$1,200 double.* **Rooms** *202.* **Credit** *AmEx, DC, MC, V.* **Map** *p334* 43

The Swiss-Grand Resort & Spa may do a mean imitation of a wedding cake (all gleaming white columns and tiered levels), but it's still the classiest hotel to be found in Bondi – which says something about the state of the area's accommodation, since parts of the building are starting to look a little on the tired side. But change is in the air: seven new private courtyard suites (with their own barbecues) are now open, along with six family suites. Rooms are spacious, with two TVs, separate bath and shower, minibar and bathrobes. There's a rooftop pool and an indoor lap pool, a very good fitness centre, and the renowned Samsara Day Spa, offering Balinese treatments. The Epic Brasserie serves decent seafood, while the classiest of the three bars (the outdoor Deck Bar) rustles up tasty barbecue.

Bars (3). Business centre. Concierge. Disabled-adapted rooms. Gym. Internet (high-speed shared terminal). No smoking. Parking ($15). Pools (1 indoor, 1 outdoor). Restaurants (2). Spa. Room service. TV (cable/pay movies).

Moderate

Coogee Bay Hotel

Corner of Arden Street & Coogee Bay Road, Coogee Beach, NSW 2034 (9665 0000/www.coogeebayhotel. com.au). Bus 372, 373, 374. **Rates** *$130-$330 double.* **Rooms** *74.* **Credit** *AmEx, DC, MC, V.*

Hughenden Hotel.

The award-winning Coogee Bay Hotel has been operating on the same site since 1873 – though it's had a few face-lifts in that time. Not exactly a quiet beachside retreat, this complex is very big and very busy. The brasserie serves hearty fare for breakfast (included in the room price), lunch and dinner seven days a week, and there are several different bars (*see p185*) including a spacious 'sports bar' whose big-screen aesthetic is offset with a tapas menu ('to attract a female crowd'). The Boutique wing has spacious and modern rooms with marble bathrooms, balconies and, in some rooms, kitchenettes. The Heritage wing is more basic. Rooms have been recently refurbished throughout with a crisp white, blue and natural timber beachside effect.
Bars (6). Disabled-adapted rooms. Internet (high-speed). No smoking. Parking (free). Restaurant. TV (cable/VCR/in-house movies).

Dive Hotel

234 Arden Street, opposite the beach, Coogee Beach, NSW 2034 (9665 5538/www.divehotel.com.au). Bus 372, 373, 374. **Rates** $165-$280 double. **Rooms** 16. **Credit** MC, V.
A smart and elegant guesthouse, the Dive Hotel's contemporary design centres on bold colours, polished wood and clean, crisp bedlinen. Its cosy, sun-filled breakfast room looks out on to a bamboo-bordered garden, while views of the ocean from some of the rooms are equally wonderful. All rooms are en suite, with a microwave, fridge, TV and VCR, and while the bathrooms may be small, they are stylishly fitted out with mosaic tiles and stainless steel sinks. The annex – a three-bed house two blocks from the beach – accommodates families. Dive is a disarmingly welcoming place, thanks to its gracious owners Terry Bunton and Mercedes Mariano and their poodle (Babe), retriever (George) and cat (Bob) who help take the sharpness off the style. At the time of writing, the addition of a 17th (luxury) guest room was planned.
Internet (wireless/high-speed). No smoking. Parking ($20). TV (cable).

Hotel Bondi

178 Campbell Parade, at Curlewis Street, Bondi Beach, NSW 2026 (9130 3271/www.hotelbondi.com.au). CityRail Bondi Junction then bus 333, 380, 381, 382/bus 333, 380. **Rates** $105-$165 double. **Rooms** 50. **Credit** AmEx, MC, V. **Map** p334 ⑥
The fun never stops at Hotel Bondi, where a bewildering array of distractions are on offer to guests, from snacking at the Bondi Grill restaurant to partying at the vast open-plan Starfish, Sand or Bombora bars. It may not be cutting-edge, but it's very convenient – plus there are pool tables, a gaming room, big-screen TVs showing sporting events, two bottle shops, a beer garden and, of course, guest rooms. Many have beach views, others have verandas, and most are en suite with air-conditioning. And fear not: all rooms are soundproofed.
Bars (3). No smoking. Parking (free). Restaurant. TV.

Ravesi's

118 Campbell Parade, at Hall Street, Bondi Beach, NSW 2026 (9365 4422/www.ravesis.com.au). CityRail Bondi Junction then bus 333, 380, 381, 382/bus 333, 380. **Rooms** 12. **Credit** AmEx, DC, MC, V. **Map** p334 ⑰
Ravesi's is known primarily for its noisy street-level bar, but upstairs you'll also find this chic boutique hotel. All rooms have private bathrooms and are impeccably furnished: the designs, courtesy of renowned abstract artist Dane van Bree, use a palette of Aboriginal colours – mainly black, copper and bronze. The split-level suites have private terraces and superb sea views.
Bars (2). Internet (high-speed/wireless). No smoking. Parking ($8 per 24hrs). Restaurant. Room service. TV (cable/DVD).

Budget

Lamrock Lodge

19 Lamrock Avenue, at Consett Avenue, Bondi Beach, NSW 2026 (9130 5063/www.lamrocklodge.com). CityRail Bondi Junction then bus 333, 380, 381, 382/bus 333, 380. **Rates** $23-$45 dorm; $54-$80 double/twin. **Rooms** 55. **Credit** AmEx, MC, V. **Map** p334 ⑱
A good bet for the more mature backpacker looking for somewhere cheap and not too raucous to stay. The Lamrock is located on a quiet street 100m from Bondi Beach, and it's a very clean, well-maintained place, now sporting funky new bamboo flooring. All rooms have TVs, microwaves and fridges, and there are four-bed dorms with rates that get better the longer you stay. Furniture and decor are in typical hostel style (bedlinen, quilts and pillows are supplied), and there are plenty of vending machines (in addition to the kitchen and laundry). Friendly, helpful staff and 24-hour security help to create a genuinely relaxed and easy-going vibe.
Internet (pay terminal, wireless). No smoking. TV (cable).

Inner West

Moderate

Tricketts Luxury B&B

270 Glebe Point Road, opposite Leichhardt Street, Glebe, NSW 2037 (9552 1141/www.tricketts.com.au). LightRail Jubilee Park/bus 431, 434. **Rates** $198-$245 double. **Rooms** 7. **Credit** AmEx, DC, MC, V.
A haven for antiques lovers, Tricketts has spared no detail, from the ornate moulded ceilings and imposing original cedar staircase to the cut-crystal glassware in the bedrooms and persian rugs, to establish its periods credentials. Practically everything you can see is a collectable. A wealthy merchant's house in the 1880s, a boys' home in the 1920s and then a children's courthouse, 270 Glebe Point Road has been many things to many people, but as

Jonah's.

a B&B it may have finally found its ultimate role. The seven guest rooms (one king-, five queen- and one twin-bedded room) are decorated in different styles, but all are en suite, and two are aimed at honeymooners (that is, they have four-poster beds). In summer breakfast is served on the rear deck; in the cooler months it is in the conservatory.

Internet (high-speed/wireless). No smoking. Parking (free). TV.

Budget

Alishan International Guesthouse

100 Glebe Point Road, between Mitchell Street & St Johns Road, Glebe, NSW 2037 (9566 4048/ www.alishan.com.au). LightRail Glebe/bus 370, 431, 432, 433, 434. **Rates** $25-$33 dorm; $99-$115 double. **Rooms** 19. **Credit** AmEx, MC, V. **Map** p328 B9 ⑲

Conveniently located among the cafés, bookshops and restaurants that line Glebe Point Road, this converted century-old mansion is a good Inner West option for those on a budget. The spacious lounge-diner sports a smart stone floor and rattan furnishings, and the very large commercial-grade kitchen is for guests to use (no meals are provided). There are dorms, simple single, double and family rooms, plus a Japanese-style twin room with low beds and tatami mats. Some of the rooms do come with private bathrooms but note that none of them have air-conditioning or an in-room phone.

Disabled-adapted rooms. Internet (pay terminal/high-speed wireless). No smoking. Parking ($5 dorm guests; free other guests). TV (DVD/TV room).

Australian Sunrise Lodge

485 King Street, between Camden & Alice Streets, Newtown, NSW 2042 (9550 4999/www.australian sunriselodge.com). CityRail Newtown. **Rates** $99-$119 double. **Rooms** 22. **Credit** AmEx, DC, MC, V. **Map** p334 ㊿

Established in 1990, this friendly, family-run inn is cosy and surprisingly quiet (given its location on King Street – Newtown's main drag). In 2007, a much-needed renovation spruced the place up with a new reception area, leather sofas in the lounge, new carpet throughout and a spanking new kitchen. Guest rooms have a TV, fridge, microwave, tea and coffee facilities, and kitchen utensils. Some have balconies overlooking a courtyard and are en suite, but none have a telephone or air-con (though there are ceiling fans). The lodge is recommended by Sydney University for off-campus accommodation, so expect a distinctly studenty clientele.

Disabled-adapted rooms. No smoking. Parking (free). TV.

Billabong Gardens

5-11 Egan Street, at King Street, Newtown, NSW 2042 (9550 3236/www.billabonggardens.com.au). CityRail Newtown. **Rates** $23-$25 dorm; $69-$89 double. **Rooms** 36. **Credit** MC, V. **Map** p334 ㊿

Bohemian, bright and arty, the decor at this Newtown hostel-motel is a patchwork of bright colours, exposed brick and crazy patterns. Set just off the bustling environs of King Street, it attracts artists and musos, even offering special deals for visiting bands, including space to store their equipment. The place is clean and all rooms have ceiling fans and wireless internet. Some rooms have TVs

North Shore

Expensive

Rydges North Sydney

54 McLaren Street, between Miller & Walker Streets, North Sydney, NSW 2060 (1300 857 922/9922 1311/www.rydges.com). CityRail North Sydney. **Rates** $350-$370 double. **Rooms** 166. **Credit** AmEx, DC, MC, V.

North Sydney, with all its office towers and corporate headquarters, means business. So it's no surprise that the Rydges caters mostly to business travellers. All rooms have a private bath and shower, and many of the deluxe rooms and suites have beautiful views over the harbour. There are also 18 'iRooms' with a computer and unlimited internet access, as well as executive boardrooms, video-conferencing facilities and even a conference concierge service. The hotel has spent millions of dollars on its new back-friendly 'dream beds', so at least there's a good night's kip to look forward to after a hard day at the office.

Bar. Business centre. Internet (high-speed). No-smoking floors. Parking ($15). Restaurant. Room service. TV (cable/pay movies).

Budget

Glenferrie Lodge

12A Carabella Street, between Peel Street & Kirribilli Avenue, Kirribilli, NSW 2061 (9955 1685/www. glenferrielodge.com). Ferry Kirribilli. **Rates** $40-$60 dorm; $109-$189 double. **Rooms** 70. **Credit** MC, V. **Map** p334 ⊕

A swish, three-star, harbour-front B&B just seven minutes by ferry from Circular Quay, this pretty, rambling house boasts spotless facilities and ample bathrooms. Air-conditioning may not be installed in the guest rooms – at least that means your sinuses won't dry out – but they do have ceiling fans and there's a lovely harbour breeze to ensure that the nights never get too stuffy. The guest lounge offers cable TV and wireless internet access, and the dining room serves dinner five nights a week. The pet-friendly policy means the critters can come too.

Internet (wireless/high-speed). No smoking. TV (cable).

Northern Beaches

Deluxe

Jonah's

69 Bynya Road, between Norma & Surf Road, Palm Beach, NSW 2108 (9974 5599/www.jonahs.com.au). Bus 190, L90. **Rates** $449-$799 double. **Rooms** 12. **Credit** AmEx, DC, MC, V.

You'll have a whale of a time at Jonah's – provided, that is, you can afford room rates that verge on the leviathan. Everything here is geared to the big

and fridges, but note that none of them have air-conditioning. Other pluses include a large modern kitchen, laundry, solar-heated pool, TV room and a lovely, leafy courtyard. Staff are extremely friendly and more than willing to help guests with everything from organising tours to finding work on an organic farm via the World Wide Opportunities on Organic Farms association.

Internet (wireless). No smoking. Parking ($5). Pool (outdoor). TV (TV room).

Y Hotel City South

179 Cleveland Street, at Regent Street, Chippendale (1800 300 882/8303 1303/www.yhotel.com.au). CityRail Central/LightRail Central. **Rates** $30 dorm; $118-$125 double. **Rooms** 60. **Credit** AmEx, DC, MC, V. **Map** p334 ⊕

Close to Sydney University, Prince Alfred Park (with its great pool), Broadway, Glebe and Newtown, this architect-designed new boutique hotel is quite a find. It's run by the YWCA (*see p39*) and is a joy to stay in, as evidenced by its diverse clientele – everyone from low-key backpackers and families through to business people. In-room broadband, air-conditioning and chic contemporary decor make for comfortable surroundings, while a decent gym, outdoor terrace, rooftop garden, secure on-site parking and the usual laundry and kitchen facilities are added bonuses. If you're feeling flush (or have up to five in your party), the tranquil and very comfortable apartment, with two large bedrooms, two bathrooms, courtyards, fully equipped kitchen, living and dining area, is wonderful.

Gym. Internet (kiosk/wireless broadband). No smoking. Parking ($7). TV.

spenders – the hotel was incorporated into the exclusive Relais & Chateaux group at the end of 2007. All of the dozen suites (including the particularly luxurious penthouse) are plushly furnished in contemporary style and have stunning views over Whale Beach from their private balconies. King-sized beds, limestone bathrooms with whirlpool spas and Bulgari toiletries are just some of the pampering touches you can expect. Friday and Saturday rates include the unmissable dinner and breakfast at the renowned restaurant (see p169), and if you really want to put the rubber stamp of luxury on the whole experience, why not skip the car journey and fly up by seaplane from Rose Bay?

Bar. No smoking. Parking (free). Pool (outdoor). Restaurant. Room service. TV (cable/DVD).

Expensive

Manly Pacific Sydney

55 North Steyne, between Raglan & Denison Streets, Manly, NSW 2095 (9977 7666/www.accorhotels. com.au). Ferry Manly. **Rates** $397-$482 double. **Rooms** 214. **Credit** AmEx, DC, MC, V. **Map** p334 ⑤4

Formerly known as the Manly Pacific Parkroyal, this four-star hotel overlooking Manly Beach was bought out by the multinational Accor chain in 2003. Since then, 52 courtyard rooms have been added, and various refurbishments undertaken. A heated outdoor pool, a rooftop fitness centre, sauna and spa ensure that guests get plenty of opportunities to burn off any of the calories they might have gained at the hotel's restaurant, Zali's, which provides an upmarket café menu in the evenings and a Mediterranean buffet on Saturday evening and Sunday lunch. Alternatively, the Corso, Manly's pedestrian shopping and café strip, is within easy walking distance, and central Sydney is only a half-hour ferry ride away.

Bars (2). Business Centre. Concierge. Disabled-adapted rooms. Gym. Internet (high-speed/wireless). No smoking. Parking ($18-$25). Pool (outdoor). Restaurant. Room service. Spa. TV (cable/in-house movies).

Moderate

Barrenjoey House

1108 Barrenjoey Road, opposite Palm Beach Wharf, Palm Beach, NSW 2108 (9974 4001/www.barren joeyhouse.com.au). Bus 190, L90. **Rates** $180-$220 double. **Rooms** 7. **Credit** AmEx, DC, MC, V.

The atmosphere at the Barrenjoey is relaxed and beachy, with white-painted walls, white furniture and the odd touch of rattan or bamboo, all punctuated by colourful sprays of fresh-cut flowers. A guesthouse since 1923, it has three en suite rooms and four with shared bathrooms – all are spotless and comfortable. The front rooms are best, as they overlook sparkling Pittwater. The café-restaurant, with its convivial terrace in summer and roaring fire

in colder months, is a perennial meeting spot for both locals and tourists drawn to the sights of Palm Beach. Unsurprisingly, given the decor of the hotel, the restaurant's speciality is seafood.

Bar. No smoking. Restaurant. TV (TV room).

Newport Arms Hotel

Corner of Beaconsfield & Kalinya Streets, Newport, NSW 2106 (9997 4900/www.newportarms.com.au). Bus 188, L88, 190, L90. **Rates** $160-$170 double. **Rooms** 9. **Credit** AmEx, DC, MC, V.

To mark its 127th birthday, the Newport Arms was given a complete face lift in 2007, but despite its swish new look, it remains a firm favourite with local families for its child-friendly restaurant and playgrounds. On the shores of Pittwater, which is about a 40-minute drive from the CBD or 15 minutes from Palm Beach, the Newport is close, but thankfully not too close, to the action. There are eight doubles, all with basic furniture and private bathrooms, and one family room that sleeps six. The hotel also houses a very popular pub (see p187), with cheap drinks and live music. The waterfront beer garden features the new Garden Bistro, two new bars and an all-weather dining area.

Bars (5). No smoking. Parking (free). Restaurants (3). TV.

Periwinkle Guest House

18-19 East Esplanade, at Ashburner Streeet, Manly, NSW 2095 (9977 4668/www.periwinkle.citysearch. com.au). Ferry Manly. **Rates** $137-$195 double. **Rooms** 18. **Credit** MC, V. **Map** p334 ⑤5

Perched above the waters of tranquil Manly Cove, within walking distance of the ferry wharf, this 1895 Federation building has iron-lace verandas and lots of period charm without feeling in any way stuffy. The 18 colourful bedrooms have ceiling fans, fireplaces and cane furniture; 12 of them are en suite. Heaters and electric blankets are provided in the winter. Guests can use the kitchen and laundry, and there's a courtyard with seating.

No smoking. Parking (free). TV (TV room).

Budget

Pittwater YHA

Morning Bay, Pittwater, NSW 2105 (9999 5748/ www.yha.com.au). Reception open 8-11am, 5-8pm daily. Ferry/water taxi Halls Wharf then 15min walk. **Rates** $25-$28 dorm; $65-$72 double. **Rooms** 8. **Credit** MC, V.

If you're looking for a real Australian bush experience within the city limits of Sydney, then head here. Overlooking pretty Morning Bay, this recently refurbished stone-and-wood hillside lodge is hidden in the trees in Ku-ring-gai Chase National Park. You can't get here by car, but it's worth the arduous journey – an hour's bus to Church Point, a ferry to Halls Wharf, then a steep, 15-minute climb through the bush – because the wildlife all around is breathtaking. Red and green rosellas, laughing kookaburras, wallabies, possums and goannas are just a few of the native Aussie animals you're likely to spot here. Guests can hire canoes and kayaks or swim in the bay, and there are women-only massage workshops once or twice a year. It's BYO food (there are no shops) and bedlinen, or you can hire the latter subject to water availability; no sleeping bags are allowed. It's incredibly popular, so advance bookings are essential. There are also kitchen and laundry facilities and, of course, a barbie. **Photo** *p52.* *No smoking.*

Sydney Beachhouse YHA

4 Collaroy Street, at Pittwater Road, Collaroy, NSW 2097 (9981 1177/www.yha.com.au). Bus 188, L88, 190, L90. **Rates** $23-$39 dorm; $63-$100 double. **Rooms** 60. **Credit** MC, V.

Who needs the glamour and glitz of Palm Beach when Collaroy's got charm to burn and much, much lower prices? This YHA hostel is one of the best budget options in the northern beaches, with bright, clean rooms and plenty of extras (check out the hilarious inflatable surf machine). There are four-person dormitories, twins and family rooms, free surfboards, boogie boards and bicycles to borrow, and a compact, solar-heated outdoor pool. You won't be bored – other facilities include a kitchen, a barbecue area, arcade games, pool table and internet café. *Disabled-adapted room (family). Internet (pay terminals). No smoking. Parking (free). Pool (outdoor). TV (cable/DVD/free movies/TV room).*

The South

Expensive

Novotel Brighton Beach

Corner of Grand Parade & Princess Street, Brighton-le-Sands, NSW 2216 (1300 656 565/ 9556 5111/www.novotelbrightonbeach.com.au). CityRail Rockdale then bus 475, 478, 479/bus 303, X03. **Rates** $219-$429 double. **Rooms** 296. **Credit** AmEx, DC, MC, V.

The family-friendly Novotel Brighton Beach is full of extras that help to make up for its rather uninspiring decor – an overhead walkway to the beach, a pool with outdoor slide for the kiddies, tennis court, fitness centre and a spa offering all the usual treatments. The Baygarden restaurant, on the third floor with a swanky, brand-new terrace, has views over the bay and serves modern Australian cuisine, and the cocktail bar also has a fine prospect. The hotel is five minutes from Sydney International Airport (25 minutes from downtown), thus making it a convenient option for stopover travellers. All rooms have private bathrooms and balconies with views inland or over Botany Bay. *Bar. Business centre. Concierge. Disabled-adapted rooms. Gym. Internet (high-speed/wireless). No smoking. Parking ($20). Pool (1 indoor, 1 outdoor). Restaurant. Room service. Spa. TV (pay movies).*

Periwinkle Guest House.

Head into the bush at **Pittwater YHA**. *See p50*.

Rydges Cronulla

20-26 Kingsway, at Gerrale Street, Cronulla, NSW 2230 (1300 857 922/9527 3100/www.rydges.com). CityRail Cronulla. **Rates** $339 double. **Rooms** 84. **Credit** AmEx, DC, MC, V.

Overlooking Cronulla Beach and the picturesque sweep of Gunnamatta Bay, this mid-range option is good for the naturalist, being close to the great bush-walking trails and wildlife of Royal National Park. All rooms have en suite bathrooms and at least one balcony, plus a desk and TV. Other facilities available include a pool, sauna, spa and beauty salon. At the time of writing, the hotel's restaurant was undergoing a large-scale refurbishment.

Bar. Business Centre. Disabled-adapted rooms. Internet (dataport/wireless). No-smoking floors. Parking (free). Pool (outdoor). Restaurant. Room service. Spa. TV (in-house movies/cable).

Serviced apartments

Somewhere in between a hotel suite and a rented apartment, these used to be strictly the domain of the business traveller. But no more. These days, many holidaymakers can't get enough of the comforts of home – more space, more flexibility, in-built kitchens and other conveniences, such as washing machines.

Apartment One

*297 Liverpool Street, Darlinghurst, NSW 2010
(9331 2881/www.contemporaryhotels.com.au). Bus
311, 333, 352, 373, 377, 378, 380, 392, 394, 396.*
Rates $385-$485. **Apartments** 1. **Credit** AmEx,
DC, MC, V. **Map** p329 H8 ⑤⑥
This gloriously hip two-level apartment is part of
the Contemporary Hotels group. There are three outdoor terraces and lovely designer touches everywhere you look. Long-stay rates are available.
Internet (dataport). Parking (free). TV (DVD).

Clarion Southern Cross Harbour Suites

*Corner of Harbour & Goulburn Streets, Darling
Harbour, NSW 2000 (1800 888 116/9268 5888/
www.southerncrosssuites.com.au). CityRail Central/
LightRail Paddy's Markets/Monorail Paddy's
Markets.* **Rates** $185-$345. **Apartments** 67.
Credit AmEx, DC, MC, V. **Map** p329 E8 ⑤⑦
The immediate location may not be very inspiring,
but this block is conveniently sandwiched between
Darling Harbour and Chinatown. The complex
includes two restaurants, a nightclub and karaoke
bar, an outdoor pool and a volcano-shaped jacuzzi.
*Concierge. Disabled-adapted apartments. Gym.
Internet (broadband). No-smoking apartments.
Parking ($36). Pool (outdoor). Restaurants (2). Room
service. Spa. TV (VCR).*

Harbourside Apartments

*2A Henry Lawson Avenue, McMahons Point, NSW
2060 (9963 4300/www.harboursideapartments.
com.au). Ferry McMahons Point.* **Rates** $275-$495.
Apartments 82. **Credit** AmEx, DC, MC, V.
Map p327 E1 ⑤⑧
The Harbourside's sweeping views of the Bridge
and Opera House are fantastic (so be sure to ask for
an apartment overlooking the water). The apartments themselves are now looking much slicker
than in previous years, with white walls, modern
furniture and fully equipped kitchens.
*Internet (high-speed). No-smoking apartments. Parking
(free). Pool (outdoor). Restaurant. TV (cable).*

Medina Executive Sydney Central

*2 Lee Street, at George Street, Haymarket, NSW
2000 (8396 9800/www.medinaapartments.com.au).
CityRail/LightRail Central.* **Rates** $300-$540.
Apartments 98. **Credit** AmEx, DC, MC, V.
Map p329 E9 ⑤⑨
Choose from one- and two-bed apartments, lofts and
studios, most with full kitchens, housed in the Parcel
Post building. There's a grocery delivery service and
a new bar and café. Laundry facilities too.
*Bar. Gym. Internet (high-speed broadband). Parking
(indoor). Pool (indoor). TV (cable/DVD).*

Meriton World Tower

*World Tower, 91-95 Liverpool Street, at George
Streets, CBD, NSW 2000 (1800 214 822/8263
7500/www.meritonapartments.com.au). CityRail
Central or Town Hall/Monorail World Square/
LightRail Central.* **Rates** $178-$1,000. **Apartments**
152. **Credit** AmEx, DC, MC, V. **Map** p329 E/F8 ⑥⓪

World Tower, part of the new World Square development, is the tallest residential building in the city.
Studios and one-bed apartments are on levels 18-36,
and two- and three-bed apartments on levels 62-74;
the higher you go, the better the views.
*Business centre. Concierge. Disabled-adapted
apartments. Gym. Internet (high-speed). No-smoking
apartments. Parking ($35). Pool (indoor). Room
service. Spa. TV (cable/DVD).*

Quay Grand Suites Sydney

*61 Macquarie Street, East Circular Quay, NSW
2000 (9256 4000/www.mirvachotels.com.au).
CityRail/ferry Circular Quay.* **Rates** $550-$800.
Apartments 68. **Credit** AmEx, DC, MC, V.
Map p327 G3 ⑥①
Near the Opera House, this five-star complex of one-
and two-bedroom apartments delivers the goods –
spacious suites (twice the usual size) with balconies
and views over the harbour, en suite bathrooms,
well-equipped kitchens, two TVs and plenty more.
*Bar. Business Centre. Gym. Internet (high-speed
broadband/wireless). No-smoking suites. Parking
($30). Pool (indoor). Restaurant. Room service. TV
(cable/DVD).*

Regents Court Hotel

*18 Springfield Avenue, off Victoria Street, Potts
Point, NSW 2011 (9358 1533/www.regentscourt.
com.au). CityRail Kings Cross.* **Rates** $275-$385.
Apartments 30. **Credit** AmEx, DC, MC, V.
Map p330 J7 ⑥②
This swish boutique hotel of studio suites is
favoured by film and arty types – they even have a
writer/artist-in-residence programme. The rooftop
terrace has great skyline views and there's free tea,
coffee and *biscotti* at reception.
*Bar. Internet (high-speed/wireless). No-smoking
apartments. Parking ($15). TV (cable/DVD).*

Saville 2 Bond Street

*Corner of George & Bond Streets, CBD, NSW 2000
(1800 222 226/9250 9555/www.savillesuites.com.au).
CityRail Wynyard.* **Rates** $340-$1,300. **Apartments**
170. **Credit** AmEx, DC, MC, V. **Map** p327 F5 ⑥③
Located in the heart of the financial district, these
apartments have full business services and well-
equipped kitchens. There are three penthouses and
a small rooftop pool.
*Concierge. Gym. Internet (high-speed/wireless). No-
smoking floors. Parking ($35). Pool (outdoor). Room
service. Spa. TV (cable/in-house movies).*

Wyndham Vacation Resort

*Corner of Wentworth Avenue & Goulburn Streets,
Surry Hills, NSW 2000 (9277 3388/www.wyndham
vrap.com). CityRail Museum.* **Rates** $180-$300.
Apartments 120. **Credit** AmEx, DC, MC, V.
Map p329 F8 ⑥④
Just south of Hyde Park, apartments on offer vary in
size (taking from two to six people) but all are well
equipped and furnished in smart contemporary style.
*Disabled-adapted rooms. Gym. Internet (dataport).
No-smoking apartments. Parking ($30). Restaurant.
TV (cable/DVD).*

Sightseeing

Features

Martin Place. *See p78.*

Introduction

Touring Sydney can be as serene, heart-stopping or decadent as you like.

Although the centre of Sydney is relatively small and easy to navigate, the rest of the city sprawls. Add in the complications provided by that stunning harbour and many lose the plot. But it's not as hard as it looks – honestly. The historic Harbour Bridge separates the north from the south, east and west, while the much newer suspension bridge, the Anzac Bridge, connects the city with the western suburbs.

Arranged by area, our Sightseeing chapters start with **Central Sydney**. This begins at Circular Quay and the Rocks area, and passes through the CBD (Central Business District) with its high-rise spires, shops and historic sights; then on to Chinatown, family-friendly Darling Harbour, gay-central Darlinghurst and neighbouring Surry Hills, colourful and seedy Kings Cross, smarter Potts Point, Woolloomooloo with its slick wharf conversion and up-and-coming ruffians Redfern and Waterloo. Next, in **Eastern Suburbs**, share the glamour grounds of the city's movers, shakers and just plain rich. Here you can shop till you drop in the boutiques of Paddington, Double Bay and Woollahra, and eat and drink yourself silly in a plethora of the hippest bars, cafés and restaurants. The area extends via picturesque harbourside suburbs all the way to South Head, taking in Bondi Beach, the closest ocean beach to the centre and a unique combination of city frenzy and 'no worries' seaside languor.

Moving west is the **Inner West**, covering one-time slums renovated into quaint cottages in waterfront Balmain, new-age chic in Glebe, a feisty Italian quarter in Leichhardt and gay, studenty, innovative Newtown.

The **North Shore** crosses the Harbour Bridge to survey well-heeled Kirribilli, Milsons Point and McMahons Point with their 'dress circle' views of the Bridge and Opera House, and the high-end suburbs of Cremorne, Mosman and Balmoral. North Sydney, the city's second business district, is also here. Manly takes us into the **Northern Beaches** as the first of a string of glorious ocean beaches, inaccessible by train, running all the way up to Palm Beach, playground of millionaires.

Parramatta & the West heads out into greater Sydney and the geographic centre of the city, Parramatta. There are a few historic sites here, thanks to the first colonial governors

choosing it for their country retreat, although sports and music fans will be more interested in the Olympic Park complex in Homebush Bay. Next comes the **South**, including historic Botany Bay, the site of James Cook's landfall in 1770. But today's gem of the south is Cronulla: despite some unfortunate recent history it's a burgeoning seaside suburb with the feel of a Queensland sunshine resort.

Finally comes **Sydney's Best Beaches**, a chapter devoted to the pick of the city's surfing, swimming and sunbathing spots.

WHERE TO START

If you've come by plane, you may already have glimpsed the Opera House majestically sited on Sydney's crenellated harbour. If you're one of the chosen few arriving on a ritzy cruise ship, you'll probably wake up slap bang next to it. In any case, it is this icon that most visitors gravitate towards first and, fortuitously, it's a good place to get your bearings.

The Opera House is on the east side of Circular Quay and next to the main entrance to the Royal Botanic Gardens. From Circular Quay you can catch ferries over to the north shore and Manly with its ocean beach, or other destinations on the south side of the harbour, including Darling Harbour, Balmain and Watsons Bay. The cute gold-and-green ferries are a great way to see the city; tickets cost a little more than the bus or train, but the journey is a delight. Also at Circular Quay is a CityRail station for trains, and numerous bus stops for routes throughout the city.

The best way to start your exploration, though, is on foot. Begin around the Quay, the neighbouring Royal Botanic Gardens, and past the Quay's west side to the Museum of Contemporary Art and the Overseas Passenger Terminal with its cool bars and restaurants. Behind the latter two places is the historic area of the Rocks, where you can find the more obvious souvenirs and visit the Harbour Bridge. Next, jump on a harbour cruise – there are numerous options (*see p60*) – to see around the harbour and spot some of the city's more desirable waterfront homes.

Now you can dive into the CBD. From Circular Quay a series of parallel roads lead through Sydney's commercial and shopping areas to the Town Hall. They are serviced by buses and trains, and at some points by the

Don't miss The best of Sydney

Sightseeing

Marvel at a wonder of the world

The **Sydney Opera House** (see p72) is the city's deserved icon and can be enjoyed in a number of ways. Splash out on a full opera ticket, take in a tour or sit under its sublime roof sails with a cold beer in your hand.

Bop till you drop

You can dance the night away in clubs to suit every bent. Best of the burgeoning bunch are **Arq Sydney** (see p221), **Moulin Rouge** (see p222), **Sapphire Suite** (see p223), **Lady Lux** (see p222) and **Tank** (see p223).

Circle the harbour

Sail beneath the noble **Harbour Bridge** (see p67) on one of **Sydney Ferries**' green-and-gold vessels (see p294).

Discover park life

Witness Australia's most exciting flora and fauna in the **Royal Botanic Gardens** (see p77), go horse-riding around the gentile bridle paths of **Centennial Park** (see p93), check out the views from the **Domain** (see p72) or go bushwalking in the **Royal National Park** (see p133).

Delight in alfresco arts

Enjoy your culture outdoors at **OpenAir** or **Moonlight Cinema** (for both, see p230), the **Sydney Festival** (see p215) or **Sculpture by the Sea** (see p214).

Feel the animal magic

Get up close and personal with sharks, rays, crocs, spiders and seals at **Sydney Aquarium** (see p85) and **Sydney Wildlife World** (see p85). For critters check out the apes, giraffes and koala bears at **Taronga Zoo** (see p116).

Ride the waves

Learn to surf, use a boogie board or paddle in the tide at the beaches of **Bondi** (see p137), **Manly** (see p139), **Maroubra** (see p139), **Collaroy** (see p140), **Newport** (see p140) or **Palm Beach** (see p140).

Sample world class cuisine

Taste the top tucker of some of the culinary wizards of Oz at **Aria** (see p146), **Bécasse** (see p145), **Bilson's** (see p145), **Rockpool (fish)** (see p149), **Guillaume at Bennelong** (see p146), **Billy Kwong** (see p155), **Glass** (see p146) and **Tetsuya's** (see p147).

Sydney Harbour.

Metro Monorail (an expensive, tourist-oriented service that circles the CBD at first-floor level), but are also easily walkable: a slowish walk including a bit of window-shopping from the Quay to the Town Hall will take about 30 minutes. From here you can walk west to bustling and very touristy Darling Harbour or catch a train or bus to Kings Cross, the city's sinful heart, or a host of other suburbs.

TRANSPORT AND INFORMATION

The CityRail system is, in general, easy to understand and services most of the main points of interest – apart from Manly (best reached by ferry or JetCat) and Bondi Beach (by bus from Bondi Junction or Circular Quay). Better, though, are the buses, partly because you can look out of the window (much of the train line is underground) and partly because they go everywhere and are more frequent. The ferries are the best – and most fun – way to get to the north shore and other harbourside spots.

There are lots of good-value travel passes covering a combination of transport types or specific areas or journeys. If you're pressed for time, consider one of the two **Explorer** buses (*see p59*): with these you can visit most of the sights in quick succession and pile a lot into a day. A **SydneyPass** (*see p60*) offers even more options. For details on all methods of public transport, *see p293*.

Also visit the information desk at Circular Quay, next to the CityRail station, or the **Sydney Visitor Centre** in the Rocks. You could call at nearby **Cadman's Cottage** (for both, *see p307*) to learn about Sydney's impressive national parks. There's a map of **Sydney by Area** on p325.

Tours

Tickets for many tours are available from **Australian Travel Specialists** (9211 3192, www.atstravel.com.au), which has outlets at Wharf 6 at Circular Quay and next to the Convention Centre in the Harbourside Shopping Centre at Darling Harbour. The **Opera House** (*see p72*) runs its own guided tours.

For a look at Sydney's seamier side, try an evening walking tour through the Rocks with **Ghost Tours** (1300 731 971, www. ghosttours.com.au), which cater to individuals, couples or groups, or a drive in a 1960s Cadillac hearse with **Destiny Tours** (9943 0167, www.destinytours.com.au), whose itineraries include the likes of Weird Sydney, Spooky Sydney and Sexy Sydney.

General

See Sydney & Beyond Smartvisit Card

1300 661 711/www.seesydneycard.com. **Rates** *1-day* $69; *2-day* $129/$169; *3-day* $159/$215; *7-day* $219/ $285; reductions for 4-15s. **Credit** AmEx, DC, MC, V. This swipe card plus guide booklet gives you free entry to over 40 attractions across Sydney and the Blue Mountains. It's certainly handy, but you'll need to cram in a lot to save money, so check what's on offer first. The higher-priced rates also include free transport on ferries, buses and CityRail.

On foot

The **Australian Architecture Association** (8297 7283, www.architecture.org.au) runs occasional architecture walks, plus cruise and bus tour options, some led by local architects. There are also excellent leaflets outlining eight historic self-guided walking tours that explore Sydney's past. The leaflets are available at tourist offices or you can download copies from www.cityofsydney.nsw.gov.au/aboutsydney – click on 'Visitor Guides and Information'.

Aboriginal Heritage Tour

Depart from Moore Room, Royal Botanic Gardens, CBD (9231 8134/www.rbgsyd.nsw.gov.au). CityRail Circular Quay. **Tours** 2pm Fri. **Tickets** $25; $13 reductions. **Credit** AmEx, MC, V. **Map** p327 G4.

The Rocks.

Join Aboriginal Education Officer Clarence Slockee to uncover the Royal Botanic Gardens' rich Aboriginal heritage – experience traditional music, dance and artefacts, and sample some staple bush foods. The tour runs for roughly 60 minutes.

Sydney Architecture Walks

Depart from Museum of Sydney, corner of Bridge & Phillip Streets, CBD (8239 2211/www.sydney architecture.org). CityRail/ferry Circular Quay. **Tours** 10.30am Wed, Sat. **Tickets** (incl entry to the Museum of Sydney) $25; $20 reductions. **Credit** AmEx, MC, V. **Map** p327 F4.

These two-hour tours conducted by young architects reveal the diversity of Sydney's architecture, from its gritty industrial past to controversial contemporary structures. There are two regular tours – 'Sydney' on Wednesdays and 'Utzon' (the Opera House) on Saturdays – plus the less-frequent 'Harbourings', and 'Public: Art, Place & Landscape', which includes a dip in the Andrew (Boy) Charlton Pool and is held on request (call for further details).

Rocks Pub Tour

Depart from Cadman's Cottage, 110 George Street, at Argyle Street, The Rocks (1800 067 676/9240 8788/www.therockspubtour.com). CityRail/ferry Circular Quay. **Tours** 4.50pm daily. **Tickets** $34.50. **Credit** MC, V. **Map** p327 F3.

A civilised alternative to a pub crawl, this 105-minute tour pops into some of Sydney's heritage pubs for a cleansing ale and a dose of local history. No under-18s allowed. The price includes three drinks.

Rocks Walking Tours

Depart from 23 Playfair Street, Rocks Square, The Rocks (9247 6678/www.rockswalkingtours.com.au). CityRail/ferry Circular Quay. **Tours** 10.30am, 12.30pm, 2.30pm Mon-Fri; 11.30am, 2pm Sat, Sun. **Tickets** $25; $11-$20 reductions; $61 family. **Credit** AmEx, MC, V. **Map** p327 F3.

Discover the secrets of one of Sydney's most historic areas in this lively 90-minute guided tour.

By bike

Bonza Bike Tours

Depart from Circular Quay (9331 1127/www.bonzabiketours.com). CityRail/ferry Circular Quay. **Tickets** $89-$123.50; $69-$107 reductions. **Credit** MC, V. **Map** p327 F4.

Bonza's most popular tour, the half-day Sydney Classic, takes in the major sights including the Opera House, Darling Harbour, Chinatown, Hyde Park and the Botanic Gardens. There's also the shorter Sydney Highlights tour, plus day-long options: to Manly and North Head, and a Harbour Bridge ride. Bike rental, food, drink, a helmet and a guide are all included. If you'd prefer to explore solo, you can also hire bikes ($55 per day).

By bus

Sydney Buses

13 1500/www.sydneybuses.info.

The government-run Sydney Buses offers a great range of tourist services. For more information on travelling by bus, *see p293.*

DayTripper *1-day* $16; $8 reductions.

This one-day pass gives you access to ordinary rail, bus and ferry services, but not premium services such as the Explorer buses or Manly JetCat.

Sydney Explorer *1-day* $39; $19 reductions; $97 family.

This red bus offers unlimited travel around the highlights of Sydney. The route covers Sydney Cove, the Opera House, the Royal Botanic Gardens, Mrs Macquarie's Chair, the Art Gallery of NSW, Kings Cross, Chinatown, the Powerhouse Museum, Star City Casino, Darling Harbour, beneath the Harbour Bridge, Queen Victoria Building, the Rocks and more. Jump on and off as you please. Services (every 20 minutes or so) start at Circular Quay, but can be picked up at any of the red stops en route. The full circuit takes about 100 minutes. You can buy tickets from the driver (no credit cards).

Bondi Explorer *1-day* $39; $19 reductions; $97 family.

A blue bus, concentrating on the eastern side of town, stopping at Kings Cross and Rose Bay Convent before hitting the beaches of Bondi, Bronte, Clovelly and Coogee. A short run northwards takes in Watsons Bay and the Gap. The bus departs daily every 30 minutes from Circular Quay, but you can board anywhere you see the blue signs and buy tickets from the driver (no credit cards).

Sydney Explorer & Bondi Explorer *2-day* $68; $34 reductions; $170 family.
Allows unlimited travel on both the Sydney Explorer and Bondi Explorer buses for any two days in a seven-day period.
SydneyPass *3-day* $110; $55 reductions; $275 family. *5-day* $145; $70 reductions; $360 family. *7-day* $165; $80 reductions; $410 family.
Unlimited access to the Sydney Explorer, the Bondi Explorer and all Sydney Ferry cruises, as well as standard bus, ferry and CityRail services and return travel on the AirportLink train.

By coach

Gray Line Tours
Depart from various locations including Wharf 4, Circular Quay (1300 858 687/9252 4499/www. grayline.com.au). CityRail/ferry Circular Quay. **Tickets** $32-$290. **Credit** AmEx, DC, MC, V. **Map** p327 F4.
Gray Line offers a variety of sightseeing tours in and around Sydney, including the Blue Mountains, Hunter Valley and a trip combined with a wildlife park sortie in which you can cuddle a koala.

Sydney by Diva
Depart from outside Oxford Hotel, Taylor Square, at Oxford Street, Darlinghurst (9360 5557/www.sydney bydiva.com). Bus 311, 333, 352, 373, 377, 378, 380, 392, 394, 396. **Tours** 2pm, 5pm, 8pm daily. **Tickets** $100. **Credit** AmEx, MC, V. **Map** p329 G/H9.
Climb aboard for an outlandish three-hour comedy tour of Sydney's tourist spots, hosted by one (or two) of the city's top drag queens. There's a minimum of 20 travellers needed unless it's Mardi Gras, when the bus usually does a round for smaller groups.

By boat

Perhaps Sydney's greatest attraction is its harbour, and the best way to see it is from the water. For more on travelling by ferry, *see p294*; for visits to the harbour islands, *see p86* **Island hopping**.

Captain Cook Cruises
Depart from Wharf 6, Circular Quay (1800 804 843/ 9206 1100/www.captaincook.com.au). CityRail/ferry Circular Quay. **Tickets** $25-$378. **Credit** AmEx, DC, MC, V. **Map** p327 F4.
One of Sydney's biggest cruise operators, with over 20 sightseeing and dining tours departing daily. Options range from the basic Coffee Cruise (10am and 2.15pm, $46) to the Opera Dinner cruise (Sunday only, $109, with live on-board arias included) and a two-night cruise where you sleep in cabins.

Matilda Cruises
Depart from Wharf 6, Circular Quay (9264 7377/ www.matilda.com.au). CityRail/ferry Circular Quay. **Tickets** $25-$63; $12-$55 reductions. **Credit** AmEx, DC, MC, V. **Map** p327 F4.

The one-hour Highlight Cruise ($25) hugs the shore of the Eastern Suburbs, running under the Harbour Bridge and back past the Opera House. The Rocket Harbour Explorer ($29) makes eight stops with the option of getting off and back on at each point.

Tribal Warrior Association
Depart from Eastern Pontoon, Circular Quay (1800 067 676/9699 3491/www.tribalwarrior.org). CityRail/ferry Circular Quay. **Tours** 12.45pm Tue-Sat. **Tickets** $55; $45 reductions. **Credit** AmEx, DC, MC, V. **Map** p327 F4.
Owned and run by Aboriginal people and aimed at educating tourists about Aboriginal culture, this 100-minute cruise opens with a traditional welcoming ceremony before whisking visitors around the harbour on a century-old ketch, visiting Clark Island and various Aboriginal settlements en route.

By air

Sydney's love affair with the ocean extends to aviation, with the harbour's Rose Bay serving as a natural runway for seaplanes. From there, numerous outfits offer aerial sightseeing trips and hops up the coast to Palm Beach or Cottage Point for a posh lunch, or to the Hunter Valley for a spot of wine tasting. Operators include **Sydney Harbour Seaplanes** (1300 732 752, 9388 1978, www.seaplanes.com.au) and **Sydney by Seaplane** (1300 720 995, 9974 1455, www.sydneybyseaplane.com).

Cloud Nine Balloons
1300 555 711/www.cloud9balloonflights.com. **Credit** AmEx, MC, V.
Lifting off at dawn from Parramatta Park, enjoy a one-hour balloon ride with views over the city followed by a champagne breakfast. Prices from $260.

Sydney HeliTours
9317 3402/www.avta.com.au/sydney. **Credit** AmEx, MC, V.
Flit over Sydney Harbour, skim the northern beaches or zoom along the coast with the doors off. Prices start at $169; departures are from Kingsford Smith Airport, but they can collect you from your hotel.

By motorbike

Take your pick from **Rolling Thunder Motorcycle Tours** (1800 427 539, www. rollingthunder.com.au) or **Easy Rider Motorbike Tours** (1300 882 065, 9247 2477, www.easyrider.com.au), which offer everything from a quick 15-minute thrill for $35 to overnight outback adventures.

With added adrenaline

For more white-knuckle harbour rides, *see p68* **Wet and wild**.

BridgeClimb: a long way down (and up), but the views are worth it.

BridgeClimb

*5 Cumberland Street, between Argyle & George
Streets, The Rocks (8274 7777/www.bridge
climb.com). CityRail/ferry Circular Quay.* **Tickets**
$179-$295; $109-$195 reductions. No under-10s.
Credit AmEx, MC, V. **Map** p327 F3.
The three-and-a-half-hour climb to the top of the
Harbour Bridge is, thankfully, less arduous and much
safer than it appears. At 134m (440ft) above sea level,
the views from the top of the arch are stunning.
Climbs, which last three and a half hours, leave every
ten to 20 minutes daily from early morning to night,
with dawn climbs during the summer. Night-before
revellers should note that all climbers are breath-
tested and must have a blood alcohol level under 0.05
per cent. Fear of heights? Don't let it deter you: you're
attached to a static line throughout the climb, and
climb leaders are specially trained to help acrophobes.

Harbour Jet

*Depart from Convention Centre Jetty, between
Convention Centre & Harbourside shopping centre,
Darling Harbour (1300 887 373/9280 4662/
www.harbourjet.com). CityRail Town Hall/ferry
Darling Harbour/Monorail/LightRail Convention.*
Tickets $65-$95; $45-$70 reductions; $198-$297
family. **Credit** AmEx, MC, V. **Map** p326 D6.
If you haven't whizzed about on a 420-horsepower
jet boat before, be prepared for some serious high-
speed fun. Choose from a 35-minute Jet Blast
Adventure, a 50-minute Sydney Harbour Adventure
– both departing three times a day – and an 80-
minute Middle Harbour Adventure departing once
a day. Life jackets are provided for the wild (and
very wet) ride, which is pumped up with rock music.

Ocean Extreme

*Depart from Convention Centre Jetty, between
Convention Centre & Harbourside shopping centre,
Darling Harbour (1300 887 373/www.ocean
extreme.com.au). CityRail Town Hall/ferry Darling
Harbour/Monorail/LightRail Convention.* **Tickets**
$75-$95. **Credit** AmEx, MC, V. **Map** p326 D6.
Take a spin around the harbour in 'Australia's only
commercially operated Special Forces vessel'.
There's the 45-minute Extreme Blast Tour or, for
real thrill seekers, the 60-minute Rush Hour.

Skywalk

*Centrepoint Podium Level, Sydney Tower, 100
Market Street, between Castlereagh & Pitt Streets,
CBD (9333 9222/www.skywalk.com.au). CityRail St
James or Town Hall/Monorail City Centre.* **Tours**
9.30am-8.45pm daily. **Tickets** $64.50; $44.50
reductions. **Credit** AmEx, MC, V. **Map** p327 F6.
Skywalk takes you to the top of the tallest building
in town, Sydney Tower. You'll stand on a glass platform 260m (850ft) above the ground with great
views of the CBD, and potential vertigo. But don't
worry: you're clipped to a safety rail at all times. As
with BridgeClimb, you'll be breath-tested for alcohol.

Sydney Harbour Parasailing

*Depart from near Manly Wharf, Manly (9977 6781/
www.parasail.net). Ferry Manly.* **Tickets** $79 solo;
$129 tandem; $55 8-in-tandem. **Credit** AmEx, MC, V.
Map p334.
Get strapped into a harness and flung 150m (490ft)
above the water while being towed along by a
speedboat for ten minutes. The season runs from
November to April with several departures a day.

Sightseeing

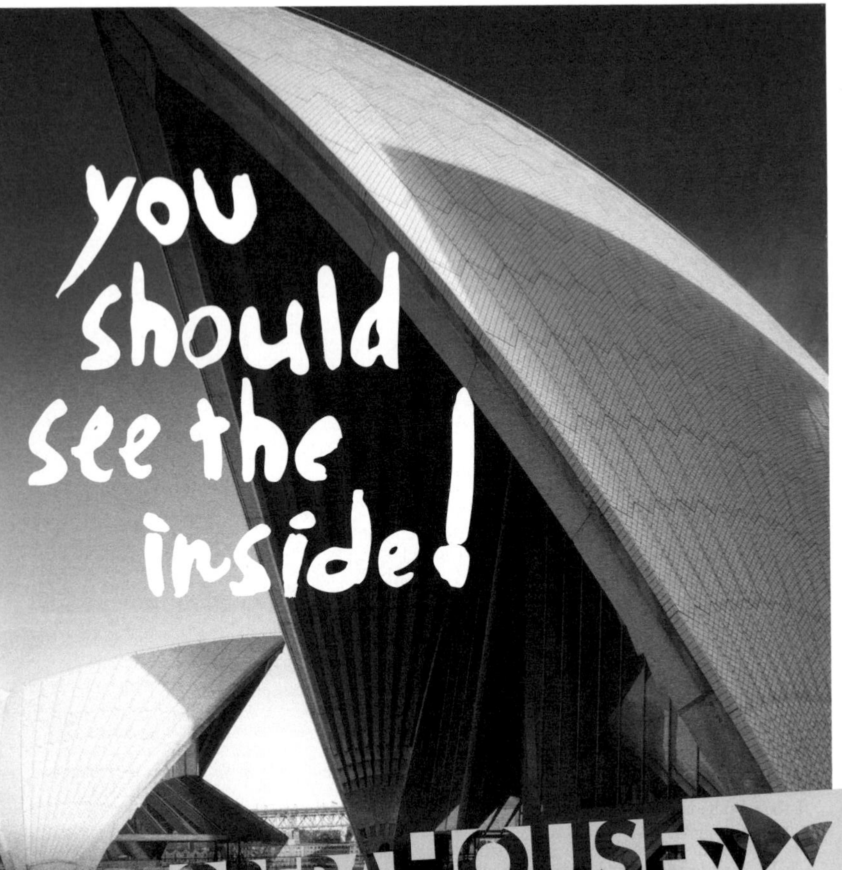
you should see the inside!

Central Sydney

Harbour and city meet at Sydney's spectacular heart.

There's nothing quite like **Circular Quay**, the heart of central Sydney, where boats, buses and trains meet and the solid iron struts of the Sydney Harbour Bridge (*see p67*) watch over the gentle undulating sails of the Opera House (*see p72*). It will take your breath away time and time again.

The **CBD** (Central Business District) has had a bit of a revival with locals in recent years. The historic **Rocks** is no longer the preserve of tourists thanks to some cool pubs and bars opening up, and Circular Quay is just as popular, with Opera Bar (*see p253*) on the eastern side pulling in alfresco drinkers and diners nightly, plus the Overseas Passenger Terminal (*see p69*) on the west side, with its wealth of swish eating and drinking spots, a welcome addition for the 'it crowd'. Indeed, gentrification is spreading all over central Sydney – even **Redfern** and **Waterloo** are getting in on the act thanks to an urban renewal programme and a wealth of new apartment blocks redefining the areas aesthetically. While **Kings Cross**, **Darlinghurst** and **Surry Hills** retain their edge, the CBD boasts elegant Macquarie Street and Martin Place reaching out to the Royal Botanic Gardens (*see p77*), giving a sense of the history of the city and how it was shaped by the colonial settlers.

Circular Quay, which wraps around Sydney Cove and is bookended by the Harbour Bridge and Opera House, is your starting point in this city, a perpetually bustling nexus for tourists and Sydneysiders alike. As you arrive here, preferably on one of the city's much-loved green-and-cream ferries, mull over how things have changed since the First Fleet set up shop in 1788. That said, the societal split that arose in those early days of the colony – the bigwigs in their grand sandstone buildings to the east, the convicts and carousing sailors in their tumbledown cottages and seedy drinking dens in the Rocks to the west – is still evident today. Yet little remains of the Cadigal people, the cove's original inhabitants, save for displays at various museums.

The evolution of the Rocks from inner-city slum to tourist-friendly precinct set the blueprint for other parts of central Sydney to smarten up their act. **Darling Harbour** and the adjacent CBD have both benefited from major refurbishments and building

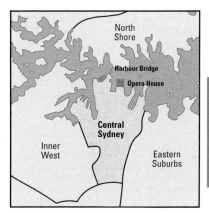

programmes over the last decade. Some might bemoan that the CBD is becoming simply a gusty midtown Manhattan with its sprouting skyscrapers (of which World Tower is the largest), but there's no denying that the previously morgue-like atmosphere at night and at weekends has been replaced by the vibey buzz of party-goers and diners in search of the next big Sydney restaurant. None of this has hurt the established party strips of neighbouring **Potts Point**, Darlinghurst and Surry Hills, ground zero for Sydney's gay and Bohemian communities, all of which are more vibrant than ever.

The CBD is easily walkable, or there are CityRail trains travelling underground around the City Circle loop – covering Central, Town Hall, Wynyard, Circular Quay, St James and Museum stations.

The CBD

Map pp326-330. **Transport** *Ferry Circular Quay/CityRail Circular Quay, Martin Place, Museum, St James, Town Hall or Wynyard/Monorail City Centre, Galeries Victoria, Paddy's Markets or World Square/LightRail Capitol Square or Paddy's Markets.*

The Rocks & around

In January 1788, after an eight-month voyage from Plymouth, England, the First Fleet stumbled ashore (after a short visit to Botany Bay) at Sydney Cove. Their brief was to 'build where you can, and build cheap'. Hence, the Rocks. Named after its rough terrain, the area survived as a working-class district for almost two centuries until the 1960s, when it was nearly demolished to create an Australian

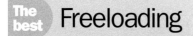

Cool sounds

Jazz fans should head to the Domain in January for the annual free jazz festival and its host of international and local stars, part of the Sydney Festival (*see p215*) and an intrinsic part of the city's summer.

Bridge walk

In a car it costs you $3, a little less on the train and a whole lot more if you take on the mighty BridgeClimb (*see p61*). But you can soak up the glorious views of Sydney Harbour Bridge, and expend considerably less energy, by simply walking across it from the Rocks to Milson's Point and back.

Drag queen glamour

You don't need to stake your place along the Mardi Gras parade route to catch the city's most daring drag queens. Instead, go along to Fair Day, part of the Gay & Lesbian Mardi Gras festival (*see p217*), where the queens give free performances and the scene is set for a relaxed and eminently gay day out.

Big bangs

Sydney's annual New Year's Eve fireworks are a sight to behold. For where to catch them gratis, *see p216* **Free seats for NYE fireworks**.

Classical music

Discover the music stars of tomorrow in the Wednesday lunchtime recitals put on by the students at the **Sydney Conservatorium of Music** (corner of Macquarie & Bridge Streets, CBD, 9351 2222). Sit back and enjoy the perfect surroundings of this historic building.

Commune with Bacchus

OK, so you'll need to get there, but once you're in the Hunter Valley (*see p280*), an hour and a quarter from Sydney, the wine really does flow. Wend your way from one vineyard to the next (by bicycle if you're feeling fit), tasting at the cellar doors as you go.

Manhattan. Civic protest saved the day and the 'birthplace of the nation' was finally restored for posterity in the mid-1970s. Now safe under the wing of the Sydney Harbour Foreshore Authority, the Rocks still has to pay its own way, and many historic buildings have been turned to commercial use.

The resulting combination of period buildings, tourist shops, restaurants and pubs, along with harbourside vistas, has made the Rocks one of the city's major sightseeing attractions. As a result, locals used to shun the area, but a clutch of new pubs, some fine restaurants and the pull that in this part of town you can always get a cab home has changed all that. The slick development of the Walsh Bay Finger Wharves is another attraction.

Head first for the excellent **Sydney Visitor Centre in the Rocks Centre** (corner of Argyle & Playfair Streets; *see p307*), where you'll also find the new **Rocks Discovery Museum** (*see p67*). Across George Street – the Rocks' central thoroughfare – is **Cadman's Cottage**, one of the nation's oldest houses. Now home to the **Sydney Harbour National Park Information Centre** (*see p307*), it's the place for info on getting to some of the harbour's islands (*see p86* **Island hopping**).

The **Rocks Market** (*see p193*) appears like magic every weekend, with souvenir stalls selling all manner of arts and crafts, puppeteers and other street performers. For a taste of Sydney's eastern cuisine, there's **Yoshii** (*see p145*) and David Thompson's **Sailors Thai** (*see p143*). If you'd like a cocktail with your view, try the **Blue Horizon Bar** on the 36th floor of the Shangri-La Hotel (*see p32*) on Cumberland Street.

Historic buildings include the handsome sandstone **Garrison Church** (9247 1268, www.thegarrisonchurch.org.au, open 8.30am-6pm daily), on the corner of Argyle and Lower Fort Streets. Officially named the Holy Trinity Church, this was the colony's first military church; regimental plaques hang on the walls and there's a brilliantly colourful stained glass window overlooking the pulpit. You can also take a peek at how 19th-century working-class families lived at the **Susannah Place Museum** (*see p67*), a row of four brick terraces on Gloucester Street.

Still, much has been lost. The site of Sydney's first hospital, which struggled to care for 500 convicts who disembarked from the Second Fleet in 1790 suffering from typhoid and dysentery, is now an unprepossessing row of shops. Several galleries, including that of well-known Aussie artist Ken Done, now occupy the site of the **Customs Naval Office** (100 George Street), where one of the colony's most

Sydney Harbour Bridge. Big and ugly according to James Michener. *See p67.*

flamboyant customs officers, Captain John Piper, made money from mismanaging taxes. He went on to build Sydney's finest mansion of its day at Eliza Point – now Point Piper – where he held extravagant parties until his maladministration came to light. He then had his crew row him beyond the Heads and play a Highland lament as he threw himself overboard. To his embarrassment, they dragged him from the sea and he died, impoverished, in 1851.

Off the main drag, under the thundering Bradfield Highway that feeds the **Sydney Harbour Bridge** (*see p67*) and towards Walsh Bay and Millers Point, the area has a quieter and gentler feel, with tiny cottages, working wharves and a few pubs vying for the honour of Sydney's oldest: the **Lord Nelson Brewery Hotel** (*see p180*) on Kent Street, the **Hero of Waterloo** (81 Lower Fort Street, 9252 4553, www.heroofwaterloo.com.au) and the **Palisade** on Bettington Street, which also has a fine restaurant (*see p146*). **Glover Cottages** (124 Kent Street) – built by stonemason and surveyor Thomas Glover in the 1820s – were the first example of terraced housing in the colony. The charming Victorian **Sydney Observatory** (*see p69*), perched on the hill of the same name, offers views of the heavens above and the harbour below. Immediately below the observatory, **Argyle Place** has the air of an English village green and is one of the most picturesque and least touristy parts of the Rocks.

From Windmill Street, walk down the Windmill Steps past the striking modern sculpture of a giant egg in a nest to Hickson Road and **Walsh Bay**, where the first wharves were built by a South Sea Islands trader in 1820. The area's grandest vision was realised by the Sydney Harbour Trust from 1901-22 when Hickson Road was carved through the sandstone, a massive sea wall was built and buildings and piers were erected. As shipping methods changed, however, the Walsh Bay wharves became obsolete and were finally abandoned in the 1970s.

The area's revitalisation is now well under way, having kicked off back in the 1980s with the development of Piers 4/5 to house various cultural institutions, including the **Sydney Theatre Company** (*see p268 and p271*). An additional 850-seat theatre for the company – the **Sydney Theatre** (*see p270*) – opened in 2004 in an artfully converted bond store on Hickson Road. All the piers have now been developed, and there's the chichi wine bar **Firefly** (*see p179*), the **Hickson Road Bistro** (No.20, 9250 1990), attached to the theatre and serving the well-heeled residents of the swish waterside apartments, plus a number of restaurants, including the flamboyant **Ottoman** (*see p149*).

A public boardwalk now stretches from Pier 1 – where the **Sebel Pier One** hotel (*see p35*) has prime position – to Piers 8/9. So you can walk along the foreshore from Circular Quay,

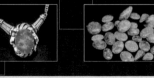

past the Museum of Contemporary Art, behind the Overseas Passenger Terminal, in front of the celebrity-favoured **Park Hyatt Hotel** (*see p32*), under the Harbour Bridge, around Dawes Point Park, then past the piers all the way to Millers Point.

Dawes Point Park contains the remains of Dawes Point Battery, Sydney's first permanent fortification. Built in 1790 against a feared Spanish invasion, it was rebuilt in 1820 by pioneer architect Francis Greenway and renovated in the 1850s and '60s. The battery was demolished in 1925 when the Harbour Bridge was built, but excavation has uncovered some remains. These include the floor of the original powder magazine, the circular battery with evidence of four gun emplacements, underground magazines, a stone ramp and the footings of the officers' quarters.

Rocks Discovery Museum

The Rocks Centre, Kendall Lane, at Argyle Street, The Rocks (1800 067 676/9251 8804/www.rocks discoverymuseum.com). CityRail/ferry Circular Quay. **Open** 10am-5pm daily. **Admission** free. **Map** p327 F3.

Housed in a restored 1850s coach house, this new museum covers the Rocks' history from the time of the indigenous Cadigal people to the 1970s demonstrations that saved many of the historic buildings from avaricious developers. It's a small space, but there's quite a bit packed in; amid the broken crockery and and tarnished jewellery look out for a mummified rat with a curious collar of Chinese newsprint, a remnant of the Rocks' less sanitary past.

SH Ervin Gallery

National Trust Centre, Watson Road, next to the Observatory, The Rocks (9258 0173/www.nsw. nationaltrust.org.au/ervin.html). CityRail Circular Quay or Wynyard/ferry Circular Quay. **Open** 11am-5pm Tue-Sun. Closed mid Dec-mid Jan. **Admission** $6; $4 members/reductions. **Credit** AmEx, DC, MC, V. **Map** p327 E3.

A spectacular setting on Observatory Hill and an impressive line-up of annual exhibitions and themed shows are the drawcards at the National Trust gallery. It specialises in Australian art (painting, sculpture and works on paper) both historical and contemporary in nature. Perhaps the gallery's strongest selling point is its popular annual shows: these include the 'Salon des Refusés', a selection of rejected works from the high-profile Archibald and Wynne art competitions. In November and December, 'The Year In Art' surveys works seen in Sydney galleries throughout the year.

Susannah Place Museum

58-64 Gloucester Street, at Cumberland Place Steps, The Rocks (9241 1893/www.hht.nsw.gov.au). CityRail/ferry Circular Quay. **Open** 10am-5pm Sat, Sun (daily in Jan). **Admission** $8; $4 reductions; $17 family. **Credit** (over $10) MC, V. **Map** p327 E4.

Built in 1844, this terrace of four houses – including a corner shop, original brick privies and open laundries – gives an idea of what 19th-century community living was really like. Entry to the museum is by guided tour only; tours leave every half hour from 10am, with no tour at 1.30pm; book ahead if possible. Note that steep, narrow stairs are involved.

Sydney Harbour Bridge & Pylon Lookout

Bridge & Pylon Lookout accessible via stairs on Cumberland Street (9240 1100/www.pylonlookout. com.au). CityRail/ferry Circular Quay. **Open** 10am-5pm daily. **Admission** *Pylon Lookout* $9.50; $4-$6.50 reductions; free under-7s. **Credit** AmEx, DC, MC, V. **Map** p327 F3.

Long before the Opera House was built, Sydney had 'the coat hanger' as its icon. Locals had dreamed for decades of a bridge to link the north and south harbour shores before construction of the 'All Australian Bridge' began in 1924, by which time Sydney's ferries were struggling to carry 40 million passengers a year. The winning design came from English firm Dorman, Long & Co, but used Australian steel, stone, sand and labour. Families within the path of the new bridge and its highways were displaced without compensation, and 800 houses were demolished. A total of 1,400 workers toiled on the structure, which is 134m (440ft) high and 1,149m (3,770ft) long, and was the world's largest single-span bridge when it was constructed. It took eight years to build, and workers grafting without safety rails took great risks: 16 died. The opening ceremony in 1932, broadcast around the world, was interrupted by a lone horseman – disaffected Irishman Francis de Groot – who galloped forward and slashed the ribbon with his sword, declaring the bridge open in the name of 'the King and all the decent citizens of New South Wales'. De Groot's organisation, the New Guard, resented the fact that a representative of the King hadn't been asked to open the bridge. After the police had removed him (he was later fined £5), the ribbon was retied, and the ceremony resumed.

The refurbished Pylon Lookout, in the south-east pylon, is well worth a visit. Climb 200 steps, past three levels of exhibits celebrating the history of the bridge and its builders. Stained-glass windows feature a painter, riveter, stonemason, rigger, concreter and surveyor. Original bridge memorabilia from the 1930s is also on display; more up-to-date souvenirs are available in the shop on level two. And the open-air views from the top are magnificent. The more intrepid can take a guided tour to the top of the bridge itself, with only a harness between you and a plunge into the harbour.

The bridge has been declared 'one of the seven wonders of the modern world' – though not everyone admires it. Writer James Michener commented in the 1950s that it was 'big, utilitarian and the symbol of Australia... But it is very ugly. No Australian will admit this.' *Photo p65.*

Sightseeing

Wet and wild

Thrill seeking on the harbour is reaching fever pitch as rival companies bring out bigger, better and faster jet boats to circle the waters at high speeds, performing 360° spins and heart-stopping power brake stunts under the Harbour Bridge, around the Opera House and out into the blue. Alternatively, you can take to the water with a frisson of style in an Italian wooden speedboat, or make like a champion and cruise in a yacht built for the America's Cup.

The mighty **Jetcruiser** (8296 7255, www. jetcruiser.com.au) is a 1,300 horsepower thrill machine. Trips are 40 to 45 minutes long, leave from Jetty 6 at Circular Quay and cost $50 ($25 reductions). When it's not speeding at 35 knots – the spin between the Heads is pretty dizzying – you get some gentler cruising.

With its unmistakeable gnashing shark teeth logo painted onto the brow of its vessels, **Oz Jet Boating** (1300 556 111, 9808 3700, www.ozjetboating.com; *photo below*) prides itself on top-notch stops, spins and wave riding. Not for the faint-hearted, the rides peak at a ridiculous 45 knots. Go for broke with the 45-minute Sydney Spin ride at $80 ($55 reductions), leaving from the Eastern Pontoon at Circular Quay. For more jet boat rides try **Harbour Jet** (*see p61*), **Ocean Extreme** (*see p61*), **Thunder**

Jet Down Under (9299 0199, www.thunder jetboat.com.au), **Sydney Jet** (9807 4333, www.sydneyjet.com.au) and Matilda Cruises' **WildCAT** thrill rides (9264 7377, www. matilda.com.au).

For a more debonair take on the harbour spin, jump aboard **La Dolce Vita**, the perfectly named, handmade mahogany diesel-engine speedboat (complete with walnut dash), courtesy of the Italian Wooden Speedboat Company (0410 529 903, www.waterlimo. com.au). Prices start at $250 per hour and there's room for four on board. The boat is berthed at Woolloomooloo Finger Wharf and owned by jazz muso David Paquette, who will also put together gourmet packages – dropping passengers off at a nearby island with a picnic hamper or for a meal at a harbourside restaurant.

And finally, if you really want to feel the wind in your hair and taste some proper sailing, get on board the **Spirit** (8456 7777, www.adrenalin.com.au), a dreamy yacht built for the 1992 America's Cup in San Diego. For $95 per person ($66 reductions) you can cruise the harbour for around three hours under the yacht's majestic sails, with sandwiches and soft drinks provided. The *Spirit* leaves Pyrmont wharf at 1.30pm on Fridays and 9.30am and 1.30pm on Saturdays, subject to numbers.

Oz Jet Boating.

Sydney Observatory

Watson Road, off Argyle Street, Observatory Hill, The Rocks (9921 3485/www.sydneyobservatory. com.au). CityRail/ferry Circular Quay. **Open** *Museum* 10am-5pm daily. **Admission** *Museum & gardens* free. *Day tours* $7; $5 reductions; $20 family. *Night tours* $15; $10-$12 reductions; $45 family. **Credit** MC, V. **Map** p327 E3.

Built in 1858, Sydney Observatory gained international recognition under Henry Chamberlain Russell, government astronomer from 1870 to 1905, who involved Sydney in the International Astrographic Catalogue, the first complete atlas of the sky. The Sydney section alone took 80 years to complete and filled 53 volumes. Increasing air pollution made the observatory ineffective, and it became a museum in 1982. Interactive displays include a virtual-reality tour over the surfaces of Venus and Mars, and there are lessons on how telescopes work. Night tours (booking essential) include a talk and tour, 3-D Space Theatre session and viewing through a 40cm (16in) reflecting telescope.

Circular Quay

Circular Quay (more of a semi-circle, in fact) is the hub of Sydney's ferry system, where the charming green-and-cream vessels leave for all points around the harbour. Commuters and day-trippers board and disembark from a constant stream of ferries, JetCats, RiverCats and water taxis at the Quay's five wharves, while tourists and teenagers idle in the cafés drinking cappuccinos, listening to buskers and admiring the view. Fast-food kiosks abound, but you'll also find **City Extra** (9241 1422), one of the few 24-hour restaurants in town, and the delicious *gelati* of **Gelatissimo** (9241 1566). Information stands proffer free literature, and sightseeing cruises and tours leave from here. The view back to the city is blocked by the CityRail Circular Quay station and Cahill Expressway, but the view out over the harbour is particularly lovely at night, when the Opera House, the Harbour Bridge, the Overseas Passenger Terminal and Fort Denison are all lit up.

On the west side of the Quay, with the Rocks stretching behind, is the grand sandstone façade of the **Museum of Contemporary Art** (*see p71*), housed in the deco-style former Maritime Services Board Building. Just beyond it is the striking **Overseas Passenger Terminal**, where international cruise liners dock. Not only an award-winning piece of architecture, the terminal is also one of the city's coolest night-time hangouts with its clutch of restaurants and bars, including Mod Oz specialists **Quay** (*see p147*), **Ocean Room** (*see p146*), buzzy **Wildfire** (8273 1222, www.wildfiresydney.com) and **Cruise** (9251 1188, www.cruiserestaurant.com.au).

On the opposite side of the quay is East Circular Quay, a bland strip of modern buildings dubbed 'the Toaster' by wags during their construction phase several years ago. Nonetheless, it's a popular spot, not least because of its anchor tenant, the arty cinema **Dendy Opera Quays** (*see p227*), various shops and a string of popular restaurants including elegant **Aria** (*see p146*) and the high-rise **ECQ** (61 Maquarie Street, 9256 4000) on the third floor of the Quay Grand building.

As you walk around the Quay, look out for a series of round metal plaques set into the promenade, each one dedicated to a famous writer. Forming **Writers' Walk**, these offer brief quotations on Sydney and human nature. Many (but not all) of the writers are Australian, including Germaine Greer, Peter Carey, Barry Humphries and Clive James.

Sydney Opera House (*see p72*), the city's modern icon, stands in lone majesty on Bennelong Point at the tip of the eastern side of Circular Quay. All the photos in the world cannot prepare you for how stunning it is. The site is where Governor Phillip provided a hut for an Aboriginal man, Bennelong, in 1790. Phillip had captured Bennelong – one of the governor's more foolish moves – and planned to use him as a mediator. Some of the key events in Bennelong's sorry life are depicted in a series of paintings by Donald Friend on display in the Opera House. From the steps in front you can walk east along the harbour foreshore and into the Royal Botanic Gardens.

Behind the Quay, across Alfred Street, is the city-owned **Customs House** (*see p71*), which has a fantastic modern interior housing both Sydney's main public library and swish restaurant and cocktail bar **Café Sydney** (9251 8683, www.cafesydney.com.au) sitting majestically on the fifth floor. Two blocks over, on the corner of Albert and Phillip Streets, is the **Justice & Police Museum** (*see p71*). Look up and you'll spy the terracotta spine and wrapped-glass front of the 41-storey **Aurora Place**, designed by Italian architect Renzo Piano and one of Sydney's most appealing modern buildings. Opposite Aurora Place is **Chifley Tower** on one corner and **Governor Phillip Tower** on the other.

Architecturally, these are three of the more interesting late 20th-century additions to the skyline and, sitting so close together, are a reminder that this is the so-called 'big end' of town. Governor Phillip Tower stands on the site of the first Government House, and inside is Trevor Weeke's towering bust of Governor Macquarie. The excellent and informative **Museum of Sydney** (*see p71*), which also has a very good shop and café, is in front of it.

Sightseeing

Customs House

31 Alfred Street, between Loftus & Young Streets,
Circular Quay (9242 8551/www.cityofsydney.
nsw.gov.au/customshouse). CityRail/ferry Circular
Quay. **Open** 8am-midnight Mon-Fri; 10am-midnight
Sat; 11am-5pm Sun. **Map** p327 F4.

Built in 1885, Customs House was one of government
architect James Barnet's finest works. Its double-
pillared colonnade, wrought-iron panels and long
clean lines give it a feeling of space and majesty,
underlined by the open area in front. The building
is heritage-listed, but its use continually changes:
today it houses a highly stylish public library – with
decor slick enough to make boutique hotel junkies
drool – and some local businesses. There's a fantastic scale model of the city under glass on the ground
floor, as well as the library's newspaper, magazine and
computer room (including lots of foreign publications), and the tasty pizzeria and café Young Alfred.
Fashionable eaterie Café Sydney retains its enviable
location on level five, with amazing views.

Justice & Police Museum

Corner of Albert & Phillip Streets, Circular Quay
(9252 1144/www.hht.net.au). CityRail/ferry Circular
Quay. **Open** 10am-5pm Sat, Sun (daily in Jan).
Admission $8; $4 reductions; $17 family.
Credit (over $10) MC, V. **Map** p327 G4.

Fittingly, the Justice & Police Museum has been
a Water Police Court (1856), Water Police Station
(1858) and plain old Police Court (1886). Death masks
of some of Australia's more infamous crims are
on display, as well as mugshots, assorted deadly
weapons and newspaper reports of sensational
wrongdoings. Also on view is a recreated 1890s
police charge room, a dark and damp remand cell,
and a restored Court of Petty Sessions with its notorious communal dock, which could hold up to 15
prisoners at a time.

Museum of Contemporary Art

140 George Street, between Argyle & Alfred Streets,
Circular Quay (9245 2400/24hr recorded information
9245 2396/www.mca.com.au). CityRail/ferry Circular
Quay. **Open** 10am-5pm daily. *Tours* 11am, 1pm
Mon-Fri; noon, 1.30pm Sat, Sun. **Admission** free.
Credit AmEx, DC, MC, V. **Map** p327 F4.

The MCA is the only major public gallery in Sydney
with a serious interest in contemporary art. It has
fared well under the directorship of Elizabeth Ann
Macgregor, a feisty and inspirational Scot who has
spearheaded the museum's renaissance. As well as
the always interesting temporary shows, many from
key overseas institutions and artists, the MCA has
added a new gallery on level four to display its permanent collection. At the time of writing Macgregor
had just booked the work of Danish-born artist
Olafur Eliasson, whose mist show mimicking the
Earth's atmosphere wowed visitors at London's
Tate Modern a few years back; the exhibition will
be put on in 2009. The MCA Café (*see p171*), facing
Circular Quay, is worth a look.

Museum of Sydney

Corner of Bridge & Phillip Streets, CBD (9251
5988/www.hht.net.au). CityRail/ferry Circular Quay.
Open 9.30am-5pm daily. **Admission** $10; $5
reductions; $20 family. **Credit** AmEx, MC, V.
Map p327 F4.

Where the hip is happening. **Museum of Contemporary Art**.

This modern building stands on one of the most historic spots in Sydney, site of the first Government House, built in 1788 by Governor Arthur Phillip and home to the first nine governors of NSW. In 1983 archaeologists unearthed the original footings of the house, which had survived since the building's 1846 demolition: these remains are now a feature at the museum. Run by the Historic Houses Trust and opened in 1995, the MOS offers a mix of state-of-the-art installations and nostalgic memorabilia – it's definitely worth a visit. A giant video spine spans the full height of the building and charts the physical development of the city; elsewhere a trade wall features goods on sale in Sydney in the 1830s. This area was the first point of contact for the indigenous Cadigal people and the First Fleet, so the museum also explores colonisation, invasion and contact. The Cadigal Place gallery honours the clan's history and culture, while outside the museum the Edge of the Trees sculpture by Fiona Foley and Janet Laurence symbolises that first encounter as the Cadigal people hid behind trees and watched officers of the First Fleet struggle ashore.

Sydney Opera House

Bennelong Point, Circular Quay (box office 9250 7777/information 9250 7111/tours 9250 7250/ www.sydneyoperahouse.com). CityRail/ferry Circular Quay. **Admission** $32; $23 reductions; $74 family. **Tours** every 30mins 9am-5pm daily. **Credit** AmEx, DC, MC, V. **Map** p327 G3.

Set in a heavenly harbour, its cream wings reminiscent of the sails of the First Fleet, the Sydney Opera House is the city's most famous asset. It took 14 troubled years and $102 million to build – $95 million more than was anticipated. In true Aussie style, the shortfall was met by lotteries. The cultural cathedral has never been visited by its creator, Danish architect Jørn Utzon, who resigned halfway through the project following a clash with the Minister of Public Works. On its opening night on 20 October 1973, an impromptu appearance was made onstage by two small possums.

In its five auditoria the Opera House holds 2,400 opera, concert, theatre, film and dance performances every year, attended by some 1.5 million people. The first performer was Paul Robeson who, in 1960, at the invitation of the militant builders' union, sang *Old Man River* at the construction site. The building recently received World Heritage recognition as an architectural wonder of the world.

Attend a performance if you have the chance; otherwise, book one of the daily guided tours, which include a two-hour backstage tour and a one-hour 'essential' tour. The Opera House is also a wonderful place to while away a few hours: eateries range from the haute-cuisine (and haute-priced) Guillaume at Bennelong (*see p146*) to the very stylish Opera Bar (*see p253*), with indoor and outdoor seating and live entertainment, and the family-friendly Sidewalk Café. For more information on concerts, *see p254*; for theatre events, *see p270*.

Macquarie Street, Royal Botanic Gardens & Hyde Park

Tree-lined Macquarie Street – named after Lachlan Macquarie, the great reformist governor of NSW, who served from 1809 to 1821 – is the closest thing the CBD has to a boulevard. It fairly drips with old money and resonates with history: on one side you'll find Sydney's main public buildings, on the other handsome apartment blocks belonging to medicos, the well-heeled and the 'squatocracy' (a sarcastic term for Australia's 'landed gentry'). A notable addition is Norman Foster's **Deutsche Bank Place** on the corner of Hunter and Phillip Streets, a sleek, 39-storey tower that is instantly recognisable by the triangular-shaped lattice structure on top.

To the west of Macquarie Street, the 30 broad green hectares (74 acres) of the **Royal Botanic Gardens** (*see p77*) – site of **Government House** (*see p75*), the home of NSW governors – form a green and pleasant rump to the city, leading down to the water at **Farm Cove**. This was the site of Australia's first vegetable patch; you can still see the spot where, two centuries ago, Governor Arthur Phillip first planted his big yams. In summer a huge screen rises from the water on the cove's eastern side, and seating is erected in the gardens so that locals can catch a movie at the **OpenAir Cinema** (*see p228*).

South of the Botanic Gardens, across Cahill Expressway, is another spacious green retreat, the **Domain**. Home to Sunday soap-box orators, the Domain has long been the place for civic protest: huge crowds gathered in 1917 to protest against World War I conscription, more than 100,000 demonstrated in 1931 against the governor's dismissal of Prime Minister Jack Lang, and in 2003 up to 50,000 demonstrated against the invasion of Iraq. It is also the site of one of the key public events on the city's annual calendar, the free Symphony & Jazz in the Domain concerts, part of January's **Sydney Festival** (*see p215*). If you're in town at this time, don't miss these fabulous communal picnics and concerts, topped off by fireworks.

The Domain is also where you'll find the **Art Gallery of New South Wales** (*see p75*) and memorials to poets Robert Burns and Henry Lawson. The park itself, mainly open space, offers few surprises, but hold your breath for the final sensational view: **Mrs Macquarie's Chair** overlooking the harbour. The Domain used to be Governor Macquarie's private park, and its tip was the favourite spot of his wife, Elizabeth. A seat has been shaped in the rock – hence the name – and the view is still one of Sydney's finest. On the Woolloomooloo Bay

Andrew (Boy) Charlton Pool.

side of the Domain is **Andrew (Boy) Charlton Pool** (*see below*), a popular outdoor lap pool for city workers, and a favoured sunbaking spot for trim gay men.

Heading south down Macquarie Street stands a row of impressive historical buildings: the **State Library of New South Wales** (*see p78*), **Parliament House** (*see p76*), **Sydney Hospital** (*see p78*), the **Mint** (*see p76*) and the **Hyde Park Barracks Museum** (*see p75*). Notable churches include **St James** (corner of King and Phillip Streets, 8227 1300, www.sjks. org.au), designed by Francis Greenway and the oldest church in Sydney (completed 1824), and **St Stephen's Uniting Church** (197 Macquarie Street, 9221 1688, www.ssms.org.au).

At Macquarie Street's southern end, between Elizabeth and College Streets, is gracious **Hyde Park**, named after its much larger London counterpart. It used to have a rowdy reputation, and was more a venue for sideshows, wrestling and boxing matches than a park; until the late 1820s it also served as Sydney's racecourse. Now it's a tranquil green space and fitting home to elegant Australian memorials, including the famous art deco **Anzac Memorial** (*see p75*), and the graceful **Archibald Fountain**, commemorating the Australian-French Alliance of 1914-18.

During the Sydney Festival, the park erupts with free entertainment and, in summer, office workers flop down on the grass, while ibis pick their long-legged way around the supine bodies. Hyde Park is a fine sight at night, with fairy-lights in the trees and possums scampering up trunks and foraging among the plants. The main avenue of Hills fig trees running north through the park is especially striking, though less so since 2005, when 34 of them had to be removed after being blighted by disease and decay. On Saturday afternoons you may catch Sydney's goth community gathering for their weekly get-together.

On the College Street side of the park are **St Mary's Cathedral** (*see p78*), the **Australian Museum** (*see p75*), **Sydney Grammar School** and **Cook & Phillip Park** (*see p258*), an enormous aquatic and sports centre. Even if you don't fancy a dip, at least pop in to see Wendy Sharpe's wonderful murals above the 50m pool depicting the life of 19th-century swimming star Annette Kellerman, who went on to become Australia's first Hollywood movie star. On Elizabeth Street, facing Hyde Park, sits the elaborate **Great Synagogue** (*see p75*).

Opposite the south-eastern corner of Hyde Park on Liverpool Street is the block-long **Mark Foy's Building** (143-147), with its distinctive gold trim and green turrets. Once a department store, completed in 1917, it was converted to a court complex in 1991: you'll often see a huddle of lawyers, clients and, depending on the case, members of the Fourth Estate gathering outside. Francis Foy, one of the seven siblings who established the original store, took his architect to look at department stores around the world before settling on the design: the lower levels feature a special glazed brick shipped from Scotland. Unable to decide whose name the store should carry, the Foys settled the dispute by naming it after their father, Mark.

Andrew (Boy) Charlton Pool

Mrs Macquarie's Road, The Domain (9358 6686/ www.abcpool.org). Bus 411. **Open** 6am-7pm daily (till 8pm daylight saving time). **Admission** $5.50; $3.60-$3.80 reductions; $15 family. **Map** p330 H5.
A $10 million refurbishment has made this harbour-side pool the place for inner-city summer swimming. It was a popular bathing spot long before the British arrived, and public sea baths first opened here in 1860. In the early 1920s famous Aussie swimmer Andrew 'Boy' Charlton achieved many of his tri-umphs here – including, aged just 16, beating European champ Arne Borg, setting a new world record in the process. Today, the baths offer an eight-lane, heated 50m pool, learners' and toddlers' pools, a sundeck and a café. The pool's harbourside edges are glazed, allowing swimmers unparalleled views across the sparkling bay.

Visit all three for the one great price.

No visit to Sydney is complete without experiencing three of Australia's best attractions, all within walking distance of Darling Harbour, and now you can see all of them for a special all-in-one price. The Discovery Sydney Value Pass allows you to walk amongst the sharks, cuddle up to a koala and pat a python, see Sydney's best views plus buckle up for the ultimate Australian virtual reality ride! And the Discovery Pass is valid for 3 months, so you can take your time to enjoy your savings, and extend the fun at Sydney's favourite attractions. Sydney Aquarium and Sydney Wildlife World, Aquarium Pier Darling Harbour. Sydney Tower, Centerpoint Podium Level, 100 Market St, Sydney. 02 8251 7800 www.discoverypass.com.au

Anzac Memorial

Hyde Park, between Park & Liverpool Streets, CBD (9267 7668). CityRail Museum. **Open** 9am-5pm daily. **Admission** free. **Map** p329 F7.

Sydney architect Bruce Dellit was only 31 when he won the 1930 competition to design this beautiful grey-pink granite memorial to the Australian and New Zealand troops who fell in World War I, particularly those involved in the bloody battle for the Gallipoli peninsula. His art deco vision caused a sensation when it opened in 1934. The striking bas-reliefs are by Rayner Hoff, who also made the central bronze sculpture in the 'Well of Contemplation' of a Christ-like naked figure held aloft on a shield by three women, symbolising the sacrifices of war. Around $2.4 million is being spent to shore up the monument in time for its 75th anniversary in 2009. An act of remembrance is held here at 11am daily and guided tours can be arranged at the reception desk in the monument's base, where you'll also find a small museum dedicated to Australia's military.

Art Gallery of New South Wales

Art Gallery Road, The Domain (9225 1700/www. artgallery.nsw.gov.au). CityRail Martin Place or St James then 10mins walk/bus 441. **Open** 10am-5pm Mon, Tue, Thur-Sun; 10am-9pm Wed. **Admission** free; charges for some exhibitions. **Credit** AmEx, MC, V. **Map** p327 H6.

NSW's main art gallery moved to its present site in 1885. It includes a solid collection of 19th- and 20th-century Australian artists, as well as Aboriginal and Torres Strait Islander art, big names in European art history and international contemporary artists, plus a fine Asian art collection. There are also regular blockbuster touring shows from overseas galleries. One of its most popular and controversial exhibitions is the annual Archibald Prize, a portraiture competition, which is complemented by the Wynne (landscape and sculpture) and Sir John Sulman (best 'subject/genre paintings' and murals) competitions. Wednesday is late-opening night, with free talks, debates and performances, and there are regular events for kids. Tours of the general collection are held two or three times a day.

Australian Museum

6 College Street, at William Street, CBD (9320 6000/ www.austmus.gov.au). CityRail Museum or St James. **Open** 9.30am-5pm daily. **Admission** $10; $5 reductions; $25 family. **Credit** AmEx, MC, V. **Map** p329 G7.

The Australian Museum (established 1827) houses the nation's most important animal, mineral, fossil and anthropological collections, and prides itself on its innovative research into Australia's environment and indigenous cultures. Displays cover the Pacific Islands, Asia, Africa and the Americas, with items ranging from Aboriginal kids' toys to a tattooed chalk head from the Solomon Islands. Any serious museum-tripper should see a few of the local stuffed animals, and the displays should answer all your questions about Australian mammals. If you're at all interested in Aboriginal culture and beliefs, visit the Indigenous Australia section, which tackles such contentious issues as the 'stolen generation', deaths in custody and problems facing indigenous people today. Around 1,000 Aboriginal objects of a secret and/or sacred nature are held separately from the main collection: access to these can be arranged through the Aboriginal Heritage Unit.

Government House

Royal Botanic Gardens (9931 5222/www.hht.net.au). CityRail Circular Quay or Martin Place/ferry Circular Quay. **Open** *House* guided tour only; every 30mins 10.30am-3pm Fri-Sun. *Garden* 10am-4pm daily. **Admission** free. **Map** p327 G3/4.

Designed in 1834 by William IV's architect, Edward Blore, the plans for Government House (the official residence of the NSW governor) had to be modified to take account of local conditions, such as the Australian sun being in the north rather than the south. However, the original Gothic Revival concept remained, and today's visitors can still enjoy the crenellated battlements and detailed interiors. Past governors have dabbled in redecorating and extensions with mixed results, but the marvellously restored State Rooms are now the best example of Victorian pomp in the country. The current governor doesn't live here, but it's still used for state and vice-regal functions. Don't miss the exotic gardens.

Great Synagogue

166 Castlereagh Street, between Park & Market Streets. Entry for services 187A Elizabeth Street, CBD (9267 2477/www.greatsynagogue.org.au). CityRail St James or Town Hall. **Open** *Services* 5.30pm (winter), 6.15pm (summer) Fri; 8.45am Sat. *Tours* noon Tue, Thur. **Admission** $5; $3 reductions. **Map** p329 F7.

Sydney's Jewish history dates back to convict times – there were around 16 Jews in the First Fleet – and the Great Synagogue, consecrated in 1878, is deemed the mother congregation of the Australian Jewry. Designed by Thomas Rowe, the building is a lavish confection of French Gothic with large amounts of Byzantine thrown in. The superb front wheel window, facing on to Hyde Park, repeats the design of the wrought-iron gates outside, while inside the cast-iron columns holding up the balcony where women sit are capped with intricate plaster designs. The ceiling, deep blue with gold-leaf stars, depicts the Creation. Twice-weekly tours (entry from the back of the synagogue on Castlereagh Street) include a short video about the history of both the synagogue and Australia's Jewish community. A small museum is also open before and after tours.

Hyde Park Barracks Museum

Queens Square, corner of Macquarie Street & Prince Albert Road, CBD (8239 2311/www.hht.net.au). CityRail Martin Place or St James. **Open** 9.30am-5pm daily. **Admission** $10; $5 reductions; $20 family. **Credit** MC, V. **Map** p327 G6.

Designed by convict architect Francis Greenway, the barracks were completed in 1819 to house 600 male convicts, who were in government employ until

When Harry met Sydney

He's known as 'the father of modern Australian architecture' and his buildings can be seen commanding Sydney's skyline wherever you look. Harry Seidler died in 2006 aged 82, but his spirit most certainly lives on. The great man never got to see his last project, the **Ian Thorpe Aquatic Centre** in Ultimo (see p258), which opened to huge acclaim in late 2007. Its white wave-shaped roof – with echoes of Utzon's Opera House – is striking enough, but it's inside that the real wonder starts.

The Olympic-sized pool looks as if it's caught in the curve of a huge rolling wave. 'The entry was deliberately kept low to heighten the experience of the grand space,' says John Curro, who worked with Seidler at his firm, the still active Harry Seidler & Associates. He says that Harry predicted patrons would be bowled over at the sight of the pool – and he wasn't wrong.

It seems particularly fitting that Seidler's last gift to Sydney should be a public space for locals to enjoy, not to mention one that embraces the city's growing commitment to green initiatives: using hydraulical roof vents for natural ventilation and harnessing rainwater for internal amenities such as toilets and sprinkler systems.

1848. Subsequently used as an immigration depot and an asylum for women, they eventually metamorphosed into a museum. On the top level are re-created convict barracks: rough hammocks hang side by side in the dormitories, while recorded snippets of conversation surround you. A computer database allows visitors to follow the official records of convicts, from conviction via flogging to rehabilitation. The women's section on level two is no less thought-provoking – these (mostly Irish) women were escaping an awful existence to start what must have been an equally burdensome new life in a harsh colony. The courtyard houses a pleasant café for a moment of quiet contemplation.

Mint

10 Macquarie Street, between Queens Square & Martin Place, CBD (8239 2288/www.hht.net.au). CityRail Martin Place or St James. **Open** 9am-5pm Mon-Fri. **Admission** free. **Map** p327 G6.

This attractive building with its yellow façade and two-storey, double-colonnaded veranda was built between 1811 and 1816 as the southern wing of the Sydney Hospital. It turned into a coin-making operation – the first branch of the Royal Mint outside London – in the 1850s, following the discovery of gold in NSW, and continued to churn out money until 1926. There aren't any coins to gawp over, just a small historical exhibit and an upstairs café overlooking Macquarie Street. The building also houses the headquarters of the Historic Houses Trust.

Parliament House

6 Macquarie Street, opposite Hunter Street, CBD (9230 2111/tours 9230 3444/www.parliament. nsw.gov.au). CityRail Martin Place or St James. **Open** 9am-5pm Mon-Fri. *Tours* (groups) 9.30am, 11am, 12.30pm, 2pm, 3pm, 4pm non-sitting days; 1.30pm Tue sitting days. Individual tours available. **Admission** free. **Map** p327 G5.

The inspirational architect was born in Vienna in 1923 and fled to England in 1938 to escape persecution by the Nazis. After the war he studied architecture at Harvard and arrived in Sydney in 1948. The first building he designed in the city was his parents' home – the **Rose Seidler House** (*see p117*), now a Historic Houses Trust museum. With this building, Seidler started on an incredible journey that saw him creating ultra-modern architecture celebrating the optimism and energy of Australia and especially Sydney. This is most tellingly demonstrated in his **Horizon tower** in Forbes Street, Darlinghurst, a glitzy 42-storey apartment block with curved balconies jutting out from a central column. The tower can be seen from all over central Sydney gleaming in the sunlight, a streak of bright white against the blue sky, and needless to say the views from the apartments are breathtaking.

Other Seidler buildings include **Australia Square**, the **MLC Centre**, and the contentious **Blues Point Tower** at the bottom of Blues Point Road in McMahons Point. Seidler was known as a man of passion who took on bureaucrats and local councils with gusto, and his legacy to the city is a series of buildings pulsating with that same passion.

Known to locals as the Bear Pit, the New South Wales Parliament is said to be the roughest, toughest parliament in the country. Its impressive sandstone home was built between 1811 and 1814 as the northern wing of the Rum Hospital, but was commandeered in 1829 to house the new colony's decision makers. Only the Legislative Assembly (lower house) existed until 1850s, when the parliament became bicameral. The Legislative Council (upper house) meets in a building that was originally intended for use as a church; the cast-iron prefab was being shipped from Glasgow to Victoria when it was diverted mid-voyage to Sydney. The parliament is largely modelled on its mother in London: there's a Speaker and Black Rod, and even the colour scheme follows the British tradition of green for the lower chamber and red for the upper chamber. Legislative sessions are open to the general public, with viewing from a public gallery; booking is essential for the guided tours.

Royal Botanic Gardens

Mrs Macquarie's Road, CBD (9231 8111/weekends 9231 8125/www.rbgsyd.nsw.gov.au). CityRail Circular Quay, Martin Place or St James/ferry Circular Quay. **Open** *Gardens* 7am-sunset daily. *Visitor Information* 9.30am-4.30pm daily. *Tropical Centre* 10am-4pm daily. *Shop* 9.30am-5pm daily. **Admission** *Gardens* free. *Tropical Centre* $4.40; $2.20 reductions. **Credit** (shop only) AmEx, MC, V. **Map** p327 G/H3/5.

The beautiful Royal Botanic Gardens, established in 1816, make a sweeping green curve from the Opera House to Woolloomooloo Bay. It's a gorgeous spot, full of majestic trees, spacious lawns, bird-filled ponds and ornamental flowerbeds. The Domain surrounds the gardens: in colonial times this land acted as a buffer between the governor's home and the penal colony, but by 1831 roads and paths had been built to allow public access, and it has remained a people's place ever since. The Palm Grove area is a good place to start: there's a shop and visitor information counter, café, restaurant and toilets. Highlights include the Tropical Centre, spectacular rose gardens, cacti collection, the large colony of fruit bats (aka flying foxes) near Palm Grove, and the 'living fossil' Wollemi pine, one of the world's rarest species, discovered in 1994 by a ranger in the Blue Mountains. The Fleet Steps provide a classic Opera House photo-op.

There are free guided walks (10.30am daily) – or you can take the 'trackless train' ($10, $5 reductions), which stops at areas of interest around the gardens, ending up at the Opera House. To learn more about Aboriginal life in the area, visit the Cadi Jam Ora garden or book a walk with an Aboriginal guide (9231 8134, $25; $13 reductions).

St Mary's Cathedral

Corner of College Street & Cathedral Square, CBD (9220 0400/www.stmaryscathedral.org.au). CityRail St James. **Open** 6.45am-6pm Mon-Fri; 9am-6.30pm Sat; 7am-6.30pm Sun. *Tours* 10.30am Sun; also by arrangement. **Admission** free. **Map** p327 G6.

St Mary's Cathedral is the seat of the Roman Catholic archbishop of Sydney (currently the controversial Cardinal George Pell) and stands on the site of Australia's first Catholic chapel. William Wilkinson Wardell's design replaced the original cathedral, ruined by fire in 1865. Constructed from local sandstone, it's the largest Gothic cathedral in the southern hemisphere – 106m (348ft) long with a 46m (150ft) central tower – dwarfing many of the European models from which it took inspiration. Wardell's original twin spires, initially not erected due to funding problems, were lowered into place by helicopter in 1999. Don't miss the cathedral's crypt, which is decorated with a beautifully designed terrazzo floor depicting the six days of Creation.

State Library of New South Wales

Corner of Macquarie Street & Cahill Expressway, CBD (9273 1414/www.sl.nsw.gov.au). CityRail Martin Place. **Open** 9am-8pm Mon-Thur; 9am-5pm Fri; 10am-5pm Sat, Sun. *Tours* 11am Tue; 2pm Thur. **Admission** free. **Map** p327 G5.

The State Library is essentially two libraries in one: the modern General Reference Library (GRL) provides access to five million books, CD-Roms and other media stored over five floors below ground, while the 1910 Mitchell Wing (closed Sundays) holds the world's greatest collection of Australiana, including James Cook's original journals and the log book of Captain Bligh. The latter wing has fine bronze bas-relief doors depicting Aboriginal peoples and European explorers, a grand mosaic and terrazzo vestibule, stained-glass windows and extensive amounts of Australian stone and timber. Its Shakespeare Room is a fine example of mock-Tudor style, with a ceiling modelled on Cardinal Wolsey's closet in Hampton Court and stained glass windows depicting the 'seven ages of man'. The GRL's very popular Family History Service offers free courses

to help people trace their family history, and changing exhibitions highlight the library's large and fascinating collection of historic paintings, photos, manuscripts and rare books. There are free guided tours of both libraries.

Sydney Hospital & Sydney Eye Hospital

8 Macquarie Street, opposite Martin Place, CBD (9382 7400/www.sesahs.nsw.gov.au/sydhosp). CityRail Martin Place. **Open** *Museum* 10am-3pm Tue. **Admission** *Museum tour* $6. *Historical tour* $8. *Both* $12. **Map** p327 G5/6.

Originally known as the Rum Hospital because its construction was paid for by government-controlled rum sales, Sydney Hospital is the city's only early institutional building still performing its original function. The current structure is a grandiose, late Victorian edifice, which thoughtlessly replaced the centre of what was once an eye-catching trio; cast your eyes to Parliament House on one side and the Mint on the other to get an idea of what the hospital originally looked like. Outside stands the Il Porcellino bronze boar sculpture, a copy of the famous original in Florence; its snout is shiny from people rubbing it for good luck. Inside, the marble floors, magnificent windows and colour scheme have been carefully restored. The lobby lists those who donated to its construction and the respective amounts – Dame Nellie Melba kicked in £100, as much as some of the business giants of the day. You can't just walk into the hospital itself, but you can book two weeks ahead for guided tours (groups only, minimum eight). The Lucy Osburn-Nightingale Foundation Museum is open to the public on Tuesdays, while the courtyard is open to all and has a very good café, with views over the Domain and an elaborate and colourful cast-iron fountain commemorating British comedian Robert Brough, who endeared himself to Australian audiences in the 19th century.

Martin Place, Centrepoint & Town Hall

Squashed between the green spaces of the Domain and Hyde Park and the waterside promenades of Darling Harbour is the CBD proper. Apart from walking, one of the best ways of getting around this central area, as well as to Darling Harbour and Chinatown, is on the elevated Monorail system.

The CBD's historic epicentre is **Martin Place**, a pedestrian boulevard lined with monumental buildings running west from Macquarie Street to George Street. The largest non-garden open space in the CBD, it houses the **Cenotaph** – which commemorates Australian lives lost in World War I – and, in December, a Christmas tree wilting in the Sydney sun. Lunchtime concerts and a fountain make this

The centre of the centre. **Martin Place**.

bar (*see p180*) and **est.** restaurant (*see p146*) – and the newly renovated **Hilton Sydney** hotel (*see p32*), with its fashionable **Zeta Bar** (*see p180*) and Luke Mangan-helmed **Glass** restaurant (*see p145*), have introduced a fresh after-hours vigour. Much of this resurgence in the CBD's party status can be credited to Justin Hemmes, the young dynamo behind the Establishment as well as the trendy bars and bistro of the **Hotel CBD** (corner of York and King Streets, 8297 7000, www.merivale.com), and the **Slip Inn** (*see p222*). His most ambitious venture, a pleasure complex of bars (one with a pool), restaurants and clubs called the **Ivy** was opening at 320-330 George Street at the time of writing.

The main shopping district of the CBD – roughly bounded by Hunter, Elizabeth, George and Park Streets – orbits Sydney's two department stores, modern **Myer** (*see p190*) and majestic **David Jones** (*see p189*). Nearby are the grandiose **State Theatre** (*see p270*) and the stately **Queen Victoria Building** (*see p81*). Pedestrianised **Pitt Street Mall** is always jammed with shoppers and has lots of buskers but never enough seats. Make sure you take a turn through the elegant **Strand Arcade** (*see p191*), packed with designer fashion and gift shops.

The **Sydney Tower** (*see p82*) – also known as Centrepoint after the shopping centre that it crowns and as the AMP Tower after the ad sign on its turret – rises 305 metres (1,000 feet) between Pitt Street Mall and Castlereagh Street, making it the tallest structure in the city. Despite its spindly appearance, the tower, which is held in place by 56 cables, is capable of withstanding earthquakes and extreme wind conditions – as the publicity blurb goes, 'if the strands of these cables were laid end to end, they would reach from Sydney to New Zealand'. In 2005 the tower underwent a glitzy revamp, adding OzTrek, a virtual-reality adventure tour, and Skywalk, a heart-thumping open-air walk around the roof.

The intersection of George, Park and Druitt Streets is a major crossroads surrounded by the QVB, the chic **Galeries Victoria** shopping mall (*see p190*) and **Sydney Town Hall** (*see p82*). Beneath them all is bustling Town Hall train station and a warren of subterranean shopping alleys linking up the various above-ground buildings. It's a hectic area, particularly during the day when office workers and students gather on the Town Hall steps to chat, eat lunch and wait for buses. Next door is the Anglican **St Andrew's Cathedral** (*see p81*).

If Sydney's mayor Clover Moore and her council colleagues have their way, this area will see striking changes in the coming decade: they

an outdoor mecca for office workers, and huge screens are often erected here during big sporting and cultural events.

At the George Street end of Martin Place you'll find the grand **General Post Office** (*see p81*), outside which crowds gathered to celebrate the end of the two world wars. This very fine Victorian building has been wonderfully renovated: in the basement you'll find several good restaurants, a sushi bar and an upmarket food court. The upper floors contain showy retail outlets and a rather formal luxury/business hotel, the **Westin Sydney** (*see p33*). The sandstone banks and office buildings erected along the southern edge of Martin Place during the economic boom of wool and wheat now jostle with the odd elegant skyscraper and modern monstrosities such as the **MLC Centre**, which houses designer shops, a huge electrical store and some great outdoor cafés. North of Martin Place, on the western side of George Street, is **Wynyard Station**, the main train and bus interchange for travelling across the Harbour Bridge to the north shore and northern beaches.

At night the CBD used to be quite dull, but twenty- and thirtysomething hangouts like the **Establishment** complex – home of **Tank** nightclub (*see p223*), **Hemmesphere** cocktail

Sightseeing

7th day free* with Avis

Rent any car with Avis in Sydney for 7 or more consecutive days and receive one day free* of the time and kilometre charges.

Include coupon number **TPPA031** in your reservation.

Offer valid on rentals commenced prior to 31 July 2010.

*Travelling to an unfamiliar city?
Add Avis' portable GPS^ to you rental.*

Visit www.avis.com.au or call Avis Reservations on 136 333

We try harder.

are on a mission to buy up the George Street block facing the Town Hall so that it can eventually be demolished to create a grassy public square. Currently, it's a far from pretty part of town. The multiplex cinema on George Street, surrounding burger bars and late-night pubs keep folk hanging out well into the early hours: be prepared to jostle with teenagers streaming in to play video games at several louche amusement arcades, and rowdy backpackers and boozers heading for drinking dens such as the perpetually lively, round-the-clock Irish bar **Scruffy Murphy's Hotel** (43-49 Goulburn Street, 9211 2002, www.scruffymurphys.com.au).

One more authentic pocket is the 'Spanish quarter', the tiny stretch of Liverpool Street between George and Sussex Streets, where you can have tapas and a cerveza at the **Spanish Club** (No.88, 9267 8440, www.spanishclub.com.au) or take home some Spanish chorizo, olives and rioja from the **Torres Cellars & Delicatessen** (No.75, 9264 6862, www.torresdeli.com.au).The area was once quite down at heel, but a clean-up has encouraged previously lacklustre restaurants to lift their game; best of the crop is the upmarket **Don Quixote** (545 Kent Street, 9264 5903), serving good Spanish food and jugfuls of sangria.

A few doors down, **Tetsuya's** (one of Sydney's superstar restaurants – *see p147*) hides behind the **Judges House** (531 Kent Street), built in 1827 and a rare example of a colonial Georgian bungalow with verandas. It's now occupied by an office, but you can admire it from the street.

The area immediately south of Liverpool Street has been transformed by **World Square**, a mega shopping, office, residential and hotel complex that takes up a whole city block. Large-scale musicals and the like are often playing at the **Capitol Theatre** (*see p268*) on Campbell Street. A block further south lies **Central Station**, Sydney's main train and bus nexus, surrounded by backpacker hostels and internet cafés.

General Post Office

1 Martin Place, between George & Pitt Streets, CBD (9229 7700/www.gposydney.com). CityRail Martin Place or Wynyard. **Map** p327 F5.

The GPO's foundations were laid in 1865, but workers' strikes and complications from building over the Tank Stream (the colony's first water supply) meant that it didn't open until 1874. The grand clocktower was added in 1891, its chimes based on London's Big Ben, with both the clock mechanism and bells made in England. The building's Italianate flourishes dominated the young city's skyline for decades before it fell into neglect; by 1989 the building was no longer adequate for the needs of Australia Post

and in 1990 it was boarded up. A deal between the city authorities and the Westin Hotel group rescued the building, restoring the original cast-iron staircase, the clocktower and two ballrooms, and transforming the offices into hotel rooms. The GPO hall is now a light-drenched atrium that forms part of the hotel lobby and leads down to a classy food court and collection of restaurants. The colonnaded Martin Place entrance is flanked by upmarket shops. Much of the GPO's beauty is in the details: the stencilling on the walls, the moderne windows and the gold leaf ceiling patterned with leaves – spot the English rose and the Irish shamrock, as well as the Australian wattle and gum. The Tank Stream viewing room is open daily to visitors.

Queen Victoria Building (QVB)

455 George Street, between Market & Druitt Streets, CBD (9264 9209/www.qvb.com.au). CityRail Town Hall/Monorail Galeries Victoria. **Open** *Tours* 2.30pm daily. **Admission** $10. **Credit** AmEx, MC, V. **Map** p327 E6.

Designed by George McRae to resemble a Byzantine palace, the QVB occupies an entire block on George Street, and once dominated the Sydney skyline with its dramatic domed roof – an inner glass dome encased by a copper-sheathed outer one. Completed in 1898 to celebrate Queen Victoria's golden jubilee, it originally housed street markets. It has suffered (and gamely survived) long periods of neglect, and demolition threats were finally quashed in the 1980s when a $75 million budget restored the building to its former grandeur. It now houses 200 outlets, including shops, cafés and restaurants. Of particular note are the coloured lead-light wheel windows, the cast-iron circular staircase and the original floor tiles and lift. The ballroom on the third floor is now the Tearoom. On the hour, shoppers gather on gallery two to watch the Royal Automata Clock display a moving royal pageant. The execution of Charles I regularly goes down a storm.

St Andrew's Cathedral

Sydney Square, corner of George & Bathurst Streets, CBD (9265 1661/www.cathedral.sydney.anglican.asn.au). CityRail Town Hall. **Open** 10am-3pm. *Tours* by arrangement daily. **Admission** free. **Map** p329 E7.

This huge late-Gothic edifice, the oldest cathedral in Australia, was started with astonishing confidence by Governor Macquarie (who named it after the patron saint of his native Scotland) when Sydney was still the size of a small village. The first stone was laid in 1819, and the cathedral was consecrated in 1868. Three architects contributed to it, the most notable being Edmund Blacket, city architect between 1849 and 1854. Special elements link the cathedral to the motherland, including intaglio tiles made by Mintons and two stones from the Palace of Westminster. Military commemorations honour the landings at Gallipoli and the prison camp at Changi in Singapore. Recent conservation work has restored the interior (altered in the 1950s) to its original glory.

Sydney Tower

Centrepoint Podium Level, 100 Market Street, between Castlereagh & Pitt Streets, CBD (9333 9222/www.sydneytoweroztrek.com.au/www.skywalk. com.au). CityRail St James or Town Hall/Monorail City Centre. **Open** *Tower & OzTrek* 9am-10.30pm Mon-Fri, Sun; 9am-11.30pm Sat. *Skywalk* 9.30am-8.45pm daily. **Admission** *Tower & OzTrek* $24.50; $14.50-$18.50 reductions; $43-$72 family; free under-4s. *Skywalk* $64.50; $44.50 reductions. **Credit** AmEx, DC, MC, V. **Map** p327 F6.

Three high-speed lifts take approximately 40 seconds to travel to the golden turret of this well-known city symbol, which provides two levels of restaurants, a coffee lounge and an observation deck 250m (820ft) above ground, with 360° views. Skywalk, the latest of the city's thrill tours, opened in 2005, allowing visitors to wander around the outside of the turret. Harnessed to a range of skyways and viewing platforms, participants have the whole of Sydney at their feet: on a clear day you can see distant headlands up and down the coast, and as far west as the Blue Mountains. You're only just above the observation deck and safe at all times, but being outside is a definite buzz – it's a good alternative to BridgeClimb. Vertigo sufferers might prefer OzTrek, a virtual-reality ride through Australia's cultural history and geography, including climbing Uluru, a game of Aussie Rules footy and a tussle with a saltie (saltwater crocodile).

Sydney Town Hall

Corner of George & Druitt Streets, CBD (9265 9189/ concert information 9265 9007/www.cityofsydney. nsw.gov.au). CityRail Town Hall. **Open** 8.30am-6pm Mon-Fri. **Map** p329 E7.

Built on a graveyard and completed in 1889, Sydney Town Hall is an impressive High Victorian building, topped by a clocktower with a two-ton bell. It has retained its original function and interiors, including the council chamber and lord mayor's offices. The stunning vestibule, its colourful domed ceiling hung with a huge crystal chandelier, has some of the earliest examples of Australian-made stained glass. Behind this, Centennial Hall is dominated by a magnificent 8,000-pipe organ: with a capacity of 2,048, it was once the largest concert hall in the world, and it is still used for organ recitals and other musical events. At the time of writing it was undergoing major renovations, and was due to reopen midway through 2009.

Chinatown & Haymarket

Chinese people have been in Sydney since the First Fleet landed in 1788: two of the ships' cooks were said to be Chinese. By 1891 the Chinese population had reached 14,000, but dwindled to 4,000 as the 'White Australia' policy peaked in the 1950s. Today, Chinese migrants make up the third-largest group of immigrants coming to New South Wales.

Vietnamese refugees (including many of Chinese descent) arrived in the wake of the Vietnam War, while dissident students sought asylum after the 1989 Tiananmen Square debacle. In the years leading to the handover of Hong Kong to China, many Hong Kong Chinese also left for Australia.

When you hit Chinatown, the vitality and energy of the Chinese community is obvious. Sino-Sydneysiders do not live in a ghetto – there are also established surburban enclaves in Strathfield, Willoughby and Ashfield, and many are simply integrated into the community – but Chinatown is the commercial and culinary hub. Once confined to Dixon Street, a somewhat tacky pedestrianised mall created in the 1980s, it continues to expand and change at a phenomenal rate. It now extends well into Haymarket, over Hay Street, down Thomas and Ultimo Streets, and across George Street.

Around the ornate gates in Dixon Street, soil, sand and rock from Guangdong province has been buried. For the Chinese, it symbolises that Australia is their home and they can be buried there. Sussex Street has now taken over from Dixon Street as the main strip; the brightly lit section from Goulburn Street to Hay Street – where **Paddy's Markets** (*see p193*) and the **Market City** shopping centre reside – bustles with activity from early morning to late at

Go high at the **Sydney Tower**.

night. There are restaurants, supermarkets, shops, Chinese-language cinemas and some well-hidden gambling spots, and this is one of the few places in Sydney where you can get a meal and a drink at 2am.

In daylight hours, chic shops sell (real and ersatz) Agnès B and Katharine Hamnett watches, Versace and Romeo Gigli perfumes, Jean-Paul Gaultier bags and a range of bewilderingly hip gear: the Chinese community is not only growing in size, it's also increasingly affluent. The days of wall-to-wall sweet-and-sour pork have been left far behind; nowadays, little Chinatown diners serve Peking-style dumplings, others specialise in handmade noodles and barbecued duck or seafood, and grand Hong Kong-style dining rooms with over-the-top chandeliers are always packed with Chinese and Anglos choosing delicacies from *yum cha* (dim sum) trolleys. For standout restaurants in the area, *see p149*.

Darling Harbour, Pyrmont & Ultimo

Map p326, pp328-329. **Transport** Darling Harbour *Ferry Darling Harbour/CityRail Central or Town Hall/Monorail Convention, Darling Park or Harbourside/LightRail Convention or Exhibition/bus 443.* **Pyrmont** *Ferry Pyrmont Bay/LightRail Fish Market, John St Square, Pyrmont Bay or Star City/bus 443, 449.* **Ultimo** *CityRail Central/Monorail/LightRail Exhibition or Paddy's Markets.*

The reclaimed waterfront of Darling Harbour, on the western side of the CBD, boasts some acclaimed modern architecture (courtesy of architect Phillip Cox) and a huge retail complex (courtesy of global capitalism). The area is geared very much towards tourists, and can feel pretty soulless compared to other parts of town. There are many attractions here – among them the **Sydney Aquarium** (*see p85*), the **Australian National Maritime Museum** (*see p84*), the **Chinese Garden of Friendship** (*see p84*), the **Sydney Entertainment Centre** (*see p249*) and the **IMAX cinema** (*see p227*) – that it's easy to overlook the most basic one of all: the view of the western cityscape from the Pyrmont side of Darling Harbour, one of the best in Sydney. And it's free. There's also the **Harbourside** shopping centre (*see p190*), a bit of a tourist trap, but good for souvenirs if you don't want to search too hard and, for the thrill seeker, boasting the **Flight Experience**, a Boeing 737 jet simulator on level three.

Darling Harbour hosts a stream of free festivals, concerts and other events at weekends and in school holidays throughout the year.

New Year's Eve and Australia Day, in particular, are occasions for giant parties: call the **Darling Harbour Information Line** for details (1902 260 568, www.darling harbour.com.au). There's also a branch of the **Sydney Visitor Centre** (*see p307*), behind the IMAX cinema.

Cockle Bay Wharf (so named because of its original abundance of shellfish), on Darling Harbour's eastern shore, houses an array of cafés, restaurants and clubs spread across an epic space designed by populist American architect Eric Kuhne, who also designed the public areas in adjoining Darling Park (and the enormous Bluewater development in Kent, England). Initially written off by many as a failure, Cockle Bay has become a hugely successful entertainment precinct and a fun place to dine and hang out. By day, it's a haven for teens and families; at night, tourists and twentysomethings move in, many heading for the sail-like glass building of superclub **Home** (*see p221*).

Further north, past the Sydney Aquarium, the party continues along the newly created **King Street Wharf** at yet more restaurants, cafés and a clutch of waterside apartments. A good place to be on a sweltering summer's night – if you're under 30, that is, is the **Cargo Bar** (*see p221*), a rowdy outdoor venue with pumping music and great waterside views, or stylish bar **Loft** (*see p180*) at the far end of the promenade.

Pyrmont, to the west of Darling Harbour (reached by the pedestrian Pyrmont Bridge), was once a mix of working-class cottages, refineries, quarries and engineering works. Now it is filling with apartment buildings and office blocks (including the Fairfax media empire and Channel Seven TV) as the city spreads ever westward. It is also home to **Star City** (*see p84*), Sydney's casino – a gaudy, vulgar, Las Vegas-like creation (also by Phillip Cox) with a deluxe hotel (*see p39*). **Jones Bay Wharf**, at the top end of the peninsula, has undergone a sleek renovation into classy offices, topped off with the fabulous seafood restaurant **Flying Fish** (*see p151*).

Pyrmont's biggest draw is undoubtedly the **Sydney Fish Market** (*see p85*), widely regarded as one of the best in the world, on the edge of Blackwattle Bay. From its auction rooms premium-grade tuna goes to Japan, and a dozen or more outlets sell fresh-off-the-boat seafood. Browse among enticing mounds of salmon, snapper and yabbies (freshwater crustaceans), then pick up some rock oysters and find a sunny wharfside seat at which to picnic. But watch out for the pelicans: they're partial to seafood too.

Sightseeing

Ultimo – south of Pyrmont and west of Chinatown, which is creeping towards it – has evolved into a strange meeting place of media, academic and museum life. Once notorious for some of Sydney's most squalid housing, and later the site of the municipal markets, it's now home to the sprawling **University of Technology**, the headquarters of the **Australian Broadcasting Corporation** and the masterfully converted **Powerhouse Museum** (*see below*). The 2007 opening of the **Ian Thorpe Aquatic Centre** (*see p258*) has added to the growing chic of this area. Housing various pools, a sauna, fitness centre and café, the centre was one of the last works by top Sydney architect Harry Seidler, who died in 2006 (*see p76* **When Harry met Sydney**).

Australian National Maritime Museum

2 Murray Street, Harbourside, Darling Harbour (9298 3777/www.anmm.gov.au). Ferry Darling Harbour or Pyrmont Bay/LightRail Pyrmont Bay/Monorail Harbourside/bus 443. **Open** 9.30am-5pm daily (6pm Jan). **Admission** free; $15-$30 for special exhibits & vessels. **Credit** AmEx, MC, V. **Map** p326 D6.

For a city whose history has always been entwined with its harbour, the sea and water travel, it comes as no surprise that this museum is one of the finest and most unabashed when it comes to maritime treasures. An exhibition traces the history of the Royal Australian Navy, but the biggest exhibits are the vessels themselves, among them the 1888 racing yacht *Akarana*, 1950s naval destroyer HMAS *Vampire* and traditional Vietnamese junk *Tu Duo* ('Freedom'), which sailed into Darwin in 1977 with 39 refugees. A café offers seafood-oriented, open-air eating at the water's edge, while the shop sells books, nautical knick-knacks and, if you really want to splash out, sailing packages with qualified skippers.

Chinese Garden of Friendship

Corner of Pier & Harbour Streets, Darling Harbour (9281 6863/www.chinesegarden.com.au). CityRail Central or Town Hall/Monorail Paddy's Markets or World Square/LightRail Paddy's Markets. **Open** 9.30am-5pm daily. **Admission** $6; $3 reductions; $15 family. **No credit cards**. **Map** p329 E8.

Unless you're prepared to arm-wrestle for your share of tranquil spots, avoid this place at the weekend when it's full of grimly determined tourists. Designed in Sydney's Chinese sister city, Guangzhou, to commemorate the 1988 bicentenary, the Garden of Friendship symbolises the bond between the two. The dragon wall features two dragon heads, one in gold for Guangzhou, one in blue for NSW, with a pearl in between. There are waterfalls, weeping willows, water lilies, 'wandering galleries' and wooden bridges. Head up to the tea room balcony, order a cup of tea and enjoy the best view of all: the entire park reflected in the Lake of Brightness. Not surprisingly, the garden is a big hit with wedding parties.

Powerhouse Museum

500 Harris Street, between William Henry & Macarthur Streets, Ultimo (9217 0111/www.powerhousemuseum.com). CityRail Central/Monorail/LightRail Paddy's Markets. **Open** 10am-5pm daily. **Admission** $10; $5-$6 reductions; $25 family. **Credit** AmEx, DC, MC, V. **Map** p328 D8.

This former power station opened as a fun and funky museum in 1988 and is the largest in Australia, with a collection of 385,000 objects, 22 permanent and five temporary display spaces, and more than 250 interactive exhibits. It covers science, technology, creativity, decorative arts and Australian popular culture, resulting in such diverse exhibitions as Tokyo street style and childhood memories of migration. Also here is the Boulton & Watt steam engine (1785).

Star City

80 Pyrmont Street, at Foreshore Road, Pyrmont (9777 9000/www.starcity.com.au). LightRail Star City/Monorail Harbourside/bus 443, 449. **Open** 24hrs daily. **Map** p326 C6.

Opened in 1997, Star City is both slick and tacky – marble toilets, cocktails, champagne, fine dining, then fish and chips, beer and miles of pokies. There are 1,500 slot machines, a huge sports betting lounge and sports bar, and 200 gaming tables featuring everything from blackjack and roulette to Caribbean stud poker. Elsewhere are invitation-only private gaming rooms for the high-rollers, many of whom fly in from Asia. The Lyric Theatre (*see p269*) and

Chinese Garden of Friendship.

Star Theatre stage glittery shows, Astral restaurant offers great views alongside its French food, and there's a revamped luxury hotel with spa.

Sydney Aquarium & Sydney Wildlife World

Aquarium Pier, Wheat Road, Darling Harbour (8251 7800/www.sydneyaquarium.com.au). Ferry Darling Harbour/CityRail Town Hall/Monorail Darling Park. **Open** 9am-10pm daily. *Seal sanctuary* 9.30am-sunset daily. **Admission** $28.50; $14.50-$19.50 reductions; $34-$80 family. **Credit** AmEx, DC, MC, V. **Map** p326 D6.

This fantastic aquarium comprises a main exhibition hall, two floating oceanariums – one dedicated to the Great Barrier Reef (and the largest collection of sharks in captivity), the other a seal sanctuary – and two touch pools. Watch out for the saltwater crocs in the northern river section and those elusive platypuses in the southern. Underwater viewing tunnels mean visitors can watch sharks and rays gliding past, or spot seals frolicking close up. Alternatively, the new glass-bottom boat Shark Explorer ride is another way to raise your heart beat.

Sydney Fish Market

Corner of Pyrmont Bridge Road & Bank Street, Pyrmont (9004 1100/www.sydneyfishmarket. au). LightRail Fish Market/bus 501. **Open** 7am-4pm daily. **No credit cards. Map** p326 C6.

This working fishing port – with trawlers in Blackwattle Bay, wholesale and retail fish markets, shops, a variety of indoor and outdoor eateries, and picnic tables on an outdoor deck – is well worth the trek to Pyrmont. Get up early and catch the noisy wholesale fish auctions; they start at 5.30am, with the public allowed in from 7am. It's the largest market of its kind in the southern hemisphere, and you won't find more varieties of fish on sale anywhere outside Japan: it trades more than 100 species a day and over 15 million kilos of fish a year. The affiliated Sydney Seafood School (9004 1111) offers a wide range of classes in handling and cooking seafood (from $75), some held by well-known local chefs.

Sydney Wildlife World

Aquarium Pier, Wheat Road, Darling Harbour (9333 9288/www.sydneywildlifeworld.com.au). Ferry Darling Harbour/CityRail Town Hall/Monorail Darling Park. **Open** 9am-10pm daily. **Admission** $28.50; $14.50-$19.50 reductions; $34-$80 family. **Credit** AmEx, DC, MC, V. **Map** p326 D6.

Opened in late 2006, this wildlife park on three levels is perfectly placed next to Sydney Aquarium (*see above*) for those families seeking an animal-oriented day out. There are over 100 Australian animal species on site and a huge variety of uniquely bizarre plant life. The ethos of the park is to tell each species' story on an evolutionary timeline within its own habitat, including elements of the Aboriginal dreamtime and conservation issues. Koalas naturally top the list, but the park is also home to wallabies, echidnas, reptiles, amphibians and more. The butterfly collection is truly amazing.

East Sydney & Darlinghurst

Map pp329-330. **Transport** Kings Cross side *CityRail Kings Cross/bus 311, 324, 325, 326, 327.* **Oxford Street side** *CityRail Museum/bus 333, 352, 378, 380, 382.*

Stand with your back to Hyde Park at Whitlam Square facing down Oxford Street towards Paddington, and you're on the edge of the CBD and the inner city. The lower end of Oxford Street up to and around Taylor Square attracts a colourful crowd of down-and-outs and all-night hedonists. It's also the eastern-suburbs hub of gay Sydney, and as night falls the street fills with perfectly pumped boys in regulation tight Ts and high-haired drag queens flitting between shows in the huddle of pubs and clubs along the 'Pink Strip'. This area is lively well into the early hours and can get a little edgy, and most recently has been subject to a troubling crime wave targetting the gay community. For the moment, the word on the street is not to go out alone and to use the many safe houses of gay-friendly pubs, clubs and shops on Oxford Street if you feel under threat.

As with the rest of Sydney, apartment blocks are forever popping up between the trad Victorian terraces, and with them an influx of cashed-up DINKs (double income no kids). Consequently, the previously drab retail options have perked up – the clothes shops are more innovative and there are even more coffee stores. Still, Darlinghurst and East Sydney are not yet a second Paddington or Double Bay – the wonderfully queer-centric **Bookshop Darlinghurst** (*see p194*) proudly stamps its identity on the Strip, as do the wig and fetish-wear shops and tattoo parlours.

Some consider **Taylor Square** the heart of gay Sydney and the epicentre of the Strip, though there's not a lot to see here save for a pocket patch of greenery (dubbed Gilligan's Island, after the US TV show), some arty bollards (several vandalised) containing local memorabilia and a lacklustre fountain – all courtesy of a slightly disappointing upgrade in 2003. City planners have now turned their attention to the Oxford Street strip itself, widening the pavements and planting trees.

Just beyond Taylor Square, on the north side of Oxford Street, **Darlinghurst Road** begins its downhill run to Kings Cross. The Victorian and art deco mansions here give a good idea of what the area used to be like, while the Harry Seidler-designed **Horizon** residential tower, looming over it all, typifies the present face. Take the time to wander through the old **Darlinghurst Gaol**, a magnificent collection of sandstone buildings dating from the 1820s,

Sightseeing

Island hopping

Port Jackson, as Sydney Harbour is properly called, is sprinkled with islands. Some, such as tiny Spectacle Island, a domain of the Royal Australian Navy, and Goat Island, one-time nerve centre of port operations, are currently off limits to the general public. On others, however, you can cast yourself away, or take a historical tour.

The largest island, at 18 hectares (44 acres), is **Cockatoo Island**, managed by the Sydney Harbour Federation Trust (8969 2100, www.cockatooisland.gov.au). The trust runs informative one-and-a-half-hour walking tours on Sundays ($18; $14 reductions; $60 family), which depart from Circular Quay and must be pre-booked. Cockatoo Island was once a convict prison and later an enormous shipbuilding and repair operation: structures associated with both these eras still stand like ghostly sentinels to an alternately dark and industrious past. There's a spanking new camping ground with 135 sites for tents (bring your own or rent one on the island), eight electric BBQs, four sinks and seating and tables for 80 people, plus solar-powered hot showers, toilets and a laundry, with internet access planned soon. Great for tourists is the full camping package ($75 per night), which includes site and tent hire, two self-inflating mattresses, two camp chairs and a lantern. All you need to bring is a sleeping bag. The site boasts amazing

Shark Island.

views across the Parramatta River to Hunters Hill, plus there's the Muster Station café and plans to open a bar.

The other islands that can be visited are under the auspices of the National Parks & Wildlife Service (NPWS; 9247 5033, www.nationalparks.nsw.gov.au), which

---

now a campus for the Sydney Institute of Technology and one of the city's best art schools. Incongruously, it also houses a butchery school, so don't be surprised to see arty types one minute and men in bloodied aprons the next.

Back then, instead of negotiating the hustling hordes and screeching traffic of Darlinghurst Road, you'd have reached Kings Cross by scrambling through scrub and sand drifts, past farms and sandstone quarries, before clambering down wooden ladders to Woolloomooloo Bay. The Darlinghurst ridge, where the Coca-Cola sign now stands at the top of William Street, was once the site of the city's windmills – walk past on a blustery August day and you'll see why. Another place worth visiting is the **Sydney Jewish Museum** (*see below*): Jewish immigrants have played a vital part in Australia's history and their story is told here.

Running roughly parallel to Darlinghurst Road on its east side is **Victoria Street**, a lively mix of cafés, restaurants, shops and a few

residential homes. The restaurants here and on Darlinghurst Road are generally better than those on Oxford Street. For a great French night out, head to **Sel et Poivre** (No.263, 9361 6530); for ice-cream and sorbet, queue up at the popular **Gelato Messina** (No.241, 8354 1223) – one spoonful and you're hooked. To find the beautiful people, seek out the **Victoria Room** cocktail bar (*see p182*) or the stylish boutique hotels **Medusa** (*see p40*) and **Kirketon** (*see p41*). Also nearby is that Sydney breakfast and lunch institution, **Bills** (*see p173*).

Sydney Jewish Museum

148 Darlinghurst Road, at Burton Street, Darlinghurst (9360 7999/www.sydneyjewish museum.com.au). CityRail Kings Cross/bus 311, 378, 380, 389. **Open** 10am-4pm Mon-Thur, Sun; 10am-2pm Fri. **Admission** $10; $6-$7 reductions; $22 family. **Credit** (shop only) MC, V. **Map** p330 H8.
After World War II, over 30,000 survivors of the Holocaust emigrated to Australia, settling mainly in Sydney and Melbourne. This museum opened in 1992

Sightseeing

has an office at Cadman's Cottage (*see p64*) in the Rocks. **Fort Denison**, just off Mrs Macquarie's Point, served as an open-air prison and was once called Pinchgut Island thanks to the starvation rations – bread and water for a week – served to its inmates. Its first resident, Thomas Hill, was marooned

here for seven days in 1788 as punishment for stealing biscuits. In 1862 a fort with a distinctive Martello tower was added and the island was renamed Fort Denison after then-governor William Denison. It's accessible by pre-booked tours ($17; $10-$16 reductions) on Matilda Cruises (9264 7377, www. matilda.com.au), leaving from Pier 26, Darling Harbour or No.6 Jetty, Circular Quay.

Shark Island, off Point Piper – named for its shape, not the creatures that lurk beneath – now has its own daily ferry service. It's great for picnics, as there are large grassy areas, lots of trees, picnic shelters, a gazebo and a wading beach. Toilets are on hand but there's no café, so bring your own tucker. Matilda Cruises (*see above*) leave from Pier 26, Darling Harbour or No.6 Jetty, Circular Quay ($16; $13.50-$14.50 reductions; $53 family), or you can hire your own water taxi.

Popular with wedding parties who like to hire their own island exclusively, **Clark Island**, near Darling Point, and **Rodd Island**, west of the Harbour Bridge in Iron Cove, are open to day-trippers year-round, with a $5 landing fee per person. Visitor numbers are limited, and you must book in advance with the NPWS and arrange your own transport by private boat, chartered ferry or water taxi from a NPWS list of licensed operators. Boats are allowed to drop off and pick up at the island wharfs, but not to tie up.

in Maccabean Hall, originally built to commemorate the Jews of NSW who had served in World War I. The hall has been the centre of Jewish life in Sydney ever since, so it seemed right to transform it into a permanent memorial to victims of both wars. There are two permanent displays – 'Culture and Continuity' and 'The Holocaust' – plus excellent touring exhibitions.

Surry Hills

Map p329. **Transport** *CityRail/LightRail Central/ bus 301, 302, 303, 352.*

South of Oxford Street is Surry Hills, an increasingly des-res area and nirvana for Sydney foodies and imbibers – a dozen new cafés, restaurants and revamped bars seem to open here every week. Its main thoroughfare is north-south **Crown Street**, an interesting mix of the very cool and the tatty. At night the vibe is heady and laid-back, with watering holes to suit every taste and pocket. The Oxford Street

end is a tad more chic; witness the **Dolphin on Crown** pub (No.412, 9331 4800, www.dolphin hotel.com.au). Opposite is **Medina on Crown** (No.359) a smart, serviced apartment block popular with short-stay business types, beneath which you'll find hip restaurants **Billy Kwong** (*see p155*) and **Marque** (*see p156*).

Moving a block further south, the very stylish **White Horse Hotel** (Nos.381-385, 8333 9999, www.thewhitehorse.com.au) is providing strong competition to the long-established **Clock Hotel** (No.470 Crown Street, 9331 5333, www.clockhotel.com.au), with its dining room and wraparound balcony.

The **Shannon Reserve**, a tiny park between these two hotels, hosts a lively flea market on the first Saturday of the month, but all through the week shoppers are well served by established premises such as the oriental curio shop **Mrs Red & Sons** (No.427, 9310 4860) and **Mondo Luce** (No.439, 9690 2667, www.mondoluce.com), one of a number of modish lighting shops. The **Book Kitchen** (*see p174*), one of Sydney's best combined book and café operations, and the **Bourke Street Bakery** (*see p174*), on the corner of Devonshire and Bourke Streets, are delicious and highly popular new additions.

Bourke Street itself, running parallel to Crown a block to the east, remains largely residential but is also sprouting some interesting shops and restaurants, spurred on by the transformation of the old St Margaret's maternity hospital into a swanky apartment complex that also includes coffee shops and restaurants, the **Object Gallery** and its great shop **Collect** (*see p208*), health point **Uclinic** (*see p208*), Ferdinando de Freitas's lush florists **Garlands** (9357 7900, www.garlands.net.au) and a rather chic **Woolworths** (No.417, 9326 0100). All this activity is gradually and inevitably gentrifying Surry Hills, as happened to previously funky Paddington, now too chichi for words. Bourke Street is also the site of the **Brett Whiteley Studio** (*see below*), a museum dedicated to the acclaimed Sydney-born artist.

Brett Whiteley Studio

2 Raper Street, off Davies Street, Surry Hills (9225 1740/recorded info 9225 1790/1800 679 278/www.brettwhiteley.org). CityRail Central then 10mins walk/bus 301, 302, 303, 352. **Open** 10am-4pm Sat, Sun. **Admission** free. **Credit** AmEx, MC, V. **Map** p329 G11.

Brett Whiteley was one of Australia's most exciting artists. In 1985 he bought a warehouse in Surry Hills and converted it into a studio, art gallery and home in which he lived from 1988. Following Whiteley's death in 1992 – in the motel room in which he was rumoured to have fuelled his drug and alcohol habit – the studio was converted into a museum. Managed by the Art Gallery of NSW, it offers a singular insight into the artist through photos, personal effects, memorabilia and changing exhibitions of his work.

Redfern & Waterloo

Transport Redfern *CityRail Redfern/bus 305, 308, 309, 310, 352.* **Waterloo** *Bus 301, 302, 303, 343, 355.*

Surry Hills peters out in the west at Central Station (just beyond the rag-trade centre on and around Foveaux Street) and in the south at Cleveland Street, the border with Redfern. Aboriginal people from rural areas started moving into Redfern in the 1920s because of its proximity to Central Station, cheap rents and local workshops offering regular work. More arrived during the Depression of the 1930s, and by the '40s the area had become synonymous with its indigenous population. Following

the 1967 national referendum, which gave indigenous people citizenship rights, Redfern's Aboriginal population increased to 35,000, causing mass overcrowding.

In the decades that followed, government programmes (some helpful, some not) have disseminated the area's indigenous people, and today it is undergoing intensive reinvention, with some pockets hurtling upmarket. But the central patch of run-down terraces in a one-hectare area bounded by Eveleigh, Vine, Louis and Caroline Streets – which make up the **Block**, the beleaguered heart of a black-run Aboriginal housing co-operative – remains an indigenous enclave.

The area's problems – poverty, drugs and alcoholism – haven't gone away, but there's an increasingly smarter edge to Redfern as artists' galleries take up residence, and those who can't quite afford Surry Hills turn their eyes south of the Cleveland Street border looking for residential bargains. The City of Sydney is pouring money in too, with a $50 million infrastructure programme for Redfern, Waterloo, Darlington and Eveleigh. This includes an $11 million revamp of **Prince Alfred Park**, between Central Station and Cleveland Street, with a 50-metre outdoor pool (*see p260*), as well as an already-underway $19 million restoration of **Redfern Park** and its stadium, training ground of the South Sydney Rabbitohs rugby league team.

In neighbouring Waterloo, development is also running rife. **Danks Street**, at the heart of a previously industrial area, is now brimming over with a fine range of eateries and interior design shops, plus art gallery complex 2 Danks Street and top-quality Italian grocers **Fratelli Fresh** with its delicious **Café Sopra** (*see p206 and p174*). Further south, in Zetland, if all goes to plan (and it's a 20-year plan), Green Square – focused around the Green Square train station and bordered by Botany Road and Bourke Street – is slated to house over 5,000 people in 2,800 new apartments and houses, plus parks, shops and recreation centres, all part of Australia's single largest development project.

Kings Cross, Potts Point & Woolloomooloo

Map p330. **Transport** *CityRail Kings Cross/bus 311, 324, 325, 326.*

Kings Cross, formed by the intersection of Darlinghurst Road and Victoria Street as they cross William Street, has long been the city's sex quarter, although today it's dominated as much by drugs as by prostitution. The seedy action is pretty much confined to 'the Strip', stretching along Darlinghurst Road from William Street to the picturesque El Alamein fountain, although visitors should stick to the main streets, especially at night when the winding roads leading back towards Potts Point and the Cross tend to become drug alleys. Along Darlinghurst Road you'll find Australia's first legal 'shooting gallery', a monitored, fully staffed injecting room opened in 2001. Despite much controversy, the centre has remained open, and many in the know say it has reduced the number of heroin deaths in the area while providing desperately needed support for the growing number of users.

Community and local government efforts in recent years to clean up Kings Cross, spurred on by the influx of cashed-up residents to the swanky new apartments that have been created on the sites of several of the area's former hotels, have made a difference. Today's Cross is a pale hangover from the days of the Vietnam War, when thousands of US soldiers descended for R&R with fistfuls of dollars and the desire to party the horrors of war out of their systems. Their appetites tended towards the carnal, and the dreary parade of seedy strip clubs and massage parlours – now frequented mostly by suburbanites, out-of-towners and international sailors – is evidence of how they got their kicks. Nonetheless, the Cross's neon lights still pull in hordes of backpackers, sustained by a network of hostels, internet cafés and cheap and cheerful restaurants. The good news for tourists is that there are plenty of police on the beat, and when the night turns ugly, as it inevitably does for some, you needn't get caught in the trouble.

The Cross officially starts from underneath the Coca-Cola sign at the intersection of William Street and Darlinghurst Road. Here you'll also find a cavernous underground **Coles** supermarket as well as perhaps the only bona fide straight sauna in the area – the **Ginseng Bathhouse** (*see p211*), a traditional Korean bathhouse with an impressive range of therapeutic treatments. Branching off Darlinghurst Road is Victoria Street, where you'll find the **Holiday Inn** (9368 4000, www.ichotelsgroup.com) and, from 2008, the **Chifley Potts Point** (1300 650 464, www.constellationhotels.com.au), an upmarket refurb of the former Crest Hotel. Another smart new hotel sprucing up the area is the Eight Hotels Group **Diamant** in Bayswater Road (*see p41*). Back in Darlinghurst Road is the **Bourbon** (*see p184*): previously the legendary Bourbon & Beefsteak Bar, this used to be the chosen watering-hole for stalwart locals, sailors and some of the area's more colourful characters, but is now aiming for the youth style set with a slick glass-and-white refit.

Beyond the El Alamein fountain you're into Potts Point proper. In contrast to the Kings Cross Strip's wall-to-wall neon lighting, Macleay Street, with its columns of cool plane trees, is made for slow strolling and offers architectural and culinary pleasures. Tall, impregnable apartment buildings such as the neo-Gothic **Franconia** (No.123) offer a glimpse of the grandeur of the old Cross. Orwell Street, running west off Macleay, houses one of Sydney's finest art deco buildings, the old Minerva theatre, now called the **Metro** (Nos. 26-30), while at 3 Manning Street the Royal Australian Institute of Architects (RAIA; 9356

Woolloomooloo.

2955, www.architecture.com.au) was pivotal in helping rescue **Tusculum**, a grand villa dating from the 1830s.

Potts Point has many fine eateries and good coffee shops, and it's a far cry from the desperate world of the Strip. You seem to be on another planet: one populated by chic, wealthy Sydneysiders. If you turn off Macleay Street and into Challis Avenue (also dotted with cafés), you'll soon come to the northern end of Victoria Street and a handful of the grand 19th-century terraces that formerly made it one of the city's most elegant thoroughfares. Victoria Street backs on to a cliff that drops down to Sydney's oldest suburb, Woolloomooloo, which stands partly on land filled with the remains of scuttled square-riggers, and is now a mix of public housing (incorporating many original buildings) and swish new developments.

You can walk down from Victoria Street via Horderns, Butlers or McElhone Stairs. Alternatively, **Mezzaluna** (123 Victoria Street, 9357 1988, www.mezzaluna.com.au), serving Italian food, offers a spectacular view over Woolloomooloo Bay to the city skyline. **Embarkation Park**, atop a navy car park at the corner of Victoria Street and Challis Avenue, provides an equally magnificent vista, particularly midweek around twilight when the office towers are lit up.

Macleay Street becomes Wylde Street, which runs out of puff at the **Garden Island Naval Base** on Woolloomooloo Bay, where you are greeted by the surreal sight of the Royal Australian Navy's fleet moored at the side of the road. The US Navy also regularly docks here, disgorging fodder for the strip joints and massage parlours of the Cross. The newly opened **Royal Australian Navy Heritage Centre** (*see below*) is at the very tip of the base on Garden Island – although you can't access it on foot; instead you have to catch a ferry from Circular Quay.

Woolloomooloo was named by the Womerah people who lived here before European colonisation. The area's Aboriginal roots are celebrated in several colourful street murals, although you should wander with care around this public housing estate: it doesn't have Sydney's best reputation for safety. Jutting into the bay is **Woolloomooloo Wharf** (also called Cowper Wharf; *photo p89*), constructed in 1910 as a state-of-the-art wool and cargo handling facility. Over the years the wharf fell into disuse, and it seemed destined to crumble into the harbour until former Premier Bob Carr slapped a conservation order on the site.

In 2000 a stylish mix of eateries, apartments, an upmarket hotel (formerly the W, now **Blue**; *see p41*) and private marinas opened. Those

who can't afford to eat in the snazzy restaurants that line the finger wharf instead promenade up and down the boardwalk in the sun. And just up Cowper Wharf Road is **Harry's Café de Wheels** (*see p175*), Sydney's most famous pie cart, here since World War II and practically an obligatory fuel stop after a night's boozing in the Cross or 'Loo.

Opposite the wharf is **Artspace** (*see below*), an extraordinary government-run art gallery, and, on the corner of Bourke Street, the **Woolloomooloo Bay Hotel** (No.2, 9357 1177, www.woolloomooloobayhotel.com.au). This traditional pub with outdoor seating, restaurants, a balcony and bands is always lively, and from Thursday nights onwards it's packed with old neighbourhood faces and rowdy youngsters who don't care for the Blue bar peacocks over the road. Around the corner on Nicholson Street the **Tilbury Hotel** has a great restaurant and a stylish bar that's popular with a gay crowd on Sunday nights (*see p240*).

Artspace

The Gunnery, 43-51 Cowper Wharf Road, between Forbes & Dowling Steets, Woolloomooloo (9356 0555/www.artspace.org.au). CityRail Kings Cross then 10mins walk/bus 311. **Open** 11am-5pm Tue-Sat. **Admission** free. **Credit** MC, V. **Map** p330 H6. This government-funded contemporary art gallery presents edgy, experimental and challenging work. Five galleries and 12 studios (for local and international artists) are housed in the historic Gunnery building. Prepare to be 'shocked, stimulated, inspired and entertained' – or so the gallery claims.

Royal Australian Navy Heritage Centre

Garden Island (9359 2003/www.navy.gov.au/ranhc). Ferry Garden Island. **Open** 9.30am-3.30pm daily. **Admission** free. *Special Exhibition Gallery* $5; free under-16s. **No credit cards. Map** p330 K3. For close on a century Garden Island, home to the Royal Australian Navy (RAN), has been off-limits to the general public. In late 2005 the very tip of the one-time island, long since connected to Potts Point, was reopened, with the only access via a five-minute ferry ride from Circular Quay. It's worth a visit, if only to enjoy the relative quiet of the grounds and the odd collection of monuments and giant naval objects, including radars, a propeller and 21in torpedoes, which constitute a bizarre outdoor sculpture exhibition. The view from the former Main Signal Building is spectacular – it's easy to see why this was the nerve centre for controlling the movement of naval vessels around the harbour. The Heritage Centre, occupying what was the Gun Mounting Workshop (dating from 1922) and an ex-boat shed (1913), includes an oceanic range of items that provides plenty of insight into navy life. Bring a picnic or enjoy lunch or afternoon tea at the Salthorse Café with a lovely view across Elizabeth Bay.

Eastern Suburbs

Life is more than just a beach for those chasing the good life east.

Over the past 20 years the eastern suburbs have been completely transformed by a young, go-getting moneyed set who want to live the high life close to the city. The east has always had a certain cachet – the back streets of **Woollahra**, **Double Bay**, **Vaucluse**, **Darling Point**, **Rose Bay** and **Centennial Park** are lined with grand colonial mansions that have housed generations of Sydney's wealthiest. But **Paddington**, **Bondi**, **Tamarama**, **Watsons Bay** and **Coogee** are where the nouveau riche are staking their claim.

Old-timers recall the beachside suburbs as largely working class enclaves and Paddington as a slum, but all that is ancient history. Today the 'it crowd' has taken over, transforming Paddington's tiny terraced houses into TARDIS-like structures – iron balconies and crowded porches on the outside, open plan with glass backs, spiral staircases and marble bathrooms on the inside, and yards with narrow lap pools out back. And in Bondi – at the Junction and around the famous beach – ritzy apartment blocks are increasingly dominating the skyline, with rents and house prices at a record high.

The magnetism of the east lies with its easy proximity to the city and its natural beauty. The water – be it ocean or harbour – is never far away, and in many suburbs it's the main view. There is a host of pretty beaches with something for everyone, from family-centric Nielsen Park to sunbathers' haven Tamarama, surf paradise Bondi or peaceful Parsley Bay. Add to this great shops – Paddington is the appointed home of the city's fashion designers, many trading from terraced homes – plus enough restaurants, cafés and bars to keep locals busy, and, even if you're just spending a few hours here, it's pretty clear why the east has become the place to settle.

Paddington

Map p332. **Transport** *Bus 333, 352, 378, 380, 389.*

There's nowhere in Sydney quite like Paddington and it's not hard to see why the area has attracted a wealth of young, trendy professionals, all eager to pay high rents in exchange for the aspirational zip code. Unlike Darlinghurst and Surry Hills, its neighbours to the west, Paddo has managed to create a fashionable chic without a seedy underside,

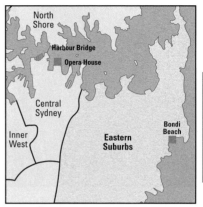

but hasn't gone so far as its easterly neighbours Woollahra and Centennial Park in becoming so overpriced that the young and impressionable can't afford to live there.

Walking up the main drag of **Oxford Street**, with the city behind you, Paddington proper starts just after **Taylor Square**, the heart of gay Sydney. The scene gets straighter (but no less fabulous) the further up the hill you go until you reach Centennial Park at the top. Banks, bottle shops, boutiques and beautiful boys and girls happily co-exist on Oxford Street, and it's a great place to spend a few hours just walking and taking in the buzzing atmosphere.

Just past South Dowling Street are two of Sydney's best art-house cinemas, the Palace chain's **Academy Twin** and **Verona** (for both, *see p226*). Nearby are two of the city's finest bookshops, **Berkelouw Books** (*see p194*) and **Ariel** (*see p193*), open late for pre- and post-movie browsing.

Further along, on the south side of Oxford Street, is **Victoria Barracks** (*see p93*). Built by convicts to house soldiers and their officers, the complex predates most of Paddington, and its Georgian lines bring a sense of grandeur to the area's rows of terraces. From the Barracks to Centennial Park, Paddington's best-dressed come out in force in the ever-changing mix of designer shops, one-off boutiques and chain stores. The cafés, pubs, bars and gift shops get their fair share of trade too.

Paddington Market.

Paddington Town Hall & Library (1891) on the corner of Oatley Road and **Paddington Post Office** (1885) provide an elegant edge, and are reminders of the days when such grand Victorian buildings dominated the skyline and steam trams rattled up Oxford Street – the Town Hall is in typical Classical Revival style with a 32.5m (107ft) clock tower. Next to the Post Office is the delightful **Juniper Hall** (1824), probably the oldest surviving villa in Australia. Built as a family home for gin distiller Robert Cooper, it was named after the berry used in making the drink. Cooper, nicknamed 'Robert the Large' for his size, was a colourful character, a convict who smuggled wine from France, fathered 28 children and founded Sydney College, which later became Sydney Grammar School. In 1984 the property was restored by the National Trust and is now privately leased to local businesses.

The imposing **Paddington Inn** (338 Oxford Street, 9380 5913, www.paddingtoninn.com.au) is the area's best-known pub. It has good bar-bistro food and a heaving mix of locals, tourists and members of the transitory overseas population that washes through Paddo. The **Light Brigade** on the corner of Jersey Road (2A Oxford Street, 9331 2930, www.lightbrigade. com.au) is also worth checking out for its recently refurbished upstairs restaurant and cocktail lounge.

Each Saturday you can sample the wares at the popular **Paddington Market** (*see p193*), on the corner of Oxford and Newcombe Streets. You'll find an assortment of local crafts and reasonably priced clothing (a number of Sydney designers started out here), plus fortune tellers, masseurs and purveyors of just about every other knick-knack you could hope for.

The streets off Oxford Street also hold much of interest. William Street, to the north just before the Paddington Inn, has a cluster of Sydney's best local fashion designers. Duck down and check out **Collette Dinnigan** (*see p195*), **Leona Edmiston** (*see p197*), the **Corner Shop** (*see p198*) and **Sylvia Chan** (No.20, 9380 5981). Back towards the city, opposite the Barracks, is Glenmore Road, flanked by the boudoir-style **Alannah Hill** boutique (*see p195*) on one corner and **Scanlan & Theodore** (*see p198*) on the other. You'll also find **Kirrily Johnston** (*see p197*) a few doors down and the super-trendy **sass & bide** (*see p198*) back around the corner on Oxford Street. Further down Glenmore Road – past a smattering of art galleries and yet more high-class boutiques – you'll find some of the area's most extravagantly and expensively refurbished Victorian terraces. Don't be fooled by the cramped exteriors: behind the front doors and delicate, iron-laced balconies so typical of Paddington, interior designers have gone to work creating bright, modern spaces with the use of the odd skylight or spiral staircase thrown in for good measure.

Over the roundabout on the left is the **Royal Hospital for Women Park**, a patch of green beloved by dog walkers because of its 'off-leash' status (there are only ten local parks where dogs are allowed to run free). The park sits behind the chi-chi **Paddington Green** housing development, a swanky conversion of the original Royal Hospital for Women buildings. There are a few benches and lots of sun (sunbathers catch the last rays of the day here), and the park also features some of the original sandstone blocks from the historic hospital.

Five Ways, which is indeed the junction of five roads surrounding a mini-roundabout, is the popular villagey heart of the area and has recently benefitted from a long-overdue pavement widening project. You're spoilt for choice for somewhere to eat here. There's the excellent Japanese restaurant **Wasavie** (*see p158*); terraced tapas spot **Tapenade** (corner of Broughton Street and Glenmore Road, 0488 198099); two French bistros, **Vamp's** (227 Glenmore Road, 9331 1032) and **L'Etoile** (*see p161*); upmarket fish 'n' chips den **A Fish Called Paddo** (No.239, 9326 9500); and **Plumer at Five Ways** (No.226, 9361 6131), a popular hangover stop where you can get your teeth into burgers and roast chook. Overseeing the lot is the majestic **Royal Hotel** (*see p186*), built in 1888 in a grand classical style. On the ground floor is a busy pub with pokies and TV screens; upstairs there's a restaurant with a popular wrap-around balcony.

If you carry on down Glenmore Road you'll find **White City Tennis Club** (9360 4113) on your left, and eventually **Trumper Park** with its cricket oval. Behind is native bush, plus a steep walkway up to Edgecliff on the left and Woollahra – via the Palms Tennis Centre – on the right.

Victoria Barracks

Oxford Street, between Greens & Oatley Roads (9339 3170). Bus 352, 378, 380, L82. **Open** *Museum* 10am-3pm Sun. *Tour with museum entry* 10am Thur. Closed Christmas holidays. **Admission** *Museum* $2 donation. *Tour* free. **Map** p332 J10.
Built with local sandstone between 1841 and 1849, the Regency-style Victoria Barracks were designed by Lieutenant-Colonel George Barney, who also built Fort Denison and reconstructed Circular Quay. Sydney's first barracks had been at Wynyard Square, where the soldiers of the 11th (North Devonshire) Regiment of Foot had been able to enjoy all the privileges of living in the city: the pubs, the eating houses and the brothels. So there were groans of despair when they were uprooted to the lonely outpost that was Paddington. The site had been chosen because it had borehole water and was on the line an attacker from the east might use, but its main feature was scrub: heath, swamp and flying sand from the adjacent dunes, which caused conjunctivitis (known as 'Paddington pink-eye'). And while the main building and parade ground were (and still are) quite stunning, the soldiers' quarters were cramped, and British regiments dreaded being posted to Australia. Nowadays, the old barracks is used as a military

planning and administration centre. The museum is housed in the former 25-cell jail, also home to a ghost, Charlie the Redcoat, who hanged himself while incarcerated for shooting his sergeant.

Centennial Park & Moore Park

Map pp332-333. **Transport** Centennial Park *Bus 333, 352, 355, 378, 380.* **Moore Park** *Bus 339, 373, 374, 376, 377, 392, 393.*

If it's greenery you're after, head to the top of Oxford Street where **Centennial Park** (*see p94*) awaits. It's hard to believe that such a huge and lush expanse of breathing space and picnic spots lies so close to the inner city. Filled with artificial lakes, fields, bridle paths and cycle tracks, the park attracts a mix of families looking for the perfect spot for a toddler's birthday party, outdoor fitness fanatics and casual strollers. Rolling all the way down to Randwick Racecourse and across to Queens Park and Moore Park (home to Sydney's first zoo), Centennial Park was created in the 1880s on the site of the Lachlan Swamps as part of the state celebrations to mark the centenary of the landing of the First Fleet. The three parks (Centennial, Moore and Queens) encompass 3.8 square kilometres (1.5 square miles) and are collectively known as Centennial Parklands.

The former Royal Agricultural Society Showground on the west side of Centennial Park has been controversially and expensively redeveloped by Fox Studios Australia into a film studio and entertainment complex, the **Entertainment Quarter** (*see p94*). Next to

Royal Hospital for Women Park.

Centennial Park.

the complex (approached from Moore Park Road or Driver Avenue), the huge white doughnuts that form **Sydney Cricket Ground (SCG) & Sydney Football Stadium (SFS)** (*see p261*) light up the skyline for miles around at night. South of the cricket ground, **Moore Park Golf Course** (*see p257*) is one of the best and most popular public courses in the city.

Centennial Park

Between Oxford Street, York, Darley, Alison & Lang Roads (9339 6699/www.cp.nsw.gov.au). Bus 333, 352, 355, 378, 380. **Open** *Pedestrians* 24hrs daily. *Vehicles* Sunrise to sunset daily. Car-free days last Sun in Mar, May, Aug, Nov. **Map** pp332-333.

A weekend trip to Centennial Park, especially in summer, reveals Aussies at their leisurely best. There's an outdoor fitness station, and you can hire rollerblades and bikes or even go horse riding. Cyclists used to be a bit of a menace, but these days most adhere to the 30km/hr (18.6mph) speed limit and will dodge a pedestrian if at all possible. But don't be scared off by all this activity: the park is also teeming with those just looking for a shady spot to snooze or read a good book. Even in peak season, when it seems every Sydneysider wants a piece of the park, the vast lawns mean that there's always a secluded spot to claim as your own. Statues, ponds and native Australian flowers make it one of the prettiest places to spend a day, and there's a great restaurant and café. Ranger-led walks include Tree Tours, Frog Pond Workshops and the night-time Spotlight Prowl, and keep your eyes peeled for the Moonlight Cinema (*see p228*) from December to March.

Entertainment Quarter

Driver Avenue, Moore Park (8117 6700/www.entertainmentquarter.com.au). Bus 355, 373, 374, 376, 377, 391, 392, 396. **Map** p332 J/K12.

Fox Studios Australia (www.foxstudiosaustralia.com) opened in May 1998. Since then, Sydneysiders have become used to having US movie stars in their city; some, such as Keanu Reeves and Kate Bosworth, have become regular visitors. Regrettably, Australia's first (and only) Hollywood-style film studios are not open to the public any more, even for tours. What the public gets instead is the super-slick Entertainment Quarter complex, with cinemas, shops, a barrage of eateries and some huge entertainment spaces. There's a weekend crafts market and a farmers' market on Wednesdays and Saturdays (both open 10am-4pm). Kids will have a ball at the two state-of-the-art playgrounds, seasonal ice-rink, ten-pin bowling centre, crazy golf course and the popular Bungy Trampoline. The Forum music venue is also found here.

Woollahra

Map p333. **Transport** *Bus 200, 389.*

If a long day of being fashionable on Oxford Street proves too much, you'll find a welcome escape opposite the Paddington Gates of Centennial Park. **Queen Street** is the closest thing in eastern Sydney to an old-fashioned English high street, and the villagey feel will make you think the city is hours rather than minutes away. Pricey antique shops, galleries, delis, homeware stores and boutiques line the first stretch, leading down to the upmarket, if rather twee, suburb of Woollahra. The antique shops are not for the bargain hunter, but are surprisingly rich in wares.

Walking along Queen Street, turn left at the traffic lights onto Moncur Street at French restaurant **Bistro Moncur** (*see p159*), past posh deli **Jones the Grocer** (*see p207*), round to the right into Jersey Road and you'll come to the **Lord Dudley Hotel** (No.236, 9327 5399, www.lorddudley.com.au). The Dudley is an oasis for nostalgic Poms looking for a touch of home; it positively screams English pubdom, from its ivy-clad exterior down to its cosy bar with British beers on tap. It's also popular with mature moneyed locals and revellers from the nearby **Palms Tennis Centre** (Quarry Street, Trumper Park, 9363 4955) and **Paddington Bowling Club** (2 Quarry Street, 9363 1150), who meet at the pub for a post-match tipple.

A walk from the east end of Queen Street via Greycairn Place and Attunga Street to **Cooper Park** – which runs east into the suburb of Bellevue Hill – is a pleasure in the jacaranda season (late November to December), when the streets are flooded with vivid purple blossoms. At the east end of Cooper Park, across Victoria Road, you'll find small **Bellevue Park**, which has some unbeatable views of the harbour.

The eastern suburbs, from Woollahra to Double Bay, Bellevue Hill, Bondi Junction and Bondi, are home to Sydney's Jewish community. On Friday evenings and Saturday mornings the streets are alive with the devout walking to and from the various synagogues dotted throughout the area, including the liberal **Temple Emanuel** in Woollahra (7 Ocean Street, 9328 7833, www.emanuel.org.au) and the beautifully designed, light-filled **Central Synagogue** in Bondi Junction (15 Bon Accord Avenue, 9389 5622, www.centralsynagogue.com.au).

Bondi Junction

Map p333. **Transport** *CityRail Bondi Junction/bus 200, 333, 352, 378, 380.*

While the almost mythical appeal of Bondi Beach is what draws the crowds to this part of Sydney, Bondi is in fact its own sprawling suburb, made up of four distinct and individual areas. Bondi Junction is the buzzing shopping and transport mecca bordering Paddington, Woollahra and Queen's Park to the west. Bondi proper is really just Bondi Road, the suburban and commercial road that links the Junction to Bondi Beach. That famous beach heads north by way of its main drag, Campbell Parade, and leads straight into the quieter area of North Bondi, home of many an expat veteran Sydneysider and the Bondi Golf Course.

While it's the beach that is the focus for most, the Junction, with its monster mall – the **Westfield Bondi Junction** (*see p191*) – has become the place to shop in eastern Sydney, if you don't mind crowds. It boasts every brand-name shop from Oxford Street and the city, plus supermarkets, restaurants, a multi-screen cinema and even a state-of-the-art gym with great views over Sydney. The proximity of the city by train or bus has turned Bondi Junction into a booming residential and commercial hub, and although the older parts look relatively shabby in the shadow of the Westfield, on the whole the place has finally come into its own.

From the Junction, there are two roads that lead to Bondi Beach. Old South Head Road turns away from the ocean and winds north to Watsons Bay, so take the turn-off at O'Brien Street or Curlewis Street. It tends to be quieter than the other route, Bondi Road, which can be thick with buses; in summer, when the crowded vehicles trundle at a snail's pace, it's often quicker to walk (about 30 minutes).

Snaking through Waverley into Bondi (increasingly called 'Bondi Heights' by estate agents keen to exploit its trendiness), Bondi Road is a mixed bag of alternative shops and international restaurants. **Kemeny's Food & Liquor** (Nos.137-147, 13 8881, www.kemenys.com.au) is the best place to buy fine wine on the cheap, and you can take your pick from a variety of casual eateries, including well-known fish restaurant **The One That Got Away** (No.163, 9389 4227).

Bondi Beach to Coogee Beach

Map p334. **Transport** Bondi Beach *CityRail Bondi Junction then bus 333, 380, 381, 382, 389/bus 333, 380, 389.* **Coogee Beach** *CityRail Bondi Junction then bus 313, 314/bus 372, 373, 374, X73.*

Bondi Beach is anything but a romantic, stroll-in-the-moonlight sandy spot. It's the closest ocean beach to the city and at first glance could easily be dismissed as a tacky tourist trap. But don't be fooled: there's a reason that some die-hard Sydneysiders wouldn't live anywhere else, local to the extent that they venture out only when they absolutely have to.

The main thoroughfare is noisy, four-lane **Campbell Parade**, which runs parallel to the beach and is lined with restaurants, cafés and souvenir shops, all of them usually packed at weekends. Below that is dinky **Bondi Park** – housing the 1928 **Bondi Pavilion** and the **Bondi Surf Bathers' Life Saving Club** (the first of its kind in the world) – and after that the sand itself. Bondi is a good surfing beach, and there are plenty of places to hire wetsuits and surfboards along Campbell Parade; check out **Bondi Surf Co** (*see p201*), which provides info on surf lessons too. Summer nights bring in punters by the carload, particularly around Christmas and on New Year's Eve, when Bondi is best given a wide berth.

Key restaurants on the thumping, pumping Parade include **Sean's Panaroma** (*see p163*), a Bondi secret, although many eateries are merely reasonable rather than remarkable. To get a feel for why some people live and die in Bondi, you need to look around the corners.

Sightseeing

Walk 1: Bondi to Coogee

Character Dramatic ocean views.
Length 5km (3 miles) one way.
Difficulty Easy, some uphill climbs and steps.
Transport CityRail Bondi Junction then bus 333, 380, 381, 382.

This coastal walk through some of the prettiest beaches in suburban Sydney takes about two and a quarter hours. You don't have to go all the way to Coogee – you can stop at any of the beaches en route – and you can, of course, do the walk in reverse.

Start at the southern end of Bondi Beach, where steps take you up to Notts Avenue and past the stylish Icebergs clubhouse and outdoor pool (*see p98*). The path starts to the left of Notts Avenue, dropping down then up some steep steps to Marks Park on the spectacular cliff-top Mackenzies Point, with its 180° views along miles of coastline.

This first stretch – as far as Tamarama Beach – is the site of the annual Sculpture by the Sea festival in November (*see p214*). It's a fantastic sight but attracts occasionally overwhelming crowds. After another headland the path drops down to Tamarama, which has a park, a little café next to the beach and plenty of surfers.

At the southern end of Tamarama, steps lead up to the road, which after a few hundred coast-skirting metres takes you to Bronte Beach. Bronte is popular with surfers and families (especially the southern end, around the outdoor pool), and good for picnics and barbecues. There are also shower and toilet blocks and a kiosk (prices go up on Sundays), plus a cluster of cafés and restaurants on the road just behind the beach.

Walk through the car park and take the road uphill via steps through Calga Reserve to Waverley Cemetery. Spreading over the cliffs, the cemetery is a tranquil, well-kept area, and the view out to sea makes this a fitting resting place. Take the oceanside path through the adjoining Burrows Park to the warm welcome of Clovelly Beach. Equipped with a café and a pub just up the hill, this is one of the prettiest of the walk's beaches and a great place to stop for a bite to eat or a swim. It's at the end of a long, narrow inlet, meaning that the waves are small and manageable, making it popular with families.

Continuing on around the next headland, the last patch of sand before Coogee is Gordon's Bay; there's not much in the way of a beach, but the view over the water is stunning. Then comes Dunningham Reserve, where a sculpture commemorates those who died in the 2002 Bali bombings. Two plaques nearby list the victims from Sydney: six from the local Dolphins rugby league club and 20 from the eastern suburbs. Then it's down to Coogee Beach. At the far end is South Coogee, where you'll find Wylie's Baths,

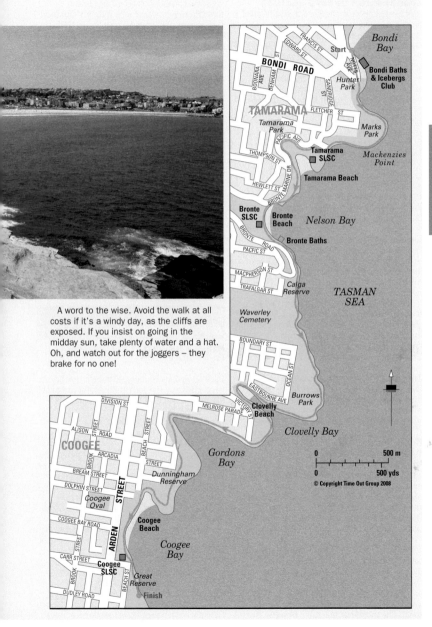

A word to the wise. Avoid the walk at all costs if it's a windy day, as the cliffs are exposed. If you insist on going in the midday sun, take plenty of water and a hat. Oh, and watch out for the joggers – they brake for no one!

Bondi Bay

Start

Bondi Baths & Icebergs Club

FRANCIS ST

EDWARD ST

BONDI ROAD

BOONARA AVE

DENHAM

Hunter Park

SANDRIDGE ST

FLETCHER ST

TAMARAMA

Marks Park

Tamarama Park

PACIFIC AVE

THOMPSON ST

Tamarama SLSC

Mackenzies Point

BRONTE MARINE DR

HEWLETT ST

Tamarama Beach

Bronte SLSC

Bronte Beach

Nelson Bay

BRONTE ROAD

Bronte Baths

PACIFIC ST

MACPHERSON ST

TRAFALGAR ST

Calga Reserve

TASMAN SEA

Waverley Cemetery

BOUNDARY ST

OCEAN ST

EASTBOURNE AVE

Burrows Park

MELROSE PARADE

VICTORY ST

Clovelly Beach

DIVISION ST

Clovelly Bay

ALISON ROAD

STREET

BEACH STREET

ARCADIA

Gordons Bay

COOGEE

BROOK STREET

STREET

BREAM STREET

DOLPHIN STREET

Dunningham Reserve

0   500 m
0   500 yds
© Copyright Time Out Group 2008

Coogee Oval

COOGEE BAY ROAD

ARDEN STREET

Coogee Beach

Coogee Bay

CARR STREET

BROOK STREET

BEACH ST

Coogee SLSC

Great Reserve

DUDLEY ROAD

Finish

enjoying a mid-afternoon beer, but give it a miss if you're hoping to meet anyone local. Australians prefer the Beach Road Hotel, previously known as the Regis and still called that by genuine Bondi-ites. On the corner of Hall Street, hotel **Ravesi's** (*see p47*), with its new cocktail bar Drift, is still a fashionable flame drawing the pretty people in from the suburbs to drink and get merry.

The north end of the beach has its fair share of cafés and eating establishments – including the hugely popular **North Bondi Italian Food** (*see p161*) – but a quieter vibe. The outdoor gym, which is really just a collection of bars set up for pull-ups, is now generally acknowledged as the number one spot for tanning, posing and mutual admiration among Sydney's gay men.

Further on is the pricey Ben Buckler headland and the shops of North Bondi. Beyond is the small but pretty **Bondi Golf Course**, site of some Aboriginal rock carvings, and **Williams Park**, a favourite spot with North Bondi residents hoping to watch the sunset or the New Year fireworks. Watch out, though: civilised North Bondi has an occasional unpleasant side when the smell from the sewage treatment plant – visible as a large chimney on the headland – drifts down. Gunk from the plant runs via a network of tunnels to an outlet five kilometres (three-and-a-half miles) into the ocean.

Bondi is also home to the famous **Bondi Icebergs Club** (*see below*), housed in a strikingly modern, four-storey building at the southern end of the cove. Throughout the winter, members of the club (formed in 1929) gather every Sunday morning for their ritual plunge into the icy waters of the outdoor pool. The club also houses the upmarket **Icebergs Dining Room** (*see p161*) and its bar on the third floor – both ideal for panoramic views over the beach.

Past the Icebergs complex is the start of a stunning walk along the cliffs to **Tamarama Beach**, **Bronte Beach** and beyond (*see p96* **Walk 1: Bondi to Coogee**). The views are fabulous from Bondi's southern headland, which turns inwards to show off Bondi Beach in all its glory. Past **Waverley Cemetery**, the coastal walk continues south to lovely **Clovelly Beach** and then on to dramatic **Coogee Beach**, with its historic **Wylie's Baths** and the deservedly popular women's pool.

Generally acknowledged to be Bondi's poorer cousin in terms of fashion, restaurants, bars and even its beach, Coogee has raised its game in the past few years. Although still littered with backpackers – who find the cheaper rates preferable to overpriced Bondi – it's answered a need for more palatable eating and drinking spots. The travellers' faves, the **Coogee Bay**

Hotel (*see p45*) and the **Beach Palace Hotel** (169 Dolphin Street, 9664 2900, www.beachpalacehotel.com.au), are still thumping every weekend, but trendy **Cushion Bar** (corner of Carr and Arden Street, 9315 9130) provides a slightly swankier spot for a drink. **A Fish Called Coogee** (229 Coogee Bay Road, 9664 7700) is a casual-looking gem, and there are also Indian, Thai and Japanese restaurants, plus breakfast spots aplenty.

Bondi Icebergs Club

1 Notts Avenue, Bondi Beach (café 9130 3120/gym 9365 0423/pool 9130 4804/www.icebergs.com.au). CityRail Bondi Junction then bus 333, 380, 381, 382. **Open** *Bar* 10am-late daily. *Café* 11am-10pm Mon-Fri; 8am-10pm Sat, Sun. *Gym* 6am-8.30pm Mon-Fri; 8am-5pm Sat, Sun. *Pool* 6am-6.30pm Mon-Fri; 6.30am-6.30pm Sat, Sun. **Admission** *Gym* $15. *Pool* $4.50; $2.50 reductions; $10 family. **Map** p334.

Although most famous for its all-weather swimming club, Icebergs houses a number of other attractions. There's a pool, gym, sauna and deck on the ground floor, all open to the public, plus the national head-quarters of Surf Life Saving Australia and a small museum on the first floor. The stunning Italian restaurant and cocktail bar are on the top floor, but you can get equally good views (and cheaper booze and nosh) from the Icebergs Club bar and Sundeck Café on the second floor.

Elizabeth Bay & Rushcutters Bay

Map p330. **Transport** *CityRail Kings Cross/ bus 200, 311, 323, 325.*

Back on Sydney Harbour, Elizabeth Bay begins beyond Fitzroy Gardens at the southern end of Macleay Street. Gone are the backpackers and crowded streets: here the calm, quiet roads are lined with residences that date from the 1930s. Worth a peek are **Elizabeth Bay House** (*see p100*) and **Boomerang** (corner of Ithaca Road and Billyard Avenue), a 1930s Alhambra-esque fantasy that has been home to some of Sydney's highest flyers – and fastest fallers. On the edge of Elizabeth Bay is **Beare Park**, one of many little green Edens that dot the harbourside.

The next inlet east is the romantically named **Rushcutters Bay** (*photo p100*), so called because of the convicts who really did cut rushes here: two of them were the first Europeans to be killed by the local Aboriginal inhabitants, in May 1778. There's now a large and peaceful park lined with huge Moreton Bay figs. The bay is also home to the **Cruising Yacht Club of Australia (CYCA)** on New Beach Road: its marinas are a frenzy of activity every December when the club is the starting point

Hall Street is the villagey heart of Bondi Beach, with such everyday necessities as banks, a post office and travel agents, as well as a gaggle of cafés and restaurants that have changed it from a daytime strolling location to a funky nightlife strip. The new vibe has spread to the surrounding streets: visit **Hurricanes** (126 Roscoe Street, 9130 7101, www.hurricanes grill.com.au) for steaks, and **Brown Sugar** (106 Curlewis Street, 9130 1566) for its famous breakfast eggs blackstone. Gould Street has a small but significant collection of designer shops, many of whose keepers started selling their wares at the famous **Bondi Market** (*see p193*), which takes place every Sunday.

Bondi is popular with backpackers for good reason: it's loud, crowded and anything goes. Most of the budget accommodation is on or around Campbell Parade, Hall Street and nearby Lamrock Avenue and Roscoe Street. Further north is the favourite drinking spot of all out-of-towners, **Hotel Bondi**. It has guest rooms (*see p47*) and is a fun and feisty spot for watching sport, dancing into the wee hours or

Secret gardens

Between and behind the million-dollar homes, the eastern suburbs hide a number of outdoor gems. From a tiny maze and a suburban creek to a hallowed beach and a picture-postcard cemetery, these haunts are not to be missed.

Harbourview Park
Entrance from either Harkness Street, Russell Street or Bathurst Street, Woollahra. **Map** p333 O10.
There's no harbour view from this shady park, but it's quite a find. A steep descent through a canopy of mature trees leads to a cool leafy oasis with a creek running through it – all this in the centre of residential Woollahra. This is where locals retreat to walk their dogs and come for picnics. There's a lovely shaded playground, tables and seating and even a basketball hoop. It's also a longish 'shortcut' on the walk from Bondi Junction to Double Bay.

Paddington Maze
Next door to Sarah Cottier Gallery, 3 Neild Avenue, Paddington. **Map** p330 K8.
Nestled between a Victorian terrace and the Sarah Cottier Art Gallery in the labyrinthine backs streets of Paddington is this mini maze – no bigger than a large house plot – which delights local children. 'It's a magical hideaway of thigh-high hedge fun,' says Sarah Cottier, who saw the place transformed in 1990 from a rundown playground to its current glory. Walk the maze or sit on the bench at the back and take in the view.

Parsley Bay Reserve
Bottom of Horler Road, Vaucluse.
The real secret to this grassy coastal haven is finding it. With that solved, devotees return again and again. It's most easily accessed by car at the bottom of the steep and winding Horler Road, where there's a convenient car park. But if you're on foot, you can also approach the Reserve from the Crescent and Hopetoun Avenue. There's no parsley, but there is plenty of other flora and fauna. The Bay itself is a narrow inlet of the Harbour with a foot bridge connecting one side to the other. There's a sandy beach, parkland, a bijou kids' playground and even toilets. The 20-minute bushland walking trail is well worth the effort.

Waverley Cemetery
Corner of St Thomas & Trafalgar Streets, Bronte.
The iconic cortege gates with their intricate iron work and stone walls open on to one of the world's most picturesque cemeteries, with stunning ocean views throughout. As a final resting place for 86,000 people so far, this 130-year-old, 40-acre cemetery is a landmark close to the hearts of many Sydney families. Eminent residents include poets Henry Lawson and Dorothea Mackellar (whose famed *My Country* has become a national favourite) and cricketer Victor Trumper. In December 2007 the gates were awarded a $185,000 preservation grant courtesy of the National Trust of Australia (NSW).

Rushcutters Bay. *See p98.*

for the Sydney Hobart Yacht Race. If you fancy trying your hand at some sailing, or simply want to sit back, glass of wine in hand, while someone else steers you around the harbour, **Eastsail** (d'Albora Marinas, New Beach Road, 9327 1166, www.eastsail.com.au), close to the CYCA, will make life easy for you.

Elizabeth Bay House

7 Onslow Avenue, Elizabeth Bay (9356 3022/ www.hht.net.au). CityRail Kings Cross/bus 311, 312. **Open** 9.30am-4pm Fri-Sun. **Admission** $8; $4 reductions; $17 family. **Credit** (over $10) MC, V. **Map** p330 K6.

No expense was spared on this handsome Greek Revival villa, designed by John Verge for NSW colonial secretary Alexander Macleay in 1839: it boasted the first two flushing toilets in the country, the finest staircase in Australian colonial architecture, and breathtaking views of Elizabeth Bay and the harbour. But Macleay's extravagance proved fatal, and his debt-ridden family were forced to move out. Over the years the grand old house was vandalised, partly demolished and finally divided into 15 studio flats, garrets for the artists who flocked to Kings Cross. From 1928 until 1935 it acted as a kind of cheap boarding house for the Sydney 'Charm School' artists, who included Wallace Thornton, Rex Julius and Donald Friend. The gardens, on which Macleay lavished so much love, have long since gone to property developers, but the beautiful house (now run by the Historic Houses Trust) still breathes noblesse, wealth and good taste. Rooms are furnished as they would have been in its heyday, 1839-45.

Darling Point & Double Bay

Map p331. **Transport** Darling Point *Ferry Darling Point/bus 324, 325, 326, 327.* **Double Bay** *Ferry Double Bay/bus 324, 325, 326, 327.*

Bordered by Rushcutters Bay Park to the west and Edgecliff to the south, Darling Point is another of Sydney's most salubrious suburbs, with spectacular views as standard – the best of these can be sampled free from **McKell Park** at the northern tip of Darling Point Road. Head south down the street to the corner of Greenoaks Avenue to see **St Mark's Church**, designed by the acclaimed Gothic Revival architect Edmund Blacket, consecrated in 1864 and still de rigueur for flash society, showbiz and celebrity weddings.

The next suburb to the east is Double Bay, also known as 'Double Pay' as it is home to Sydney's luxury shopping precinct. Migration after World War II turned 'the Bay' into a sophisticated European-style village of cafés, restaurants, delicatessens and ritzy boutiques. Don't wander through here unless you look the part: you'll feel out of place in less than a well-put-together outfit and will have to cope with scathing looks and bad service in cafés.

It's no surprise that cosmetic surgeons prosper in the area – take a look at the ladies who lunch and you'll see the results. Despite the snob quota being fairly high, it's still a good place to grab a coffee or a bite to eat amid the pretty streets and lanes. The stunning purple blooms of the jacaranda tree set Double Bay ablaze in springtime, and for good reason: Michael Guilfoyle, one of the area's earliest professional gardeners, whose own nursery of exotic plants could be found on the corner of Ocean Avenue in the mid 1800s, was responsible for first acclimatising the Brazilian species to Australia.

New South Head Road is the main thoroughfare through the Bay. The **Golden Sheaf Hotel** (*see p44*) is a popular watering hole with drinkers of all ages and tastes. The bistro is exceptional, and the busy beer garden is especially fun on Sunday afternoons when bands perform. At the western end of New South Head Road you'll find real estate agents, upmarket tea specialist **Taka Tea Garden** (No.320, 9362 1777, www.takateagarden.com.au) and the **Sharon-Lee Studios** (Nos.308-310, 1300 769 011, www.sharon-lee.com.au), base of Sydney's eyebrow plucker to the stars.

There are also two beaches at Double Bay, but only one of them is suitable for swimming. The beach next to Steyne Park sadly isn't, but it's a nice place to wander and is always bustling with yachties. On summer weekends you can see the famous 18-foot sailing boats that compete in the annual Sydney-to-Hobart race rigging up and practising their moves, ready for battle. The **Australian 18 Footers League** club (77 Bay Street, 9363 2995, www.18footers.com.au), located just to the left of the beach, is something of a local secret. From October to the end of March, 25 or so skiffs race on the harbour every Sunday, with the club running a spectators' ferry, leaving the wharf at 2.15pm ($15 per head). It's a thrilling outing and you can kick back and indulge in an iconic Aussie pie served on board, or dine in style beforehand at **Alruth**, the club restaurant, which overlooks the water.

If you do want to swim in Double Bay, continue east for ten minutes on New South Head Road to **Redleaf Pool** (a shark-netted swimming area) and **Seven Shillings Beach**. This adorable little harbour beach is well hidden from the road, has a lovely garden setting and welcomes everyone. Behind the beach, next to Blackburn Gardens, is the attractive Woollahra municipal council building. On the other side of the gardens is **Woollahra Library** (548 New South Head Road, 9391 7100), undeniably the quaintest library in Sydney: it's a good place to read the newspapers for free.

Point Piper, Rose Bay, Vaucluse & Watsons Bay

Map p331. **Transport** Point Piper *Bus 323, 324, 325.* **Rose Bay** *Ferry Rose Bay/bus 323, 324, 325.* **Vaucluse & Watsons Bay** *Ferry Watsons Bay/bus 323, 324, 325, 380, 386, 387.*

Even if you can't match the hefty wallets of the people who live in these stunning harbourside suburbs, they are still easily enjoyed on the cheap. By ferry from Circular Quay you can take in Darling Point, Rose Bay and Watsons Bay – though not every ferry stops at every destination, and there's no service to Darling Point at weekends.

From Double Bay, small harbour beaches dot the shore up to Point Piper, which is full of stunning high-walled mansions. You can enjoy the multi-million-dollar views for free from the tiny **Duff Reserve** on the edge of the harbour, a good picnic spot if you can beat the crowds.

Lyne Park in Rose Bay is where the city's seaplanes land. You can watch them in more comfortable surroundings at the bayside restaurants **Catalina** (*see p163*) and **Pier** (*see p163*) – both great (and expensive) places to eat. On the other side of New South Head Road is **Woollahra Golf Course**, which is very charitably open to the general public, unlike the snooty **Royal Sydney Golf Course** right next door.

The streets from Rose Bay to Vaucluse feature yet more millionaire mansions: for the jealously inclined, the hidden jewels of the **Hermitage Foreshore Reserve** and an arm of **Sydney Harbour National Park**, which run around the peninsula, come as compensation. They are reached by a walking track that starts at Bayview Hill Road, below the imposing stone edifice of **Rose Bay Convent**, and offer fine views of the Harbour Bridge, as well as picnic spots aplenty and glimpses of the lifestyles of the rich and comfortable. The walk emerges at **Nielsen Park** (*see p102*), off Vaucluse Road, where there is an enclosed bay, **Shark Beach** – particularly beautiful on a summer evening – and the popular **Nielsen Park Café & Restaurant** (9337 7333, www.npk.com.au).

Dramatic **Watsons Bay**.

Sightseeing

Further along, on Wentworth Road, the estate that became **Vaucluse House** (*see below*) was bought by newspaperman and politician William Charles Wentworth in 1827. It's open to the public, along with its fine tearooms. Next to Vaucluse Bay, **Parsley Bay** is a lesser-known, verdant picnic spot popular with families.

It is claimed that **Watsons Bay** (*photo p101*) was the country's first fishing village. Now largely the province of **Doyles on the Beach** seafood restaurant (11 Marine Parade, 9337 2007, www.doyles.com.au) and rowdy weekend pub the **Watsons Bay Hotel** (*see p186*) – it has stunning views back across the harbour to the city, particularly at night, and retains vestiges of its old charm, including original weatherboard houses and terraces. These are best seen by walking north to the First Fleet landing spot at **Green Point Reserve** and on to **Camp Cove** and **Lady Bay** beaches, and the **Hornby lighthouse** on the tip of South Head.

On the other (ocean) side of the peninsula from Watsons Bay beach is the bite in the sheer cliffs that gives the **Gap** its name – and from which many have jumped to their doom. **Gap Park** is the start of a spectacular cliff walk that runs south back into Vaucluse. Along the way, hidden high above the approach to Watsons Bay at the fork of the Old South Head Road, is another fine Blacket church, **St Peter's** (331 Old South Head Road, 9337 6545, www.stpeterswb.org.au), home to Australia's oldest pipe organ, which dates from 1796 and was once loaned to the exiled Napoleon. The church gates commemorate the Greycliffe ferry disaster of 1927 when 40 people (including many schoolchildren) died in a collision at sea.

Nielsen Park

Greycliffe Avenue, Vaucluse (9337 5511/www.national parks.nsw.gov.au). Bus 325. **Open** 5am-10pm daily.
Generations of Sydneysiders have been flocking to Nielsen Park for family get-togethers since the early 1900s. They sit on Shark Beach or the grassy slopes behind or climb the headlands either side for a great view across the harbour. With its abundance of shady trees, gentle waters, panoramic views and the excellent Nielsen Park Café & Restaurant (*see p101*), it's the perfect picnic spot. It's also a favourite New Year's Eve viewing point for the harbour fireworks. Nestled in the grounds to the rear of the grassy slopes lies Greycliffe House, a Gothic-style mansion built in 1862 as a wedding gift from the co-founder and first editor of the *Australian* newspaper, William Charles Wentworth, for his daughter Fanny and her husband John Reeve. In 1913 it became a baby hospital, then a home for new mothers. Nowadays it's a NSW National Parks & Wildlife Service office, providing information on parks in the state. Watch out for the seaplanes that take off in neighbouring Rose Bay and begin their ascent over the waters of Shark Bay.

Vaucluse House

Vaucluse Park, Wentworth Road, Vaucluse (9388 7922/www.hht.net.au). Bus 325. **Open** *House* 9.30am-4pm Fri-Sun. *Grounds* 10am-5pm Tue-Sun. **Admission** $8; $4 reductions; $17 family. **Credit** (over $10) MC, V.
The oldest 'house museum' in Australia nestles prettily in a moated 19th-century estate, surrounded by ten hectares (28 acres) of prime land, with its own sheltered beach on Vaucluse Bay. From 1827-53 and 1861-62 this was the opulent home of William Charles Wentworth. The house originally stood in a much larger estate, and 26 servants were required to look after the master's seven daughters and three sons, not to mention his vineyards, orchards and beloved racehorses. The Historic Homes Trust has endeavoured to keep the place as it was when the Wentworths were in residence. In the kitchen a fire burns in the large grate and hefty copper pans line the walls; a tin bath, taken on European travels, still displays its sticker from London's Victoria Station; the drawing room is sumptuously furnished, and has a door that hides a secret (just ask a guide to open it for you).

Randwick & Kensington

Map p323. **Transport** Randwick *Bus 314, 316, 317, 371, 372, 373, 374, 376, 377.* **Kensington** *Bus 391, 392, 393, 394, 395, 396, 397, 399.*

For a flutter on the horses or just an excuse to get dressed up for a day, head to the **Royal Randwick Racecourse** (*see p264*). It's on Alison Road bordering Centennial Park, and the Spring Carnival in November is especially popular, giving all the fillies – both on and off the track – a chance to show off their finery. Check www.ajc.org.au for race dates. In November 2007 the course was famously shut down because of the devastating bout of equine flu that broke out in Sydney, but was quickly back up and running once the bans were lifted later in the year. The **University of NSW campus** lies south of the racecourse, while, across the road, the **National Institute of Dramatic Art (NIDA)** – alma mater of such stars as Nicole Kidman and Mel Gibson – has its headquarters and theatre.

Anzac Parade is one long highway, but will lead you to **Grotta Capri Seafood Restaurant** (Nos.97-101, 9662 7111, http://grottacapri.com.au). Hardly convenient for the city, the only reason to make the trip out is to gaze in wonder at the decor of this bizarre but wonderful eatery. Decked out like an undersea fantasy, it's well worth the taxi ride. Just up the road is the pinkest department store you'd ever hope to see, **Peter's of Kensington** (*see p190*). Avoid it like the plague at Christmas or during sale season, unless you like to queue.

Inner West

A Bohemian playground beyond the city and its beaches.

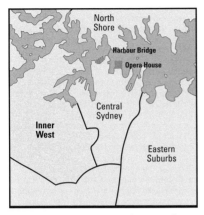

North Shore

Harbour Bridge

Opera House

Central Sydney

Inner West

Eastern Suburbs

Despite the usual attempts to clean up and gentrify the more fashionable suburbs in this underrated area, the inner west is a mix of grunge and glamour. At one extreme is the alternative hub of **Newtown** – home to goths, punks, musos, artists, writers, gays and lesbians – and the university student hangout of **Glebe**; at the other end, the cafés and restaurants of harbourside **Balmain** and trendy **Leichhardt** attract yuppie out-of-towners. Foodies also flock to **Rozelle**, **Haberfield** and **Petersham** to pick up delicacies from multicultural delis and bakeries, many of which remain local secrets.

Property prices are almost as high as the eastern suburbs, and there's plenty of modernisation, but much of the inner west likes to pretend it's still down-to-earth and 'real' by comparison. Overall it holds on to its status as an intriguing Bohemian village, but you have to look a bit harder than you once did to find the cheap and quirky gems that make it so special.

Balmain, Birchgrove & Rozelle

Map p326. **Transport** Balmain *Ferry Balmain, Balmain West or East Balmain/bus 442, 434.* **Birchgrove** *Ferry Birchgrove/441.* **Rozelle** *Bus 432, 433, 434, 440, 441, 442, 500.*

Snuggled in the inner west's harbour, a six-minute ferry ride from Circular Quay or a 20-minute bus trip from the city centre, Balmain was settled in the 1830s by boatbuilders; today it's increasingly home to on-the-make moneyed types. **Darling Street** – the spine of the area – starts at **Balmain East Wharf** and curves uphill past the sandstone **Watch House** (built in 1854, it was once the police lock-up and is now the headquarters of the Balmain Historical Society). For an easy ferry-and-food experience, walk a couple of minutes up from the wharf to **Relish at Balmain Bug** (55 Darling Street, 9810 5510). Housed in a cute stone cottage, this restaurant concocts traditional Australian food with an Asian edge.

Further up in central Balmain, Darling Street is lined with yet more food options interspersed with homeware and clothing shops, all winding along in a pleasingly low-key, two-storey way. A cluster of impressive Victorian buildings – the **Post Office**, **Court House**, **Town Hall** and **Fire Station** – are testament to Balmain's prosperity in the 1880s. **Balmain Market** (*see p193*), held on Saturdays in the grounds of **St Andrew's Church**, opposite Gladstone Park, is worth a browse, as is **Bray Books** (No.268, 9810 5613).

Pockets of urban cool include **Chopsticks** (No.264, 9818 3551), a dark, devil's-lair dining spot that serves pho, laksa and noodles at good prices. **Kazbah on Darling** (No.379, 9555 7067, www.kazbah.com.au) transports you to Morocco, while **Tuk Tuk Real Thai** (No.350, 9555 5899) offers fast and funky Thai food. **Blue Ginger** (No.241, 9818 4662) specialises in modern Asian cuisine, and newcomer **Efendy**, just off the main drag (79 Elliott Street, 9810 5466, www.efendy.com.au), serves modern Turkish food in a contemporary setting.

Cafés abound too, including the modern and spacious **Canteen Café** (No.332, 9818 1521) and current fashion hotspot **Bertoni Casalinga** (No.281, 9818 5845, www.bertoni. com.au), with its crates-on-the-footpath seating and high-quality Italian food. **Circle Café** (No.344, 9555 9755) recalls Balmain's simpler 1970s period: it houses a Uniting Church service on Sunday mornings. To create your own meal, head to French bakery **Victoire** (No.285, 9818 5529), a 25-year-old institution with a loyal following, for sourdough baguettes, outrageously good pastries and fresh cheeses, or **Dockside Seafood** (No.314, 9810 6587) to order mandarin scallops or spicy prawns.

Pubs are still the lifeblood of Balmain. Glamour couples head for the refined surroundings of the **London Hotel** (234 Darling Street, 9555 1377), or the **Exchange Hotel** (corner of Beattie and Mullens Streets, 9810 1171) – never mind the incongruity of a ping pong tournament and Martini club on Thursday nights. Ageing funsters patronise the **Unity Hall Hotel** (292 Darling Street, 9810 1331), while the **Town Hall Hotel** (No.366, 9818 8950) hovers oddly between pleasing pool sharks and house music lovers. Meanwhile, a variety of bands play the ever-popular **Cat & Fiddle Hotel** (*see p250*).

On the northern side of Darling Street is Birchgrove, flanked on three sides by water. The somewhat ramshackle **Sir William Wallace Hotel** (31 Cameron Street, 9555 8570) features a large autographed poster of a kilted Mel Gibson in *Braveheart* mode. Locals claim that Gibson, who lived in the area as an up-and-coming actor, was first inspired by the Scottish patriot while drinking at their bar. On Sundays the owners throw a free barbecue lunch. There's also the **Riverview Hotel** (29 Birchgrove Road, 9810 1151), for years owned by legendary Olympic gold medal-winning swimmer Dawn Fraser; her name lives on at the carefully restored harbourside pool at the edge of charming **Elkington Park**. The park overlooks **Cockatoo Island**, the largest of the harbour's islands and a former prison and shipyard.

Another park can be found at the tip of the narrow finger of **Louisa Road**, which is lined with half-hidden, multi-million-dollar homes. The peninsula was originally an abattoir of sorts, where Aboriginal people used to kill kangaroos. Its name was officially changed from Long Nose Point to **Yurulbin Point** in 1994 to reflect its indigenous heritage, but most people still use its former name. The wharf at its end is where the Birchgrove ferries arrive.

To reach Rozelle, simply continue west along Darling Street. If you're driving, let the overall-clad lads fill 'er up at Balmain's oldest service station, **Bill's Garage** (418 Darling Street, 9810 2611), established in 1915 and still featuring its original fixtures. For years the weekend Rozelle Market (Rozelle Public School) was about the only thing that brought people here, with bargain stalls selling CDs, plants, ceramics and collectables. That was, of course, until food became such an integral part of Sydney life.

The first figure to make local folk think beyond lentils was Tetsuya Wakuda, the internationally renowned Japanese chef, who opened his first restaurant (now closed) in the area. These days there are two hulking hangars that have become monuments to modern cuisine. First to arrive was **Barn Café**

& Grocery (731 Darling Street, 9810 1633), mixing a restaurant, a café and a 'supermarket' of hard-to-find, beautifully packaged and rather pricey ingredients. Next came **About Life** (No.605, 8755 1333), a self-styled 'natural marketplace' – a posh mix of café, caterer and naturopath. Across the road, the **Organic Trading Company** (No.584, 9555 9991) is a toned-down rival selling yet more organic lotions and funky baby clothes.

The rest of this stretch of Darling Street is a smattering of cafés, nurseries, antique stores and gift shops. Chocolatier **Belle Fleur** (*see p206*) injects some wicked indulgence into the somewhat earnest, upmarket-hippie scene. But it's **Orange Grove Farmers' Market**, held on Saturdays at Orange Grove Public School (at the junction of Darling Street and Balmain Road) that has the last word, with its organic produce and multinational cuisines (Ethiopian, Japanese, Dutch), all of them good (and cheap) enough to lure even Bondi dwellers across town.

Back out along Victoria Road to the north, the **Balmain Leagues Club** (138-152 Victoria Road, 9556 0400), one of two venues belonging to local rugby battlers the Wests Tigers, is a good place for a cheap steak and beer, rivalled only by the **Red Lion Hotel** (726 Darling Street, 9555 7933), which caters to travelling backpackers. Bringing back a smidge of Tetsuya glamour to this part of the strip is **La Grande Bouffe** (758 Darling Street, 9818 4333), a modern take on the classic French bistro. Back down Victoria Road towards the city is new arrival the Restaurant at Three Weeds (197 Evans Street, 9818 2788), serving modern European flavours. Housed in the Three Weeds Hotel, a former rock haven, it's a revamped, remodelled testimony to redemption.

Glebe

Map p328. **Transport** *LightRail Glebe/bus 431, 432, 433, 434.*

Directly to the west of central Sydney and shaped by its proximity to Sydney University on Parramatta Road, Glebe is an incongruous but atmospheric mix of grand, turn-of-the-20th-century mansions flanking quaint terraces and drab 1970s flat lets, with most streets still sporting their original rusty street signs. There are probably more cheap takeaway joints per square mile than anywhere else in Sydney – Glebe is the land of the $5 pad Thai.

The main drag is **Glebe Point Road**. Walking along it you find yourself weaving in and out of students and travellers, who are well catered for by several budget hotels, including the **Alishan International Guesthouse**

Sightseeing

Glebe Market. *See p106*.

(*see p48*) and the large and leafy hostel **Glebe Village Backpackers** (256 Glebe Point Road, 9660 8133). Become as one with them at the **Toxteth Hotel** (No.345, 9660 2370) or bond with Brits at **British Sweets & Treats** (No.85, 9660 9912), which has helpfully collected together all the faves needed to console homesick Poms.

You will never go hungry in Glebe, with its overwhelming array of Indian, Chinese, Thai and Vietnamese eateries – expect quick-fill, rather than gourmet. But the retail landscape is changing, home to the likes of the **Sonoma Baking Company** (No.215A, 9660 2116), which offers brilliant baked-on-the-premises spelt breads. For organic takeaway, try Moby's favourite Sydney haunt **Iku** (*see p166*) – think brown rice, miso, tofu and tahini-type offerings wrapped up in little paper parcels. And it's worth opening your wallet to try out modern European newcomer **Restaurant Atelier** (*see p165*) and oyster specialist the **Boathouse on Blackwattle Bay** (*see p166*).

For bestsellers and books to impress, head to **Gleebooks** (*see p194*), something of a literary institution, with user-friendly extended opening hours and two branches. Duck next door for a cheaper browse in **Sappho Books** (*see p194*), which peddles second-hand tomes and has the added lure of fresh coffee. You'll probably find cheaper still across the road on Saturdays at **Glebe Market** (*see p193*); sprawling out through school grounds, it deals in everything from clothes to CDs, with a small army of Asian food stalls to keep you going.

Traditional pubs include the British-style **Nag's Head Hotel** (162 St John's Road, 9660 1591), and Irish pub the **Friend in Hand Hotel** (58 Cowper Street, 9660 2326), which is stuffed with street signs, number plates and even a surfboat hanging from the ceiling, and hosts live crab races every Wednesday night.

For a feel of what Sydney used to be like before the money took over, visit **Wentworth Park Greyhound Track** (*see p264*), Sydney's premier dog-racing venue, which has meets every Monday and Saturday night. It's a great night out – there are bars and a bistro – and the betting ring here is about the only place where you'll still see pork-pie hats worn without a trace of irony.

At the Rozelle Bay end of Glebe Point Road is the large expanse of **Jubilee Park** and **Bicentennial Park**, plus adjoining **Harold Park Raceway** (*see p264*), home of 'the trots'; it also has camel racing planned for November and December 2008 following a successful season during the devastating equine flu outbreak the previous year. The park area has undergone a major face-lift to become

Camel racing at **Harold Park Raceway**.

a pleasantly marshy play zone with canoes and watercraft at its edge. Construction has also begun on a two-kilometre (1.2-mile) foreshore walk from the Bicentennial Park round to the fish markets in Pyrmont.

If you're in town in November, look out for the one-day **Glebe Street Fair** (see p215), the city's longest-running street party.

Annandale

Map p322. **Transport** Bus 436, 437, 438, 440, 470.

Annandale was once earmarked as a model township, hence the look of its main throughfare: broad, tree-lined Johnston Street (named after Lieutenant George Johnston, the first man to step ashore from the First Fleet in 1788 – albeit on the back of a convict). Located between Glebe and Leichhardt, it soon became a predominantly working-class district. These days it's gradually upping its foodie quotient on Booth Street to cope with the growing influx of residents decamping from the east.

Opened in late 2007, the rustic Italian **Vicini** (No.37, 9660 6600) is run by locals Natalie and George, who previously owned the Palace restaurant in Darlinghurst and Mars Lounge in Surry Hills, while head chef Massimiliano Borsato hails most recently from the central Summit restaurant. Providing a quick fix for those seeking sustenance in its red-chair surrounds is **Bar Asia** (No.101, 9571 9919), where it's noodles, rice and curry in a box to eat in or take away. **Bar Sirocco** (No.62, 9660 3930) picks up the pieces with brilliant breakfasts after a night out at the **North Annandale Hotel** (corner of Booth and Johnston Streets, 9660 7452).

Relaxed to the point of being horizontal, Annandale has a gentle vibe that smacks of parents with two-point-five kids. However, at the Parramatta Road end of the district, the **Annandale Hotel** (see p249) punks up the atmosphere with some of Australia's best rock bands, plus low-budget 16mm movie screenings on Monday nights.

Leichhardt

Map p322. **Transport** Bus 436, 437, 438, 440.

Further west still lies Leichhardt. Formerly known as the 'Little Italy' of the west, it's long outgrown that title, and the suburb's main thoroughfare, Norton Street, now pumps with a whole new nightlife vibe, although with young, slick Italians still having a firm grip on the territory.

Two stalwarts of the Italian dining scene are the recently revamped **Elio** (159 Norton Street, 9560 9129), which offers an elegant modern take on old favourites, and **Grappa** (see p165), which has barn-like proportions that would happily house the entire crew from *The Sopranos* – proper big-night-out stuff.

Get down with old Med boys at **Bar Italia** (see p176) to snap up cheap focaccia and great ice-cream. Drive the kids into **Café Gioia & Pizzeria** (No.126, 9564 6245), housed in a renovated service station, or visit the **Italian Forum** shopping mall: the architecture isn't to everyone's taste, but the enclosed piazza is a blessing for parents with wandering offspring – they can eat and watch at the same time. **La Cremeria Sorbetteria** (No.106, 9564 1127), still shifts great gelati, while **Glace** around the corner (27 Marion Street, 9569 3444) sexes it up with champagne sorbet. For a serious caffeine hit, you can always rely on **Bar Sport** (2A Norton Street, 9569 2397).

A cluster of Australian heritage buildings on Norton Street includes the two-storey **Leichhardt Town Hall** (No.107), built in 1888, which often hosts visiting art exhibitions, the former **Post Office** (No.109) and **All Souls Anglican Church** (No.126). But it's the **Palace Norton Street Cinema** (No.99), a four-screen art-house specialist with a licensed bar, a restaurant, a café and even a CD shop that pulls the crowds. Readers, meanwhile, should look to **Berkelouw Books** (see p194) across the road for a great selection of titles and a decent café to read them in.

Haberfield

Map p322. **Transport** Bus 436, 437, 438, 440.

Situated to the west of Leichhardt, Haberfield is the more recently discovered 'Little Italy' of the west – 'little' being the operative word. Yet despite its size, Haberfield remains the true heartland of homeland authenticity.

Foodies make a beeline for the main thoroughfare, Ramsay Street, where you'll find delicatessen **Paesanella** (No.88, 9799 8483), offering arguably the best antipasti and cheeses in Sydney; **Haberfield Bakery** (No.153, 9797 7715) with its staggering array of bread; and **A&P Sulfaro Pasticceria** (No.119, 9797 0001) boasting ice-cream, biscotti and handmade chocolates.

Trattoria **Il Locale** (No.94A, 9797 8966) is a newcomer to the scene. A simple tiled shell with wooden tables, its pizza is proving popular with the masses – book ahead or prepare to queue. Also recently opened is **Dolcissimo** (Nos.96-98, 9716 4444); choose from the bright

Sightseeing

café or the smarter, low-lit restaurant, although it's something of a bloodsport trying to get a seat in either. And still going strong is old favourite **Napoli in Bocca** (73 Dalhousie Street, 9798 4096): the red-checked tablecloths and pizza and pasta menu are as much of an institution as the bustling, old-style service.

Newtown, Erskineville & Enmore

Map p334. **Transport** Newtown *CityRail Newtown/bus 422, 423, 426, 428, 352.* **Erskineville** *CityRail Erskineville.* **Enmore** *CityRail Newtown/bus 426, 428.*

You can throttle it with renovators and young families, you can tart up the rough edges with smart shops, but Newtown somehow manages to remain stubbornly and comfortably down-at-heel, like an old drag queen in her glitter rags. Lying to the south of Annandale and Glebe, Newtown has it all: few other areas accommodate so many subcultures – grungy students from the nearby University of Sydney, young professional couples, goths, spiky punks, gays and lesbians – and in such apparent harmony. See the community in all its glory during the **Newtown Festival** (*see p214*) in November.

You could easily spend a day wandering along the main drag, King Street (and it's faster to stroll than drive, since the traffic can be horrendous). Intriguing and often eccentric specialist shops include one dedicated solely to buttons, another to ribbons and braids. A major player in the area is the **Dendy Newtown** four-screen cinema (No.261-263); next door is a good dance and alternative music shop, **Fish Records** (*see p212*), which opens late, as does bookshop **Better Read Than Dead** (No.265, 9557 8700). There's also **Goulds** (*see p194*), one of the largest and most popular second-hand bookshops in the city. Maybe it's because of the wild mix of humanity that makes up Newtown, but it's the perfect place to find anything for anyone. **Pentimento** (No.249, 9565 5591) has an exquisite range of books, homewares and handbags, while **Eastern Flair** (No.319, 9565 1499) offers exotic jewellery and furnishings. For divine teas, visit **T2** (No.173, 9550 3044), and for funky bags of all kinds stop in on **Crumpler** (No.305, 9565 1611).

You'll have no trouble finding somewhere to linger over a cappuccino – every second shopfront houses a café, and new places seem to open every week. Try **Astino's** (No.284, 9565 5238) for organic coffee, and **El Basha Café** (No.233, 9557 3886) for top-notch Lebanese sweets and pastries.

The restaurants on the strip veer towards pan-Asian bland, but are satisfying for the price. **Thanh Binh** (No.111, 9557 1175) is a stand-out Vietnamese, while **Sumalee Thai** (No.324, 8568 1988), at the back of the revamped **Bank Hotel** (No.324, 9557 1692), injects authenticity into its dishes – although at time of writing the pub was undergoing a major makeover. For a quick dinner, try funky **Simply Noodles** (No.273, 9557 4453) or **Italian Bowl** (No.255, 9516 0857), which offers a nifty, choose-your-own selection of pastas and sauces. For a contemporary take on Australian cuisine, book well in advance for **Oscillate Wildly** (*see p166*), just off King.

Newtown also has no shortage of pubs, each with its own distinctive slant. Check out bands at the **Sandringham Hotel** (*see p250*), still adorned with its original green and yellow tiles. New on the block for jazz and blues is the **Vanguard** (*see p250*) – more of a moody club than a pub, with sit-down dining during performances. The Newtown Hotel, a popular gay haunt, closed at the end of 2007, but still on the scene is the tarted-up **Marlborough Hotel** (No.145, 9519 6500), which has a wide art deco balcony upstairs. For near-24-hour comfort, try **Zanzibar** (No.323, 9519 1511): with a rooftop bar, pool downstairs and a cushion room upstairs, it relies on low lighting and beads to fulfil its name's exotic promise.

The bottom end of King Street, south of the railway station, has always been heaven for fans of antiques, junk and second-hand clothes, but edgy fashion shops are now beginning to predominate – look for **Dragstar** (No.535A, 9550 1243) and **Zukini** (No.483, 9519 9188), while kids get the star treatment at **Shorties** (No.537, 9550 5003). **Fiji Market** (No.591, 9517 2054) offers Indian and Pacific Islander produce as well as cheap sari fabrics and fabulously kitsch Hindu icons and posters. For a coffee break, locals head to the grungily hip **Chocolate Dog Café** (No.549, 9565 2526). Get the total Lebanese experience at **Arabella's** (No.489-491, 9550 1119), where a small clutch of Beirutians seem to be in permanent celebration mode; on Friday and Saturdays there's also bellydancing.

While in Newtown it's also worth ducking off King Street to the two 'E' suburbs, Erskineville and Enmore. To reach the former – which is rapidly expanding into a crowd-puller in its own right – turn off King Street at Erskineville Road and keep walking. You may recognise the landmark art deco **Imperial Hotel** (35 Erskineville Road) from *Priscilla, Queen of the Desert*. If drag shows are your thing, head here on Thursday to Saturday nights to see one of the best. It was closed as this guide went to press, but expected to reopen in 2008.

On Swanson Street – a continuation of Erskineville Road – is music club the **Rose of Australia** (*see p250*), which has been revved up to become a bar and restaurant with pavement seating. Across the road, **Stir Crazy** (128 Erskineville Road, 9519 0044) is creating its own noise with tasty twists like pumpkin stir-fry and chilli jam seafood. For well-priced, good all-round grub, try the **Tart Café** (106 Erskineville Road, 9557 9448) before heading down for a seriously strong espresso at **Café Sofia** (7 Swanson Street, 9519 1565). It's worth walking a little further down the road (which changes its name again, to Copeland Street) for the gourmet **Bitton Café** (*see p176*). Despite its somewhat out-of-the-way location, Bitton

has thrived under French-born chef David Bitton and his Indian wife, Sohani. You can buy sauces, dressings and oils to take home, and David also offers cookery classes.

To get to Enmore, return to Newtown and then turn off King Street on to Enmore Road. Bands and DJs occupy the renovated **@Newtown RSL** (No.52), two levels of slink with beads, funky wallpaper and chandeliers. Also check out the **Enmore Theatre** (*see p248*), a renovated deco-style theatre popular with local and international rock bands and stand-up comedy acts. For a pre-gig dinner, try out any of the Thai restaurants – **Banks Thai** (91 Enmore Road,

Italian Forum. *See p107.*

Quirky pub comps

With such an eclectic population of creative types and uni students, the inner west knows that alcohol is no longer enough to pull in the punters. Many of the area's pubs are famous for their crazy events, with venues falling over themselves to dream up the next outlandish comp.

One of the best-known activities is **crab racing**, which takes place on Wednesdays at 7.30pm at the **Friend in Hand** (58 Cowper Street, Glebe, 9660 2326, www.friendinhand. com.au). Patrons can purchase a crustacean for around $5, name it and send it off to race against other crabs in a series of heats and finals to win prizes.

In Enmore, the **Sly Fox** hotel (199 Enmore Road, 9557 1016) plays host to **YourSpace**, a night of free live music and performance every Thursday. Each week an average of ten acts hits the stage, from experienced artists

to the rawest of first-timers. Expect everything from bands and solo singers to comedians, spoken word artists, spoon players, poets and storytellers. Enter the raffle to win jugs of beer or suitably silly items such as electric mug warmers.

On Monday nights, the **Sandringham Hotel** (387 King Street, Newtown, 9557 1254) has an open mic night, **Club Stand Up**, held upstairs from 8pm, and **Popheads Music Trivia** downstairs; both are great fun.

Drunken Spelling Bee is one of the latest events on the calendar, first held in Australia at **Bar Broadway** (2 Broadway, Broadway, 9211 2321, www.barbroadway.com.au) in January 2008. Participants have to knock back a shot before attempting to spell a word. While it's not a regular night yet, it's bound to make a comeback soon, so keep an eye on the entertainment and gig pages.

Sightseeing

9550 6840) is one of the best. More food can be found at late-opening **Saray Turkish Pizza** (No.18, 9557 5310), and there are plenty of high-quality Lebanese restaurants on the street: try **Fifi's** (*see p166*) or head off the main track to **Emma's** on Liberty. Perhaps one of the oddest yet coolest additions to the Sydney nightlife scene is the **Sly Fox** (199 Enmore Road, 9557 1016); the music varies nightly, alternating between house, electro, techno, drum 'n' bass, rock and goth, while Wednesday brings Sydney's lesbians and drag kings out in force.

Petersham

Map p322. **Transport** *CityRail Petersham/ bus 428.*

Petersham lies north-west of Enmore; if you're driving, turn right off Enmore Road into Stanmore Road, which becomes New Canterbury Road, the main thoroughfare. Until very recently the neighbourhood was home to the **Oxford Tavern** that hulks at its gateway, flashing '24 hour lingerie waitresses' in screaming neon. It took some time to see that within the cloud of choking fumes of the main road, a 'Little Portugal' had already been born. It's a tiny strip that lacks the glamour of Leichhardt or the more villagey vibe of Haberfield, both just over Parramatta Road to the north, but makes up for it with authenticity.

A fleet of excellent traditional Portuguese restaurants and patisseries line the few blocks

of New Canterbury Road from Audley Street to West Street. Picking up occasional honours is **Gloria's Café** (82 Audley Street, 9568 3966), which serves homely Portuguese bites (pork and clam stew or cod cakes) both indoors and out on the pavement seating. There's often a trail of prettily-dressed Portuguese families heading into **Silvas Portuguese Traditional Charcoal Chicken** (82-86 New Canterbury Road, 9572 9911). At first glance it looks like a Portuguese McDonald's with alcohol, but scratch the surface and you'll find seafood specialities and table service alongside the takeaway chook and chips. At the sweetly named **Honeymoon Patisserie & Coffee Lounge** (No.96, 9564 2389) elderly Iberian gents gather for Portuguese snacks, while the barn-like **Petersham Liquor Mart** (No.41, 9560 2414) offers shelves of red, white and rosé wines imported from Portugal. To experience the full flavour of the area's cuisine and culture, be sure to visit during Audley Street's annual **Bairro Português** festival, which is held on a Sunday in March.

Finally, don't miss Petersham's main claim to fame on the food front – even though it's Greek, not Portuguese. Modern Taverna **Perama** (*see p165*) has soaked its way so completely into the touchy taste buds of Sydney's foodie elite that they don't mind the trek out to plane-traffic territory. Its signature dish of crisp kataifi pastry with bastourma, warm ricotta and figs is regularly eulogised on critics' lists of the best eats in Sydney.

North Shore

Safe, comfortable and family friendly – not to mention stunning.

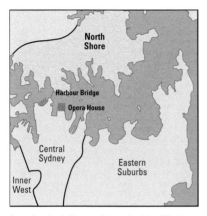

Crossing the bridge to the north side of Sydney has always meant joining the comfortable set. North Sydney itself is a business centre for insurance, publishing and especially advertising, so it's no surprise that many of the homes in the surrounding area are middle-class family mansions. Such a community has shaped the landscape here, establishing quaint villagey hubs hugging the jaw-dropping coastline. This makes it a good place to visit – there's always a café, restaurant, deli or ice-cream parlour nearby, and most of them are on or close to the water.

Another pull here is the child-friendly double whammy of funfair Luna Park Sydney (*see p113*) and Taronga Zoo (*see p116*), both on the family must-do list. From this side of the city you also get postcard views of the Harbour Bridge and the Opera House – the best, of course, is from the prime minister's home in Kirribilli (*see p112*). The current PM Kevin Rudd only uses it on weekends, residing in Canberra during the week, where he must be constantly dreaming of that dress circle vista. Other dreamy spots include Cremorne foreshore (*see p115*), where kookaburras and rainbow lorikeets nestle in weeping figs, and Balmoral beach (*see p116*), Sydney's most sophisticated oceanside suburb.

Note that the 'north shore' is not an officially designated area: rather, it's a term to lump together the suburbs on the north side of the harbour that are south and/or west of the

northern beaches. Many of these suburbs are not actually on the shore, nor are they especially interesting to tourists, being suburban enclaves. Those that are worth visiting – **Kirribilli**, **North Sydney**, **McMahons Point**, **Milsons Point**, **Mosman**, **Balmoral** and **Cremorne** – are all on the water.

Getting around the north shore isn't easy. Its size and sprawl mean that you're best off in a car, and many of its hidden beaches can only be reached by car, on foot (if you're prepared for the hills) or by charter boat (if you're not). But there is public transport available in the form of the north shore CityRail train line from North Sydney to Hornsby, a wide range of buses and the green-and-gold ferries from Circular Quay. The latter offer the most picturesque way to travel and capture the area's vibe perfectly as they visit the lower north shore suburbs.

Today the north shore is largely the homeland of Sydney's well-heeled, with the original Aboriginal population long since having been squeezed out. The early north shore settlers in the early 1800s were land dealers, among them Billy Blue, James Milson and Edward Wollstonecraft, and its development into a place of white estates and family homes stems from that time. More recently the area has become increasingly multicultural, with first and second generation immigrants from Japan, China, Korea and South Africa all settling in now and calling the area home.

The Cammeraygal and Wallumedegal tribes who inhabited the area when the First Fleet arrived at Sydney Cove in 1788 had largely been driven out of the region by the 1860s. The Cammeraygal, recorded as being a powerful and numerous tribe, 'most robust and muscular', lived along the foreshore, in the bushland and cliffs, and in rock shelters. Places such as Berry Island, Balls Head, Kirribilli, Cremorne and Cammeray are dotted with cultural remnants of the tribe's heyday.

Kirribilli

Transport *Ferry Kirribilli.*

The north shore starts at Kirribilli and Milsons Point, tiny suburbs nestled on either side of the Harbour Bridge and boasting sweeping vistas of the city and the Opera House. Despite the apartment blocks that have sprung up in between the old houses, both suburbs are Victorian in feel, with many original buildings still standing.

The southern tip of Kirribilli is home to the official Sydney residences of the prime minister (Kirribilli House) and the governor-general (**Admiralty House**), where British royals and other foreign dignitaries also stay. The latter is the most impressive, a classic colonial mansion built in 1844 to 1845 by the collector of customs, Lieutenant-Colonel Gibbes. Originally called Wotonga, it was bought in 1885 by the NSW government to house admirals of the fleet, hence its name today.

Next door, **Kirribilli House**, with its rolling, manicured lawns, was built in 1855 in a Gothic Revival style by a rich local merchant. After a series of owners it was acquired by the government in 1956 for use by the prime minister, his family and important guests. Unlike his predecessor, the current prime minister Kevin Rudd has opted to revert to the official protocol of making his ministerial residence the lodge in the nation's capital Canberra, but he does retain Kirribilli House as a weekend retreat and place to entertain foreign dignitaries. To get the best views of Kirribilli House and Admiralty House (neither are open to the public), hop on a ferry from Circular Quay (*see p69*).

There's a distinctly villagey feel to Kirribilli, and its good-life residents continue to fill the cafés and restaurants around the hub of Fitzroy, Burton and Broughton Streets. Try sitting down to a meal of excellent seafood at **Garfish** (*see p168*) or great Thai noodles at **Stir Crazy** (1 Broughton Street, 9922 6620). There's also laid-back **Freckle Face** (32 Burton Street, 9957 2116) and the justly renowned **Kirribilli Hotel** (35 Broughton Street, 9955 1415) with its lovely outdoor terrace. Once bodily needs are catered to, turn your mind to cultural pursuits at the famous and well-patronised **Ensemble Theatre Company** (*see p267*), built over the water at Careening Cove, which serves up dramatic treats both contemporary and classic.

A particularly good time to visit Kirribilli is on the fourth Saturday of the month, when one of Sydney's oldest bric-a-brac, fashion and antiques markets is held in **Bradfield Park**, on the corner of Burton and Alfred Streets.

Milsons Point, McMahons Point & North Sydney

Transport Milsons Point *CityRail/ferry Milsons Point*. **McMahons Point** *Ferry McMahons Point*. **North Sydney** *CityRail North Sydney*.

On a sunny day, treat yourself to a ferry trip from Circular Quay wharf 4, gliding past the Opera House to Milsons Point wharf (Alfred Street South). From here, you can take the harbourside walk in either direction. The ferry pulls up right in front of the grinning face and huge staring eyes of the **Luna Park Sydney** funfair (*see p113*). To the right (with your back to the water) is the historic **North Sydney Olympic Pool** (*see p115*), which must be the top contender for the 'most stunningly located swimming pool in the world' award: it's on the water's edge, beneath the northern pylon of the Harbour Bridge. The pool also houses a couple of snazzy eateries that are popular with the media and advertising crowd that works in North Sydney. The less formal restaurant **Ripples** (corner of Alfred Street and Olympic Drive, 9929 7722) is right next to the pool and has outdoor tables. On the other side, in a glass box overlooking the pool, is the pricey **Aqua Dining** (*see p167*). The same people run both restaurants, and both are open for lunch and dinner.

Walking along the boardwalk in front of the pool, it's possible to peek in through the bay windows at the swimmers and sunbathers, while the colourful art deco façade has fabulous mouldings of frogs and cockatoos. Carry on under the bridge and continue past the green lawns of Bradfield Park with its rather ugly

North Sydney Olympic Pool.

Australian Angel, the Swiss cultural contribution to an exhibition of sculpture and graphic art at the 2000 Olympics. There's also a plaque commemorating the deaths of 51 people from typhus aboard the quarantined ship the *Surry*, which was anchored here in 1814. Third Mate Thomas Raine was the only officer to survive, and his grandson Tom Raine founded the wealthy Sydney estate agents Raine & Horne – a fitting north shore tale. The foreshore walk ends at **Mary Booth Lookout**, a patch of green with a great view that's perfect for picnics.

In the other direction from Luna Park the foreshore walk winds around **Lavender Bay**: it's especially dazzling at sunset when the city lights shimmer in the golden glow. Walk up the Lavender Bay Wharf steps to Lavender Street, turn left and after another couple of minutes you'll reach **Blues Point Road**, which slices down from North Sydney through the heart of McMahons Point. It's one of Sydney's great people-watching strips, and there are numerous cafés, pubs, delis and restaurants from which you can take in the view; try **Blues Point Café** (No.135, 9922 2064), which serves Italian food, or the **Commodore Hotel** (No.206, 9922 5098, www.commodorehotel.com.au), a rowdy after-work haunt with a large outdoor terrace. Allow time to walk down to **Blues Point Reserve**, a swathe of open parkland at the southern tip of Blues Point that provides a great photo op for that obligatory Sydney Harbour holiday snap.

The northern end of Blues Point Road merges into **Miller Street**, dominated by North Sydney office blocks and constituting Sydney's main business district after the CBD. A little way up on the left-hand side of Miller Street is Mount Street and the bizarre **Mary MacKillop Place** (*see p114*). This homage to Australia's only saint stands on the site of her former convent and is worth a visit if only for its zany exhibition; at the time of writing, local Catholics were also hoping that Pope Benedict XVI might drop in while he's in Sydney for World Youth Day 2008. To get a sense of the history of the area, visit the nearby **Don Bank Museum** (*see below*), located inside one of North Sydney's oldest houses. Further up Miller Street is **North Sydney Oval**, one of the oldest cricket grounds in Australia (established 1867), now used for rugby (league and union) as well as cricket matches and, on summer evenings, the alfresco **Starlight Cinema** (*see p228*).

The main commercial centre of the lower north shore is **Military Road**, a low-slung, seemingly endless and faceless strip of shops, cafés and restaurants that heads east through Neutral Bay to Balmoral. At No.118, in Neutral Bay, is the popular **Oaks** pub (*see p187*) with its tree-covered courtyard, a hangout for local movers and shakers who order steaks and fish by the kilo and then make for the outdoor barbecue to cook up a storm. Further up the road is the unmissable **Pickled Possum** pub (No.254, 9909 2091), a diminutive outback-style boozer in the centre of the city where stubbies are served straight from an ice box.

Don Bank Museum

6 Napier Street, off Berry Street, North Sydney (9955 6279). CityRail North Sydney. **Open** *Museum 1-4pm Wed, Sun. Garden 7am-7pm daily.* **Admission** $1; 50¢ reductions. **No credit cards.** It's not known exactly when this house was built, but parts are thought to date from the 1820s. Originally called St Leonards Cottage (most of North Sydney as it is now was once called St Leonards), it was part of the Wollstonecraft Estate granted to Edward Wollstonecraft in 1825. The house was bought by North Sydney Council in the 1970s and restored with assistance from heritage groups: it is now a community museum. As well as visiting exhibitions, its permanent displays include kitchen objects from the times of the early settlers and other historical items. The building itself is significant: it's one of the few surviving examples of an early timber-slab house.

Luna Park Sydney

1 Olympic Drive, at the foreshore, Milsons Point (9033 7676/www.lunaparksydney.com). CityRail/ ferry Milsons Point. **Open** *11am-6pm Mon-Thur;*

Luna Park Sydney.

Walk 2: Cremorne Point

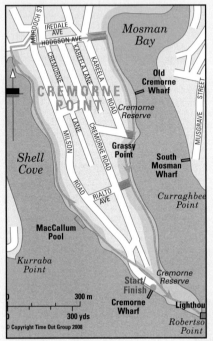

Character Harbour views and bush.
Length 3km (2-mile) loop.
Difficulty Easy.
Transport Ferry Cremorne Point/bus 225.

The paved track around Cremorne Point is hardly taxing, but the spectacular vistas are breathtaking, and if the idea of picnicking to the laughter of kookaburras against a backdrop of Sydney red gums appeals, this is definitely one for you. Various signs chart the history of the area, from its Aboriginal roots as Wulwarrajeung to the efforts to return indigenous flora and fauna to the area.

The walk is signposted from Bogota Avenue down to Cremorne Point wharf and then back up. Transport-wise it's easiest to catch a ferry to the wharf and start from there. The path dives off to the left, leading north past a series of landscaped lawns and the backs of properties on Milson Road, a mix of federation, art deco and modern styles. Don't miss the side path to historic **MacCallum Pool**, a narrow harbourside pool designed in the 1920s with views towards the Harbour Bridge and a timber deck that's perfect for sunbathing. The pool is closed for cleaning once a week, usually Thursday or Friday.

11am-11pm Fri; 10am-11pm Sat; 10am-6pm Sun (later in school holidays). **Admission** *Entry* free. *Rides* individual rides vary. *Unlimited ride pass* $20-$43; free children under 85cm (3ft). **Credit** AmEx, DC, MC, V. **Map** p327 F1.

The huge laughing clown's mouth that marks the entrance to Luna Park is visible from Circular Quay. Walk through that mouth and you'll find Sydney's venerable funfair back in full stomach-churning swing after a few troubled decades. The park opened in 1935 on the site of the Dorman Long workshops used to build the Harbour Bridge, and its heyday lasted until well into the 1950s. A slow decline during the 1970s ended in sudden closure in 1979 following a fatal fire on the ghost train. Reopening in 1982, the park then closed again in 1988 for extensive renovations. After an abortive 1990s relaunch, a new plan in 2000 saw the park finally opening again in 2004. Now Luna Park lives once more, this time as a 1930s-style fun park and performance venue. Some of the park's original rides and sideshows are still around, and there's no shortage of fixes for addicts of high speeds and vertigo.

Mary MacKillop Place

7-11 Mount Street, between Edward & William Streets, North Sydney (8912 4878/www.mary mackillopplace.org.au). CityRail North Sydney.
Open 10am-4pm daily. **Admission** $7.50; $3-$5 reductions; $15 family. **Credit** MC, V.

Mary MacKillop (1842-1909) was the founder of the Sisters of St Joseph, an order initially devoted to educating poor Australian children. Often referred to as 'the people's saint', MacKillop's pioneering work lead to her beatification in 1995 when the Pope visited and blessed the site, giving Australia its first – and only – saint to date. She died on 8 August 1909, and the eighth day of each month has become one of pilgrimage to the museum for devout Catholics. It includes MacKillop's home, Alma Cottage, and the chapel housing her tomb. A curious mix of humble 19th-century artefacts and high-tech wizardry, the displays of MacKillop's possessions – including crucifixes, rosary beads, figurines and scraps of her habits – are jazzed up with talking dioramas, videos and other surprisingly cool special effects, all of which take you on a journey through the saint's life.

Sightseeing

At the top of **Shell Cove** there's a couple of hundred metres of tarmac to cross to the other side of the peninsula: turn right on to Bogota Avenue, go up the hill, cross over Murdoch Street and walk along Hodgson Avenue to its end, where you'll find steps taking you down to **Mosman Bay**.

After **Old Cremorne Wharf** there's an uphill stretch to **Grassy Point** and its views, which account for this being the site of the **Laurels**. This is one of Sydney's best examples of the early 20th-century federation style. You'll then pass the **Lex & Ruby Graham Gardens**, first maintained by this local couple and now taken on by the National Trust. You may also see magpies, kookaburras, lizards and rainbow lorikeets.

The finger of land down at the bottom of the peninsula is **Robertson's Point**, named after the Scottish watchmaker who lived here in the first half of the 19th century. Pleasure gardens, with a shooting gallery, fireworks and masked balls, operated here in the 1850s. Walk down to the whitewashed 1904 lighthouse at its end and gaze west to Kurraba Point and Kirribilli, south to the city and Woolloomooloo, and east to Double Bay and Watsons Bay, looking over Taronga Zoo. Take advantage of the toilets, children's play area and picnic tables here before the short walk back to the ferry wharf.

Cremorne Point Lighthouse.

North Sydney Olympic Pool

4 Alfred Street South, at the foreshore, Milsons Point (9955 2309/www.northsydney.nsw.gov.au). CityRail/ ferry Milsons Point. **Open** 5.30am-9pm Mon-Fri; 7am-7pm Sat, Sun. **Admission** *Pool* $5.50; $2.80-$4.50 reductions. *Sauna, spa & swim* $16. **Credit** AmEx, DC, MC, V. **Map** p327 F1.

This unique outdoor swimming pool, situated between the Harbour Bridge and Luna Park, holds a special place in the hearts of many a Sydneysider. Built on the site where much of the construction work for the bridge was carried out, it opened in 1936. Hailed as 'the wonder pool of Australasia' because of the high standard of its facilities and the sophistication of its filtration system – at the time one of the most advanced in the world – the building has wonderful art deco stylings and decorative plasterwork, most of it still intact. Art aside, a total of 86 world records have been set here by such swimming greats as Jon Konrads, Shane Gould and Michelle Ford. Today a slick 25m indoor pool, state-of the-art gym, spa and sauna have been added to the famed 50m heated outdoor pool. The views from

the pool itself and from the terraced concrete seating above it are stupendous. There are two onsite eateries to provide post-swim sustenance.

Cremorne, Mosman, Balmoral & the Spit Bridge

Transport Cremorne *Ferry Cremorne Point then bus 225/bus 247, L88 to Neutral Bay then bus 225.* Mosman *Ferry South Mosman, Old Cremorne or Mosman Bay/CityRail Milsons Point then bus 228, 229, 230.* Balmoral *Ferry Taronga Zoo then bus 238.*

If you continue east along Military Road (an extension of the busy main route that links the suburbs of the lower north shore), you will arrive at some of Sydney's richest suburbs: Cremorne, Mosman and Balmoral, where the heavily moneyed live in conspicuous splendour.

Cremorne Point, a sliver of a peninsula, offers one of the finest panoramas of Sydney Harbour. It's the perfect setting for a scenic harbourside

Zoo with a view: the new Wild Asia area at **Taronga Zoo**.

stroll (*see p114* **Walk 2: Cremorne Point**). You can then hop back on the ferry to Mosman Bay wharf, where an uphill walk or bus will take you into Mosman village (alternatively, the Cremorne Point walk leads around Mosman Bay). Further east lies **Taronga Zoo** (*see below*), which occupies a splendid vantage point overlooking Bradleys Head. North of the zoo, Mosman's commercial centre runs along Military Road – a good place to people-watch and shop, if your wallet can cope.

But there's more to Mosman than shopping. **Sydney Harbour National Park** is a local secret that is winning new fans thanks to the opening of **Ripples Chowder Bay** (*see p167*). This sister restaurant to Ripples at Milson's Point (Olympic Drive, Milsons Point, 9929 7722) is in one of the city's most divine locations and is consequently packed for breakfast, lunch and dinner. Surrounded by the rugged green slopes of the National Park (a favourite power-walking and jogging spot), and with views over Chowder Bay wharf and way out to Port Jackson, this place feels a million miles from suburban Mosman; if walking to it seems like an unfair hike, go on a weekday when the 244 bus runs down Chowder Bay Road.

Over on the 'Middle Harbour' side of Mosman is Balmoral, one of Sydney's prettiest harbour suburbs. Boasting not one but two beaches, lots of green space and a curiously Romanesque bandstand (the venue for many local events), this is also a place to eat with a few excellent restaurants – **Watermark** (2A The Esplanade, 9968 3433, www.watermarkrestaurant.com.au) and **Bathers' Pavilion** (*see p169*) are among the best to be found in the city, while **Bottom of the Harbour** (21 The Esplanade, 9969 7911) is a fish and chip shop serving a decent promenade snack.

The two arcs of sand, **Edwards Beach** and **Balmoral Beach**, are separated by Rocky Point, and part of Edwards is protected by a shark net. If you come on a Saturday before 10am you're likely to spy members of the **Balmoral Beach Club** pounding the water. This family-friendly club is a local institution and has been using Balmoral's outdoor baths since 1914.

Head further north and you hit the Spit Bridge, the beautiful bottleneck faced by those wanting to head towards Manly and the northern beaches (*see p118*). The view driving down Spit Road from Military Road is one of Sydney's most amazing, with boats bobbing in the marina either side of the narrow causeway and swanky mansions clinging to the rocky cliffs. Traffic comes to a halt when the bridge lifts to let boats pass beneath.

Taronga Zoo

Bradleys Head Road, Mosman (9969 2777/www. zoo.nsw.gov.au). Ferry Taronga Zoo/bus 247. **Open** 9am-5pm daily. **Admission** *Zoo only* $37; $18-$23 reductions; $93 family; free under-4s. *Zoopass* $44; $30-$21.50 reductions; $117 family. **Credit** AmEx, DC, MC, V.

Only 12 minutes by ferry from Circular Quay, the 'zoo with a view' covers 17.5 hectares (43 acres) on the western side of Bradleys Head. The zoo contains 2,600 animals of more than 340 species: best of all, especially for foreigners, are the native ones, including koalas, kangaroos, platypuses, echidnas, Tasmanian devils and lots of colourful, screechy birds (follow the Wild Australia Walk to see them all). Visitors are no longer allowed to cuddle koalas, but a 'koala encounter' (11am-2.45pm) lets you have your photo taken beside one of the sleepy critters.

Other highlights at Taronga include the Free Flight Bird Show, the Seal Show, Giraffes in Focus – where you can meet the giraffes face to face, listen to a keeper talk and grab a close-up photo – the huge Komodo Dragon, named Tuka, in the Serpentaria exhibit, and the Gorilla Forest. Backyard to Bush is a journey from an Aussie back garden through an adventure-packed farmyard and into a bush wilderness, while the new Asian Elephant Rainforest is a sight to behold with its deep swimming pool waterfall and mud wallows. The elephant exhibit is part of a new area called Wild Asia, which includes a 2.3km (1.4-mile) stretch where the elephants interact with other species including gorillas, penguins and kodiak bears. The zoo also offers sleepovers and classes aimed at addressing phobias of spiders and snakes. All in all, a truly delightful place.

Waverton

Transport *CityRail Waverton.*

While it's true that the north shore's most spectacular vistas are found on the harbour foreshore, there are a couple of other areas worth visiting for something a little different. A train ride across the Harbour Bridge to Waverton (one stop past North Sydney) will deliver you to **Balls Head Reserve**, a thickly wooded headland overlooking the start of the Parramatta River. Turn left out of the station down Bay Road, which runs into Balls Head Road; it's a five- to ten-minute walk. From here you can look west to Gladesville, south to the city, Balmain and Goat Island, and east to McMahons Point and beyond. Until 1916 this area was the home of a local Aboriginal community – a carving of a six-metre (20-foot) whale with a man inside is still preserved – but during World War I the Australian army claimed the land and a Quarantine Depot (still standing) was established. Wildlife is abundant, and on summer nights you might see flying foxes feeding on the Port Jackson fig trees, dragon lizards, geckos, brush-tailed possums and around 70 bird species. There are free barbecues, so you can take your own steak or prawns and dine out at one of the finest window seats in Sydney. (Check there isn't a fire ban in place first though, especially in summer.)

West of Balls Head, around the next cove, **Berry Island Reserve** is the best place to see remnants of the north shore's Aboriginal heritage. The island was originally a camping area for Aboriginal communities, and evidence of their way of life – including shell middens, axe grindings and a rock hole that would have stored water – are still visible. In the early 19th century Edward Wollstonecraft attached the island to his land by building a stone causeway over mud flats (now reclaimed as lawns); the area became a public nature reserve in 1926.

Wahroonga

Transport *Wahroonga CityRail Wahroonga.*

Wahroonga is a quiet, leafy suburb on the north-west fringe of the north shore, and the place where you'll find **Rose Seidler House** (*see below*). This was the first building that the late Viennese-born architect Harry Seidler (*see p76* **When Harry met Sydney**) designed in Australia. He went on to become one of Sydney's most celebrated architects, and his unusual buildings around the city continue to provoke admiration and controversy in equal measure. The house itself is impressive enough on its own, but do check out the amazing panoramic views of **Ku-ring-gai Chase National Park** from almost every window – you'll soon see why Seidler chose this spot.

Rose Seidler House

71 Clissold Road, at Devon Street, Wahroonga (9989 8020/www.hht.nsw.gov.au). CityRail Wahroonga.
Open 10am-5pm Sun; also by appointment.
Admission $8; $4 reductions; $17 family.
No credit cards.
Harry Seidler built this house, his first commission, between 1948 and 1950 for his parents, Rose and Max. The ambitious architect came over from New York, where he had been working for Bauhaus guru Marcel Breuer, specifically to build the house; it was the first local instance of 'mid-century modern' domestic architecture. In basic terms, the house is a flat single-storey box resting on a smaller box, with a section cut out to form a sun deck and floor-to-ceiling windows. The open-plan interior is divided into two distinct zones: the living or public areas, and the sleeping or private areas. The original 1950s colour scheme has been restored, and the furnishings are by important post-war designers such as Charles Eames and Eero Saarinen. The kitchen had all mod cons – the very latest refrigerator, stove and dishwasher, plus a waste-disposal unit and exhaust fan – which were then utterly new to Australia and added to the house's allure locally. Max and Rose Seidler lived in the house until 1967. It's now run by the Historic Houses Trust, and guided tours are available on request.

Northern Beaches

Where the living is easy and the surfing is serious.

Sightseeing

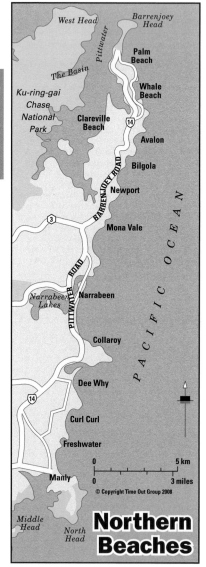

West Head
Barrenjoey Head
Pittwater
Palm Beach
The Basin
Whale Beach
Ku-ring-gai Chase National Park
Clareville Beach
14
Avalon
BARRENJOEY ROAD
Bilgola
Newport
3
Mona Vale
PITTWATER ROAD
PACIFIC OCEAN
Narrabeen Lakes
Narrabeen
Collaroy
Dee Why
14
Curl Curl
Freshwater
0   5 km
0   3 miles
© Copyright Time Out Group 2008
Manly
Northern Beaches
Middle Head
North Head

Beyond the environs of the city lies Sydney's secret – the seemingly endless stretch of surf beaches that lines the north coast like a string of pearls. This is a wonderful place and the locals know it – which is why they have fiercely protected the northern beaches from tourist overload. It's not for nothing that this area is dubbed 'the insular peninsula'.

The northern beaches start over the Spit Bridge, which crosses Middle Harbour and connects Mosman to Seaforth and Manly. Busy, touristy **Manly**, where there is a plethora of hotels, kicks off the run of beaches, but it's the more distant suburbs such as **Collaroy**, **Narrabeen**, **Newport**, **Avalon**, **Whale Beach** and **Palm Beach** that set the tone for the area, which is lush, laid-back and totally devoted to living well in the great outdoors.

The secret of the northern beaches' character lies in their relative inaccessibility: there's no suburban train line servicing the area. This means that residents of the northern beaches must either drive to the city in the crawling rush-hour traffic, sit on a sweaty bus or charter their own boat, seaplane or helicopter (which many do); either that, or they stay at home.

Nevertheless, the area has changed over the years and continues to expand as more and more rich Sydneysiders snap up their own piece of paradise, with many opting to work from a seaside home rather than a city office. This has brought a greater variety of businesses, cafés and restuarants to the area, as well as amenitites from gift and gourmet food shops to office supply stores and computer warehouses.

The beaches themselves remain largely untouched, with deep pink sand, crashing waves and fresh sea air. Take the 190 or the faster L90 bus from Wynyard up Pittwater Road (the easiest way to tour the northern beaches if you don't have a car). Sit back and marvel at one beach after another, interspersed with lush parkland and oceanside golf courses, and peppered with boys and girls with huge surfboards tucked under their arms. It's not long before the chilled northern vibe has washed the city's worries from your system.

> ► For more details on some of the beaches mentioned here, *see pp134-140* **Sydney's Best Beaches**.

Manly

Map p334. **Transport** *Ferry Manly*.

A summery explosion of shops, restaurants, cafés, surfboards, people and colour, this famous beachside suburb nestles on its own peninsula, boasting both ocean and harbour beaches, plus views from every corner. Since its first days as a resort in the 1920s, Manly's catchphrase has been 'seven miles from Sydney and a thousand miles from care' – actually an advertising slogan coined by the once-famous Port Jackson & Manly Steamship Company. Hearing it might cause the locals to cringe a little these days, but the sentiment still stands.

The suburb was given its name by Arthur Phillip, the first governor of New South Wales, when he saw a number of 'manly' Aboriginal men of the Kay-ye-my clan on the shore of what he later called Manly Cove. Now it's a centre for such macho pursuits as surf lifesaving, bodysurfing, kayaking and the Australian Ironman Championships, so the name still fits.

Just a few years ago Manly was slipping into decline and had the feel of a fading British seaside resort, but it has since rejuvenated itself and is now a vibrant and dynamic suburb with a bevy of amenities and some good festivals that attract major crowds. For all that, Sydneysiders have mixed feelings about Manly, but its perennial holiday atmosphere and one-and-a-half kilometres (one mile) of tree-lined ocean beach are irresistible to visitors. The tourists who head to Manly are a curious mix of the well-heeled (who stay at the area's expensive hotels), a burgeoning (predominantly British) backpacker brigade holing up in cheap hostels and pubs, and day-trippers delivered by ferry from the Sydney suburbs.

To get to Manly, take one of the large Manly ferries (30 minutes) or the pricier but faster JetCats (15 minutes) from Circular Quay to the slickly refurbished **Manly Wharf** with its cafés, pubs and restaurants on **Manly Cove**. Here you'll also find a peaceful patch of harbourside sand (though no surf, and the water is a tad murky for swimming). Stop in at the **Visitor Information Centre** (*see p120*) in front of the wharf for maps and brochures. The **Manly Wharf Hotel** (*see p169*) is one of Sydney's finest waterside eating and drinking spots, but it does get extremely busy. Nearby, at the western end of the cove, is popular **Oceanworld Manly** (*see p121*), **Manly Art Gallery & Museum** (*see p120*) and **Manly Waterworks** (9949 1088, www.manlywater works.com), a small water park that's open from September to April. Further west is the start of a fine ten-kilometre (6.2-mile) walk through bushland and along clifftops to Spit Bridge (pick up a self-guided walk leaflet at the Visitor Information Centre).

The main pedestrian precinct, the **Corso**, links Manly Wharf with Manly Beach, and is lined with restaurants, surf shops, fast-food

Manly beach.

joints and tourist shops. Here you'll find a clutch of high-street chains, plus cool clothing and footwear stores amid a myriad of cafés and restaurants; **Bacino** (No.1A, 9977 8889) is a corner coffee spot popular first thing in the morning. The Corso's amphitheatre is used regularly for live entertainment and has been known to draw enormous crowds, particularly for the **Manly Jazz Festival** (*see p214*) in October and the **Food & Wine Festival** in June. The **Manly Arts & Crafts Market**, worth a browse for handmade jewellery and souvenirs, is held every weekend on the lower end of Sydney Road, just off the Corso.

The suburb's main attraction, though, is **Manly Beach** itself, a long crescent of sand and ocean surf, fringed by a promenade lined with giant Norfolk pines that is a mecca for surfers, sunbathers, cyclists, in-line skaters and beach volleyball enthusiasts. The pines were planted in the 1850s by Henry Gilbert Smith, a wealthy English immigrant who decided to turn Manly from a tiny fishing village into a holiday resort for Sydneysiders. The services of Eddie and Joe Sly, the first lifesavers to patrol the beach, were soon needed, as the holidaymaking crowds failed to understand the danger of the surf. Today, surfboards, wetsuits and beach umbrellas are available for hire on the beach, and novice surfers can hone their skills with the **Manly Surf School** (9977 6977, www.manlysurfschool.com).

Head south along the beachfront road to find a row of laid-back bars and cafés with lovely ocean views on **South Steyne** – busy most of the time, they are perfect spots in which to enjoy a meal or a coffee, or just watch the world cruise by. Some of the most popular spots include **Blue Water Café** (No.28, 9976 2051), **Manly Fish Café** (No. 25, 9976 3777), with its sublime grilled octopus, and **Rouge Mediterranean Café** (No.33, 8966 9872). There's also the chic **Manly Ocean Beach House** (Ocean Promenade, North Steyne, 9977 0566) slap bang in the middle of the promenade.

A must is the 15-minute walk to **Shelly Beach**. Potter south along the beachfront from Manly Beach to **Marine Parade** and follow the winding path around the headland known as **Fairy Bower**, passing magnificent cliff-top homes along the way. Watch out for the beautiful and carefully hidden sea-themed artworks of the **Sculpture Walk** sited en route, and feel free to stop in at a couple of decent eateries: the **Bower Restaurant** (7 Marine Parade, 9977 5451) is a good spot for breakfast, lunch or an early dinner, while the sandstone **Le Kiosk** at Shelly Beach (1 Marine Parade, 9977 4122) is a smart restaurant with a cheaper takeaway booth next door.

Also unmissable is the spectacular view from **North Head**, the northern of the two Heads that form the gateway to Sydney Harbour. It's a five- to ten-minute drive via Darley Road (running south-east from the middle of the Corso) and North Head Scenic Drive. North Head is also home to the historic **North Head Quarantine Station** (*see p121*) and **North Fort** (*see below*). You can take bus 135 from Wentworth Street, but be aware that the service operates in the daytime only. Keep your eyes peeled on the walk down towards the harbourside: you might spot some of Sydney's famous fairy penguins, tiny versions of their Antarctic cousins, living in the heart – and the heat – of the city. Don't approach them, though, as they're a protected species.

Manly Art Gallery & Museum

West Esplanade (9976 1420/www.manlyaustralia. com.au/manlyartgallery). Ferry Manly. **Open** 10am-5pm Tue-Sun. Closed public holidays. **Admission** free. **Map** p334.

Although Manly isn't exactly synonymous with high culture, you can pop into this small gallery/museum if all the surfer lingo starts to curdle your brain. Opened in 1930, it has an 845-strong collection of paintings by Australian artists, more than 2000 historic photographs of the northern beaches area, some impressive ceramics and exhibitions by local students and photographers. The museum is devoted to the history of Manly and has a marvellously kitsch collection of beach memorabilia, including vintage swimming costumes. The shop sells leaflets describing two Heritage Walks around Manly.

Manly Visitor Information Centre

Manly Wharf (9976 1430/www.manlytourism.com). Ferry Manly. **Open** 9am-5pm Mon-Fri; 10am-4pm Sat, Sun (5pm summer). **Map** p334.

Situated at the front of the wharf, this is the place to find brochures, bus timetables, free maps and lots of information about what's going on.

North Fort

North Fort Road, off North Head Scenic Drive (9976 6102/www.northfort.org.au). Ferry Manly then bus 135. **Open** 9am-4pm Wed-Sun. **Admission** $11; $5-$8 reductions; $25 family. **Credit** MC, V.

The remote location of North Fort means its landscape has changed little since early colonial paintings of the spot. Wind-blown sand dunes cover the headland, with hillside 'hanging' swamps among the coastal shrub. Today it is home to the Royal Australian Artillery National Museum, once part of the School of Artillery, constructed between 1935 and 1938 in the shadow of war and the need to defend Sydney Harbour from naval attack. You can still tour the fortifications, underground tunnels and a memorial walkway – the latter undergoes continual upgrades as more and more inscribed paving stones honouring nationals who have served in the defence of Australia are added.

North Head Quarantine Station

*North Head Scenic Drive (9976 6220/www.
q-station.com.au). Ferry Manly then bus 135.*
Open (pre-booked tours only) *Day tour* 3pm-5pm
Sat; 10am-noon, 3pm-5pm Sun. *Adults' ghost tour*
8pm-11pm Wed-Sun. *Family ghost tour* 6.30pm-
8.30pm Thur, Sun. **Admission** *Day tour* $25; $19
reductions; $70 family. *Adults' ghost tour* $34; $32
reductions. *Family ghost tour* $25; $19 reductions;
$70 family. **Credit** MC, V.

The ghost tours at North Head Quarantine Station
are possibly the creepiest sightseeing you'll ever do.
Built in 1828, the station was the prison – and burial
place – of scores of unfortunate souls, who were quarantined here for a minimum of 30 days if their ship
was suspected of carrying an infectious disease such
as smallpox, bubonic plague or influenza. The station
was overcrowded, the treatment often degrading and
many who died were buried in unmarked graves.
Closed in 1972 (though, incredibly, it was used as
emergency housing for Vietnamese orphans in 1975),
the station is currently a top attraction for ghoulish
tourists. They are led through its black streets, old
fumigation rooms, shower blocks and cemetery by a
guide with a kerosene lamp. Several visitors claim to
have seen the resident ghosts – a moustachioed man
in a three-piece suit and a stern matron – and others
have reported feeling nauseous after getting a whiff
of putrid and inexplicable smells. If you take a night
tour, bring a torch and wear flat shoes.

Oceanworld Manly

*West Esplanade (8251 7877/www.oceanworld.
com.au). Ferry Manly.* **Open** 10am-5.30pm daily.
Admission $17.95; $9.50-$12.95 reductions; $29.95-
$43.95 family; 15% discount after 3.30pm. **Credit**
AmEx, MC, V. **Map** p334.

Located a couple of hundred metres from Manly's
ferry terminal, Oceanworld is about as good as
aquaria get. The three-level attraction has a floor
devoted to dangerous Australian creatures (poisonous snakes, funnel-web spiders, giant monitor
lizards, crocodiles) and another to tropical fish,
corals and venomous sea creatures. The main attraction, on the lower level, is the oceanarium, which
holds the largest sharks in captivity in Australia,
plus giant rays and sea turtles – all seen via a 110m
(360ft) underwater viewing tunnel. Fish and sharks
are fed at 11am on Mondays, Wednesdays and
Fridays, and there's a Dangerous Australian
Animals show at noon daily. Other attractions
include the 'touch pool', where you can get up close
and personal with hermit crabs and starfish. For the
really adventurous there's Shark Dive Xtreme ($180-
$245), a chance to dive with huge grey nurse sharks.

Freshwater to Whale Beach

Transport Dee Why, Collaroy, Narrabeen &
Mona Vale *Bus 188, 190, E83, E84, E86, E87,
E88, E89, L88, L90.* **Newport & Avalon** *Bus 188,
190, E88, E89, L88, L90.* **Whale Beach** *Bus 190,
L90 then bus 193.*

From Manly, the beaches get less crowded
and more spectaculour, with names like
Freshwater, Curl Curl, Dee Why, Collaroy,
Narrabeen, Newport and Avalon slipping off
the tongue like a surfer off the crest of a wave.
You are now entering serious surfing territory,
with Sydney's pros limbering up along the
coast on a daily basis. Here the air smells of sea
salt and coconut oil, and it seems as if every

Your destination, you know it: **Avalon beach**.

Sightseeing

second teenager hides under a mop of matted bleached blond hair, surfboard in tow.

The best way to explore is by car, allowing you to stop, take in the view, and swim at leisure at whichever beach you fancy. Otherwise, the L90 bus from Wynyard will take you all the way to Palm Beach – the journey takes about 90 minutes if you don't stop – calling in at various beaches (but not Manly) en route. The road becomes steeper and more winding after you've passed Newport and the views get increasingly breathtaking.

You can pick up the useful and informative Sydney's Northern Beaches Map, produced by the Northern Beaches Visitors Association, from **Sydney Beachhouse YHA** (*see p51*), located on Collaroy beach; much of the same information is on the association's website, www.sydneybeaches.com.au. Also useful is www.sydneynorthernbeaches.com.au.

If you want to try one of the best meat pies in Sydney head for **Upper Crust** (1003 Pittwater Road, 9971 5182) at the crest of the hill in Collaroy. Sylvia and Fran's legendary pies have amassed such a devoted following that there's always a jostle for a parking spot outside the shop: be prepared to fight for your place in the queue with barefooted surfers who dash across the busy street for a bite between waves. And for a cool beer in spectacular surroundings pop into the **Surf Rock Hotel** (1062 Pittwater Road, 9982 3924), with its balcony overlooking the seashore and sensational interior design.

Visitors with a car can take a detour to **Garigal National Park** (9451 3479, www.nationalparks.nsw.gov.au), which links Sydney's north shore suburbs with the northern beaches. Covering more than 20 square kilometres (nearly eight square miles) of rugged bush, sandstone outcrops and waterways, it's divided into various sections. The western section hugs **Middle Harbour Creek**, which leads into Sydney Harbour; a walking track by the creek offers much historical interest (and four picnic areas), plus some rare native ash and stringybark trees.

Further north is the much larger Ku-ring-gai Chase National Park (*see p124*), on the south-eastern edge of which, inland from Mona Vale, is a striking domed white building. This is the **Bahá'í House of Worship** (173 Mona Vale Road, Ingleside, 9998 9221, www.bahai.org.au), a temple for members of the Bahá'í faith, a religion founded in the 19th century that has five million members worldwide. The temple's design, with nine sides and nine entrances, represents the unification of the human race under one God. Whatever your religious views, it's a lovely spot, with beautiful grounds and great views of the ocean.

North of Mona Vale is Newport, worth a stop for its great delicatessen, **Tongue Teasers** (339 Barrenjoey Road, 9997 3557) – a top spot to load up for a picnic – and the **Newport Arms Hotel** (*see p187*), a much-loved pub with a fantastic beer garden overlooking the tranquil ocean inlet of Pittwater.

The final community before Palm Beach is Avalon, once something of a secret but now a thriving shopping centre and booming

Collar the sun at **Collaroy beach**.

residential village, and getting bigger by the year. It's approached via an unnervingly steep and winding road, which offers dramatic ocean views for whoever is in the passenger seat but one hairy ride for the driver. On the right you'll pass the shockingly steep decline that leads to **Bilgola Beach**: take time to turn off, follow signs for the beach and drive around the breathtaking bends – the road's not called the Serpentine for nothing – that lead you down and then back up the hillside. Just before you rejoin the main road, the lookout point on **Bilgola Head** is well worth a stop – it offers unique views down the coastline towards Bondi and up to Barrenjoey Lighthouse at Palm Beach.

On the upward ascent into Avalon, look out for the traditional birthday and anniversary greetings that locals pin to the trees. **Avalon Beach** is down the hill on the right. This beautiful surf spot was once considered as a possible location by the makers of *Baywatch*, but the locals weren't having any of it, and Avalon surfers still jealously guard their waters; they're in their combies from dawn until dusk, waiting for that perfect wave. The town itself has two main strips: **Avalon Parade**, which runs from the beach up towards the Pittwater side of the peninsula, and the **Old Barrenjoey Road**, which crosses Avalon Parade and leads to Palm Beach in one direction and Sydney in the other.

On Avalon Parade, chic new licensed café, deli and gelateria **'Allo 'Allo** (No.24, 9973 4785) is popular with locals who sit outside on the bentwood furniture, while on Old Barrenjoey Road there's a longstanding favourite, the **Ibiza Café** (No.47, 9918 3965), which does a roaring trade: it's got an open pavement area for the summer and a warm, friendly feel in winter. **Bookoccino** (No.37A, 9973 1244) is one of the best bookshops on the northern beaches, with an excellent range of children's books, cookery books, biographies, history, Australiana and much more; as the name suggests, there's a café here too.

To get to the idyllic stretches of **Clareville Beach** on the calm shore of Pittwater, sheltered from the ocean waves, head up Avalon Parade with the post office on your left. Avalon Parade becomes Hudson Parade and hooks left to run parallel to Pittwater; when you reach the bottom of the hill, turn right into Delecta Avenue – 20 minutes' walk from Avalon, or a few minutes in the car. The sandy beach is not good for swimming, but it's popular with locals for meet-and-greet Sunday barbecues; many also moor their boats here. **Clareville Kiosk** (27 Delecta Avenue, 9918 2727, www. clarevillekiosk.com), a delightful beach-house-style restaurant, is open from Wednesday

through to Sunday for dinner and on Saturday and Sunday for lunch. Be sure to book ahead.

There's one more treasure to be seen before you reach Palm Beach, the end of the northern beaches road. For many locals, **Whale Beach** is closer to paradise than glitzier Palm. Its inaccessibility helps, making it a definite 'those in the know' bolt-hole. You can get there by bus – the 193 from Avalon Parade in Avalon – or by walking from the L90 bus stop on Careel Head Road. From there, turn left on to Whale Beach Road and continue until you reach the beach itself; it's a roughly half-hour and suitably hilly trek through roads lined with wonderful beach houses, but it's worth the effort. The pink sand, rugged surf and rocky headland have a quality all of their own, and there's an oceanside swimming pool. The **Whale Beach Kiosk** (corner of Surf Road and The Strand) serves up freshly-made rolls, antipasti plates, fish and chips, and much more.

If you want something more substantial and you're feeling flush, then stop in at the lovely **Jonah's** (*see p169*), where the area's swankier denizens enjoy five-star food on a coastal hilltop; there are guest rooms too (*see p49*). You might want to bring a change of clothes, though – beachside gear won't cut it here.

Palm Beach & around

Transport Bus 190, L90.

Finally to Palm Beach, the well-heeled tip of the northern beaches, where you'll find more multi-million-dollar mansions than seagulls. The area is a luxurious home to a high concentration of the rich and famous keen on living outside of Sydney's glaring limelight, including tennis star Lleyton Hewitt and former rugby league champion Matthew Johns.

It wasn't always thus. In 1900, all the land except Barrenjoey Headland (which had been purchased by the government in 1881) was divided into 18 large blocks and offered for sale. None sold. Today the average price of a Palm Beach property is a cool $3 million and every ocean view is taken; as a result, there aren't as many cabbage tree palms around as there were when they gave the place its name.

Palm Beach is worth at least a day's exploration. The community itself is reserved and somewhat haughty, but there are lots of restaurants and cafés worth stopping in at and masses of watersports on offer. If you haven't time for the road trip from the city, splash out and do it in style by seaplane. Planes fly from Rose Bay to Pittwater on the sheltered western side of the Palm Beach peninsula and companies offer sightseeing and gourmet tours.

Sightseeing

Don't mistake Palm Beach Wharf on the western side of the peninsula for the main beach. **Palm Beach** proper is on the eastern, ocean side. At the southern end of the beach – the safest place to swim – the colonial-style buildings of the **Palm Beach Surf Club** and private **Palm Beach Pacific Club** sit majestically, their picturesque wooden balconies surrounded by stately palms. It was this beautiful corner of Australia that Governor Arthur Phillip first passed in his cutter before entering Broken Bay in 1788; a plaque commemorates his voyage. Now Palm Beach Surf Club is the club to join for wannabe socialites in Sydney – and as a result one of the pickiest, with half the applicants turned down every year and more failing to get through the first year's strict initiation. The reason is that membership also grants you access to the prestigious **Cabbage Tree Club** and **Palm Beach Pacific Club** next door, the hangouts of Sydney's real movers and shakers, where Krug is the resident tipple and banking is the common profession.

Soap fans might want to head further up to **North Palm Beach**, where, if you're lucky, the kids from *Home and Away* will be filming by the **North Palm Beach Surf Club** (ironically, one of the easiest surf clubs to join, as it's at the unfashionable end of Palmy). When the 'Summer Bay SLSC' sign is hanging on the side of the building, the Seven Network crew are in business and you may well spot wily old Alf Stewart (aka actor Ray Meagher) ordering a latte from the kiosk, or younger cast members learning their lines. Right at the top of the peninsula is **Barrenjoey Head** and its historic **lighthouse**, which can be reached by a short but steep walk (*see below* **Walk 3: Barrenjoey Lighthouse**).

If the sun gets too hot – there's not much shade, particularly at the southern end of the beach – head to the wharf and take a boat trip instead. The **Palm Beach Ferry Service** (9947 2411, www.palmbeachferry.com.au) runs every day (including Christmas Day) across Pittwater to the Basin, an area within **Ku-ring-gai Chase National Park** (*see below*) where you can ponder some excellent Aboriginal rock carvings. Cool off afterwards with a swim in the spookily dark and seriously deep bay that gave the Basin area its name thanks to its shape. **Palm Beach & Hawkesbury River Cruises** (0414 466 635, www.sydneyscenic cruises.com) offers a trip that crosses Pittwater into Broken Bay, stopping at **Patonga** (a pleasant beach village) and then cruising up the beautiful lower Hawkesbury River into Cowan Waters, stopping at **Bobbin Head** for lunch. The boat leaves Palm Beach daily at 11am, returning at 3.30pm, with more cruises on weekends and during school holidays. Alternatively, splash out with **Peninsula Water Taxi** (0415 408 831), which offers bespoke cruises for up to six people.

Ku-ring-gai Chase National Park

NPWS office 9472 8949/www.nationalparks.nsw. gov.au. **Open** sunrise-sunset daily. **Admission** $3 arriving by boat/ferry; $2 reductions; $11 per vehicle. **Map** p321.

Occupying nearly 15,000 hectares (37,000 acres) of dense forest, hidden coves and sheltered beaches where the Hawkesbury River meets the sea, Ku-ring-gai Chase was designated a national park in 1894. It is located in one of Sydney's wealthiest municipalities, stretching from the suburbs of St Ives North and Wahroonga in the south to Broken Bay in the north. Every visitor to Sydney should take in the West Head lookout, with its views over the mouth of the Hawkesbury, the beginning of the Central Coast, Barrenjoey Lighthouse and Palm Beach. Walking tracks lead to significant examples of Aboriginal rock art. Guided walks and canoe and boat tours can also be arranged.

Walk 3: Barrenjoey Lighthouse

Character Rugged bushland and incredible ocean views.
Length 700m (2,300ft) one way.
Difficulty Moderate.
The starting point, at the northern end of Barrenjoey Beach (on the Pittwater side), is marked by a sign next to a rust-coloured shed. There's a choice of routes to the top: the left-hand one, the Service Road, is the less steep of the two and has the best views back over Palm Beach. But don't let the short distance mislead you – you'll work up quite a

sweat climbing to the grassy summit plateau. From here, a panoramic vista takes in the Pacific Ocean, Pittwater, Palm Beach and Lion Island, a deserted rocky outcrop that guards the entrance to Broken Bay. The 1881 lighthouse, built from Hawkesbury sandstone, is 113 metres (370 feet) above sea level and visible from 35 kilometres (22 miles) out at sea. It's open only on Sundays (11am-3pm) for guided tours, weather permitting (9472 8949, $3; $2 reductions). The downhill trip takes less puff, but can be hard on knees.

Parramatta & the West

Get in touch with true multicultural Sydney.

If you want to get to Sydney's multicultural heart you'll need to head west. Although the area is not on the typical Sydney tourist trail, and has been tarred in recent years by sensational news stories of riots and gang warfare, it's still well worth a wander.

Once you do, you'll wonder what all the fuss was about: **Parramatta** is a sedate, friendly town that is forging an identity for itself in the arts with council grants for artists and its Riverside Theatres complex (*see p270*) snapping up the best of local theatre, while also quietly acknowledging and celebrating its heritage as Australia's second European settlement and building up its status as Sydney's second CBD. The fascinating spread of cultures that is represented in these often misunderstood suburbs – which sprawl out from the inner city to the foothills of the lush Blue Mountains – underlines the reality of modern Sydney and Australia in general.

Back in the 19th century, the area now called Greater Western Sydney was a series of rural farming communities, which is why some of the oldest white settlement buildings can be found there. These days, however, the 'settlement' story is very different: the western suburbs cover more than two thirds of the metropolitan area and house a third of the city's population (1.4 million), with a mix of blue-collar Aussies, Asians, Eastern Europeans, Latinos and others making up the numbers. The melting pot of the west also attracts three-quarters of the 50,000 people who migrate to Sydney each year, making it the fastest growing area of the city. According to local government estimates, the west will house more than two million people by 2031, by which time Sydney's population will be around the 5.3 million mark.

Parramatta – the 'capital' of the west – boasts a historic importance that rivals any area in Sydney, and also lays claim to the city's second business district. Closer in to town, the Sydney Olympic Park (*see p127*) in **Homebush Bay** was where the Aussies proudly held their 2000 Olympic Games, and they haven't forgotten it. The area has since been turned into a family-oriented sports complex, with adjacent Newington (a new suburb that was created from the athletes' Olympic Village) feeding the facilities with people, cash and the retail outlets to go with it. Further west is the Asian centre of **Cabramatta**, a food and clothes shopper's delight that draws visitors with its vibrant market life.

The so-called 'Westies' are often snobbishly dismissed by their eastern suburb cousins as unsophisticated, beer-guzzling gamblers, but in compensation they enjoy more spacious surroundings and greater value for money in their property. Racial tensions may challenge future community leaders, but the tourist areas remain unaffected by such issues.

For a map of Greater Sydney, *see p321*.

Parramatta

Transport *CityRail/RiverCat Parramatta.*

Parramatta may be the gateway to the west, but it's also the geographic centre of the Sydney sprawl. There are various ways of getting here: the nicest is by RiverCat ferry from Circular Quay along the pristine **Parramatta River** (a laidback and very beautiful journey taking just under an hour; *photo p126*). Those in more of a hurry can travel by train (25 to 30 minutes) or car (35 to 40 minutes).

Historically, western Sydney belonged to the Dharug, Dharawal and Gandangara people before the white settlers moved in, and the word Parramatta is, like many Sydney place names, Aboriginal in origin. In fact, the Aboriginal warrior Pemulwuy kept the white people of Parramatta in fear of their lives for more than a decade before he was eventually killed in 1802 and his head sent to England. At the last census of the Parramatta population just 1,201 Aboriginal and Torres Strait Islanders were counted – that's 0.8% of the city's inhabitants – and the majority of these were under 50, thanks to the drastically reduced life expectancy of the Aboriginal community. And while 86 per cent of the city's population was comprised of Australian citizens, English was spoken in just just under 50% of Parramatta homes, with Arabic, Cantonese, Mandarin, Korean and Hindi being the next most common languages.

It wasn't always like this, and Parramatta's heritage as Australia's second-oldest white settlement makes it a popular stop for historically-minded tourists. You can learn more about the area at the **Parramatta Heritage & Visitor Information Centre**

Sightseeing

Easy does it: taking the **RiverCat ferry** makes for a gentle day out. *See p125.*

(*see p127*), on the north bank of the river next to **Lennox Bridge**, which was built by convict labour in the 1830s. The centre is a short stroll from the ferry wharf via the **Riverside Walk**, designed by Aboriginal artist Jamie Eastwood and exploring the story of the Parramatta River and the traditions of the Burramatta people, Parramatta's first inhabitants.

Once known as the 'cradle city', Parramatta is the site of many Australian firsts: its first jail, land grant, successful farm (which saved the First Fleet from starvation in 1788), orchard, train line to Sydney and wool mill. Many of the first settlers were buried in **St John's Cemetery**, on O'Connell Street between **St John's Cathedral** and **Parramatta Park**.

Parramatta also contains New South Wales' second-largest business district (after the CBD to the east), itself a dynamic mix of old and new, with towering skyscrapers next door to heritage-listed huts. **Elizabeth Farm** (*see p127*), built in 1793 by wool pioneer John Macarthur and named after his wife, is the oldest colonial home still standing in Australia. Nearby is **Experiment Farm Cottage** (*see p127*), a beautiful colonial cottage built on the site of Australia's first land grant.

Also open for viewing is **Old Government House** (*see p127*), the oldest public building in Australia. Standing in the grounds of

spacious Parramatta Park, the spot was chosen by the colony's founding governor, Arthur Phillip, within months of the establishment of the penal settlement at Sydney Cove in January 1788, and was used by NSW governors until the new residence opened in the centre of Sydney in 1845. Old Government House and Experiment Farm Cottage are both run by the National Trust (www.nationaltrust.org.au); buy a combined admission to both and you'll also get a ten per cent discount in the visitor shops and restaurant.

Parramatta was also the site of Australia's first recorded race meeting and its first legal brewery – and Westies still love a beer and a bet. **Rosehill Gardens Racecourse** (*see p264*) on Grand Avenue is a citadel of both pursuits, particularly during the **Autumn Carnival**, when the $2 million Golden Slipper – the world's most rewarding race for two-year-olds – is held.

Cultural attractions include the **Parramatta Riverside Theatres** (*see p270*), three well-patronised venues that host stand-up comedy, various arts events and part of the Sydney Festival each January, as well as local plays from all over Australia. The **Roxy** (69 George Street, 9687 4219) is a hip hangout for local DJs and their fans. **PJ Gallagher's Irish Pub** (74 Church Street, 9635 8811) prides itself on being the finest drinking hole in the west (it's not, but it's not bad), while other old Parramatta pubs with character include the **Woolpack** (19 George Street, 9635 8043), which is said to be Australia's oldest licensed hotel and dating back to 1796 (though it was on a different site until 1821), the **Commercial Hotel** (2 Hassall Street, 9635 8342) and the **Albion Hotel** (135 George Street, 9891 3288), which boasts an enormous garden bar.

Those seeking retail therapy during their tour of the west should head to the gargantuan mall **Westfield Parramatta** on Church Street, near the station. Pretty much everything is here – there are 528 outlets – including an 11-cinema complex popular with local teens.

Elizabeth Farm

70 Alice Street, between Arthur & Alfred Streets, Rosehill (9635 9488/www.hht.net.au). CityRail Parramatta then 15mins walk. **Open** 9.30am-4pm Fri-Sun. **Admission** $8; $4 reductions; $17 family. **Credit** MC, V.
Elizabeth Farm is notable both for being the birthplace of the Australian wool industry – John Macarthur imported merino sheep for breeding at the site – and for the farm's main building. With its deep, shady verandas and stone-flagged floors, it became the prototype for the Australian homestead, and parts of the original 1793 construction – the oldest surviving European building in Australia – remain. The interior has been restored to its 1830s condition, with a recreated Victorian garden to match, while the museum's genteel tearooms are open from 11am to 3pm. The farm is run by the Historic Houses Trust, which looks after various museums and historic sites in Sydney.

Experiment Farm Cottage

9 Ruse Street, Harris Park (9635 5655/www.nsw. nationaltrust.org.au). CityRail Harris Park then 10mins walk/RiverCat Parramatta then 20mins walk. **Open** 10.30am-3.30pm Tue-Fri; 11am-3.30pm Sat, Sun. **Admission** $6; $4 reductions; $14 family. *Joint admission with Old Government House* $10; $7 reductions; $25 family. **Credit** (over $20) MC, V.
In 1789 Governor Phillip set up an experiment 'to know in what time a man might be able to support himself'. The guinea pig was convict James Ruse, who became wholly self-sufficient in two years and was given the colony's first land grant here as a reward, thereby becoming Australia's first private farmer. He then sold the land to a surgeon, John Harris, who built this modest cottage in 1793. *Photos p129.*

Old Government House

Parramatta Park, Parramatta (9635 8149/ www.nsw.nationaltrust.org.au). CityRail/RiverCat Parramatta then 15mins walk. **Open** 10am-4pm Mon-Fri; 10.30am-4pm Sat, Sun. **Admission** $8; $5 reductions; $18 family. *Joint admission with Experiment Farm Cottage* $10; $7 reductions; $25 family. **Credit** MC, V.

Set in 105 hectares (260 acres) of parkland, Old Government House was built between 1799 and 1818 on the foundations of Governor Phillip's 1790 thatched cottage, which had collapsed, and is Australia's oldest public building. At times serving as everything from a vice-regal residence to a boarding house for local schoolboys, the building has been restored to its former glory by a multi-million-dollar revamp. It also boasts the nation's most important collection of Australian colonial furniture, while the ghost tours on the third Friday evening of every month are a hoot.

Parramatta Heritage & Visitor Information Centre

346A Church Street, next to Lennox Bridge, Parramatta (8839 3311/www.parracity.nsw.gov.au). CityRail/RiverCat Parramatta then 10mins walk. **Open** 9am-5pm daily.

Homebush Bay

Transport *CityRail Olympic Park/RiverCat Sydney Olympic Park.*

If you've got even the tiniest sporting spark in your body, be sure to visit the site of the triumphant 2000 Olympic Games. **Sydney Olympic Park** (*see below*) is in Homebush Bay, eight kilometres (five miles) east of Parramatta. The site features a huge range of sporting and entertainment facilities, including the mammoth **Acer Arena** (*see p248*) and the **Sydney Showground** (9704 1111, www.sydneyshowground.com.au), which plays host to the annual **Big Day Out** music festival (*see p246*) and other major events.

An arm of the Parramatta River, the bay is surrounded by 1.8 square kilometres (0.7 square miles) of wetlands, woodland and grassland, which provide sanctuary for 160 bird species. **Bicentennial Park** (open from sunrise to sunset daily), the largest of the bay's five main parkland areas, is one of the best places to go for specialist birdwatching excursions. A waterbird refuge and salt marsh are out on the water, with a fine viewing tower at their north-easterly tip. You may recognise the **Brickpit**, at the park's heart, as Mad Max's Thunderdome. There's a café and restaurant, and it's also a pleasant spot for picnics.

Sydney Olympic Park

Visitor Centre *1 Showground Road, at Murray Rose Avenue (9714 7888/www.sydneyolympic park.com.au). CityRail Olympic Park/RiverCat Sydney Olympic Park then bus 401.* **Open** 9am-5pm daily.
If you're time-rich, hop on the most scenic route to Olympic Park: the RiverCat ferry from Circular Quay to Sydney Olympic Park (50 minutes). Bus No.401 meets the boat and takes you to the visitor centre. If you prefer to travel by train, the station you want

Sightseeing

is Olympic Park, bang in the middle of the complex – but be warned: frustratingly, there are few direct CityRail services (even when an event is being staged); your best bet is to go to Lidcombe and pick up the Sprint train from there.

To see the stadia rising out of the flat landscape as you approach is awe-inspiring. The size and scope of the biggest – ANZ Stadium – dwarfs everything else in the vicinity. The park is big but easily walkable if the weather isn't too hot; even better, you can explore by bike (for hire at the visitor centre). At the Aquatic Centre you can go for a dip, marvel at the indoor water slides and get a faint tingle of what it must be like to perform before thousands of cheering spectators (swim meets continue to be held here). It's free to visit the Sports Centre and stroll down the gallery's Hall of Champions, covering athletes from the 1890s to the present. To get into the other key venues, you'll need to take an organised tour (there are many – ask at the visitor centre). The one-hour ANZ Stadium 'Explore' tours are particularly good, including the new interactive tour, in which you follow in the footsteps of heroes of the 2000 games. Check out the website before you go; it's packed with information.

Blacktown & around

Transport *CityRail Blacktown.*

Blacktown, located 11 kilometres (seven miles) north-west of Parramatta, earned its name from being home to the Native Institution, established by the early colonial authorities to educate Aboriginal children. Today, 2.3 per cent of the local population is Aboriginal – that's just over 7,000 people.

For a unique insight into Australian taste through the years, head north of Blacktown to historic **Rouse Hill House & Farm** (*see below*). You can only visit the house as part of a guided tour (which don't run if the weather's bad) – it's wise to book in advance. And if you want to see native wildlife, including a face-to-face encounter with a koala, visit the excellent, family-run **Featherdale Wildlife Park** (*see below*), home to strange-looking cassowaries and scary-looking owls.

In keeping with local tastes, western Sydney boasts more social clubs than any other suburb. League clubs, golf clubs, bowling clubs, workers' clubs, returned servicemen's clubs – they're absolutely everywhere, providing community services, cheap food and drink, and live entertainment, subsidised by row upon row of poker machines. Two of the biggest and best around here are **Blacktown Workers Club** on Campbell Street (9830 0600, www.bwcl. com.au) and **Rooty Hill RSL Club** (9625 5500, www.rootyhillrsl.com.au) on the corner of Sherbrooke and Railway Streets, in Rooty Hill.

Public transport is generally poorer in the west than in the east, so Westies tend to have a special attachment to their cars. Rev-heads love **Eastern Creek Raceway** (Brabham Drive, Eastern Creek, 9672 1000, www.eastern-creek-raceway.com), which regularly hosts touring car, motorbike and drag races.

Featherdale Wildlife Park

217-229 Kildare Road, Doonside (9622 1644/ www.featherdale.com.au). CityRail Blacktown then bus 725. **Open** 9am-5pm daily. **Admission** $19.50; $9.75-$15.50 reductions; $57.50 family; free under-3s. **Credit** AmEx, DC, MC, V.
Kangaroos, koalas and Tasmanian devils all feature in this well-kept wildlife park, which houses one of Australia's largest collections of native animals. The huge diversity of birds includes the bizarre cassowary (which lives in the rainforests in the tropical far north, but is rarely spotted by locals).

Rouse Hill House & Farm

Guntawong Road, off Windsor Road, Rouse Hill (9627 6777/www.hht.net.au). CityRail Riverstone then bus 741R or taxi. **Tours** 9.30am-4.30pm Wed-Sun. Closed in bad weather. **Admission** $8; $4 reductions; $17 family. **Credit** MC, V.
This two-storey Georgian sandstone house, set in a 15 hectare (37 acre) estate, was the home of the Rouse family for six generations. Free settler Richard Rouse built the original house between 1813 and 1818, and his last direct descendant left in 1993. There are also some 20 outbuildings, ranging from a pretty Victorian summerhouse to a corrugated iron cottage annex, and a very early 'dry weather' garden.

Cabramatta & Bankstown

Transport Bankstown *CityRail Bankstown.* **Cabramatta** *CityRail Cabramatta.*

Cabramatta, Bankstown and their neighbours comprise the country's multicultural heartland. Given Sydney's dominance over Australia's other state capitals, it's hardly surprising that it remains the most popular destination for immigrants entering Australia, and the vast majority of them go to live in the western suburbs. In some south-western suburbs, more than half the population was born overseas, with residents hailing from Italy, Greece, Vietnam, Cambodia, the Philippines, China, Serbia, Croatia, Poland, Latin America, Lebanon and the Pacific Islands.

One of the consequences of this multicultural mix is that there's high-quality, inexpensive dining to be had – Cabramatta in particular has developed a name for itself as the culinary centre of the western suburbs. It also suffers from a reputation as heroin central in Sydney thanks to the proliferation of Asian gangs, and tends to hit the headlines for drug- and gang-

Experimental Farm Cottage. *See p127.*

related deaths. For a grittily honest portrayal of the lives of the homeless and disadvantaged in the Asian centre of Sydney, check out local director Khoa Do's no-holds-barred film *The Finished People* (2003), or the more recent star-studded, downbeat drama *Little Fish* (2005), starring Cate Blanchett and Hugo Weaving. For all that, it's important to keep things in perspective when visiting Cabramatta. True, as a casual tourist, you should remain vigilant and savvy when wandering about – it's better to visit during the day than after dark – but don't let the negative press cloud your own opinion.

If you like dining and shopping, don't miss the area's exotic mix of Aussie suburbia. From Cabramatta CityRail station, cross over the road to Arthur Street and pass through the ornate Pai Lau Gate into **Freedom Plaza**, the main marketplace. It's like stepping into Asia itself, with the authentic flavours of Thai, Laotian, Cambodian, Filipino and Chinese cuisines on offer at numerous stalls. There are plenty of discount fabric, clothing and jewellery dealers too: on Park Road, John Street, Hughes Street and around the main plaza, direct importers and wholesalers ply their wares for all their worth in typical Asian bazaar fashion (haggling is the norm). Other attractions are the nearby **Tien Hau** and **Kwan Zin** Buddhist temples.

The best time to visit is when the Chinese and Vietnamese communities hold their New Year celebrations (around February), with wild dragon parades and more firecrackers than you can shake a match at. Some lucky visitors may experience the annual Moon Festival, held on the 15th day of the eighth lunar month – August or September, depending on the year.

Sport is a key feature of life in the west too. It's thanks to the high number of immigrants that soccer is a bigger sport than rugby in this part of the city. Sydney soccer fans follow their teams with a fiery passion based along ethnic lines, and the games can be boisterous and spectacular affairs. Local teams in the NSW premier league include the Parramatta Eagles, Marconi Stallions, Blacktown City Demons and Bankstown City Lions. Bankstown is also the home town of the famous cricketing Waugh brothers, and boasts an impressive cricket team, which you can catch on summer weekends at the **Bankstown Oval** (corner of Chapel Road South and Macauley Avenue).

Penrith

Transport *CityRail Penrith.*

At the foot of the Blue Mountains and perched on the banks of the Nepean River, Penrith lies 50 kilometres (31 miles) west of central Sydney.

It's a sprawling modern suburb distinguished by beautiful rural and bushland scenery as well as history and modern culture.

At its heart is Panthers, Australia's largest licensed club, and the rugby league team it supports. The huge **Panthers World of Entertainment** on Mulgoa Road (4720 5555, www.panthersworld.com.au) resembles an Antipodean Butlins resort; you'll find not only a vast array of 24-hour bars, gaming facilities, restaurants, nightclubs and live music performances, but also a motel, swimming pools, water-skiing, water slides, tennis courts, beach volleyball, a golf driving range and more. This staggering creation rakes in more than $100 million a year, with the profits being ploughed back into the rugby club and the community. You might catch the Panthers training at winter weekends in **Penrith Park**, just opposite the club centre. Or try to attend one of their home games in **Penrith Stadium** against one of the western suburbs' other first-class rugby league teams, the Parramatta Eels, the Bulldogs or the Wests Tigers.

Penrith also offers dogs and trots at **Penrith Paceway** (corner of Ransley and Station Streets, 4721 2375, www.harness.org.au/penrith). On a more cultural note, there's the long-running and well-respected **Q Theatre Company** (www.railwaystreet.com.au), with which Toni Colette made her professional stage debut in 1990; the company moved into its new home, the striking, glass-fronted **Joan Sutherland Performing Arts Centre** (597 High Street, 4723 7611, www.jspac.com.au), at the end of 2005. Also worthy of your time is the beautiful **Penrith Regional Art Gallery** (86 River Road, Emu Plains, 4735 1100, www.penrithregionalgallery.org).

If you want to get away from urban life for a bit, you'll find a waterborne solution in the form of the historic paddle-wheeler **Nepean Belle** (The Jetty, Tench Avenue, 4733 1274, www.nepeanbelle.com.au), which offers lunch and dinner cruises up the spectacular **Nepean Gorge**. The Penrith area is also home to several vineyards, among them **Vicary's Winery** in Luddenham (The Northern Road, 4773 4161, www.vicaryswinery.com.au): Sydney's oldest working winery, it runs wine tastings (9am-5pm Tue-Fri, 11am-5pm Sat, Sun) and uses a converted woolshed for weekend bush dances ($48-$57, book well in advance).

North of Penrith, the Nepean River becomes the **Hawkesbury River**, which forms the lifeline of another unique part of western Sydney. For the historic towns of Richmond and Windsor, the **Ku-ring-gai Chase National Park**, and more on the delights of the Hawkesbury, *see p279.*

The South

Family, food and fast cars down on the sands.

As Sydneysiders search for their own piece of beachside paradise, the south is coming into its own. Here houses are bigger, prices are lower and there's more of a family vibe.

The south technically starts at Greek community hub **Brighton-le-Sands** in the district of Rockdale before extending into a very cliquey district known as 'the Shire' and inhabited by people who call themselves 'the locals'. **Cronulla** is the stronghold of the Shire, championing a lifestyle of sun, sea, surf and anything (preferably motorised) that allows you to travel on water. After an incident in late 2005 in which boys 'of Middle-Eastern appearance' (as the news labelled them) supposedly roughed up two volunteer lifesavers, Cronulla erupted in what were beamed around the world as 'race riots', leaving Australia to debate its own cultural tolerance, or lack thereof.

Languishing across Port Hacking from Cronulla, oblivious to any tension, is the former artists' colony of **Bundeena**. Here, inside the Royal National Park (*see p133*), life carries on as normal – with private picnics, swimming spots and much home- and pool-building.

Brighton-le-Sands

Map p321. **Transport** Kurnell *CityRail Cronulla then bus 987.* **Brighton-le-Sands** *CityRail Rockdale then bus 475, 478, 479.*

From the air, the first thing you notice about Brighton-le-Sands is the oversized pyramid of the **Novotel** (*see p51*). Set on the west side of Botany Bay, just below the airport, this hulking hotel doesn't look much prettier from the ground. Fortunately, the swankier end of the Greek community is bent on transforming the car-laden beachfront drag of **Grand Parade** into, well, a grand parade, and has so lined it with sleek cafés – anyone familiar with the coastline near Athens will have some idea what they're aiming for. On Friday and Saturday evenings and all day Sunday, Grand Parade is bumper to bumper with traffic and crowds visiting the eating and drinking establishments of 'Little Athens'. The stretch starts at the north end with **Gecko** (No.18, 9567 3344), a chic indoor and outdoor café. Nearby is **Mezes** (No.36, 9567 2865), equal parts café, restaurant and ice-cream bar and understandably popular with a young crowd. Further down, **Eurobay**

(No.86, 9597 3300) goes for an ultra-smooth, Greco-Italian blend of food and style, while nearby restaurant and café **Kamari** (No.82, 9556 2533) is more rustic, with whitewashed walls and sleek terracotta floors.

The cafés and restaurants along Bay Street around the corner attract a slightly older and more glamorous Greek crowd. There's **One Bay** (Shop 1, 376 Bay Street, 9599 5775) and **Zande Brasserie** (Shop 2, 376 Bay Street, 9567 6475). The most upmarket restaurant (price-wise, if not style-wise) is **Le Sands** (Grand Parade, 9599 2128) with its panoramic views of Botany Bay – never mind the planes landing to the left and the pipes and towers of the oil refinery to the right.

To learn more about the beginnings of colonial Australia, head south around the bay to the tip of **Kurnell Peninsula**, where the British first landed in 1770. Under the command of James Cook, and with botanist Joseph Banks leading a party of scientists, the crew of HMS *Endeavour* spent a week exploring the area and recording information on the flora and fauna they found (hence the bay's name). **Captain Cook's Landing Place** is now a regular school excursion: on weekdays it's crowded with children visiting the **Cook Obelisk**, **Cook's Well** and **Landing Rock**. To find out more about the history of the area and the young colony, visit the **Discovery Centre** (Captain Cook Drive, Botany Bay National Park, 9668 9111, 11am-3pm Mon-Fri, 10am-4.30pm Sat, Sun, $7 per car).

Cronulla

Map p321. **Transport** *CityRail Cronulla.*

It helps to have 'the look' when you're visiting Cronulla Beach. This largely revolves around a tan, blonde hair and as little clothing as modesty will allow – imagine the love children of Jessica Simpson and David Hasselhoff. If that doesn't describe you, you might find it more comforting to hang with the multicultural Sunday crowd picnicking beneath the trees. And don't let the legacy of the 2005 riots put you off – the locals are a friendly bunch.

Cronulla is a much longer beach than its more famous city counterparts Bondi, Coogee, Clovelly and Maroubra. It takes at least four hours to walk its length from South Cronulla

Worth the hike: beachside bliss at **Wattamolla**.

northwards to Green Hills and beyond. There's also a walking track that starts at the end of South Cronulla and wends its way southwards around the cliff of **Port Hacking**, past sea pools to **Darook Park**, where you can swim in calm, clear water. Halfway along the track is **Bass and Flinders Point**: from here you can stare across the water to **Jibbon Beach** in Bundeena on the edge of the Royal National Park (*see p133*).

Serious surfers like to head to the northern end, to **Eloura**, **Wanda** and **Green Hills** beaches, where there's often the background churn of 4WDs playing on the sand dunes behind the beach. Revs are big in these parts – especially on the water. Jet skis, speedboats and waterskiers create chaos in the otherwise sleepy arms of the Port Hacking river every weekend. For more water action, contact **Cronulla Surf School** (9544 0895, www.cronullasurf.com.au)

for surfing lessons, or **Pro Dive** (9544 2200, www.prodivecronulla.com) to discover what lies beneath the waves.

In Cronulla itself, the pedestrianised strip of **Cronulla Street** is jammed with surf shops. For great coffee and corn cakes, duck into gourmet deli **Surfeit** (2 Surf Road, 9523 3873) – you might even see swimming supremo Ian Thorpe having breakfast here. Better coffee still can be found closer to the beach at **Grind** (20-26 the Kingsway, 9527 3100).

If your wallet stretches to city prices, head to **Summer Salt** (Elouera Surf Club, 66 Mitchell Road, 9523 2366) for uninterrupted beach views and a mix of tapas and seafood. More city chic can be found at Mod Oz mecca the **Nun's Pool** (103 Ewos Parade, 9523 3395), named after a little rock pool across the road through Shelley Park. On the Kingsway, views can be found at mid-market prices at **Stonefish** (Nos.8-18, 9544

3046), which offers a mix of stir-fries, steaks and seafood, while **Bella Costa** (9544 3223), in the same complex, specialises in modern Italian. The **Naked Grape** on Gerrale Street just off the Kingsway (Nos.59-65, 9527 7729) is becoming a hit with local foodies who come for its swish contemporary cuisine. It's also worth hiking up the road to **Peter Michael's Seafood** (No.47, 9544 0033) for first-rate seafood kebabs and grills; if you're in the mood for Lebanese food, opposite the train station is the top-notch **Cedars Corner** (138 Cronulla Street, 9527 0488).

On summer nights the electric-coloured interiors of **Northies Cronulla Hotel** (corner of Elouera Road and the Kingsway, 9523 6866, www.northies.com.au) spill over with energy. For a slower vibe, try **Brass Monkey** (115A Cronulla Street, 9544 3844), which hosts live jazz and blues bands.

Bundeena & around

Map p321. **Transport** *CityRail Cronulla then ferry Bundeena.*

A 20-minute ferry ride from Cronulla's Tonkin Street wharf across Port Hacking delivers you to Bundeena, a small township (population 2,300, of which about a quarter is under 18 years old) that spreads out along the top of the north-eastern section of the **Royal National Park** (*see below*). Established in 1879, this was Australia's first national park – and only the second in the world after Yellowstone in the US. Covering 150 square kilometres (58 square miles) on the southern boundary of the Sydney metropolitan area, it offers stunning coastline, rainforest, open wetlands, estuaries and heath.

Bundeena, which means 'noise like thunder' in the local Aboriginal language, was named after the sound of the surf pounding on the east coast. The Aboriginal Dharawal people used the area as a camping ground, and were sometimes joined by other large clans for feasting and ceremonies. In the 1820s white settlers arrived in 'the Village', as locals call Bundeena, to build a few fishing shacks. More came during the 1930s Depression, but it was only after World War II that a substantial number of permanent houses and holiday homes began to appear.

There are three main beaches, two of which fall within the national park. The main strip of sand is **Hordens Beach**, which you'll see to your right as you approach by ferry. If you walk up the hill from the wharf you'll find a small supermarket, a newsagent, a couple of inexpensive cafés and a fish and chip shop. To reach **Jibbon Beach**, walk left from the ferry,

past a toilet block and the **RSL club**, which serves very cheap drinks with brilliant views and where head chef Wayne Walsh serves up Med fare in the rather civilised restaurant **SaltBush** (open noon-4pm, 6-10pm Fri-Sun) and equally tasty treats in the accompanying brasserie (open noon-9pm daily; both 9527 7850). Follow the road to its end, turn downhill and through a cutting to the magnificent orange-sand beach. At the far end, hop up the rocks and take the track through the bush to **Jibbon Head**, about 20 minutes away, where there are awe-inspiring views out to sea. A sign en route points to Aboriginal rock carvings of whales and fish. From Jibbon Head you can walk further down the coast on a well-worn track; it's about a three-hour return walk to **Marley Beach**, or six hours to **Wattamolla**. Take plenty of water, sunscreen and insect repellent in summer.

The third beach, **Bonnie Vale**, is to the right just before you leave the village; you can walk to it in about 15 minutes via Bundeena Drive. Edged by swamp and ponds, it's an exceptionally long and pristine beach, with very shallow water that's ideal for kids.

The ferry to Bundeena leaves Cronulla every hour on the half-hour between 5.30am and 6.30pm on weekdays (there's no 12.30pm service), returning on the hour from 6am to 7pm. On weekends, the first ferry leaves at 8.30am and the last returns at 7pm. It costs $5.40 ($2.70 reductions) each way. It's around a 20-minute drive to Bundeena through the national park if you come by road – about an hour in total from the city.

Royal National Park
9542 0648/www2.nationalparks.nsw.gov.au. **Open** *Park* 7am-8.30pm daily. *Visitor centre* 9.30am-4.30pm Mon-Fri; 8.30am-4.30pm Sat, Sun. **Admission** $11 per vehicle.
You can get to the Royal by following walking paths from various nearby CityRail stations – Engadine, Heathcote, Loftus, Otford, Waterfall – but driving is the easiest way to explore its vast expanse. The park's nerve centre is at Audley, on the Hacking River, once the heart of the park's Victorian 'pleasure gardens'. There you'll find the main visitor centre, spacious lawns, an old-fashioned dance hall and a causeway. You can hire a canoe or rowing boat from the Audley boathouse and head upstream to picnic spots at Ironbark Flat or Wattle Forest. If you're a surfer, Garie Beach provides the waves, while further south is Werrong Beach, which is located among littoral rainforest and is the park's only authorised nude bathing spot. At secluded Wattamolla Beach you can often see migrating whales. Walking trails include Lady Carrington Drive, an easy 10km (six-mile) track along the Hacking River, and the more arduous 26km (16-mile) Coast Track, which hugs the coastline from Bundeena to Otford.

Sydney's Best Beaches

Come on in, the water's lovely.

Summer, winter, after school, after work, with a bunch of mates or just plain solo, beaches are where Sydneysiders head to chill out. And with more than 50 beaches along Sydney's coastline, from posey Palm Beach in the north to family magnet Cronulla in the south, each one has its own character. The protected harbour beaches inside the Heads are smaller and have no surf, but are great for views and picnics – after heavy rain they're not ideal for swimming though, as pollution floats in through the storm pipes. Instead, locals often take their daily dip in the outdoor seawater pools cut into the rocks on many beaches – both harbour and ocean. The bigger, bolder ocean beaches attract hordes of surfers and serious swimmers.

From September to May nearly all Sydney's ocean beaches are patrolled at weekends by local volunteer lifesavers and during the week by lifeguards – hours vary with the beach and time of year. The famous surf lifesavers wear red and yellow uniforms and an unmistakeable skullcap. The council-paid lifeguards (who are sometimes also hired on harbour beaches) wear different colours – usually a more sober blue or green – and in surfing hot spots such as Bondi and Manly work 365 days a year.

Rules on Sydney's beaches are stringent: alcohol and fires are banned, and on many beaches ball games, skateboards, in-line skaters, kites and frisbees are also illegal. Smoking is also forbidden on many beaches, including Bondi, Tamarama, Bronte, Manly and the northern beaches up to Palm Beach, and the beaches on the north side of the harbour. That said, rules are regularly flouted by 'no worries' regulars, especially off-season. Locals love to fish on the beach, but you need a licence and there are catch limits. Dropping rubbish is also an offence – 'Don't be a tosser, take your rubbish with you!' is the motto – and recycling is a must in the bins provided. Don't expect to find deckchair touts, donkeys or even an ice-cream seller, because Sydneysiders are fiercely protective of the fact that their beaches are unspoilt – and they intend to keep them that way.

WATER TEMPERATURES

The water at Sydney beaches can turn icy without warning, so take the following as a guide only. As a general rule, the water temperature lags a couple of months behind the air temperature. So when the weather is warming up in October and November, the ocean is still holding its winter chill of 16-17°C (61-63°F). Only in December does the sea become a nicely swimmable 18-19°C (64-66°F). The ocean is a balmy 20-21°C (68-70°F) from February to April, sometimes until May. It can even reach 23-24°C (73-75°F) if there's a warm current running from the north.

Below are Sydney's best beaches: the harbour beaches are listed from east to west; the northern ocean beaches heading north; and the southern ocean beaches heading south. Orange numbers given in this chapter correspond to the location of each beach as marked on the Greater Sydney map on p321 or the Sydney Harbour map on pp322-323. There's also a more detailed map of the northern beaches on p118.

For more information on many of the beaches listed here, see the relevant Sightseeing chapters. For information on the latest surfing conditions, visit www.coastalwatch.com.

Harbour beaches

South

Shark Beach
Nielsen Park, Vaucluse Road, Vaucluse. Bus 325. **Map** p323 ③④
Locals swim in the smooth warm waters of this sheltered harbour inlet all year round. In summer it's as packed as an Australian beach can get, with families swarming the narrow 300m beach or picnicking in the shade of the Moreton Bay fig trees on the grassy slopes. Part of leafy Nielsen Park, the beach also boasts fabulous views of Manly, Shark Island (hence its name) and, from the upper parklands, the Harbour Bridge. If you don't swim, you can watch the ferries, yachts, kayakers, seaplanes and oil tankers vie for space in the harbour, or you could just grab a bite to eat. Nielsen Park (9337 7333), an Italian restaurant that's been serving since 1914, offers trattoria fare when it's not booked out for a wedding. More informal is its licensed café next door, which serves pizzas, wraps, ice-creams and excellent coffee – just be prepared to queue.
Services *Café. Changing rooms. Child-friendly. No dogs. Parking. Picnic area. Restaurant. Shade. Shark net (Sept-May). Showers. Toilets.*

Parsley Bay
Horler Avenue, Vaucluse. Bus 325. **Map** p323 ㉙

Barbecue etiquette

Aussies are well known for worshipping the fiery altar, throwing snags (sausages), prawns, whole snapper and even vegetables and fruit (especially bananas) on the hallowed coals. Sydneysiders are no different and while the universal barbie may seem the most casual of dining events, there is a certain etiquette to every occasion, plus some rules that must be obeyed.

● At public electric or gas barbecues (those in picnic areas, by beaches and in parks) first check you haven't jumped a queue – you'll usually know from the primal roar emanating from milling throngs you'd hardly noticed. After use, always clean down your bbq surface – and this means clean, no burnt offerings, no slimy grease spots, and absolutely no rubbish. Then retire to a nearby spot leaving the bbq for the next person.

● If you're invited to a home barbie, always turn up with chilled tinnies, stubbies or chardy, and a plate. No not just your Willow Pattern dish to eat off…a plate of meat/fish/vegeburgers to be barbecued, preferably marinated, or a substantial salad for the table. And on no account touch the tongs. An Aussie man's castle is ruled by his Weber – keep a respectful distance.

● If you fancy lighting up your own portable barbie on the roadside, in a park or on a beach, first check the signs. Many beaches and parks do not allow barbecues. Next check if there's a fire ban in place – which there often is in the hot summer months.

● Be ready to participate in barbecue games however full/tired/drunk/bored you are. Best of the bunch is a gentle game of boules – worst is spin the (empty) bottle!

It's the grass, not the tiny beach, that is the big draw here. Nestled at the foot of a steep (and sometimes treacherous) road of million-dollar mansions, the bay is part of a 5.7-hectare (14-acre) nature reserve with its own ranger and an abundance of birds, fish and insects. It's great for small children, who can play safely on the lawns and in the well-equipped recreation area, and there are excellent walks through the bush and even across a rickety suspension bridge over the water. The small crescent-shaped beach (roughly 70m long) leads into what are often murky waters: after heavy rain, rubbish floats into the bay from storm pipes. Nevertheless, the millpond-like swimming area is popular with snorkellers and scuba divers thanks to its array of tropical fish.
Services *Café (closes 4pm). Changing rooms. Child-friendly (play area). No dogs. Parking. Picnic area. Shade. Shark net (removed for repairs 1mth winter). Showers. Toilets.*

Camp Cove

Victoria Street, Watsons Bay. Ferry Watsons Bay/bus 324, 325, 380, L24. **Map** p323 ❹
Serious sun-seekers love this 200m strip of bright yellow sand, which runs in a thin curve against a backdrop of designer cottages. The beach is not particularly great for surfing, but it's a fine place for a

dip and provides fabulous views of the city's skyscrapers. At the southern end of the upper grasslands is the start of the South Head Heritage Trail. Camp Cove has one small kiosk serving sandwiches, coffee and ice-creams. Although the beach does have a dedicated parking area, spaces are at a huge premium; far better to come by ferry to Watsons Bay and walk around the corner.
Services *Café (Oct-May). Lifesavers (Oct-May). No dogs. Parking. Toilets.*

Lady Bay Beach

Victoria & Cliff Streets, Watsons Bay. Ferry Watsons Bay/bus 324, 325, 380, L24. **Map** p323 ❷
Sydney's first nudist beach, Lady Bay is just below South Head and a short walk along the South Head Heritage Trail from Camp Cove. Steep iron steps lead down to the 100m beach, which is reduced to virtually nothing when the tide comes in: you're better off sunbathing on one of the rocks. It's popular as a pick-up place for gay men, but Lady Bay offers scenic as well as sexual thrills, including spectacular views of the city and, if you walk around the headland to Hornby Lighthouse, the open sea to the east (it's actually the last southern beach inside the harbour).
Services *No dogs. Toilets (located on the clifftop above beach).*

Clontarf Beach is ideal for families and sailors.

North

Balmoral Beach

The Esplanade, Balmoral. Ferry South Mosman (Musgrave Street) then bus 233/ferry Taronga Zoo then bus 238. **Map** p323 ●

Home to Sydney's seriously rich, Balmoral has been a popular bathing spot since the late 1900s. Its beach promenade and Bathers' Pavilion (now one of Sydney's most sought-after eateries, *see p165*) were both built in the late 1920s and retain a genteel air from that era. Hundreds of families flock here at weekends to enjoy the sheltered waters of its two large sandy beaches, which together stretch for about a mile. The beaches are separated by Rocky Point, a tree-covered picnicking island accessible by a footbridge. To the south, Balmoral Beach has an enclosed swimming area surrounded by boardwalks and is excellent for children; to the north, Edwards Beach is bigger and less protected, but has interesting rock pools with shells, fish and anemones. You can hire boats from Balmoral Boathouse. The white rotunda which is often used for weddings also acts as a stage for Shakespeare By The Sea, a short season of the Bard's work performed on summer evenings (www.shakespeare-by-the-sea.com).
Services *Boat hire. Cafés. Changing rooms. Child-friendly (play area). Danger: underwater rocks. No dogs. Parking. Picnic areas. Shade. Shark nets. Shops. Showers. Toilets.*

Chinamans Beach

McLean Crescent, Mosman. Bus 175, 178, 185, 229, 249. **Map** p323 ●

A real Sydney secret, Chinamans Beach in Middle Harbour is stumbled upon through dunes on the edge of the Rosherville bushland reserve. It's a quiet paradise, with 300m of beautiful sand, gently lapping waters and huge, strikingly designed homes perched on the hills above. Located right opposite busier Clontarf Beach (*see below*), Chinamans has plenty of recreational facilities – a play area, picnic tables nestled under pepper trees, and rolling lawns where you can play ball games – but no shop, café or restaurant. Children love the mass of barnacle-encrusted rock pools at the southern end, but there's a $500 fine for taking any crustaceans home.
Services *Changing rooms. Child-friendly (play area). No dogs. Parking. Picnic area. Shade. Showers. Toilets.*

Clontarf Beach

Sandy Bay Road, Clontarf. Bus 171, E71. **Map** p323 ●

With around 600m of sand, a large grassy picnic area, an excellent playground, an outdoor netted pool and all the facilities you might need, Clontarf is a very popular beach location for families. It's situated right opposite the Middle Harbour Yacht Club, so there are good views of the Spit Bridge with boats sailing underneath and cars racing over the top. It's worth stopping at Balgowlah Heights en route to pick up a picnic – the fantastic Balgowlah Heights Deli on Beatrice Street (No.122, 9949 3969) is open from 7am to 7pm daily.
Services *Barbecues. Café. Changing rooms. Child-friendly (play area). No dogs. Parking. Picnic area. Pool. Restaurant (closed July). Shade. Shark net (Sept-May). Showers. Toilets.*

Ocean beaches

South

Bondi Beach

Campbell Parade, Bondi Beach. CityRail Bondi Junction then bus 380, 381, 382, 333, X84/ bus 222, 380, 389, 333. **Map** p323 ❷

Australia's most famous beach, Bondi is believed to have been named after an Aboriginal word meaning 'the sound of breaking waves'. Today its crashing breakers attract a huge fraternity of urban surfies as well as ubiquitous Britpackers and new-generation hippies strumming guitars on the sand. At the height of summer, the beach draws up to 40,000 people per day, but, and you'll be hard put to believe this if you arrive when it's crowded, there are times in the week when it's relatively empty. The elegant Bondi Pavilion, built in 1929 as a changing area, houses showers, toilets, a community centre and cafés. Two lifesaving clubs patrol the half-mile beach – 'Ready Aye Ready' is the motto of the North Bondi Surf Life Saving Club. The central area near the Pavilion is the safest swimming area; surfers favour the southern end, with its strong rips. Also at this end is a skateboard ramp and the famous Bondi Icebergs' pool and club. Be vigilant: 'Thieves go to the beach too', warn big NSW police signs. Lockers are available in the Pavilion – use them. For a local area map, *see p334.*

Services *Barbecues. Cafés. Changing rooms. Child-friendly (play area). Lifeguards/savers. No dogs. Parking. Picnic area. Pool. Restaurants. Shark net (Sept-May). Shops. Showers. Toilets.*

Tamarama Beach

Pacific Avenue, Tamarama. CityRail Bondi Junction then bus 361. **Map** p323 ❹

A 100m sheltered cove, Tamarama Beach is neither easy to get to by public transport nor to park at should you decide to drive there. Not only that, once you arrive, it's not particularly accessible either: you have to climb down 40 steep steps to reach the water. And with its tricky surf and deep rip, it's not a swimming spot. That said, it's got a serious fan base of macho surfers who like to live dangerously and equally dedicated sun-seekers (there's absolutely no shade to be found on the sand). Britpackers play Sunday soccer matches on the large grassy picnic area and volleyball is the sport on the beach itself. The small children's play area with swings and a slide is within eyeshot of the excellent Tama Café (9130 2419), which serves wonderful gourmet vegetarian and non-vegetarian sandwiches as well as refreshing power juices and coffee.

Services *Barbecue. Café. Changing rooms. Child-friendly (play area). Danger: underwater rocks. Lifeguards/savers (Sept-May). No dogs. Parking. Picnic area. Shark net (Sept-May). Showers. Toilets.*

Bronte Beach

Bronte Road, Bronte. CityRail Bondi Junction then bus 378. **Map** p323 ❸

Bronte is absolute bliss for local parents – pack the kids, the swimsuits and the boogie boards, and this 300m stretch of sand (complete with cute kids' train) will babysit all day long. Though the water has a strong rip and is great for surfing, the outdoor Bronte Baths at the southern end – and the adjacent community centre – are the preserve of kids. There's plenty of shade under the sweeping sandstone rocks and scores of covered picnic benches (some with inlaid chessboards) on which to enjoy the traditional Aussie tucker served at the Bronte Kiosk on the beach – meat pies and hot chips aplenty. For more sophisticated dining options there's a stretch of decent eateries behind the beach along Bronte Road, which run the gamut from sushi to gourmet salads, and from fish and chips to Mediterranean treats.

Services *Barbecues. Cafés. Changing rooms. Child-friendly (play area). Danger: underwater rocks. Lifeguards/savers (Sept-May). No dogs. Parking. Picnic area. Pool. Restaurants. Shade. Shark net (Sept-May). Shops. Showers. Toilets.*

Clovelly Beach

Clovelly Road, Clovelly. CityRail Bondi Junction then bus 360/bus 339, X39. **Map** p323 ❾

Once known as Little Coogee, tucked as it is around the corner from the more famous Big Coogee (which is now simply Coogee Beach; *see below*), Clovelly is an idyllic spot, swathed in natural beauty. The tiny square of sand slopes into a long inlet of calm water, surrounded by a boardwalk and a concrete promenade with chic barbecue pavilions and picnic tables. It's a favourite with scuba divers and snorkellers, but it's the wheelchair access that weaves the real magic. The Clovelly Bay boardwalk boasts specific entry points to the water with locking devices for a submersible wheelchair, on loan from the Beach Inspector's office (weekdays) or the SLSC (weekends). On the south promenade sits a chic 25m three-lane lap pool, built in 1962 and nicely revamped in 2002. There's also a good café, Seasalt (9664 5344), which serves fish and chips at the takeaway kiosk and more exotic fare at the tables.

Services *Barbecues. Café. Changing rooms. Child-friendly. Lifeguards/savers (Sept-May). No dogs. Parking. Picnic area. Pool. Restaurant. Shade. Showers. Toilets. Wheelchair access.*

Coogee Beach

Beach Street, Coogee. CityRail Bondi Junction then bus 313, 314/bus 372, 373, 374, X73, X74. **Map** p323 ⑫

This excellent family swimming beach is 400m long, with old-fashioned pools carved into the rocks at both ends. In 1929 it was declared Australia's first shark-proof beach when nets were introduced. It's not great for surfing, but at least you don't have to worry about getting hit by boards. There are fast-food restaurants aplenty, cafés and places to picnic, and it's very much a tourist attraction. In 2003 the

Sightseeing

Sea safety

TO THE RESCUE

Each year Sydney's famed surf lifesavers carry out countless rescue operations. A disproportionate number of these rescues are of foreigners who have underestimated the 'rips' (currents) in the surf. Waves at Sydney's ocean beaches can be up to four metres (13 feet) high and conceal powerful rips. More often, they are less than one metre; at Bondi and Manly, they're somewhere in between.

To be safe, always swim between the red and yellow flags that the lifesavers plant in the sand each day. If you stray outside the flags, the lifesavers will blow whistles and scream through megaphones at you. And don't think shallow water is completely safe. 'Dumpers' are waves that break with force, usually at low tide in shallow water, and can cause serious injury. Waves that don't break at all (surging waves) can knock swimmers over too and drag them out to sea. Finally, remember that alcohol and water don't mix – most of the adults who drown in NSW are under the influence.

If you do get caught by a rip and you're a confident swimmer, try to swim diagonally across the rip. Otherwise, stay calm, stick your hand in the air to signal to a lifeguard and float until you're rescued: don't fight the current by swimming toward shore.

SHARK THINKING

Shark attacks are very rare. In the past 20 years only one person in all NSW has been killed by a shark attack, and the last fatal attack in Sydney harbour was in 1963. It's true there have been more sharks seen in recent years, but this is because better sewage methods have made the beaches much cleaner and so more palatable to sharks. That said, the closest most people get to a shark is in an aquarium: since beach swimming became popular, sharks have tended to shy away.

A lot of Sydney's beaches are shark-netted. The nets are usually around 150 metres long, seven deep and are anchored to the sea floor within 500 metres of the shore. You won't spot them because they are always dropped in ten metre-deep water ensuring three metres (ten feet) of clearance for swimmers and surfers. The nets are meant not so much as a physical block to sharks but to prevent them establishing a habitat close to shore.

They are moved from time to time to keep the sharks guessing.

If by some quirk of fate you do see a shark while swimming, try not to panic: just swim calmly to shore. Easier said than done, yes, but keep in mind that sharks are attracted to jerky movements. 'However,' say the experts at Taronga Zoo, 'if a shark gets close then any action you take may disrupt the attack pattern, such as hitting the shark's nose, gouging at its eyes, making sudden movements and blowing bubbles.' Scared? Honestly, it hardly ever happens.

STINGERS

Two kinds of jellyfish are common on Sydney's beaches in summer. The jimble (a less potent southern relative of the deadly box jellyfish) is box-shaped with four pink tentacles. It is often found at the harbour beaches. On the ocean beaches you're more likely to come across bluebottle jellyfish (aka Portuguese man-of-war), which has long blue tentacles and tends to appear only when an onshore wind is blowing.

Jimbles can deliver a painful sting but are not dangerous; bluebottles are nastier, causing an intense, longer-lasting pain, red, whip-like lesions and, occasionally, respiratory problems. Even dead bluebottles on the beach can sting, so don't touch them.

Treatment for each is different. If stung by a jimble, wash the affected area with vinegar (lifeguards and lifesavers keep stocks of it) – or, if you can, pee on it – gently remove any tentacles with tweezers or gloves, and apply ice to relieve the pain. If stung by a bluebottle, leave the water immediately, don't rub the skin and don't apply vinegar; instead use an ice pack or anaesthetic spray.

northern headland was renamed Dolphin Point in memory of the six Coogee Dolphins rugby league players who were killed in the Bali bombings. Two memorial plaques, plastered with photographs, list the 26 victims from the local community (from a total Australian death toll of 88).

Services *Barbecues. Cafés. Changing rooms. Child-friendly. Lifeguards/savers. No dogs. Parking. Picnic area. Pools. Restaurants. Shade. Shark net (Sept-May). Shops. Showers. Toilets.*

Maroubra Beach

Marine Parade, Maroubra. CityRail Bondi Junction then bus 317, 353. Bus 376, 377, 395, 396, X77, X96. **Map** p321 🟢

Maroubra Beach was chosen as the new headquarters for Surfing NSW in 2003 – which didn't come as much of a surprise, since the waves are huge here and it's long been a top surf spot. All the outfit's coaching, judging, educational and safety programmes are conducted at the 1.1km (0.7-mile) beach. The Safe Surf School (9365 4370, www.safesurfschools.com.au) is a perfect place for children to learn how to surf away from all the crowds. Much less touristy than neighbouring Coogee, it's also a favourite with beach sprinters who run through the shallows in their Speedos. There are a few local shops, showers and toilets, a well-equipped kids' play area and a sizeable skateboard park (which is packed when school's out) located next to the beach's windswept dunes.

Services *Barbecues. Cafés. Changing rooms. Child-friendly (play area). Lifeguards/savers. No dogs. Parking. Picnic area. Pool. Restaurants. Shark net (Sept-May). Shops. Showers. Toilets.*

Cronulla Beach

Mitchell Road, Cronulla. CityRail Cronulla. **Map** p321 🟢

A vast sandy beach more than 6km (3.75 miles) long, Cronulla had a flash of worldwide notoriety in December 2005 as a battleground between groups of white and Middle Eastern Australians. To Sydneysiders, though, it has long been the south's most popular surfing and swimming spot. Cronulla isn't actually one beach but a whole series, running from Kurnell on Botany Bay at the northern end through Wanda, Elouera, North Cronulla, South Cronulla snd on down to Shelly and Port Hacking in the south. On the surfing front Cronulla Point has lots of breaks off three reef ledges and experts like to attempt Shark Island, the area's most notorious break. It has the feel of a big Queensland resort with its high-rise apartments and hotels, bars, steakhouses and carloads of young rev-heads. The southern end, a half-moon patch of sand around 100m long, is patrolled by a lifeguard all year round; with less of a rip, this is family territory for bathing, fossicking in the rock pools or swimming indoors at the Cronulla Sports Complex (located next to the lifesavers' hut). The much longer northern end of the beach has a fiercer undertow and views of a not-so-pretty oil refinery. There's a huge grassy picnic area

Shelly Beach is good for swimming.

with plenty of tables and an esplanade walkway. Getting to Cronulla from the city, it takes about 50 minutes by train or an hour by car.

Services *Cafés. Changing rooms. Child-friendly (play area). Lifeguards/savers (south all year round; north Sept-May). No dogs. Parking. Picnic area. Pools. Restaurants. Shade. Shark net (Sept-May). Shops. Showers. Toilets.*

North

Shelly Beach

Marine Parade, Manly. Ferry Manly. **Map** p323 🔵

A ten-minute stroll south of Manly, small Shelly Beach is a family delight with yellow sand, gentle waters and a grassy picnic area. As you stroll south along the promenade from Manly, don't miss the Fairy Bower ocean pool, an excellent outdoor rock pool with spectacular views of the coastline and its famous sculptures (*Sea Nymphs* by artist Helen Leete). Set in Cabbage Tree Bay, Shelly Beach is best known for its good swimming conditions, but it is also popular with novice scuba divers testing the deep and for seekers of quality surf; Shelly is the paddle out spot for the Bower – one of Australia's better big wave locations.

Services *Barbecue. Café. Changing rooms. Child-friendly. No dogs. Parking. Picnic area. Restaurant (closed winter Sun-Mon). Shade. Showers. Toilets.*

Manly Beach

Manly. Ferry Manly. **Map** p323 🔵

Jumping aboard a Sydney ferry is a must and a trip to Manly is the perfect excuse. Take one of the trusty old yellow-and-green giants from Circular Quay to Manly Wharf in Manly Cove, where there's a small harbour beach (about 250m long) and a netted swimming area. To reach the open sea, head across the busy pedestrianised street, the Corso, to the 1.5km (mile-long) crescent of sand known as Manly Surf

Beach, but actually comprising Queenscliff in the north, followed by North Steyne, South Steyne and Manly Beaches. A mecca for mums, surfies and international tourists, Manly has all the facilities of a big resort and on a hot day attaracts up to 50,000 visitors. It also has plenty of history: in 1903 it was one of the first beaches to permit daylight swimming, but the crowds didn't understand the danger of the surf – there are rips along the entire length of the beach – and so fishermen Eddie and Joe Sly set up Manly's first lifesaving patrol. It's not all about surf, you can snorkel, dive, sail, fish – and the beach volleyball nets are in almost constant use. Cyclists and in-line skaters can enoy the bike track along the shore, from Burnt Bridge Creek to Shelly Beach. For a local area map, *see p.334*.

Services *Cafés. Changing rooms. Child-friendly. Lifeguards/savers. No dogs. Parking. Picnic area. Pool (at Queenscliff). Restaurants. Shade. Shark net (Sept-May.) Shops. Showers. Toilets.*

Collaroy Beach

Pittwater Road, Collaroy. Bus 188, 190, E83, E84, E86, E87, E88, E89, L88, L90. **Map** p321 ❹
North of Manly lies a stretch of magnificent surfing beaches with wonderfully ludicrous names such as: Curl Curl, Dee Why, Long Reef, Narrabeen. At Collaroy, which lies directly south of Narrabeen, there's a 1km (half-mile) stretch of honey-coloured sand pounded by huge waves. It's also got an excellent, large ocean pool, plus a toddler pool at its southern end. The Bruce Bartlett Memorial Playground to the rear is shaded and has masses of fun equipment. The Surf Rock Hotel is right on the beach and had an impressive modern revamp in 2005. The Deck is the place to be for al fresco beers and light meals, right on the sand with the waves in front of you. This is a true local hangout and be prepared for the whole area to get thumping at night.

Services *Barbecues. Cafés. Changing rooms. Child-friendly (play area). Danger: underwater rocks. Lifeguards/savers (Sept-May). Parking. Picnic area. Pools. Restaurants. Shark net (Sept-May). Shops. Showers. Toilets.*

Newport Beach

Barrenjoey Road, Newport. Bus 188, 190, E88, E89, L88, L90. **Map** p321 ⑫
This half-mile of windswept beach offers good surf with easy access to a busy main road of shops, cafés and restaurants. Its accessibility makes it very popular with locals keen to catch a quick wave. There's a well-equipped, fenced-off play area in the grassland to the rear, but at dusk the beach can get rowdy and is no place for youngsters.

Services *Barbecues. Cafés. Changing rooms. Children's play area. Danger: underwater rocks. Lifeguards/savers (Sept-May). No dogs. Parking. Picnic area. Pool (south end). Restaurants. Shark net (Sept-May). Shops. Showers. Toilets.*

Avalon Beach

Barrenjoey Road, Avalon. Bus 188, 190, E88, E89, L88, L90. **Map** p321 ❶

This sandy and sophisticated half-mile beach gets pretty busy in the summer, especially with surfers, who arrive by the carload to tackle the generous waves. There's also good swimming and an excellent ocean pool at the southern end, and the whole beach is backed by grassy sand dunes.
Services *Barbecues. Changing rooms. Children's play area. Lifeguards/savers (Sept-May.) Parking. Picnic area. Pool. Shark net (Sept-May). Showers. Toilets.*

Whale Beach

The Strand, Whale Beach. Bus 190, L90 to Avalon then bus 193. **Map** p321 ⑮
Approached via a precariously steep road, this 700m stretch of salmon-pink sand offers big surf and a rugged coastline. There's a 25m ocean pool at the southern end: take care when the tide comes in as the waves crash over the pool and surrounding rocks. Unlike nearby Palm Beach, Whale tends to remain crowd free and is something of a local hideaway. There's a kiosk on the beach serving freshly made rolls, juices and hot food, while more elaborate cafés and restaurants turn a trade back up Whale Beach Road: the Olive and Rose café (9974 1383, open Wednesday to Sunday) is well worth a visit.
Services *Barbecues. Café (closed July). Changing rooms. Child-friendly (play area). Danger: underwater rocks. Lifeguards/savers (Sept-May). Parking. Picnic area. Pool. Restaurants. Shade. Shark net (Sept-May). Showers. Toilets.*

Palm Beach

Barrenjoey Road, Palm Beach. Bus 190, L90. **Map** p321 ⑬
Situated at the northernmost tip of the northern beaches peninsula, Palm Beach is a local paradise. Don't be fooled by Palm Beach Wharf, a busier beach on the west side that you come to first. Keep on driving up the hill and around the bend to get to the real deal on the east side: you won't be disappointed. Palm Beach is home to Sydney's rich and famous; colonial-style mansions set on the hillside possess breathtaking views of foaming ocean and more than a mile of caramel-coloured sand. The southern end, known as Cabbage Tree Boat Harbour, is the safest spot to swim and surf. If you find the sea too daunting, there's the excellent Jack 'Johnny' Carter outdoor pool, named after the man who spent 50 years teaching local kids to swim. The Sugar Palm Restaurant on Ocean Road (No.24, 9974 4410), right in the heart of Palm Beach proper, is a new and very popular addition to the many eateries here: try to catch the evening wine and tapas served from 4pm to 9pm for a taste of the local high life. Further back on North Palm Beach keep an eye out for young Aussie actors on a tea break – this is where the hit soap *Home and Away* is filmed.
Services *Barbecues (in the play area). Café. Changing rooms. Child-friendly (play area is in the adjacent Governor Phillip Park). Lifeguards/savers (Sept-May). Parking. Picnic area. Pool. Restaurant. Shade. Shark net (Sept-May). Shops. Showers. Toilets.*

Eat, Drink, Shop

Features

Bite Me. *See p153.*

Restaurants

Sydney's chefs are cooking up an international storm.

Eat, Drink, Shop

Sydney's restaurant scene is fast, glitzy and ever-changing. Sydneysiders tend to eat out a lot – and add to this the tourists and you have a public eager to be fed. But honing the perfect dish or venue isn't so easy, as the local chefs discover daily. The 'it' crowd is fickle and this is a city that thrives on the latest culinary novelty, rather than the classic.

In New South Wales close to one in five restaurants closes its doors every year, which is a pretty scary prospect if you're a fledgling chef longing to share your fare. This was felt most keenly recently when one of Sydney's most admired chefs Peter Conistis went bankrupt when his fine dining venture Omega hit trouble. He lost his house, his business and a lot of pride, and shocked the hell out of Sydney's foodies. Why? Perhaps he was too caught up in the food – it happens here. Much as normal folk love fresh new tastes and combinations, for the majority, eating out is about relaxing with friends, impressing a date, dining with a water view and, yes, tantalising those tastebuds (but probably in that order!). Fortunately, Conistis is back on track with a low-key but exciting venture, which only goes to prove that Sydneysiders do still recognise culinary wizardry – they just don't want to pay the earth for it or have to dress up to the nines. Such a lesson has been heeded across town and prices are better than ever, with many truly fine eateries keeping main courses below $30. Quite something when you compare costs with London, Tokyo and New York.

But in terms of the food on the plate, most of Sydney's top restaurants wouldn't be out of place in Manhattan or Mayfair. While they make the best of local produce, they belong to that light, inventive, produce-driven cuisine common to the Western world's finest, albeit with a keener understanding of the flavours of Asia and fewer ties to French technique. Native ingredients appear on some menus and indeed are the focus of some restaurants, but they're regarded in much the same terms as, say, Native American foods in the States or Welsh food in the UK: more a diversion than a serious component of contemporary dining. You can eat crocodile and kangaroo and wattleseed in Sydney, but the native ingredients you'll see in the city's better restaurants tend to run more along the lines of Coffin Bay scallops, Yamba prawns, West Australian crayfish and Tasmanian oysters than Skippy and co.

And there lies one of Sydney's great strengths: seafood. It's diverse, plentiful, fresh and of excellent quality. Just as importantly, perhaps, people know how to cook it: that is, not very much – or at all. Minimal interference between hook and plate keeps the natural qualities of the fish to the fore.

Many of the city's best seafood restaurants happen to make the most of the city's other great asset, the harbour. It's another distinctive facet of Sydney dining: true, there is no shortage of waterside places that will strip your wallet in return for food and service distinguished only by their ordinariness, but a significant fraction of the view-restaurants are worth visiting for more than the eye candy – in some instances grandly so.

Nowhere else in Australia is the country's proximity to Asia better expressed on the plate. While good and authentic Cantonese, Thai, Vietnamese, Japanese, Korean and Malaysian food is readily available (truly outstanding Indian, Pakistani and Sri Lankan is another matter, however), the modern Asian restaurants make a much better fist of things than their Western counterparts, dispensing with the ugly forced unions of 'fusion' food in favour of dishes that remain true to their ethnic roots even while dressing them up for the cocktail-and-couture set at the same time.

On the plus side, the bring-your-own (BYO) tradition is alive and kicking: even some of the more high-flying establishments allow it. But it often extends only to bottled wine, so call ahead if you plan to bring a few bottles of beer. Some restaurants offer BYO in the week, but go in-house-only on busier nights. A small corkage fee is usually charged, either by the head or bottle. In the listings below we've indicated whether the restaurant is licensed, BYO, both or doesn't allow alcohol at all. We've also given the price range for main courses at dinner.

Tipping, meanwhile, is something Sydneysiders do to reward exceptional service, not to keep angry waiters at bay. Ten per cent

---

❶ Purple numbers given in this chapter correspond to the location of each restaurant as marked on the street maps. *See pp326-334.*

Dive in for sensational seafood at **Rockpool (fish)**. *See p149.*

on top of the bill is the local standard, but no one's likely to be offended if you up the ante, and equally they're not likely to chase you down the street if you don't tip at all (though we're mindful of the New York bartenders' mantra – if you can't afford to tip, you can't afford to drink. Or eat).

Finally, bear in mind that it's illegal to smoke in any restaurant in Sydney. You may be allowed to smoke outdoors – the decision rests with individual establishments – but even then there may be a no smoking policy early in the evening to allow alfresco diners to enjoy their meals smoke-free.

The CBD & the Rocks

Asian

Azuma
Level 1, Chifley Plaza, 2 Chifley Square, corner of Phillip & Hunter Streets, CBD (9222 9960/www. azuma.com.au). CityRail Martin Place. **Open** noon-2.30pm, 6-10pm Mon-Fri; 6-10pm Sat. **Main courses** $27-$66. **Licensed/BYO. Credit** AmEx, MC, V. **Map** p327 F5 ❶ Japanese
The deluxe skyscraper setting will have you squinting and pretending you're in Roppongi Hills or some other moneyed Tokyo setting, but the lightness and boldness of the kitchen's way with traditional Japanese flavours will tell you otherwise. When

Azuma-san suggests you try sashimi with a squeeze of lemon rather than the ubiquitous soy, follow his advice and experience raw fish perfection.

Chat Thai
Food Avenue, 500 George Street, between Market & Park Streets, CBD (9264 7109/www.chatthai. com.au). CityRail Town Hall/Monorail City Centre. **Open** 9am-8pm Mon-Wed, Fri-Sun; 9am-9pm Thur. **Main courses** $7-$9. **BYO. No credit cards.** **Map** p329 F7 ❷ Thai
The queues wind halfway down the street and nearly everybody dining in the restaurant is Thai. With a stylish room and dishes like redfish mousse fritters and an excellent version of chicken rice with bitter melon soup, you can see why.

Sailors Thai Canteen & Restaurant
106 George Street, opposite Mill Lane, The Rocks (9251 2466). CityRail/ferry Circular Quay. **Open** *Canteen* noon-10pm Mon-Sat. *Restaurant* noon-2pm, 6-10pm Mon-Fri; 6-10pm Sat. **Main courses** *Canteen* $21-$28.50. *Restaurant* $29-$39.50. **Licensed. Credit** AmEx, DC, MC, V. **Map** p327 F3 ❸ Thai
Chef David Thompson now spends most of his time running Nahm, his Michelin-starred Thai restaurant in London. Here you can eat food every bit as dynamic and thrilling, but for a fraction of the cost. Upstairs is more casual, serving the usuals like pad thai and som tum, while the ground-floor restaurant is a little more fancy (and expensive). The Thai sweets are particularly special – try the coconut custard.

wagamama

delicious noodles ı **rice dishes**
freshly squeezed juices
wine ı **sake** ı **japanese beers**

king street wharf ı **bridge street**
the galeries victoria ı **crown street**
sydney international airport

positive eating + positive living

wagamama.com.au

Sushi Tei

1 Chifley Square, corner of Phillip & Hunter Streets, CBD (9232 7288). CityRail Martin Place. **Open** 11.30am-2.30pm, 5.30-9.30pm Mon-Sat. **Main courses** $9-$20. **Licensed**. **Credit** AmEx, DC, MC, V. **Map** p327 F5 ❹ Japanese
For inexpensive Japanese food in the middle of the city, look no further than this newcomer, which rather cheekily mushroomed apparently overnight across the road from the smooth operators and Japanese restaurant to the stars, Azuma (*see p143*). Order the edamame and gyoza and don't miss the sea urchin roe – it's spectacular.

Sydney Madang

371A Pitt Street, between Bathurst & Liverpool Streets, CBD (9264 7010). CityRail Museum. **Open** 11.30am-1am daily. **Main courses** $12-$25. **Licensed**. **Credit** MC, V. **Map** p329 F8 ❺ Korean
Korean food is taking over the world. Well, Pitt Street, at least. The service here is outstanding, and the kim chi pancake tasty as hell. The fried dumplings with rice vinegar are other must-orders, while the little sides of pickle, fish cake and tofu will leave you feeling virtuous from the inside out.

Takeru

Shop 10, 339 Sussex Street, between Bathurst & Liverpool Streets, CBD (9283 3522). CityRail TownHall or Central. **Open** noon-9.30pm Mon-Wed, Sun; noon-10pm Thur-Sat. **Main courses** $8.50-$16.50. **BYO**. **Credit** AmEx, DC, MC, V. **Map** p329 E7 ❻ Japanese
Expect plenty of kooky Japanese takes on Western food at this attractive space. Pizza, for instance, sees chicken pieces and puffed rice sharing the same base topped with mayonnaise. Try the noodle soup with slices of pork and fried garlic in a rich both.

Yoshii

115 Harrington Street, between Essex & Argyle Streets, CBD (9247 2566/www.yoshii.com.au). CityRail/ferry Circular Quay. **Open** 6-9.30pm Mon, Sat; noon-2pm, 6-9.30pm Tue-Fri. **Set menu** $80; $110 tasting menu. **Licensed**. **Credit** AmEx, DC, MC, V. **Map** p327 E4 ❼ Japanese
Ryuichi Yoshii's father was a sushi chef, and the genes have run true in his offspring, with young Yoshii-san offering the finest sashimi in the land. Sit at the bar and watch him at his work or take a table for exquisitely cooked treats like the *chaud-froid* of egg and sea urchin roe. This is culinary inventiveness at the bleeding edge, presented in cosy but utterly civilised surrounds.

European

Bécasse

204 Clarence Street, between Druitt & Market Streets, CBD (9283 3440/www.becasse.com.au). CityRail Town Hall. **Open** noon-2.30pm, 6-10pm Mon-Fri; 6-10pm Sat. **Main courses** $42-$49. **Licensed**. **Credit** AmEx, DC, MC, V. **Map** p327 E6 ❽ French

Justin North is one of the city's brightest young chefs, and with a French-based menu bursting at the seams with delights such as john dory with scallops or the seriously protein-punched rib-eye, it's especially big with the lunchtime business crowd. The stunning room is decked out in muted mushrooms, heavy curtains and hula hoop chandeliers.

Bilson's

Radisson Plaza Hotel, 27 O'Connell Street, at Hunter Street, CBD (8214 0496/www.bilsons. com.au). CityRail Wynyard. **Open** 6pm-late Tue-Thur, Sat; noon-3pm, 6pm-late Fri. **Set menu** $120-$150. **Main courses** $45. **Licensed**. **Credit** AmEx, DC, MC, V. **Map** p327 F5 ❾ French
Tony Bilson is something of a legend in these parts, having cooked in Australian kitchens for over 30 years. The unashamedly francophile elder statesman of Sydney dining creates marvels, whether turning his hand to spanner crab with chilled almond gazpacho or an assiette of Angus beef. Order the *dégustation* for the full Bilson's experience. The wine list is pretty spectacular.

Bistro CBD

Level 1, CBD Hotel, 52 King Street, at York Street, CBD (8297 7010/www.merivale.com). CityRail Wynyard. **Open** noon-3pm, 6-10pm Mon-Fri. **Main courses** $31-$37. **Licensed**. **Credit** AmEx, DC, MC, V. **Map** p327 E6 ❿ French
Throw a bread roll at lunch here and you're likely to incur the wrath of one of Sydney's top CEOs: the white-collar brigade love Bistro CBD for its pace, sirloin with Café de Paris butter, and buzz. The rest of us love the 'Your usual, sir?' service, the consistency and the exemplary fish cooking.

Civic Dining

388 Pitt Street, at Goulburn Street, CBD (8080 7040/www.civichotel.com.au). CityRail Central/ Lightrail Capitol Square. **Open** noon-2.30pm Mon; noon-2.30pm, 6pm-late Tue-Fri; 6pm-late Sat. **Main courses** $32-$35. **Licensed**. **Credit** AmEx, DC, MC, V. **Map** p329 F8 ⓫ Greek
Peter Conistis is one of Sydney's most applauded chefs, and the whole city quaked when his Omega restaurant hit the skids in late 2006. At the Civic he's back on form, creating modern Greek delicacies, only this time catering to a less hoity-toity clientele. The food is still inspiring and includes his signature dishes of scallop moussaka and rabbit pie. Yum!

Forty One

Level 42, Chifley Tower, 2 Chifley Square, corner of Phillip & Hunter Streets, CBD (9221 2500/ www.forty-one.com.au). CityRail Martin Place. **Open** 6pm-late Mon, Sat; noon-2pm, 6pm-late Tue-Fri. **Set menu** $130-$150. **Licensed**. **Credit** AmEx, DC, MC, V. **Map** p327 F5 ⓬ Modern European
While the talk of the views from the urinal in the men's room (it's glass from the waist up, with 41 floors below) is a constant, so too is the quality of chef/owner Dietmar Sawyere's cuisine. Try the Murray cod fillet with ragoût of duck confit.

Glass

2nd Floor, Hilton Sydney, 488 George Street, between Park & Market Streets, CBD (9265 6068/ www.glassbrasserie.com.au). CityRail Town Hall/ Monorail City Centre. **Open** 6am-3pm, 6pm-late Mon-Fri; 7-11am, 6pm-late Sat, Sun. **Main courses** $30.50-$59. **Licensed. Credit** AmEx, DC, MC, V. **Map** p327 F6 ⑬ French

Yes, it's one of those hotel dining rooms dreamed up by the damned. The same panel may have also thought that yoking culinary whizz Luke Mangan to a steak-frites-and-soufflés brasserie-by-numbers menu was a good idea. Sadly, the schismatic result does little service to either, but the room is seriously splashy and real effort has been made in the wine department. The wine bar (*see p180*) is nice too.

Modern Australian

Aria

1 Macquarie Street, East Circular Quay (9252 2555/www.ariarestaurant.com.au). CityRail/ferry Circular Quay. **Open** noon-2.30pm, 5.30-11pm Mon-Fri; 5-11.30pm Sat; 6-10.30pm Sun. **Main courses** $44-$56. **Licensed. Credit** AmEx, DC, MC, V. **Map** p327 G3 ⑭

TV's Matt Moran is much more than just another celebrity chef. He really can cook. Few compare to the service, the wine list is multi-award winning and the stylish room makes for a special evening. The five-spice duck consommé is a highlight, as is the slow-roasted pork belly. And that's before you even mention the view of the Opera House.

Café Sydney

5th Floor, Customs House, 31 Alfred Street, Circular Quay (9251 8683/www.cafesydney.com). CityRail/ferry Circular Quay. **Open** noon-11pm Mon-Fri; 5-11pm Sat; noon-4pm Sun. **Main courses** $28-$39. **Licensed. Credit** AmEx, DC, MC, V. **Map** p327 F4 ⑮

The setting is the draw here. Stepping out of the glass elevator, you enter a light-filled room with a dreamy vista over the harbour. There's a cool cocktail bar and a restaurant (where the quality of the view depends on the table you get). The menu is dominated by fresh fish and seafood, which are undoubtedly the highlights – meat dishes can be a little pedestrian for the price.

Dome

Arthouse Hotel, 275 Pitt Street, CBD (9284 1230/ www.thearthousehotel.com.au). CityRail St James or Town Hall/Monorail Galeries Victoria. **Open** noon-3pm, 6-10pm daily. **Main courses** $28-$36. **Licensed. Credit** AmEx, DC, MC, V. **Map** p329 F7 ⑯

This classy restaurant inside the Arthouse Hotel is headed up by talented head chef Tim Michels, whose take on Mod Oz cuisine is winning fans. On a Wednesday or Friday, Sydney icon Franca Manfredi serves up her sensational pasta dishes: don't miss the mushroom ragoût with tagliatelle.

Est.

Level 1, Establishment Hotel, 252 George Street, between Bridge Street & Abercrombie Lane, CBD (9240 3010/www.merivale.com.au). CityRail Circular Quay or Wynyard/ferry Circular Quay. **Open** noon-2.30pm, 6-10pm Mon-Fri; 6-10pm Sat. **Main courses** $42-$49. **Licensed. Credit** AmEx, DC, MC, V. **Map** p327 F4 ⑰

To step out of the lift and into the bright, colonnaded Est. dining room is to enter a bubble of total assurance. Peter Doyle's menu is flawlessly executed, skilfully cooked and hits its mark every time. And what you'll lose in pocket change, you'll gain in pure joy per bite. Amateur botanists, take note: manager Frank Moreau can tell you the name of every flower in the restaurant.

Guillaume at Bennelong

Sydney Opera House, Bennelong Point, Circular Quay (9241 1999/www.guillaumeatbennelong. com.au). CityRail/ferry Circular Quay. **Open** 5.30-11.30pm Mon-Wed, Sat; noon-3pm, 5.30-11.30pm Thur, Fri. **Main courses** $38-$90. **Licensed. Credit** AmEx, DC, MC, V. **Map** p327 G3 ⑱

Given the following that Guillaume Brahimi picked up while working with Joël Robuchon in Paris, it's tempting to call his food French (not least his rendition of the great Robuchon's Paris mash). But there's a lightness that is pure Sydney in his signature dish of tuna infused with basil, for example, or the crab sandwiches that are the mainstays of the bar menu. Wine and service are of a similarly high order, and the Opera House is a nonpareil setting.

Ocean Room

Ground Level, Overseas Passenger Terminal, West Circular Quay (9252 9585/www.oceanroomsydney. com). CityRail/ferry Circular Quay. **Open** noon-3pm, 6-11pm Mon-Thur; noon-3pm, 6pm-midnight Fri, Sat. **Main courses** $36-$50. **Licensed. Credit** AmEx, DC, MC, V. **Map** p327 F3 ⑲

Japanese chef Raita Noda's wilfully out-there Japanese fusion cuisine had a loyal following at Darlinghurst's Rise (*see p152*), but something has been lost in the translation to this gastro-barn by the water. Noda's work is in there somewhere, along with some superb seafood, but a throw-everything-at-the-wall-and-see-what-sticks approach from the management means you'll be as likely marooned and confused as riding high on waves of inspiration.

Palisade Hotel

Corner of Bettington & Argyle Streets, Millers Point (9251 7225/www.palisadehotel.com). CityRail/ferry Circular Quay. **Open** noon-3pm, 6-10pm Tue-Fri; 6-10pm Sat. **Main courses** $32-$36. **Licensed. Credit** AmEx, DC, MC, V. **Map** p326 D3 ⑳

A hidden gem, the upstairs dining room in this lovely old pub is certainly worth the fossick. Brian Sudek crafts food that sings with freshness, balance and simplicity. Service can be as laid back as the atmosphere, but that's not necessarily a bad thing. Be warned – the bridgeside location doesn't necessarily translate to views for all.

The best Restaurants

For fresh fish
Neil Perry's latest venture, **Rockpool (fish)** (*see p149*), is the place for thrilling combinations; simple and suburban **Garfish** (*see p169*) celebrates the nation's spectrum of species, while **Flying Fish** (*see p151*) brings its own cool urban edge. When it comes to don't-miss dishes, try the squid at **East Ocean Restaurant** (*see p149*), a plate of shellfish at **Nick's Bar & Grill** (*see p151*) or the oysters at Glebe's **Boathouse on Blackwattle Bay** (*see p166*).

For water views
Dine with the sound of water lapping at Turkish **Ottoman** (*see p149*) right next to the Harbour Bridge. Spot the late-night surfers from **Icebergs Dining Room** (*see p161*) on Bondi Beach and **Jonah's** (*see p169*) above Whale Beach. Drink in the beauty of the Harbour from the swanky **Guillaume at Bennelong** (*see p146*) and **Café Sydney** (*see p146*).

For relaxed dining
At the laid-back **La Brasserie** (*see p152*) you'll be channelling Edith Piaf before you can say 'moules-frites'. Communal dining comes into its own at **Longrain** (*see p155*), home of some of the city's most dynamic Asian cooking, and pasta specialist **A Tavola** (*see p152*). On Bondi Beach sits the simple

and popular **North Bondi Italian Food** (*see p161*), while **Ripples at Chowder Bay** (*see p167*) is the place for an outdoor lunch that won't break the bank.

For eastern promise
Asian flavours abound in Sydney. Some of the best dishes can be found at David Thompson's **Sailors Thai Canteen & Restaurant** (*see p143*), **Yoshii** (*see p145*) and **Wasavie** (*see p158*). For south-east Asian curries, try **Jimmy Liks** (*see p157*); for Vietnamese street food head to **Phamish** (*see p152*), and for Chinese yum cha it has to be **Marigold Citymark** (*see p149*).

For carnivores
Bite into a juicy steak at **Prime** (*see p149*) in the city, try some offal French-style at **Tabou** (*see p156*), or a Peruvian meat platter at **La Cocina Peruana** (*see p163*).

For a cool crowd
Join the 'it' crowd shooting the breeze at the hot new **Flying Squirrel Tapas Parlour** (*see p161*). Alternatively, there's **Sean's Panorama** (*see p163*), a firm favourite with thirty- and fortysomethings who know their food. City swingers head for Darlinghurst's **Onde** (*see p152*) and Christine Manfield's new **Universal** (*see p153*). And in Kings Cross, **Bayswater Brasserie** (*see p158*) and **Hugo's Bar Pizza** (*see p163*) are full of pretty people.

Quay
Upper Level, Overseas Passenger Terminal, Circular Quay West (9251 5600/www.quay.com.au). CityRail/ferry Circular Quay. **Open** 6-10pm Mon, Sat, Sun; noon-2.30pm, 6-10pm Tue-Fri. **Set menu** $145. **Licensed**. **Credit** AmEx, DC, MC, V. **Map** p327 F3 ㉑

Peter Gilmore's food roves the world, making this one of Sydney's greatest dining experiences. Try the mud crab congee or ravioli of slow-cooked rabbit, rare-breed pig belly with green-lipped abalone or the eight-hour slow-braised Flinders Island milk-fed lamb. What's more, there's not a bad seat in the house – they all offer beautiful views of the harbour. Such perfection comes at a price, naturally.

Summit
Level 47, Australia Square, 264 George Street, between Bond Street & Curtain Place, CBD (9247 9777/www.summitrestaurant.com.au). CityRail Wynyard. **Open** noon-3pm, 6-10pm Mon-Fri; 6-10pm Sat, Sun. **Licensed**. **Credit** AmEx, DC, MC, V. **Map** p327 F5 ㉒

Generally the revolving restaurant is the one to avoid, but Summit lifted its game with a fantastic relaunch in 2007. Chef Michael Moore worked at Bluebird in London, as well as a clutch of top-notch eateries in Sydney, and his experience is paying off. He uses plenty of local fresh fish and seafood, and gives an Asian frisson to dishes like blue swimmer crab with red chilli salt and coriander. Heartier fare such as pork with thick crackling keeps the traditionalists happy. The view is a further reason to visit – Sydney in its glory, from every angle.

Tetsuya's
529 Kent Street, between Bathurst & Liverpool Streets, CBD (9267 2900/www.tetsuyas.com). CityRail Town Hall/Monorail Galeries Victoria. **Open** 6-10pm Tue-Fri; noon-3pm, 6-10pm Sat. **Tasting menu** $195. **Licensed/BYO**. **Credit** AmEx, DC, MC, V. **Map** p329 E7 ㉓

You must eat here. No, no arguments. Yes, it's a lot of money to hand over for a meal. But, given that Tetsuya Wakuda is a culinary Olympian of the order of France's Alain Ducasse and the USA's

YOU ARE HERE

to taste it all

Cafés
Baia San Marco   9283 3434
Blackbird Café   9283 7385
CMC   9283 3393
Lindt Chocolat Café   9267 8064
Nick's 103   9267 4404

Restaurants
Chinta Ria   9264 3211
Coast   9267 6700
I'm Angus Steakhouse   9264 5822
Nick's Seafood Restaurant 9264 1212

Bars
Home Bar   9266 0600
Pontoon Bar   9267 7099
Wallaby Bar   9267 4118

Nightclub
Home   9266 0600

Function Centres
Dockside   9261 3777
L'Aqua   8267 0300

COCKLE BAY WHARF

www.cocklebaywharf.com

Thomas Keller, it's actually a bargain of sorts. Don't be put off by the numerous (ten) courses in the fixed menu: each is so light and small you're guaranteed to leave groaning only with pleasure. And, fear not: everyone ends up eating the entire dish of butter whipped with black truffle and parmesan that accompanies the bread. They'd worry if you didn't. Winner of the Good Food Guide's Restaurant of the Year in 2008 (see p161 **Hats off to…**).

Other

Ottoman
Pier 2, 13 Hickson Road, Dawes Point (9252 0054). CityRail/ferry Circular Quay. **Open** noon-3pm, 6-10pm Tue-Fri; 6-10pm Sat. **Main courses** $29-$40. **Licensed. Credit** AmEx, DC, MC, V. **Map** p327 E2 ㉔ Turkish
Sister restaurant to Ottoman Cuisine in Canberra, this newcomer opened with a few coughs and splutters. Service was slow and faltering, and prices seemed high. But matters have improved since then, and the food here is worth the wait – the Persian spices sing through each dish and the fresh tang of citrus is never far away. Don't overdo the dips or you'll have no room for the signature dish – salmon dolma (salmon, minced prawns and crayfish wrapped in vine leaves). The setting on a deck of a finger wharf at Dawes Point is sublime too.

Prime
Lower Ground Floor, GPO Sydney, 1 Martin Place, between George & Pitt Streets, CBD (9229 7777/ www.gposydney.com). CityRail Martin Place or Wynyard. **Open** noon-3pm, 6-10pm Mon-Fri; 6-10pm Sat. **Main courses** $30-$58. **Licensed. Credit** AmEx, DC, MC, V. **Map** p327 F5 ㉕ American
The closest Sydney gets to a big, New York-style steakhouse, this designer basement in the old GPO building is all about the blokey business of heavy stone, big-dollar blockbuster reds, and meat – thick slabs and quivering haunches of the stuff. The red wine sauces are finger-lickin' great, and the knives are made from German surgical steel.

Rockpool (fish)
107 George Street, between Alfred & Argyle Streets, The Rocks (9252 1888/www.rockpool.com). CityRail/ferry Circular Quay. **Open** noon-2.30pm, 6-11pm Mon-Fri; 6-11pm Sat. **Main courses** $29-$140. **Licensed. Credit** AmEx, DC, MC, V. **Map** p327 F4 ㉖ Fish
For 18 years Neil Perry's Rockpool was one of Sydney's finest. Then in 2007 he did a brave thing and recreated his star as a more casual seafood diner. His culinary creations are still a delicate combination of Asian-inspired Mod Oz but seafood is now the main focus. The snapper poached in coconut and garam masala broth is inspirational in its combination of flavours, as are the freshly shucked live scallop with black bean and chilli dressing entrée. There are meat and vegetarian options, too, but really it's all about the fish. **Photo** p143.

Chinatown & Haymarket

Asian

East Ocean Restaurant
88 Dixon Street, at Liverpool Street, entrance at 421-429 Sussex Street, Haymarket (9212 4198/ www.eastocean.com.au). CityRail Central/Monorail Paddy's Markets or World Square/LightRail Capitol Square or Paddy's Markets. **Open** 10am-midnight Mon-Fri; 9am-2am Sat, Sun. **Main courses** $15-$35. **Licensed/BYO. Credit** AmEx, DC, MC, V. **Map** p329 E2 ㉗ Cantonese
East Ocean Restaurant comes across as a slick Hong Kong-style eaterie. The salt and pepper squid is particularly good, as are the baby abalone steamed with ginger and spring onion. The yum cha, meanwhile, is among the city's finest, with impressive diversity and freshness. The downside of this is that the news has spread, so be prepared to queue at weekends.

Emperor's Garden BBQ & Noodles
213 Thomas Street, between Ultimo Road & Quay Street, Haymarket (9281 9899). CityRail Central/Monorail Paddy's Markets/LightRail Capitol Square or Paddy's Markets. **Open** 9.30am-11pm daily. **Main courses** $9.50-$25. **Licensed/BYO. Credit** AmEx, DC, MC, V. **Map** p329 E9 ㉘ Cantonese
There are other establishments in Chinatown that dispense barbecue that's nearly as good as the Emperor's, but for the hardcore of roast and barbecue pork fanciers (and their pigeon and soy chicken loving brethren), Westerners and Cantonese alike, there is only one place to go for their regular fix. The Garden also does faithful renditions of stir-fried asparagus with garlic, ma po bean curd and the usual classic Cantonese dishes.
Other locations 96-100 Haymarket, CBD (9211 2135).

Golden Century
393-399 Sussex Street, between Goulburn & Hay Streets, Haymarket (9212 3901). CityRail Central/ Monorail World Square/LightRail Capitol Square. **Open** noon-4am daily. **Main courses** $16-$30. **Licensed/BYO. Credit** AmEx, DC, MC, V. **Map** p329 E8 ㉙ Chinese
Although the printed menu is fine, many regulars bypass it completely and flag down a member of the famously surly staff for steamed fish with ginger and spring onion, salt and pepper prawns and the restaurant's top-notch signature Peking duck. After 10pm the restaurant switches down a gear, offering cheaper, one-bowl meals for owls, drunks, waiters, chefs and other miscreants.

Marigold Citymark
Level 4 & 5, 683 George Street, between Hay Street & Ultimo Road, Haymarket (9281 3388/www. marigold.com.au). CityRail Central/LightRail Capitol Square. **Open** 10am-3pm, 5.30pm-midnight daily. **Main courses** $15-$30. **Licensed. Credit** AmEx, DC, MC, V. **Map** p329 E8 ㉚ Cantonese

Eat, Drink, Shop

Marigold Citymark. *See p149.*

Some argue that this is the best yum cha in Sydney. You'll be swayed by the dumplings (their har gau can't be beaten) as well as the flat rice noodles fried and served with dark and light sesame sauce.

Pasteur

709 George Street, between Ultimo Road & Valentine Street, Haymarket (9212 5622). CityRail/LightRail Central. **Open** 10am-9.30pm daily. **Main courses** $6-$12. **BYO**. **No credit cards**. Map p329 E9 ③①
Vietnamese

Hands down the best place for phô – the beef noodle soup that is Vietnam's lifeblood – in Chinatown. Should the soups (beef or chicken, no part of the beast left unturned) not grab you, try the excellent vermicelli or grilled pork salad.

Red Chilli

51 Dixon Street, entrance on Little Hay Street, Haymarket (9211 8122). CityRail Central/Monorail Paddy's Markets/LightRail Paddy's Markets. **Open** 11.30am-3.30pm, 5.30-11pm daily. **Main courses** $15. **Licensed/BYO**. **Credit** AmEx, DC, MC, V. **Map** p329 E8 ③② Sichuanese

Abandon hope all ye who fear spice, for this is not the place for thee: Red Chilli is one of only a handful of Sichuan restaurants in the whole of Australia – and one of the best. The signature deep-fried chicken served with its weight in chilli (balanced in the mouth by the cool burn of Sichuan pepper, of course) is famous for good reason.

Zilver

Level 1, 477 Pitt Street, entrance on Hay Street, Haymarket (9211 2232/www.zilver.com.au). CityRail Central/LightRail Capitol Square. **Open** 10am-3.30pm, 5.30-11pm Mon-Fri; 9am-3.30pm, 5.30-11pm Sat, Sun. **Main courses** $16.80-$38.80. **Licensed/BYO**. **Credit** AmEx, DC, MC, V. **Map** p329 E8 ③③
Chinese

With its crisply uniformed staff and attractive dark tones, this place is just about impossible to get into around Chinese New Year. The yum cha here is a notch above your usual fare, but be sure to try the flat rice rolls or the congee too. It's best to arrive around noon.

Darling Harbour & Pyrmont

Asian

Malaya

39 Lime Street, King Street Wharf, Darling Harbour (9279 1170/www.themalaya.com.au). CityRail Town Hall/ferry Darling Harbour/Monorail Darling Park. **Open** noon-3pm, 6pm-late Mon-Sat; 6-9pm Sun. **Main courses** $21-$31. **Licensed**. **Credit** AmEx, DC, MC, V. **Map** p326 D6 ③④
Malaysian

The Malaya looms large in the recent history of Sydney restaurants, having been responsible, over the course of 30-odd years and several changes of location, for introducing local palates to galangal, lemongrass and other Asian flavours. It might not be the cutting edge for Malaysian food any more, but the laksa and fish curry still delight in this airy establishment boasting water views.

Zaaffran

Level 2, 345 Harbourside Shopping Centre, Darling Harbour (9211 8900/www.zaaffran.com.au). CityRail Town Hall/ferry Darling Harbour/Monorail Harbourside. **Open** noon-2.30pm, 5.30-9.30pm Mon-Thur, Sun; noon-2.30pm, 5.30-10.15pm Fri, Sat. **Main courses** $18.50-$39.50. **Licensed**. **Credit** AmEx, DC, MC, V. **Map** p326 D6 ③⑤ Indian

Free-range chickens issuing from the tandoor? Semolina-crusted barramundi with turmeric, lime, ginger and chilli? It's an Indian restaurant, Jim, but not as we know it. And while you might not want to make your way to Darling Harbour just to visit it, if you're here already it's a superior dining option.

European

Coast

Roof Terrace, Cockle Bay Wharf, Darling Harbour (9267 6700/www.coastrestaurant.com.au). CityRail Town Hall/ferry Darling Harbour/Monorail Darling Park. **Open** noon-2.30pm, 6-10pm Mon-Fri; 6-10pm Sat. **Main courses** $34-$46. **Licensed**. **Credit** AmEx, DC, MC, V. **Map** p326 D6 ③⑥ Italian

Traditional Italian food in stunning, breezy surrounds high above Darling Harbour, with timber decking and slanting glass windows. The menu is slick, with deluxe salumi (cured meats), oysters, pastas, meat and fish, plus a 'market menu' that showcases seasonal ingredients. The wine list has some interesting by-the-glass options.

Seafood

Flying Fish

Lower Deck, Jones Bay Wharf, 19-21 Pirrama Road, Pyrmont (9518 6677/www.flyingfish.com.au). LightRail Star City/bus 443. **Open** 6.30-10.30pm Mon; noon-2.30pm, 6.30-10.30pm Tue-Fri; 6-10.30pm Sat; noon-3.30pm Sun. **Main courses** $44-$48. **Tasting menu** $130. **Licensed**. **Credit** AmEx, DC, MC, V. **Map** p326 C4 ③⑦ Seafood

Seafood from the tank is the forte here, with Tasmanian scallops and mighty Queensland mud crabs. Peter Kuruvita's menu also features Sri Lankan curries, raw fish dishes, chargrilled wagyu beef and some of the best chips in town.

Nick's Bar & Grill

King Street Wharf, Darling Harbour (9279 0122/www.nicks-seafood.com.au). CityRail Town Hall/ferry Darling Harbour/Monorail Darling Park. **Open** noon-3pm, 6-10pm Mon-Sat; noon-10pm Sun. **Main courses** $27.50-$78. **Licensed**. **Credit** AmEx, DC, MC, V. **Map** p326 D6 ③⑧ Seafood

You can eat brilliantly at Nick's or you can not. The trick is easy: order fish from the extensive selection (don't ever pass up an opportunity to eat red emperor) and get it cooked as simply as possible.

Hungry? **Phamish**ed?

Rise

23 Craigend Street, at Royston Street, Darlinghurst (9357 1755/www.riserestaurant.com.au). CityRail Kings Cross. **Open** 6-10pm Tue-Sun. **Main courses** $20-$35. **Tasting menu** $42; $60. **Licensed**. **Credit** AmEx, DC, MC, V. **Map** p330 J8 ㊶ Asian
Deep-fried soft-shell crab tacos? Chicken teriyaki with potato salad? Fasten your seatbelt and make sure you've got a firm grip on your chopsticks: Rise's Japanese chefs take the food of their homeland as their departure point and then proceed deftly to interweave international influences at a fierce rate of knots. The seven-course tasting menus offer great value.

European

A Tavola

348 Victoria Street, between Liverpool & Surrey Streets, Darlinghurst (9331 7871/www.atavola. com.au). **Open** 6pm-late Mon-Thur, Sat, Sun; noon-2.30pm, 6pm-late Fri. **Main courses** $22-$37. **Licensed/BYO**. **Credit** AmEx, MC, V. **Map** p330 J8 ㊷ Italian
Pasta is the speciality here. The communal marble table packs in around 25 people – just enough to serve comfortably with everyone getting the right attention from the very cool waitresses. The *olive all'ascolana* (olives wrapped in pork mince then deep fried – a bit like Italian Scotch egg) are spectacular, while orecchiette with broccoli is a stunning rendition of a homey Italian classic.

La Brasserie

118 Crown Street, Darlinghurst (9358 1222/ www.labrasserie.com.au). Bus 324, 325, 326, 327. **Open** noon-3pm, 6-10pm Mon-Fri; 6-10pm Sat, Sun. **Main courses** $24-$48. **Licensed**. **Credit** AmEx, MC, V. **Map** p329 G7 ㊸ French
La Brasserie is, you guessed it, a classic Parisian brasserie serving rich French fare such as escargots, tripe, confit of duck and cassoulet in the perfect Gallic environs – La Vache Qui Rit poster on the wall and long bar at the front. Normandy-born co-owner Philippe Valet's grandfather once owned famous Parisian brasserie and nightclub Chez Castel, and there's something of that sparkle here. The chef is an Aussie – David Bransgrove – but his cooking is Gallic through and through.

Onde

346 Liverpool Street, between Womerah Avenue & Victoria Street, Darlinghurst (9331 8749). CityRail Kings Cross. **Open** 5.30-11pm Mon-Thur; 5.30-11.30pm Fri, Sat; 5.30-10pm Sun. **Main courses** $17.50-$26. **Licensed**. **Credit** AmEx, DC, MC, V. **Map** p330 J8 ㊹ French
At times this seems not so much a restaurant as the part-time dining room of half of swinging Darlinghurst. Thankfully, Onde is unpretentious, buzzy, well-priced and friendly. Think classic bistro food in space-age environs: you'll find yourself in the large polished concrete room faced with choices such as fried lamb's brains or duck pâté.

Eat, Drink, Shop

East Sydney & Darlinghurst

Asian

Phamish

354 Liverpool Street, at Boundary Street, Darlinghurst (9357 2688). CityRail Kings Cross. **Open** 6-9.30pm Tue-Sat; 5.30-9.30pm Sun. **Main courses** $12.50-$19.50. **BYO**. **Credit** AmEx, DC, MC, V. **Map** p330 J8 ㊴ Vietnamese
Part of the movement to upgrade Vietnamese cuisine and place it firmly square on the city's cuisine, Phamish takes plenty of southern Vietnamese standards and places them in the context of a very buzzy, shiny, Darlinghurst no-bookings BYO. The food won't always knock your socks off (although the crunchy take on the rice-paper roll is intriguing, and the chilli tamarind prawns are fun), but it's never bad and the price is right for groups.

Rambutan

96 Oxford Street, between Crown & Palmer Street, Darlinghurst (9360 7772/www.rambutan.com.au). Bus 311, 333, 352, 373, 377, 378, 380, 392, 394, 396. **Open** 6pm-late daily. **Main courses** $18-$30. **Licensed**. **Credit** AmEx, MC, V. **Map** p329 G8 ㊵ Thai
Rambutan is one of the most promising establishments to have opened on the Pink Strip for what seems like ages. The highlights are the wagyu shin with rice noodles, and the tea-smoked quail. Make sure you head to the downstairs bar for a cocktail before going on to hit the nosh pit.

Verde

115 Riley Street, at Stanley Street, Darlinghurst (9380 8877/www.verde.net.au). **Open** 6pm-midnight Tue, Sat; noon-midnight Wed-Fri. **Main courses** $32-$37. **Licensed**. **Credit** AmEx, DC, MC, V. **Map** p329 G7 ④⑤ Italian

Verde's bar upstairs is excellent, with a huge selection of Italian beers, including a few lesser known brews including some from Sardinia. Downstairs is a modern Italian restaurant featuring the likes of cured pork belly and fresh pasta.

Modern Australian

Universal

Republic, 2 Courtyard, Palmer Street, between Burton & Liverpool Streets, Darlinghurst (9331 0709/www.universalrestaurant.com). **Open** 6-10pm Mon-Thur, Sat; noon-3pm, 6-10pm Fri. **Main courses** $19-$28. **Licensed**. **Credit** AmEx, MC, V. **Map** p329 H8 ④⑥

Sydney star chef Christine Manfield is back after a northern hemisphere stint in London, and she has

The new burger meister

Australian hamburgers, served from milk bars all over the nation, traditionally come with rebel additions such as beetroot and even pineapple. But Sydneysiders are relishing the arrival of a new generation of chic burger joints that echo America's 1950s hamburger heyday but boast health-conscious menus with 21st-century tastes. The slickest of the pack is **Bite Me**, the brainchild of Brit entrepreneur and Las Vegas casino tycoon David Michaels, who models himself on Richard Branson and aims to 'make the world a burger place'. The menu includes beef, fish, lamb, seafood and chicken burgers with monikers like Beef Encounter ($15.50), Lambtastic ($14) and Salmon Chanted Evening ($24.50, only at Bondi Beach). Chips come in cute miniature shopping trolleys, and the most kitsch things on the menu are the mini bites – baby burgers from $5 a pop. Ingredients are prime quality, although the crusty wood-fired sourdough buns take a bit of getting used to.

Below we've listed some of the slickest burger places in the city. Tuck in!

Bite Me

340 Oxford Street, Paddington (9331 1916/ www.bitemeburgerco.com). Bus 333, 352, 378, 380. **Open** noon-10pm Mon-Thur, Sun; noon-late Fri, Sat. **BYO**. **Credit** AmEx, MC, V. **Map** p332 K10.
Other locations 108 Campbell Parade, Bondi Beach (9300 6566).

Burger Edge

Shop 1, 157 Curlewis Street, Bondi Beach (9300 9961). CityRail Bondi Junction then bus 389. **Open** 11am-10pm daily. **Unlicensed**. **Credit** AmEx, MC, V. **Map** p334.
Healthy chain originating in Melbourne, with a taste of trad in the Okker (beef, bacon, egg, cheese, pineapple, beetroot relish and aioli).

Burger Fuel

172 King Street, Newtown (9519 4700/ www.burgerfuel.com). CityRail to Macdonaldtown or bus L23. **Unlicensed**. **Credit** MC, V. **Map** p334.
The New Zealand chain boasts an extensive menu with plenty of extras.

Burgerlicious

Shop 2, 107-111 Oxford Street, Darlinghurst (9356 4608/www.burgerlicious.com.au). Bus 311, 352, 371, 373, 377, 378. **Open** 11am-midnight Mon-Wed, Sun; 11am-1am Thur; 11am-4am Fri, Sat. **BYO**. **Credit** AmEx, MC, V. **Map** p329 G8.
Patties, wraps, nachos and a bunless burger.

Burgerman

116 Surrey Street, Darlinghurst (9361 0268). CityRail to Kings Cross. **Open** noon-10pm daily. **Licensed/BYO**. **No credit cards**. **Map** p330 J8.
Healthy burgers – beef, lamb and vegetarian. They even have wheat-free spelt buns.

Eat, Drink, Shop

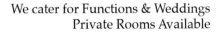

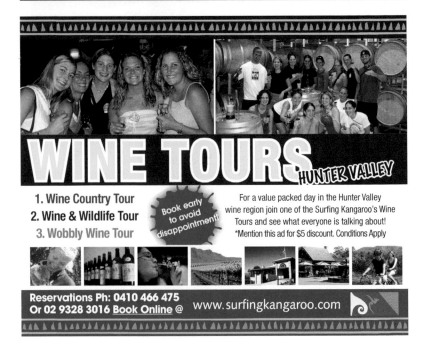

come back with all guns blazing. Universal is a small-plates-only establishment with a technicolour fit-out to match the food. The flavours are big and often Asian-inspired (jasmine tea-soaked duck, turmeric lemongrass broth), the crowd is cool and the cocktails are potent.

Surry Hills

Asian

Billy Kwong
355 Crown Street, between Albion & Foveaux Streets (9332 3300). CityRail/LightRail Central then 10min walk/bus 301, 302, 303, 374, 376, 391. **Open** 6-10pm Mon-Thur; 6-11pm Fri, Sat; 6-9pm Sun. **Main courses** $18-$42. **Licensed/BYO** (wine only). **Credit** AmEx, MC, V. **Map** p329 G9 ❼
Modern Chinese
It's loud, you can't book, you eat elbow-to-chopstick with other diners on three-legged stools – and it's utterly fabulous. Celebrity chef Kylie Kwong takes the food of her Cantonese ancestry and sexes it up, keeping the emphasis on freshness, flavour and lightness. The stir-fries rock, the kingfish sashimi sings with sweet crispness and the crisp duck with blood plums has a well-deserved following.

Longrain
85 Commonwealth Street, at Hunt Street (9280 2888/www.longrain.com). CityRail Central or Museum/LightRail Central. **Open** noon-2.30pm, 6-11pm Mon-Fri; 6-11pm Sat; 5.30-10pm Sun. **Main courses** $23.50-$40.50. **Licensed. Credit** AmEx, DC, MC, V. **Map** p329 F8 ❽ Thai
The restaurant is hip and gorgeous and so is the crowd along its communal tables. Think the food's going to have less depth and integrity than your waiter's lipgloss? Think again. Witness big, mostly Thai flavours dressed up for a big night out. Peanut curry of braised wagyu beef with chilli and thai basil is curry gone glam, and the betel leaves with prawn, peanuts and pomelo are frequently imitated but seldom bettered. The bar is a must-visit too (*see p182*).

Maya Da Dhaba
431 Cleveland Street, between Baptist & Bourke Streets (8399 3785/www.mayamasala.com). Bus 301, 302, 303, 372, 393, 395. **Open** 11am-3pm, 5.30-10.30pm daily. **Main courses** $8.90-$16.90. **BYO. Credit** DC, MC, V. **Map** p329 G11 ❾
South Indian
Spawn of the city's increasingly common Maya Indian sweet shops. But where the other Maya outlets typically only augment their dessert sales with the odd masala dosai and other vegetarian snacks, Dhaba has a full – and very attractive – menu of meaty delights from the subcontinent's south.

Red Lantern
545 Crown Street, between Lansdowne & Cleveland Streets (9698 4355/www.redlantern.com.au). Bus 301, 302, 303. **Open** 12.30-3pm, 6.30-10.30pm

Tue-Fri; 6.30-10.30pm Sat, Sun. **Main courses** $20-$25. **Licensed. Credit** AmEx, DC, MC, V. **Map** p329 G11 ❿ Vietnamese
The chef might be a white guy, but the combination of his skills and the knowledge and experience of the restaurant's young Vietnamese owners raise Red Lantern above most other purveyors of the cuisine, while the funked-up look and democratic prices give it an uncommon edge.

Spice I Am
90 Wentworth Avenue, between Campbell & Commonwealth Streets (9280 0928/www.spice iam.com). CityRail Central or Museum/LightRail Central. **Open** 11.30am-3.30pm, 6-10pm Tue-Sun. **Main courses** $13.90-$25.95. **BYO. Credit** AmEx, DC, MC, V. **Map** p329 F8 ❺❶ Thai
Spice they certainly are: this unremarkable-looking bolt-hole on (appropriately enough) a fume- and backpacker-loaded street serves the most authentic Thai food in Sydney. If you want to dice with some serious chilli, just ask your waitress to take down your order in Thai. That way the kitchen will do your green mango salad, your mussel and chilli pancakes and sour curries without concession to local tastes. Be warned – food this good is addictive, and so is the value: witness the ever-present queue of would-be diners waiting for a table.

Uchi Lounge
15 Brisbane Street, between Goulburn & Oxford Streets (9261 3524). CityRail Museum. **Open** 6.30-11pm Mon-Sat. **Main courses** $15-$21. **Licensed/BYO** (wine only). **Credit** AmEx, MC, V. **Map** p329 G8 ❺❷ Japanese
Downstairs will get you some edamame or spiced almonds and a sake cocktail, upstairs will get you the likes of lightly-seared salmon sushi blocks and aubergine with sweet soy paste topped with parmesan. For dessert, you can't look past the green tea and cinnamon crème brûlée. The food is fairly priced and it's plenty of fun on a Friday night.

European

Café Mint
579 Crown Street, between Devonshire & Cleveland Streets (9319 0848/www.cafemint.com.au). CityRail/LightRail Central then 10min walk/bus 301, 302, 303. **Open** 7am-4pm Mon, Sat; 7am-9.30pm Wed; 7am-10.30pm Thur, Fri. **Main courses** $16-$27. **BYO. No credit cards. Map** p329 G11 ❺❸
Mediterranean
A cool yet inexpensive caff-cum-restaurant, Café Mint is tucked away down at the uncool end of Crown Street. The food from chef/owner Hugh Foster is great – try the spicy lamb with houmous – and the almond and grapefruit frappé is an exceptional hangover-buster. It's a tiny space, note.

Emmilou
413 Bourke Street, between Campbell Street & Church Lane (9360 6991/www.emmilou.com.au). Bus 311, 333, 352, 373, 377, 378, 380, 392, 394,

396. **Open** noon-3pm, 6pm-1am Tue-Sat. **Set menu** $40-$90. **Tapas** $3.50-$21. **Licensed**. **Credit** AmEx, MC, V. **Map** p329 H9 🟤 Spanish

A new offering for Bourke Street, Emmilou is a mix of tasting plates like white anchovies and chargrilled octopus, plus heftier offerings such as vongole wrapped in shoelaces of ham. A good one if you're out late and need a little ballast.

Marque

Shops 4-5, 355 Crown Street, between Albion & Foveaux Streets (9332 2225/www.marquerestaurant. com.au). CityRail/LightRail Central then 10min walk/bus 301, 302, 303, 374, 376, 391. **Open** 6.30-10.30pm Mon-Sat. **Main courses** $42-$47. **Licensed/BYO**. **Credit** AmEx, DC, MC, V. **Map** p329 G9 🟤 French

Chef Mark Best trained in some of France's finest kitchens and has one eye on the pioneering work done by Spain's gastronomic wizards, yet the food at his quietly luxurious restaurant manages to be at once at the bleeding edge and utterly his own. Beetroot tarte (almost a tatin) with horseradish foam sits cheek-by-jowl with sweetbreads paired with sea urchin roe and samphire on one of the country's most exciting menus. The outstanding – and out-there – wine list rolls with every punch.

Pizza Mario

417-421 Bourke Street (9332 3633/www.pizza mario.com.au). Bus 311, 333, 352, 373, 377, 378, 380, 392, 394, 396. **Open** 6pm-late daily. **Main courses** $11-$25. **Licensed**. **Credit** AmEx, MC, V. **Map** p329 H9 🟤 Pizza

These guys have the Verace Pizza Napoletana stamp of approval, which is a licence to say that they make pizza properly. Pretty much everything they do is done the way it is in the old country. Try the killer potato, sea salt and rosemary pizza and don't neglect the excellent antipasto.

Restaurant Assiette

48 Albion Street, at Mary Street (9212 7979/ www.restaurantassiette.com.au). CityRail/LightRail Central. **Open** noon-3pm Fri; 6-10.30pm Tue-Sat. **Main courses** $33. **Licensed**. **Credit** AmEx, DC, MC, V. **Map** p329 F9 🟤 French

Marco Pierre White-trained chef Warren Turnbull may dabble a little in the dark arts of progressive cuisine, but for the most part it's solid cooking with some lovely French flavours at excellent prices. Restaurant Assiette really is the place where you'll find Sydney's best-value fine dining.

La Sala

23 Foster Street, between Hunt & Campbell Streets (9281 3352/www.lasala.com.au). CityRail Central or Museum/LightRail Central. **Open** 6-11pm Mon-Wed, Sat; noon-3pm, 6-11pm Thur, Fri. **Main courses** $32-$39. **Licensed**. **Credit** AmEx, DC, MC, V. **Map** p329 F8 🟤 Italian

La Sala is an Italian restaurant with a rather unexpected hint of the British Isles thrown in. The menu features bone marrow served with toast, and corned

Bentley Restaurant & Bar.

beef brisket, although you'll also find more usual Italian staples such as risotto made to order and crudités of crisp raw veg with smooth aioli on the side. Good service is a further bonus.

Lo Studio

53-55 Brisbane Street, at Commonwealth Street (9212 4118/www.lostudio.com.au). CityRail Central or Museum/LightRail Central. **Open** noon-3pm, 6pm-late Mon-Fri; 6pm-late Sat. **Main courses** $22-$37. **Licensed**. **Credit** AmEx, DC, MC, V. **Map** p329 F8 🟤 Italian

The old Paramount Studios building is a fittingly deco home for this paean to chic 1950s Italy. Think *The Talented Mr Ripley*, only with better food and cocktails (the Corleone with fresh nectarine is an offer you really shouldn't refuse).

Tabou

527 Crown Street, between Devonshire & Lansdowne Streets (9319 5682). Bus 301, 302, 303. **Open** noon-2.30pm, 6.30-10pm Mon-Fri; 6-10.30pm Sat, Sun. **Main courses** $26-$35. **Licensed/BYO** (wine only, Mon-Thur, Sun only). **Credit** AmEx, DC, MC, V. **Map** p329 G11 🟤 French

Tabou is, to all appearances, a classic French bistro with all the trimmings – glass mirrors with the menu scribbled on them, wooden chairs, the works. And the menu is what you'd expect, too, from steak-frites to brains and brawn. However, sufferers of noise fatigue should be wary – it may be a comfy, sweet little space but it's also loud as they come.

Vini

*Shop 3, 118 Devonshire Street, at Holt Street
(9698 5131). CityRail/LightRail Central.* **Open**
noon-midnight Tue-Fri; 5pm-midnight Sat. **Main
courses** $24-$28. **Licensed. Credit** DC, MC, V.
Map p329 F10 ⑥ Italian
A tiny restaurant with a whole lotta style, Vini plays
off the brevity of its excellent Italian menu – two
starters, two mains, two desserts and some snacks
– with the richness and variety of its blackboard of
Italian wines. The value on both counts is bang-on.

Modern Australian

Bentley Restaurant & Bar

*320 Crown Street, at Campbell Street (9332 2344/
www.thebentley.com.au). Bus 311, 333, 352, 373,
377, 378, 380, 392, 394, 396.* **Open**
6-11pm Tue-Sat. **Main courses** $29-$36. **Tasting
menu** $95. **Licensed. Credit** AmEx, DC, MC, V.
Map p329 G9 ⑫
This popular restaurant in a heritage pub is the
work of chef Brent Savage and sommelier Nick
Hildebrandt, who complements the food with matching wines from an unbelievably comprehensive list
(including lots by the glass). Try some of the progressive tapas, or go the whole hog and do the tasting menu. The dishes here are always surprising,
which keeps regulars coming back for more. Winner
of Good Living's Best New Restaurant Award and
Sommelier Award in 2007 (*see p161* **Hats off to…**).

Bistrode

*478 Bourke Street, between Foveaux & Phelps
Streets (9380 7333). Bus 301, 302, 303.* **Open**
6-10.30pm Tue-Thur, Sat; noon-3pm, 6-10.30pm
Fri. **Main courses** $27-$33. **Licensed. Credit**
AmEx, DC, MC, V. **Map** p329 G10 ⑬
Don't let the bistro setting in a heritage butcher's
shop put you off. To some, Jeremy and Jane Strode's
food may seem simple, but this is real art on the
plate. Dishes like fried duck egg with sourdough
crumbs and pine mushrooms show why three things
on a plate are better than six. There's a French inspiration to some dishes, plus a well-priced wine list.

Other

Erciyes

*409 Cleveland Street, between Crown & Bourke
Streets (9319 1309). Bus 372, 393, 395.* **Open**
10am-midnight daily. **Main courses** $12-$30.
Licensed/BYO. Credit AmEx, MC, V.
Map p329 G11 ⑭ Turkish
'Err-chee-ehs'. It's really not that hard to pronounce,
but it seems to elude most non-Turkish speakers for
some reason. But no one seems to have a problem
wrapping their tongue around the spicy sausage-
topped Turkish pizzas, the cabbage rolls or smoky
kebabs. Hit the dips and breads hard and don't leave
without a Turkish coffee. Saturdays see the ante
upped by gyrating belly dancers.

Kings Cross, Potts Point & Woolloomooloo

Asian

Aki's

*1 Woolloomooloo Wharf, Cowper Wharf Road,
opposite Forbes Street, Woolloomooloo (9332 4600/
www.akisindian.com.au). CityRail Kings Cross then
10min walk or bus 311.* **Open** noon-3pm, 6-10pm
Mon-Fri, Sun; 6-10pm Sat. **Main courses** $18.80-
$35.80. **Licensed. Credit** AmEx, DC, MC, V.
Map p327 H6 ⑮ Indian
Sydney's Indian dining scene doesn't have the
sophistication of London or Manchester, let alone
the old country. But it does have Sydney Harbour,
as seen from Aki's – and that's got to count for something. Enjoy artfully presented (mostly Southern)
Indian food while the water laps gently at the edge
of Woolloomooloo Wharf.

Bay Bua

*Ground Floor, 2 Springfield Avenue, Potts Point
(9358 3234/www.baybua.com.au).* **Open** 5.30-
10.30pm Mon-Thur; 5.30-11pm Fri-Sun. **Main
courses** $11.50-$15.50. **Licensed. Credit** AmEx,
MC, V. **Map** p330 J7 ⑯ Vietnamese
Affordable fine dining from Sydney restaurateur
Mai Tran. Try the delectable boneless chicken
stuffed with pork, sweet little rice cakes topped with
pork mince and tomato, and crisp pancake with
green onion. And to top it all off there's a kooky little bar right in the middle of the restaurant.

Jimmy Liks

*186-188 Victoria Street, between Darlinghurst
Road & Orwell Street, Potts Point (8354 1400/
www.jimmyliks.com). CityRail Kings Cross.* **Open**
5-11pm daily. **Main courses** $27-$35. **Licensed.
Credit** AmEx, DC, MC, V. **Map** p330 J7 ⑰
South-east Asian
Jimmy Liks has copped some flak in the past for not
treating its customers particularly well. And in
terms of service, it's a fair cop. But don't let that keep
you from sampling the good cocktails, nor, for that
matter, the full-flavoured takes on the street food of
South-east Asia. The mussaman curry of veal shank
with peanut betel leaf and ar-jard dipping sauce is
inspired. *See also p185.*

European

Fratelli Paradiso

*12-16 Challis Avenue, at Macleay Street, Potts
Point (9357 1744). CityRail Kings Cross.* **Open**
7am-11pm Mon-Fri; 7am-5pm Sat, Sun. **Main
courses** $29-$32. **Licensed. Credit** AmEx, DC,
MC, V. **Map** p330 J6 ⑱ Italian
All-Italian menu, all-Italian wine list, all-Italian waiting staff. If the restaurant's packed (it invariably is),
the waiter will stand out front and recite the menu.
Take ten mates and order everything.

Eat, Drink, Shop

Nove

9 Woolloomooloo Wharf, Cowper Wharf Road, opposite Forbes Street, Woolloomooloo (9368 7599/www.otto.net.au). CityRail Kings Cross then 10min walk/bus 311. **Open** noon-midnight Tue-Sun. **Main courses** $22-$29. **Licensed. Credit** AmEx, DC, MC, V. **Map** p330 H5 ⑥⑨ Pizza

Buzz, buzz, buzz. What's that? No, it's not bees around a honeypot, it's a scene. Look one way and you'll see celebs and water views. Turn your head to the other for an eyeful of today's pizza (square-cut, Roman-style) and a blackboard full of clipped, thoughtful Italian treats. And it's not a bad spot for just a mid-afternoon Peroni or Aranciata Rossa.

Otto

8 Woolloomooloo Wharf, Cowper Wharf Road, opposite Forbes Street, Woolloomooloo (9368 7488/www.otto.net.au). CityRail Kings Cross then 10min walk/bus 311. **Open** noon-3pm, 6pm-late daily. **Main courses** $35-$140. **Licensed. Credit** AmEx, DC, MC, V. **Map** p330 H5 ⑦⓪ Italian

Don't ask to speak to Otto – it's Italian for 'eight', the address of this celebrity magnet. If you can fight your way through the air-kissing and attract the attention of the charming but wildly inconsistent waiters, you might be in for some outstanding cucina moderna. Or you might not – it's that sort of place. But you'll have fun either way.

Penny's Lane

Corner of Penny's Lane & Kings Cross Road, Darlinghurst (9356 8177/www.pennyslane.com.au). CityRail Kings Cross. **Open** 7am-3pm, 6-10pm daily. **Main courses** $28. **Licensed. Credit** MC, V. **Map** p330 J7 ⑦① Italian

Simple, pared-back bistro fare in the heart of the Cross. The confit chicken leg with cavolo nero and blue eye cod with two types of artichoke are perfectly executed. Well-priced wine list too.

Modern Australian

Bayswater Brasserie

32 Bayswater Road, at Ward Avenue, Kings Cross (9357 2177/www.bayswaterbrasserie.com.au). CityRail Kings Cross. **Open** 5pm-late Mon-Thur; noon-late Fri; 5-10pm Sun. **Main courses** $27-$38. **Licensed. Credit** AmEx, DC, MC, V. **Map** p330 J7 ⑦②

An air of cultured hedonism lingers at this exceedingly pleasant landmark. Enjoy great oysters and other French brasserie classics in the front, and cocktails and luxe bar snacks – foie gras on toast, say – in the hopping bar (*see p184*) out the back.

Lotus

22 Challis Avenue, at Mcleay Street, Potts Point (9326 9000/www.merivale.com). CityRail Kings Cross. **Open** 6-10.30pm Tue-Sat. **Main courses** $30-$35. **Licensed. Credit** AmEx, DC, MC, V. **Map** p330 J6 ⑦③

Beware: the cocktails here are the stuff of legend, and with good reason. But Lauren Murdoch's smart,

upbeat, well-executed Mod Oz menu is another reason to stay the course. The restaurant proper is insanely loud, so try to bag a seat outside if you can, but don't miss a glimpse of the stunning Florence Broadhurst wallpaper lining the walls of the bar.

Salon Blanc

2-6 Cowper Wharf Road, Woolloomooloo (9356 2222/www.salonblanc.com.au). CityRail Kings Cross then 10min walk/bus 311. **Open** noon-3pm, 6-11pm Mon-Sat; noon-4pm, 6-9pm Sun. **Main courses** $36-$49. **Licensed. Credit** AmEx, DC, MC, V. **Map** p330 H5 ⑦④

This bright white newcomer to the smart Woolly wharf eating strip has become a firm favourite with the 'it-crowd'. But there's more to this place than its cool decor. It won a chef's hat for Alex Ensor at the 2007 Good Living awards (*see p161* **Hats off to...**) and blends French, Spanish and Italian flourishes with fresh Australian produce. Try the yabbie ravioli with caramelised figs or the loin of roast venison atop a turnip cake.

Other

Fish Face

132 Darlinghurst Road, between Liverpool & Burton Streets, Kings Cross (9332 4803/www.fishface.com.au). CityRail Kings Cross/bus 389. **Open** 6-10pm Mon-Sat; 6-9pm Sun. **Main courses** $28.50-$34.50. **Licensed/BYO. Credit** AmEx, MC, V. **Map** p330 H8 ⑦⑤ Seafood

Give Steve Hodges a fish and he'll tell you where and when it was caught and its mother's name. He's just as talented at cooking (or not – they also do sushi and sashimi). But really it's the plain fish and chips you should come for – sublime.

Eastern Suburbs

Asian

Wasavie

8 Heeley Street, at Glenmore Road, Paddington (9380 8838). Bus 333, 352, 378, 380, 389. **Open** 6-10pm Mon-Thur; noon-3pm, 6-10pm Fri-Sun. **Main courses** $18-$27. **BYO. Credit** AmEx, MC, V. **Map** p332 K9 ⑦⑥ Japanese

This minimal little local is living proof that good, cheap Japanese food isn't a paradox. You can sear your slices of raw fish on a hot stone for a bit of theatre, abandon yourself to the pleasures of the flesh in the form of the sumptuously sticky braised pork belly with hot mustard, or walk on the wilder side with Japanese/Mod Oz experiments.

European

Bistro Moncur

Woollahra Hotel, corner of Moncur & Queen Streets, Woollahra (9363 2519/www.woollahrahotel.com.au). Bus 378, 380, 389. **Open** 6-10.30pm

Of course it's cool. **Icebergs Dining Room**. *See p161.*

Mon; noon-3pm, 6-10.30pm Tue-Sun. **Main courses** $29-$40. **Licensed**. **Credit** AmEx, DC, MC, V. **Map** p333 M10 ⑰ French
Bistro Moncur isn't as cheap as its name might suggest, but then it's been a long time since anyone went into a bistro expecting a cheap meal. However, Bistro Moncur is one of the finest examples of a smart-casual restaurant in Sydney that really gets it right, balancing near-boisterous conviviality with food that is as satisfying as it is seductive. Damien Pignolet is the god of (seemingly) simple culinary things done exceptionally well. Bistro classics such as provençal fish soup with rouille, pork sausages with lyonnaise onions and sirloin steak with Café de Paris butter are near-perfect every time.

Buon Ricordo
108 Boundary Street, at Liverpool Street, Paddington (9360 6729/www.buonricordo.com.au). CityRail Kings Cross/bus 389. **Open** 6.30-10.30pm Tue-Thur; noon-2.30pm, 6.30-10.30pm Fri, Sat. **Main courses** $39.50-$49.50. **Tasting menu** $120. **Licensed**. **Credit** AmEx, DC, MC, V. **Map** p330 J8 ⑱ Italian
You might think Armando Percuoco a chef, but he's actually hospitality on two legs. Watch him: clapping a back here, kissing a hand there, his big sandpaper voice booming one minute, confidential the next. And yet he somehow runs a tight kitchen too, with Buon Ricordo's luxe fare earning it a swag of best-Italian awards over the past decade. Go all out with the *fettuccine al tartufovo*, a rich explosion of house-made pasta with soft-poached truffled egg, or spare your arteries and delight your palate with the excellent seared beef carpaccio.

Buzo
3 Jersey Road, at Oxford Street, Woollahra (9328 1600). Bus 333, 352, 378, 380, 389. **Open** 6.30pm-late Mon-Sat. **Main courses** $27-$32. **Licensed**. **Credit** AmEx, DC, MC, V. **Map** p332 L10 ⑲ Italian
The atmosphere of this classy osteria in Woollahra is fostered by the rustic simplicity of the blackboard menu, pricing that is relatively modest for the quality and the crush of locals who storm the place. Antipasti are a highlight – the salad of celery, white anchovy and parsley for example – as are faves such as the Sicilian roast lamb and the vincisgrassi, which interleaves porcini mushrooms, prosciutto, pasta and truffle oil in a luxurious lasagne.

Claude's
10 Oxford Street, between Queen Street & Jersey Road, Woollahra (9331 2325/www.claudes.org). Bus 333, 352, 378, 380, 389. **Open** 7.30-10pm Tue-Sat. **Set menu** $135; $165 tasting menu. **Licensed/BYO**. **Credit** AmEx, DC, MC, V. **Map** p332 L11 ⑳ French
The room is classic and beautiful. The location is a terrace in Paddington. The service is attentive and the dishes are intriguing – caramel roasted Aylesbury duck, and sour sweet quail. Chui Lee Luk does wonderful things with food. No surprise therefore that it is a stalwart of the Sydney dining scene.

L'Etoile
211 Glenmore Road, Paddington (9332 1577/ www.letoilerestaurant.com.au). Bus 389. **Open** 6pm-late Mon-Thur; noon-3pm, 6pm-late Fri; 10am-3pm, 6pm-late Sat, Sun. **Main courses** $28-$32. **Licensed**. **Credit** AmEx, MC, V. **Map** p332 K9 ㉛ French

Eat, Drink, Shop

Classic, ultra-French food brought to hungry Sydnesiders from within the civilised surrounds of Paddington. Scallops with boudin noir (blood sausage) sees plump, bouncy scallops perched on rounds of rich sausage, while the roast garlic and hazelnut soup is creamy, smooth and soothing. They make a very good martini too.

Flying Squirrel Tapas Parlour

249 Bondi Road, Bondi (9130 1033/www.flying squirreltapasparlour.com.au). CityRail Bondi Junction then bus 333, 380, 381, 382/bus 333, 380. **Open** 6pm-midnight daily. **Tapas** $8-$15. **Licensed**. **Credit** MC, V. Spanish
The Flying Squirrel Tapas Parlour is the place to hang with the über-trendy Bondi-ites. Try the salt and pepper squid and chargrilled beef tenderloin, or stay old-school with the chorizo. And why not throw in a bloody caesar on the side (they import their own Clamato juice from Canada).

Hats off to…

Sydney may be the nation's fickle party city, but a hallowed hush descends when the foodies start to pontificate and then to judge, which they do every year for the *Good Food Guide*. This weighty tome, produced by *Sydney Morning Herald*'s critics, hands out its coveted chef's hats like Oscars to a throng of trembling restaurateurs et al on an awards night that frequently ends with steak knives drawn. Duels aside, the critics – more than 30 unannounced diners, who visit 300-plus restaurants across the city – are held in grudgingly high esteem, which is why this event holds such clout. Supreme achievers get three hats, chefs who are hot in the kitchen get two, while those who have done well get one. In the 2008 guide the classy and highly innovative **Tetsuya's** (*see p147*) was, as expected, winner of Restaurant of the Year, but **Guillaume at Bennelong** (*see p146*), the Opera House's fine-dining jewel, surprisingly dropped a hat to a two-hat posting, and **Pier** (*see p163*) went from two to one, causing much gnashing of teeth.

In the run up to the winners being announced at the beginning of spring, there's a sense of fraternal rivalry between the chefs and their critics, although there's a serious side too: with fine dining feeling the pinch in this town, a chef's hat can mean the difference between staying afloat or going under.

Icebergs Dining Room

1 Notts Avenue, at Campbell Parade, Bondi Beach (9365 9000/www.idrb.com). CityRail Bondi Junction then bus 333, 380, 381, 382/bus 333, 380. **Open** noon-3pm, 6.30-10.30pm Tue-Sat; noon-3pm, 6.30-9pm Sun. **Main courses** $38-$48. **Licensed**. **Credit** AmEx, DC, MC, V. **Map** p334 ⑫ Mediterranean
Bondi Beach-flavoured eye candy and visiting celebs are the order of the day at this roost styled by the highly talented Maurice Terzini. Fortunately, the food more than matches the location. Salt-crusted suckling lamb, melt-in the mouth ox fillet, light crab and soft polenta – it's all excellent. The adjoining bar (*see p186*) is fabulous at dusk, and the building also houses the famous Icebergs winter swimming club. *See also p260.* **Photo** *p159.*

Lucio's

Corner of Windsor & Elizabeth Streets, Paddington (9380 5996/www.lucios.com.au). Bus 380, 382, 389. **Open** 12.30-3pm, 6.30-11pm Mon-Sat. **Main courses** $39-$44. **Licensed**. **Credit** AmEx, DC, MC, V. **Map** p332 L10 ⑬ Italian
Love art and food? Lucio's – where the myth of the starving artist is exploded – is the answer. The walls are festooned with works by many of Australia's foremost painters of the past 50 years, while the plates come adorned with two decades' worth of modish Italian eats. Head chef David Dale cooks up traditional Ligurian fare such as duck neck filled with its own liver. It ain't cheap, but it sure is tasty.

North Bondi Italian Food

118-120 Ramsgate Avenue, at Campbell Parade, North Bondi (9300 4400/www.idrb.com). CityRail Bondi Junction then bus 333, 380, 381, 382/bus 333, 380. **Open** 5-10.30pm Mon, Tue; noon-4pm, 6.30-10.30pm Wed-Sat; noon-4pm, 6.30-10pm Sun. **Main courses** $24-$29. **Licensed**. **Credit** AmEx, DC, MC, V. **Map** p334 ⑭ Italian
Yes, it can get a bit noisy; no, you can't book; and, no, it isn't as cheap as menus printed on disposable paper place mats may suggest. But this place, run by Icebergs' Maurice Terzini (*see p161*), is fabulous – fabulously busy, fabulously simple, a fabulously stylish setting by the beach, with Coopers Pale Ale and red wine on tap, and tripe with cotechino sausage, borlotti beans and peas in its own tripe section (*see* the menu). Be sure to taste the spaghetti arrabiatta with crab cooked in a paper bag. **Photo** *p162.*

Pompei

Corner of Roscoe & Gould Streets, Bondi Beach (9365 1233). CityRail Bondi Junction then bus 333, 380, 381, 382/bus 333, 380. **Open** 3-11pm Tue-Thur; 11am-11pm Fri-Sun. **Main courses** $17-$23. **Licensed/BYO** (wine only). **Credit** AmEx, MC, V. **Map** p334 ⑮ Pizza
It's a matter of fierce debate: is the greatest thing about Pompei the creamy, all-natural gelato that comes in a range of drool-worthy flavours – or is it the pizza, Neapolitan-thin and available topped with everything from seasonal delights, like the pizza

North Bondi Italian Food. *See p161.*

Caffè
freddo
$3.50

bianco with fresh artichoke, to the timeless margherita? It's a question that is probably best examined in person, as frequently as possible.

Restaurant Balzac

141 Belmore Road, at Avoca Street, Randwick (9399 9660/www.restaurantbalzac.com.au). Bus 371, 372, 373, 376, 377, X73, X77. **Open** 6-10pm Tue-Thur, Sat; noon-2.30pm, 6-10pm Fri. **Main courses** $26-$35. **Licensed/BYO. Credit** AmEx, DC, MC, V. Modern French

Matt Kemp does the Franglais thing (mixing up French and British cuisine) better than anyone in town. The saddle of lamb with olive crust is a stand-out. And there's a special *dégustation* menu ($95) on the last Sunday of every month. The value is sound, and that's before you try the famous pre-Ritz special – two courses for $50. C'est magnifique, innit?

Sugo

10 Elizabeth Street, off Oxford Street, Paddington (9331 2962). Bus 333, 352, 378, 380. **Open** noon-3pm, 6-10.30pm Mon-Sat. **Main courses** $25-$33. **Licensed/BYO** (wine only). **Credit** AmEx, MC, V. **Map** p332 L10 ⑯ Pizza

This new restaurant in calm and serene Paddington is serving up traditional woodfired pizza including one with *'nduja* (a type of spicy sausage from Calabria) as well as a very good margherita. A bunch of nice old Italian dudes run the floor and it's only a hop-skip from Oxford Street.

Modern Australian

Catalina

Lyne Park, off New South Head Road, Rose Bay (9371 0555/www.catalinarosebay.com.au). Ferry Rose Bay/bus 323, 324, 325. **Open** noon-10pm Mon-Sat; noon-9pm Sun. **Main courses** $40-$99. **Licensed. Credit** AmEx, DC, MC, V.

Arriving by boat has a certain cachet, yes, but to really nail the sense of occasion there's really nothing that beats pulling up in a seaplane. Catalina is pricey, showy and not immune to occasional attitude attacks. That said, the juxtaposition of so-Sydney water views and superb wine is pretty special, and the food itself is slick. You won't go wrong by ordering gutsy French classics like pig's head with sauce gribiche. Whitebait fritters with fried duck egg is a winner, as is the sushi platter.

Hugo's Bar Pizza

Level 1, 33 Bayswater Road, Kings Cross (9357 4411/www.hugos.com.au). CityRail Kings Cross. **Open** 6pm-late Mon-Sat; 3pm-late Sun. **Main courses** $22-$35. **Licensed. Credit** AmEx, DC, MC, V. **Map** p330 J7 ⑰

Chef Peter Evans brings some serious glamour to the menu at this super-trendy eaterie. Italian is the go – the meatballs are melt-in-the-mouth. The pizzas are gourmet, with toppings including belly pork and baked aubergine, but the seafood stew in a tomato broth is sheer heaven.

Sean's Panaroma

270 Campbell Parade, at Ramsgate Avenue, Bondi Beach (9365 4924/www.seanspanaroma.com.au). CityRail Bondi Junction then bus 333, 380, 381, 382/bus 380, 333. **Open** 6.30-9.30pm Wed, Thur; noon-3pm, 6.30-9.30pm Fri, Sat; noon-3pm Sun. **Main courses** $26-$45. **Licensed/BYO. Credit** MC, V. **Map** p334 ⑱

Sean's Panorama is pure Sydney – if you can handle forking out top dollar for three (sometimes two) elements on a plate (perhaps you're paying for what they have the good sense to leave off). Chef Sean Moran waxes herbal at times, but his baseline is good-quality, local ingredients treated with maximum integrity. And with the new addition of a tasting menu (fantastic Queensland mud crab served with a sauce made from crushed arborio rice), there's even more reason to make your way to Bondi.

Other

Churrasco

240 Coogee Bay Road, between Arden & Brook Streets, Coogee (9665 6535/www.churrasco.com.au). Bus 372, 373, X73. **Open** 6-10.30pm Mon-Sat; noon-4pm, 6-10.30pm Sun. **Set menu** $35. **Licensed. Credit** MC, V. Brazilian

Six words: All. You. Can. Eat. Brazilian. Barbecue. Churrasco serves much that once walked or trotted, from sausages to hunks of lamb, all skewered on giant sword-like things and cooked over hot coals. It's TOO LOUD for conversation, so concentrate on the carnivorous carnage and drink a mojito.

La Cocina Peruana

103 Avoca Street, between Alison Road & Francis Street, Randwick (9326 4344/www.bgtrading. com.au). Bus 371, 372, 373, 376, 377, X73, X77. **Open** noon-3pm, 6-10pm Mon-Fri; noon-4pm, 6pm-late Sat, Sun. **Main courses** $15.50-$19.50. **BYO. Credit** AmEx, MC, V. Peruvian

La Cocina Peruana is a bright Peruvian restaurant that serves up meat platters alongside purple corn drinks and Incan cola. Try the platter with a mix of deep-fried pork, chicken, sweet potato served with a battery of sauces and cured onions.

Pier

594 New South Head Road, opposite Cranbrook Road, Rose Bay (9327 6561/www.pierrestaurant. com.au). Bus 323, 324, 325. **Open** noon-3pm, 6-10pm Mon-Sat; noon-3pm, 6-9pm Sun. **Main courses** $44-$49. **Licensed. Credit** AmEx, DC, MC, V. Seafood

Pier offers sheer delight on a plate, with smooth service and a waterside setting to boot. Floor-to-ceiling windows produce great views looking out over Rose Bay. Greg Doyle and Grant King's menu is centred on seafood, with the odd meat dish on the side; the pan-roasted barramundi is poetry, as are Katrina Kanetani's desserts. The verdict? Far from cheap, but close to perfect. For smaller, less expensive offerings, try the adjoining Tasting Room.

Eat, Drink, Shop

Inner West

Asian

Faheem's Fast Food

196 Enmore Road, between Metropolitan & Edgware Roads, Enmore (9550 4850). CityRail Newtown. **Open** 5pm-midnight daily. **Main courses** $10-$19. **Unlicensed. No credit cards.** Indian/Pakistani
Faheem may be the man, but we reckon that haleem is responsible for all the repeat business. In a menu of brilliant halal and vegetarian subcontinental cheap treats, haleem – a Pakistani curry of four different kinds of lentils and boneless beef cooked to seriously flavoursome mush – still stands out. How many dishes earn a subtitle, much less one as high-falutin' as 'the king of curries'? Super cheap too.

Pomegranate

191 Darling Street, between Ann & Stephen Street, Balmain (9555 5693). Bus 434, 442. **Open** 5.30-10pm Tue-Thur; 12.30-3pm, 5.30-10pm Fri-Sun. **Main courses** $23-$35. **Licensed/BYO. Credit** AmEx, DC, MC, V. **Map** p326 A3 ⑳ Thai
The best Thai in Balmain. Betel leaves with whitebait and soft-shell crab with a side of pomegranate salad are the best choices, but save room for the salty-sweet Thai desserts.

European

Bistro Ortolan

134 Marion Street, between Flood & Edith Streets, Leichhardt (9568 4610). Bus 436, 437, 438, L38, L39. **Open** 6-10pm Tue-Sat. **Main courses** $28-$36. **Licensed** (Fri, Sat)/**BYO** (wine only, Tue-Thur). **Credit** AmEx, DC, MC, V. French
This sweet little restaurant gets plenty right, with straight bistro food in stylish surrounds and smart service. Try the steak tartare served with a teeny weeny quail's egg nested in the raw mince. Capers, tomato and wasabi are arranged on the plate like little accoutrement soldiers. There's a very snappy wine list, too, with interesting rieslings by the glass.

Ecco

2 St George's Crescent, corner of Park Avenue, Drummoyne (9719 9394/www.ecco.com.au). Bus 500, 501, 502, 503, 504, 505, 506, 507, 508, 509. **Open** noon-3pm; 6-10pm Tue-Fri; 6-10pm Sat, noon-3pm Sun. **Main courses** $32-$36. **Licensed. Credit** AmEx, DC, MC, V. Italian
The views are extraordinary, the staff are all incredibly friendly and the food is smart Italian. What else can we ask for? The orecchiette with peas and pancetta is a winner, while the zabaglione with tiny sugared doughnut balls is sensational.

Grappa Ristorante e Bar

267-277 Norton Street, at City West Link, Leichhardt (9560 6090/www.grappa.com.au). Bus 440, 445, L40. **Open** 6-10pm Mon; noon-3pm, 6-10pm Tue-Thur; noon-3pm, 6-11pm Fri; 6-11pm Sat; noon-3pm, 6-9.30pm Sun. **Main courses** $28-$39. **Licensed/BYO** (wine only). **Credit** AmEx, DC, MC, V. Italian
From toddlers sucking on strands of linguine with chilli and roasted tomato to couples exchanging looks over slices of pizza to tables of old whipper-snappers hoeing into the whole salt-baked snapper, punters of all ages and stripes find something to tempt on this barn-like restaurant's menu.

Peasant's Feast

121A King Street, between Missenden Road & Elizabeth Street, Newtown (9516 5998/www.peasantsfeast.com.au). CityRail Newtown. **Open** 6-10pm Tue-Sat. **Main courses** $16-$26.50. **BYO. Credit** AmEx, MC, V. **Map** p334 ㉚ Pan-European
King Street's dining scene is a bit of a sham: restaurants, restaurants everywhere, but nothing good to eat. So dining at the Feast comes as a pleasant surprise. Organic produce is brought to the fore, but flavour and presentation are strong too. Check out the gnocchi with a ragoût of aubergine and mushrooms, or the organic cassoulet. The good prices also help.

Perama

88 Audley Street, between New Canterbury Road & Trafalgar Street, Petersham (9569 7534/www.perama.com.au). CityRail Petersham. **Open** 6-10.30pm Tue-Sat. **Main courses** $25-$29. **Licensed/BYO** (wine only). **Credit** MC, V. Greek
The whitewash and retsina are in place, yes, but there's something unusual about this Greek restaurant. That's right, it's the food: from favourites such as falling-off-the-bone lamb or rabbit pie to adventures in food such as honey-peppered figs – it's really interesting, and really good. Super-warm service, as well as superb baklava ice-cream, seal the deal.

Il Piave

639 Darling Street, between Merton Street & Victoria Road, Rozelle (9810 6204). Bus 432, 433, 434, 442, 445. **Open** 6-10pm Tue-Sat. **Main courses** $28-$34. **Licensed/BYO** (wine only, Tue-Thur). **Credit** AmEx, DC, MC, V. Italian
Rozelle and Balmain have more than their fair share of Italian restaurants, but this one is a cut above. It's the fresh pastas like the ravioli that pull in the crowds, not to mention the pork belly.

Restaurant Atelier

22 Glebe Point Road, between Parramatta Road & Francis Street, Glebe (9566 2112/www.restaurantatelier.com.au). Bus 431, 432, 433. **Open** 6pm-late Tue-Thur, Sat; noon-2pm, 6pm-late Fri. **Main courses** $28-$34. **Licensed/BYO** (wine only). **Credit** MC, V. **Map** p328 B/C10 ㉛ Modern European
Glebe Point Road has a knack for killing off restaurants that try to reach for the stars, so let's hope the curse passes the door of this modest-looking house. Darren Templeman cut his teeth in the Michelin-starred restaurants of the UK, and his command of technique is clear in everything from Berkshire pork rillettes with pickles and a 'lasagne' of blue swimmer crab, shellfish oil, basil and olives.

Modern Australian

Glebe Point Diner

407 Glebe Point Road, between Cook & Forsyth Streets, Glebe (9660 2646). Bus 431, 434. **Open** 6-9pm Wed, Thur; noon-2.30pm, 6-9pm Fri, Sat; noon-3pm Sun. **Main courses** $18-$30. **Licensed.** **Credit** MC, V. **Map** p328 A7 ❷

Organic roast chicken, house-made pasta and Scharer's lager on tap. And we'll be damned if that isn't a suckling pig. This is the best Glebe has on offer – and the most crowd-pleasing place to have opened in recent years.

Oscillate Wildly

275 Australia Street, between King Street & Hoffman Lane, Newtown (9517 4700). CityRail Newtown. **Open** 6-10pm Tue-Sat. **Main courses** $27-$29. **BYO** (wine only). **Credit** AmEx, MC, V. **Map** p334 ❸

It's not every day you run across a restaurant named after a Smiths track, but it almost makes sense in Newtown. The restaurant doesn't share Morrissey's devotion to vegetarianism, however, as the pork belly and duck confit on white bean purée or the fish pie attest. Tiny, and pitched at those on a bargain budget, it's not the most formal and refined of dining experiences, but there's plenty of heart.

Other

Boathouse on Blackwattle Bay

Blackwattle Bay end of Ferry Road, Glebe (9518 9011/www.boathouse.net.au). Bus 431, 432, 433, 434, 370. **Open** noon-3pm, 6.30-10.30pm Tue-Thur, Sun; noon-3pm, 6-10.30pm Fri, Sat. **Main courses** $34-$45. **Licensed. Credit** AmEx, DC, MC, V. **Map** p328 B7 ❷ Seafood

At Boathouse on Blackwattle Bay – and how about that for a name – it's all about the oysters. Order lots of them – there are typically at least six kinds – and lash out on some quality bubbles. Now marvel at the oysters' freshness, their diverse tastes and textures, how well they go with brown bread and champagne – and at the unique glory of this most relaxing of top-tier Sydney restaurants. Crab, flown in fresh from the Northern Territory, gets minimal mucking about, cracked and tossed in a wok just long enough and with just enough salt, pepper and spring onion to bring out the meat's clean sweetness.

Fifi's

158 Enmore Road, between Metropolitan & Simmons Roads, Enmore (9550 4665). CityRail Newtown. **Open** 5.30am-midnight Tue-Sun. **Main courses** $11-$25. **Licensed/BYO** (wine only). **Credit** AmEx, MC, V. Lebanese

The best falafels outside Lakemba can be found at this Enmore restaurant. The little room is packed every night and waitresses barge through the throng with plates heaving with houmous, tabouleh and rice. They also have Lebanese cola, which tastes a lot like plum juice, and some pretty tasty baklava.

Guzman y Gomez

175 King Street, corner of O'Connell Street, Newtown (9517 1533/www.guzmanygomez.com). CityRail Newtown. **Open** 11.30am-10pm Mon-Sat; 11.30am-9pm Sun. **Main courses** $6-$10.90. **BYO. Credit** AmEx, MC, V. **Map** p334 ❺ Mexican

It may look like little more than fast-food joint, but it ain't so. This is the most authentic Mexican food in the city: the corn chips are legendary and the pork adobado burrito is the bomb.

Other locations 1A Bronte Road, Bondi Junction (9388 0369); Corner of Bayswater Road & Penny's Lane, Kings Cross (9322 2245).

Iku Wholefood Kitchen

25A Glebe Point Road, between Parramatta Road & Francis Street, Glebe (9692 8720/www.iku.com.au). Bus 370, 431, 432, 433, 434. **Open** 11am-9pm Mon-Fri; 11am-8pm Sat; noon-7.30pm Sun. **Main courses** $7-$9.50. **BYO. No credit cards.** **Map** p328 C10 ❻ Vegan

Vegetarians, vegans, macro-eaters and diet-conscious individuals flock to Iku's sharp-looking establishments in search of nourishment that is entirely vegetable. Pleasing tastes and textures don't always rule, but specialities such as the lime leaf curry laksa and the rice balls have dedicated followings.

Other locations throughout the city.

North Shore

Asian

Ju Ge Mu/Shimbashi

246-248 Military Road, between Waters Road & Winnie Street, Neutral Bay (9904 3011). Bus 169, 175, 178, 180, 247. **Open** noon-2pm, 6-9.30pm Tue-Sat; 6-9.30pm Sun. **Main courses** $12-$28. **Licensed. Credit** MC, V. Japanese

One half of the restaurant (Ju Ge Mu) is an *okonomiyaki* (a kind of Japanese pancake) and teppanyaki house, whereas the other half (Shimbashi) is all about the handmade soba noodles.

Mino

521 Military Road, between Gurrigal & Harbour Streets, Mosman (9960 3351). Bus 169, 175, 178, 180, 247. **Open** 6-10pm Tue-Sun. **Main courses** $15-$50. **Licensed/BYO** (wine only). **Credit** AmEx, MC, V. Japanese

Military Road's many Japanese eateries range from very ordinary mass-market sushi joints to the well-hidden charms of this little restaurant. Not much to look at from the outside, Mino is quite nice once you're through the door – and though the à la carte options are wide-ranging, regulars all seem happy to put their faith in the chef's kaiseki menu.

Shinju Teppanyaki

51 Berry Street, North Sydney (9957 6511). CityRail North Sydney. **Open** noon-3pm, 6-10pm Mon-Thur; noon-3pm, 6-11pm Fri; 6-11pm Sat; 6-10pm Sun. **Main courses** $19.50-$27. **Licensed. Credit** AmEx, DC, MC, V. Japanese

Food that makes waves. **Ripples at Chowder Bay**.

This restaurant is a North Sydney stalwart on the teppanyaki circuit. It provides the whole kit and caboodle, with flying fried eggs, fish and rice, and punters trying their very best to catch it all, with varying degrees of success.

European

Alchemy 731

731 Military Road, between Gouldsbury Street & Delmore Road, Mosman (9968 3731/www.alchemy 731.com.au). Bus 169, 175, 178, 180, 247. **Open** 6-9.30pm Tue-Thur, Sat; noon-2pm, 6-10pm Fri. **Set menu** $30-$40 lunch; $55-$65 dinner; $80 tasting menu. **Licensed**. **Credit** AmEx, DC, MC, V.
Modern European
European-style dining in all its glory can be found on the busy main drag of Mosman. The set lunch menu includes the likes of gravalax and saltimbocca, while the tasting menu comes with vegetarian options. Service is personable, and the wine list and value make this a local standout.

Ripples at Chowder Bay

Deck C, Chowder Bay Road, Mosman (9960 3000/ www.aquadining.com.au). Bus 244. **Open** 9am-11am, noon-3pm, 6-9.30pm Mon-Fri; 8am-10.30am, noon-4pm, 6-9.30pm Sat, Sun. **Main courses** $22-$29. **Licensed/BYO** (wine only). **Credit** AmEx, DC, MC, V. Italian

A rare restaurant in Sydney – food that stands up to the view. Try the skewers of pork, polenta and cabbage or perhaps the fregolone (that's Italian for little balls of pasta). This 140-seater restaurant with beautiful views and a breeze to boot is the perfect place to while away a Saturday afternoon and turn lunch into dinner.

Modern Australian

Aqua Dining

North Sydney Pool, corner of Paul & Northcliff Streets, North Sydney (9964 9998/www.aqua dining.com.au). CityRail/ferry Milsons Point. **Open** noon-2.30pm, 6.30-10.30pm Mon-Sat; noon-2.30pm, 6-10pm Sun. **Main courses** $48-$49. **Licensed**. **Credit** AmEx, DC, MC, V. **Map** p327 F1 ⓪
Aussies with childhood memories of standing barefoot and dripping by the deep end while clutching a meat pie slathered in tomato sauce may be thrown by the setting of this hip diner. But there's something very appealing about looking out over North Sydney's lovely Olympic pool and across the harbour as you dine. The food isn't amazing or cheap, but that view is something else.

Bathers' Pavilion

4 The Esplanade, between Awaba Street & Mandolong Road, Balmoral Beach (9969 5050/ www.batherspavilion.com.au). Ferry Taronga Zoo

Eat, Drink, Shop

Bathers' Pavilion. *See p167.*

Eat, Drink, Shop

then bus 238/ferry Mosman South then bus 233.
Open *Café* 7am-late daily. *Restaurant* noon-2.30pm,
6.30-9.30pm daily. **Main courses** *Café* $15.50-$32.
Set menu *Restaurant* $95-$115. **Licensed**. **Credit**
AmEx, DC, MC, V.

Serge Dansereau is one of the big men of Australian
cuisine. Big, that is, in terms of his contribution to
Sydney dining, helping to usher in the idea of sea-
sonality (witness his chestnut soup) and an
Australian style of cooking. This beautiful beachside
restaurant highlights the best of his philosophy. The
prices may send us out the back to wash the plates,
but this is a popular choice with locals and tourists.

Other

Garfish

*Corner of Burton & Broughton Streets, Kirribilli
(9922 4322/www.garfish.com.au). CityRail/ferry
Milsons Point.* **Open** 8-11am, noon-3pm, 6-9.30pm
Mon-Sat; 9-11am, noon-3pm, 6-8.30pm Sun. **Main
courses** $22-$32. **Licensed/BYO** (wine only).
Credit AmEx, MC, V. Seafood

These guys are really into their fish. Working hand-
in-fin with one of Sydney's leading seafood suppli-
ers, they focus on freshness. And it's great to see the
fish choice going beyond the usual clichés of salmon
and tuna. Try the likes of aromatic kingfish curry
with aubergine pickle or choose one of the day's
catch from the blackboard, select a cooking method
and garnish and await satisfaction.

Vera Cruz

*314 Military Road, between Winnie Street & Langley
Avenue, Cremorne (9904 5818). Bus 169, 175, 178,
180, 247.* **Open** 6-10pm Mon-Sat. **Main courses**
$15-$26. **Licensed/BYO**. **Credit** AmEx, MC, V.
Mexican

'True Cross', maybe, but it's not true Mexican cuisine – that great gap in the Australian culinary landscape. Nonetheless, the food on offer at this very
designer boîte isn't aiming for authenticity so much
as a crowd-pleasing lightness and clarity of flavour
– no bad thing, either. A couple of *cervezas* don't go
amiss with the killer chicken mole, for that matter.

Northern Beaches

European

Alhambra Cafe & Tapas Bar

*54 West Esplanade, opposite Manly Wharf, Manly
(9976 2975). Ferry Manly.* **Open** 6-10.30pm Tue;
noon-3pm, 6-10.30pm Wed-Sun. **Main courses** $22-
$29. **Licensed/BYO** (wine only). **Credit** AmEx, DC,
MC, V. **Map** p334 ➒ Moroccan/Spanish

Moorish by theme, moreish by nature, this loud, fun
restaurant does a kickin' line in tapas, as well as
spiced tagines, fluffy jewelled couscous and luscious
pastilla – shredded braised chicken in light, crisp
pastry dusted with sugar. The outdoor seating and
wild flamenco on Saturday nights up the ante.

Pilu at Freshwater

*Freshwater Beach, Moore Road, Harbord (9938
3331/www.piluatfreshwater.com.au). Ferry Manly
then bus 136, 139.* **Open** 6-9.30pm Tue; noon-3pm,
6-9.30pm Wed-Sat; noon-3pm Sun. **Main courses**
$35-$44. **Licensed**. **Credit** AmEx, DC, MC, V.
Sardinian

The Freshwater in question is the beach of the same
name, while the Pilu is talented Sardinian-born chef
Giovanni Pilu. For eastern feasters it's a bit of a mission to get to, but the *gnochetti sardi* with goat
ragoût, the sweet honey and ricotta ravioli, and the
roast suckling pig are worth the trip.

Modern Australian

Jonah's

*69 Bynya Road, between Norma & Surf Roads,
Palm Beach (9974 5599/www.jonahs.com.au). Bus
190, L90.* **Open** 8-11am, noon-3pm, 6.30-9.30pm
Mon-Thur, Sun; **Open** 8-11am, noon-3pm, 6.30pm-
late Fri, Sat. **Main courses** $36-$48. **Licensed**.
Credit AmEx, DC, MC, V.

California-born but now an Aussie maestro, George
Francisco cooks up roasted marrow bone with garlic croûtons and Murray cod in this lovely setting,
but the snow crab is a highlight, as is the soufflé
with mixed berries. For a complete blow-out, catch
the seaplane over from Rose Bay.

Manly Wharf Hotel

*Manly Wharf, East Esplanade, Manly (9977 1266/
www.manlywharfhotel.com.au). Ferry Manly.* **Open**
noon-midnight Mon-Sat; noon-10pm Sun. **Main
courses** $16-$26. **Licensed**. **Credit** AmEx, DC,
MC, V. **Map** p334 ➒

The slick Manly Wharf development is a divine (if
loud) place to meet for a drink, but it's also a really
lovely spot to rendezvous for more solid sustenance.
While the steaks, duck potsticker dumplings with
pineapple relish and suchlike are good, the seafood
is, fittingly enough for the waterside location, a big
highlight. You can go à la carte – open lobster ravi-
olo with scallops and asparagus for example – or
why not just opt for the enormous seafood platter,

Parramatta & the West

Asian

Pho An

*27 Greenfield Parade, between Chapel Road & Neville
Lane, Bankstown (9796 7826). CityRail Bankstown.*
Open 7am-9pm daily. **Main courses** $8.70-$11.80.
Unlicensed. **No credit cards**. Vietnamese

There's plenty of dissent over who does what best
in Sydney's Vietnamese restaurants. But not when
it comes to phô. The beef noodle soup (and the chicken version too) dispensed at this Bankstown landmark is the very coriander-accented nectar of the
gods, and the toppings, from steak slices (prosaic)
to wobbly bits (exciting), are without peer.

Eat, Drink, Shop

Tan Viet

100 John Street, between Railway Parade &
Hill Street, Cabramatta (9727 6853). CityRail
Cabramatta. **Open** 9am-7pm daily. **Main courses**
$10-$17. **BYO**. **No credit cards**. Vietnamese

The poultry versions of phô, the great Vietnamese
soup, tend to be overshadowed by the beef style that
is the nation's lifeblood. But not here: chicken gets
celebrated in soup as well as some very fine fried
incarnations, while the duck phô is a rare treat.

Temasek

71 George Street, between Church & Smith Street,
Parramatta (9633 9926). CityRail Parramatta.
Open 11.30am-2.30pm, 5.30-10pm Tue-Sun. **Main**
courses $10-$25. **BYO**. **Credit** AmEx, DC, MC, V.
Malaysian

Long held to be the purveyor of Sydney's finest
curry laksa, this plastic-tableclothed palace also
takes top honours in the beef rendang and Hainan
chicken stakes. Call ahead for house specialities such
as fishhead curry and chilli crab.

Thanh Binh

52 John Street, between Railway Parade & Smith
Street, Cabramatta (9727 9729/www.thanhbinh.
com.au). CityRail Cabramatta. **Open** 9am-9pm daily.
Main courses $8-$30. **BYO**. **No credit cards**.
Vietnamese

John Street is full of buzzy Vietnamese restaurants,
but Angie Hong's Thanh Binh is pretty much universally accepted as the mothership. The choice is
typically broad, but, atypically, almost everything
on the menu is interesting, with many dishes unique
to this establishment. The Newtown branch fights
the good fight, but the original is still best.
Other locations 111 King Street, Newtown
(9557 1175).

Woodland's

238 George Street, Liverpool (9734 9949). CityRail
Liverpool. **Open** 11.30am-2.30pm, 6-9.30pm Tue-Sun.
Main courses $9.50-$18. **BYO**. **Credit** AmEx, MC,
V. South Indian

Consider the masala dosai: is there a bigger commonly available foodstuff? And why hasn't anybody
invented plates large enough not to be dwarfed by
these vast, crisp, South Indian pancakes? You may
not find any answers here, but you will find bliss-
fully light examples of the dosai genre.

Other

Sofra

35-39 Auburn Road, at Queen Street, Auburn (9649
9167). CityRail Auburn. **Open** 7am-midnight daily.
Main courses $7-$16. **Unlicensed**. **No credit**
cards. Turkish

In the very Turkish suburb of Auburn is this very
Turkish eaterie. Forget rugs on the walls and belly
dancers – the look here is tiles and fluoro strips –
Sofra's cred is down to its very good charcoal-grilled
kebabs and fluffy pide. And the baklava rocks.

Summerland

457 Chapel Street, between Ricard & French Streets,
Bankstown (9708 5107). CityRail Bankstown. **Open**
noon-10.30pm Tue-Sun. **Main courses** $13-$22.
Licensed/BYO (wine only). **Credit** AmEx, MC, V.
Lebanese

Thirty-five bucks and a big appetite will take you
far at this most hospitable of Lebanese restaurants.
One of its many drawcards is a focus on seafood. It
goes well beyond the usual whitebait – a breadth not
common in Lebanese eateries in Australia and something we'd love to see emulated elsewhere.

The South

Asian

Ocean King House

247 Princes Highway, at English Street, Kogarah
(9587 3511/www.oceankinghouse.com.au). CityRail
Carlton. **Open** 11am-3pm, 5.30-11pm Mon-Fri; 10am-
3pm, 5.30-11pm Sat, Sun. **Main courses** $11.80-
$26.80. **Licensed/BYO**. **Credit** AmEx, DC, MC, V.
Chinese

It may be a rickety old house on the edge of the highway, but it's also the place of places to spend Chinese
New Year. Eat oysters as big as your fist, but be sure
not to miss the legendary yum cha.

Shanghai Yangzhou House

177 Forest Road, at Rose Street, Hurstville (9580
9188). CityRail Hurstville. **Open** 11am-3.30pm,
5.30-10pm daily. **Main courses** $9.50-$38.50.
BYO. **No credit cards**. Chinese

'The number one dish in the world' – which happens
to be fried rice squares with vegetable and tomato
sauce – may have the coolest name, but the soup
filled dumplings are our favourites.

European

Blackwater

Shop 1, 8 Water Street, Sans Souci (9529 4893/
www.blackwaterrestaurant.com.au). CityRail Rockdale
then bus 477/bus 303. **Open** 6-9.30pm Tue; noon-
2.30pm, 6-9.30pm Wed-Fri, Sun; 6-9.30pm Sat. **Main**
courses $25-$38. **Licensed/BYO**. **Credit** AmEx,
MC, V. Italian

Traditional Italian food hits Sans Souci with the help
of chef Riccardo Roberti who dishes up firm, thumb-
sized gnocchi with hand-pounded pesto and light-
as-a-feather pear sorbet in stylish surrounds.

Chez Pascal

250 Rocky Point Road, at Ramsgate Road, Ramsgate
(9529 5444). Bus 476. **Open** 7-9.30pm Tue-Sat.
Main courses $16-$26.50. **BYO** (wine only).
Credit DC, MC, V. French

Hankering for some old-school French fun? Make a
beeline for Chez Pascal: in a room decorated with
murals of a can-can chorus line you can indulge in
gloriously unreconstructed coq au vin, super-rich
saucisson lyonnais and garlic-laden snails.

Cafés

Take your best shot in a coffee culture explosion.

After a brief flirtation with tea, coffee is back on the menu in Sydney's cafes, and the baristas are all charged up for a battle: who can craft the best design in your froth, and who will go the extra mile and give you a free biscuit or double shot with your drink?

Italianate terms and style pervade – there are short blacks, flat whites and long blacks, but you can't go wrong ordering an espresso, a latte or, more contemporarily, a macchiato or a retro-credible cappuccino. Unlike Italy, however, prices remain the same whether you stand, sit inside or sit outside. Table service is the norm, and, contrary to other Australian states, many cafés here aren't licensed to sell or serve alcohol.

Starbucks and other chains are tempting a slice of the CBD's office business and the young and gullible but, thankfully, independent cafés still abound along caffeine arteries such as Darlinghurst's Victoria Street, Paddington's Oxford Street, King Street in Newtown and Glebe Point Road in Glebe.

Central Sydney

The CBD & the Rocks

Bambini Trust Restaurant & Café

185 Elizabeth Street, between Park & Market Streets, CBD (9283 7098/www.bambinitrust.com.au). CityRail Museum or St James/Monorail City Centre. **Open** 7am-11pm Mon-Fri; 5.30-11pm Sat. **Licensed.** **Credit** AmEx, DC, MC, V. **Map** p329 F6 ❶
Designed with echoes of Milan in its wooden Venetian blinds and dark timber against crisp linen and white tiles, this is the canteen for Sydney's media elite, not least the editors of the Australian Consolidated Press stable, whose building it adjoins and who can usually be seen monopolising the back corner banquettes. The coffee is great, the food is OK, but the buzz is the real deal.

GG Espresso

175 Pitt Street, between Martin Place & King Street, CBD (9221 1644/www.georgegregan.com). CityRail Martin Place or Wynyard. **Open** 6.30am-5.15pm Mon-Fri. **Unlicensed.** **Credit** AmEx, DC, MC, V. **Map** p327 F6 ❷
That's GG as in George Gregan. Not content with making his mark in the world of rugby union, the former Wallabies' champ has set about making his initials synonymous with good coffee in the city. Basic food, but the espresso has plenty of oomph. **Other locations** throughout the city.

The best Cafés

For art-isans
Book Kitchen (*see p174*), **MCA Café** (*see below*), **MoS Café** (*see below*) and **Tropicana** (*see p173*).

For a beaut brunch
Bills (*see p173*), **Café Sopra** (*see p174*), **Danks Street Depot** (*see p174*), **Flat White** (*see p175*) and **Plan B** (*see p172*).

For coffee & cake
Bourke Street Bakery (*see p174*), **La Renaissance Pâtisserie** (*see p172*) and **Tea Room** (*see p172*).

For a classic Italian vibe
Bacino Bar (*see p177*), **Bar Coluzzi** (*see p173*), **Bar Italia** (*see p176*) and **Café Sopra** (*see p174*).

For people watching
Dee Bee's (*see p175*), **Jackie's** (*see p176*) and **Lumiere** (*see p174*).

MCA Café

Museum of Contemporary Art, 140 George Street, between Argyle & Alfred Streets, The Rocks (9241 4253/www.mca.com.au). CityRail/ferry Circular Quay. **Open** noon-3pm Mon-Fri; 10am-11.30pm Sat, Sun. **Licensed.** **Credit** AmEx, DC, MC, V. **Map** p327 F3 ❸
Not for the MCA the glam styling of the eateries at the Guggenheim in Bilbao, say, or New York's MOMA. The deco design takes its cues more from the building's deco days when it housed the Maritime Services Board, while the food is light Mod Oz fare. There's also a nice deck at the front of the museum.

MoS Café

Museum of Sydney, corner of Phillip Street & Bridge Street, CBD (9241 3636/www.moscafe.com.au). CityRail/ferry Circular Quay. **Open** 6.30am-9pm Mon-Fri; 8.30am-5pm Sat, Sun. **Licensed.** **Credit** AmEx, DC, MC, V. **Map** p327 F4 ❹

❶ Green numbers given in this chapter correspond to the location of each café as shown on the street maps. *See pp326-334.*

Eat, Drink, Shop

La Renaissance Pâtisserie.

The trad porridge with thick slices of poached apricots and peaches is a favourite with the money men, while lunch sees tourists move in for Grant Gordon's set menus of a decent main, a side of chips, salad, bread and a coffee, starting at (a rather hefty) $32.50.

Plan B

204 Clarence Street, CBD (9283 3450). CityRail Town Hall/Monorail Galeries Victoria. **Open** 8am-4pm Mon-Fri. **Unlicensed. No credit cards. Map** p327 E6 ⑤
This cute hole-in-the-wall café next to its big brother, fine-dining restaurant, Bécasse (*see p145*), is a great place for a mouth-watering lunch. The wagyu burger is a no-nonsense deal of beef, fresh roasted beetroot, cheddar and tomato, although the coronation chicken sandwich is an excellent second choice.

La Renaissance Pâtisserie

47 Argyle Street, off George Street, The Rocks (9241 4878/www.larenaissance.com.au). CityRail/ ferry Circular Quay. **Open** 8.30am-6pm daily. **Unlicensed. Credit** AmEx, MC, V. **Map** p327 F3 ⑥
This family business established in 1974 is highly recommended for its gateaux made daily by a team of pastry chefs, which can be savoured in the lovely courtyard. Afterwards, check out the aboriginal and contemporary art in the Gannon House Gallery located just down the street.

Speedbar

27 Park Street, between Castlereagh & Pitt Streets, CBD (9264 4668). CityRail Town Hall/Monorail Galeries Victoria. **Open** 7am-6pm Mon-Fri; 8am-2pm Sat. **Unlicensed. No credit cards. Map** p329 F7 ⑦

It's not much too look at, but the focus here is coffee, done right, done fast and done consistently. You want to lounge in an armchair over a dry double hazelnut frappuccino, there's a Starbucks up the street, pal. The rest of us are trying to drink coffee.

Tea Room

Level 3, Queen Victoria Building, 455 George Street, between Market & Druitt Streets, CBD (9283 7279/ www.thetearoom.com.au). CityRail Town Hall/ Monorail Galeries Victoria. **Open** 11am-5pm Mon-Fri, Sun; 10am-3pm Sat. **Licensed. Credit** AmEx, DC, MC, V. **Map** p327 E6 ⑧
Grandmothers sip single-estate Darjeelings and attack three-tiered platters of pretty cakes and finger sandwiches, while the CBD business set takes advantage of the widely spaced tables to talk shop over white tea, pinot noir and Mark Holmes's light, contemporary food.
Other locations Gunners' Barracks, Suakin Drive, off Middle Head Road, Mosman (8962 5900).

Pyrmont

Concrete

224 Harris Street, at Pyrmont Bridge Road (9518 9523). LightRail Fish Market or Wentworth Park/ bus 111, 443, 501. **Open** 7am-4pm Mon-Sat; 8am-4pm Sun. **Licensed. Credit** AmEx, DC, MC, V. **Map** p326 C6 ⑨
Although the decor is as modern and industrial as the name suggests, there's nothing cold about Concrete on a sunny day. The Pyrmont peninsula's advertising and dotcom types swing by for their fresh juices, while pram-pushers seek out the superior scrambled eggs and sandwiches.

East Sydney & Darlinghurst

Bar Coluzzi
*322 Victoria Street, between Surrey & William
Streets, Darlinghurst (9380 5420). CityRail Kings
Cross.* **Open** 5am-7pm daily. **Unlicensed**.
No credit cards. Map p330 J8 ⑩
Decorated with old boxing memorabilia, Bar Coluzzi
is one of Sydney's oldest coffee shops. The macchiato is excellent, but they also make a mean chocolate milkshake. You'll see lots of old Italian men
sitting on the squat wooden stools outside, smoking
and eyeing up the ladies.

Bills
*433 Liverpool Street, at West Street, Darlinghurst
(9360 9631/www.bills.com.au). CityRail Kings
Cross/bus 389.* **Open** 7.30am-3pm, 6-10.30pm
Mon-Sat; 8.30am-3pm Sun. **Licensed. Credit**
AmEx, MC, V. **Map** p330 J8 ⑪
Chef Bill Granger has an ever-expanding empire of
cookbooks and TV appearances, but this café is still
the finest of his achievements. Its communal table
plays host to his famous creamy scrambled eggs,
sunrise drink and toasted own-made coconut bread
at breakfast, while lunch sees the simplicity of steak
sandwiches with garlic cream and chicken club
sandwiches with roasted tomatoes. If you want
(slightly) shorter queues, try the sister cafés.
Other locations 359 Crown Street, Surry Hills
(9360 4762); Queen's Court, 118 Queen Street,
Woollahra (9328 7997).

Ecabar
*128 Darlinghurst Road, at Liverpool Street,
Darlinghurst (9332 1433). CityRail Kings Cross.*
Open 7am-3pm Tue-Fri; 7.30am-4pm Sat; 8.30am-
4pm Sun. **Unlicensed. Credit** AmEx, MC, V.
\Map p330 H8 ⑫
It's all about the coffee. Not that the scrambled eggs
with pesto or the sliced boiled egg with tomato and
avocado on rye aren't great. And not to make light
of the brilliant fresh pear, apple and lime juice. It's
just that the joe at this popular, sunny sliver of a
venue is really, really outstanding.

Forbes & Burton
*252 Forbes Street, Darlinghurst (9356 8788/
www.forbesandburton.com.au).* **Open** *Café* 7am-3.30pm Mon-Fri; 8am-
3.30pm Sat; 9am-4pm Sun. *Restaurant* 6.30-10pm
Tue-Sat. **Licensed. Credit** AmEx, MC, V.
Map p330 H8 ⑬
Dave Pegrum's food is pitched just right for the East
Sydney crowd that comes for excellent juices and
the likes of figs, goat's curd and honey on toast with
great coffee for brekkie, or the likes of skate and puy
lentils for dinner. The sandstone room transforms
from cool café by day to stylish restaurant by night.

Kings Lane Sandwiches
*28 Kings Lane, between Palmer & Bourke Streets,
Darlinghurst (9360 8007). CityRail Museum/bus
311, 373, 377, 378, 380, 392, 394, 396, 399.*
Open 8am-2.30pm Mon-Fri; 10am-2pm Sat.
Unlicensed. No credit cards. Map p330 H8 ⑭
A longtime favourite with inevitable lunchtime
queues eager for the gigantic constructions served
here. Top-quality ingredients, great bread and inventive condiments make for Sydney's best sandwiches,
including a vegetarian offering of walnut houmous
that's good enough to tempt any carnivore.

Latteria
*320B Victoria Street, between Surry & William
Streets, Darlinghurst (9331 2914). CityRail Kings
Cross.* **Open** 5.30am-7.30pm daily. **Unlicensed**.
No credit cards. Map p330 J8 ⑮
Want a caffè just like mamma used to make? Check
out Latteria, next door to Bar Coluzzi (*see above*). The
coffee and panini are pure Italian, sure, but it's the
incredible efficiency with which the limited space
is used that really makes you think you're just off
the Via Tornabuoni.

Le Petit Crème
*118 Darlinghurst Road, between Farrell Avenue
& Liverpool Street, Darlinghurst (9361 4738).
CityRail Kings Cross.* **Open** 7am-2.30pm Mon-Sat;
8am-2.30pm Sun. **Unlicensed. No credit cards.**
Map p330 H8 ⑯
Everything here, from the crêpes to the coffee to the
1980s film posters, is pure Paris. Pull up a bentwood
chair and dive into an enormous Gallic breakfast.
The milkshakes, made with French-style *chocolat
chaud* as their base, can't be beat.

Ten Buck Alley
*185A Bourke Street, corner of William Street,
East Sydney (9356 3000). CityRail Kings Cross/
bus 389.* **Open** 7am-3pm Mon-Fri. **BYO**. **Credit**
AmEx, MC, V. **Map** p329 H7 ⑰
Named for the nearby shady Darlo street (where
anything's yours for a price) is this hole-in-the-wall
café serving what might be the best java in the city.
When it comes to food, keep it simple with a sandwich or salad. Iced coffee is a speciality in summer.

Tropicana
*227 Victoria Street, between Surrey & William
Streets, Darlinghurst (9360 9809/www.tropicana
caffe.com). CityRail Kings Cross.* **Open** 5am-11pm
daily. **Licensed/BYO. No credit cards.**
Map p330 J7/8 ⑱
Forget agents and casting calls: this is where the real
business of Sydney's film and theatre industries
takes place. Against a background of reasonable coffee, adequate café food and capable service, deals
are done and names are made. Immortalised in the
name of Tropfest, the country's leading short film
showcase, the Tropicana has an energy – and a
clientele – like no other.

Una's
*340 Victoria Street, at Surrey Street, Darlinghurst
(9360 6885/www.unas.com.au). CityRail Kings
Cross.* **Open** 7.30am-10.30pm Mon-Sat; 8am-10.30pm
Sun. **Licensed/BYO** (wine only). **No credit cards.**
Map p330 J8 ⑲

Eat, Drink, Shop

It's *Heidi* meets *Queer as Folk* at this wood-panelled Victoria Street stayer. Lederhosen-wearing waiters flit between tables of guys fuelling up on the menu's big, meaty mainstays of schnitzel, stews, rösti, wurst and sauerkraut. Una's is cheap, no one leaves hungry and the upstairs bar is worth its weight in weird. **Other locations** 135 Broadway, Ultimo (9211 3805); 372 New South Head Road, Double Bay (9327 7287).

Surry Hills & Waterloo

Book Kitchen

255 Devonshire Street, at Bourke Street, Surry Hills (9310 1003/www.thebookkitchen.com.au). CityRail/ LightRail Central then 10min walk/bus 301 303, 355. **Open** 8am-4pm Mon, Sun; 8am-4pm, 6.45-10pm Wed-Sat. **Licensed/BYO. Credit** AmEx, MC, V. **Map** p329 G11 ⑳
The idea of a bookshop as a café has currency, so why not a café selling books? Better yet, why not a café selling cookbooks? You can browse shelves of new, imported and second-hand cooking titles here while you wait for excellent hand-cut chips or own-made baked beans cooked with ham hock.

Bourke Street Bakery

633 Bourke Street, at Devonshire Street, Surry Hills (9699 1011). CityRail/LightRail Central then 10min walk/bus 301, 303, 355. **Open** 7am-6pm Mon-Fri; 8am-5pm Sat, Sun. **Unlicensed. No credit cards. Map** p329 G11 ㉑
It's hard to swing a ciabatta here, let alone a cat. Yet this slightly scruffy corner bakery still finds room to pack shelves with ace chocolate cookies, pork and fennel sausage rolls, pastries rich with tomato and olive, and all sorts of wonderful bread. Get in early to score one of the few seats in the window. **Other locations** 130 Broadway, Ultimo (9281 3113).

Café Sopra

1st Floor, Fratelli Fresh, 7 Danks Street, between Young & Bourke Streets, Waterloo (9699 3174/ www.fratellifresh.com.au). Bus 301, 302, 303, 355. **Open** 10am-3pm Tue-Fri; 8am-3pm Sat. **Licensed/BYO. Credit** AmEx, MC, V.
Sopra is Italian for 'upstairs', and this coffeehouse is located above Fratelli Fresh, the warehouse headquarters of one of Sydney's top importers of Italian foodstuffs. Simplicity is the watchword, and sparkling fresh produce and the warehouse's peerless dry goods are at the fore in dishes such as *papa al pomodoro*, the luscious peasant soup.

Danks Street Depot

2 Danks Street, at Young Street, Waterloo (9698 2201/www.danksstreetdepot.com.au). Bus 301, 302, 303, 355. **Open** 7.30am-4pm Mon-Wed; 7.30am-11pm Thur, Fri; 8am-11pm Sat; 9am-4pm Sun. **Licensed. Credit** AmEx, MC, V.
Jared Ingersoll's laid-back café/bar is where you want to be on a lazy weekend. Go for breakfast and have the sardines on toast or slow-cooked broccoli and eggs. Or sit back in the evening with a kir royale and some salt and vinegar potatoes.

Kafa

224 Commonwealth Street, between Foveaux & Albion Streets, Surry Hills (9280 2624). CityRail/ LightRail Central. **Open** 7am-4pm Mon-Fri. **Unlicensed. No credit cards. Map** p329 F9 ㉒
A fine example of how designer smarts can make a Kmart budget look a million bucks. A single large round table fills the room; above it hangs an enormous chandelier constructed of large bucket-like… buckets. Just the thing to ponder while you knock off breakfast treats from the menu.

Lumiere

Shop 13, 425 Bourke Street, Surry Hills (9331 6184). Bus 311, 333, 373, 377, 378, 380, 392, 394, 396, 397, 399, L94. **Open** 7.30am-5pm Mon-Fri; 8am-5pm Sat, Sun. **Unlicensed. Credit** AmEx, MC, V. **Map** p329 G9 ㉓
This smart pâtisserie/coffee/lunch joint is located in the St Margarets development. Sit outside for Sunday brunch with your paper amid the cool crowd in designer T-shirts. Lunch options include a mammoth ribeye beef baguette for hearty appetites, plus plenty of healthy snacks for waistline watchers.

Single Origin

60-64 Reservoir Street, between Elizabeth & Mary Streets, Surry Hills (9211 0665/www.singleorigin. com.au). CityRail Central/LightRail Central. **Open** 7am-4pm Mon-Fri. **Unlicensed. No credit cards. Map** p329 F9 ㉔
The guys who work the bean down at Single O are trippers. On caffeine, that is. You might visit for the selection of cakes and muffins, but you stay for the coffee (the beans are roasted in the behemoth they call Boris the Roaster). Have a heart-starting ristretto and follow up with a more calming flat white to get a good grip on the magic these fellas weave.

Wah Wah Lounge

1 Danks Street, at Young Street, Waterloo (9699 3456). Bus 301, 302, 303, 355. **Open** 7.30am-4pm daily. **Licensed/BYO** (wine only). **Credit** MC, V.
Comfortable banquettes and a wealth of smoothies and frappés make this a popular healthy morning treat for Waterloo's smooth set. At lunch the menu opens up with everything from sandwiches to salads to salmon and mash.

Kings Cross, Potts Point & Woolloomooloo

Café Hernandez

60 Kings Cross Road, between Ward Avenue & Roslyn Street, Kings Cross (9331 2343/www.cafe hernandez.com.au). CityRail Kings Cross. **Open** 24hrs daily. **Unlicensed. Credit** MC, V. **Map** p330 J7 ㉕
A favourite among strong-coffee drinkers, this Spanish-inflected, 24-hour establishment just off the Kings Cross strip is also one of the few places in the city where you'll find non-alcoholic entertainment after the witching hour.

Harry's Café de Wheels

Cowper Wharf Road, opposite Brougham Street, Woolloomooloo (9357 3074/www.harryscafede wheels.com.au). CityRail Kings Cross/bus 222, 311. **Open** 8.30am-2am Mon-Thur; 8.30am-4am Fri; 9am-4am Sat; 9am-12.30am Sun. **Unlicensed. No credit cards. Map** p330 J6 ㉖
This shiny snack van has been supplying late-night meat pies with gravy, mash and mushy peas to locals, visitors, sailors, cab drivers and drunks for more than 50 years. The 3am stagger to Harry's is almost a Sydneyside rite of passage.

Toby's Estate

129 Cathedral Street, at Palmer Street, Woolloomooloo (9358 1196/www.tobysestate.com.au). CityRail Kings Cross. **Open** 7am-5.30pm Mon-Fri; 8am-4pm Sat; 9am-2pm Sun. **Unlicensed. Credit** AmEx, DC, MC, V. **Map** p329 H7 ㉗
Although Toby's beans are widely available, coffee obsessives come to this Cathedral Street roastery-cum-espresso bar to worship at the scant few tables that surround the roasting machinery. Textbook espresso is guaranteed, and there are some nice teas. **Other locations** 32-36 City Road, Chippendale (9211 1459); corner of Manning & Macleay Streets, Potts Point (8356 9264).

Uliveto

33 Bayswater Road, between Kellett Street & Ward Avenue, Kings Cross (9357 7331). CityRail Kings Cross. **Open** 7am-5pm Mon-Sat; 8am-5pm Sun. **BYO. No credit cards. Map** p330 J7 ㉘

Dreamy **Danks Street Depot**.

Uliveto occupies a nice indoor/outdoor slice of Bayswater Road between a gym and a strip club. Handily enough for both crowds, in addition to fine breakfast staples it does a wonderful heart-starter smoothie that's ideal if you're feeling a little dented.

Zinc

Corner of Macleay Street & Rockwall Crescent, Potts Point (9358 6777). CityRail Kings Cross. **Open** 7am-4pm Mon; 7am-4pm, 6.30-10pm Tue-Sat; 8am-4pm Sun. **Licensed/BYO. Credit** MC, V. **Map** p330 J6 ㉙
Perhaps Zinc's popularity with the beautiful people is connected to the prominent role that mirrors play in its design. Or maybe it's just that the city's lovelies have a taste for just-squeezed blood orange juice, good coffee and superb, fresh Italian-style salads.

Eastern Suburbs

Alimentari

2 Hopetoun Street, at William Street, Paddington (9358 2142). Bus 333, 352, 378, 380. **Open** 7am-6pm Mon-Fri; 8am-5pm Sat. **Unlicensed. Credit** AmEx, MC, V. **Map** p332 K9 ㉚
Tucked away at the end of fashion central William Street under the frangipani trees is this little piece of Italy in Paddo. A slick revamp has made this the hangout for locals in the know as they feast on hand-made Italian delicacies, rich coffee and paninis.

Blue Orange

49 Hall Street, between Jacques & Consett Avenues, Bondi Beach (9300 9885/www.blueorangerestaurant. com.au). CityRail Bondi Junction then bus 380, 381, 382, 333/bus 380, 333. **Open** 7.30am-4pm, 6.30pm-midnight Wed-Fri; 7am-4.30pm, 6.30pm-midnight Sat, Sun. **Licensed/BYO** (wine only). **Credit** AmEx, MC,V. **Map** p334 ㉛
Intimate and woody, Blue Orange is a sultry restaurant by night, but its daytime incarnation as a café offers the most mileage. If a ricotta and passion fruit soufflé somehow isn't your cup of tea first thing, try your luck with the smoked salmon pancakes.

Dee Bee's

27 Knox Street, Double Bay (9327 6696). Bus 324, 325, 326. **Open** 7.30am-1.30am Mon-Fri; 7.30am-2am Sat, Sun. **Licensed/BYO. Credit** AmEx, MC,V. **Map** p331 N8 ㉜
Dee Bee's is always packed with Double Bay's own versions of Paris Hilton and paparazzi trying to catch a shot of celebs staying at the Stamford hotel around the corner. Service is friendly and the sandwiches are above average.

Flat White

98 Holdsworth Street, at Jersey Road, Woollahra (9328 9922). Bus 200, 389. **Open** 7am-4pm Mon-Sat; 8am-4pm Sun. **BYO. Credit** MC, V. **Map** p333 M10 ㉝
Gruyère and ham brioche toastie? Yes please. The space isn't huge (and, between us, neither are the portions), but everything here is skewed towards the

Eat, Drink, Shop

perfectly formed – including the clientele. European is the slant, eggs are a favourite, and the milk coffees are as good as you'd hope with a name like this.

Gusto Deli Café
Corner of Broughton & Heeley Street, Paddington (9361 5640). Bus 389. **Open** 7am-7.30pm daily. **Unlicensed. Credit** MC, V. **Map** p332 K9 ❹
A Paddington institution with limited seating inside but a number of tables outside precariously perched on the Five Ways hills. The coffee is excellent but most people come for the healthy range of spicy salads, substantial rolls and sandwiches. There's deli food to go, plus cold cuts and fresh bread.

Jackie's
1C Glenmore Road, at Oxford Street, Paddington (9380 9818) Bus 352, 378, 380, 333. **Open** 7.30am-3.30pm Mon, Tue, Sun; 7.30am-3.30pm, 6-11pm Wed-Sat. **Licensed. Credit** MC, V. **Map** p332 J9 ❸
This place, which used to be in Bondi Beach, has relocated to the designer fashion hub now collecting around this corner of Glenmore Road and Oxford Street. It's a great spot for breakfast before shopping – vanilla ricotta pancakes with maple syrup are the go – and popular with ladies who lunch.

Micky's Café
268 Oxford Street, Paddington (9361 5157/www. mickyscafe.com.au). Bus 352, 378, 380, 333. **Open** 8am-midnight daily. **BYO. Credit** AmEx, MC, V. **Map** p332 K10 ❸
It's all about the ambience here. Paddo's fun young crowd chow down on BLTs, nachos, big hangover breakfasts with fresh frappés and shakes, and coffee with a biscuit or Mars Bar cheesecake on the side.

Parc
30 Clovelly Road, between Darley Road & Avoca Street, Randwick (9398 9222). Bus 339, X39. **Open** 7am-4pm Tue-Fri; 8am-3pm Sat, Sun. **BYO. Credit** MC, V. **Map** p333 N14 ❸
Toast made with bread from the Infinity Sourdough Bakery is just the beginning. The set menu is solid – try the salad of smoked trout with orange, baby cos lettuce and fried capers – while daily specials such as tomato and smoked ham soup thickened with arborio rice keep things interesting. Popular with cyclists from nearby Centennial Park.

Inner West

Badde Manors
37 Glebe Point Road, at Francis Street, Glebe (9660 3797/www.baddemanorscafe.com). Bus 431, 432, 433, 434. **Open** 7.30am-midnight Mon-Fri; 7.30am-1am Sat; 8.30am-midnight Sun. **Unlicensed. Credit** MC, V. **Map** p328 C9 ❸
Maybe they're just living up to the name, but the manners of the waiters here can, at times, be a little eccentric. But, just like the staunchly vegetarian food, the quirky wooden booths and the ice-cream vending window, it's all part of charm.

Bar Italia
169 Norton Street, at Macauley Street, Leichhardt (9560 9981). Bus 436, 437, 438, 440, 445, L40. **Open** 9am-midnight Mon-Thur, Sun; 9am-1am Fri, Sat. **BYO. No credit cards**.
Many Sydneysiders got their first taste of *gelato* within these very walls, and many more still make the pilgrimage as soon as the weather gets even a little warm. The savoury stuff is nothing special – Bar Italia is all about the coffee, the vibe and the double scoop of pistachio and tiramisu that's slowly trickling down your fingers.

Bitton Café
36-37 Copeland Street, between Newton Street & Mitchell Road, Alexandria (9519 5111/www. bittongourmet.com.au). CityRail Erskineville. **Open** 7am-7pm Mon, Tue; 7am-9pm Wed, Thur, Fri; 7am-5pm Sat, Sun. **Unlicensed. Credit** AmEx, MC, V.
A liberal splash of Gallic charm colours everything in this friendly café, from the repartee of the waiters and kitchen staff to the divine crêpes with orange jelly. Bitton also trades in jams, sauces, oils and anything else that can be bottled or put in a jar.

Campos
193 Missenden Road, at Longdown Street, Newtown (9516 3361/www.camposcoffee.com). Bus 352, 370, 422, 423, 426, 428, L23, L28. **Open** 7am-4pm Mon-Fri; 8am-5pm Sat. **Unlicensed. Credit** MC, V. **Map** p334 ❸
These guys are serious about their coffee, but it is bloody good and they don't even cringe when you ask for a flat white. There are a couple of seats, but you're probably better off taking your coffee away and sitting somewhere in the park.

Giulia Café
92 Abercrombie Street, between Meagher & Little Queen Streets, Chippendale (9698 4424/www. cafegiulia.com). CityRail Central/bus 352. **Open** 6.30am-4pm Tue-Fri; 8am-3pm Sat, Sun. **Licensed. Credit** AmEx, DC, MC, V. **Map** p328 D10 ❹
Set in a 100-year-old butchery, Giulia is packed every Saturday morning with people queuing out the door for breakfasts, shakes, juices and bagels. The long counter groans with breads, pastries and glossy mags, plus a huge espresso machine.

Kopitiam
594 Harris Street, Ultimo (9282 9883). CityRail Central/Monorail/LightRail Haymarket. **Open** noon-3pm, 6-10pm daily. **Unlicensed. No credit cards.** **Map** p328 D9 ❹
This tiny blink-and-you'll-miss-it café on screaming Harris Street serves an unbelievably good roti, along with all the usual Malaysian hawker favourites. Get your fix of Malaysian TV while you're at it.

Sonoma Café
215 Glebe Point Road, between Bridge Street & St Johns Road, Glebe (9660 2116/www.sonoma.com.au). Bus 370, 431, 432, 433, 434. **Open** 8am-4pm Mon-Sat; 9am-2pm Sun. **Unlicensed. No credit cards.** **Map** p328 A9 ❹

Eat, Drink, Shop

If you haven't tried the organic sourdough bread from these guys, you're missing out on some of the best buns this side of San Francisco. They also do decent coffee and pastries, and sell delicious breads such as walnut and raisin and soy and linseed.

Vargabarespresso
Corner of Wilson Street & Erskineville Road, Newtown (9517 1932). CityRail Newtown. **Open** 7am-6pm Mon-Fri; 8am-5.30pm Sat, Sun. **BYO. No credit cards. Map** p334 ⓐ
Forget café-laden King Street, the coolest coffee in Newtown is just off the beaten track. Friendly staff serve thoughtful, interesting eats in the mould of American diner-style meatball sandwiches with grilled cheese, and hangover-helpers such as iced liquorice tea or Berocca frappé.

North Shore

Awaba
67 The Esplanade, at Awaba Street, Balmoral (9969 2104/www.awabacafe.com.au). Bus 233, 238, 247, 257. **Open** 7.30am-3pm Mon-Wed; 7.30am-3pm, 6-9.30pm Thur-Sat; 7.30am-5pm Sun. **Licensed/ BYO. Credit** AmEx, MC, V.
This white-on-white sunny space makes sunglasses a necessity. No need to shield your eyes from the menu, however: what's on offer is pretty upmarket fare. The buttermilk flapjacks with maple syrup and berry compote are a winner.

Delicado Foods
134 Blues Point Road, McMahons Point (9955 9399/www.delicadofoods.com.au). CityRail North Sydney. **Open** 7am-5pm Mon, Sun; 7am-8.45pm Tue-Sat. **BYO** (wine only). **Credit** AmEx, MC, V.
Ben Moechtar was the star sommelier at Wildfire but now imports the city's finest Spanish *jamón* and lots of fine South American fare. The coffee is good and strong and lunchtime treats include freshly-made soup served inside or on the streetside tables in the shade of the trees.

Northern Beaches

Bacino Bar
Shop 1A, the Corso, at Darley Road, Manly (9977 8889/www.bacinobar.com). Ferry Manly. **Open** 6am-6pm Mon-Thur; 6am-10pm Fri, Sat; 7am-10pm Sun. **Licensed/BYO. No credit cards. Map** p334 ⓐ
People line up for their morning fix from this Italian corner café. The Little Italy blend coffee is rich and addictive and there's a selection of well-stuffed paninis and tramezzini too.

Chelsea Tea House
48 Old Barrenjoey Road, Avalon (9918 6794). Bus 188, 190, E88, L88, L90. **Open** 8.30am-4pm daily. **Licensed/BYO. No credit cards.**
Lucienne Francisco's wagyu beef brisket sandwich with house-made barbecue sauce is so good you won't care about the extra juice dripping down your

chin and collecting on the table. And your lap. In fact, you'll want an extra piece of bread to mop it up. If beef isn't your thing, there'll be something else on the (short) menu to tempt you.

Cook's Larder
Shop 1, 21-23 Old Barrenjoey Road, near Avalon Parade, Avalon (9973 4370/www.thecookslarder. com.au). Bus 188, 190, E88, L88, L90. **Open** 8am-4pm Mon-Thur, Sat; 8am-4pm, 6.30pm-late Fri; 8am-3.30pm Sun. **BYO. Credit** AmEx, MC, V.
The cake here is legendary. But that's not all: there's also a delicious menu stuffed with goodies from buttermilk pancakes to house-made baked beans to chargrilled lamb. There are deli items to go, and the people who run the place also host cookery classes. And to top it all, it's just two minutes from the beach.

Ground Zero
18 Sydney Road, at Central Avenue, Manly (9977 6996). Ferry Manly. **Open** 8am-5pm daily. **BYO. Credit** MC, V. **Map** p334 ⓐ
Sun, surf and… short blacks? The coffee at Ground Zero – a loungey establishment just a hop and a skip from the sand of Manly Beach – is among the best in Sydney. The fresh salmon is always succulent.

Swelter
1112 Barrenjoey Road, Palm Beach (9974 3169). Bus 190, L90. **Open** 8am-4pm Tue, Wed, Sun; 8am-4pm, 6-10pm Thur-Sat. **Licensed/BYO. Credit** MC, V.
The blackboard menu running the length of the room, covered with a list including the likes of panini, steak sandwiches and organic fizzies, encapsulates the easy, no-nonsense Aussie/Italian vibe at this stylish new addition to Barrenjoey Road.

The South

Allpress Espresso
58 Epsom Road, between Dunning & Mentmore Avenues, Rosebery (9662 8288/www.allpress espresso.com.au). CityRail Green Square/bus 309, 310, 343, 345, 370. **Open** 7am-3pm Mon-Fri; 8am-?pm Sat. **Unlicensed. Credit** MC, V.
Allpress reflects the evolution of this neighbourhood, with industrial machinery juxtaposed with gentrified customers and the swish look of the café itself. The coffee is outstanding, while the breads and pastries, from sister company Brasserie Bread, are a must. Make ours a vitello tonnato roll to go, thanks.

Nuns' Pool
103 Ewos Parade, Cronulla (9523 3395/www. thenunspool.com). CityRail Cronulla then bus 985. **Open** 8am-4pm Tue-Sun. **Licensed. Credit** AmEx, MC, V.
Walking in to the Nun's Pool is like entering a sun-drenched living room. Breakfasts include modern takes on fry-ups, such as poached eggs with asparagus, while the lunch menu features the likes of sautéed mushrooms with prosciutto and thyme, and grilled scampi with angel hair pasta.

Bars & Pubs

Gaze at the stars while drinking in the city's new bar culture.

Sydney's a thirsty town. Always has been, always will be. Most of that neck oiling goes on in big pubs, hotels and clubs in the company of gambling, but change is afoot. New laws spearheaded by Lord Mayor Clover Moore are set to change the landscape of the city's pubs and bars, and the future looks good. Now small hole-in-the-wall venues can afford the previously exorbitant liquor licences, and the aim of creating a sophisticated, European-style bar culture looks realistic. In truth, the change had already started happening when the indoor smoking ban, which kicked in mid 2007, forced drinkers who smoke outdoors, making pub and bar owners follow suit, resulting in glorious

The best **Bars**

For celeb spotting
The **Ivy** (see p180), the **Zeta Bar** (see p180), **Hemmesphere** (see p180), the **Icebergs Bar** (see p186) and the **Water Bar @ Blue** (see p185).

For old-fashioned pub style
The **Australian Hotel** (see p179), the **Lord Nelson Brewery Hotel** (see p180), the **Hollywood Hotel** (see p182), the **Cricketers Arms** (see p182), the **Nag's Head Hotel** (see p187), **Oaks** (see p187) and the **East Sydney Hotel** (see p184).

For smart bar food
Café Pacifico (see p182), the **Victoria Room** (see p182), the **Lincoln** (see p185), the **Courthouse Hotel** (see p186), the **Bennelong Bar** (see p179), **Foveaux Restaurant + Bar** (see p182) and the **Mars Lounge** (see p182).

For water views
The **Opera Bar** (see p180), the **Orbit Bar** (see p180), the **Bennelong Bar** (see p179), the **Watsons Bay Hotel** (see p186), **Drift** (see p180), the **Loft** (see p180) and the **Newport Arms Hotel** (see p187).

For wine
Vini (see p184), **Aperitif** (see p184) and the **Glass Bar** (see p180).

under-the-stars drinking spots popping up all over town (see p183 **Alfresco addicts**).

Cocktail bars are the latest fad (see p181 **The best: Mixologists**). But pubs – confusingly known as 'hotels' for historical reasons, although precious few in the city still offer rooms for the night – continue to do a roaring trade too. And whether they're of the million-dollar-refit type or defiantly unreconstructed, the primary trade is in beer. Cold draught beer is bought in middies (a 285ml glass, close to a half-pint) and, more commonly, 425ml schooners. Boutique Australian beers such as Coopers, James Boag's, Cascade and James Squire are increasingly popular, and imported brands are widely available, but the bulk of beer drunk tends to be the big domestic names. They once divided fiercely down state lines, with Reschs and Tooheys beers being the big deal in Sydney and NSW, but lately VB (Victoria Bitter), brewed by Foster's, has become almost ubiquitous. Foster's Lager itself, it should be mentioned, rarely gets a look-in at Sydney bars – except when tourists order it.

Central Sydney

The CBD & the Rocks

Argyle
12-18 Argyle Street, at Playfair Street, The Rocks (9247 5500/www.theargyle.biz). CityRail/ferry Circular Quay. **Open** 10.30am-3am Mon-Sat; 10.30am-midnight Sun. **Credit** AmEx, DC, MC, V. **Map** p327 F3 ❶
This 1826 wool store built around a grand sandstone outdoor courtyard has become the chosen place for smart drinkers on a weekday night. There are many levels here and it's easy to get separated from your bunch, but seek out the cocktail quarter with fab red daybeds and you can't go wrong.

Attic Bar
2nd Floor, Arthouse Hotel, 275 Pitt Street, between Park & Market Streets, CBD (9284 1200/www.thearthousehotel.com.au). CityRail St James or Town Hall/Monorail Galeries Victoria. **Open** 5.30pm-late Thur-Sat. **Credit** AmEx, DC, MC, V. **Map** p329 F7 ❷

> ❶ Pink numbers given in this chapter correspond to the location of each bar or pub as marked on the street maps. *See pp326-334.*

Argyle.

Almost hidden atop three levels of suits drinking Becks and domestic fizz, the Attic is an eyrie of good drinking. Champion bartender and self-styled 'cocktail chef' Ben Davidson now oversees all of the Arthouse Hotel's bars, so you'll be lucky to get him in person, but his staff are well drilled in the ways of the negroni and manhattan, and his list is still full of curve-balls worthy of your extra time.

Australian Hotel

100 Cumberland Street, at Gloucester Street, The Rocks (9247 2229/www.australianheritagehotel.com). CityRail/ferry Circular Quay. **Open** 11am-midnight Mon-Sat; 11am-10pm Sun. **Credit** AmEx, DC, MC, V. **Map** p327 E4 ❸
Locals and tourists flock to this old-school pub just by the Harbour Bridge. There's no view to speak of, but the neighbourhood is very much olde Sydney towne, yet happily a step away from backpacker ground zero. It's a great place to play two-up on Anzac Day, or to tuck into the superior pizzas. It also offers accommodation.

Bennelong Bar

Sydney Opera House, Bennelong Point, Circular Quay (9241 1999/www.guillaumeatbennelong.com.au). CityRail/ferry Circular Quay. **Open** 5.30pm-late Mon-Sat. **Credit** AmEx, DC, MC, V. **Map** p327 G3 ❹
Being situated in the smallest sail of the Sydney Opera House does give Bennelong Bar something of an unfair advantage. The soaring ceiling is stunning, the harbour views rock, the superb wine list

and service make you feel grown-up and sexy, and the Saarinen chairs are God's gift to lounging. The bar is in the top level of classy restaurant Guillaume at Bennelong (*see p146*).

Ember

Overseas Passenger Terminal, Circular Quay West, The Rocks (8273 1222/www.wildfiresydney.com). CityRail/ferry Circular Quay. **Open** noon-1am Mon-Fri; 6pm-2am Sat; 6pm-midnight Sun. **Credit** AmEx, DC, MC, V. **Map** p327 F3 ❺
It's all about the manhattans. Quite fitting, really, for a bar that adjoins Wildfire, a big, brash, American-style restaurant. We'll take the bar over the mothership any day. Kick back and crunch some popcorn shrimp while you peruse the selection of infused bourbons and the distinguished cocktail list.

Firefly

Pier 7, 17 Hickson Road, Walsh Bay (9241 2031/ www.fireflybar.net). CityRail/ferry Circular Quay then 10min walk/bus 343, 431, 432, 433, 434. **Open** *Apr-Nov* noon-10pm Mon-Sat. *Dec-Mar* noon-10pm Mon-Sat; 3-10pm Sun. **Credit** AmEx, MC, V. **Map** p327 E3 ❻
We reckon they picked the name on the strength of this spot being so small and shiny. Not the sort of place you'd want to be kicking back at during, say, a gale or one of Sydney's rare snap frosts, Firefly's indoors-outdoors shtick runs to fine coffee all day and good cocktails and small, smart, snacky plates of an upmarket order after dark. It's absolutely sublime on a balmy evening.

Glass Bar

2nd Floor, Hilton Sydney, 488 George Street, between Park & Market Streets, CBD (9265 6068/ www.glassbrasserie.com.au). CityRail Town Hall/ Monorail City Centre. **Open** noon-11pm Mon-Fri; 6-11pm Sat, Sun. **Credit** AmEx, DC, MC, V. **Map** p327 F6 **7**

Shimmering with designer gimmicks such as towering shelves of wine, and with a stunning view of the Queen Victoria Building's architectural curlicues, this cool wine bar is everything a big-city hotel bar should be – offering assured cocktail service, good snacking and an outstanding wine experience for greenhorns and connoisseurs alike. Upstairs is glam Zeta Bar (*see below*).

Hemmesphere

Level 4, Establishment Hotel, 252 George Street, between Bridge Street & Abercrombie Lane, CBD (9240 3040/www.merivale.com). CityRail Wynyard or Circular Quay/ferry Circular Quay. **Open** 5.30pm-late Mon-Thur; 3pm-late Fri; 6pm-late Sat. **Credit** AmEx, DC, MC, V. **Map** p327 F5 **8**

On the ground floor of the enormous Establishment building, lots of guys – and girls – in near-identical suits shout orders for pricey beers and stare blankly at the talent. Upstairs sees a much rosier picture: couples lounge around a high-ceilinged bar, sipping luxe cocktails and discussing the various absinthe drinks on offer. Celeb-spotting is a bonus; the downside is that you (on the whole) need to book in advance. Sushi e, adjoining the lounge, serves fabulous modern Australian fare.

Ivy

320-330 George Street, at Angel Place, CBD (9240 3000/www.merivale.com.au). CityRail Wynard. **Open** 11am-late Mon-Sat. **Credit** AmEx, DC, MC, V. **Map** p327 F5 **9**

At the time of writing the Ivy's pleasure dome was slowly unfolding. The exterior was still a concrete work in progress and you had to pick your way through rubble to get inside, but at the top of the grand staircase is an oasis of lush, airy, Miami-meets-Dubai chic. With candy-striped yellow and white throughout, Lloyd Loom chairs and a mass of scatter cushions and opulent sun umbrellas in the open central courtyard, it feels as though you're in a six-star hotel in the desert. The open air means smokers can puff away with impunity, while food outlets on the side allow the opportunity to graze with your booze; upstairs promises yet more suites, bars and restaurants. Whatever locals think of the Ivy's maestro – playboy entrepeneur Justin Hemmes (*see p221* **The pleasure principle**) – this place is hitting a new and very exciting note in Sydney.

Lord Nelson Brewery Hotel

Corner of Argyle & Kent Streets, Millers Point (9251 4044/www.lordnelson.com.au). CityRail/ferry Circular Quay. **Open** 11am-11pm Mon-Sat; noon-10pm Sun. **Credit** AmEx, DC, MC, V. **Map** p327 E3 **10**

Real ale fans, rejoice – the Lord Nello is one of the best places to explore the joys of Sydney's varying microbrews. Anyone else will enjoy admiring the pub's colonial stonework and tucking into the seriously hearty bar plate – pickled onions, cheese, pickles, doorstop wedge of bread and all. Keep an eye out for Nelson's Blood, the pub's signature beer.

Opera Bar

Lower Concourse Level, Sydney Opera House, Bennelong Point, Circular Quay (9247 1666/ www.operabar.com.au). CityRail/ferry Circular Quay. **Open** 11.30am-late daily. **Credit** AmEx, DC, MC, V. **Map** p327 G3 **11**

Loved by Sydneysiders and visitors alike, the Opera Bar is one of those multi-purpose venues that actually gets it right. It offers better-than-it-needs-to-be lunch for quayside rubberneckers; a lovely environment for an afternoon beer; quick, reasonably priced dinners for the pre-theatre crowd; and live music (*see p253*) and cocktails most nights for people looking to shake a little booty. The views are particularly pretty at dusk, and the prices are reasonable.

Orbit Bar

Level 47, Australia Square, 264 George Street, between Hunter & Bond Streets, CBD (9247 9777/ www.summitrestaurant.com.au). CityRail Wynyard. **Open** 5pm-late Mon-Thur, Sun; noon-late Fri, Sat. **Credit** AmEx, DC, MC, V. **Map** p327 F5 **12**

Do not adjust your set, and don't worry, your drink hasn't been spiked: it's the bar itself that's spinning. And, 47 floors up, you get a fat eyeful of the city in plush retro-modern surrounds. The drinks are decent and the cheese twists suitably twisty, but the bill can make you dizzy if you're not careful. The building itself is a city landmark, designed by Harry Seidler, Sydney's original modernist architect.

Zeta Bar

4th Floor, Hilton Sydney, 488 George Street, between Park & Market Streets, CBD (9265 6070/www. zetabar.com.au). CityRail Town Hall/Monorail City Centre. **Open** 5pm-late Mon-Wed; 3pm-late Thur, Fri; 4pm-late Sat. **Credit** AmEx, DC, MC, V. **Map** p327 F6 **13**

Kin to London's Zeta by virtue not only of its Hilton connection and Tony Chi design, but also the handful of London bar geezers who run the place, the Sydney Zeta has 'bright lights, big city' written all over it. It's a large space, running from glam VIP areas (yours too for a hefty minimum spend) past acres of bar to a tree-shaded terrace overlooking George Street storeys below. There's also Glass Bar (*see p180*), attached to the Glass brasserie on the hotel's second floor. Beware queues at weekends.

Darling Harbour

Loft

3 Lime Street, King Street Wharf (9299 4770/www. theloftsydney.com). CityRail Wynyard/ferry Darling Harbour/Monorail Darling Park. **Open** 4pm-1am Mon-Wed; noon-3am Thur-Sun. **Credit** AmEx, DC, MC, V. **Map** p326 D5 **14**

The Baghdad Iced Tea – cucumber Smirnoff Blue voddy, Plymouth gin, apple, mint, lime and jasmine tea – is the perfect early-evening refresher. There's much to love about the Loft in general, even if bridge-and-tunnel types pack the place out on weekends. Carved Moorish-styled ceilings, lots of squishy leather loungers, verandas opening onto water views across Darling Harbour and great tapas served late will all conspire to keep you smiling.

East Sydney & Darlinghurst

The heart of gay Sydney (and therefore gay Australia), the 'Golden Mile' of Oxford Street stretches from mixed, occasionally sleazy business down at the Hyde Park end, becoming noticeably flasher as it goes art-house with cinemas and bookshops between Taylor Square and the Paddington Town Hall, and then much straighter and glossier in the land of moneyed boutiques and collar-up pubs for private-school kids between there and Centennial Park.

The area around Taylor Square – the locals know it as Gilligan's Island for the number of fools who find themselves hopelessly marooned there – can be a bit of a zoo on weekends, as it's the meeting point for Surry Hills cool kids, Darlinghurst hipsters, suburbanites up for a lark, bottom-feeding eastern suburbs wannabes and every flavour of homosexuality. The bars cater for all types and are, by and large, quite mixed and open. Thirst and a willingness to pay to cater to it are the common denominators.

For more gay bars, *see p238*.

Burdekin Hotel
Corner of Oxford & Liverpool Streets, Darlinghurst (9331 3066/www.burdekin.com.au). CityRail Museum/bus 333, 378, 380. **Open** 4pm-4am Tue-Thur; 4pm-6am Fri; 5pm-6am Sat; 4pm-midnight Sun. **Credit** AmEx, DC, MC, V. **Map** p329 G8 ⑮
One of the best Sydney bars of the early 1990s, the Burdekin Hotel may have aged, but it still has a great bone structure. A range of upstairs rooms offers a world of dance options at the weekend, while

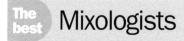
The best Mixologists

Here's a quick guide to the movers and shakers currently stirring up the cocktail set.

Charlie Ainsbury, Bayswater Brasserie
Charlie Ainsbury (*pictured*) won the 2007 Barman of the Year award from *Bartender Magazine*, beating hundreds of shakers from across the state. Why? It's all in the foreplay. Ainsbury prepares ingredients well in advance to ensure the strongest flavours in his cocktails. Try his complex Italiano Sour No.2 – Campari and Strega (an Italian herbal liqueur), shaken hard with fresh grapefruit juice, soured with lemon and sweetened with passion fruit syrup. It works! *See p184*.

Grant Collins, Zeta Bar
With sidekick UK-trained Mikey Enright, Grant Collins has made Zeta Bar one of the coolest hangouts for cocktail aficionados, which is quite something considering it's in the Hilton Hotel. The classic martini, made by Collins with a wash of vermouth, icy-cold gin and an olive, is perfection. *See p180*.

Brad Cullen, Opera Bar
Do cocktails taste better in the open air? Bartender Brad Cullen thinks so, and he has a point when you consider that the al fresco seating in question is harbourside, with the Coathanger centre-frame. Try the Dirty Carpet

Disco – Chambord and Absolut Vanilia with wild strawberry liqueur over macerated redcurrants and raspberries, finished with apple juice and soda. A veritable taste explosion. *See p180*.

the ground-floor bar feels like an upmarket pub. The tiny tiled art deco Dugout Bar in the basement, with its speakeasy cred, is the coolest bet.

Café Pacifico

1st Floor, 95 Riley Street, between Stanley & William Streets, East Sydney (9360 3811/www. cafepacifico.com.au). CityRail Kings Cross/bus 389. **Open** 6pm-late Tue-Sun. **Credit** AmEx, DC, MC, V. **Map** p329 G7 ⑯

Yes, it's part of the same chain that operates Café Pacificos in London, Paris and Amsterdam; no, the Tex-Mexican food here isn't far above Sydney's relatively low standard – but Pacifico has a rockin' bar scene and the kind of random crowd mix on any given evening that makes it pleasingly unpredictable. Or maybe that's just the nation's broadest range of tequilas talking. Muy bien.

Darlo Bar

Corner of Liverpool Street & Darlinghurst Road, Darlinghurst (9331 3672). CityRail Kings Cross/bus 389. **Open** 10am-midnight Mon-Sat; noon-midnight Sun. **Credit** AmEx, DC, MC, V. **Map** p329 H8 ⑰

More properly known as the Royal Sovereign Hotel, the Darlo Bar has been a local institution for the past decade: in gay-friendly Darlinghurst it's distinguished by its reputation for being the number-one straight pick-up joint. Sure, there's plenty of boy-boy, girl-girl is to be had over its pool tables, mismatched second-hand furniture and adequate drinks, but the ease with which happy young heteros hook up here is almost freakish.

Victoria Room

Level 1, 235 Victoria Street, between Liverpool & William Streets, Darlinghurst (9357 4488/www. thevictoriaroom.com). CityRail Kings Cross. **Open** 6pm-midnight Tue-Thur; 6pm-2am Fri; 2pm-2am Sat; 1pm-midnight Sun. **Credit** AmEx, DC, MC, V. **Map** p330 J8 ⑱

Victoria Street goes truly Victorian with this dim and sexy space harking back to the Raj, with much in the way of heavy baroque furnishings and classic cocktails. There's plenty to like in the way of tom collinses and old fashioneds, but no shortage of ginger and vanilla martinis and their ilk should you wish to travel back to the future. There's a Mediterranean/Middle East-inflected restaurant too.

Surry Hills

Cricketers Arms

106 Fitzroy Street, at Hutchinson Street (9331 3301). CityRail Central then 10min walk/bus 339, 374, 376, 391. **No credit cards. Map** p332 H10 ⑲

In addition to being one of the finest places in the city to down beers, the Cricketers is everything that's good about Surry Hills in microcosm, remaining poised between unreconstructed flavour (read grime and the occasional thug) and moving with the times (read decent grub, a good range of beers and quality tracks issuing from the decks by the bar). The beer garden is the ideal ground on which to mount a late-afternoon assault on sobriety.

Foveaux Restaurant + Bar

65-67 Foveaux Street, between Commonwealth & Belmore Streets (9211 0664/www.foveaux.com.au). Bus 339, 374, 376, 391. **Open** 6pm-late Tue-Thur, Sat; noon-3pm, 6pm-late Fri. **Credit** AmEx, MC, V. **Map** p329 F9 ⑳

Darrell Felstead makes mean snacks upstairs and Julian Serna (ex Hemmesphere) mixes something else altogether in the dungeon-like downstairs. Try the Señor Papa cocktail or maybe the Ode to Van Gogh. The menu constantly changes as Felstead experiments with miniature toffee apples, popcorn and pork in all its guises.

Gaslight Inn

278 Crown Street, between Oxford & Campbell Streets (9360 6746). Bus 311, 333, 352, 373, 377, 378, 380, 392, 394, 396. **Open** noon-midnight Mon, Tue; noon-1.30am Wed, Thur; noon-3am Fri, Sat; noon-10pm Sun. **No credit cards. Map** p329 G8 ㉑

Prop up the bar downstairs for some peace and quiet and a well-poured schooner, or stake a claim at one of the tables in the little-known courtyard upstairs.

Hollywood Hotel

Corner of Foster & Hunt Streets (9281 2765/www. hotelhollywood.com.au). CityRail Central or Museum/bus 301, 302. **Open** 11am-midnight Mon-Wed; 11am-3am Thur, Fri; 6pm-3am Sat. **No credit cards. Map** p329 F8 ㉒

This Surry Hills stalwart has outlived, out-shone and out-sung half the pubs in the area and with bags more style and all the original fittings still in place. It also does a decent cheese plate.

Longrain

85 Commonwealth Street, at Hunt Street (9280 2888/www.longrain.com.au). CityRail Central or Museum/bus 301, 302. **Open** noon-2.30pm, 5.30pm-midnight Mon-Fri; 5.30pm-midnight Sat. **Credit** AmEx, DC, MC, V. **Map** p329 F8 ㉓

Now this is a bar. It's also a restaurant, for that matter, but the bar is so much part of the leading edge of Sydney nightlife that it commands equal footing with the famed Thai diner (*see p155*). Taste the greatness in the Bloody Longrain – a mix of vodka, red chilli, nahm jim, cucumber and coriander – and then settle back on a low stool to contemplate the beauty of the century-old converted warehouse.

Mars Lounge

16 Wentworth Avenue, between Oxford & Goulburn Streets (9267 6440/www.marslounge.com.au). CityRail Museum/bus 333, 378, 380. **Open** 5pm-midnight Wed, Thur; 5pm-3am Fri; 7pm-3am Sat; 7pm-1am Sun.* **Credit** AmEx, DC, MC, V. **Map** p329 G8 ㉔

Sunday night is the new Saturday. Or at least it is in this neighbourhood. Fed up with Oxford Street and its surrounds being overrun by the suburban hordes on Fridays and Saturdays, many locals now

Alfresco addicts

Smokers in Sydney may feel like social pariahs thanks to the stringent NSW laws banning puffing in their traditional haunt of pubs, bars and clubs, but they don't have to give up the habit just yet if they don't want to. Keen to hang on to this lucrative sector of their business, drinking holes are falling over themselves to provide enticing outdoor settings to lure smokers in, and keep on the right side of the law. Here are a few that go the extra mile.

In the east is the recently opened and hugely popular **Moncur Terrace** (116 Queen Street, Woollahra, 9327 9777), on the first floor of the Woollahra Hotel. Chow down on one of the most expensive wagyu burgers in town, then puff away on the classy indoor terrace. In fine weather, the retractable roof is pulled back and the blue skies or twinkling stars revealed. When the roof is closed, smokers can retreat to the front balcony. Eastern 'burbers also flock to **Icebergs Bar** (*see p186*), where the outdoor terraces at the front and the side of this square glass establishment often prove to be the most windswept smoking spots in the city. Still, at least you get to watch the surfers as you puff. And there's the glorious, if pricey,

Gazebo Wine Garden (2 Elizabeth Bay Road, Elizabeth Bay, 9357 5333, www.gazebo winegarden.com.au), a wine bar at the foot of one of the city's more flashy apartment blocks. In Darlinghurst, the refurbished **Beauchamp Hotel** (267 Oxford Street, 9331 2575, www.thebeauchamp.com.au) is in the heart of the gay strip and has a lovely private courtyard on the first floor. Heaters and awnings keep the place open and useable in winter, and thanks to the latter you can even smoke in a downpour. In the CBD, the Hilton's **Zeta Bar** (*see p180*) has a large outdoor smoking terrace complete with trees and great views of the city and the Queen Victoria Building. And let's not forget the **Opera Bar** (*see p180*), where you can smoke under the sails of the grand lady.

More urban, edgy and a tad grungy is Surry Hills' **Café Lounge** (277 Goulburn Street, 9356 8888), with its courtyard of retro seating and DJ on some nights, and the **Annandale Hotel** (*see p250*), with its beer garden with retro umbrellas. On the northern beaches, meanwhile, you can't beat the cavernous garden at the **Newport Arms Hotel** (*see p187*) where you can chain smoke all night.

Sightseeing

Favela is not your average shanty town.

save much of their partying for Sundays. Foremost among the Sunday-nighters, the dark and spacious red-and-black Mars Lounge is famed for its mixed crowd and extensive selection of premium vodkas.

Vini

Shop 3, 118 Devonshire Street, at Holt Street (9698 5131). CityRail Central/Lightrail Central. **Open** noon-midnight Tue-Fri; 5pm-midnight Sat. **Credit** DC, MC, V. **Map** p329 F10 ❷

The choice is yours: there's an old shipping container on the side, which doubles as the wine bar's makeshift cellar, or there's the main *enoteca* – only just big enough to swing a kitten, and serving well-executed dishes to go with the all-Italian wine list.

Kings Cross, Potts Point & Woolloomooloo

The Tilbury (*see p240*) in Woolloomooloo is a popular gay haunt, particularly on Sundays, but its beer garden is lovely any time.

Aperitif

7 Kellett Street, at Bayswater Avenue, Kings Cross (9357 4729). CityRail Kings Cross. **Open** 5.30pm-3am Mon, Wed-Sat; 5.30pm-midnight Sun. **Credit** AmEx, DC, MC, V. **Map** p330 J7 ❷

With a courtyard set under a massive old fig tree and dotted with rickety tables lit by candles, this is balmy summer sipping at its best. Ex-MG Garage sommelier Charles Leong tends bar from the back end of an old terrace, running an all-French wine and champagne list, mixing great martinis and doing a mean trade in, you guessed it, wonderful aperitifs.

Bayswater Brasserie

32 Bayswater Road, at Ward Avenue, Kings Cross (9357 2177/www.bayswaterbrasserie.com.au). CityRail Kings Cross. **Open** 5pm-late Mon-Thur; noon-late Fri; 5-10pm Sun. **Credit** AmEx, DC, MC, V. **Map** p330 J7 ❷

In the 1980s, before the Fringe Benefits Tax effectively killed off the Australian version of the three-martini lunch, the Bayz was better known as 'the Office'. And while the zenith of the expense-account days may have passed, the Harry's-esque bar at the back still retains a whiff of that three-o'clock-be-damned spirit, with great drinks, informed bartenders and a notable tequila selection.

Bourbon

24 Darlinghurst Road, at Macleay Street, Kings Cross (9358 1144/www.thebourbon.com.au). CityRail Kings Cross. **Open** 10am-6am Mon-Fri; 9am-6am Sat, Sun. **Credit** AmEx, DC, MC, V. **Map** p330 J7 ❷

The former Bourbon & Beefsteak opened in the 1960s to cater to visiting US sailors on leave during the Vietnam war. It stayed decidedly idiosyncratic until a makeover a few years ago rendered it designer-bland cookie-cutter contemporary. It remains, however, very broad in the scope of drinkers it attracts, and is a fine last resort for a night out in the area. It also has its own club, the Cross (*see p222*).

East Sydney Hotel

Corner of Cathedral & Crown Streets, Woolloomooloo (9358 1975/www.the-east sydneyhotel.com.au). CityRail Kings Cross/bus 200. **Open** 10am-late Mon-Sat; noon-midnight Sun. **Credit** MC, V. **Map** p330 H7 ❷

With signs proudly bearing the news that it's a poker-machine-free establishment, the East Sydney Hotel marks itself out as a breed apart. And if the friendly bar staff, roaring darts tournaments and generally genial air of this old-fashioned pub, complete with pressed-tin ceilings, are any guide, it's a breed that should really be encouraged.

Favela

1 Kellett Way, at Roslyn Street, Kings Cross (9357 1640/www.favela.com.au). CityRail Kings Cross. **Open** 6pm-midnight Wed, Thur; 6pm-3am Fri, Sat; 7-11pm Sun. **Credit** AmEx, DC, MC, V. **Map** p330 J7 ③⓪

This newish bar/nightclub/restaurant is hitting all the right notes with Sydney's generally demanding twentysomething nightbirds. Fresh fruity cocktails are the thing, along with a menu of rather expensive but trendy snacks with an Asian flair. Lighting is low and if you manage to get a chair it'll be a padded cube or bench with cushions, but generally there's a lot of standing involved.

Hugo's Lounge

Level 1, 33 Bayswater Road, between Ward Avenue & Kellett Street, Kings Cross (9357 4411/www.hugos.com.au). CityRail Kings Cross. **Open** 7pm-3am Thur-Sat; 8pm-3am Sun. **Credit** AmEx, DC, MC, V. **Map** p330 J7 ③①

Most people come here for the drinks. The drinks and the babes, that is. Male and female, they tend towards the blonde, corn-fed, moneyed (or money-hungry) end of the spectrum and prowl the Lounge's broken-glass bar, dim banquettes and canopied veranda. Mere mortals come for the peerless fresh mango daiquiris or to gaze in wonder at the blonde-dom on display. Downstairs is Hugo's pizzeria.

Jimmy Liks

186-188 Victoria Street, between Darlinghurst Road & Orwell Street, Potts Point (8354 1400/www.jimmyliks.com). CityRail Kings Cross. **Open** 5pm-midnight daily. **Credit** AmEx, DC, MC, V. **Map** p330 J7 ③②

You've gotta love a list that features a drink called the Kyoto Protocol, especially when it also offers some of the finer Asian-accented cocktails in town. Chilli, saké, nahm jim, ginger and more find their way into Jimmy Liks' concoctions. Service is famously uneven, so arrive early, pull up a pew on the street or slide on to a stool at the long, elegant bar, and bat those lashes extra hard. *See also p157.*

Lincoln

36 Bayswater Road, at Ward Avenue, Kings Cross (9331 2311/www.thelincoln.com.au). CityRail Kings Cross. **Open** 6pm-midnight Wed; 6pm-3am Thur, Sat; 5pm-3am Fri; 4pm-midnight Sun. **Credit** AmEx, DC, MC, V. **Map** p330 J7 ③③

Bar manager George Nemec is mixing it up. Take a classic (say a tom collins) give it a bit of a twist like adding watermelon juice and kaffir lime leaves and you have yourself a cocktail, Lincoln style. There's also a great line in bar snacks like Welsh rarebit.

Lotus

22 Challis Avenue, at Macleay Street, Potts Point (9326 9000/www.merivale.com). CityRail Kings Cross. **Open** 6pm-1am Tue-Sat. **Credit** AmEx, DC, MC, V. **Map** p330 J6 ③④

You'll probably be bouncing off the snakeskin-padded walls here, the cocktails are so good. It's a small and perfectly formed place, and with the oriental decor and comfy ottomans, you think you've died and gone to some sort of Susie Wong heaven.

Melt Bar

Level 3, 12 Kellett Street, at Bayswater Road, Kings Cross (9380 6060/www.meltbar.com.au). CityRail Kings Cross. **Open** 8pm-late Thur-Sat; 9pm-late Sun. **Credit** AmEx, MC, V. **Map** p330 J7 ③⑤

Here, the walls are covered in murals, the lighting is virtually non-existent, tatty couches and milk crates make up the furnishings, and DJs mix everything they can get their grubby little hands on.

Old Fitzroy Hotel

129 Dowling Street, at Cathedral Street, Woolloomooloo (9356 3848/www.oldfitzroy.com.au). CityRail Kings Cross/bus 200. **Open** 11am-midnight Mon-Fri; noon-midnight Sat; 3-10pm Sun. **No credit cards.** **Map** p330 H7 ③⑥

Theatre, laksa, beer. Not uncommon to encounter them all during a night on the town, but finding them all under one roof is rare. Best of all? Even without the cheap and reasonable Asian noodle soups and the talents of the Tamarama Rock Surfers, one of the city's more daring theatre troupes, the pub has a rollicking charm rare for this neck of the woods. For information on the theatre, *see p269.*

Water Bar @ Blue

Blue, Woolloomooloo Wharf, 6 Cowper Bay Road, opposite Forbes Street, Woolloomooloo (9331 9000). CityRail Kings Cross then 10min walk or bus 311. **Open** 4-10pm Mon, Sun; 4pm-midnight Tue-Sat. **Credit** AmEx, DC, MC, V. **Map** p330 H6 ③⑦

The guys at this trendy dark hangout in the Blue hotel know how to mix a drink. Let them show you what they can do, or just muddle your way through the way too extensive list and hope for the best.

Eastern Suburbs

Coogee Bay Hotel

Corner of Arden Street & Bay Road, Coogee (9665 0000/www.coogeebayhotel.com.au). Bus 372, 373, 374. **Open** *Beach Bar* 9.30am-3am daily. *Sports Bar* 9am-4am Mon-Thur; 9am-6am Fri, Sat; 9am-10pm Sun. *Arden Bar & Arden Lounge* noon-1am daily (summer only). *Nightclub* 9pm-late Thur-Sat. **No credit cards.**

Seating 500 people (most of them visiting from the UK), the Coogee Bay's beer garden is truly a thing to behold, and with a cool ocean breeze waving the palms, and Coogee Beach spread before you, it's a contender for the best of its ilk in the east. Other bars within the pub itself – which is enormous – offer sports, DJs, a pool, a brasserie and live music.

Sightseeing

Drift

Ravesi's, 118 Campbell Parade, at Hall Street,
Bondi Beach (9365 4422/www.ravesis.com.au).
CityRail Bondi Junction then bus 333, 380, 381,
382/bus 333, 380. **Open** 5pm-1am Mon-Fri; 3pm-
1am Sat; 3pm-midnight Sun. **Credit** AmEx, MC, V.
Map p334 ⓷⓷
This incredibly popular drinking haunt opened in
late 2007 and has been overflowing with prettysome-
things ever since. Upstairs at Ravesi's hotel, slap
bang on Campbell Parade, it's a chic glass and soft
furnishings hangout, and guests fight for the seats
at the front with views across to the beach.

Icebergs Bar

1 Notts Avenue, at Campbell Parade, Bondi Beach
(9365 9000/www.idrb.com). CityRail Bondi Junction
then bus 333, 380, 381, 382/bus 333, 380. **Open**
noon-midnight Mon-Sat; noon-10pm Sun. **Credit**
AmEx, MC, V. **Map** p334 ⓷⓽
This utopian bar embodies Sydney drinking –
understated urban cool colliding with nature.
Carved into the Bondi rockface and with stunning
ocean views, Icebergs is a natural wonder, but the
extra yard comes in the form of dashingly-dressed
bartenders schooled in the art of giving customers
what they need before they know it. So whether it's
a soul-soothing glass of Fernet-Branca or a heroic
local beer, Icebergs has you covered.

Light Brigade

2A Oxford Street, at Jersey Road, Woollahra (9331
2930/www.lightbrigade.com.au). Bus 333, 352, 378,
380, 389. **Open** *Downstairs* noon-late daily. *Upstairs*
5pm-late Tue-Sat. **Credit** AmEx, DC, MC, V.
Map p332 L10 ⓸⓪
On the one hand a beautiful old pub, on the other –
as its name suggests – something of a battleground.
In the trenches (ie downstairs), owner Dean Haritos
is going more for a blaring sports bar than a lounge
bar. But over the top (upstairs) it's all about plush
privacy and original features and cocktails. Head
bartender Percy Small mixes playful concoctions
like his Apple and Grapefruit Sling. Chaaarge!

Royal Hotel

237 Glenmore Road, at Five Ways, Paddington
(9331 2604/www.royalhotel.com.au). Bus 389. **Open**
10am-midnight Mon-Sat; 10am-10pm Sun. **Credit**
AmEx, DC, MC, V. **Map** p332 K9 ⓸⓵
Paddington is ground zero for strapping lads and
lasses who love their rugby, and lots of them love
the Royal too. Three levels of well-heeled conviviality are divided between the ground-floor bar, the
quite reasonable Mod Oz restaurant on the first floor,
and the top floor's Elephant Bar, which is stuffed
with pachyderm knick-knacks and young upwardly mobiles enjoying cosmopolitans and caipiroskas.

Watsons Bay Hotel

1 Military Road, at Cliff Street, Watsons Bay (9337
5444/www.watsonsbayhotel.com.au). Ferry Watsons
Bay/bus 324, 325, 380. **Open** 10am-midnight daily.
Credit AmEx, DC, MC, V.

The fish and chips are so-so. The drinks aren't
thrilling or cheap. But the Watto, as it's known, is
an eastern suburbs institution, and still on most
Sydneysiders' list of top pubs. There really is something to be said for watching the sun sink over the
harbour from the comfort of its capacious veranda,
surrounded by other beer-swilling day-trippers.

Inner West

Clare Hotel

20 Broadway, between Regent & Abercrombie
Streets, Ultimo (9211 2839). CityRail Central. **Open**
9.30am-midnight Mon-Wed; 9.30am-1am Thur, Fri;
6.30pm-3am Sat. **No credit cards. Map** p328 D10 ⓸⓶
It was the bike couriers who first colonised this place
anew a few years back. Soon their Lycra-clad bums
were being crowded off the shared-house couches
by students from the nearby University of
Technology, and now the Clare runs the gamut from
blow-ins here for the music to late teens to beer-lov-
ing twentysomethings.

Courthouse Hotel

Corner of Australia & Lennox Streets, Newtown
(9519 8273). CityRail Newtown. **Open** 10am-
midnight Mon-Sat; 10am-10pm Sun. **No credit**
cards. Map p334 ⓸⓷
Counter meals are on offer to go with your fine
schooner of beer (the stout is especially good) plus
there's one of the nicest courtyards in Sydney, popular in fair weather but never unpleasantly crowded thanks to the pub's relative seclusion from the
hustle and bustle of King Street.

Leichhardt Hotel

95 Norton Street, between Parramatta Road &
Marion Street, Leichhardt (9569 6640/www.95
norton.com). Bus 436, 437, 438, 440, 445. **Open**
10am-midnight Mon-Thur, Sun; 10am-3am Fri, Sat.
Credit AmEx, MC, V.
A two-storey-high reproduction of Caravaggio's
Bacchus makes the business of this ostentatiously
renovated open space all too clear. In the midst of
Norton Street's Italian red-sauce merchants, the
Leichhardt is a shiny beacon of things done with an
eye away from the Old Country. Downstairs you'll
find cheap Asian food, upstairs darkness and a
range of devastating shots.

Madame Fling Flong

Level 1, 169 King Street, at O'Connell Street,
Newtown (9565 2471/www.madameflingflong.
com.au). CityRail Newtown or Macdonaldtown. **Open**
4pm-late daily. **No credit cards. Map** p334 ⓸⓸
In a cosy room, perched above a restaurant you
wouldn't cross the street for, hides a bar space kitted out with retro furnishings and tatty chaises
longues accommodating a big corner bar. It's easy
to see why MFF has become the bar *du jour* for
renaissance slackers in the inner west, keeping
things eclectic with vintage movie nights, smooth
Sunday sounds and crackerjack cocktails all night.

Nag's Head Hotel

Corner of St Johns Road & Lodge Street, Glebe (9660 1591/www.nagshead.com.au). Bus 412, 413, 436, 437, 438, 434, 440. **Open** 9am-midnight Mon-Sat; 10am-midnight Sun. **Credit** MC, V. **Map** p328 A9

One of the closest approximations to a proper British pub to be found in Sydney, the Nag's Head Hotel has what too many wannabe boozers can't seem to rustle up however much they spend on refits: charm. It's got all ye olde glass, woody bits and Mother Country draught beers that any real ale fan could want, and its situation – away from the main drag of Glebe Point Road – keeps the mix of young students, old whippersnappers and locals fresh.

Town Hall Hotel

326 King Street, between Newman & Wilson Streets, Newtown (9557 1206). CityRail Newtown. **Open** 9am-2.30am Mon; 9am-3.30am Tue-Thur; 9am-4.30am Fri, Sat; 10am-midnight Sun. **No credit cards**. **Map** p334

Along with the Zanzibar (née Oxford) and Bank Hotel, the Town Hall forms what the locals affectionately refer to as the Devil's Triangle of pubs near the junction of King Street and Enmore Road. All three are popular with students, the pierced, tattooed, dyed and branded, as well as the just plain reckless, but there's a kind of mojo at work at the Townie that sees its two floors of undistinguished wooden furniture and framed train-wreck photos play host to the sort of two-fisted drinking mayhem that make it a thing of beauty unto itself.

From little acorns mighty **Oaks** grow.

North Shore

Oaks

Corner of Military & Ben Boyd Roads, Neutral Bay (9953 5515/www.oakshotel.com.au). Bus 175, 178, 180, 243, 246, 247, 249, 263. **Open** 10am-midnight Mon-Wed; 10am-1.30am Thur-Sat; noon-midnight Sun. **Credit** AmEx, DC, MC, V.

Sydney's biggest pub? Quite possibly. A North Shore institution, the Oaks is beloved of locals young and old. The cook-your-own barbie may or may not be regarded as a plus, but the huge spreading namesake tree in the beer garden is lovely, and the fireplaces, bistro, pizzeria, innumerable bars and various other nooks are put to good use.

Northern Beaches

Manly Wharf Hotel

Manly Wharf, East Esplanade, Manly (9977 1266/ www.manlywharfhotel.com.au). Ferry Manly. **Open** *Main bar* 11.30am-midnight Mon-Fri; 11am-midnight Sat; 11am-10pm Sun. *Harbour bar* noon-midnight Mon-Sat; noon-10pm Sun. *Jetty bar* noon-10pm daily. *Lounge bar* 5pm-midnight Thur-Sat; 3-10pm Sun. **Credit** AmEx, DC, MC, V. **Map** p334

From the bamboo-screened cocktail bar to the main bar opening on to the large timber deck and the open-air jetty bar, the Manly Wharf Hotel is all about light, water and a fresh, contemporary look. There's a good range of well-priced margarita variants, summery stick drinks and classics. The Mod Oz restaurant is worth a gander too.

Newport Arms Hotel

Corner of Beaconsfield & Kalinya Streets, Newport (9997 4900/www.newportarms.com.au). Bus 188, 190, L88, L90. **Open** 10am-midnight Mon-Sat; 10am-10pm Sun. **Credit** AmEx, DC, MC, V.

This Newport landmark (est. 1880) has a mammoth beer garden out the back with a spectacular view over Pittwater and the eucalyptus-clad hills of Ku-ring-gai Chase National Park. It's the perfect spot for a post-beach beer and to contemplate your sunburn. Three restaurants, a vast outdoor screen and guest rooms are further attractions.

Shore Club

36-38 South Steyne, between the Corso and Wentworth Street, Manly (9977 6322/www. shoreclub.com.au). Ferry Manly. **Open** *Sand bar* 11.30am-midnight Mon-Wed; 11.30am-2am Thur-Sat; noon-midnight Sun. *Sound bar* 8pm-2am Fri, Sat; 7pm-midnight Sun. *Sun deck* 4pm-midnight Mon-Wed; 4pm-2am Thur, Fri; noon-2am Sat; noon-midnight Sun. **Credit** AmEx, MC, V. **Map** p334

The list is designed by bar guru Alex Swainston. The sun deck is as breezy, laid back and as cool a place as you can drink in. Get the Pimm's jug for $28 – bargain – or, if you're feeling serious and need a lift, the Mexican Pony Ride (tequila, orange blossom and chilli). Manly's looking up in bar land.

Shops & Services

Cool new designers are putting Sydney's shopping on the map.

Shopping is the latest sport to take hold in Sydney. Gone are the days when the city shifts to the beach at the weekend: nowadays, smart, sohisticated urbanites fill the streets and malls in search of chic new threads, cool homewares, jewels and bags.

Fortunately, the backbone of this burgeoning shopping boom is not the blood-sucking chain store, but a host of local talents prepared to put themselves on the line. Their lights shine most brightly in the rag trade, where old favourites like **Collette Dinnigan** (*see p194*), **Lisa Ho** (*see p194*) and **Akira Isogawa** (*see p195*) have paved the way for daring young designers such as **Kirrily Johnston** (*see p197*), **Jayson Brunsdon** (*see p197*) and the super-successful Sarah-Jane Clarke and Heidi Middleton of **Sass & Bide** (*see p198*).

The **CBD** is where visitors gravitate on their first visit, and where you'll find the biggest concentration of shops. A labyrinth of arcades and malls snakes around the centre via the corner of Bathurst and Kent Streets through to Town Hall Square, connecting George, Pitt

and Market Streets. Pedestrianised Pitt Street Mall (the section of Pitt Street between Market and King Streets) is a focal point, and leading department stores **David Jones** (*see p189*) and **Myer** (formerly Grace Bros; *see p190*) battle for supremacy on Market Street. A shiny new mall inside the **World Square** development (*see p191*) has boosted options near Chinatown.

If it's traditional souvenirs and duty-free you're after, head to the historic but touristy **Rocks** district, where upmarket fashion labels and didgeridoo shops line up for 21st-century tourist dollars – a far cry from the original slums and sluice of the 19th-century immigrants who used to live in this area.

City insiders make for Oxford Street, an epically long road that acts as a spine to surrounding Darlinghurst, Surry Hills and Paddington. The city end of Oxford Street, in **Darlinghurst**, is queer Sydney central with fetish and wig shops and music shops. In the **Paddington** area you'll find the flagships of the fashion chain stores, and at Glenmore Road and William Street, pretty boutiques harbouring smaller designers who have escaped being swallowed up by bigger brands. On Crown Street, heading south towards **Surry Hills**, offbeat clothing stores sit among the numerous restaurants and arty cafés.

In **Double Bay**, ladies who lunch browse middle-of-the-road designer fashion in between stops at the area's many good eateries. **Woollahra**'s Queen Street boasts some excellent antique shops, upmarket clothes shops and delicatessens, the high prices reflecting the privilege of living in the postcode. Across the Harbour Bridge, **Neutral Bay** and **Mosman** have everything a middle-class family could need, including homewares, high-end fabric shops, kids' clothes and fashion.

On the west side of the CBD lie the suburbs of Balmain, Rozelle, Leichhardt and Glebe, all of which have become increasingly gentrified as families move out of the eastern suburbs in the hunt for reasonably priced property. Darling Street is **Balmain**'s main drag and caters for the area's funky, upwardly mobile young families. Further up Darling Street in **Rozelle**, the spending changes gear with interesting bric-a-brac stores and organic produce. In **Leichhardt**, revel in Italian fashion on Norton

The best Shops

For all-in-one shopping
David Jones (*see p189*), Queen Victoria Building (*see p191*) and Westfield Bondi Junction (*see p191*).

For cool cossies
Lisa Ho (*see p197*), Rip Curl (*see p201*) and Zimmerman (*see p198*).

For foodies
David Jones' food hall (*see p189*), Fratelli Fresh (*see p206*) and Simon Johnson Quality Foods (*see p206*).

For funky jewellery
Dinosaur Designs (*see p208*), Melissa Harris Jewellery (*see p202*) and Family Jewels (*see p203*).

For the latest international mags, comics and newspapers
Borders (*see p194*) and Kinokuniya (*see p190*).

Street and at the **Italian Forum** (*see p190*) complex of shops and eateries.

Backpacker-friendly Glebe Point Road in **Glebe** has numerous second-hand booksellers amid cafés, pubs and health-food shops. Further south, King Street is the main thoroughfare in studenty, multicultural **Newtown**, and home to well-priced furniture shops, great vinyl outlets and loads of vintage clothing shops.

For the best swim- and surfwear head over to **Bondi Beach** and **North Bondi**, where you can also find good vintage clothing shops and ultra-trendy boutiques. Nearby Bondi Junction offers an entirely different vibe, centred around the massive **Westfield Bondi Junction** mall (*see p191*). It's got the major brands and a few exclusives, plus a multi-screen cinema and an excellent food court with sensational views of the Harbour. The Westfield overshadows the shops that were here before the development, but some are still worth checking out – there's a good cobbler on Oxford Street and other stores geared towards budget-conscious families. Look out for cheap second-hand furniture and electrical goods in the area too.

OPENING HOURS

Shops open between 9am and 10am and close between 5.30pm and 6pm Monday to Friday, except for Thursday, when most mainstream shopping areas stay open until around 9pm. On Saturday most places tend to shut pretty sharpish between 5pm and 6pm. Sunday trading is the norm, with most shops open between 11am and 4pm, or 5pm in the summer – though hours can vary quite a bit.

Sale time is usually at the end of summer and of winter, but department stores also hold sales to coincide with public holidays. The big ones to watch out for are David Jones's twice-yearly clearances at the end of June and after Christmas, and Myer's Boxing Day sale.

What you see on the price tag is what you pay; it includes GST (Goods & Services Tax). For details of how to reclaim your GST when you fly out, *see p304*.

General

Department stores

David Jones

Market Street, at Castlereagh Street; Elizabeth Street, at Market Street, CBD (9266 5544/www. davidjones.com.au). CityRail St James or Town Hall/Monorail City Centre. **Open** 9.30am-6pm Mon-Wed; 9.30am-9pm Thur; 9.30am-7pm Fri; 9am-7pm Sat; 10am-6pm Sun. **Credit** AmEx, DC, MC, V. **Map** p327 F6.

Opened in 1838 by its Welsh-born namesake, David Jones is the oldest department store in the world still to be trading under its original name. The flagship city-centre store is on two sites at the junction of Market and Castlereagh Streets, linked by a first-floor walkway. The Market Street store has three

Perfect pitch: leading department store **David Jones**.

Eat, Drink, Shop

enswear, plus furniture, homewares and
goods. There's a gourmet food hall with an
nt noodle bar, a champagne and oyster bar, a
bar and much more on the lower ground floor
well as a stationer's and a cosmetics section
although the main one is on the ground floor, along
with jewellery and accessories). More cosmetics, perfumes, jewellery and accessories are on the ground
floor of the Elizabeth Street store. Above them are
four floors of women's fashion, including a good
range of international designers.
Other locations Westfield Bondi Junction (9619
1111); see website for other suburban locations.

Myer

*436 George Street, at Market Street, CBD (9238
9111/www.myer.com.au). CityRail St James or Town
Hall/Monorail City Centre.* **Open** 9am-6pm Mon-
Wed, Sat; 9am-9pm Thur; 9am-7pm Fri; 10am-6pm
Sun. **Credit** AmEx, DC, MC, V. **Map** p327 F6.
In 2004 Sydney institution Grace Bros changed its
name to Myer in one of the biggest rebrandings in
Australian history, although it had been owned by
Coles Myer since 1983. Sidney Myer was a penniless
Russian immigrant who opened his first store in
Bendigo, Victoria. Now, along with David Jones (*see
p189*), Myer is one of the two leading department
stores in the country. It positions itself as providing
something for everyone, stocking a good range of
clothes, homewares, electrical goods and cosmetics.
The brands tend to be a little cheaper than at David
Jones, but everything is good quality and some
designer brands are still there.
Other locations Westfield Bondi Junction (9300
1100); Westfield Parramatta (8831 3100); see website
for other suburban locations.

Peter's of Kensington

*57 Anzac Parade, between Todman Avenue &
Alison Road, Kensington (9662 1099/www.petersof
kensington.com.au). Bus 390, 391, 392, 393, 394,
395, 396, 397, 398, 399.* **Open** 9.30am-5.30pm
Mon-Fri; 9.30am-5pm Sat. **Credit** AmEx, DC, MC, V.
This suburban emporium in a bubblegum-pink
building first opened its doors in 1977 and has been
winning fans ever since. Step inside and you'll see
it's packed to the rafters (literally) with homewares,
collectibles, luggage, high-class funky cookware,
trad children's toys, stationery and a good cosmetics section. Everything is at highly competitive
prices (eat your heart out, David Jones and Myer).

Malls

Chifley Plaza

*2 Chifley Square, corner of Hunter & Phillip Streets,
CBD (9221 6111/www.chifleyplaza.com.au). CityRail
Martin Place.* **Map** p327 F5.
Chic business workers shop at this New York-style
tower complex, which sells designer labels such as
MaxMara, Pierucci and Leona Edmiston. There's
also a food court, not to mention the excellent
Japanese restaurant Azuma (*see p143*).

Kinokuniya at **Galeries Victoria**.

Galeries Victoria

*500 George Street, at Park Street, CBD (9265
6888/www.tgv.com.au). CityRail Town Hall/
Monorail Galeries Victoria.* **Map** p329 F7.
Designed by the award-winning firm of Sydney
architects, Crone Associates, the Tokyo-esque four-
level Galeries Victoria is a welcome relief from the
nearby identikit Pitt Street malls. Here you'll find
Mooks, MNG and Freedom Furniture, as well as cosmetics boutique Mecca Cosmetica and a branch of
Wagamama. Worth a special trip, particularly for
language students, is Kinokuniya, on Level 2,
Sydney's largest cross-cultural book shop, with titles
in English, Japanese, Chinese, French and German.

Harbourside

*Darling Drive, Darling Harbour (9281 3999/
www.harbourside.com.au). CityRail Town Hall/
ferry Darling Harbour/Monorail Harbourside.*
Map p326 D6.
This glitzy shopping centre on the Pyrmont side of
Darling Harbour has been refurbished with a slick
fresh food precinct and food court. The shops,
including a good clutch that sell Australian products, are open until 9pm daily to attract as many
tourists as possible after a day's sightseeing – but
don't expect to nab a bargain. The new entertainment floor on Level 3 includes a 20-lane Kingpin
Bowling Lounge (www.kingpinbowling.com.au)
and Australia's first Boeing 737-800 airplane flight

simulator, Flight Experience (www.flightexperience.
com.au). You get two hours free parking if you spend
$40 at any of the shops in the centre.

Imperial Arcade
*168 Pitt Street Mall, between King & Market Streets,
CBD (9233 5662/www.imperialarcade.com.au).
CityRail Martin Place, St James or Town Hall/
Monorail City Centre.* **Map** p327 F6.
One of four arcades running off pedestrianised Pitt
Street Mall (the others are the Mid City Centre,
Skygarden and Strand Arcade), Imperial Arcade has
three levels of fashion, accessories, jewellery, cafés,
hair, beauty and services. Check out super-cheap
teenage-chic fashion at Supre and bargain basics at
Cotton On. There's also an Angus & Robertson
bookshop and Lincraft for haberdashery and crafts.

Italian Forum
*23 Norton Street, between Parramatta Road &
Marion Street, Leichhardt (9518 3396/www.the
italianforum.com). Bus 435, 436, 437, 438, 440,
445, L38, L40.*
A mall modelled on an Italian village complete with
Romanesque piazza? Not as bad as it sounds, in fact.
This suburban square of upmarket shops, restaurants, cafés and apartments does a good job of con-
juring up an authentic taste of Italy. Check out the
Merchant of Venice, where everything, from carnival masks to Murano glass, is imported from Venice,
and Marles Jewellers, with Italian white and yellow
gold pieces and Zoppini stainless steel jewellery
from Florence. For the cultural consumer, there's a
statue of Dante in the main piazza.

Queen Victoria Building (QVB)
*455 George Street, between Market & Druitt Streets,
CBD (9264 9209/www.qvb.com.au). CityRail Town
Hall/Monorail Galeries Victoria.* **Map** p327 E6.
The elegant, airy Victorian halls of this historic
building pull in the tourist dollars, but there are plenty of places for Sydneysiders to shop as well. You'll
find designer labels, fashion chain stores, shoe
shops, florists and chocolate shops on the ground
floor, and arts, antiques and Australiana on level
two. The lower ground level links through to the
Town Hall Square shops and station, along with the
Galeries Victoria shopping centre.

Skygarden
*77 Castlereagh Street, between King & Market
Streets, CBD (9231 1811/www.skygarden.com.au).
CityRail Martin Place, St James or Town
Hall/Monorail City Centre.* **Map** p327 F6.
Sportsgirl and a decent-sized Borders bookshop are
the main draws on the ground floor of this centre
running between Pitt Street Mall and Castlereagh
Street. The first and second floors are home to some
quality shoe shops and men's tailoring establish-
ments – for a bit of panache in your pinstripe, try
Antons on Level 1. You can also connect to the
Glasshouse arcade, which houses Pacific East India
Co, stocking exotic homewares, and where glam
girls will love the Holly Golightly boutique.

Strand Arcade
*412-414 George Street, between King & Market
Streets, CBD (9232 4199/www.strandarcade.
com.au). CityRail MartinPlace, St James or Town
Hall/Monorail City Centre.* **Map** p327 F6.
This beautiful arcade is as historic as the Queen
Victoria Building, but a hundred times cooler. There
are the all-but obligatory touristy shops, such as
Haigh's Chocolates and Strand Hatters, on the
ground floor, but venture upwards and you'll discover the darlings of the Australian fashion scene,
including Leona Edmiston, Lisa Ho, Wayne Cooper,
Third Millennium, Bettina Liano, Zimmermann,
Little Joe by Gail Elliott, Terry Biviano and Dinosaur
Designs. The prices continue to escalate as you
move up again – check out the divine Alex Perry
and sleek Jayson Brunsdon.

Sydney Central Plaza
*450 George Street, at Market Street, CBD (8224
2000/www.westfield.com.au). CityRail Town Hall or
St James/Monorail City Centre.* **Map** p327 F6.
Department store Myer (*see p190*), which was formerly known as Grace Bros, dominates Sydney
Central Plaza, but there are plenty of other decent
shops worth visiting. For fashion, check out Sydney
designer Morrissey, as well as Saba and the excellent chain store Witchery. The international food
court on the lower ground floor is one of the city's
best, and stays open until 10pm on Thursdays.

Westfield Bondi Junction
*500 Oxford Street, at Grosvenor Street, Bondi
Junction (9947 8000/www.westfield.com.au).
CityRail Bondi Junction/bus 333, 352, 378, 380.*
Map p333 P11.
Love it or hate it, you can't ignore the Westfield
Bondi Junction (popularly known as the WBJ, of
course), Sydney's largest and chicest shopping cen-
tre. Its roster of shops includes department stores
Myer and David Jones, supermarkets Coles and
Woolworths, chain stores Target, Country Road,
Borders and the Body Shop, plus around 450 spe-
ciality shops, an 11-screen cinema, 3,300 car park-
ing spaces and a food court with some of the best
views of Sydney Harbour. Phew!

World Square
*Corner of Liverpool, George, Goulburn & Pitt
Streets, CBD (8669 6900/www.worldsquare.com.au).
CityRail Central or Town Hall/LightRail Central.*
Map p329 E/F8.
This office, residential, hotel and retail development,
which covers an entire block at the Central Station
end of the CBD, has more than 90 fashion, lifestyle
and homeware shops, medical centres, travel agents,
bars and restaurants, and a big Coles supermarket.
The emphasis here is generally on commercial
affordability rather than top-of-the-range designer
chic, so there's Pulp Footwear, Hype DC teenage
fashion, Rebel Sport and some mid-range furniture
stores like Dare Gallery. You'll also find a Toni &
Guy hairdressers and Napoleon Perdis Cosmetics.

40 RESTAURANTS, 12 PUBS, 10 BARS EAT HAPPILY EVER AFTER

The Rocks

A STORY AROUND EVERY CORNER

THEROCKS.COM

The Rocks is home to some of Sydney's newest, best restaurants in Sydney's oldest, best location. Explore everything from artefacts found in archaeological dig sites to museums and modern art galleries. Crafts, fashion, speciality shops and even high adventure – all of this surrounded by the most beautiful harbour in the world.

Markets

Most Sydney markets are held in schools or church grounds. Be prepared to try things on in the toilets, and leave your credit cards at home as cash is preferred.

Balmain

St Andrew's Church, corner of Darling Street & Curtis Road, Balmain (9555 1791/www.balmain market.com). Ferry Balmain or Balmain East/bus 442, 445. **Open** 8.30am-4pm Sat.
Artists sell paintings and ceramics in this pretty market in the grounds of a charming 19th-century church. You'll also find good-quality vintage jewellery, hammocks, naturally-made cosmetics and organic fruit and veg. Check out the enamelled organ pipes inside the church before you leave.

Bondi Beach

Bondi Beach Public School, corner of Campbell Parade & Warners Avenue, Bondi Beach (9315 8988/www.bondimarkets.com.au). CityRail Bondi Junction then bus 333, 380, 381, 382/bus 380, 333. **Open** 10am-5pm Sun. **Map** p334.
The beautiful Bondi primp and pose among the stalls of the emerging generation of Aussie fashion designers. The market can get crowded and hot, but it's worth a visit if you're after either new or vintage clothing, and there's also an excellent flower stall.

Glebe

Glebe Public School, Glebe Point Road, between Mitchell Street & Parramatta Road, Glebe (4237 7499). Bus 370, 431, 432, 433, 434. **Open** 10am-4pm Sat. **Map** p328 B9.
This used to be the most feral of Sydney's markets, but it's becoming smarter as the area gentrifies. All the same, it still features second-hand clothing, kooky jewellery and New-Agey stalls with lots of crystals, plus some good crafts and bookshops. The food stalls are excellent too.

Kirribilli

Bradfield Park, Alfred Street, at Burton Street, Milsons Point (9922 4428/www.kncsydney.org). CityRail/ferry Milsons Point. **Open** 7am-3pm 4th Sat of the mth; extra markets on 1st & 3rd Sat in Dec.
This monthly market specialises in bric-a-brac and antiques, but you'll also find some great vintage dress stalls and original jewellery.

Paddington

Paddington Uniting Church, 395 Oxford Street, at Newcombe Street, Paddington (9331 2923/www.paddingtonmarkets.com.au). Bus 333, 352, 378, 380. **Open** 10am-4pm Sat. **Map** p332 L10.
This is the centre of Paddo shopping activity on a Saturday. Many a big-name fashion designer began by selling here. There are also masses of jewellery makers, ceramicists and artisans selling their wares, plus multicultural food stalls. The market makes a nice break from the air-conditioned stores on Oxford Street, but it does tend to get packed.

Paddy's

Market City, corner of Hay & Thomas Streets, Haymarket (1300 361589/www.paddysmarkets.com.au). CityRail Central or Town Hall/Monorail/LightRail Paddy's Markets. **Open** 9am-5pm Thur-Sun. **Map** p329 E8.
Paddy's covered labyrinth of more than 1,000 stalls caters to bargain-hunting families and backpackers. Expect kooky Asian clothing, shoes, CDs, electronics and fruit and veg – all at cheap, cheap prices.

Rocks

North Precinct, George Street & Playfair Street, The Rocks (Sydney Harbour Foreshore Authority 1300 655995/www.rocksmarket.com). CityRail/ferry Circular Quay. **Open** 10am-5pm Sat, Sun. **Map** p327 F3.
Mainly quality arts, crafts, homewares, antiques and collectibles, with lots of stalls selling indigenous craft and souvenirs. You might spot a bargain or two in among the tourist prices.

Surry Hills

Shannon Reserve, corner of Crown Street & Foveaux Street, Surry Hills (9310 2888). CityRail/Light Rail Central. **Open** 10am-5pm 1st Sat of mth. **Map** p329 G10.
Still the hippest of all of the city's many weekend markets. There's lots to catch the eye in the form of clothes, accessories and good junk. This is also where you'll find retro revivals before anyone else realises they are fashionable.

Specialist

Books & magazines

Dymocks (www.dymocks.com.au) is Sydney's best-established bookshop chain, and also features excellent stationery and travel sections. It has branches all over town, including a big one at 424 George Street (between King & Market Streets, CBD, 9235 0155). There are also a number of outlets of the nationwide chain **Angus & Robertson** (www.angusrobertson.com.au), including one on the Corso in Manly (No.24, 9976 3188).

Ariel

42 Oxford Street, between Barcom Avenue & West Street, Paddington (9332 4581/www.arielbooks.com.au). Bus 333, 352, 378, 380. **Open** 9am-midnight daily. **Credit** AmEx, DC, MC, V. **Map** p329 H9.
Situated opposite NSW University College of Fine Art, Ariel stocks gorgeous hardback art, design, photography, fashion and contemporary culture books, most of which come with price tags to match their high production values. However, the laid-back staff are happy for you to leaf through for as long as you like. The store also sells magazines.
Other locations 103 George Street, (9241 5622).

Berkelouw Books

19 Oxford Street, between South Dowling Street & Greens Road, Paddington (9360 3200/www.berkelouw.com.au). Bus 333, 352, 378, 380. **Open** 9am-11pm Mon-Thur, Sun; 9am-midnight Fri, Sat. **Credit** AmEx, DC, MC, V. **Map** p329 H9.

More or less opposite Ariel, Berkelouw has an intriguing selection of new and antique Australiana and assorted rare books. It's also right next to the Palace art-house cinemas (*see p228*) and has a café upstairs, both of which go towards making it a great place to grab a soy latte and a yummy slice of organic toasted banana bread before the movie. Note that the other branches have shorter opening hours.
Other locations 70 Norton Street, Leichhardt (9560 3200); 708 New South Head Road, Rose Bay (9371 5500); 12-14 Park Street, Mona Vale (9979 2112).

Bookshop Darlinghurst

207 Oxford Street, between Flinders & South Dowling Streets, Darlinghurst (9331 1103/ www.thebookshop.com.au). Bus 352, 378, 380. **Open** 10am-10pm Mon-Wed; 10am-11pm Thur; 10am-midnight Fri, Sat; 11am-11pm Sun. **Credit** AmEx, DC, MC, V. **Map** p329 H9.

Bookshop Darlinghurst specialises in gay and lesbian literature, but also stocks a range of rare imported books, as well as mainstream books that cater for hip inner-city dwellers. The staff are exceptionally knowledgeable.

Borders

Skygarden, 77 Castlereagh Street, between King & Market Streets, CBD (9235 2433/www.borders.com.au). CityRail Martin Place, St James or Town Hall/Monorail City Centre. **Open** 9am-7pm Mon-Wed, Fri; 9am-9.30pm Thur; 9am-6.30pm Sat; 10am-6pm Sun. **Credit** AmEx, DC, MC, V. **Map** p327 E6.

The US monster book chain is well represented in Sydney with one huge store in the city, plus others in Bondi Junction, Parramatta, Chatswood and the 'burbs. The shops are typically capacious, and many have coffee shops, not to mention Sydney's most comprehensive selection of international magazines.
Other locations Westfield Bondi Junction (9389 2200); Westfield Parramatta (9687 3388); Westfield Chatswood (9415 4800); see website for other suburban locations.

Gleebooks

49 Glebe Point Road, between Cowper & Francis Streets, Glebe (9660 2333/www.gleebooks.com.au). Bus 370, 431, 432, 433 434. **Open** 9am-9pm daily. **Credit** AmEx, DC, MC, V. **Map** p328 B9.

Highly rated Gleebooks has two branches on Glebe Point Road alone. No.191 specialises in second-hand and children's books, as well as more esoteric works on the humanities. No.49 sells everything else. The theatre shop in Walsh Bay opens around performance times to catch the luvvies.
Other locations 191 Glebe Point Road, Glebe (9552 2526); Sydney Theatre, 22 Hickson Road, Opposite Pier 6/7, Walsh Bay (9250 1930).

Map World

280 Pitt Street, between Park & Bathurst Streets, CBD (9261 3601/www.mapworld.net.au). CityRail Town Hall/Monorail Galeries Victoria. **Open** 9am-5.30pm Mon-Wed, Fri; 9am-6.30pm Thur; 10am-4pm Sat. **Credit** AmEx, MC, V. **Map** p329 F7.

As you might have guessed, Map World sells road maps for the whole of Australia, as well as travel guides, atlases and books about such outdoor activities as four-wheel-driving and rock climbing.
Other locations 136 Willoughby Road, Crows Nest (9966 5770).

Second-hand

See also above **Berkelouw Books** *and* **Gleebooks**.

Goulds

32 King Street, between Queen & Fitzroy Streets, Newtown (9519 8947/www.gouldsbooks.com.au). Bus 352, 422, 423, 426, 428. **Open** 8am-midnight daily. **Credit** AmEx, MC, V. **Map** p334.

Around 3,000m (9,000ft) of bookshelves make this the largest second-hand bookshop in Sydney. It's a librarian's nightmare, but worth the rummage; you never know what serendipity might reveal. And it's open until midnight. It specialises in Australian history and politics, plus general Australiana.

Sappho Books

51 Glebe Point Road, between Cowper & Francis Streets, Glebe (9552 4498/www.sapphobooks.com.au). Bus 370, 431, 432, 433, 434. **Open** 8am-9pm Mon-Sat; 9am-7pm Sun. **Credit** AmEx, DC, MC, V. **Map** p329 B9.

A popular, friendly and immaculately catalogued second-hand bookshop that offers something for every bookworm – from Australian first editions and leather-bound tomes to art books and the latest kiddie's classic. There's also a comfortable café at the rear, with a lovely big courtyard.

Children

Fashion

Bonds (www.bonds.com.au), **Gumboots** (www.gumboots.com.au) and **Fred Bare** (www.fredbare.com) are good Australian brands; look for them at David Jones (*see p189*) and Myer (*see p190*). **Cotton On** (www.cottonon.com.au) also has very cute children's clothes at great prices. Or try the markets (*see p193*) for something more original – Bondi, Balmain and Paddington markets are particularly good.

Toys

Both **David Jones** (*see p189*) and **Myer** (*see p190*) have good toy departments.

Electronics

Isenberg M10 Handy

347 Oxford Street, at William Street, Paddington (9331 4689/www.mitre10.com.au). Bus 333, 352, 378, 380. **Open** 7.30am-5.30pm Mon-Fri; 8am-4pm Sat; 9am-4pm Sun. **Credit** AmEx, MC, V. **Map** p332 K10.

Compact version of the huge Mitre 10 chain, which has most of what you need for home improvements and caters to electrical work of any kind.

Fashion

Australian designers

For the latest Aussie fashion names, *see p198* **From rags to riches**.

Akira Isogawa

12A Queen Street, at Oxford Street, Woollahra (9361 5221/www.akira.com.au). Bus 333, 352, 378, 380. **Open** 10.30am-6pm Mon-Wed, Fri; 10.30am-7pm Thur; 10am-6pm Sat; 11am-4pm Sun. **Credit** AmEx, MC, V. **Map** p332 L11.

Akira is known for his romantic, other-worldy multi-layering of transparent fabrics and bold colours. The shop has been in Woollahra since 1993, and his garments are now sold in fashion epicentres across the globe. If you're a follower of original and high-end designs, he's well worth checking out.
Other locations Strand Arcade, CBD (9232 1078).

Alannah Hill

118-120 Oxford Street, at Glenmore Road, Paddington (9380 9147/www.alannahhill.com.au). Bus 333, 352, 378, 380. **Open** 10am-6pm Mon-Wed, Fri, Sat; 10am-8pm Thur; 11am-6pm Sun. **Credit** AmEx, DC, MC, V. **Map** p332 J9.

Melbourne designer Alannah Hill has cornered the market in flirty feminine styles. The vintage-doll-like shop assistants look like they're having as much fun trying on the rich fabrics, velvet trims, lace and feathered hats as the customers. A good place to buy race-day accessories.
Other locations Strand Arcade, CBD (9221 1251), Westfield Bondi Junction (9389 3066); Chatswood Chase Shopping Centre, Chatswood (9413 2755).

Charlie Brown

178 Oxford Street, opposite Victoria Barracks, Paddington (9360 9001/www.charliebrown.com.au). Bus 333, 352, 378, 380. **Open** 10am-6pm Mon-Wed, Fri, Sat; 10am-8pm Thur; 11am-5pm Sun. **Credit** AmEx, DC, MC, V. **Map** p332 J9.

American-born Charlie Brown provides flamboyant, innovative clothes for women who are sick and tired of trying to fit in to the stick-insect sizes provided by other designers. She's one of the doyennes of Australia's fashion scene, and both Jade Jagger and Jerry Hall have modelled at her shows. Also stocked are the Howard Showers label, plus vintage accessories and costume jewellery.

Fun, flirty styles at **Alannah Hill**.

Kidstuff

126A Queen Street, between Moncur & Ocean Streets, Woollahra (9363 2838/www.kidstuff. com.au). Bus 389. **Open** 9am-5.30pm Mon-Sat; 9am-4pm Sun. **Credit** AmEx, MC, V. **Map** p333 M10.

Wooden toys and doll's houses that are likely to last considerably longer than today's plastic tat, as well as educational toys for children of all ages.
Other locations 774-776 Military Road, Mosman (9960 3222).

Electronics & photography

Cameras & photo developing

Paxtons

285 George Street, at Hunter Street, CBD (9299 2999/www.paxtons.com.au). CityRail Wynyard. **Open** 8am-6pm Mon-Wed, Fri; 8am-8pm Thur; 9am-4pm Sat; 10am-3.30pm Sun. **Credit** AmEx, DC, MC, V. **Map** p327 F5.

Sydney's largest independent camera retailer stocks a fine range of digital cameras, SLRs, video cameras, lenses, audio gear and more. Don't be shy about asking for a discount: staff are keen to outprice competitors. Processing also available.
Other locations Westfield Bondi Junction (9389 6100); Westfield Chatswood (9413 1144); Westfield Parramatta (9635 9696); see website for other suburban locations.

Collette Dinnigan

*33 William Street, off Oxford Street, Paddington
(9360 6691/www.collettedinnigan.com.au). Bus 333,
352, 378, 380.* **Open** 10am-6pm Mon-Sat; noon-5pm
Sun. **Credit** AmEx, DC, MC, V. **Map** p332 K10.
Models about to get married and celebs in need of a
sensational gown to wear on the red carpet love
Dinnigan's exquisite beading and sensual embroi-
dery. Collette has recently launched a children's
range, which is very cute if money is no object.

Easton Pearson

*18 Elizabeth Street, between Oxford & Underwood
Streets, Paddington (9331 4433/www.eastonpearson.
com). Bus 333, 352, 378, 380.* **Open** 10am-6pm
Mon-Sat. **Credit** AmEx, MC, V. **Map** p332 L10.
Beautiful fabrics and unusual textiles are the go with
dynamic design duo Pamela Eston and Lydia
Pearson, who take their influences – and a lot of their
materials – from India, Africa, Mexico and
Polynesia. Their attention to the smallest details –
buttons, stitching – is what defines their special
style. You can wear one of their shirts or skirts for
years and it will always look new and surprising.

Jayson Brunsdon

*Strand Arcade, 412-414 George Street, between
King & Market Streets, CBD (9233 8891/www.
jaysonbrunsdon.com). CityRail MartinPlace, St James
or Town Hall/Monorail City Centre.* **Open** 9.30am-
5.30pm Mon-Wed, Fri; 9.30am-8pm Thur; 9.30-4pm
Sat. **Credit** AmEx, DC, MC, V. **Map** p327 F6.
He may seem like the new kid on the block, but
Brunsdon has been in the fashion industry for 20
years, first as an illustrator and fashion editor, then
as creative director of Morrissey; he then went on to
launch his own label. He likes to work with bold
colours and shapes that accentuate a woman's figure and stand out in a crowd – the resulting creations are real event pieces.

Kirrily Johnston

*6 Glenmore Road, at Hopewell Lane, Paddington
(9380 7775/www.kirrilyjohnston.com). Bus 333,
352, 378, 380.* **Open** 10am-6pm Mon-Wed, Fri, Sat;
10am-7pm Fri; 11am-5pm Sun. **Credit** AmEx, MC,
V. **Map** p332 J9.
Kirrily Johnston stormed onto the Australian fashion scene a few years back. Her bold sassy use of
colour and lush fabrics blend with genuinely comfortable designs meaning you don't have to be a
stick model to wear her clothes. But watch out: the
price tag can carry quite a sting.

Ksubi

*82 Gould Street, between Hall & Curlewis Streets,
Bondi Beach (9300 8233/www.ksubi.com). CityRail
Bondi Junction then bus 380, 381, 382, 333/bus
222, 380, 333.* **Open** 10am-6pm Mon-Wed, Fri, Sat;
10am-7pm Thur; 11am-6pm Sun. **Credit** AmEx, MC,
V. **Map** p334.
Sydney surfer boys Dan Single, George Gorrow and
Gareth Moody launched their brand (then called
Tsubi) at Australian Fashion Week 2001. Since then

they've made a name with ultra-cool jeans and Ts,
while making headlines with quirky shows.
Other locations 16 Glenmore Road, Paddington
(9361 6291).

Leona Edmiston

*88 William Street, off Oxford Street, Paddington
(9331 7033/www.leonaedmiston.com.au). Bus 333,
352, 378, 380.* **Open** 10am-6pm Mon-Fri; 10am-5pm
Sat; noon-4pm Sun. **Credit** AmEx, DC, MC, V.
Map p332 K10.
Sydneysider Leona Edmiston once teamed up with
Morrissey, but she set up on her own in 2001. Now
her designs couldn't be more different, with a fun
and flirty collection of pretty frocks and fabulous
accessories. Chic and cheeky femininity is the thing
here, with delicate prints and flattering cuts.
Other locations throughout the city.

Lisa Ho

*Corner of Oxford & Queen Streets, Woollahra (9360
2345/www.lisaho.com.au). Bus 333, 352, 378, 380.*
Open 10am-6pm Mon-Wed, Fri; 10am-8pm Thur;
10am-5pm Sat; 11am-5pm Sun. **Credit** AmEx, MC,
V. **Map** p332 L11.
If the prices at Collette Dinnigan seem a little steep,
try equally luxurious Lisa Ho. When Australian
actress Sarah Wynter wore one of Ho's creations to
the Emmy awards ceremony back in 2004, regard
for the designs became international. Stretch fabrics,
silk and sheer chiffon are beaded and pleated with
gorgeous results. Great swimwear too.
Other locations Strand Arcade, CBD (9222 9711);
Chatswood Chase Shopping Centre, Chatswood (9411
8442); Castle Towers Shopping Centre, Castle Hill
(9659 9459).

Morrissey

*372 Oxford Street, between Elizabeth Street & Jersey
Road, Paddington (9380 7422/www.morrissey.
net.au). Bus 333, 352, 378, 380.* **Open** 9.30am-
5.30pm Mon-Wed, Fri, Sat; 9.30am-8pm Thur; 11am-
5pm Sun. **Credit** AmEx, MC, V. **Map** p332 L10.
Peter Morrissey began his fashion career with Leona
Edmiston (*see above*), and together they created the
Morrissey Edmiston label, a hit for 14 years. His
designs are classically styled, with vibrant colours.
Good contemporary tailoring for men and women.
Other locations throughout the city.

RM Williams

*389 George Street, between King & Market Streets,
CBD (9262 2228/www.rmwilliams.com). CityRail
Martin Place, St James or Town Hall/Monorail City
Centre.* **Open** 8.30am-6pm Mon-Wed, Fri; 8.30am-
9pm Thur; 9am-5pm Sat; 11am-5pm Sun. **Credit**
AmEx, DC, MC, V. **Map** p327 E/F6.
Reginald Murray Williams and his pardner Dollar
Mick started out as a 'bush outfitters' in South
Australia in the early 1930s. Now their clothes are
more likely to be seen on urban cowboys than the
hard-riding jackaroos they were first designed for.
Boots and moleskins are the staple, but you can also
get good-quality shirts, knits and shorts for men.
Other locations throughout the city.

Eat, Drink, Shop

Sass & Bide

132 Oxford Street, between Glenmore & Shadforth Streets, Paddington (9360 3900/www.sassand bide.com.au). Bus 333, 352, 378, 380. **Open** 10am-6pm Mon-Wed, Fri, Sat; 10am-8pm Thur; 11am-5pm Sun. **Credit** AmEx, DC, MC, V. **Map** p332 J9.

Sarah-Jane 'Sass' Clarke and Heidi 'Bide' Middleton started selling clothes on London's Portobello Road, but struck gold when they made international headlines with their sexy, skinny low-rise jeans. This concept store is one of two in the world devoted to their label (the other is in Brisbane), though you'll find their clothes in department stores and boutiques.

Scanlan & Theodore

122 Oxford Street, at Glenmore Street, Paddington (9380 9388/www.scanlantheodore.com.au). Bus 352, 378, 380, L82. **Open** 10am-6pm Mon-Wed, Fri; 10am-8pm Thur; 10am-5.30pm Sat; noon-5pm Sun. **Credit** AmEx, DC, MC, V. **Map** p332 J9.

If you love fashion and can only make it to one Aussie designer, make it Scanlan & Theodore. Gary Theodore and Fiona Scanlan use outrageously luxurious fabrics with creative but classy colours. **Other locations** Chatswood Chase Shopping Centre, Chatswood (9410 1711).

Wheels & Doll Baby

259 Crown Street, at Goulburn Street, Darlinghurst (9361 3286/www.wheelsanddollbaby.com). CityRail Museum/bus 373, 374, 377, 378, 380. **Open** 10am-6pm Mon-Wed, Fri, Sat; 10am-8pm Thur; 11am-5pm Sun. **Credit** AmEx, DC, MC, V. **Map** p329 G8.

Melanie Greensmith started her vampy fashion label in 1987. Her clothes became synonymous with all things rock when Michael Jackson came in browsing for a customised leather jacket for his Bad tour. Now rockers such as Debbie Harry and the Black Crowes wear her styles on stage.

Zimmermann

387 Oxford Street, opposite William Street, Paddington (9357 4700/www.zimmermannwear. com). Bus 333, 352, 378, 380. **Open** 10am-6pm Mon-Wed, Fri; 10am-8pm Thur; 10am-5pm Sun. **Credit** AmEx, DC, MC, V. **Map** p332 K10.

Sisters Nicole and Simone Zimmermann launched this very successful label in the early 1990s. Swimwear has always been their calling card – bright, bold, contemporary designs for hip bodies – but they have cute dresses and tops too. **Other locations** Strand Arcade, CBD (9221 9558); Westfield Bondi Junction (9387 5111).

Boutiques

Belinda

8 Transvaal Avenue, off Cross Street, Double Bay (9328 6288/www.belinda.com.au). Ferry Double Bay/bus 323, 324, 325, 326. **Open** 10am-6pm Mon-Fri; 10am-5pm Sat. **Credit** AmEx, DC, MC, V. **Map** p331 N7.

The pick of the crop of exquisite fashion and beautiful accessories, both local and overseas, selected by the store's stylish namesake Belinda Seper, who was a model and is now an Australian fashion queen. Marni, Lanvin, Stella McCartney, Jimmy Choo, Dries Van Noten all feature. **Other locations** 39 William Street, Paddington (9380 8728); MLC Centre, CBD (9233 0781); Shoe Salon, 14 Transvaal Avenue, Double Bay (9327 8199).

Ben Sherman

Shop 3, 255C Oxford Street, between Oatley Road & William Street, Paddington (9360 3770/www. bensherman.com). Bus 333, 352, 378, 380. **Open** 10am-5.30pm Mon-Wed, Fri, Sat; 10am-8pm Thur; 11am-5pm Sun. **Credit** AmEx, MC, V. **Map** p332 K10.

The Brit Mod-inspired designer brings his unique brand of shirts and jackets to Sydney in a large and always busy funky flagship store. **Other locations** Sydney Arcade, 400 George Street, CBD (9222 1903).

Calibre

398 Oxford Street, between William & Elizabeth Streets, Paddington (9380 5993/www.calibreclothing. com.au). Bus 333, 352, 378, 380. **Open** 9.30am-6pm Mon-Wed, Fri; 9.30am-8pm Thur; 10am-6pm Sat; 11am-5pm Sun. **Credit** AmEx, MC, V. **Map** p332 K10.

Started from one shop in Melbourne, Calibre is a stylish menswear store stocking its own label alongside international brands. It's not all about the beautifully cut suits, however: look also at the cool knits and slick casualwear. **Other locations** 139 Elizabeth Street, CBD (9267 9321); Sydney Central Plaza, CBD (9223 8988); Westfield Bondi Junction (9369 2885).

Corner Shop

43 William Street, off Oxford Street, Paddington (9380 9828). Bus 333, 352, 378, 380. **Open** 10am-6pm Mon-Wed, Fri, Sat; 10am-7pm Thur; 10am-5.30pm Sun. **Credit** AmEx, DC, MC, V. **Map** p332 K10.

For this eclectic fashion venture, the Belinda team (*see above*) scours the world's international fashion fairs to bring back the hippest and brightest of the up-and-coming designers. It's also a good place to catch the newest Aussie names. **Other locations** Strand Arcade, CBD (9221 1788).

Ed Hardy

108 Oxford Street, between Hopewell Street & Glenmore Road, Paddington (9357 3150/www. edhardy.com.au). Bus 333, 352, 378, 380. **Open** 10am-7pm Mon-Wed, Fri, Sat; 10am-9pm Thur; 10am-6pm Sun. **Credit** AmEx, DC, MC, V. **Map** p332 J9.

A favourite with rock and pop stars around the world, the Ed Hardy store might be something of a Sydney newcomer, but it is already much-loved. Christian Audigier's T-shirts, jeans and children's clothes, based on the tattoo art of Ed Hardy, are all over the local party people.

Marcs

QVB, 455 George Street, between Market & Druitt Streets, CBD (9267 0823/www.marcs.com.au). CityRail Town Hall/Monorail Galeries Victoria. **Open** 9am-6pm Mon-Wed, Fri, Sat; 9am-9pm Thur; 11am-5pm Sun. **Credit** AmEx, DC, MC, V. **Map** p327 E6.

The Marcs label launched in the 1980s, when two designers had the idea to make men's shirts out of women's fabrics. Now it's a massively successful chain selling fashions for both sexes. It offers cool fashion basics using lots of colour, plus imports including Diesel and Citizens of Humanity.

Other locations 645 Military Road, Mosman (9968 1298); 270 Oxford Street, Paddington (9360 5238); Westfield Bondi Junction (9369 1733).

Paul & Joe

Westfield Bondi Junction, 500 Oxford Street, Bondi Junction (9386 0902/www.paulandjoe.com). CityRail Bondi Junction/bus 333, 352, 378, 380. **Open** 9.30am-7pm Mon-Wed, Fri, 9.30am-9pm Thur; 9.30am-6pm Sat; 10am-6pm Sun. **Credit** AmEx, DC, MC, V. **Map** p333 P11.

Parisian designer Sophie Albou's fashion label, named after her two sons, has a huge fan base over here, so she opened her own store in 2007. Sydney's cool set just can't get enough of her chic shirts and cool dresses. And the shop itself is like a little slice of the Rive Gauche, transplanted to the south.

Chain stores

Sydney has large branches of womenswear chain stores like **Country Road** (142 Pitt Street, CBD, 9394 1818, www.country road.com.au), which is excellent for basics; cheap and cheerful **Dotti** (356 Oxford Street, Paddington, 9332 1659, www.dotti.com.au); the funky, unique chain **Seduce** (Shop 1, The Ivy, 320-348 George Street, CBD, 9233 1888, www.

From rags to riches

More than anything else, it's the fashion industry that's booming in Australia. It's not due to cheap imports, but rather a groundswell of inspirational local talent. Australian designers like **Collette Dinnigan** (*see p194*) and **Lisa Ho** (*see p194*) have been creating a buzz in the front rows of global fashion shows for a while now, and Dinnigan even has her own London boutique in Chelsea. But it's in the high streets that these stars of the southern hem are really making their mark, with ultra-trendy department stores such as London's Harvey Nichols and New York's Bloomingdale's stocking up on Sydney's **Wheels & Doll Baby** (*see p198*), **Sass & Bide** (*see p198*) and **Ksubi** (*see p197*). Then there's **Alex Perry** (*see p101*) following in the footsteps of **Akira Isogawa** (*see p195*), cutting a swathe through Kuwait, Saudi Arabia, Hong Kong and Indonesia. Of course, international recognition (and the resulting lucrative global market) is what every young designer dreams of, but on their way to the top it's also exciting for Sydneysiders (and visitors) to be the first to snap up their designs. So start talent-spotting!

The heart of creative Australian fashion beats in Melbourne, but label lovers visiting Sydney for the first time are often surprised at the diversity of home-grown designers found here too. The CBD's **Strand Arcade** (*see p191*) is home to many of these names. For high-high-end party frocks, head to Alex Perry or **Jayson Brunsdon** (*see p197*), whose Audrey Hepburn-esque eveningwear is already a couture staple. Also in the arcade are some of the coolest names, including quirky **Leona Edmiston** (*see p195*), jeans goddess **Bettina Liano** (*see p191*) and super-sexy **Zimmermann** (*see p198*).

Newer to the scene are a clutch of designers who are on the brink of global recognition, but are still driving the fashion industry forward in their home country. The **Corner Shop** (*see p198*) in Paddington is a good starting point as it specialises in emerging Australian designers: it stocks Marnie Skillings' ladylike creations and Josh Goot's slinky jersey knits for men and women. Alice McCall's hippy-dippy floaty numbers and fab jeans are stocked at **David Jones** (*see p189*), while Lover can be found at hip boutiques like Darlinghurst's **Alfie's Friend Rolfe** (Shop 1, 221 Darlinghurst Road, 9361 0220). Also worth checking out are **Kirrily Johnston** (*see p197*), with bold silk frocks in her own store on Glenmore Road, and the feminine creations of **Fleur Wood**, in the Strand Arcade and also at 464 Oxford Street, Paddington (9380 9511).

The annual Rosemount Australian Fashion Week trade shows (Spring/Summer, held in April/May, and the Transseasonal shows in October) are key events for new designers. If you're in town at the time, it's worth checking out the fashion columns of the newpapers to discover the new hot young things

Eat, Drink, Shop

seduce.com.au); **Cue** (323 George Street, CBD, 9299 9933, www.cue.cc), stocking reliable work clothes, and **Sportsgirl** (Skygarden, 77 Castlereagh Street, CBD, 9223 8255, www. sportsgirl.com.au), where many girls spend their first pay cheque before graduating to the more grown-up **David Lawrence** (Westfield Bondi Junction, 9386 5583, www.david lawrence.com.au). **Witchery** (332 Oxford Street, Paddington, 9360 6934, www. witchery.com.au) offers well-priced designs that often copy the latest catwalk releases.

Fetish

House of Fetish
93 Oxford Street, between Crown & Riley Streets, Darlinghurst (9380 9042/www.houseoffetish. com.au). Bus 222, 311, 373, 377, 378, 380, 392, 394, 396, 397, 399. **Open** 10am-7pm Mon-Sat; noon-5pm Sun. **Credit** AmEx, DC, MC, V. **Map** p329 G8.
For purist goths and S&M dabblers. Here you'll find a great array of corsetry, latex, hosiery, men and women's clothing, plus spiky shoes and jewellery.

Radical Leather
Basement, 20 Hutchinson Street, Surry Hills (9331 7544/www.radical-leather.com). Bus 373, 377, 392, 394, 396, 397, 399. **Open** noon-6pm Wed-Fri; noon-4pm Sat. **Credit** AmEx, MC, V. **Map** p329 H10.
Sydney's leading leather bondage manufacturer and retailer of all things dungeon has been around since 1982 and offers the full works from gauntlets and hoods to meat tenderisers and harnesses.

Tool Shed
81 Oxford Street, between Crown & Riley Streets, Darlinghurst (9332 2792/www.toolshed.com.au). Bus 222, 311, 373, 377, 378, 380, 392, 394, 396, 397, 399. **Open** 10am-1am Mon-Thur, Sun; 10am-2pm Fri, Sat. **Credit** AmEx, DC, MC, V. **Map** p329 G9.
Should you feel the need for an extra-sexual accessory, head for Tool Shed, which stocks a vast range of appliances, protuberances and fetish wear. **Other locations** Basement, 191 Oxford Street, at Taylor Square, Darlinghurst (9360 1100).

Surfwear & swimwear

Aussie Boys
102 Oxford Street, between Crown & Palmer Streets, Darlinghurst (9360 7011/www.aussieboys.com.au). Bus 333, 352, 378, 380. **Open** 10am-6pm Mon-Wed, Fri, Sat; 10am-9pm Thur; 11am-5pm Sun. **Credit** AmEx, DC, MC, V. **Map** p329 G8.
A fun, friendly store selling beach towels from the cute Aussie Boys label, Dolce & Gabbana bathers and Bonds T-shirts; there's even a hair stylist downstairs. It's a one-stop shop for all that the smart gay man needs at the beach, and there are all sorts of underwear and jockstraps to investigate too.

Between the Flags
Opera Quays, East Circular Quay (9241 1603). CityRail/ferry Circular Quay. **Open** 9am-9pm Mon-Fri; 10am-9pm Sat, Sun. **Credit** AmEx, DC, MC, V. **Map** p327 G3/4.
Have fun on the beach and give something back to those iconic Aussie lifesavers. Ten per cent of the takings of these innovative swimwear shops goes to the Bondi Surf Bathers' Life Saving Club. The Opera Quays store has some fantastic maritime memorabilia, while the wood-lined Bondi branch has a ceiling in the shape of a boat's hull.
Other locations throughout the city.

Big Swim
74 Campbell Parade, between Lamrock Avenue & Hall Street, Bondi Beach (9365 4457/www.bigswim. com.au). CityRail Bondi Junction then bus 333, 380, 381, 382/bus 222, 333, 380. **Open** *Summer* 9.30am-6pm daily. *Winter* 9.30am-5pm daily. **Credit** AmEx, DC, MC, V. **Map** p334.
An Aladdin's cave of bikinis, tankinis, one-pieces, G-strings and bandeau tops. It's perhaps the best place in Sydney for women to buy swimwear: rack after rack of well-priced stuff in loads of different styles and cup sizes, plus bags, towels, sarongs and footwear. The shop is across the road from the beach.
Other locations 51 The Corso, Manly (9977 8961); Warringah Mall, Brookvale (9907 3352).

Billabong
393 George Street, between King & Market Streets, CBD (9262 2878/www.billabong.com.au). CityRail St James or Town Hall/Monorail City Centre. **Open** 9am-6.30pm Mon-Wed, Sat; 9am-9pm Thur; 10am-5pm Sun. **Credit** AmEx, DC, MC, V. **Map** p327 F6.
Billabong founder Gordon Merchant was responsible for designing the first surfboard with a tucked-under edge, and the first surfboard leg-rope. In 1973 he began producing homemade boardshorts that soon became favourites with the surfers in Queensland, and, before long, around the globe. Step over the threshold of this massive Sydney store and you'll find yourself in surfie heaven. There's gear for the beach – cute bikinis and short shorts for the girls, and über-cool board shorts, Ts and more for the guys. Trendy streetwear completes the picture.
Other locations 63 The Corso, Manly (9976 3763).

Bondi Surf Co
72 Campbell Parade, between Lamrock Avenue & Hall Street, Bondi Beach (9365 0870). CityRail Bondi Junction then bus 333, 380, 381, 382/bus 222, 333, 380. **Open** *Summer* 9am-7pm daily. *Winter* 10am-6pm daily. **Credit** AmEx, MC, V. **Map** p334.
Sales, hire, repairs, surfboards, bodyboards and wetsuits for the serious surfer. Plus surfie clothing, sunglasses, watches and other accessories.

Mambo
80 Campbell Parade, between Lamrock Avenue & Hall Street, Bondi Beach (9365 2255/www.mambo. com.au). CityRail Bondi Junction then bus 333, 380, 381, 382/bus 222, 333, 380. **Open** 9am-7pm daily. **Credit** AmEx, DC, MC, V. **Map** p334.

Rip Curl for the surfer girl.

Launched in 1984, this flamboyant surf/skatewear label has become an institution. Founder Dare Jennings employed radical artist Reg Mombassa of the band Mental As Anything to create his trademark gnarly designs. Pick up shorts, T-shirts, swimwear, sunnies, caps and wallets.
Other locations 80 The Corso, Manly (9977 9171).

Rip Curl
61-63 Market Street, between Pitt & Castlereagh Streets, CBD (9264 6777/www.ripcurl.com). CityRail St James or Town Hall/Monorail City Centre. **Open** *Summer* 9am-7pm daily. *Winter* 9am-6pm daily. **Credit** AmEx, DC, MC, V. **Map** p327 E/F6.
In the late 1960s Doug 'Claw' Warbrick and Brian 'Sing Ding' Singer decided to start a surfboard-shaping company from their garage in Torquay, Victoria. When they began making wetsuits for surfers of the icy Victorian waters, Rip Curl became big business. The designs may be more 'street' today, but the company hasn't lost its roots. Stock up on boards, boardies and everything else.
Other locations 82 Campbell Parade, Bondi Beach (9130 2660); 98-100 The Corso, Manly (9977 6622); 105 George Street, The Rocks (9252 4551).

Used & vintage

Blue Spinach Recycled Designer Clothing
348 Liverpool Street, at Womerah Avenue, Darlinghurst (9331 3904/www.bluespinach.com.au). CityRail Kings Cross/bus 389. **Open** 10am-6pm Mon-Wed, Fri, Sat; 10am-7pm Thur. **Credit** AmEx, DC, MC, V. **Map** p330 J8.
If your idea of recycled clothing is more about last season's Missoni than musty-smelling cast-offs, head down to this fashion-insider spot. Run by Mark and Jayne Thompson, it's the most innovative and upmarket recycled clothing joint in town. The building is bright blue, so you can't miss it.

Puf'n Stuff
96 Glenayr Avenue, at Blair Street, North Bondi (9130 8471). CityRail Bondi Junction then bus 333, 380, 381, 382/bus 333, 380. **Open** 11am-6pm Mon-Fri; 10am-6pm Sat, Sun. **Credit** DC, MC, V.
If you want to fit in with the hip Bondi crowd, you need to make the short walk from the beach to this shop, which sells cowboys boots, floaty dresses and envy-inducing vintage accessories. If you're quick you can snap up a 1950s or '70s original.

Rokit Gallery
Metcalfe Arcade, 80-84 George Street, The Rocks (9247 1332/www.rokit.com.au). CityRail/ferry Circular Quay. **Open** 10am-5.30pm daily. **Credit** MC, V. **Map** p327 F3.
This treasure trove of vintage clothing and jewellery in immaculate condition is like a glittering museum. Most of the stock is from the 1930s to '50s, ranging from dresses, coats, skirts and blouses to cigarette cases, magazines and watches. Expect to be served by a shop assistant made up in full '50s eyeliner and powder, with clothes to match. Wonderful.

Route 66
255-257 Crown Street, at Goulburn Street, Darlinghurst (9331 6686/www.route66.com.au). Bus 301, 302, 303, 352. **Open** 10.30am-6pm Mon-Wed, Fri, Sat; 10.30am-8pm Thur; noon-5pm-Sun. **Credit** AmEx, MC, V. **Map** p329 G8.
Rockabilly heaven. A huge range of second-hand Levi's, 1950s chintz frocks and more Hawaiian shirts than you can swing a lei at.

Fashion accessories & services

Bags & hats

Mimco
436 Oxford Street, between Elizabeth Street & George Street, Paddington (9357 6884/www.mimco.com.au). Bus 333, 352, 378, 380. **Open** 10am-6pm Mon-Wed, Fri, Sat; 10am-8pm Thur; 11am-5pm Sun. **Credit** AmEx, MC, V. **Map** p332 L10.

Highly original funky bags, luggage, fantastic sun-hats and up-to-the-minute jewellery and wallets. Owner Amanda 'Mim' Briskin is an Aussie success story, and her gear sells all over the world. **Other locations** throughout the city.

Strand Hatters
Strand Arcade, 412-414 George Street, between King & Market Streets, CBD (9231 6884/www. strandhatters.com.au). CityRail Martin Place, St James or Town Hall/Monorail City Centre. **Open** 8.30am-6pm Mon-Wed, Fri; 8.30am-8pm Thur; 9.30am-4.30pm Sat; 11am-4pm Sun. **Credit** AmEx, MC, V. **Map** p327 F6.

While Akubras pull the crowds in, you can also top off your look with an authentic panama or fedora, or even a replica of the pith helmet worn by dapper soldiers at Rorke's Drift in 1879.

Jewellery

Apart from the establishment listed below, it's also worth making a stop at the super-elegant **Melissa Harris Jewellery** (Shop 14, 2-16 Glenmore Road, 9331 8817, www. melissaharrisjewellery.com), which has some fabulously unusual designs. If that doesn't

Where I shop
Deni Hines, singer

Ed Hardy
I've been fortunate to be given most of my clothes by Ed Hardy, although I did buy a pair of their jeans about six moths ago, which are still going strong, despite the fact that I wear jeans *a lot*. I went to their first store opening in Melbourne and got cut by Adam, their Hollywood cutter to the stars. Ever since, I've loved the clothing and many people make comments. *See p198.*

Tree of Life
320 King Street, Newtown (9557 8820/ www.treeoflife.com.au). CityRail Newtown. **Open** 10am-6pm Mon-Wed, Sat; 10am-8pm Thur; 10am-7pm Fri; 11am-5pm Sun. **Credit** AmEx, MC, V. **Map** p334.
The Tree is like a lolly shop for me, it has so many great things. I mainly get my incense, candles and the odd crystal here. But like most people, I do walk out with something else I don't plan on. It has the hippy vibe I like and it helps me to zone out and relax.

Frenchs Forest Organic Market
Parkway Hotel, 5 Frenchs Forest Road East, Frenchs Forest (9999 2226). Bus 169. **Open** 9am-1pm Sun.
Over the years I've got to know most of the growers here. All the produce is great – so fresh and organic. I make sure I buy what's in season and of good texture.

Iku Wholefood
25A Glebe Point Road, Glebe (9692 8720/ www.iku.com.au). Bus 370, 431, 432, 433, 434. **Open** 11am-9pm Mon-Fri; 11am-8pm Sat; noon-7.30pm Sun. **Unlicensed. No credit cards. Map** p328 B9.

This is my place for real 'fast food' – biodynamic, organic goodness. The tofu fritters and wraps are fantastic.

Camilla
132A Warners Avenue, Bondi Beach (9130 1430/www.camilla.com.au). Bus 333, 380, 381. **Open** 8.30am-6.30pm Mon-Fri; 10am-7pm Sat, Sun. **Credit** AmEx, MC, V. **Map** p334.
This is where I go when I need clothes for work. Designer Camilla Franks' kaftans are so sexy.
Deni Hines & James Morrison's album The Other Woman *was released 13 October 2007 by MRA Entertainment.*

Eat, Drink, Shop

exhaust either desire and bank account, then a look at the jewellery sold at gift shop **Dinosaur Designs** (*see p208*) is very much in order. If you're in the market for opals – a popular Australian souvenir, as 95 per cent of the world's supply comes from here – be sure to check that the retailer is a certified member of the Jewellers' Assocation of Australia (www.jaa.com.au): look for the JAA 'pink diamond' in the shop.

Family Jewels
46 Oxford Street, between West & Comber Streets, Paddington (9331 6647/www.thefamily jewels.com.au). Bus 333, 352, 378, 380. **Open** 10am-6pm Mon-Wed, Fri, Sat; 10am-7.30pm Thur; 11am-5.30pm Sun. **Credit** AmEx, DC, MC, V. **Map** p329 H9.
The cheekily named Family Jewels sells silver jewellery from all over, plus fun designs from hot local designers and sparkly costume jewellery.
Other locations 48 Oxford Street, Paddington (9360 1215); 393A Oxford Street, Paddington (9331 3888); Sydney Central Plaza, CBD (9231 0009).

Lingerie & underwear

Some department stores also have excellent lingerie sections: try **David Jones** (*see p189*) and **Myer** (*see p190*). For sexy sleepwear, visit **Peter Alexander** (Pitt Street Mall, 9223 3440, www.peteralexander.com.au).

Arianne on Oxford
310 Oxford Street, between Perry Lane & William Street, Paddington (9331 4820). Bus 333, 352, 378, 380. **Open** 10am-6pm Mon-Wed, Fri, Sat; 10am-8pm Thur; 11am-5pm Sun. **Credit** AmEx, MC, V. **Map** p332 K10.
High-end, handmade underwear that has obviously been crafted with seduction in mind. There's a good selection of nightwear too.

Dirty Pretty Things
225 Glenmore Road, at Heeley Street, Paddington (9331 2066/www.dirtyprettythings.com.au). Bus 333, 352, 378, 380. **Open** 10am-6pm Mon-Wed, Fri; 10am-7pm Thur; 10am-5pm Sat. **Credit** AmEx, DC, MC, V. **Map** p332 K9.
Like a burlesque-style Parisian boudoir, this place specialises in racy European brands including Chantal Thomass, Buttress & Snatch and Bela's Dead. To help unwind, sip a glass of bubbly from a vintage flute as you shop.

Dress Me Darling
305 Darling Street, between College & Mort Streets, Balmain (9810 8818). Bus 433, 434, 442, 445. **Open** 10am-6pm Mon-Sat; 11am-5pm Sun. **Credit** AmEx, MC, V.
As its name suggests, this boutique is basically an enormous walk-in wardrobe full of decadent buys. There's a well-picked selection of undies veering on the cutesy side, making it perfect for girlie girls.

Gary Castles. Shoes fit for palaces too.

Shoes

Apart from the shops listed below, *see also* **p189 Department stores**.

Gary Castles
Strand Arcade, 412-414 George Street, between King & Market Streets, CBD (9232 6544/www. garycastlessydney.com). CityRail Martin Place, St James or Town Hall/Monorail City Centre. **Open** 9.30am-6pm Mon-Wed, Fri, Sat; 9.30am-8.30pm Thur; 11am-5pm Sun. **Credit** AmEx, MC, V. **Map** p327 F6.
Smart, gorgeous, sophisticated styles in great colour combinations. Wait for the sales if you find the prices too close to international designer levels.
Other locations 45A Bay Street, Double Bay (9327 5077); 112 Queen Street, Woollahra (9327 5611).

Midas
QVB, 455 George Street, between Market & Druitt Streets, CBD (9261 5815/www.midasshoes.com.au). CityRail Town Hall/Monorail Galeries Victoria. **Open** 9am-6pm Mon-Wed, Fri, Sat; 9am-9pm Thur; 11am-5pm Sun. **Credit** AmEx, MC, V. **Map** p327 E6.
A great destination for well-priced, well-made and gorgeous footwear for women. It sells fun bags, belts hats and scarves to coordinate with your shoes too.

Other locations Glasshouse on the Mall, 135 King Street, CBD (9221 5620); 17 Knox Street, Double Bay (9363 3977); Westfield Bondi Junction (9388 9359).

Mollini

302 Oxford Street, between Underwood & William Streets, Paddington (9331 1732/www.mollini. com.au). Bus 333, 352, 378, 380. **Open** 10am-6pm Mon-Wed, Fri; 10am-8.30pm Thur (8pm in winter); 9.30am-6pm Sat; 11am-5pm Sun. **Credit** AmEx, DC, MC, V. **Map** p332 K10.

Wedges, flats, round-toes, point-toes, boots, kitten heels, mid-heels, sandals, stilettos and platforms, plus bags and belts from around the world – phew. They come in fashionable shapes and designs, in various finishes (plaited leather, ponyskin, sequins, metallic). A fix for shoe addicts.
Other locations throughout the city.

Nine West

308 Oxford Street, between Oatley Road & William Street, Paddington (9331 8481/www. ninewest.com.au). Bus 333, 352, 378, 380. **Open** 9.30am-6pm Mon-Wed, Fri, Sat; 9.30am-8pm Thur; 10am-5pm Sun. **Credit** AmEx, DC, MC, V. **Map** p332 K10.

The US shoes and bag chain first came to Australia in 1995 and now boasts 45 stores nationwide. While the designs are not always the most dynamic, the reasonable prices are very attractive in a city where shoes seem to cost way too much.
Other locations throughout the city.

Platypus Shoes

47 The Corso, between Whistler Street & Sydney Road, Manly (9977 1500/www.platypusshoes.com). Ferry Manly. **Open** 9am-6pm Mon-Sat; 10am-5.30pm Sun. **Credit** AmEx, DC, MC, V. **Map** p334.

Hip brands like Diesel, Onitsuka Tiger, Crocs, Vans and Birkenstock, at reasonable prices. Plus loads of cool trainers, as well as hats, sunglasses and more.
Other locations throughout the city.

Food & drink

Asian

Lucky Food Stores

37 Ultimo Road, between Quay & Thomas Streets, Haymarket (9211 1763). CityRail Central/Monorail Paddy's Markets/LightRail Capitol Square, Central or Paddy's Markets. **Open** 10am-6pm daily. **No credit cards. Map** p329 E9.

A fabulous store for Thai foodstuffs. Where else will you find ten brands of fish sauce? Plus 25kg sacks of Thai rice, enormous bags of fresh beansprouts, pink and white lime paste and bottles of chilli paste.

TQC Burlington Supermarket

Corner of Thomas & Quay Streets, Haymarket (9281 2777/www.tqc-burlington.com.au). CityRail Central/Monorail Paddy's Markets/LightRail Capitol Square, Central or Paddy's Markets. **Open** 9am-7pm daily. **Credit** AmEx, MC, V. **Map** p329 E9.

A huge emporium of Chinese and other Asian groceries, including fruit and veg, and a butcher.
Other locations 285-289 Penshurst Street, Willoughby (9417 2588).

Butchers

Jim's Butchery

211 Oxford Street, between Taylor Square & South Dowling Street, Darlinghurst (9331 1678). Bus 333, 352, 378, 380. **Open** 7am-5.30pm Mon-Fri; 7am-1pm Sat. **No credit cards. Map** p329 H9.

An old-fashioned butcher reminiscent of the days when now-busy Darlinghurst was just a village, Jim's has been selling meat since 1962. If you're heading to the city for a rooftop barbecue, this is the place to pick up a juicy steak or plump lamb chop.

Chocolates

Belle Fleur

658 Darling Street, off Victoria Road, Rozelle (9810 2690/www.bellefleur.com.au). Bus 432, 433, 434, 440, 445. **Open** 9am-6pm Mon-Fri; 9am-4pm Sat; 10am-4pm Sun. **Credit** AmEx, MC, V.

Where confectionery meets art. Jan and Lynne ter Heerdt are third-generation chocolatiers from Belgium who set up in Sydney 20 years ago. The chocolates are made fresh every day. **Photo** *p206.*

Just William

4 William Street, at Oxford Street, Paddington (9331 5468/www.justwilliam.com.au). Bus 333, 352, 378, 380. **Open** 10am-6pm daily. **Credit** AmEx, MC, V. **Map** p332 K10.

This diminutive store, filled to the rafters with chocolate-covered delights, is a chocoholic's fantasy. The glass cabinets boast beautifully-presented trays of dark, milk and white chocolates with every filling imaginable, as well as glistening pyramids of jellies and nut-encrusted morsels.

Max Brenner

437 Oxford Street, between Centennial Park & Elizabeth Street, Paddington (9357 5055/www. maxbrenner.com). Bus 333, 352, 378, 380. **Open** 9am-11pm Mon-Thur; 9am-midnight Fri, Sat; 10am-10.30pm Sun. **Credit** AmEx, DC, MC, V. **Map** p332 L10/11.

There's a café at the front and a shop at the back of this branch of the international chain. Drink frozen chocolate cocktails or steaming cups of hot choc, or gorge on strawberries dipped in melted chocolate.
Other locations Manly Wharf, Manly (9977 4931); 15 Knox Street, Double Bay (9328 2555).

Delis & gourmet foods

Fine Food Store

595 Darling Street, between Wise & Norman Streets, Rozelle (9810 2858/www.finefoodstore.com). Bus 432, 433, 434, 440. **Open** 8.30am-7pm Mon-Fri; 9am-5pm Sat; 10am-4pm Sun. **Credit** AmEx, MC, V.

Belle Fleur. *See p205.*

Belle Fleur
Smooth hazelnut
with a hint of
fresh orange

Despite Fine Food Store being a chic gourmet food store – not something that often produces cheeriness – staff are surprisingly friendly and approachable. The shop's motto is 'food is our passion', and it does live up to what it says on the label, selling pasta, frozen dim sum and tins of English golden syrup of excellent quality. There's also a cheese room. **Other locations** Rocks Centre, The Rocks (9252 1196).

Fratelli Fresh

7 Danks Street, between Young & Bourke Streets, Waterloo (1300 552 119/www.fratellifresh.com.au). Bus 301, 302, 303. **Open** 10am-6pm Tue-Fri; 8am-4pm Sat. **Credit** AmEx, MC, V.
Sydney's top restaurants have long benefitted from Fratelli Fresh's produce, so when the owners opened a store for the public the response from the locals was rightfully enthusiastic. Foodies from all over make the pilgrimage to Danks Street for its warehouse market full of top-quality Italian and Australian produce – fruit, veg, meat, salami, poultry, dry goods, dairy, bread – even flowers.

Jones the Grocer

68 Moncur Street, at Queen Street, Woollahra (9362 1222/www.jonesthegrocer.com). Bus 389. **Open** 7.30am-5.30pm Mon-Sat; 9am-5pm Sun. **Credit** AmEx, MC, V. **Map** p333 M10.
Known for fine cheeses, sausages, cakes and high-quality grocery, Jones the Grocer is also a great place to just hang out and have a coffee.

Other locations 91-93 Macleay Street, Potts Point (9358 3343); 166 Military Road, Neutral Bay (8905 0150).

Provedore Pelagios

235 Victoria Street, between Liverpool & Surrey Streets, Darlinghurst (9360 1011). CityRail Kings Cross/bus 311, 389. **Open** 9am-8pm Mon-Sat; 10am-7pm Sun. **Credit** AmEx, DC, MC, V. **Map** p330 J8.
Established in 1926, this traditional Italian grocer prides itself on its knowledgeable and enthusiastic staff. The bread is divine and there are also salads, cold cuts, cheeses, organic veg and gourmet pasta. The chocolate counter at the checkout is especially tempting at Easter. You can also have a coffee in the small lounge area at the front.

Simon Johnson Quality Foods

55 Queen Street, between Oxford & Moncur Streets, Woollahra (9328 6888/www.simonjohnson.com). Bus 389. **Open** 10am-6.30pm Mon-Fri; 9am-5pm Sat; 10am-4pm Sun. **Credit** AmEx, MC, V. **Map** p333 M10.
Esteemed foodie Simon Johnson has set himself up as the nation's leading provider of Australian and imported gourmet foods. His produce comes from more than 50 key sources, all vetted for quality. This shop has a great kitchenware section, a pleasingly odorous cheese room and plenty of sweet offerings. **Other locations** 181 Harris Street, Pyrmont (9552 2522); 24A Ralph Street, Alexandria (8244 8220).

Sweet Art
96 Oxford Street, between Kidman Lane &
Hopewell Street, Paddington (9361 6617/www.
sweetart.com.au). Bus 333, 352, 378, 380. **Open**
10am-5pm daily. **Credit** AmEx, DC, MC, V.
Map p332 J9.
Creativity at its best. Check out the window displays
of sculptured cakes, made to whatever shape or
design you desire. Sweet Art is also a florist and an
event management service – useful if you want to
organise a wedding, christening or party.

Health foods

Bayside Natural Health Centre
30-36 Bay Street, between Cooper & Cross Streets,
Double Bay (9327 8002). Ferry Double Bay/bus 323,
324, 325, 326. **Open** 9am-6pm Mon-Sat; 11.30am-
5.30pm Sun. **Credit** AmEx, DC, MC, V.
Map p331 N7/8.
Lots of organic fresh and dried produce, including
bread and a small deli section. A few well-placed
stone buddhas and oil burners create a calming
ambience in which to splurge on the herbal reme-
dies, natural skincare cosmetics and therapeutic
massages (book in advance) on offer.

Health Emporium
263 Bondi Road, between Denham & Castlefield
Streets, Bondi (9365 6008). CityRail Bondi Junction
then bus 333, 380, 381, 382/bus 333, 380. **Open**
8.30am-7pm Mon-Fri; 8.30am-6pm Sat, Sun. **Credit**
AmEx MC, V.
As well as stocking earth-friendly cosmetics including Jurlique, Dr Hauschka and Weleda, this shop
also has a good organic and grocery section and as
many vitamins and supplements a vegan could
need. You can also buy eco-safe detergents and 'eth-
ical' coffee from the small takeaway deli.

Macro Wholefoods Market
31-37 Oxford Street, at Ruthven Street, Bondi
Junction (9389 7611/www.macrowholefoods.com.au).
CityRail Bondi Junction then bus 333, 378, 380,
389/bus 333, 378, 380, 380. **Open** 7.30am-8pm
Mon-Fri; 7.30am-7pm Sat; 8am-7pm Sun. **Credit**
AmEx, MC, V. **Map** p333 N11.
The mecca for macrobiotic, vegan, vegetarian and
organic food. These people are serious about their
natural clean, fresh produce, and the prices aren't
bad either. You can even buy organic pet food.
Other locations 13-19 Willloughby Road, Crows
Nest (9004 1240).

Gifts & souvenirs
There is an unsettling whiff of Disneyland
about the historic Rocks area near Circular
Quay, but it is still a quaint and interesting
place to spend a day. There's plenty of kitsch
Australiana for sale, but also genuinely decent
souvenirs in stores large and small, at a
reasonable range of prices.

Didj Beat Didjeridoos (corner of Argyle
& Harrington Streets, 9251 4289, www.didjbeat.
com) sells didgeridoos, Aboriginal art and
artefacts from all over Australia. Staff can teach
you how to play a didgeridoo and tell you about
the Aboriginal artists the shop buys from.
Naturally Australian (43 Circular Quay
West, 9247 1531, www.naturallyaust.com.au)
specialises in native timber furniture and craft,
while **Craft NSW** (104 George Street, 9241
5825) is operated by the Society of Arts &
Crafts NSW (www.artsandcraftsnsw.com.au)
and has a wide selection of ceramics,
handwoven, hand-spun and hand-knitted
garments, as well as glass and woodwork.
Natural Selection Souvenirs (Metcalfe
Arcade, 82-84 George Street, 9247 9174) sells
Driza-Bone coats and Ugg boots. Head to
Flame Opals (119 George Street, 9247 3446,
www.flameopals.com.au) for opal jewellery.
Check www.therocks.com for more options.

The **Museum of Contemporary Art** (*see
p71*) has a good gift shop, as do the **Museum
of Sydney** (*see p71*), the **Powerhouse
Museum** (*see p84*) and the **Sydney Opera
House** (*see p254*). The latter has shops both in
the foyer and a new separate store with funky
artefacts on the Lower Concourse.

Fratelli Fresh. It is.

Collect

Object Gallery, St Margarets, 417 Bourke Street,
Surry Hills (9361 4511/www.object.com.au). Bus
371, 373, 377, 380, 396. **Open** 11am-6pm Tue-Sun.
Credit AmEx, MC, V. **Map** p329 H9.
Located beneath Object Gallery (which shows the
work of Australian designers), this shop sells collectible glass and ceramics, plus Australia-made
homewares and jewellery. A not-for-profit organisation, it supports the local artistic community.

Dinosaur Designs

Strand Arcade, 412-414 George Street, between
King & Market Streets, CBD (9223 2953/www.
dinosaurdesigns.com.au). CityRail Martin Place, St
James or Town Hall/Monorail City Centre. **Open**
9.30am-5.30pm Mon-Wed, Fri; 9.30am-8pm Thur;
10am-5pm Sat; noon-4pm Sun. **Credit** AmEx, MC, V.
Map p327 F6.
Founded in 1985 by three former art students,
Dinosaur Designs makes bright, glowing resin
bowls, vases, jugs, plates and other household items,
as well as chunky jewellery, with ranges inspired by
artists as well as by natural forms.
Other locations 339 Oxford Street, Paddington
(9361 3776).

Gavala Aboriginal Cultural Centre

Harbourside Centre, Darling Drive, Darling Harbour
(9212 7232/www.gavala.com.au). CityRail Town
Hall/ferry Darling Harbour/Monorail Harbourside.
Open 10am-9pm daily. **Credit** AmEx, MC, V.
Map p327 D6.
Established in 1995, Gavala is Aboriginal-owned
and staffed, and is a top spot to buy arts, crafts and
souvenirs made by Aboriginal artists. Expect
clothes, jewellery, boomerangs, didgeridoos and
more, including paintings in the separate art gallery.

Opus Designs

344 Oxford Street, between William & Elizabeth
Streets, Paddington (9360 4803/www.opusdesign.
com.au). Bus 333, 352, 378, 380. **Open** 10am-6pm
Mon-Wed, Fri; 10am-7.30pm Thur; 9am-6pm Sat;
11am-5pm Sun. **Credit** AmEx, DC, MC, V.
Map p332 K10.
This Paddo institution has been open since the
1960s, selling a kitsch collection of novelties, funky
ashtrays, photo frames, beach bags, clocks and drag-
queen greetings cards, plus other homewares,
kitchenwares and stylish furniture.
Other locations Octopus Design, 260 King Street,
Newtown (9565 4688).

Health & beauty

Complementary medicine

Complete City Health

Level 14, National Mutual Building, 44 Market
Street, at York Street, CBD (9299 1661/www.
completecityhealth.com.au). CityRail St James or
Town Hall/Monorail City Centre. **Open** 8am-6pm
Mon-Fri. **Credit** MC, V. **Map** p327 E6.

One of the first centres in Sydney to bring together
all major healthcare professions, with the philosophy that the body only works when it is well as a
whole. You'll find a GP and dentist, as well as chi-
ropractors, naturopaths, massage therapists, reflex-
ologists and more.

A Natural Practice

161A Glebe Point Road, between Mitchell Street
& St Johns Road, Glebe (9660 7308/www.anatural
practice.com.au). Bus 431, 432, 433. **Open** 10am-
6pm Mon-Sat; also by appointment. **Credit** MC, V.
Map p328 B9.
A Natural Practice has been running for 20 years
and has experts in acupuncture, homeopathy, iridol-
ogy, shiatsu, reflexology, reiki, remedial massage,
naturopathy, osteopathy, psychotherapy and more.
Detox programmes are also on offer.

Uclinic

Level 1, 421 Bourke Street, between Church Lane
& Albion Street, Surry Hills (9332 0400/www.
uclinic.com.au). Bus 371, 373, 377, 392, 394,
396, 397, 399, 890, L94. **Open** 8am-6pm Mon-
Fri; 8am-2pm Sat. **Credit** AmEx, DC, MC, V.
Map p329 G9.
Professor Kerryn Phelps, former chairman of the
Australian Medical Association, has done a brave
thing stepping outside the confines of her western
medicine training to set up this fully complementary
health clinic. All are welcome here and the emphasis is on achieving a healthy body and lifestyle.
Practitioners include acupuncturists, naturopaths
and Chinese medicine specialists, and there's a 24-
hour physio service available.

Cosmetics

Jurlique

Strand Arcade, 412-414 George Street, between
King & Market Streets, CBD (9231 0626/www.
jurlique.com.au). CityRail Martin Place, St James or
Town Hall/Monorail City Centre. **Open** 9am-5.30pm
Mon-Wed; 9am-9pm Thur; 9am-6pm Fri; 9am-5pm
Sat; 10am-4pm Sun. **Credit** AmEx, DC, MC, V.
Map p327 F6.
This small company based in South Australia is
making big news at home and overseas. It might not
be cheap, but this is the real deal when it comes to
gorgeous 'aromatherapeutic' natural toiletries.
Other locations throughout the city.

Mecca Cosmetica

126 Oxford Street, opposite Victoria Barracks,
Paddington (9361 4488/www.meccacosmetica.
com.au). Bus 333, 352, 378, 380. **Open** 10am-6pm
Mon-Wed, Fri, Sat; 10am-8pm Thur; 11am-5pm Sun.
Credit AmEx, DC, MC, V. **Map** p332 J9/10.
A chic cosmetic boutique with overseas brands such
as Nars, Stila and Philosophy. Some branches have
pedicure and make-up services too.
Other locations David Jones, Westfield Bondi
Junction (9389 4406); Galeries Victoria, CBD
(9261 4911).

Opus Designs.

Eat, Drink, Shop

Tasteful takeways

It doesn't have to be a koala in a can or a boomerang that doesn't come back. Here are a few suggestions of genuinely Australian-made gifts that will raise a smile rather than a groan.

● A Robert Foster jug, cup and bowl from the **Sydney Opera House Shop** (*see p254*). Foster's F!nk Water Jug became an immediate design classic in 1994, and since then he has exhibited and sold all over the world. His homewares are minimalist gems.

● A luminous table lamp created by Alex Noble, from his concept stall at **Paddington Markets** (*see p193*). Noble is one of Sydney's hottest young designers – his use of shape and colour will blow your mind.

● A resin platter or vase, a jug or a plate from **Dinosaur Designs** (*see p208*). This trio of artists uses organic colours and shapes inspired by land- and seascapes. The results are soothing.

● A Florence Broadhurst overnight bag. The flamboyant portfolio of the late Sydney grande dame of lush wallpaper and prints has been resurrected by local entrepreneurs David and Helen Lennie. Head to **Signature Prints**, Unit 2, 3 Hayes Road, Rosebery (8338 8400, www.signatureprints.com.au).

● Billabong board shorts from the **Billabong Store** (*see p200*). These are *the* must-have attire for beach, beer and board lubbers. Pure Australiana – and drip-dry too!

Napoleon Perdis Make-up Academy

74 Oxford Street, between Comber & Hopewell Streets, Paddington (9331 1702/www.napoleon cosmetics.com). Bus 333, 352, 378, 380. **Open** 9am-6pm Mon-Sat; 9am-5pm Sun. **Credit** AmEx, DC, MC, V. **Map** p332 J9.

Founded by Napoleon Perdis, an Australian-born Hollywood make-up artist, this shop has its own cosmetics brand and in-house make-up artists.
Other locations Sydney Central Plaza, CBD (9221 6277); World Square, CBD (9262 7733).

Perfect Potion

QVB, 455 George Street, between Market & Druitt Streets, CBD (9286 3384/www.perfectpotion. com.au). CityRail Town Hall/Monorail Galeries Victoria. **Open** 9am-6pm Mon-Wed, Fri; 9am-9pm Thur; 9am-6pm Sat; 11am-5pm Sun. **Credit** AmEx, MC, V. **Map** p327 E6.

These people are serious about their holistic aromatherapy and offer a good skincare range made from essential oils, infused plant oils, cold-pressed vegetable oils, organically grown herbal extracts and other plant-derived ingredients.
Other locations Strand Arcade, CBD (9238 0203); Westfield Bondi Junction (9389 6120).

Hairdressers & barbers

Raw Anthony Nader

30 Burton Street, between Little Burton & Crown Streets, Darlinghurst (9380 5370/www.rawhair. com.au). Bus 222, 311, 373, 377, 378, 380, 392, 394, 396, 397, 399. **Open** 10am-5pm Tue, Wed; 10am-8pm Thur; 10am-9pm Fri; 10am-6pm Sat. **Credit** AmEx, MC, V. **Map** p329 G8.

There's a good reason why the A-list wait in line for Anthony Nader, the founder of this chic salon: this is a man who knows about hair. He specialises in sophisticated, natural styling, and the salon is a genuine delight to visit, with its chandeliers, dramatic native flora and candelit basement.

Toni & Guy

255 Oxford Street, between Oatley Road & William Street, Paddington (9380 2299/www.toniandguy. com.au). Bus 333, 352, 378, 380. **Open** 9am-6pm Mon-Wed; 9am-8pm Thur; 9am-7.30pm Fri; 9am-5.15pm Sat. **Credit** AmEx, DC, MC, V. **Map** p332 K10.

The global chain, well established in Oz, is a good place to get a quality cut. There are lots of salons around town but this branch, with fully reclining and massaging chairs, is something special.
Other locations throughout the city.

Opticians

K Optica

432 Oxford Street, between Elizabeth & Jersey Streets, Paddington (9331 3400/www.koptica. com.au). Bus 333, 352, 378, 380. **Open** 9am-6pm Mon-Wed, Fri; 9am-8.30pm Thur; 9.30am-6pm Sat; 11am-5.30pm Sun. **Credit** AmEx, DC, MC, V. **Map** p332 L10.

A popular eyewear shop with an ever-changing collection of the latest frames, including designer lines. There's also an on-site optician service.

OPSM

183 Maquarie Street, corner of Chifley Square, CBD (9232 7995/www.opsm.com). CityRail Martin Place. **Open** 7.30am-5pm Mon-Wed, Fri; 8am-5pm Thur. **Credit** AmEx, DC, MC, V. **Map** p327 F5.

One of the country's biggest chains, with a good selection of designer frames.
Other locations throughout the city.

Eat, Drink, Shop

Pharmacies

There are very few 24-hour pharmacies in Sydney, but many trade into the evening.

CBD Pharmacies

92 Pitt Street, at Martin Place, CBD (9221 0091). CityRail Martin Place or Wynyard. **Open** 7.45am-6.45pm Mon-Fri. **Credit** AmEx, DC, MC, V. **Map** p327 F5.

Centrally located chemist open weekdays for troubled city staff, with an affiliated medical centre just up the road (open 8am-5pm Monday to Friday).

Spas & salons

Detail For Men

6 O'Connell Street, between Hunter & Bent Streets, CBD (9231 5999/www.detailformen.com). CityRail Wynyard. **Open** 9am-7pm Mon-Wed, Fri; 9am-8.30pm Thur; 9am-6pm Sat. **Credit** AmEx, DC, MC, V. **Map** p327 F5.

Aimed at city boys, this salon provides a premium hairdressing and day spa service designed for 'today's modern man'. Services include waxing, facials, haircuts, shaves and massages.

Ginseng Bathhouse

1st Floor, Crest Hotel, 111 Darlinghurst Road, off Victoria Street, Kings Cross (9356 6680/www. ginsengbathhouse.com.au). CityRail Kings Cross. **Open** 9.30am-9pm Mon-Fri; 9am-9pm Sat, Sun. **Credit** AmEx, DC, MC, V. **Map** p330 J7.

This traditional Korean bathhouse offers steam treatments, ginseng baths, scrubs and masterly massage. Separate baths for men and women.

Nail Spa

David Jones, Lower Ground Level, 86-108 Castlereagh Street, CBD (9266 5544). Market Street, at Castlereagh Street; Elizabeth Street, at Market Street, CBD. **Open** 9.30am-6pm Mon-Wed; 9.30am-9pm Thur; 9.30am-7pm Fri, Sat; 10am-6pm Sun. **Credit** AmEx, DC, MC, V. **Map** p327 F6.

Give those tired summer feet a makeover or indulge in some serious hand care at Nail Spa. Remember to wear open-toe sandals if you've booked in for a pedicure, however, or you'll be sent shuffling back into the well-dressed crowds outside in a pair of monstrously ugly paper flip-flops.

Zen Day Spa

116-118 Darlinghurst Road, between William & Liverpool Streets, Darlinghurst (9361 4200/www. zendayspa.com.au). CityRail Kings Cross. **Open** 9am-9pm Mon-Fri; 8am-8pm Sat; 10am-7pm Sun. **Credit** AmEx, MC, V. **Map** p329 H8.

Serenity is the name of the game at this day spa, a sanctuary in the heart of bustling Darlinghurst. Options include massage, aromatherapy sessions, and skincare treatments using Dermalogica products, as well as waxes, manicures and pedicures. **Other locations** 118-122 Queen Street, Woollahra (9328 1656).

Tattoos & piercing

Inner Vision Tattoo

334 Crown Street, at Campbell Street, Surry Hills (9361 4376/www.innervisiontattoo.com.au). Bus 301, 302, 303. **Open** 11am-7pm daily. **No credit cards. Map** p329 G9.

A clean and smart place offering top-quality service (including great follow-up advice). The other branch has a wider range of options, such as full body, facial and genital piercing, and also sells jewellery. **Other locations** 251 Crown Street, Surry Hills (9360 3179).

Steel Lotus Body Arts

174 Crown Street, at Chapel Street, Darlinghurst (9326 0555/www.steellotus.com). Bus 324, 325, 326, 327. **Open** 11am-7pm Tue, Wed, Fri, Sat; 11am-8pm Thur. **Credit** AmEx, DC, MC, V. **Map** p329 G7.

The five tattooists and one body piercer here take time and care to create custom-made work for their clients. Not surprisingly, they're all booked well in advance by a broad clientele of body-art devotees. Jewellery is also stocked.

House & home

For reasonably priced, brand-new contemporary furniture from sofas through to beds with stops for bookcases and tables along the way, a couple of good, first-stop options are **Freedom** (1300 135 588, www.freedom.com.au) or **Fantastic Furniture** (9663 4588, www. fantasticfurniture.com.au), which are both located in Moore Park's **Supacenta** (corner of South Dowling Street and Todman Avenue). Should the desire for a little Swedish style prove overwhelming, then trek out to **IKEA** (8002 0400, www.ikea.com.au) at Homebush.

There are heaps of second-hand furniture emporiums that sell (when you arrive) and buy (when you leave) all types of furniture, from lamps to sofas, beds to washing machines. Two reliable outlets are **Bondi Furniture Market** (2 Jacques Avenue, Bondi Beach, 9365 1315) and **Peter Foley's Furniture** (93 Bronte Road, Bondi Junction, 9387 3332).

Music & entertainment

Sydney's megastores are **Virgin** (343 George Street, CBD, 9347 0300) and **Sanity** (Imperial Arcade, Pitt Street Mall, 9239 0050, www.sanity.com.au).

Ashwood's Music & Books

129 York Street, between Market & Druitt Streets, CBD (9267 7745). CityRail Town Hall/Monorail Galeries Victoria. **Open** 9.30am-6pm Mon-Wed, Fri; 9.30am-8pm Thur; 9.30am-5pm Sat; noon-4pm Sun. **Credit** MC, V. **Map** p327 E6.

This basement music emporium opposite the QVB has traded since 1932 and is a great place to find obscure CDs or vinyl. It's also good for second-hand music books and DVDs, and vintage sheet music.

Birdland

231 Pitt Street, between Market & Park Streets, CBD (9267 6881/www.birdland.com.au). CityRail St James or Town Hall/Monorail City Centre. **Open** 10am-5.30pm Mon-Wed, Fri; 10am-8pm Thur; 9am-4.30pm Sat. **Credit** AmEx, DC, MC, V. **Map** p329 F7.
Birdland is the best jazz and blues shop in the city – some claim it's one of the best in the world.

Central Station Records

46A Oxford Street, between Hyde Park & Crown Street, Darlinghurst (9361 5222/www.central station.com.au). CityRail Museum/bus 373, 377, 378, 380, 333. **Open** 10am-6pm Mon-Wed, Fri, Sat; 10am-9pm Thur; noon-5pm Sun. **Credit** MC, V. **Map** p329 G8.
Want to buy that track you heard in the club last night on vinyl? Central Station's vast basement shop houses the very latest in import and domestic dance, house, hip hop, R&B and Mardi Gras compilations. It also produces dance compilations on its own label.

Fish Records

261 King Street, between Church & Mary Streets, Newtown (9557 3074/www.fishrecords.com.au). CityRail Newtown. **Open** 9am-10pm Mon-Sat; 9.30am-9pm Sun. **Credit** AmEx, MC, V. **Map** p334.
Next to the Dendy cinema, this branch of Fish stocks mostly Top 40 and dance music, with a good soundtrack section. The 350 George Street and QVB branches focus on classical music.
Other locations throughout the city.

Folkways Music

282 Oxford Street, between Underwood & William Streets, Paddington (9361 3980). Bus 333, 352, 378, 380. **Open** 9am-6pm Mon-Wed, Fri, Sat; 9am-8pm Thur; 11am-6pm Sun. **Credit** AmEx, DC, MC, V. **Map** p332 K10.
The standard-bearer for folk and ethnic music.

Red Eye

66 King Street, between George & York Streets, CBD (9299 4233/www.redeye.com.au). CityRail Wynyard. **Open** 9am-6pm Mon-Wed, Fri; 9am-9pm Thur; 9am-5pm Sat; 11am-5pm Sun. **Credit** AmEx, MC, V. **Map** p327 E6.
The biggest of the indie shops, Red Eye has an excellent range of Australian bands and labels, as well as a good selection of imports. There's also second-hand merchandise at this outlet, but it's the Pitt Street branch that specialises in second-hand. You can also buy tickets for gigs here.
Other locations 370 Pitt Street, CBD (9262 9755).

Op shops

Op (for 'opportunity') shops are second-hand shops, the Australian version of the UK's charity shops and the US's thrift stores.

St Vincent de Paul

292 Oxford Street, between Elizabeth & Underwood Streets, Paddington (9360 4151/www.vinnies.org. au). Bus 333, 352, 378, 380. **Open** 9.30am-6pm Mon-Wed, Fri; 9am-7.30pm Thur; 9.30am-6pm Sat; 10am-5pm Sun. **Credit** MC, V. **Map** p332 K10.
The proceeds of these shops – fondly known as 'St Vinnie's' – go to the St Vincent de Paul hospitals and help towards their charity work. This branch specialises in clothes and, thanks to the quality of the stock, turnover is quick. Look out for current-season fashion and designer labels.
Other locations throughout the city.

Salvos Store St Peters

7 Bellevue Street, off Princes Highway, St Peters (9519 1513). CityRail St Peters. **Open** 8.30am-3.30pm Mon-Fri; 8.30am-1.45pm Sat. **Credit** AmEx, DC, MC, V.
More department store than humble op shop, this warehouse-size emporium holds racks of clothes, enough furniture to fill an apartment block, plus old computers, a good collection of records and cut-price household goods. Proceeds go to the Salvation Army ('Salvos') – huge in Australia.
Other locations throughout the city.

Sport & fitness

For surf- and swimwear, *see p200*.

Kathmandu

Town Hall Arcade, corner of Kent & Bathurst Streets, CBD (9261 8901/www.kathmandu.com.au). CityRail Town Hall/Monorail Galeries Victoria. **Open** 9am-5.30pm Mon-Wed, Fri; 9am-8.30pm Thur; 9am-5pm Sat; 10am-4pm Sun. **Credit** AmEx, MC, V. **Map** p329 E7.
'Live the dream, ski it, sail it, run it, climb it, surf it, walk it, paddle it, explore it, skate it': that's the motto, and this shop means it. It has everything in here: the gear, the clothes, the gadgets.

Paddy Pallin

507 Kent Street, at Bathurst Street, CBD (9264 2685/www.paddypallin.com.au). CityRail Town Hall/Monorail Galeries Victoria. **Open** 9am-5.30pm Mon-Wed; 9am-9pm Thur; 9am-6pm Fri; 9am-5pm Sat; 10am-5pm Sun. **Credit** AmEx, DC, MC, V. **Map** p329 E7.
Bushwalker Paddy opened his first shop in the 1930s, selling lightweight camping and walking gear. The mini national chain is still going strong, with the shops stocking everything that the modern-day backpacker might want.

Travel agents

The reliable chains **Flight Centre** (66 King Street, between York & George Streets, CBD, 9262 6644, 13 3133, www.flightcentre.com.au) and **STA Travel** (855 George Street, at Harris Street, Haymarket, 9212 1255, www.statravel. com.au) have branches throughout the city.

Arts & Entertainment

Features

Festivals & Events

Join the locals and let the carnival atmosphere carry you along.

Sydney's festivals represent the city's multi-faceted personality. From the paper dragons of the **Chinese New Year** to the dancing boys of the **Gay & Lesbian Mardi Gras** and the tall sails of the **Sydney Hobart Yacht Race**, old and new traditions sit cheek by jowl and always the party spirit reigns.

Many events are free – be they stand-alone fixtures such as **Sculpture by the Sea** or elements of a major festival, like the Sydney Festival's **Symphony & Jazz in the Domain** – and these tend to command huge crowds. But with every suburb now holding its own cultural festival, there are plenty of events that attract smaller, more manageable audiences.

More film festivals are on *p230*, sports events on *pp256-265*; for public holidays, *see p307*.

Spring

Festival of the Winds

Bondi Beach (8362 3400/www.waverley.nsw.gov.au). CityRail Bondi Junction then bus 381, 382, 380, 333/bus 222, 380, 333. **Map** p334. **Date** 2nd Sun in Sept.

Australia's largest free kite-flying festival is staged outside the Bondi Pavilion on Bondi Beach and in the park behind the sands, attracting up to 50,000 people and hundreds of kites of all shapes and sizes. The competitions are only open to kite club members, but there are plenty of other activities for beginners and non-kiters, including kite-making lessons, live music and masses of stuff for kids.

Sydney Running Festival

www.sydneyrunningfestival.org. **Date** Sun in mid Sept.

First held in 2001 and incorporating the Sydney Marathon, the Running Festival is the only community event that closes the Sydney Harbour Bridge. It comprises four road races – the marathon, a half-marathon, a 9km (5.6 mile) Bridge Run and the most recent addition, a family fun run of 4km (2.5 miles). Entry is open to all, though you have to apply in advance and pay an entry fee.

Art & About

Various venues (www.cityofsydney.nsw.gov.au/artand about). **Date** Oct.

For three weeks in October the parks, squares, streets and shopping centres of the city become the canvas for events, exhibitions and workshops showcasing local artists both established and emerging. There's fashion, photography, ice sculpture, flower arrangements and more.

Good Food Month

Various venues (www.gfm.smh.com.au). **Date** Oct.

There's something for everyone to nibble at this *Sydney Morning Herald*-sponsored festival. The idea is that the city's best chefs offer their fare at affordable prices, with lunchtime specials at top restaurants and plenty of outdoor events, including the Night Noodle markets in Hyde Park and the Food and Wine Fair. Tuck in!

Manly International Jazz Festival

Manly (9976 1400/www.manly.nsw.gov.au/manlyjazz). Ferry Manly. **Map** p334. **Date** Oct long weekend.

Australia's largest and longest-running community jazz festival attracts crowds of over 20,000. Local and international artists play on the outdoor stages set along the Corso, the beach and the council forecourt opposite Manly Wharf. Along with roving bands, there are more than 60 free performances from noon till sunset, as well as indoor sessions (for which you'll have to pay) going into the night.

Sleaze Ball

Entertainment Quarter, Driver Avenue, Moore Park (9568 8600/www.mardigras.org.au). Bus 339, 373, 374, 376, 377, 393, 395, 396. **Map** p332 J12. **Date** 1st Sat in Oct.

A spectacular and, of course, very sleazy dance party organised as a fund-raiser for gay Sydney's main event, Mardi Gras (*see p217*). There's a hot new theme each year to inspire wild costumes and shows – the fantastic 2007 Zircus theme saw attendance rocket with ring masters, clowns and bearded ladies aplenty. Sleaze kick-starts the gay summer party season. For more information, *see p244*.

Sculpture by the Sea

Along the cliff walk from Bondi to Tamarama (8399 0233/www.sculpturebythesea.com). CityRail Bondi Junction then bus 381, 382, 380, 333/bus 222, 380, 333. **Map** p334. **Date** 1st 3wks in Nov.

This must surely be one of the world's most spectacular locations for an art event. For three weeks, Australia's largest free outdoor exhibition of contemporary sculpture shows off over 100 works by local and overseas artists along the coastal cliff walk from Bondi Beach to Tamarama Beach. Alongside the outdoor event, 'Sculpture Inside' exhibits smaller works by selected artists at the Bondi Pavilion Gallery and the Tamarama Surf Life Saving Club.

Newtown Festival

Camperdown Memorial Park, corner of Lennox & Australia Streets, Newtown (9519 2509/ www.newtowncentre.org). CityRail Newtown. **Map** p334. **Date** Sun in mid Nov.

Sculpture by the Sea.

Tucked behind King Street in the grounds of St Stephen's Church, this free festival boasts a dog show like no other ('Celebrity Look-a-Like', anyone?). If you're not into the pooches there's plenty of other stuff going on, with music, workshops, food and activities for kids. The festival runs from 10am to 6pm.

Glebe Street Fair

Glebe Point Road, from Parramatta Road to Bridge Road, Glebe (9281 0024/www.glebestreetfair.com.au). LightRail Glebe/bus 370, 431, 432, 433, 434. **Map** p328 A8. **Date** 3rd Sun in Nov.
Sydney's longest running street festival takes over Glebe Point Road as traffic gives way to food stalls, wine-tasting booths, arts and craft stalls, clowns, stilt-walkers and music stages. Foley Park is devoted to children's activities. Expect crowds of around 100,000. The fair runs from 10am to 5pm.

Summer

Homebake

The Domain, Mrs Macquarie's Road, Royal Botanic Gardens, CBD (9266 4800/www.homebake.com.au). CityRail Circular Quay or Martin Place/ferry Circular Quay. **Map** p327 G/H5. **Date** late Nov/early Dec.
As the name suggests, this one-day music festival features some of Australia's (and New Zealand's) best home-grown talent. Homebake celebrated its tenth anniversary in 2005 and has grown from muddy beginnings in a Byron Bay paddock to a

crowd of tens of thousands descending on the Domain for 12 hours of ear-splitting pleasure, with a cinema tent now extending the concept to up-and-coming film-makers. Book tickets well in advance.

Carols in the Domain

The Domain, Mrs Macquarie's Road, Royal Botanic Gardens, CBD (www.carolsinthedomain.com). CityRail Circular Quay or Martin Place/ferry Circular Quay. **Map** p327 G/H5. **Date** wk before Christmas.
In case you were worried that Christmas wouldn't be Christmas in all the heat, you can join the 100,000 who fill the Domain for an evening of traditional carols by candlelight. The crowds are kept in tune by a 150-strong choir and a chorus of local and celebs, and the evening is sealed by a firework display.

Christmas Day on Bondi Beach

Bondi Beach. CityRail Bondi Junction then bus 333, 380, 381, 382/bus 222, 333, 380. **Map** p334. **Date** 25 Dec.
Thousands of travellers from around the world (especially Brits) gather on Bondi Beach each year for an impromptu party, some with their own sofa and Christmas tree. Since the council introduced an alcohol ban on the beach a few years ago, this traditional festivity has become more of a family affair and the backpacker crowd instead heads to the Bondi Pavilion for an all-day dance party.

Sydney Hobart Yacht Race

Sydney Harbour (8292 7800/www.cyca.com.au). **Date** 26 Dec.
Hundreds of keen yachtsmen and supporters turn out to watch the spectacular lunchtime start of this notoriously gruelling race to Hobart. It's sobering to remember that several sailors died in the 1998 race when wild seas tore yachts apart, but the sight of hundreds of sails filling the harbour as the racers make their way out to sea is stunning. The best viewing areas are coastal cliff spots around the harbour, such as Bradleys Head, Chowder Bay and Georges Heights on the west, Vaucluse Point, South Head and the Gap on the east, and North Head in the north.

New Year's Eve Fireworks

Sydney Harbour & Darling Harbour (9265 9757/ www.cityofsydney.nsw.gov.au/nye). **Date** 9pm & midnight 31 Dec.
When it comes to pyrotechnic experiences, New Year's Eve in Sydney is in a league of its own. Each year the stakes to be the best in the world are raised, and each year Sydney usually wins. After a day of public spectacles, there are two fireworks displays, one at 9pm for families and then the midnight extravaganza. For ideas of where to watch them, *see* *p216* **Free seats for NYE fireworks**.

Sydney Festival

Various venues (8248 6500/www.sydneyfestival. org.au). **Date** Jan.
Launched in 1976 to celebrate the city and bring people into the CBD, the festival has more recently branched out to include venues in Parramatta. This

Arts & Entertainment

Free seats for NYE fireworks

Our pick of the pyrotechnics.

Bicentennial Park

Federal Road, Glebe; access via Chapman Road.
There are waterside seats to be had in this park along the industrial side of the harbour. Food is for sale, but bring your own alcohol and be prepared to join more than 5,000 Glebe locals living it up with gusto.

Blues Point Reserve

Blues Point Road, McMahons Point; access via Blues Point Road. **Map** p327 E1.
A superb site with dress circle views of the fireworks and the Opera House. The road is closed to cars and the capacity is small, but don't be deterred. Alcohol is for sale only.

Bradfield Park

Alfred Street South, Milsons Point; access via Broughton Street or Alfred Street South. **Map** p327 F1.
If you can't get into Blues Point Reserve, try neighbouring Bradfield Park. There's room for 5,000 and the slope of the hill makes viewing good for all. You can't bring alcohol, but booze and food are for sale on site.

Cremorne Point Reserve

Milson Road, Cremorne; access via Milson Road.
One of Sydney's most spectacular vantage points, the leafy setting of Cremorne is a great place for families. Rock up early with your picnic blanket and sample how the chosen few live. There's room for 1,000 and food on sale, but bring your own booze.

Embarkation Park

Victoria Street, Potts Point; access via Victoria Street or Cowper Wharf Road. **Map** p330 J5.
Staying in Kings Cross? Then this is the place to catch the fireworks. It's heavily policed and you can't bring your own alcohol but there are stalls selling food and booze. There's room for 1,800 but come early for a prime spot.

Illoura Reserve

Peacock Point, Weston Street, East Balmain; access via Weston Street or Darling Street. **Map** p326 C3.
Stake your spot mid-afternoon in this pretty park. Expect 3,000 others to join you and don't bother coming by car – public transport is great here. Food is for sale; BYOB.

McKell Park

Darling Point Road, Darling Point; access via park gate on Darling Point Road or Darling Point Wharf. **Map** p331 M5.
Cocktails at dusk followed by champagne and canapés: this is the story for the Darling Point set gathering at McKell Park, the civilised place to watch the fireworks for those 500 in the know. If you're really clever you can drive here and park in the Point's side streets.

Mrs Macquarie's Point

Mrs Macquarie's Road, the Domain; access via Art Gallery Road. **Map** p330 J3.
The grand dame of vantage points – with some 22,000 fellow revellers. Food and alcohol are for sale only and there are plenty of police on site.

North Head

North Head Scenic Drive, Manly; access on foot via North Head Scenic Drive. **Map** p334.
Manly-ites make the trek to the Head rather than the city. Be prepared for a hike in the dark; bring a torch and something to sit on.

Sydney Opera House

Bennelong Point, Circular Quay; access via Macquarie Street. **Map** p327 G3.
First time? Then go join the milling throngs of around 6,000 hugging the sails of the Opera House. There's no doubt you'll get an in-your-face view, but be prepared for a tight squeeze.

is Sydney's major cultural event: held in the three weeks leading up to Australia Day (26 January), the festival hosts dance, theatre, visual arts, opera and music, with performances from home-grown and international superstars. Ticketed events are supplemented by an impressive free outdoor programme, including the Symphony & Jazz in the Domain evenings, plus some avant-garde firework displays.

Australia Day
Various venues (9513 2000/www.australiaday. com.au). **Date** 26 Jan.
Festivities take place all over the city (and the rest of Australia) in this annual celebration of European settlement in Australia. Events focus around Hyde Park, the Rocks and Darling Harbour, with music, food, kids' entertainment and plenty of flag-waving. A morning 'Woggan-ma-gule' ceremony takes place in the Botanic Gardens to acknowledge the 'traditional owners', the local indigenous Gadigal people; the day ends with a firework display over Darling Harbour.

Ferrython
Sydney Harbour (www.sydneyfestival.org.au). **Date** 26 Jan.
Thousands of spectators watch four of Sydney's catamaran ferries race for the title of Ferry Champion, with the Harbour Bridge as the finishing line. The race, from 11am, is a traditional part of the Sydney Festival's Australia Day celebrations (*see p215*), and is followed by a prize for best-dressed ferry. Good viewpoints are Milsons Point, McMahons Point, the Botanic Gardens and Mrs Macquarie's Chair.

Chinese New Year
Chinatown, Haymarket (9265 9333/www.cityof sydney.nsw.gov.au). CityRail Central/LightRail Capitol Square/Central. **Map** p329 F9. **Date** varies, usually end Jan/early Feb.
Head to Chinatown for the traditional 15 days of Chinese New Year festivities, complete with firecrackers, markets, a colourful parade and dragonboat racing on Darling Harbour.

Autumn

Gay & Lesbian Mardi Gras
Various venues (9568 8600/www.mardigras.org.au). **Date** Feb; ends 1st Sat in Mar.
The month of February sees Sydney celebrate all things queer. The city's gay, lesbian and transgender community swells with the arrival of thousands of international visitors, who join in an extravaganza of shows, exhibitions, plays, art, film and sport. The finale is the parade, which sees marching boys and girls shimmy and strut their stuff along the 'Golden Mile' from Hyde Park down Oxford Street to the party venue at the Entertainment Quarter. *See also p243.*

Royal Easter Show
Sydney Showground, Sydney Olympic Park, Homebush Bay (9704 1111/www.eastershow.com.au). CityRail Olympic Park. **Date** from Thur before Good Fri.

The Easter Show is a Sydney institution: for two weeks every year rural Australia is packaged up for the urbanites and attracts more than a million visitors. There are competitions galore – not just livestock prizes and sheepdog trials, but also contests for bees, alpacas, rats and mice, not to mention the popular women's wood-chopping contest.

Anzac Day March
Along George Street from Martin Place to Hyde Park. CityRail Circular Quay, Martin Place, Town Hall or Wynyard/ferry Circular Quay. **Map** (Martin Place) p327 F5–p329 F7. **Date** 25 Apr.
Sydneysiders pay their respects to the Australian and New Zealand troops killed at Gallipoli and in other wars by turning out in their thousands to watch the parade of veterans and Defence Force bands. A public holiday, the day starts with a dawn service at the Martin Place Cenotaph followed at 9am by a march along George Street and a 12.30pm service at the Anzac Memorial in Hyde Park. There are dawn services throughout Sydney and Australia.

Sydney Writers' Festival
Various venues (9252 7729/www.swf.org.au). **Date** last wk in May.
From highbrow to pulp, fact to fiction, writers from around the world as well as home-grown talents come together for a week of debate and discussion. This is Sydney's biggest literary event, with readings, workshops and the chance to meet authors. Some events are free, but all require booking.

Winter

Sydney Film Festival
Various venues (9318 0999/www.sydneyfilmfestival. org). **Date** 3wks in June.
Featuring innovative and independent as well as mainstream movies, this festival of film aims to please all with cinema from Australia and around the world. In 2008 the festival became part of an official international competition circuit, with 12 films from around the globe competing for a cash prize. For more details, see p230.

Biennale of Sydney
Various venues (9368 1411/www.biennaleofsydney. com). **Date** June-Sept, even-numbered years only.
Each festival explores a specific subject or theme through the works of Australian and international artists. Alongside what is claimed to be 'the southern hemisphere's largest collection of contemporary art' there are seminars, talks and screenings.

City to Surf Fun Run
From corner of Park & College Streets to Bondi Beach (1 800 555 514/www.city2surf.sunherald. com.au). **Date** mid Aug.
This 14km (8.7-mile) community fun run starts near Hyde Park and ends at Bondi Beach. Around 60,000 runners participate, mostly amateur joggers and walkers, with at least one chicken suit guaranteed.

Children

Fun in the sun for the little ones.

There's very little that's not open to children in Sydney, which makes it family holiday heaven. Beaches form a big part of the draw, but much more is on offer too, from amusement parks to aquariums, wildlife sanctuaries, museums and watersports for every age.

For full information on children's activities, pick up a copy of *Time Out*'s weekly magazine. For more on shops that sell children's clothes, *see p194*; for toy shops, *see p194*.

Beaches

Beaches both with and without surf co-exist at **Manly** (*see p119 and p139*), which also has pleasant walks and plenty of cheap places to eat. Head north for great playgrounds at **North Steyne** and **Queenscliff**. Head south along Fairy Bower, the waterfront pathway, and you'll find a paddling pool and safe swimming at **Shelly Beach** (*see p139*); older kids may even like to take a surf lesson (*see p259*). The surf at **Bondi Beach** (*see p137*) is usually too strong and crowded for little ones, but there's a paddling pool and playgrounds at the north end, and lots of space for inline skating. At the south end is a challenging skateboarders' ramp.

South of Bondi, sheltered **Bronte Beach** (*see p137*) has a large park with barbecue facilities, a fantastic playground and a superb fish and chip shop. While the sea is too dangerous here for youngsters, there's a great natural rock pool that fills up at high tide and an ocean pool, tended in the summer by lifeguards. Next door, **Clovelly Beach** (*see p137*) is one of the safest and most tranquil in Sydney, with lots of colourful fish awaiting snorkellers. On land there are barbecue pavilions, a playground, rock pools and surrounding grassy cliffs for the perfect picnic. **Balmoral Beach** (*see p136*) on the North Shore is also good for picnics, and you can sip a drink in the café while the kids enjoy the playground or swim in a netted area.

Of the northern beaches, the best options are **Dee Why Beach**, with a good playground and various child-friendly eateries, and **Collaroy Beach** (*see p140*), with a paddling pool, large playground and barbecue facilities. Further north, secluded **Clareville Beach** (*see p123*) is a safe swimming beach on the Pittwater (western) side of the peninsula; the water's too shallow for adults, but is ideal for little kids.

Wherever you go, respect the surf and don't swim outside the marker flags. For other family-friendly beaches, *see pp134-140*.

Child-friendly pubs

In the north the historic **Newport Arms Hotel** (*see p187*) has a vast garden with views over Ku-ring-gai Chase National Park (*see p124*), three kids' playgrounds, a garden bistro and all-weather dining areas. Alternatively, the **Palm Beach RSL** (1087 Barrenjoey Road, 9974 5566, www.palmbeachrsl.com.au) has a deck area in its beer garden with lots of space for kids. In the south try **Northies Cronulla Hotel** (corner of Kingsway and Elouera Road, 9523 6866, www.northies.com.au) with its bistro and terraced bar area. In the east the **Clovelly Hotel** (381 Clovelly Road, 9665 1214, www.clovellyhotel.com.au) has a large family-friendly bistro and outdoor deck. And out west the **Rose Hotel** in Chippendale (54 Cleveland Street, 9318 1133, www.therosehotel.com.au) has a rustic beer garden serving pizzas.

Museums

As well as animal skeletons, the **Australian Museum** (*see p75*) has interactive exhibits, including Kids' Island, an indoor play and discovery area for those under six. The **Australian National Maritime Museum** (*see p84*) has a playground, plus various ships waiting to be explored.

Parks & playgrounds

For wet and wild adventures without the beach, head to **Manly Waterworks** (corner of West Esplanade and Commonwealth Parade, 9949 1088, www.manlywaterworks.com); sluicing down the gullet of the Insane Earthworm is an experience never to be forgotten.

Darling Harbour (*see p83*) is touristy, but has lots for kids of all ages. There's a giant playground at Tumbalong Park, conveniently surrounded by cafés, and also a fun water play area, paddle-boats and a merry-go-round – not to mention the Sydney Aquarium (*see p85*) and an IMAX cinema (*see p229*). At weekends and during school holidays you'll see lots of street entertainers and may well chance upon an open-air concert or dusk firework display.

The best
Kid stops

For a rainy day
The nautical but nice **Australian National Maritime Museum** (*see p218*).

For safe swimming
Net gains at **Balmoral Beach** (*see p218*).

For animal magic
Close encounters of the furred kind at **Taronga Zoo** (*see right*).

For eating outside
Alfresco fun at the **Newport Arms Hotel** (*see p218*).

The **Entertainment Quarter** (*see p94*), next to the Sydney Cricket Ground in Moore Park, also has a great playground, an enormous open area where older kids can run wild, and lots of cinemas and child-friendly restaurants. Other attractions include an ice rink (winter only) and the indoor play centre Lollipop's Playland (1300 565 547).

For older children, lovely **Centennial Park** (*see p93*) in Woollahra is big and buzzing with activity: inline skates, bikes and pedal cars can be hired from Centennial Park Cycles (*see p258*) at the corner of Hamilton and Grand Drives, and for horseriders there's the Centennial Parklands Equestrian Centre (*see p258*).

Services

Dial an Angel
1300 721 111. **Phone enquiries** 8.30am-8.30pm daily. **Credit** AmEx, MC, V.
Offers an excellent 24-hour nanny or babysitting service. All carers are carefully screened.

Theatre & concerts

The school holidays, especially Christmas, are the time for children's concerts and pantos, and there are more during the **Sydney Festival** (*see p215*) in January; check local newspapers and *Time Out*'s weekly magazine for up-to-date details. At the **Sydney Opera House** (*see p254*), the Kids at the House programme offers an introduction to music, dance and theatre.

Wildlife

Shark fans should head to **Sydney Aquarium** (*see p85*) and **Oceanworld Manly** (*see p121*). Both offer close encounters with sharks and

stingrays, as well as hands-on experiences with starfish and sea urchins. Oceanworld Manly also has an interactive 'Dangerous Australian Animals' show and sleepover nights for kids. Sydney Aquarium offers an incredible range of marine life, including fairy penguins and seals.

Harbourside, **Taronga Zoo** (*see p116*) has both native Australian and exotic animals on show. There are tours, presentations and a great petting zoo that should keep kids happy all day. The most scenic way to get there is by ferry – from the dock you can catch a cable car up the hill to the zoo's main entrance and work your way back down to the ferry.

For more home-grown creatures, head west to **Featherdale Wildlife Park** (*see p128*) near Blacktown, where kids can hand-feed a wallaby, kangaroo or emu and have their photo taken with a koala. More koala cuddling is on offer at the **Koala Park Sanctuary** (*see below*).

A colony of flapping fruit bats inhabits the spacious **Royal Botanic Gardens** (*see p77*) on the harbour – it's also an ideal picnic spot and kids love the tour by 'trackless train'.

If you want to get out into the bush, there are several easy walks in and around Sydney, in particular at **Berry Island Reserve** (*see p117*), where you'll find a short track with informative plaques about the area's Aboriginal heritage. **Manly Dam Reserve**, off King Street, Manly Vale (catch a bus from Wynyard or Manly Wharf), has easy and very scenic walks, and you can swim safely. The **NSW National Parks & Wildlife Service** runs Discovery walks, talks and tours for children (1300 361 967, www.nationalparks.nsw.gov.au).

Australian Reptile Park
Gosford exit of Sydney-Newcastle Freeway, Somersby (4340 1022/www.reptilepark.com.au). CityRail Gosford then 10min taxi ride. **Open** 9am-5pm daily. **Admission** $22.50; $15 reductions; $11.50 3-15s; $60 family of four; free under-3s. **Credit** AmEx, MC, V.
An hour's drive north of Sydney lives this collection of cold-blooded critters, creepy-crawlies and native animals including koalas, echidnas, wombats and Tasmanian devils. There are lots of noisy, colourful birds too. Interactive exhibits include Spider World and the Lost World of Reptiles.

Koala Park Sanctuary
84 Castle Hill Road, West Pennant Hills (9484 3141/ www.koalaparksanctuary.com.au). CityRail Pennant Hills then bus 632, 636. **Open** 9am-5pm daily. **Admission** $19; $9 reductions; free under-4s. **Credit** AmEx, DC, MC, V.
There's no denying that koalas are Australia's cutest animal, and what child wouldn't want to cuddle one? The main attractions are joined here by their compatriots – emus, kangaroos, echidnas, dingoes and wombats – plus there are ten acres of lush rainforest, eucalyptus groves and native gardens to explore.

Arts & Entertainment

Clubs

Get down under and party.

They go out two by two from the **Arq Sydney**.

Arts & Entertainment

There was a time when Sydney's clubs struggled to fill their biggest nights despite a wealth of gimmicks, but not anymore. Whether it's the mainstream locales of **Home** (*see p222*) and **Arq Sydney** (*see p221*), or seedy late-night haunts such as **Q Bar** (*see p223*), Sydney's club scene is alive and thriving, with a wealth of local and big-name international DJs filling their stages on a regular basis.

This return to former glories can be laid squarely at the feet of **Fuzzy**, the dance outfit that specialises in annual outdoor events. The **Parklife** festival in Centennial Park (September), **Harbourlife** at Lady Macquarie's Chair (November), **A Shore Thing** on Bondi Beach (New Year's Eve) and **Field Day** in the Domain (New Year's Day) all sell out in a matter of seconds. This erstwhile niche outfit for serious clubbers has revived the dance music scene in Sydney with a word-of-mouth buzz that's had a knock-on effect few would have predicted (its weekly club night is old favourite Sounds on Sunday, at the Greenwood Hotel in North Sydney). As a result, there's been a boom in venues both working hard to keep their crowds content – including **Moulin Rouge** (*see p222*) and **Slip Inn** (*see p223*) – plus younger talent trying its luck, such as the **Sapphire Suite** (*see p223*).

In addition, the likes of website www.inthemix.com.au and weekly clubbing bible *3D World* (available in pubs and record stores) sponsor events and stages like never before. And **Future Music** – the latest outfit taking on Fuzzy with its Future Music Festival, associated sideshows and regular club nights (the main one being Famous, at Home, on Saturdays) – only adds to the buoyancy.

The age group remains determinedly teen and twentysomething at its core, but brave thirtysomethings still try their luck. And as fashions change, so do the accessories. For older souls, the sight of fluoro sticks around teens' necks and wrists is likely to produce mild amusement, but the '80s throwbacks are here in force. And since it's Sydney, the Oxford Street strip remains a stronghold for the gay community and its partygoers.

Whether it's upstairs at the **Colombian** (*see p222*), classic night Kink at the hip **Oxford Art Factory** (*see p222*), or a hedonistically camp big name bash at Arq, Sydney's club scene has something for everybody. And everybody, it seems, is out to party hard.

Bars & clubs

Arq Sydney

16 Flinders Street, between Oxford & Taylor Streets, Darlinghurst (9380 8700/www.arqsydney.com.au). Bus 311, 333, 352, 373, 377, 378, 380, 392, 394, 396. **Open** 9pm-late Thur-Sun. **Admission** (after 10pm) $20 Fri; $25 Sat; $5 Sun. **No credit cards.** **Map** p329 H9.

The quintessential gay club par excellence bumps and grinds with wild abandon, bolstered by a regular influx of big-name local talent to pump it up. The main action takes place over two levels, with a flesh-friendly vibe throughout. Weekends remain the gay-focused nights, while weekdays are more mixed. There's a cash point for when it's too late to care.

ArtHouse Hotel

275 Pitt Street, between Park & Market Streets, CBD (9284 1200/www.thearthousehotel.com.au). CityRail St James or Town Hall/Monorail Galeries Victoria. **Open** *Verge Bar, Gallery Bar & Dome Lounge* 11am-midnight Mon-Thur; 11am-3am Fri; 5pm-6am Sat. *Attic Bar* 5pm-late Wed-Sat. **Admission** *Saturday Sessions* $25. **Credit** AmEx, DC, MC, V. **Map** p329 F7.

The Saturday Sessions transform this former 19th-century school of art – which has also been a chapel and a theatre in its day – into a 21st-century club with attitude. With an admission price about as lofty as the mile-high stilettos that the wannabe models teeter in on, it makes for an expensive night out. Dress up, think funky and praise be for dark corners to hide in, as this is a young, glamourous crowd. Great cocktails are served in the Attic Bar (*see p178*).

Beach Road Hotel

Corner of Beach Road & Glenayr Avenue, Bondi Beach (9130 7247/www.beachrdhotel.com.au). CityRail Bondi Junction then bus 380, 381, 333/ bus 380, 333. **Open** *Club* 7-11.30pm Tue-Thur; 7pm-1am Fri, Sat; 4-10.30pm Sun. **Admission** free. **Credit** MC, V. **Map** p334.

While you have to wear more than a bikini top, this Bondi institution – a favourite haunt for backpackers – is one of the few places where thongs (flip-flops) get through the door. School-night closing times keep extended frenzy under control, but it's still a club option for those who want to hop from beach to disco in just a few bounds. Resembling an ultra-glam RSL, this is a club filled with beautiful people on a mission to mingle – and, best of all, it's free to get in. Live acts perform on Tuesdays, Thursdays and Sundays, but the hotel shifts to dance mode on Friday and Saturday nights, with DJs playing anything from dub to house.

Cargo Bar

52-60 The Promenade, King Street Wharf, Darling Harbour (9262 1777/www.cargobar.com.au). CityRail Wynyard/ferry Darling Harbour/Monorail Darling Park. **Open** *Bar* 11am-late daily. *DJs* 6pm-late Thur-Sun. **Credit** AmEx, DC, MC, V. **Map** p326 D6.

Cargo Bar works hard to carry cred, and it has to: it doesn't have the coolest crowd by any means, but it does have an impressive water view. It's a bar most of the time, with DJs shifting it into club mode on weekends, and it also hosts semi-regular band nights, usually on Sundays.

Club 77

77 William Street, between Crown & Yurong Streets, East Sydney (9361 3387). CityRail Kings Cross. **Open** 8pm-late Thur-Sun. **Admission** $20. **Credit** AmEx, DC, MC, V. **Map** p329 G7.

Off the skids and very cool, Club 77 keeps it dark, underground and ultra-hip. Sydney's fashion trash turn up for the Bang Gang crew on Fridays, while the long-running Club Kooky, on Sunday nights,

The pleasure principle

Justin Hemmes is a man on a mission: the lanky, 34-year-old playboy and nightclub prince is determined to bring upscale urban glamour to Sydney's nightlife. In doing so, Hemmes is often seen cutting a dash around town – regularly photographed amid a bevy of beauties at all the glitziest parties – but there's more to this Gucci-loafered dandy than you might think.

At just 26 years old, Hemmes thrilled Sydney with his multi-level style palace **Establishment** (*see p35*), which combines restaurants, clubs, bars and even a boutique hotel without breaking a sweat. And at the dawn of 2008 Hemmes was putting his reputation and fortune on the line once more with the $150 million **Ivy** (*see p180*). This self-proclaimed 'pleasure precinct' (a stone's throw from Establishment on George Street) promises to house no less than 18 bars – from cocktail haunts and a French-style wine bar to an ale house – plus nine restaurants, nightclubs, shops, two penthouse hotel suites, a day spa and a 25-metre swimming pool bar. Licensing the joint proved an early headache for Hemmes, but he got the green light at the end of 2007 and was opening his new pad in stages at the time of writing, so keep your eyes peeled for what could be a defining moment in Sydney's nightlife.

Home.

shines its light on camp with art students a-go-go – it's also a big hit with the gay crowd (*see p240*). Bands sometimes play too.

Colombian Hotel

117-123 Oxford Street, at the corner of Oxford & Crown Streets, Darlinghurst (9360 2151). Bus 311, 333, 352, 373, 377, 378, 380, 392, 394, 396. **Open** 9am-6am daily. **Credit** AmEx, MC, V. **Map** p329 G8.
Once a Westpac bank, the Colombian has superseded its neighbour Stonewall in becoming the hottest gay bar and club on Oxford Street. The bar area downstairs looks out onto the strip, while on the dancefloor upstairs a generally gay (and occasionally more mixed) crowd jives to whatever is on offer.

The Cross

The Bourbon, 24 Darlinghurst Road, at Macleay Street, Kings Cross (9358 1144/www.thebourbon. com.au). CityRail Kings Cross. **Open** 10pm-6am Fri-Sun. **Admission** $15. **Credit** (bar only) AmEx, DC, MC, V. **Map** p330 J7.
There's something a little sad about the sleaze of Sydney giving way to the schmooze of style. The old Bourbon & Beefsteak, once the bastion of sailors on shore leave and all the Kings Cross skullduggery that accompanied them, is now simply the slick and shiny Bourbon (*see p184*), with its own club, the Cross. Leather ottomans seat a sleek clientele, there to groove to anything from R&B to relaxed, sexy house on Sundays. With the Bourbon restaurant serving medium-priced, bistro-style food, it makes for an easy night out with friends.

Home

Cockle Bay Wharf, Darling Harbour (9266 0600/ www.homesydney.com). CityRail Town Hall/Monorail Darling Park/ferry Darling Harbour. **Open** *Bar* 11am-late daily. *Club* 11pm-7am Fri; 11pm-6.30am Sat. **Admission** *Club* $25 Fri, Sat. **No credit cards**. **Map** p328 D7.
Home is one of Sydney's few old-school, large-scale clubbing experiences. It sprawls over three levels and four bars, with chill-out areas, space-age lighting and a great view over Darling Harbour. Sublime on Friday spills over with everything from house to trance to drum 'n' bass, and flips its finger at critics by remaining the longest-running club night in the city. Future Music's Famous rocks up on Saturday, and the club also hosts the self-explanatory Homosexual (*see p242*).

Lady Lux

2 Roslyn Street, between Darlinghurst Road & Ward Avenue, Kings Cross (9361 5000/www. ladylux.com.au) CityRail Kings Cross. **Open** 10pm-5am Fri, Sat; 10pm-6am Sun. **Admission** $20. **No credit cards**. **Map** p330 J7.
Lady Lux runs the gamut of what's happening in Sydney, aimed squarely at the MySpace crowd with short attention spans and egos to match. Friday nights are Bread and Butter deep house favourites. Dark lighting, bordello-style wallpaper and leather seating all keep it warm, funky and intimate, but it gets packed out and extremely hot.

Moulin Rouge

39 Darlinghurst Road, at Springfield Avenue, Kings Cross (8354 1711/www.moulinrougesydney.com.au). CityRail Kings Cross. **Open** 10pm-6am Fri, Sat; 9.30pm-6am Sun. **Admission** $10-$20. **Credit** AmEx, MC, V. **Map** p330 J7.
Think *Moulin Rouge!* the movie and you've got the gist of this club, part of the once-burgeoning burlesque scene in the city. The look is gaudy and red, while the waitresses in corsets and fishnets are matched only by the towering models this place attracts, fiercely pretty in skyscraper heels. Masks and feathers aren't unusual dress options, although the owner insists that the dress code is reasonably relaxed. The dancefloor serves almost as a stage to the three tiered cages rising above, where you can drink absinthe while listening to laid-back funky breaks and disco.

Oxford Art Factory

38-46 Oxford Street, at Pelican Street, Darlinghurst (9332 3711/www.oxfordartfactory.com). Bus 373, 377, 378, 380, 382, 391, 394, 396. **Open** 9pm-late Thur-Sun. **Admission** (after 10pm) $10 Fri, Sun; $20 Sat. **No credit cards**. **Map** p329 G8.
The hippest venue on the Oxford Street strip, Art Factory favours big-name DJs and bands, with a handful of great club nights (notably Kink, previously at ArtHouse; *see p221*). The venue is sleek, simple and roomy, with a no-frills attitude both inside and out. The cool factor, however, is always evident thanks to a hugely in-the-know crowd.

Q Bar
Exchange Hotel, Level 3, 34-44 Oxford Street, between Riley & Liverpool Streets, Darlinghurst (9360 1375). CityRail Museum/bus 311, 333, 352, 373, 377, 378, 380, 392, 394, 396. **Open** 10pm-late Wed-Sun. **Admission** $15 Fri; $20 Sat. **Credit** AmEx, MC, V. **Map** p329 G8.
The big, busy Q Bar is the seedy after-party joint for anyone and everyone. Whether it's gangsters or hipsters, there's a dancefloor that swirls with funk and house, becoming the burlesque club 34b on Friday nights with a VIP area for members offering ping-pong tables and loungers.

Sapphire Suite
2 Kellet Street, at Bayswater Road, Kings Cross (9331 0058/www.sapphiresuite.com.au). CityRail Kings Cross. **Open** 8pm-6am Thur-Sun. **Admission** (after 9pm) $15 Fri-Sun. **Credit** AmEx MC, V. **Map** p330 J7.
In a vain attempt to bring a touch of Tank-style glamour to the Cross, the Sapphire's interior designers have gone all out with a sapphire-inspired rock wall trickling with water behind the long bar. The effect is ice, ice baby – which is perhaps just as it should be for the sweaty dancers who come here for acid jazz on Thursday, live percussionists versus DJs on Friday, vocal house on Saturday and retro funk on Sunday. Arrive early on Thursday and Friday for free champagne and cheap cocktails.

Slip Inn
111 Sussex Street, at King Street, CBD (8295 9911/www.merivale.com.au). CityRail Town Hall or Wynyard. **Open** *Slip Bar* noon-midnight Mon-Thur; noon-2am Fri; 5pm-2am Sat. *Sand Bar* noon-midnight Mon-Thur; noon-3am Fri; 5pm-3am Sat. *Garden Bar* noon-midnight Mon-Fri; 5pm-midnight Sat. *Chinese Laundry* 10pm-4am Fri; 10.30pm-4am Sat. *Cave* 11pm-4am Fri, Sat. **Admission** $10-$15 Fri; $15-$25 Sat. **Credit** AmEx, DC, MC, V. **Map** p327 E6.
The Slip Inn – forever famous locally as being the place where Aussie estate agent Mary Donaldson met her future husband, the Prince of Denmark – houses three bars (Slip, Sand and Garden) and two clubs (Chinese Laundry and the smaller Cave). Chinese Laundry splits itself into two nights: Break Inn on Fridays and the pricier, pumped-up Laundry on Saturdays. Currently very popular is the Garden Bar – a huge, sun-filled courtyard at the rear that hosts a buzzing outdoor day club every Sunday. Its organisers also run other local and international events; details at www.jammusic.com.au.

Sly Fox
199 Enmore Road, between Cambridge Street & Stanmore Road, Enmore (9557 1016). Bus 423, 426, 428. **Open** 10am-4am Mon-Thur; 10am-6am Fri, Sat; 9am-midnight Sun. **No credit cards**.
One of the strangest yet hottest little happenings in town at the moment, the Sly Fox has fooled clubbers into believing it's something more than a local pub. Located at the grungier, western end of Enmore, it

Chinese Laundry at **Slip Inn**.

offers funk on Thursday, drum 'n' bass on Friday and rotating DJs on Saturday. Wednesday brings lesbians and drag kings to the popular girls' night (*see p239*). Cocktails cost $5 between 7pm and 9pm.

Tank
3 Bridge Lane, off Bridge Street, between George & Pitt Streets, CBD (9240 3000/www.tankclub.com.au). CityRail Circular Quay or Wynyard/ferry Circular Quay. **Open** 10pm-6am Fri, Sat. **Admission** $20 Fri; $25 Sat. **Credit** AmEx, DC, MC, V. **Map** p327 F4.
This high-columned über-club is the closest thing you'll get to a Studio 54 experience in Sydney. Big on style, Tank even credits the sound and lighting dudes on its website – it's nice to think the clubbers may care. The music itself has settled into comfortable funky house on Fridays and a chunkier sound on Saturdays, with loads of international DJs.

Yu at Soho Bar
Soho Bar, 171 Victoria Street, between Darlinghurst Road & Orwell Street, Potts Point (9358 6511/www.yu.com.au). CityRail Kings Cross. **Open** *Bar* 10am-4am Mon-Thur, Sun; 10am-6am Fri, Sat. *Yu* 9pm-6am Thur-Sun. **Admission** $10-$20. **Credit** (bar only) AmEx, DC, MC, V. **Map** p330 J7.
Fridays draw the shiny young set to Fight Night, while Saturdays bring Trashbags, often with international DJs. Sunday night Your Mum shifts to sophisticated grooves and a more mixed crowd. Yu is worth dressing up for, and its designers were thoughtful enough to install a sprung dancefloor.

Arts & Entertainment

Film

The movie capital of the southern hemisphere.

Putting on the glitz: the **Hayden Orpheum Picture Palace**. *See p228.*

In Sydney going to the movies is almost as popular as going surfing, having a barbecue or watching the Test series, which is a telling sign of how much the city's cultural landscape is shifting. Such passion is fuelled by local stars who have made it in Tinseltown only to then give back in a major way. *X-Men* superhero Hugh Jackman and his actress wife Deborra-Lee Furness are a perfect example. In late 2006 the couple announced plans to produce four to five films in Australia a year (a joint initiative with Fox); their company Seed Productions already produces local documentaries and TV shows, and even works in the theatre. Add to this Nicole Kidman returning home to film Baz Luhrmann's epic *Australia* (*see p225* **All that Baz**) and the multi-award winning Cate Blanchett back to take the helm at the Sydney Theatre Company (*see p271* **The Cate factor**), and there's a lot of pride in town.

Behind the glitter there's much more going on in the local film world – stand-outs include Joel Edgerton as actor and co-writer of *The Square*, directed by his brother Nash; Brendan

Cowell as a troubled cop in the edgy *Noise*; and Eric Bana (aka *The Hulk*) in Richard Roxburgh's touching *Romulus, My Father*. Local movies are supported by a clutch of well-attended film festivals all over the country, plus the Australian Film Awards and Inside Film Awards, and tend to focus on hard-hitting, soul-searching issues examining the nature of modern Australia – from Aboriginal anger to the sex trafficking of illegal immigrants. While they may not match Hollywood fare at the box office, these rites of passage still capture a devoted audience. That said, blockbuster films remain the big show-stoppers, with stars pouring into Sydney to appear at premières and push the lucrative Australian box office.

Reflecting this boom is the nature of cinema-going itself. Watching movies outdoors has become a private Sydney passion, with the hugely succesful **OpenAir Cinema** (*see p230*) and **Moonlight Cinema** (*see p230*) leading the fray. Indoors, where once there was a series of independent cinemas dotted about town, now there are virtually none. Inevitably bowing to the teen-targeted multiplexes, the heritage-listed **Ritz Cinema Randwick** (*see p226*) and **Hayden Orpheum Picture Palace** (*see p228*) both screen mainstream fare. But despite the homogenisation, Sydney has a healthy appetite for art-house cinema, found at the **Palace**, **Dendy** and **Chauvel** theatres. And the giant theatres offer a luxurious touch, with **Hoyts EQ**'s La Premiere (*see p226*) and **Greater Union Bondi Junction**'s Gold Class options (*see p226*) available at a price.

TICKETS AND INFORMATION

First-run movies open on Thursdays, with three to four premières a week. Unless it's a blockbuster, you can usually get a ticket without a problem. Prices are around $15 to $16 for adults, with reductions for children, senior citizens, students and the unemployed. Public holidays usually involve a $1 'surcharge', while Monday and Tuesday are traditionally bargain nights, when tickets are reduced to as little as $5. The major chains – Hoyts, Greater Union, Palace and Dendy – have websites with screening times, plus there are cinema ads in the entertainment sections of the *Sydney Morning Herald* and *Daily Telegraph*. Screen times are also available through the **Cinema Information Line** (1 902 263 456), albeit for a premium-rate call fee.

Cinemas

First-run

The multiplexes typically offer Hollywood blockbusters and kids' movies. Christmas, September school holidays and the Easter long weekend are key periods for distributors, who often hold back movies for that all-important opening weekend at these times.

All that Baz

Without them, Fox Studios may never have been built and it's debatable whether ballroom dancing would have enjoyed the revival it did. Such is the influence and pulling power of Baz Luhrmann and his wife Catherine Martin.

In 2007 the writer, producer and director of *Moulin Rouge!*, *Romeo + Juliet* and *Strictly Ballroom* was at it again. His epic tale *Australia*, set against the backdrop of World War II, not only saw him reunited with star Nicole Kidman, but promised to bring a massive boost for the tourism of New South Wales upon its August 2008 release, having already swelled the state's coffers during production. NSW Minister for Tourism Matt Brown proudly declared that the film – shot in NSW, Queensland, the Northern Territory and Western Australia – would be 'a stunning showcase of our country to the rest of the world' and would provide a great benefit to tourism, although he wouldn't be drawn on specific figures. Thanks to the historical epic, which co-stars Hugh Jackman, film and TV production in the state jumped from a meagre $120 million to $283 million between 2006 and 2007, an increase of 45 per cent.

Luhrmann's film – which at various stages featured the late Heath Ledger (who dropped out to film *The Dark Knight*) and Russell Crowe (who proved too expensive) – literally took over the tiny town of Bowen in

Nicole Kidman in *Australia*.

Queensland, much to the delight of the Sydney media that followed in droves. Filming drew the wrath of locals, however, when a World War I memorial was clambered over during a scene involving a cattle stampede. Due to the public outcry, the director was forced to ditch the scene from the final cut. Even Baz doesn't always get it right.

Greater Union Bondi Junction

Westfield Bondi Junction, Level 6, 500 Oxford Street, Bondi Junction (9300 1555/www.greater union.com.au). CityRail Bondi Junction/bus 333, 352, 378, 380. **Screens** 11. **Tickets** $16; $7-$12.50 reductions; $9 Tue. **Credit** AmEx, DC, MC, V. **Map** p333 P11.

This ultra-modern complex has cheery staff, digital surround sound, comfy seating, its own bar, a 'fine dining' food court right on its doorstep and harbour views to boot. Programmes feature a mix of block-busters and the mainstream end of art-house. There's free parking in the Westfield car parks for up to three hours, but be sure to factor in the half hour it takes to find a spot here. The Gold Class option ($22-$36), similar to Hoyts EQ's La Premiere (*see below*), offers plush armchairs that recline until you're almost horizontal, a separate lounge and the option of food and drink on demand.

Greater Union George Street

505-525 George Street, between Bathurst & Liverpool Streets, CBD (9273 7431/www.greater union.com.au). CityRail Town Hall/Monorail World Square. **Screens** 17. **Tickets** $16; $7-$12.50 reductions; $9 Tue. **Credit** AmEx, DC, MC, V. **Map** p329 E7.

This sprawling cinema complex shows virtually every new commercial movie release as soon as it opens. Located in the heart of George Street's garish entertainment strip, it attracts throngs of noisy kids and can get a little edgy at night, so guard your valuables. The state-of-the-art auditoria with digital surround sound and comfy (if rather narrow) seats are especially popular with teens and out-of-town-ers, as you'll see from the queues.

Hoyts Broadway

Broadway Shopping Centre, Bay Street, at Greek Street, Glebe (9211 1911/www.hoyts.com.au). Bus 370, 412, 431, 432, 433, 434. **Screens** 12. **Tickets** $15.50; $8.50-$12 reductions; $9.50 Tue. **Credit** AmEx, DC, MC, V. **Map** p328 C9.

Situated on top of a major shopping mecca, this huge complex (the largest auditorium has 379 seats) often wilts under the pressure of sheer numbers, particularly at weekends when the rowdy teen crowd descends. Three of the theatres are 'CinemaxX' standard, with high-backed seats, perfect sight lines, super-large screens and digital surround sound. As with the Palace chain's 'Babes in Arms' events, 'Mums and Bubs' sessions for movie-craving carers and their infants run twice a month.

Hoyts EQ

Bent Street, Entertainment Quarter, Driver Avenue, Moore Park (9332 1300/www.hoyts.com.au). Bus 355, 371, 372, 391, 392, 393, 394, 395, 396, 397, 399, 890. **Screens** 12. **Tickets** $15.50; $8.50-$12 reductions; $9 Tue ($8 reductions). *La Premiere* $32 ($24 seat only); $20 Tue. **Credit** AmEx, DC, MC, V. **Map** p332 K12.

Located in the Entertainment Quarter, part of the Fox Studios complex, this vast pseudo-retro cinema boasts huge screens, stadium seating (total capacity 3,000) and smart facilities, and is a refreshing change from the pushing, shoving and traffic-choked thoroughfare of George Street. A classy upgrade package, popular with first-time daters, is La Premiere: for twice the cost of a usual ticket you get a cosy, two-person sofa with unobstructed views, plus free soft drinks, tea, coffee, snacks, hot food and popcorn in the La Premiere lounge. There's also booze to buy, which you can take in with you, and single seats are available for those not in a couple.

Manly Cinemas

25/43-45 East Esplanade, opposite Manly Wharf, Manly (9977 0644/www.manlycinemas.com.au). Ferry Manly. **Screens** 2. **Tickets** $14; $7-$12 reductions. **No credit cards**. **Map** p334.

This modest two-screener opposite the wharf features quality art-house flicks and selected mainstream movies, and is a second home to Manly's many culture vultures. There's stadium seating, a recently upgraded sound system and fresh juice on sale in the foyer.

Reading Cinemas

Market City, 9-13 Hay Street, entrance on Thomas Street, Haymarket (9280 1202/www.readingcinemas.com.au). CityRail Central/LightRail or Monorail Paddy's Markets. **Screens** 5. **Tickets** $15.50; $9-$12.50 reductions; $9 Tue. **Credit** MC, V. **Map** p329 E8.

A youngish pup in the local market, the American-owned Reading chain has its Chinatown five-screens directly above Paddy's Market. Appropriately enough, it favours first-release mainstream and Asian movies (in Cantonese with English subtitles). Seats are supremely comfortable and all the screens have Dolby digital sound.

Ritz Cinema Randwick

43-47 St Paul's Street, at Avoca Street, Randwick (9399 5722/www.ritzcinema.com.au). Bus 372, 373, 376, 377. **Screens** 6. **Tickets** $10; $7-$9 reductions; $7 Tue. **Credit** MC, V.

With a distinctive art deco design restored to its former 1930s glory and an impressive sound system, the six-screen Ritz cinema is both a local landmark and an excellent venue for catching the latest mainstream releases. Signs explain the regulations – no alcohol, bare feet, smoking or skateboards – which make sense if you hit the place in the afternoon after school's out. In the evening the place attracts a different crowd, including film geeks who seek out the Ritz for its great acoustics and old-fashioned flair. Upstairs the inimitable Bar Ritz boasts a marble bar and balcony – perfect for pre- and post-film drinks.

Art house

Both the Dendy and Palace cinema chains have great-value membership schemes, which are well worth the investment if you plan to go to the cinema regularly.

Chauvel

Paddington Town Hall, corner of Oxford Street & Oatley Road, Paddington (9361 5398/ www.chauvelcinema.net.au). Bus 333, 352, 378, 380. **Screens** 2. **Tickets** $15.50; $9-$12.50 reductions; $8 Tue. **Credit** AmEx, DC, MC, V. **Map** p332 J10.

Named after the Australian film pioneer Charles Chauvel – of *Jedda* fame – this much-loved local cinema recently reopened after a period of closure. Its proscenium arch brings true grandeur to the art of film and the staff really know their stuff. Screenings tend to be seriously arty and the place also plays a part in the annual Sydney Festival (*see p230*). Be sure to seek out the lovely upstairs bar.

Cinema Paris

Bent Street, Entertainment Quarter, Driver Avenue, Moore Park (9332 1633/www.hoyts.com.au). Bus 355, 371, 372, 391, 392, 393, 394, 395, 396, 397, 399, 890. **Screens** 4. **Tickets** $15.50; $8.50-$12.50 reductions; $9 Tue. **Credit** AmEx, DC, MC, V. **Map** p332 K12.

An unassuming art-house cinema within Fox Studios' Entertainment Quarter, with a total seating capacity of 600. The Paris also hosts several film festivals including the Bollywood film fesitval.

Dendy Newtown

261-263 King Street, between Mary & Church Streets, Newtown (9550 5699/www.dendy.com.au). CityRail Newtown. **Screens** 4. **Tickets** $14; $8-$10.50 reductions; $9 Mon. **Credit** AmEx, DC, MC, V. **Map** p334.

Matching its Opera Quays sister (*see below*) for style if not setting, the Dendy Newtown offers quality first releases, 562 super-comfortable seats, big screens, Dolby digital surround sound and a bar. There's free parking for film-goers in the Lennox Street car park behind the cinema – a definite plus on the often jam-packed King Street.

Dendy Opera Quays

2 East Circular Quay, Circular Quay, CBD (9247 3800/www.dendy.com.au). CityRail/ferry Circular Quay. **Screens** 3. **Tickets** $14; $8-$10.50 reductions; $9 Mon. **Credit** AmEx, DC, MC, V. **Map** p327 G3.

A stone's throw from the Opera House, with great views to the Harbour Bridge, this luxurious complex (with a total capacity of 579) usually offers a mix of middlebrow and art-house fare, and is fully licensed. There's also disabled access to all screens.

Govinda's

112 Darlinghurst Road, between William & Hardie Streets, Darlinghurst (9380 5155/ www.govindas.com.au). CityRail Kings Cross. **Screens** 1. **Tickets** $11.90; $25.80 with meal. **Credit** AmEx, MC, V. **Map** p330 J8.

Adored by its twenty- and thirtysomething regulars, this Krishna-operated restaurant-cum-quality art-house cinema is a must-visit film experience. After you've loaded up on the generous vegetarian buffet, sit (or lie) back on the cushions and bean bags and enjoy arty films, documentaries and classics in 35mm. You can watch and not eat, but diners are

OpenAir Cinema. *See p230.*

Arts & Entertainment

Destination Sydney

It's one of the oldest of its kind in the world, but the **Sydney Film Festival** (*see p230*) has always had something of a parochial feel about it. The problem has been largely down to geography: because Australia is so far away from other Western film-making nations, the festival hasn't been able to emulate London or New York with lavish A-list premières and parties – until now.

As of 2008, the Sydney Film Festival, now in its 55th year, will be an official competition accredited by the International Federation of Film Producers Associations, with 12 films from around the world selected to compete for a cash prize of $60,000. As Marketing Manager Carmel England explains: 'We'd love to be able to get the calibre of George Clooney or Susan Sarandon out here in the future. Now, with new funding and an international judging panel, that's far more likely.'

Carmel also points out that what it lacks in glamour, the festival more than makes up for with its highly innovative programming. 'It's incredibly diverse,' she says, 'plus audience numbers (over 125,000 in 2007) are higher here than in London, which is staggering. And when you consider that 65 to 70 per cent of the films we show wouldn't otherwise be seen, what we're doing here is actually far more important.'

given entry preference and since there are only 65 seats in the cinema – roughly half the restaurant's capacity – it's best to buy your ticket early.

Hayden Orpheum Picture Palace

380 Military Road, between Winnie & Macpherson Streets, Cremorne (9908 4344/www.orpheum.com. au). Bus 143, 144, 151, 228, 229, 230, 243, 246, 247, 257. **Screens** 6. **Tickets** $15.50; $8.50-$12 reductions; $7.50-$10.50 Tue. **Credit** MC, V.
Without doubt the grandest cinema in Sydney, Cremorne's art deco picture palace is a stunning step back in time. Built in 1935 by George Kenworthy, the top theatrical architect of the period, today's version is even glitzier than the original thanks to a $2.5-million restoration some years back by owner and local TV celeb Mike Walsh. Each of the six auditoria has its own colour scheme and decor, but the 744-seat Orpheum is the true star of the show. It even has a genuine Wurlitzer cinema organ, which rises out of a stage pit on weekend evenings complete with flashing lights and a grinning organist. Expect a mix of mainstream US, British and Australian fare, with some art-house, special presentations and the occasional cabaret show. **Photo** *p224.*

Palace Academy Twin Cinema

3A Oxford Street, between South Dowling & Verona Streets, Paddington (9361 4453/www. palacecinemas.com.au). Bus 333, 352, 378, 380.

Screens 2. **Tickets** $15.50; $9-$12.50 reductions; $9.50 Mon. **Credit** AmEx, DC, MC, V. **Map** p332 H9.
The Palace-owned Academy Twin Cinema has seen better days, with its facilities in dire need of refurbishment (and a word of warning: don't go if you're tall – the seats have very little leg room). One of the city's longest-running art cinemas, it presents an eclectic mix of foreign, Australian and arty mainstream releases, plus a number of showcases including the Mardi Gras Film Festival.

Palace Norton Street Cinema

99 Norton Street, between Marion Street & Parramatta Road, Leichhardt (9550 0122/www. palacecinemas.com.au). Bus 435, 436, 437, 438, 440, 445, L38, L40. **Screens** 4. **Tickets** $15.50; $9-$12.50 reductions; $9.50 Mon. **Credit** AmEx, DC, MC, V.
Located in the heart of Little Italy, the sleek and stylish Norton Street Cinema is the cream of the Palace chain. The air-conditioning keeps you cool, the seats are plush and comfortable, and the sound and sight lines are uniformly excellent. There's not much else you could ask for from the fabric of a cinema. You'll find an intelligent mix of offbeat Hollywood releases, foreign movies and Australian art-house fare. The 'Babes in Arms' sessions on Thursday mornings are popular: the lights are turned up, the sound down and breastfeeding is everywhere.

Arts & Entertainment

Palace Verona Cinema

*17 Oxford Street, at Verona Street, Paddington
(9360 6099/www.palacecinemas.com.au). Bus 333,
352, 378, 380.* **Screens** 4. **Tickets** $15.50; $9-
$12.50 reductions; $9.50 Mon. **Credit** AmEx, DC,
MC, V. **Map** p332 H9.

Just a few doors down from the Palace Academy
Twin (*see p228*), the modern Verona is the eastern-
suburbs equivalent to Norton Street, and
Paddington's intellectuals, gays and art-house
crowds attend with glee. The four screens are on the
small side and the seats aren't quite as soft as you'd
expect, but the movies are an enticing blend of
quirky commercial, sexy foreign and Australian.

IMAX

IMAX Sydney

*31 Wheat Road, southern end of Darling Harbour
(9281 3300/www.imax.com.au). CityRail Town
Hall/ferry Darling Harbour/Monorail or LightRail
Convention.* **Tickets** $18-$25; $13-$21 reductions;
$50-$66 family. **Credit** AmEx, MC, V. **Map** p327 E6.

The giant, eye-shaped IMAX theatre sticks out on
the water in touristy Darling Harbour. The 540-seat
theatre claims to have the world's largest screen,
some eight storeys high, and shows around 12 films
a day from 10am to 10pm. Expect a mixed bag of 2D
and 3D affairs, with documentaries a common feature. Hardly essential viewing, although the sheer
impact of seeing a 3D film makes it a worthy stop
for the uninitiated.

Open-air

Given the climate, it's hardly surprising that
Sydneysiders flock outdoors whenever they
can. Open-air screenings are a firm fixture on
the summer social calendar, with three main
inner-city offerings: a picnic-on-the-grass affair
in Centennial Park, a similar set-up in North
Sydney Oval (with seats and cover if desired)
and a sensational harbourside experience in the
Domain. Weather permitting (screenings are
cancelled only in gale-force conditions), all are
great nights out. You may have to pay booking
fees on top of the prices quoted below.

Bondi Openair

*Bondi Pavilion, Queen Elizabeth Drive, Bondi Beach
(9130 1235/www.bondiopenair.com.au). CityRail
Bondi Junction then bus 333, 380, 381, 382/bus
222, 333, 380.* **Tickets** $12.90-$17. **Credit** AmEx,
MC, V. **Map** p334. **Date** mid Jan-mid Mar.

Like the beach that hosts it, Bondi Openair cinema
is wonderfully unpredictable and offers myriad
forms of entertainment. Outside the beautiful Bondi
Pavilion the bar offers a local DJ and bands plus
drinks and dinner near the ocean. When it's time for
the main feature, grab a bean bag and head to the
lawn or sit in the amphitheatre – and all this with
the ocean roaring in the background.

Palace Verona Cinema.

Arts & Entertainment

Moonlight Cinema

Belvedere Amphitheatre, Centennial Park, Woollahra (1300 511 908/www.moonlight.com.au). Bus 333, 378, 380. **Tickets** *$15-$17; $11-$14 reductions.* **Credit** *AmEx, DC, MC, V.* **Map** *p333 N11.* **Date** *early Dec-mid Mar.*

Now gone nationwide, the Moonlight's programme focuses heavily on current and recent mainstream releases, with customary classics *Grease* and *Breakfast at Tiffany's* (on Valentine's Day) popular fixtures. Films kick off at sunset and entry is via Woollahra Gate (Oxford Street) only. Bring a picnic, cushions and insect repellent, and arrive early. Limited Gold Grass tickets (at $32 a pop) guarantee a prime spot, a 'bean bed' and a glass of wine.

OpenAir Cinema

Mrs Macquarie's Chair, The Domain, CBD (1300 366 649/www.stgeorge.com.au/openair). CityRail Circular Quay or Martin Place/ferry Circular Quay. **Tickets** *$23-25; $22-$23 reductions.* **Credit** *AmEx, DC, MC, V.* **Map** *p330 J3.* **Date** *early Jan-mid Feb.*

Part of the Sydney Festival, this is the ultimate outdoor movie-going experience, with the Harbour Bridge and Opera House twinkling in the background. You get several Sydney premières of mainstream movies, as well as a pick of current and classic fare. Films start at 8.30pm but the gates open at 6.30pm – as do the stylish on-site bar and restaurant. Capacity is around 1,700. **Photo** *p227.*

Starlight Cinema

North Sydney Oval, Miller Street, North Sydney (9976 0699/www.starlightcinema.com.au). CityRail North Sydney. **Tickets** *$16-$20; $8-$17 reductions.* **Credit** *AmEx, DC, MC, V.* **Date** *mid Jan-mid Mar.*

The Starlight has a similar mix of movies to its Moonlight equivalent in Centennial Park, but with seating and covers if the weather turns nasty. There's an on-site bar and food, with waiter service and deckchairs for an additional fee. Screenings are also held at the Leichhardt Oval.

Festivals

Festival of Jewish Cinema

Date *Nov.*

The annual screening of international Jewish films organised by the Melbourne-based Jewish Film Foundation, which often provides a useful sneak peek at future Oscar contenders. Check the local press for details of venues and timings.

Flickerfest

Bondi Pavilion, Bondi Beach, NSW 2026 (9365 6888/www.flickerfest.com.au). CityRail Bondi Junction then bus 333, 380, 381, 382/bus 222, 333, 380. **Tickets** *$13-$15.* **Credit** *MC, V.* **Map** *p334.* **Date** *early Jan.*

Running for nine days after the New Year madness has subsided, Flickerfest is the only short-film festival in Australia to be recognised by the American Academy of Motion Picture Arts and Sciences as an Oscar-qualifying event. As a result, it's not only a serious event on the world film calendar, it's also one of few forums in which local short-film-makers can directly compare their work with international fare.

Mardi Gras Film Festival & queerDOC Festival

Information: Queer Screen, PO Box 1081, Darlinghurst, NSW 2010 (9332 4938/www.queerscreen.com.au). **Date** *Mardi Gras Feb; queerDOC Sept.*

Part of Sydney's month-long gay and lesbian jamboree, the Mardi Gras Film Festival features mainly international gay movies, screened at the Palace Academy Twin Cinema (*see p228*) and other venues. In September, Queer Screen also puts on the queerDOC festival, the world's first dedicated entirely to queer documentaries.

Sydney Film Festival

Information: Suite 102, 59 Marlborough Street, Surry Hills, NSW 2010 (9318 0999/www.sydneyfilmfestival.org). **Date** *early June.*

A slick, high-profile, intensive two-week orgy of international and Australian film (with up to 250 movies showing), opening on the Queen's Birthday weekend in early June. In 2008 the festival hits the world stage and will be recognised in the international film calendar (*see p228* **Destination Sydney**). Regular highlights include major retrospectives and meet-the-film-maker forums, and the main venues are the grand State Theatre (*see p270*) and the Dendy Opera Quays (*see p227*).

Tropfest

Information: 62-64 Riley Street, East Sydney, NSW 2010 (9368 0434/www.tropfest.com.au). **Date** *Sun in late Feb.*

Instigated by actor-turned-director John Polson (*Swimfan, Hide and Seek*), this free outdoor festival of short films is held every February, and was originally held at Polson's old hangout, the Tropicana café in Darlinghurst (*see p173*). The films are simulcast on giant screens in the Domain to an audience that runs into the tens of thousands, and also to other cities around Australia. The festival is heavily frequented by actors, directors and writers, and its judging panel usually includes A-list celebs who are working in town: Samuel L Jackson, Russell Crowe and John Woo have all performed judging duties in the past. All films are under seven minutes, made specially for the festival and have to contain a reference to the year's Tropfest Signature Item (past items have included a bubble, an umbrella, a kiss, a coffee bean and chopsticks).

World of Women Film Festival

Chauvel Cinema, 249 Oxford Street, Paddington (9332 2408/www.wift.org). **Date** *Oct, biennial.*

Women in Film & Television (WIFT), a non-profit outfit committed to improving the lot of women in film, organises this festival of short and feature-length work by new and established female talents.

Galleries

From graffiti to gilt frames, Sydney's art scene is a picture of good health.

How exactly do the seemingly countless art galleries in Sydney survive? The answer, quite simply, is that the art world is thriving here. Not only are artists' works snapped up by locals; public buildings, restaurants, cafés and hotels are also keen to fill their walls with the work of homegrown talents. Patrons range from serious collectors to those who save up for a piece of original art, and others who just walk past and like the look of something. It helps that prices aren't as steep as in Europe – yet – but big hitters like John Olsen, Sidney Nolan and Brett Whiteley still fetch huge sums. In 2007 Brett Whiteley's *The Olgas* – a tribute to Australian outback explorer Ernest Giles, who discovered the famous rock formation – sold for a record $3.48 million at auction. Meanwhile the market for Aboriginal works continues to flourish at galleries all over Sydney. In 2007 a painting by Clifford Possum Tjapaltjarri, one of the giants of the Aboriginal art movement, more than doubled the previous record for an Aboriginal painting sale when it was snapped up by the National Gallery in Canberra for $2.4 million, outbidding a host of foreign interests to keep the work in Australia.

The city's gallery heartland is **Paddington**, where dozens of spaces offer schmoozy opening nights and exhibitions that regularly feature the best in Australian contemporary art. This is the place to get a snapshot of what's driving the visual arts scene. In one afternoon you could see top-notch work by the likes of subversive photographer Tracey Moffatt at **Roslyn Oxley9 Gallery** (*see p235*), cutting edge new media at **Kaliman Gallery** (*see p235*), a diverse selection of Aboriginal art at **Hogarth Galleries** (*see p235*) and an engaging local or international showing at the **Australian Centre for Photography** (*see p234*).

Not that the city's art scene is restricted to the eastern suburbs. Just south of the CBD, the increasingly gentrified suburb of **Waterloo** shines brightly on the art radar. That's thanks mainly to converted warehouse complex **2 Danks Street** (*see p236*), home to several important galleries. The city centre also has its share of venues: you can see shows from likely future stars at the **Mori Gallery** (*see p232*) or sample established artists (and free drawing classes) at drinking spot-cum-exhibition space the **Arthouse Hotel** (*see below*).

Although art remains a fashionable pursuit among Sydney's most trend-conscious (and affluent) citizens, some of the scene's most vital components are free. High-profile exhibitions that meld Sydney's fabled natural beauty with local artistic talent are the most reliable crowd-pullers. Perhaps most alluring is **Sculpture by the Sea** (*see p214*), a massively popular event held each November in which artworks are displayed along the stretch of coast between Bondi and Tamarama Beaches. **Art & About** (*see p214*), held in October, has several outdoor components, including a series of oversized photographs documenting local life set amid the fig trees in Hyde Park.

Look out too for the annual Archibald Prize at the **Art Gallery of New South Wales** (*see p75*), with the winner usually announced in late March. This portraiture competition is as entertaining for the fierce division of opinion it sparks as for the always varied works on show. Nor should you miss the general collections at the Art Gallery of NSW or Sydney's other major public gallery, the **Museum of Contemporary Art** (*see p71*).

INFORMATION AND OPENING HOURS

For an excellent round-up of what's on, grab a copy of *Art Almanac* ($4, published 11 times a year, www.art-almanac.com.au) or *Art Gallery Guide Australia* ($3, published bi-monthly, www.artguide.com.au). The latter has a useful calendar of gallery openings and events. Both are available at bookshops, galleries and newsagents, as is the quarterly journal *Art & Australia* ($28.50, www.artaustralia.com), which takes a more in-depth look at visual arts news and exhibitions.

Many galleries are shut on Mondays, and also close for a period during Christmas and New Year, so call before you set out if you're in town at that time. Admission is free unless otherwise stated.

Central Sydney

Arthouse Hotel
275 Pitt Street, between Park & Market Streets, CBD (9284 1200/www.thearthousehotel.com.au). CityRail St James or Town Hall/Monorail Galeries Victoria. **Open** 11am-midnight Mon-Thur; 11am-3am Fri; 5pm-6am Sat. **Credit** AmEx, DC, MC, V. **Map** p329 F7.

This popular Sydney watering hole also doubles as an art gallery, holding about 30 shows each year. Aboriginal artist Fran Dunn is just one of the intriguing artists to have exhibited here and a permanent collection includes the work of Shona Wilson, Guy Hawson and many others. If you fancy an art lesson with your aperitif, there are free life drawing classes each Monday from 6.30pm; the model is supplied, but bring your own materials.

Birrung Gallery

134 William Street, between Bourke & Forbes Streets, Woolloomooloo (9550 9964/www.world vision.com.au/birrung). Bus 324, 325, 326, 327. **Open** 10am-5.30pm Tue-Fri; 11am-5pm Sat, Sun. **Credit** AmEx, MC, V. **Map** p330 H7.
Birrung Gallery is a World Vision initiative to raise funds for indigenous communities, especially in the areas of employment, education and leadership. Its diverse Aboriginal art offerings include works in fibre from Arnhem Land, Western Deserts paintings and various pieces from artists living on the Tiwi Islands, off Australia's north coast near Darwin.

Collins & Kent Fine Art

Shop 25, Opera Quays, 7 Macquarie Street, Circular Quay (9252 3993/www.collinskent.com.au). CityRail/ferry Circular Quay. **Open** 10am-8pm Mon-Sat; 10am-7pm Sun. **Credit** AmEx, DC, MC, V. **Map** p327 G4.
Part of Opera Quays, the smart shopping and dining strip between Circular Quay and the Sydney Opera House, this upmarket gallery shows works by European masters. Look out for originals by the likes of Chagall, Dalí, Miró, Picasso and Matisse.

Legge Gallery

183 Regent Street, between Boundary & Margaret Streets, Redfern (9319 3340/www.leggegallery.com). CityRail Redfern. **Open** 11am-6pm Tue-Sat. Closed mid Dec-early Feb. **Credit** MC, V.
Contemporary Australian painting, sculpture and ceramics make up Legge Gallery's diverse collection. The mix of young and established artists who have exhibited here include abstract painter John Bartley and Annette Iggulden, of *Softshoe Sojourn* fame.

Liverpool Street Gallery

243A Liverpool Street, between Riley & Crown Streets, East Sydney (9331 7799/www.liverpool streetgallery.com.au). CityRail Museum. **Open** 10am-6pm Tue-Sat. **Credit** AmEx, DC, MC, V. **Map** p329 G8.
Behind its impressive glass façade, Liverpool Street Gallery showcases a diversity of Australian contemporary artists alongside modern international works. Painting – whether abstract, realist or figurative – predominates but you might also find sculpture, works on paper and photography.

Martin Browne Fine Art

57-59 Macleay Street, at Challis Avenue, Potts Point (9331 7997/www.martinbrownefineart.com). CityRail Kings Cross/bus 311. **Open** 11am-6pm Tue-Sun. **Credit** MC, V. **Map** p330 J6.

This building is a landmark of Bohemian Kings Cross and one-time residence of iconic Australian artists including Brett Whiteley and Martin Sharp. Its eye-catching yellow paintwork is said to represent Van Gogh's unrealised ambition of having a home for artistic expression. Today it offers a strong selection of new work by emerging artists as well as curated exhibitions over two floors.

Mori Gallery

168 Day Street, between Bathurst & Liverpool Streets, CBD (9283 2903/www.morigallery.com.au). CityRail Town Hall/Monorail Chinatown. **Open** 11am-6pm Wed-Sat. **No credit cards**. **Map** p329 E7.
Stephen Mori's gallery shows an eclectic mix of works from established young Australian names, including Jenny Bell, Giles Alexander and conceptual artist Alana Hunt. He has also shown a talent for exhibiting an interesting selection of art by impressive 'unknowns' over the years, including new media as well as more traditional offerings.

Object Gallery

417 Bourke Street, between Campbell and Albion Streets, Surry Hills (9361 4511/www.object.com.au). Bus 311, 333, 352, 373, 377, 378, 380, 392, 394, 396. **Open** 11am-6pm Tue-Sun. **Credit** AmEx, DC, MC, V. **Map** p329 G9.
This gallery used to be in the Queen Victoria Building (*see p191*), but it seems much more suited to its new home in the edgy St Margarets development on Bourke Street. Downstairs is a great little shop, called Collect (*see p208*), selling collectible glass and ceramics, while upstairs Object passionately supports innovative craft and design, and uses its space to raise awareness of the wealth of artistic talent both at home and overseas.

Outback Centre

28 Darling Walk, 1-25 Harbour Street, Darling Harbour (9283 7477/www.outbackcentre.com.au). CityRail Town Hall/Monorail Darling Park. **Open** 10am-6pm daily. **Credit** AmEx, DC, MC, V. **Map** p329 E7.
Alongside its gift shop, the Outback Centre has a well-regarded Aboriginal art gallery, which includes works from the Central and Western Deserts, Arnhem Land and the Kimberleys.

Ray Hughes Gallery

270 Devonshire Street, between Bourke & Crown Streets, Surry Hills (9698 3200/www.rayhughes gallery.com). Bus 301, 302, 303, 352. **Open** 10am-6pm Tue-Sat. Closed 2wks after Christmas. **Credit** MC, V. **Map** p329 G11.
A colourful character on the Sydney art scene and former subject of the controversial Archibald portraiture competition held each year (entries always generate heated argument), Ray Hughes shows leading contemporary Australian and Chinese artists in his inner-city gallery. Names to look out for include landscape artist Joe Furlonger, Chinese painter Li Jin and Scottish ceramicist Stephen Bird.

Australian Art Print Network.
See p234.

Robin Gibson Gallery

278 Liverpool Street, between Forbes & Darley Streets, Darlinghurst (9331 6692/www.robingibson. net). CityRail Kings Cross. **Open** 11am-6pm Tue-Sat. **Credit** MC, V. **Map** p329 H8.

In an atmospheric three-storey Georgian sandstone house, Robin Gibson Gallery is known for varied, mainly Australian exhibitions that strike a balance between contemporary and traditional styles. The late sculptor Clement Meadmore and emerging Australian painters Gina Bruce and Catherine Fox feature on the long list of artists shown.

Watters Gallery

109 Riley Street, at Stanley Lane, East Sydney (9331 2556/www.wattersgallery.com). CityRail Museum. **Open** 10am-5pm Tue, Sat; 10am-7pm Wed-Fri. Closed mid Dec-early Jan. **Credit** AmEx, DC, MC, V. **Map** p329 G7.

Established in 1964, this Sydney institution maintains a loyal following among some of Australia's most significant artists. Among the notables are late sculptor Robert Klippel, figurative painter Vicki Varvaressos and renowned surrealist painter James Gleeson. Another Watters regular is Chris O'Doherty (aka Reg Mombassa) whose colourful, politicised images fuse fashion and art.

Eastern Suburbs

Australian Art Print Network

68 Oxford Street, between Crown & Riley Streets, Darlinghurst (9332 1722/www.aboriginalartprints. com.au). Bus 311, 352, 371, 377, 378, 380, 392, *394, 396, 397, 399.* **Open** 10am-6pm Mon-Fri; 11am-6pm Sat. **Credit** AmEx, DC, MC, V. **Map** p329 G8.

Director Michael Kershaw says that his collection of limited-edition Aboriginal and Torres Strait Islander prints is probably the largest in the world. A number of the country's best indigenous artists are represented here, among them Kimberley legend Rover Thomas and urban artist Sally Morgan. **Photo** *p233*.

Australian Centre for Photography

257 Oxford Street, between Ormond & William Streets, Paddington (9332 1455/www.acp.au.com). Bus 333, 352, 378, 380. **Open** noon-7pm Tue-Fri; 10am-6pm Sat, Sun. **Credit** AmEx, MC, V. **Map** p332 K10.

Impressive local and international photography and new media feature in the ACP gallery; innovative video works are an increasingly regular highlight. Aspiring photographers can enrol in the centre's various courses and hone their skills in its digital suite or darkroom. ACP also publishes the informative *Photofile* magazine.

Blender Gallery

16 Elizabeth Street, between Oxford & Underwood Streets, Paddington (9380 7080/www.blendercom. au). Bus 333, 352, 378, 380. **Open** 10am-6pm Tue-Sat. **Credit** MC, V. **Map** p332 L10.

Expect mainly photography and, less regularly, sculpture, painting and mixed media over two floors in a converted Paddington terraced house. The annual exhibition of photography finalists in the national Walkley journalism awards is a highlight and there are new shows every three to four weeks.

Keeping it in the family – John Olsen is one of the artists showing at **Tim Olsen Gallery**.

Coo-ee Aboriginal Art Gallery

31 Lamrock Avenue, at Chambers Avenue, Bondi Beach (9300 9233/www.cooeeart.com.au). CityRail Bondi Junction then bus 333, 380, 381, 382/bus 333, 380. **Open** 10am-5pm Tue-Sat. **Credit** AmEx, MC, V. **Map** p334.

This highly regarded Aboriginal art gallery has been around for almost 30 years. It specialises in quality artworks from indigenous communities in the Northern Territory, Western Australia and the Torres Strait Islands.

Eva Breuer Art Dealer

83 Moncur Street, between Queen Street & Jersey Road, Woollahra (9362 0297/www.evabreuerart dealer.com.au). Bus 352, 378, 380, 389. **Open** 10am-6pm Tue-Fri; 10am-5pm Sat; 1-5pm Sun. **Credit** AmEx, MC, V. **Map** p333 M10.

High-end 20th- and 21st-century Australian art is the focus here, with an emphasis on paintings by such home-grown greats as Arthur Boyd and Sidney Nolan. Its varied programme includes solo shows and arresting thematic exhibitions.

Hogarth Galleries

7 Walker Lane, between Liverpool & Brown Streets, Paddington (9360 6839/www.aboriginal artcentres.com). Bus 333, 352, 378, 380. **Open** 10am-5pm Tue-Sat. **Credit** AmEx, DC, MC, V. **Map** p332 J9.

Tucked away down a Paddington side street, this highly regarded gallery features a diversity of Aboriginal art. Geographical variety is a particular strength: artists from the far north of Queensland, the Central and Western Deserts, Arnhem Land and Western Australia are all represented. Expect bark paintings, prints, woven work and carvings.

Ivan Dougherty Gallery

Corner of Albion Avenue & Selwyn Street, Paddington (9385 0726/www.cofa.unsw.edu.au/galleries/idg). Bus 333, 378, 380. **Open** 10am-5pm Mon-Sat. **No credit cards**. **Map** p332 J9.

Part of the University of NSW College of Fine Arts, the Ivan Dougherty Gallery (or IDG for short) is known for challenging and diverse shows and a focus on professional rather than student work. Themed exhibitions often include a range of media, from design to video and sketches on paper. Those in search of quality student art will have to pick their moment – the only regular student (Master of Fine Arts) shows are in January and December.

Kaliman Gallery

56 Sutherland Street, at Cascade Street, Paddington (9357 2273/www.kalimangallery.com). CityRail Edgecliff then 5min walk or bus 389. **Open** 11am-5.30pm Tue-Sat. Closed Christmas-mid Feb. **Credit** AmEx, MC, V. **Map** p332 L9.

Expect a strong experimental flavour and works from younger Australian artists at Kaliman. Colourful painting, installation works and new media feature frequently, from artists such as Del Kathryn Barton, the Kingpins and Ms & Mr.

Rex Irwin Art Dealer

1st Floor, 38 Queen Street, between Oxford Street & Halls Lane, Woollahra (9363 3212/www.rexirwin. com). Bus 333, 378, 380, 389. **Open** 11am-5.30pm Tue-Sat; also by appointment. **Closed** mid Dec-early Feb. **Credit** MC, V. **Map** p332 L11.

This compact gallery represents several of Australian art's leading names, including landscape artist Nicholas Harding and painter Peter Booth. The gallery also deals in pieces by important Australian artists such as ceramicist Prue Venables, as well as European works including British figurative painting and prints and drawings by Picasso.

Roslyn Oxley9 Gallery

8 Soudan Lane, off Hampden Street, Paddington (9331 1919/www.roslynoxley9.com.au). CityRail Edgecliff then 5min walk or bus 389. **Open** 10am-6pm Tue-Fri; 11am-6pm Sat. Closed Christmas-late Jan. **Credit** AmEx, MC, V. **Map** p332 L9.

Top-flight Australian artists including renowned photographer Julie Rrap feature, as do sculptor James Angus, indigenous photographer Destiny Deacon and installation artist Lindy Lee. Big-name internationals such as Tracey Emin have also shown here, and the gallery encourages offshore talent.

Stills Gallery

36 Gosbell Street, between Boundary Street & Neild Avenue, Paddington (9331 7775/www.stillsgallery. com.au). Bus 324, 325, 326, 327. **Open** 11am-6pm Tue-Sat. Closed mid Dec-Jan. **Credit** AmEx, MC, V. **Map** p330 K8.

This large, bright exhibition space shows leading contemporary Australian photographers and some installation and video works. Represented artists include the noted photojournalist Narelle Autio, Trent Parke and Petrina Hicks. Every five weeks sees a Saturday discussion by the artist on show.

Tim Olsen Gallery

63 Jersey Road, at Caledonia Street, Woollahra (9327 3922/www.timolsengallery.com). Bus 333, 352, 378, 380. **Open** 10am-6pm Mon-Fri; 10am-5pm Sat; noon-5pm Sun. **Credit** AmEx, MC, V. **Map** p332 L10.

John Olsen, now in his 80s, is one of Australia's most revered painters – and he's still going strong. His work, along with a Who's Who of great and up-and-coming contemporary Australian artists, is on show (and for sale) at this new two-floor space, recently relocated from around the corner in Paddington. The gallery is run by Tim Olsen, John's son, whose sister Louise is a member of Dinosaur Designs (*see p208*).

Inner West

Aboriginal & Pacific Art Gallery

2 Danks Street, at Young Street, Waterloo (9699 2211/www.2danksstreet.com.au). Bus 301, 302, 303, 304, 339, 343. **Open** 11am-5pm Tue-Sat. Closed mid Dec-mid Jan. **Credit** AmEx, MC, V.

Under the direction of long-time indigenous art specialist Gabriella Roy, this gallery shows traditional and contemporary Aboriginal works, specialising in Arnhem Land barks and carvings. The gallery represents major artists including Kitty Kantilla, Kay Lindjuwanga and Spider Snell.

Annandale Galleries

110 Trafalgar Street, at Booth Street, Annandale (9552 1699/www.annandalegalleries.com.au). Bus 370, 470. **Open** 11am-5pm Tue-Sat. Closed mid Dec-mid Feb. **Credit** MC, V.

Australian abstract painter Guy Warren and overseas artists such as Leon Kossoff and William Kentridge are some of the names to look out for. The gallery also has a strong selection of Aboriginal work, and pieces by the likes of Chagall and Miró.

Boomalli Aboriginal Artists' Co-op

55-59 Flood Street, between Marion & Myrtle Streets, Leichhardt (9560 2541/www.boomalli. org.au). Bus 436, 437, 438, 470. **Open** 10am-4pm Mon-Fri; by appointment Sat, Sun. **Credit** AmEx, DC, MC, V.

Boomalli's focus on contemporary urban Aboriginal art sets it apart from most indigenous galleries, which tend to prefer regional works. The gallery has associations or past links with many of Australia's foremost indigenous artists, including Jeffrey Samuels and Bronwyn Bancroft.

Gallery Gondwana

7 Danks Street, at Bourke Street, Waterloo (8399 3492/www.gallerygondwana.com.au). Bus 301, 302, 303, 304, 339, 343. **Open** by appointment Tue; 10am-5.30pm Wed-Sat. **Credit** AmEx, MC, V.

In conjunction with its sister gallery in Alice Springs, Gallery Gondwana sources works from leading Aboriginal artists including Dorothy Napangardi and Walala Tjapaltjarri. Expect Central and Western Deserts paintings as well as weavings and other crafts. Two annual exhibitions, 'Big Country' and 'Divas of the Deserts', promote male and female indigenous artists respectively.

2 Danks Street

2 Danks Street, at Young Street, Waterloo (www.2danksstreet.com.au). Bus 301, 302, 303, 304, 339, 343. **Open** 11am-6pm Tue-Sat. Closed mid Dec-mid Jan. **Credit** MC, V.

In a traditionally industrial but increasingly residential (and upwardly mobile) inner-city suburb, this former warehouse boasts seven permanent galleries and three spaces devoted to temporary shows. These include Aboriginal and Pacific Art, Utopia Art Sydney, the international Conny Dietzschold Gallery and the Brenda May Gallery, which shows modern, often experimental work in a variety of media.

Utopia Art Sydney

2 Danks Street, at Young Street, Waterloo (9699 2900/www.2danksstreet.com.au). Bus 301, 302, 303, 304, 339, 343. **Open** 10am-5pm Tue-Sat. Closed mid Dec-mid Jan. **Credit** AmEx, MC, V.

Utopia Art Sydney promotes Aboriginal artists from the Northern Territory, along with work by non-Aboriginal artists including sculptor Marea Gazzard and the gallery's owner Christopher Hodges. Emily Kame Kngwarreye is among the leading indigenous artists regularly shown here.

Art for art's sake

In a city sugar-coated with commercialism, it's inspiring to see the art world leading the way when it comes to giving something back.

For 21 years art dealers Brian and Gene Sherman wooed Sydney's art-buying luvvies with stylish parties, mixing artists, celebs and patrons at their chic Paddington-based Sherman Galleries. As the wine flowed and the art lit up the walls, the Shermans time and again found themselves launching the stellar careers of artists such as Tim Storrier, Mike Parr and Janet Laurence. Throughout it all the couple's commitment to supporting and developing contemporary art was plain to see thanks to their various educational endeavours, including a respected artist-in-residency programme.

But from April 2008 the gallery's original incarnation ceased business and transformed into a not-for-profit art foundation with new and unique exhibitions planned for its airy space. The **Sherman Contemporary Art**

Foundation (16-20 Goodhope Street, 9311 1112, www.sherman-scaf.org.au) was something of a dream for Gene Sherman, whose aim was always to expand the global art world, help emerging artists and educate the public in appreciating contemporary art. At the time of writing the foundation was still very much in its infancy, but had already delivered a resounding statement of intent to help showcase 'significant works by innovative and influential artists from Asia, the Pacific and Australia through projects not easily accommodated in private galleries, contemporary spaces or the museum sector.'

In short, artists who are currently falling through the gaps will get a chance to show their work here, with four curated exhibitions planned for the first twelve months alone. And while the Sydney art community mourns the loss of the Sherman Galleries, it's clear that the couple are paving the way for a whole new generation of artists.

Gay & Lesbian

It's not all coming up roses on the pink strip.

With the largest and most vibrant gay scene in the southern hemisphere, Sydney has a lot to boast about. While it centres largely around the Oxford Street precinct, the inner-city suburbs are also places to look for action.

The grungy and alternative crew stick to the inner-western suburbs, largely **Newtown**, while the smart party crowd gathers along Darlinghurst Road and Victoria Street in **Darlinghurst**, and Macleay Street in **Potts Point**. You'll find the inner-city queer set along Crown Street in **Surry Hills** and the upper-class über gays in **Paddington**. If swimming in the city's beautiful beaches takes your fancy, go for a dip off the rocks at **North Bondi**, where Sydney's gays gather in droves. For a back-to-nature trip, head west to the **Blue Mountains**. Only an hour or so by car from Sydney, the area harbours a relaxed and casual gay scene.

Darlinghurst's Oxford Street remains at the heart of all this action, although a recent rise in incidents of homophobic violence have marred the beloved strip. Despite these issues, Sydney still acts as a magnet for gay men and lesbians from all around Australia, as well as New Zealand and Asia, drawn by the simple fact that gay life in the Emerald City is relatively hassle-free. Homosexuals and transgender people in NSW are legally protected against discrimination, as are those living with HIV or AIDS. Same-sex sex is legal (the age of consent is 16 for everyone) and the state government recognises same-sex partnerships.

Of course, part of gay Sydney's appeal, for locals and visitors alike, is the annual **Gay & Lesbian Mardi Gras**, held in late summer and culminating in a spectacular parade and even more spectacular party – for full details, *see p243* **Hoorah for the Mardi Gras!**. It's the best time for the queer tourist to visit Sydney: the clubs pump, the beaches beckon, and excitement hangs in the air. Oxford Street and its surrounding areas come into their own.

Lesbian visitors might find the venues around Darlinghurst, Surry Hills and East Sydney overwhelmingly patronised by gay men, but there are in fact loads of weekly and monthly lesbian events in the area too. Dykes will feel particularly comfortable in **Newtown**, as well as nearby **Erskineville** and **Enmore**, where there is a strong concentration of lesbians and a plethora of bars and cafés

that cater specifically to the girls. Sydney has also recently experienced a 'lesbian baby boom', so you're just as likely to find dyke couples with toddlers in tow hanging out in the inner-west cafés as in the clubs.

Newtown's gays, both male and female, copped a blow in 2007 when the much-loved Newtown Hotel, the home of Sydney's drag queen scene, closed down. The **Bank Hotel** (*see p238*) and the **Sly Fox** (*see p239*) have picked up some of the Newtown Hotel crowd, although most of the gay men and drag queens are waiting for the **Imperial Hotel** (*see p239*) to reopen in 2008, following refurbishment.

But gay Sydney's scene extends far beyond the pubs and clubs. There are lots of community groups covering every possible leisure activity, political bent, social cause or medical issue, so there's no need to be alone. For a full listing of the groups on offer, check out the website of the oldest-running gay community publication, the *Sydney Star Observer*, at www.ssonet. com.au. You'll also find up-to-date listings at www.samesame.com.au.

WHERE TO STAY

It can safely be said that any 'international' hotel in Sydney (glass front, big lobby, expensive cocktails) will be gay-friendly. A large chunk of staff at any of these places will be 'family', so you should have no hassles. If you want the full ghetto-accommodation experience, check before arriving with the US-run **International Gay & Lesbian Travel Association** (www.iglta.org). Other good online sites for travel to and within Australia, including lists of gay- and lesbian-friendly accommodation, are **Gay Australia Guide** (www.gayaustralia guide.com) and **Gay & Lesbian Tourism Australia** (www.galta.com.au).

PLAYING SAFE

While Sydney is one of the most tolerant places on earth for gays and lesbians, bashers and homophobes do exist. At night, be sensible. Stick to well-lit streets with your mates, walk quickly and with a sense of purpose and, if you're intoxicated or just nervous, play safe and catch a cab. Be aware that while the Mardi Gras season brings out huge numbers of homosexuals, it also flushes out the occasional homophobe, so don't let your guard down at this time of year.

Hanging out at the **Colombian Hotel**.

The community, with the help of local politicians, namely Sydney's mayor Clover Moore, recently established 'Drop In Safe Space' at 60 Oxford Street to support any victims of homophobic violence. It will open initially from 11pm to 5am on Friday and Saturday nights and is run by staff from the government-run Anti-Violence Project (phone them on 9206 2116 or Free Call 1800 063 060). To contact police directly call 000, or if you're near Oxford Street you can head to the local Surry Hills Police station at 241 Goulburn Street (9265 4144). If you're not comfortable speaking to a general police officer, ask to see a Gay & Lesbian Liaison Officer (GLLO). Also, on Friday and Saturday nights, trained community members known as the Generation Q Street Angels patrol the street.

If you're in trouble or feel threatened, look out for the pink triangle stickers displayed in gay-friendly businesses; they're in a conspicuous place, usually near the doorway. The programme started in 1993 after some initial concerns about violence directed against gays and lesbians.

SAFE SEX

Safe sex is a way of life here – 'if it's not on, then it's definitely not on', as the local slogan goes. Sydney is the epicentre of Australia's HIV pandemic and while a decade of safe-sex campaigns has hugely reduced the incidence of new infection, the dangers are still out there.

INFORMATION

For the latest on what's happening, ask the friendly staff at the **Bookshop Darlinghurst** (*see p194*). Alternatively, check the queer press, available in gay outlets, bottle shops, newsagents, music venues and cinemas around town. The city's two free weekly gay newspapers, *Sydney Star Observer* and *SX*, have full, up-to-the-minute 'what's on' and venue guides. Dykes will find the free monthly news magazine *Lesbians on the Loose* (www.lotl.com) and new *Cherrie* magazine (www.cherrie.e-p.net.au) required reading. For gay community groups, helplines and support networks, *see p299*.

Nightlife

Bars & pubs

Bank Hotel

324 King Street, between Newman & Wilson Streets, Newtown (8568 1900/www.bankhotel.com.au). CityRail Newtown. **Open** 10am-late daily. **Credit** AmEx, MC, V. **Map** p334.
Already one of Newtown's most popular pubs, the Bank recently underwent a multi-million dollar facelift. It draws a smattering of gays and lesbians throughout the week, but traditionally gets overrun with lesbians on Wednesday nights. The three-level venue includes great outdoor areas, casual bars, a quality cocktail lounge and DJs at night. Also try the superb in-house (but outdoor) Thai restaurant.

Colombian Hotel

117-123 Oxford Street, at Crown Street, Darlinghurst (9360 2151). Bus 311, 333, 352, 373, 377, 378, 380, 392, 394, 396. **Open** 9am-6am daily. **Credit** AmEx, MC, V. **Map** p329 G8.
This is the gay pub that more gay pubs should try to be like. Inside are two levels of fun, both decorated in an 'art deco meets Aztec' design theme that succeeds against all the odds. The ground-floor bar opens on to the street, and is excellent for people-watching, while the upstairs cocktail bar is more sedate, although boogie fever breaks out later on Friday and Saturday nights. Both floors get crowded pec-to-pec on weekends. It should also be noted that the Colombian is also one of the Golden Mile's more lesbian-friendly establishments.

Flinders Hotel

63 Flinders Street, off Oxford Street, Darlinghurst (9356 3622). Bus 311, 333, 352, 373, 377, 378, 380, 392, 394, 396. **Open** 2pm-late Mon-Fri; 3pm-late Sat, Sun.* **Credit** AmEx, MC, V. **Map** p329 H9.
The Flinders is perfect for a quiet bevvy in the afternoon, and hosts various functions for the gay community. It's the home of the Harbour City Bears on Friday nights, and also holds great monthly lesbian events (*see p244* **The L word**). There's also a great restaurant serving quality, affordable food.

Imperial Hotel

35 Erskineville Road, at Union Street, Erskineville (9519 9899/www.theimperialhotel.com.au). CityRail Erskineville or Newtown. Currently closed for refurbishment. **Map** p334.

The Imperial is featured at the beginning of the film *Priscilla, Queen of the Desert* and the pub has honoured this by staging a succession of rude but hilarious Priscilla drag shows. It closed for refurbishment in 2007, much to the dismay of Sydney's gay community, although it is expected to reopen in 2008 (for more information, see the local press or ask around).

Mars Lounge

16 Wentworth Avenue, between Oxford & Goulburn Streets, Surry Hills (9267 6440/www.marslounge. com.au). CityRail Museum/bus 311, 333, 352, 373, 377, 378, 380, 392, 394, 396. **Open** 5pm-late Wed-Fri; 7pm-late Sat, Sun. **Credit** AmEx, DC, MC, V. **Map** p329 G8.

Mars Lounge is popular with a gay, lesbian and straight crowd, particularly on Sunday nights, when it hosts top local DJs such as Alex Taylor. For lesbian night Bitch, *see p244* **The L word**.

Middle Bar

Kinselas Hotel, 383-387 Bourke Street, at Taylor Square, Darlinghurst (9331 3100). Bus 311, 333, 352, 373, 377, 378, 380, 392, 394, 396. **Open** *Hotel* 9am-6am daily. *Middle Bar* 9pm-4am Fri, Sat. **Credit** AmEx, DC, MC, V. **Map** p329 H9.

Looking for a more upmarket drinking experience? Middle Bar, located on the upper level of Kinselas Hotel, may be just the ticket. With an outdoor deck overlooking Taylor Square, it's the place to be on a hot summer night. It attracts a dressy crowd that encompasses straights, gay men and lesbians. The common denominator is a sense of style, and money: be prepared to shell out for fancy cocktails. There are plenty of plush sofas and funky DJs. The more casual, low-key bar on the ground floor is open pretty much all day and night.

Oxford Hotel

134 Oxford Street, at Taylor Square, Darlinghurst (9331 3467/www.theoxfordhotel.com.au). Bus 311, 333, 352, 373, 377, 378, 380, 392, 394, 396. **Open** *Main bar* 24hrs daily. *Basement bar* 10pm-10am Fri, Sat. *Will & Toby's* 7pm-late Wed-Sun. *Polo Lounge* 6pm-3am Tue-Sun. **Credit** AmEx, MC, V. **Map** p329 H8.

A mainstay of the 'Golden Mile' for about as long as anyone can remember, the Oxford has undergone a few changes in recent years. The ground-floor pub used to be dark and cloistered, but renovations and additions have opened it up considerably. A wooden veranda now enables outdoor drinking over Taylor Square, which is lovely in the warmer months. But the best things about the place haven't changed: the main space is still virtually a 24-hour bar, and an almost universally gay male venue. Upstairs at Will and Toby's are two sophisticated and rather ritzy lounge bars, with live entertainment and a superb cocktail list.

Slide

41 Oxford Street, between Crown & Bourke Streets, Darlinghurst (8915 1899/www.slide.com.au). Bus 311, 333, 352, 373, 377, 378, 380, 392, 394, 396. **Open** 7pm-3am Wed-Sun. **Credit** AmEx, MC, V. **Map** p329 G8.

Undoubtedly the hottest spot in town, the very slick bar/restaurant/club Slide opened its doors at the end of 2005. New gay bars in Sydney can be a risky venture, but Slide has found its niche as a more upmarket gay watering hole. French chef and venue manager Marc Kuzma (who is also drag queen Claire de Lune) oversees the popular El Circo on Sunday nights, where guests enjoy a nine-course tasting menu for $80 while watching performances. Wednesday and Thursday nights are open for a dinner and show experience. It's $60 per person for a European-inspired three-course meal, and a cabaret, jazz or pop act. Visitors are also welcome to pay to see the show only. On Friday and Saturday nights, Slide becomes a bar and club; it's $10 to get in, and the first drink is free. Sunday night is a casual industry night, featuring DJs, two-for-one cocktails and $5 beers. Corporate events for the community, such as the launch of Mardi Gras or the Queerscreen film festival, are held on Mondays and Tuesdays, when the venue is closed to the public.

Sly Fox

199 Enmore Road, between Cambridge Street & Stanmore Road, Enmore (9557 1016). Bus 423, 426, 428. **Open** 10am-4am Mon-Thur; 10am-6am Fri, Sat; 9am-midnight Sun. **No credit cards.**

Slide – poles apart.

Arts & Entertainment

From the outside, the Sly Fox looks like an average spit-and-sawdust Aussie pub, but get past security and you'll find one of Sydney's hottest bars. It's a queer and alternative venue, mostly inhabited by lesbians. Wednesday night, known as Queer Central, is the big event, with lesbians and gay men. You'll find dancing, pool, competitions, lots of drag shows and well-known DJ Sveta on the decks. This is the home of Sydney's drag king scene, so expect some wild acts.

Tilbury Hotel
12-18 Nicholson Street, Woolloomooloo (9368 1955/ www.tilburyhotel.com.au). CityRail Kings Cross then 10min walk/bus 222, 311. **Open** *8am-11.45pm Mon-Fri; 9am-11.45pm Sat; 10am-9.45pm Sun.* **Credit** *AmEx, MC, V.* **Map** *p330 H6.*
Come on a Sunday afternoon and evening, and you'll find the upstairs bar at the Tilbury swarming with a spunky and very fashionable crowd of gay men. There's a pool table and a DJ, but not much room for dancing. The place to be is on the outdoor veranda, which gets crowded with Sydney's most beautiful gay men – and don't they know it! It's a lovely venue, and perfect for a casual afternoon drink any day.

Clubs

Arq Sydney
16 Flinders Street, between Oxford & Taylor Streets, Darlinghurst (9380 8700/www.arqsydney.com.au). Bus 311, 333, 352, 373, 377, 378, 380, 392, 394, 396. **Open** *9pm-late Thur-Sun.* **No credit cards.** **Map** *p329 H9.*

Arq is the busiest club on the Sydney scene, and the first port of call for many a gay tourist. Its big nights are Saturday and Sunday, when it draws a very Oxford Street crowd of bare-chested pretty boys. With two levels and a mezzanine walkway, it holds around 900 people when full – and it always is at weekends. Head for the upper floor for sensational lighting and uptempo house and trance music, delivered via an ultra-crisp sound system; the lower floor is more chilled, with lounges, pool tables and more funky music. Shows are a speciality, whether drag or song and dance numbers from pop stars (both aspiring and actual). The club goes into overdrive on long weekends, and its recovery parties are hugely popular. Look out for the Fomo foam parties in summer.

Club 77
77 William Street, between Crown & Yurong Streets, East Sydney (9361 3387). CityRail Kings Cross. **Open** *8pm-late Thur-Sun.* **Credit** *AmEx, DC, MC, V.* **Map** *p329 G7.*
Club 77 is something of an underground institution. Conceived more than a decade ago by queer and alternative Sydney DJs Seymour Butz and Gemma, it's a space for all those people who are left cold by the constant repetition of trance remixes and Kylie numbers in most gay venues in town. The crowd is as alternative as the music, but you never know who you might spot on the dancefloor: Nick Cave, Rufus Wainwright and Jarvis Cocker have all been seen here. The roster covers a variety of nights, from gothic and fluro to gay, mainstream and rave.

Exchange Hotel
34-44 Oxford Street, between Riley & Liverpool Streets, Darlinghurst (9331 1936/www.exchange hotel.biz). CityRail Museum/bus 311, 333, 352, 373, 377, 378, 380, 392, 394, 396. **Open** *Spectrum 8pm-late Tue-Sun. Phoenix 10pm-late Thur-Sun. QBar & 34B 10pm-late Wed-Sun. Nevada Lounge 10am-6am daily.* **Credit** *(Q Bar only) AmEx, MC, V.* **Map** *p329 G8.*
There are four floors of fun in this decade-old gay fave, but Spectrum and the subterranean Phoenix are of most interest to gay and lesbian visitors. Spectrum is a quiet bar that turns into a live music venue later in the evening. Phoenix is a small, sweaty box of a club, renowned for a harder style of dirty house music and a crowd that skews a bit older and dirtier too. The fetish boys who used to frequent leather-bar Manacle before it closed down in 2007 now come to Phoenix on weekend mornings. On Saturday nights the place is overrun with shirtless gay men, although it also features lesbian DJs. QBar is a nightclub, 34B is famous for its shows (largely burlesque), while Nevada Lounge is a gaming room.

Midnight Shift
85 Oxford Street, between Riley & Crown Streets, Darlinghurst (9360 4319/www.themidnightshift. com). CityRail Museum/bus 311, 333, 352, 373, 377, 378, 380, 392, 394, 396. **Open** *Video Bar noon-late Mon-Fri; 2pm-late Sat, Sun. Club 11pm-late Fri, Sat.* **No credit cards.** **Map** *p329 G8.*

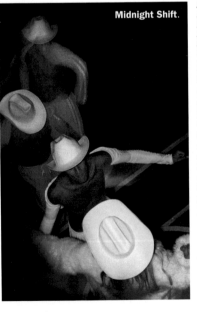

Midnight Shift.

What a drag show: Polly's Follies rock the **Stonewall Hotel**.

Another Sydney legend, but this one's really only for the boys: the 'no open-toed shoe' policy is a convenient if transparent way for women to be excluded. The Shift is two clubs in one: at street level, it's a dark but friendly video bar, with no cover charge, a wide range of punters and pool tables out the back. The large dancefloor is well utilised, particularly on Sunday evenings, when the resident DJs play feel-good retro classics. Upstairs is the packed dance club, which has an entry fee and a crowd of wall-to-wall men. If you can take your eyes off the washboard stomachs and bulging biceps, there are great lighting effects and frequent drag shows.

Palms on Oxford

124 Oxford Street, at Taylor Square, Darlinghurst (9357 4166). Bus 311, 333, 352, 373, 377, 378, 380, 392, 394, 396. **Open** 8pm-midnight Thur, Sun; 8pm-3am Fri, Sat. **No credit cards. Map** p329 H8.
This is probably gay Sydney's most tragically fun venue. Don't go expecting cutting-edge music and hipper-than-hip lighting effects, but do expect lots of Kylie/disco diva remixes and a friendly crowd out for a good time. Palms feels a bit like a 1980s gay bar – and that's just the way the punters like it.

Stonewall Hotel

175 Oxford Street, between Taylor Square & Crown Street, Darlinghurst (9360 1963/www.stonewallhotel. com). Bus 311, 333, 352, 373, 377, 378, 380, 392, 394, 396. **Open** 9.30am-5am Mon-Fri; 9.30am-7am Sat, Sun. **No credit cards. Map** p329 G9.
A large, three-level pub and dance venue, much loved and always busy. The crowd tends towards younger gay men (wearing the latest-season fashions and spiky quiffs) and those who fancy them.

The street-level bar has a chatty, pub-style atmosphere, with drag shows, the occasional talent quest, a small dancefloor and sexy male dancers on the bar on weekends. Upstairs there are two lounge areas with more bars; it's a bit like partying in somebody's living room. The hotel also hosts various events, launches and parties during Gay Pride Week in June.

Taxi Club

40-42 Flinders Street, between Taylor & Short Streets, Darlinghurst (9331 4256/www.thetaxi club.com). Bus 311, 333, 352, 373, 377, 378, 380, 392, 394, 396. **Open** 10am-2am Mon-Thur; 10am-6am Fri-Sun. **No credit cards. Map** p329 H9.
When everything else is closed on a weekend, and desperation strikes, never fear – there's always the Taxi. It provides the cheapest drinks in queer Sydney and is open until 6am at the weekend. Which is why it's a favourite with both drag queens – who stop here after a night's work – and some extremely intoxicated out-of-towners. There's also a restaurant and café on the ground floor, a gaming room, a TV area and lounge on the first floor, and a small dancefloor above that. It's a members' club, but you can get temporary membership on the door for free.

Dance parties

The highlight of the calendar is the huge **Mardi Gras** party, a 12-hour affair that includes top-name DJs, big shows, spectacular lighting and an extremely sexy crowd (*see p243* **Hoorah for the Mardi Gras!**), but there are plenty of other bashes throughout the year. Every public holiday long weekend is sure to feature at least

Arts & Entertainment

one major event, and the bigger party weekends (New Year's Eve, Mardi Gras, the October long weekend) offer several, including pre-party parties, recovery parties and (yes!) post-recovery parties.

For many years gay and lesbian community group Pride staged its annual New Year's Eve fund-raiser at Fox Studios, but declining popularity saw its cancellation in 2005. In 2007-2008, Wildlife, organised by New Mardi Gras, Fuzzy and Fag Tag, was given a run, and proved successful. Watch out for it in the coming years.

Dance parties come and go as promoters emerge or fade from the scene, the best way to keep in touch is to pick up the *Sydney Star Observer*, *SX* or *LOTL* (Lesbians on the Loose) from venues and cafés around the city. Admission ranges from about $60 for the smaller events to $150 or more for the big productions. See websites for details.

Bad Dog

www.baddog.net.au. Also check local gay press. Organised by a group of DJs and artists dismayed by the stodgy sameness of Sydney's gay clubs, the Bad Dog events, which happen every few months, are a refreshing alternative to the norm. The venues tend to be away from the Oxford Street Golden Mile, while the parties are renowned for drawing a crowd that's high on friendliness and low on attitude.

DTPM

This event, held at Tank Nightclub (3 Bridge Lane, CBD, 9420 3000), is an offshoot of London's famed DTPM (or Delirium Tremens Post Meridien). The venue is built into the site of an old tank stream, with exposed brick walls and remnants of its former state. The resident DJ is Alan Thompson, the main spinner at the London club for over a decade, and the long weekend events are packed with a fun up-for-it crowd spread out over two rooms of house and electro. Tickets can be bought from websites such as www.fagtag.com.au and www.samesame.com.au.

Fag Tag

www.fagtag.com.au. A much-needed innovation on the party scene, Fag Tag has a simple premise: each party sees a horde of lesbians and gay men descend on an otherwise straight venue and claim it for a night. But this is no guerrilla act: the venues are in on the joke, which means there's little risk of trouble from surprised regulars. Venues that have been Fag Tagged in the past few years include the Opera Bar at Circular Quay and the Eastern Hotel in Bondi Junction. Details of events are announced about two weeks ahead.

Gurlesque

www.gurlesque.com. Eight years old and showing no signs of maturity (thank goodness), the Gurlesque strip shows continues to pack out venues and leave the dykes of Sydney gasping for more. Formed by dancers who were tired of stripping for men and wanted to 'give it to the girls', the Gurlesque events encourage all women to explore and interpret the art of striptease. The results, they say, have ranged 'from hilarious comedy and drag to seriously sexy, in-your-face pussy strutting'. With stunning costumes (just waiting to come off), raunchy routines and music from DJ Sveta, Gurlesque has truly brought something unique and unrivalled to the girls' scene. The girls perform at a number of different venues, so check the website or the local gay press for details.

Harbour Party – Sol y Luna

www.mardigras.org.au. The annual open-air Harbour Party is one of the hot tickets of the year – and with good reason. Held on the weekend before Mardi Gras, it takes place at Fleet Steps, against the stunning backdrop of Sydney Harbour, and plays host to a string of top DJs. Although the party has been running for many years, since 2008 it has been known as Sol y Luna, and now forms part of the official New Mardi Gras celebrations. Tickets are available at 13 2849 or www.ticketek.com.au.

Homesexual

www.homesexual.com.au. Homesexual is the regular gay and lesbian party at mega-club Home. Often held the night after another big party (such as New Year's Eve or Mardi Gras), it can be relied on for great drag shows and a dream team of Sydney DJs. With four floors and numerous dance spaces, it caters for a diverse range of musical tastes. Some complain that it gets too packed when at its 2,200-person capacity, but organisers say they're working to improve the bottleneck areas. Don't forget to check out the balcony: sipping a cocktail while looking out over Darling Harbour and the city makes for a magical moment.

Inquisition

Entertainment Quarter, Driver Avenue, Moore Park (9319 2309/www.sydneyleatherpride.org). Bus 355, 339, 373, 374, 376, 377. **Map** p332 J12. Held in May, Inquisition brings the annual Leather Pride Week to its climax. Festivities usually include an art exhibition, workshops, the Love Muscle competition and the Forbes Street Fair (in Darlinghurst), but Inquisition is the party for punters of all kinds to fly their fetish flag for a night. Some die-hards have decried the influx of 'leather tourists' at the event, but it remains gay Sydney's premier fetish party, with a music policy that runs to the harder side of house, and some spectacular floor shows.

Queen's Birthday Ball

www.pinkmountains.com.au. And now for something completely different. A fancy-dress ball on the long weekend of Queen Elizabeth II's birthday in June (a public holiday in Australia), organised by the Three Sisters Social Group. Held in various locations around the Blue

Hoorah for the Mardi Gras!

Lots of big cities have gay pride parades, but few take them to heart like Sydney's **Gay & Lesbian Mardi Gras**. It's gaudy, bawdy, irreverent and sexy – the perfect shorthand, then, for the city.

The Mardi Gras parade started in winter 1978 as a series of demonstrations commemorating New York's Stonewall Riots, and itself turned violent when police moved in. Several years later, the parade moved to the more comfortable season of early March, and soon the Mardi Gras story was one of unparalleled growth: it became an empire, with a series of parties, a month-long arts festival and a reputation for sexual liberation that travelled around the world.

There have been glitches along the way, but the bash is now run by the New Mardi Gras group, which works hard to make it bigger and better each year – especially the main public event, the parade, with its marching boys, drag queens in limos, disco lorries, dykes on bikes and community groups such as PFLAG (Parents & Friends of Lesbians & Gays).

WHAT AND WHEN

The Mardi Gras festival takes place over three or four weeks, ending on the last weekend in February or the first weekend in March. Although it's the parade and party on the final Saturday that get the publicity, it's worth joining the locals at as many of the pre-parade events as you can fit in.

Things kick off with the **Festival Launch** (usually on a Saturday): many bring a picnic and make a night of it. Entertainment comes in the form of speeches and a few snippets from Mardi Gras festival shows.

Other celebrations include the **Mardi Gras Film Festival** (*see p228*), art exhibitions, themed parties and nightly cabaret and stage shows in venues all over Sydney. The **Fair Day** in Victoria Park, Camperdown (held on the Sunday a fortnight before the final weekend), attracts more than 60,000 people and features an excellent high-camp pet show.

The **parade** itself begins at sunset. It starts at the corner of Hyde Park and Whitlam Square, heads up Oxford Street to Flinders Street and finishes at the party venue, the Entertainment Quarter in Moore Park. Crowds have been estimated at anything up to half a million. Many stake out their territory at least six hours before the parade starts, while hotels and restaurants along the route

sell seats at ticket-only cocktail parties. Another comfortable option is the Bobby Goldsmith 'Glamstand', which seats several thousand (for tickets and information, visit www.bgf.org.au or call 9283 8666); all proceeds go to assist men, women and children living in poverty with HIV/AIDS.

After the parade comes the **party**. Attracting some 17,000 revellers, it features top DJs and performers whose identities are usually kept secret until the night (don't expect Kylie, though: she hasn't come for years). As well as the crammed dance halls and outrageous drag shows, there are plenty of places in the Entertainment Quarter complex for drinking, eating and chilling out. There's also a hefty medical presence, in case things go wrong.

INFORMATION AND TICKETS

To keep abreast of what's going on, contact **New Mardi Gras** (9568 8600, www.mardigras. org.au) or get the excellent free programme, available from January from gay-friendly venues around Oxford Street and Newtown. You'll need to book accommodation and tickets (at least for the major events) months ahead. Tickets for the main party are available from mid December and can sell out quickly, so buy them before you arrive in Sydney if possible (13 2849, www.ticketek.com.au). For more information go to www.mardigras party.org.au/party.

Arts & Entertainment

The L word

Sydney's gay scene used to be dominated by the boys, but the girls have recently started to claim back their territory. No longer banished to dingy back bars, they are increasingly spoilt for choice, with lesbian nights cropping up at all the main venues around the city.

The biggest talk on the town at the moment is the impending arrival of Candy Bar. Founder Kim Lucas, who runs two lesbian Candy Bars in the UK, has set her sights on Sydney, and is hoping to establish a venue here by the end of 2008. For the 2008 Mardi Gras, Candy Bar teamed up with **Bitch** – whose trendy girls' night is held every Friday at Mars Lounge (see p239) – to form the official girls' Mardi Gras recovery party, **Bitch Vs Candy Bar** (www.bitchnews.com.au), at the Oxford Art Factory (38-46 Oxford Street, 9332 3711, www.oxfordartfactory.com). Bitch promoter Renee Schembri also runs a fab girls' hip hop night **Bada Bing** at the Flinders Hotel (see p238) on the first Saturday of every month.

Lesbian event **Tongue Twister** (www.tonguetwister.org) also takes place during the Mardi Gras season – usually in February. Held on five floors of the Burdekin Hotel (2-4 Oxford Street, 9331 3066, www.burdekin.com.au), it has proved massively successful in recent years.

Newtown is the place to be on a Wednesday night, with the **Bank Hotel**'s (see p238) long-running and trendy lesbian event, and the Sly Fox's **Queer Central** (see p239), an alternative night of drag-king shows, performances and DJs. Inner-west lesbians also love **Mr Mary's** (106-110 George Street, Redfern, 9690 0610, www.mrmarys.com), held every night.

Arq Sydney (see p240) puts on sexy and femme girls' nights once a month, as does Slide (see p239), with its themed girls' nights **Cherrie**. And don't miss **Luscious**, which caters for a sophisticated and slightly older crowd at the Flinders Hotel (see p238) on the third Saturday of every month, sexy **Gurlesque** (see p242; photo above), or **Lemons with a Twist** at Slide (see p239) – a social night for a late 20s-50s fun-loving crowd, held on the first Friday of the month (www.sglba.com.au).

Mountains, the ball is not a dance event in the conventional sense – more an old-style camp party, with dressing-up, lots of tragic drag, dancing, silliness and merriment, attracting many locals as well as Sydney queens looking for something new.

Ruby

www.rubydance.com.au.
Sydney DJ Ruby decided to create his own dance parties back in the late 1990s, and they've grown in scope ever since. Each party is given a theme (Alice Through the Looking Glass and Enchanted Forest have been two of the more memorable), and no expense is spared in decorating the various venues. But the parties are also renowned for their stunning light displays, ferocious uptempo music and the sexiness of the crowd.

Sleaze Ball

Entertainment Quarter, Driver Avenue, Moore Park (9568 8600/www.mardigras.org.au). Bus 339, 355, 373, 374, 376, 377. **Map** p332 J12.
A Mardi Gras fundraiser, Sleaze Ball is held on the Saturday night of the October long weekend. It's an enormous party, attracting thousands of people and featuring several halls, spectacular shows and many DJs. Each year has a theme – recent ones have included Beast, HomoSutra, and Zirkus – and party-goers are urged to dress up accordingly. Don't miss it.

Summer Gay Day

www.summergayday.com.au.
The inaugural Summer Gay Day took place in 2007, on the first day of summer, 1 December, in beautiful parklands, around Kippax Lake in Moore Park.

Arts & Entertainment

Three different spaces catered for a mix of partygoers, with a funky and more mainstream party stage, a dark and dirty Manhunt stage and a live music area. The event will undoubtedly be held again in 2008: check the website for more information.

Toybox

www.toyboxparty.com.au. Also check local gay press. 'Daytime is playtime!' That's the motto of the phenomenally successful Toybox parties, which have attracted many thousands of buff party boys and girls since 2003. Held every few months in various venues, the parties start in the early afternoon and continue until late. Several have taken place at Luna Park as a recovery event after the Mardi Gras and Sleaze Ball parties, leading some of the faithful to abandon the main event and devote their energies to Toybox instead. Renowned for their awesome lighting, superior sound quality and high production values all round, these parties are a very hot ticket in gay Sydney right now.

Gyms

As in all large gay cities worthy of that mantle, there is a thriving culture of the body in Sydney. Below are two gyms popular with gay men and lesbians; also try **Bayswater Fitness** (58 Kippax Street, Surry Hills, 9211 2799, www.bayswaterfitness.com.au).

City Gym Health & Fitness Centre

107-113 Crown Street, between William & Stanley Streets, East Sydney (9360 6247/www.citygym. com.au). CityRail Kings Cross/bus 323, 324, 325, 389. **Open** 5am-midnight Mon-Fri; 6am-10pm Sat; 8am-10pm Sun. **Admission** $19.50. **Credit** AmEx, MC, V. **Map** p329 G8.
A legendary venue, popular with gay men and the serious bodybuilding crowd. Full fitness facilities, an extensive programme of classes and, for the men, a notoriously cruisy changing area (with steam room).

Gold's Gym

23 Pelican Street, between Oxford & Goulburn Streets, Darlinghurst (9264 4496/www.goldsgym.com). CityRail Museum. **Open** 5.30am-10pm Mon-Fri; 7am-9pm Sat; 8am-7pm Sun. **Admission** $19.75. **Credit** AmEx, DC, MC, V. **Map** p329 G8.
A very busy franchise of the global gym brand, with a huge gay and lesbian clientele. Classes, solarium, massage and all the usual workout facilities.

Saunas & sex clubs

Sydney has plenty of men-only sex-on-premises venues, and most of them draw particular crowds. Take along a gym membership card if you have one: many establishments offer discounts. Most venues have signed up to a code of practice organised by the AIDS Council, meaning they distribute free condoms and lube to customers. Over-18s only.

Bodyline Spa & Sauna

10 Taylor Street, at Flinders Street, Darlinghurst (9360 1006/www.bodylinesydney.com). Bus 311, 333, 352, 373, 377, 378, 380, 392, 394, 396. **Open** noon-7am Mon-Thur; 24hrs noon Fri-7am Mon. **Admission** $23; $16 gym members Mon-Thur; $12 reductions. **Credit** AmEx, DC, MC, V.
Established in 1991, Bodyline was the first lawfully established sex-on-premises gay venue in NSW, and is still gay-owned and -operated. It has a huge spa, steam room and sauna on the lower ground floor; a coffee lounge and cinema on the ground floor; private rooms and a video room on the first floor; and a great sun deck on the second floor. It's kept very clean and tends to attract the buff party crowd from many of the nearby nightclubs, including Arq.

HeadQuarters on Crown

273 Crown Street, at Campbell Street, Darlinghurst (9331 6217/www.headquarters.com.au). Bus 311, 333, 352, 373, 377, 378, 380, 392, 394, 396. **Open** 24hrs daily. **Admission** *7pm-7am Mon-Thur* $16; *7am-7pm Mon-Fri* $10; *Fri 7pm-Mon 7am* $18. **Credit** AmEx, MC, V. **Map** p329 G9.
Sprawling over three large levels, HeadQuarters specialises in 'fantasy play areas' including a pig pen, a jail room and a wet area – you get the idea. It holds frequent fetish nights (including leather, Speedo and footy shorts parties), as well as the occasional all-nude evening. There's a coffee lounge and full aircon – thank goodness.

Ken's at Kensington

83 Anzac Parade, opposite Ascot Street, Kensington (9662 1359/www.kensatkensington.com.au). Bus 391, 392, 393, 394, 395, 396, 397, 399. **Open** 11am-6am Mon-Thur; 24hrs 11am Fri-6am Mon. **Admission** $19; $13 11am-3pm Mon-Fri. **No credit cards.**
Something of a legend in gay Sydney, Ken's has been running for over 30 years, and just about everybody has trod its halls at some time or other. The upper level features a chill-out cinema, a gym and a few private booths, while the lower includes a swimming pool, a steam room, a sauna, a spa and many private rooms. Look out for the glass ceiling over the pool. The regular 'Buck Naked' nude nights are extremely popular, while DJ Seymour Butz adds to the ambience on Sunday afternoon with an appropriately sexy soundtrack.

Sydney City Steam

357 Sussex Street, at Liverpool Street, CBD (9267 6766/www.sydneycitysteam.com.au). CityRail Town Hall. **Open** 10am-6pm Mon-Thur; 24 hours 10am Fri-6am Mon. **Admission** $20; $17 reductions; $13 10am-2pm Mon-Fri. **No credit cards.** **Map** p329 E8.
Gay-owned and -run, and located in the heart of Chinatown, Sydney City Steam features four floors of action. Facilities include a spa, steam room, sauna, two cinema spaces, various 'fantasy rooms', a coffee shop area and the services of a non-sexual masseur, Gary, whose massages are legendary.

Music

To make it here, you have to play by Aussie rules.

Rock, Roots & Jazz

Rock

If live music's your thing, compose yourself for some surprising Antipodean treats. Like all major cities around the globe, Sydney has its fair share of international mega-shows from the Justin Timberlakes of this world, but there's also plenty of real flavour and attitude all of its own. Small, intimate gigs are just as common (if not more so) than the vast-scale spectaculars at venues like the 1,600-capacity **Enmore Theatre** (*see p248*), while the range of styles and scenes springing up in Sydney's pubs, clubs and concert halls is as broad as you'll find anywhere in the southern hemisphere. The city's varied and insatiable musical appetite devours rock, funk, world, jazz, classical, opera and much, much more.

Thirty years ago, the climate couldn't have been more different. Raised on a wholesome staple of TV shows *Six O'Clock Rock, Bandstand* and later *Countdown*, Aussies didn't know what to make of visiting bands they'd idolised on record but couldn't relate to in the flesh. Intimidated by the sheer bravado of overseas 'guests', audiences reacted in typical Aussie fashion: they fought back. Sinatra was famously blockaded in his hotel suite in 1974 by unions after he branded a journalist a 'whore', while an inebriated Eric Clapton slurred his way through a 1975 tour to jeers and condemnation. Pete Townshend vowed never to return after the 'humourless' reception The Who received from the media a few years earlier, and Joe Cocker was physically ejected from Australia for bad behaviour and told never to return.

Where people felt at ease – and where the heart of live music lay – was in the pubs. The Angels, Cold Chisel, Radio Birdman, Midnight Oil, and Hunters & Collectors all blossomed in beer barns that swelled with the music-hungry masses. Such behaviour dated back, interestingly enough, to the American GIs stationed in Sydney in the 1940s. They brought with them a rich tradition in song, and local dives began servicing them, creating a musical revolution of sorts in the process. By 1955, when the infamous 'six o'clock swill' (a 6pm

close that ensured mass downings of beer) had been banished, Sydney was ready to embrace homespun rock 'n' roll and an ensuing teenage rebellion. When, in 1957, Johnny O'Keefe and Col Joye and the Joy Boys tore up the Town Hall for the inaugural Rock 'n' Roll Ball, popular music had arrived.

By the late 1970s and '80s, Sydney bands were flying high – literally – around the world, with AC/DC and INXS achieving recognition on both sides of the Atlantic. But while MTV happily played Men at Work and the UK loved Kylie, the local scene suffered a recession as fire restrictions impinged and nightclubs took the place of pubs. The national passion for gambling (resulting in pubs being filled with poker machines) threatened to finish off the live scene altogether, but thanks to power acts such as You Am I, the mid- to late-1990s saw a resurgence in band power that continues unabated.

The ever-resilient inner-city scene is buoyed by Sydney's dominance of the music industry. All the major record companies (domestic and international) have their headquarters in the city, and any band worth its salt must do the Sydney circuit to have any hope of getting signed. In addition, the MTV Video Music Awards are held in April, and the ARIA (Australian Record Industry Association) awards are staged in October, both typically glitzy televised affairs. The huge success of reality TV's *Australian Idol* (the finals of which are held at Sydney Opera House) also reawakened interest – in pop, at least – with winners and finalists scoring record deals.

Annual festivals have blossomed too, with **Big Day Out** (www.bigdayout.com), held in Sydney and throughout Australia and New Zealand in January and February, continuing to be a major draw for overseas acts. The all-Aussie **Homebake** (www.homebake.com.au, *see p215*), held in the Domain in December, pulls in huge crowds; as does dance festival **Field Day** (www.fuzzy.com.au), also in the Domain, on New Years Day. Next up is **Good Vibrations** in February (www.goodvibrations festival.com.au), followed by **V Festival** (www.vfestival.com.au) and indie rock event **St Jerome's Laneway Festival** (www.lanewayfestival.com.au), which are both held in March. The **Great Escape** (www.thegreatescape.net.au) completes the set, held over Easter. As ever in this alfresco city, outdoor events are guaranteed sellouts.

INFORMATION

ABC's national youth radio network Triple J (105.7 FM) highlights new Aussie talent – past glories include Silverchair and Grinspoon, both still riding high in popularity – while FBi Radio (94.5 FM) has taken over the mantle as the underground spot on the dial.

If you're looking for music news, reviews and listings on the local music scene keep an eye open for *Drum Media*, *3D World* and *The Brag Magazine*, free publications widely distributed in pubs and record shops. On the net, check out the comprehensive www.fasterlouder.com.au which offers even more reviews and listings plus audio and video samples and downloads. The *Sydney Morning Herald*'s Metro section on Friday features news, reviews and listings, as does the pseudo-tabloid *Daily Telegraph* with its daily Sydney Live section and a more comprehensive liftout guide on Thursdays. A local version of *Rolling Stone* targets the monthly market and another glossy mag, *Australian Musician*, is published every quarter, and is available free from music stores.

Tickets often sell out far less quickly than you might expect, so it's always worth making a call even for the big acts. Note that smoking isn't allowed in any indoor venue.

Girls on top

She may wear the tiara, but there's much more to Australia's female musicians than adored pop princess Kylie Minogue. In the past few years a host of talented local singer-songwriters have held their own in the Australian charts with their impressive range of independent voices. Sydney girl **Delta Goodrem** has won the respect of the industry and public with her exceptional vocal, piano and song-writing skills. More left-of-centre musicians like the melodic, ethereal **Missy Higgins** found mainstream success, while country crooner **Kasey Chambers** packs in the crowds and has helped open up the genre to a wider audience. And waiting in the wings is the girl power of **Jade MacRae**, whose talents encompass soul and electro pop, alongside popular jazz and soul singer **Katie Noonan**. Meanwhile reality TV hit *Australian Idol* has spawned a number of new stars including hot girl group **Young Divas**, and ex-member of the group **Ricki-Lee Coulter**, who has now successfully branched out on her own. Also getting the crowds' booties shaking in a major way all over the country are Brisbane out-there twins Lisa and Jessica Origliasso, aka **The Veronicas** (pictured). Indie fans, meanwhile, have got behind **Sarah Blasko**, **Holly Throsby** and **Clare Bowditch**, all mistresses of folk tunes with heartfelt lyrics.

On the classical front, Sydney-raised opera star **Amelia Farrugia** has made waves internationally. Her debut solo album, *Joie de Vivre!*, saw the soprano compared to Dame Joan Sutherland. As part of World Youth Day 2008, hosted by Sydney, Farrugia was set to perform solo for Pope Benedict XVI during the Final Mass on 20 July.

'The Australian music and pop industry, which has been influenced by many different cultures, has opened up for female artists and we are now hearing an emergence of truly unique, individual sounds,' says Amelia. 'With the introduction of talent shows like *Australian Idol*, young women have the opportunity to receive far greater exposure, so more diverse talents are being discovered. In the last few years, Australians have embraced some beautiful and arresting voices including Paulini, Christine Anu, Ella Hooper and Vanessa Amorosi.' Sisters, in other words, are doing it for themselves.

Will & Toby's, home to **Supper Club**.

Major venues

Acer Arena

Olympic Boulevard, at Edwin Flack Avenue, Sydney Olympic Park, Homebush Bay (8765 4321/www. acerarena.com.au). CityRail Olympic Park/RiverCat Homebush Bay then bus 401. **Box office** (in person) 1hr before show. **Tickets** varies. **Credit** AmEx, DC, MC, V.

Built for the 2000 Olympics, the Acer Arena (previously called the Sydney SuperDome) boasts a whopping 21,000-seat capacity and multiple configurations for anything from rock, pop and rap to big-scale dance parties, monster truck shows, equestrian events and even the occasional audience with a psychic. Elton John, Justin Timberlake and Gwen Stefani have all played here over the years.

Big Top

Luna Park, Milsons Point (9033 7600/www.bigtop sydney.com). CityRail/ferry Milsons Point. **Box office** 9am-5.30pm Mon-Thur, Sun; 9am-8pm Fri, Sat. **Credit** AmEx, MC, V.

Used as both a mid-sized band venue (the capacity is nearly 3,000) and for glitzy awards nights, the indoor Big Top opened in 2004. Since then the likes of Nick Cave, My Chemical Romance, the Pixies, Incubus and the Scissor Sisters have all graced its stage to much acclaim. State-of-the-art sound and sight lines, great facilities and easy access all combine to make it popular with punters.

Enmore Theatre

118-132 Enmore Road, between Simmons & Reiby Streets, Newtown (9550 3666/www.enmoretheatre. com.au). CityRail Newtown. **Box office** 9am-5pm Mon-Fri; 10am-2pm Sat. **Tickets** varies. **Credit** AmEx, DC, MC, V. **Map** p334.

The most atmospheric of the inner-city venues, this 1,600-seat theatre plays host to local talent, overseas acts and big-name stand-up and theatre. Queens of the Stone Age, Kings of Leon and the Stones (doing a 'club night') have all strutted their stuff here. The acoustics are excellent, the seats are often removed for dancing, and the door and bar staff are friendly.

Factory Theatre

105 Victoria Road, Enmore (9550 3666/www.factory theatre.com.au). CityRail Newtown then bus 423, 426. **Box office** 1hr before show. **Tickets** varies. **Credit** AmEx, DC, MC, V.

Since opening in December 2006, this custom-built venue has fired up the scene with shows by local and international musicians, plus dance, cabaret and film events. It has excellent acoustics and features a bar and comfy sofa area. Past performers include Sixto Rodriguez, José González and The Necks.

Hordern Pavilion

Driver Avenue, Moore Park (9921 5333/www. playbillvenues.com.au). Bus 339, 373, 374, 376, 377, 393, 395, 396. **Box office** (in person) 2hrs before show. **Tickets** vary. **Credit** AmEx, DC, MC, V. **Map** p332 J12.

palace, built in 1929, boasts massive chandeliers, abundant statuary, an imported marble staircase and lots of gilt. It's a rococo-cum-deco delight, never short of atmosphere, and plays co-host to the Sydney Film Festival (*see p217*) in winter when gigs are scarce, movie premieres and occasional theatre pieces (*see p249*). It has a capacity of 2,000, and seating is mandatory, with dancing restricted to the aisles – if security are friendly.

Supper Club

Will & Toby's Taylor Square, Level 1, 134 Oxford Street, Darlinghurst (9331 3467/www. willandtobys.com.au). Bus 378, 343, 309, 376, 392, 397, L94. **Open** 8pm-late Thurs-Sat; 7pm-late Sun. **Admission** varies. **Credit** AmEx, DC, MC, V. **Map** p329 H9.

The classy Taylor Square hang-out of celebrated Sydney restaurateur brothers Will and Toby Osmond includes a lavishly decorated 200-capacity supper club that features sophisticated music, cabaret and comedy acts. It serves shared plates and has an impressive cocktail and wine list.

Sydney Entertainment Centre

35 Harbour Street, between Hay & Pier Streets, Darling Harbour (admin 9320 4200/www. sydentcent.com.au). CityRail Central or Town Hall/Monorail/LightRail Paddy's Markets. **Box office** (in person) 9am-5pm Mon-Fri. **Tickets** varies. **Credit** AmEx, DC, MC, V. **Map** p329 E8.

This 12,500-seater complex in Darling Harbour presents more A-list acts than any other. Built in 1983, it's a typical aircraft hangar that can accommodate crowds easily and safely and is convenient for transport and accommodation. Like most venues this size, though, it falls short on atmosphere, with heavy-handed security. Beyoncé, Bob Dylan, The Cure and the like play here to packed houses.

Sydney Opera House

Bennelong Point, Circular Quay (box office 9250 7777/admin 9250 7111/www.sydneyoperahouse.com). CityRail/ferry Circular Quay. **Box office** 9am-8.30pm Mon-Sat; 2hrs before show Sun. **Tickets** *Opera Theatre* $70-$250; $70-$195 reductions. *Concert Hall* prices vary. *Drama Theatre and Playhouse* $35-$80; $30-$60 reductions. *Studio* $25-$50; $25-$40 reductions. **Credit** AmEx, DC, MC, V. **Map** p327 G3.

The Sydney icon's acoustics tend to work better for more 'refined' acts such as Norah Jones and Michael Bublé than for louder bands. That said, the powers that be have broadened the House's remit, so the main Concert Hall now hosts anything from the final telecasts of *Australian Idol* to avant-garde artistes, while the smaller Studio opts for intimate, often acoustic-based shows. The steps are also used for music events, much to the dismay of local residents.

A barn of a venue, yet with a typically relaxed Australian vibe, the 5,500-capacity Hordern sits at the cool end of the Moore Park complex at the Entertainment Quarter. Built in 1924, it presents big-name local acts (Powderfinger, John Butler Trio) and overseas artists seeking financially viable intimacy (Oasis, Coldplay, the Strokes). The floor is usually standing only, there's tiered seating behind and on both sides, and it's air-conditioned.

Metro

624 George Street, at Central Street, CBD (9550 3666/www.metrotheatre.com.au). CityRail Town Hall/Monorail World Square. **Box office** 1hr before show. **Tickets** $20-$75. **Credit** AmEx, DC, MC, V. **Map** p329 E7.

With its tiered, standing-only set-up (the stage is always in full view), the 1,200-capacity Metro is the archetypal muso hangout. Its central location, relatively intimate size and overwhelmingly vibey ambience keeps it constantly in demand. If a hot band's in town, chances are they'll sniff out the Metro first.

State Theatre

49 Market Street, between Pitt & George Streets, CBD (admin 9373 6852/www.statetheatre.com.au). CityRail St James or Town Hall/Monorail City Centre. **Box office** (in person) 9am-5pm Mon-Fri. **Tickets** $25-$120. **Credit** AmEx, DC, MC, V. **Map** p327 F6.

The first choice for older, 'serious' artists (think Lou Reed, Brian Wilson, Elvis Costello), this opulent

Pubs & clubs

There are dozens – if not hundreds – of pubs (aka hotels) in Sydney where you can see bands perform. RSL (Returned Services League) clubs also offer regular gigs of all shapes and sizes. These have licensing laws that require all visitors, whatever their age, to show ID, so bring your passport and adhere to the dress code (no shorts, singlets or flip-flops, aka thongs) or you won't get in. Most serve good bar food too. The following are the best.

Annandale Hotel
Corner of Parramatta Road & Nelson Street, Annandale (9550 1078/www.annandalehotel. com.au). Bus 413, 435, 436, 437, 438, 440, 461, 483. **Open** 11am-10pm Mon, Tue, Sun; 11am-midnight Wed-Sat. **Admission** $10-$30. **Credit** (phone & internet bookings only) MC, V.
The legendary Annandale is the place to see hot up-and-coming bands, including visiting interstate acts, and to catch overseas talent performing 'secret' shows for fans. The sound is reasonable and the upper level at the rear is given over to tables and chairs for the terminally rocked out. A photo gallery lines the walls in the second bar, with a Thai restaurant and beer garden at the rear. The Annandale also hosts weekly cult movie nights.

Bar Broadway
Corner of Broadway & Regent Street, Haymarket (9211 2321/www.barbroadway.com.au). CityRail/ LightRail Central. **Open** 10.30am-4am Mon-Thur; noon-5am Fri, Sat; noon-4am Sun. **Admission** $10-$20. **Credit** AmEx, MC, V. **Map** p329 E9.
This wood and stainless steel bar hosts everything from acoustic to ska and funk. The intimate upstairs space, with its low ceilings, cocktail bar and chat areas, doubles as a club. The downstairs bar has lighting dim enough to fake prowess with a pool cue.

Bridge Hotel
119 Victoria Road, at Wellington Street, Rozelle (9810 1260). Bus 500, 501, 502, 504, 505, 506, 507, 508, 510, 515, 518, 520. **Open** 24hrs Mon-Sat; until midnight Sun. **Admission** $5-$30. **No credit cards.**
Blues-oriented R&B acts and cover bands play the large room here (capacity 700), along with the odd thesp revue. Retro discos spin into action on many nights after 11pm. Popular with meat-marketeers, birthday bashers and suburban gals.

Cat & Fiddle Hotel
456 Darling Street, at Elliot Street, Balmain (9810 7931/www.thecatandfiddle.net). Bus 432, 433, 434, 445. **Open** 10am-midnight Mon-Sat; noon-10pm Sun. **Admission** $8-$10. **No credit cards.**
Folk, bush, jazz and pop: all do the rounds at this seasoned, ever-reliable venue. Out-of-towners pick up work here, while old favourites often play low-key shows for faithful fans.

Gaelic Club
64 Devonshire Street, between Chalmers & Elizabeth Streets, Surry Hills (9211 1687/www.thegaelicclub. com). CityRail/LightRail Central. **Open** varies; phone for details. **Admission** $20-$55. **No credit cards.** **Map** p329 F10.

Another barn of a room, with capacity not far off the four-figure mark, this place attracts local and international acts who can't – or don't want – to play the Metro (*see p249*). Located in the band-loving area of Surry Hills, it's booked solid through much of the year, with the Strokes, the Darkness and Shane McGowan all having appeared. The lack of any air-conditioning means it heats up fast though.

Hopetoun Hotel
416 Bourke Street, at Fitzroy Street, Surry Hills (9361 5257/www.myspace.com/hopetounhotel). Bus 301, 302, 303. **Open** 2pm-midnight Mon-Sat; noon-10pm Sun. **Admission** $10-$20. **No credit cards.** **Map** p329 G10.
The other pub venue in Sydney that showcases live local talent on a weekly basis. More intimate than the Annandale (*see left*), it also tends to book more left-field acts. A basement bar is open at weekends for musos taking an audio break, plus there's an upper level for lunchtime snacks.

Lansdowne Hotel
2-6 City Road, at Broadway, Chippendale (9211 2325/www.myspace.com/lansdownehotel). Bus 370, 422, 423, 426, 428. **Open** 10am-3am Mon-Sat; noon-10pm Sun. **Admission** free. **Credit** AmEx, MC, V. **Map** p328 C10.
A good spot for a laid-back Sunday afternoon, when you can see three bands on the same bill. The best bit? Entry is free. Handy after a stroll around Glebe.

Rose of Australia
1 Swanson Street, at Charles Street, Erskineville (9565 1441). CityRail Erskineville. **Open** 10am-midnight Tue-Sat; 10am-10pm Mon, Sun. **Admission** free. **Credit** AmEx, DC, MC, V. **Map** p334.
A stayer in the pub stakes, this low-key venue often has something going on. It covers all angles, with pop, rock and cover bands, as well as jazz.

Sandringham Hotel
387 King Street, between Holt & Goddard Streets, Newtown (9557 1254/www.sando.com.au). CityRail Newtown. **Open** 10am-midnight Mon-Wed; 10am-2am Thur-Sat; 10am-10pm Sun. **Admission** $5-$15. **No credit cards.** **Map** p334.
The Sandringham's upstairs concert space is small but cosy, decked out in opulent red. Plenty of undiscovered talent rocks up to a receptive brigade hungry for fresh sounds.

Spectrum
Exchange Hotel, 34-44 Oxford Street, between Riley & Liverpool Streets, Darlinghurst (9331 1936/www. pashpresents.com). Bus 311, 371, 373, 377, 378, 380, 392, 394, 396, 397, 399, 890, X39. **Open** 8pm-late Sat; 8pm-midnight Sun. **Admission** $5-$20. **Credit** MC, V. **Map** p329 G8.
Bringing music screaming into the 'pink strip' of town, this intimate club has succeeded in showcasing hot new bands and attracting established talent who want a central location that isn't a barn. The venue also hosts popular club nights. Housed in the four-level Exchange Hotel.

Annandale Hotel.

Vanguard

42 King Street, between Queen & Fitzroy Streets, Newtown (9557 7992/www.thevanguard.com.au). Bus 352, 370, 422, 423, 426, 428. **Open** 5pm-midnight Tue-Sat; 4-10pm Sun. **Admission** $10-$30. **Credit** AmEx, DC, MC, V. **Map** p334.

Opened in late 2003, the smart yet cosy Vanguard adds to the Inner West's push to make a mark on the live music front. Expect a range of rock, jazz and blues acts, in comfortable surroundings; there's a restaurant too. The venue is often used as a showcase for local and international touring acts.

Jazz

Although its appeal lies primarily with the inner-city wine bar set, jazz enjoys an undeniably solid presence in Sydney's live music scene. Jazz audiences are fiercely loyal: 1980s hero Vince Jones – one of the few jazz all-rounders to break out into the mainstream – still sells out well in advance. Local legends Jackie Orszaczky and Tina Harrod are among the most recognised faces of the Sydney jazz scene, and, until Orszaczky's death in early 2008, were to be found at various inner-city venues on a weekly basis. Hard bop fans should catch Bernie McGann, a craggy veteran who wrings emotion from his alto sax and swings like a gorilla when hyped. Trumpeter James Morrison, meanwhile, is very much the popular face of jazz in Australia and recently put out an album with hot performer Deni Hines.

Young experimentalists work independently or in company with older but edgy players in the vein of Mike Nock, John Pochee, Mark Simmonds and Bob Bertles. These stalwarts have helped bring an array of bands to the fore, including Clarion Fracture Zone, Wanderlust, the Catholics, the Necks, Ute, Australian Creole, First Light, the Scott Tinkler Trio, Twentieth Century Dog and Engine Room, some of whom gained overseas exposure. 'Nu' jazz has also proved a popular offshoot.

The avant-garde continues to influence many bands, adding bite and a degree of wildness to a prevailing world music influence. Contemporary jazzers often earn their living in rock, funk, Latin and blues bands and have allowed these influences to colour their playing. Champion of new talent **SIMA** (Sydney Improvised Music Association; www.sima.org.au) offers up an array of innovative jazzers to watch, such as the award-winning Phil Slater Quartet. In addition, the **Jazzgroove Association** (www.jazzgroove.com) – a musicians' co-op dedicated to promoting new jazz talent – helps organise events and profile young players, including the Gerard Masters Trio, Nicholas McBride and the Nick Bowd Quartet.

More recent additions to the scene continue to keep it fresh and eclectic. Singer-songwriter Elana Stone from the Jazzgroove stable packs a punch, as does Matt Baker's Transition Project, Cin Cin, guitarist Ray Beadle and the Edwina Blush Trio. Saxophonists Mark Taylor, Dale Barlow and Tim Hopkins, vocalist Melanie Oxley, keyboardist Chris Abrahams and guitarist Ben Hughes show what can be done with melodies and instrumentation, while fans of hardcore free improvisers can get their kicks from multi-instrumentalist Jim Denley and turntable maniac Martin Ng.

Possibly the best place to see the bulk of Sydney's jazz talent, and an increasing number of top international acts besides, is the ever-expanding **Manly International Jazz Festival** (*see p214*). Held over the long weekend in October, its musical scope covers swing, blues, funk, Afro-Latin and zydeco. To get the scoop on what's happening jazz-time, tune into Eastside Radio (89.7 FM) and Jazztrack (5-7pm Saturday and Sunday ABC Classic 92.9 FM).

For a full guide to jazz on local and national radio, visit www.jazzscene.com.au.

Venues

The **Vanguard** in Newtown (*see above*) mirrors the modern-day vibe of the long-running **Basement** (*see below*) in style and content. Expect a mix of roots, blues, jazz and acoustic-based melodies at both.

Other venues with occasional jazz nights include the **Bald Faced Stag** in Leichhardt (345 Parramatta Road, 9560 7188), with jam sessions on Thursdays; and **Café Sydney** (9251 8683, www.cafesydney.com), an upmarket eaterie on the top floor of the Customs House at Circular Quay, which offers jazz, funk and classical Sunday lunchtimes (booking advised). Jazz acts also feature regularly at the popular weekend **Rocks Market** (*see p193*) to keep the tourist crowds jigging and grinning. R&B, guitar duos and the occasional classical string ensemble also mingle among the stalls.

Basement

29 Reiby Place, off Pitt Street, Circular Quay (9251 2797/www.thebasement.com.au). CityRail/ferry Circular Quay. **Open** noon-late Mon-Fri; 7pm-late Sat, Sun. **Admission** $12-$60. **Credit** AmEx, DC, MC, V. **Map** p327 F4.

One of the hippest clubs on the scene, this hugely popular jazz and blues venue near the Quay boasts a supper-club-style setting with tables, an adjacent 'blue room' and a bistro for cheap eats. Expect the likes of Tony Joe White or Roger McGuinn to turn up, along with world music maestros and established local jazz names.

El Rocco @ Bar Me

Corner of William Street and Brougham Street,
Woolloomooloo (9368 0894/www.barme.com.au).
CityRail Kings Cross. **Open** 3pm-3am daily.
Admission $5-$25. **Credit** AmEx, DC, MC, V.
Map p330 J7.
The epithet 'legendary' is over used these days, but
in the case of a venue which staged the likes of Frank
Sinatra and Elton John in its heyday, it may perhaps
be justified. These days, El Rocco is an intimate
sandstone-walled room that features cabaret, jazz,
blues, and the occasional comedy act. Good-value
meals are served mid-performance and there's also
a small, funky upstairs bar.

Macquarie Hotel

42 Wentworth Avenue, at Goulburn Street, Surry
Hills (8262 8888/www.macquariehotel.com). CityRail
Central. **Open** 9am-late Mon-Sat; 9am-midnight Sun.
Admission free. **Credit** AmEx, DC, MC, V.
Map p329 F8.
An inner-city pub that, belying the Australian ten-
dency to call just about anything a hotel, does actu-
ally double as a place to stay. Specialising in jazz,
funk and soul, it has free live sessions every night.

Opera Bar

Lower Concourse Level, Sydney Opera House,
Bennelong Point, Circular Quay (9247 1666/
www.operabar.com.au). CityRail/ferry Circular
Quay. **Open** 11.30am-midnight Mon-Wed, Sun;
11.30am-1am Thur-Sat. **Admission** free.
Credit AmEx, DC, MC, V. **Map** p327 G3.

A mix of live jazz, soul, funk and ambient DJs perform in a setting that's hard to beat anywhere in
Sydney, right on the water's edge. The sounds kick
off throughout the week from 8.30pm, and at weekends from 2pm. *See also p180.*

Sound Lounge

Seymour Centre, corner of City Road & Cleveland
Street, Chippendale (box office 9351 7940/admin
9351 7944/www.seymour.usyd.edu.au). Bus 370,
422, 423, 426, 428. **Open** from 8.30pm Fri, Sat.
Admission $15-$20; $12-$53 reductions. **Credit**
AmEx, MC, V. **Map** p328 C11.
World music, jazz, cabaret and comedy performances
are held here from Tuesday to Saturday nights, in
what was the old restaurant area of this student-
friendly arts centre. Capacity is deliberately kept low
(it's never above 100), with pub grub and drinks
served in a supper club environment.

Woollahra Hotel

Corner of Moncur & Queen Streets, Woollahra
(9327 9777/www.woollahrahotel.com.au). Bus 389.
Open noon-midnight Mon-Sat; noon-10pm Sun.
Admission free. **Credit** AmEx, DC, MC, V.
Map p333 M10.
The Woollahra isn't an ideal venue – it's on the
snobbier side of the eastern suburbs and lacks the
warmth of jazz's hallowed grounds – but its musical servings can still surprise. Come for the Jazz Juice
sessions every Sunday (6.30-9.30pm, featuring all
types of jazz) and Thursday (7.45-10.45pm, focusing
on danceable sounds such as Brazilian funk).

Cosy for tutti at Sydney Opera House's **Opera Bar**.

Classical & Opera

Sydney's flourishing classical music scene has raised its bar even higher with the news that, in January 2009, internationally acclaimed conductor and music director Vladimir Ashkenazy will be stepping in as Sydney Symphony Orchestra's principal conductor and artistic advisor, taking over the reins from Gianluigi Gelmetti. To have Ashkenazy in the city will be music to the ears of Sydney's very enthusiastic classical crowd, who flock to concerts – especially when they're laid on in an outdoor picnic-style setting.

The **Sydney Festival** (*see p215*) alleviates post-Christmas blues by running musical events throughout January – including the Sydney Symphony's free **Symphony & Jazz in the Domain**. The other main outdoor event, also free, is Opera Australia's **Opera in the Domain**, on the last Saturday in January or the first Saturday in February. The orchestral and carol-singing sit-ins in the Domain pack in tens of thousands of families every year, although connoisseurs steer clear of such mainstream fare, which tends to favour well-worn classics. ABC's TV and radio stations often broadcast live relays of opera performances, usually at weekends.

Venues

The **Eugene Goossens Hall** – named after the British composer and conductor who first suggested the idea of the Opera House back in 1954, and housed in the ABC headquarters in Ultimo – is often used by smaller ensembles playing contemporary music. **Sydney Town Hall** (*see p82*) also showcases contemporary music, plus free organ recitals, the SBS Youth Orchestra, the Sydney University Musical Society and Sydney Festival events. Churches are also popular if irregular venues for recitals, and a guide to church music can be found in the *SMH*'s Metro section. **St Andrew's Cathedral** (*see p81*) plays host to the Cathedral Singers & Orchestra, who perform choral classics, as well as jazz choirs and guest chamber music groups. The Historic Houses Trust of NSW offers classical and jazz concerts in the ballroom at **Government House** (*see p75*). Guests can stroll the grounds before the performance.

City Recital Hall

Angel Place, near Martin Place, CBD (admin 9231 9000/box office 8256 2222/www.cityrecitalhall.com). CityRail Martin Place. **Box office** 9am-5pm Mon-Fri; 3hrs before show. **Tickets** free-$90. **Credit** AmEx, MC, V. **Map** p327 F5.

The 1,200-seat City Recital Hall in the centre of the CBD gives Sydney's orchestras room to roam, as

Vladimir Ashkenazy.

well as hosting international names (including one David Helfgott). Created via a deal with the AMP Corporation, the two-tiered, horseshoe-shaped hall has a colour scheme borrowed from a Latvian baroque church (soft grey, soothing aubergine and twinkles of gold) and the architecture and acoustics have been designed for both chamber orchestras and solo performers. The acoustics are said to match Amsterdam's Concertgebouw.

Sydney Opera House

Bennelong Point, Circular Quay (box office 9250 7777/admin 9250 7111/www.sydneyoperahouse.com). CityRail/ferry Circular Quay. **Box office** 9am-8.30pm Mon-Sat; 2hrs before show Sun. **Tickets** *Opera Theatre* $70-$250; $70-$195 reductions. *Concert Hall* prices vary. *Drama Theatre and Playhouse* $35-$80; $30-$60 reductions. *Studio* $25-$50; $25-$40 reductions. **Credit** AmEx, DC, MC, V. **Map** p327 G3.

The largest shell of the Sydney icon houses the 2,700-seat Concert Hall (although it was first intended for opera productions). Thanks to its purpose-built acoustics, symphonic music can be heard with a full, rich and mellow tone. Eighteen adjustable acrylic rings (aka the 'toilet seats') are suspended above the orchestra platform to reflect some of the sound back to the musicians. The hall also has the largest mechanical tracker-action organ in the world, with 10,154 pipes. The smaller, 1,500-seat Opera Theatre is used by Opera Australia, but has its problems (it can't do a real-time set change or take a full-scale orchestra). The Studio (capacity 350) showcases anything from rap to percussion bands and spoken-word shows. The two other spaces are used for drama productions (*see p270*).

Orchestras & groups

Australian Brandenburg Orchestra

9328 7581/www.brandenburg.com.au.
Australia's first period-instrument group – baroque and classical periods, that is – has played to sell-out audiences from Tokyo to Germany. Formed by artistic director Paul Dyer in 1990, the orchestra now puts on regular seasons at the City Recital Hall. Its concerts are fashionable events – rich mixes of visual and musical experience.

Australian Chamber Orchestra

8274 3800/www.aco.com.au.
Under the flamboyant artistic directorship of high-profile violinist Richard Tognetti, the ACO has injected some excitement into classical music. Formed in 1975, the Sydney-based orchestra is relatively youthful – most performers are under 40 – and Tognetti's programming is always provocative. He likes to mix periods, offer rarely heard works and blend period-instrument soloists with contemporary instruments. The results are invariably startling.

Musica Viva

8394 6666/www.musicaviva.com.au.
Musica Viva is the world's largest chamber music organisation, touring Australian and international groups around the country. The outfit, which turns 65 in 2010, tours famous choirs and caters to a wide range of musical sensibilities. A roll-call of the world's best ensembles, including the Emerson Quartet, the Beaux Arts Trio and the Australian String Quartet, have all appeared on its impressive calendar.

Opera Australia

Opera Centre, 480 Elizabeth Street, between Devonshire & Belvoir Streets, Surry Hills (box office 9318 8200/tours 9318 8330/www.opera-australia. org.au). CityRail/LightRail Central. **Open** *Box office 9am-5pm Mon-Fri. Tours 10am, 11am, 2pm Mon-Fri.* **Tickets** *Shows* $55-$245. *Tours* $15 incl tea; 11am tour $35 incl lunch. **Credit** AmEx, MC, V. **Map** p329 F11.
Australia may be far from the great European opera houses, but the country's divas have been disproportionately represented in the ranks of global opera stars, among them Nellie Melba, Joan Hammond, Joan Sutherland, Elizabeth Whitehouse and Yvonne Kenny. And Opera Australia has the third-largest programme (after Covent Garden and the Vienna Staatsoper) of any opera company in the world. The company performs in the Opera Theatre of the Opera House for seven months of the year; from April to May and November to December, it ups sticks to Melbourne.

Brit-born Richard Hickox stepped in as music director at the beginning of 2005. For the visiting punter, there are still 175 performances of more than a dozen operas in any given year, as well as 80 performances of four different ballets. The company's touring arm, OzOpera, performs year-round across Australia.

Visitors can also go behind the scenes at OA's fascinating headquarters in Surry Hills. Tours (which must be booked about two weeks ahead) take in the costume, millinery and wig-making departments, the props and storage departments, set design and building, and rehearsal spaces for singers and musicians.

Sydney Symphony

8215 4600/www.sydneysymphony.com.au.
Under the artistic directorship of conductor Gianluigi Gelmetti (to be succeeded by Vladimir Ashkenazy in 2009), the Sydney Symphony continues to be the flagship of a network of Australian state capital city orchestras. Established in 1932 as a radio broadcasting orchestra, it has grown into the biggest and best in the country, attracting the finest soloists from Australia and abroad. The orchestra presents more than 140 events a year.

Other ensembles

Look out for the **Sydney Philharmonia Choirs** (9251 2024, www.sydneyphilharmonia. com.au), which has been going strong for nine decades and continues to stun audiences with a lusty *Carmina Burana* or luscious *Missa Solemnis* several times a year. A capella outfit the **Song Company** (8272 9500, www.song company.com.au), Australia's premier vocal ensemble, perform early operas and oratorios. Other a cappella groups include Sydney's first world music choir, **Voices from the Vacant Lot** (www.voicesfromthevacantlot.net), while the **Sydney Gay & Lesbian Choir** (9360 7439, www.sglc.org) attracts an audience broader than its selection criteria might suggest. Pianist Kathryn Selby, formerly of the Macquarie Trio that disbanded in 2008, is the artistic director of **Selby & Friends** (9969 7039, www.selbyandfriends.com.au) whose core ensemble is popular piano group TrioZ.

Ticket agencies

You can book tickets for all major venues through agencies **Ticketek** (132 849, www. ticketek.com.au) and **Ticketmaster** (136 100, www.ticketmaster.com.au), but both charge booking fees, even if you book online. For smaller shows, try **Moshtix** (1300 438849, www.moshtix.com.au) and **OzTix** (1300 762545, www.oztix.com.au). **MyTickets** (www.mytickets.com.au) is a search engine that lists what is still available and links you through to ticket agencies' websites.

Arts & Entertainment

Sport & Fitness

Blood, sweat and beers.

Sport is part of Sydney's soul – so if you don't like it, the safest thing to do is to fake it. And besides, it won't be long before even the least sporty visitors have been won over by the vast choice of activities on offer (combined with the fact that 90 per cent of sports here are played outside in the glorious sunshine). There really is something for everyone: be it kayaking, lawn bowls, tennis, rugby, swimming – you name it, they play it. So much so, in fact, that Sydneysiders have even taken the dreaded soccer to heart, turning out in their droves in 2007 to see David Beckham's US Galaxy team whipped by the local boys.

The city's pubs are usually surrounded by walls of televised action and the throbbing murmur of passionate, sport-related conversation (not to mention the guts and the glory of Oz's guilty national habit of sports-related gambling). All of which means it's handy to know at least a few basics about the national obsession. Although football, in the Pommy version, is the fastest-growing sport in Australia, the term 'footy' here generally refers to the city's game of choice, rugby league. What the British call 'football' is generally known as 'soccer'. Passion for cricket, meanwhile, is extreme, and Aussie Rules – traditionally a Victorian sport – has also soared in the local popularity stakes since the Sydney Swans triumphed in the 2005 premiership.

Participation sports

Canoeing & kayaking

There's no fresher or more original way to take in the harbour than from water level, and for as little as $20 an hour you can hire a canoe from **Sydney Harbour Kayaks** (9960 4389, www.sydneyharbourkayaks.com) in Mosman. At weekends the company also runs four-hour guided eco tours of Middle Harbour ($99 per person). Further out of town, **Bundeena Kayaks** (9544 5294, www.bundeenakayaks.com.au) offers a superb kayaking experience on the waterways of southern Sydney's Royal National Park. If you feel up to braving the choppier waters (and sharks) of the Pacific, head north to **C-Kayak Australia** (4324 2867, www.kayaktours.com.au), which is based in West Gosford.

For an overview of paddling opportunities in the state's lakes, rivers and ocean waters, contact **New South Wales Canoeing** (8116 9730, www.nswcanoe.org.au).

Climbing

Sydney's surrounding areas, especially the Blue Mountains and Hunter Valley, offer plenty of natural resources for rock climbing, abseiling and canyoning. **Outward Bound Australia** (1800 267 999, www.outwardbound.org.au) is a good first port of call for the novice, while the **Australian School of Mountaineering** (4782 2014, www.asmguides.com) caters for all levels. The latter is based in the Blue Mountains, a wilderness of canyons, plateaus and sandstone cliffs, and visits the Snowy Mountains in winter for ice-climbing trips.

Experts might want to go and talk the talk in **Paddy Pallin** (8799 2430/1800 805398, www.paddypallin.com.au), a gear shop in the CBD. The **Edge Adventure Centre** (Hudson Avenue, Castle Hill, 9899 8228, www.edge-adventure.com.au) is a good indoor centre, with climb heights up to 18.5 metres (61 feet). You'll also find climbing walls at **Climb Fit** (4/12 Frederick Street, St Leonards, 9436 4600, www.climbfit.com.au) and **City Crag** at the back of Mountain Designs (499 Kent Street, CBD, 9267 3822, www.mountaindesigns.com).

If you want to combine climbing with a range of other adventurous sports, **Bush Sports** (9630 2222, www.bushsports.com.au) tackles the lot, including climbing, abseiling, canyoning, rafting and caving, as well as survival programmes, 'Amazing Races' – based on a reality TV format – and treasure hunts.

Cycling

First things first: cycle helmets are compulsory in Sydney, and bottled water a must. Also, local councils have been slow on the uptake with cycle paths, so it's well worth visiting recreational and commuter bike group **Bicycle NSW** (Level 5, 822 George Street, 9218 5400, www.bicyclensw.org.au) for a word of advice and a copy of *Cycling Around Sydney* ($25) before putting foot to pedal.

Competitive cyclists can speak to **Cycling NSW** (9738 5850, www.nsw.cycling.org.au)

for the best information on local clubs, rides and racing, while off-roaders should approach **BMX NSW** (6367 5277, www.bmxnsw.com.au) for the latest on BMX facilities, tracks and events. For more advice on cycling and bike hire, *see p296*.

Fishing

If it involves water, Australians love it. To get involved with one of Sydney's biggest participation sports, you first need to buy a recreational licence ($6 for three days, $12 for one month, $30 for one year, $75 for three years). You can do this at various fishing shops and clubs, by phoning 1300 369 365 or online at www.dpi.nsw.gov.au/fisheries.

Next step is to seek out the best spots: you'll find information on the state government website above, or call the government helpline on 1300 550 474. Alternatively, get nattering with the staff in tackle shops – the guys at **Compleat Angler** in the CBD (3rd Floor, Dymocks Building, 428 George Street, 9241 2080, www.compleatangler.com.au) are particularly happy to share their local expertise and offer demonstrations.

For a dawn-to-midday session out in the harbour, try **Fishabout Tours** (9451 5420, www.fishnet.com.au/fishabout_tours), which runs tours of Sydney Harbour and the

Hawkesbury River. Prices range from $490 for one person to $180 each for four. Boat, licence, equipment, hot and cold snacks, and drinks are included.

At certain times in autumn and spring, big-game fishing is an option. A charter with Botany Bay-based sea dog Captain John Wright of **Game & Sport Fishing Charters** (0414 542548, www.gamefisher.com) offers a thrilling day fishing marlin, tuna, shark and other big ocean fish. Prices for up to six people range from $1,450 for game fishing and $1,200 for sport fishing. No licence is required.

Golf

Many of Sydney's abundance of golf courses are private, but public courses near the CBD include **Moore Park Golf Course** (Cleveland Street, 9663 1064, www.mooreparkgolf.com.au). Green fees range from $45-$50 for 18 holes. Club hire costs $40, lessons are around $60 per half-hour, and the course also has a three-level driving range. Also fairly central is the south-eastern suburbs' **Eastlake Golf Club** in Kingsford (Gardener Road, 9663 1374, www.eastlakegolfclub.com.au), where it's $38-$42 for 18 holes, club hire is $28, and lessons $50 for half an hour. Contact the NSW Golf Association (9505 9105, www.nswga.com.au) for more locations.

Coming to a beach near you

Beach volleyball is Sydney's perfect sport, combining sun, sand and bronzed bodies. At the 2000 Sydney Olympics, Bondi Beach was transformed into one huge volleyball court with tiered seating blocking the view of the ocean. Afterwards, the seating came down and the sand was restored to its rightful place, but a passion for the sport was ignited and now BV games – both organised and impromptu – take place on beaches all over town.

There's no uniform – most play in their board shorts or swimsuits – but there is a loose adherence to the rules of the game. Even on sand with a tatty net, this is serious sport and as with all competitive endeavours in this wide brown land, there's a winning frisson in the air. You can play doubles (two each side), four each side or in bigger teams of up to eight players. Serving is from the back of the court (usually laid out with string or a line in the sand), then it's a maximum of two touches per side before, with the third touch, the ball goes back over the net. No

player can hit the ball consecutively. Players mustn't touch the net, and the ball mustn't hit the ground. If it does, the point's over. A full game is best of three sets. The first two sets are first to 21 points, with a point gained for each rally won. The third set, if necessary, is first to 15 points. In the competitive league there is a raft of more complex rules, but these are the basics.

You'll find spontaneous games on many of the ocean beaches and most are happy for curious gamecrashers to join in. For the more serious, lessons, training sessions and organised games for all levels take place on Manly Beach, Dee Why, Maroubra Beach and Brighton-le-Sands. Visit www.beachvolleyball. com.au for details or call the Sydney Beach Volleyball School on 1300 865539. For the Northern Beaches, try the Northern Beaches Volleyball Association (www.nbva.org.au). Even if you're not likely to reach Olympic standard, it's a great way to work out, get a tan (sun cream obligatory) and have fun in the sun.

Arts & Entertainment

Gyms & sports centres

Surprisingly, in a country so fixated on the outdoors, gyms are really popular in Australia – you're never too far from all the weights, circuit training and aerobics classes you could wish for. The ubiquitous **Fitness First** (9762 1600/1300 557 799, www.fitnessfirst.com.au) is among the cheapest, and has branches all over the city. Membership, which can be used in any branch the world over, starts at $15 per week, while one-off visits cost $18. For gyms popular with gay men and lesbians, *see p245*.

Cook & Phillip Park

4 College Street, at William Street, CBD (9326 0444/www.cookandphillip.com.au). CityRail Museum or St James. **Open** 6am-10pm Mon-Fri; 7am-8pm Sat, Sun. **Admission** *All facilities* $16; $8.50 reductions. *Pool only* $6; $4.40 reductions. **Credit** AmEx, MC, V. **Map** p329 G7.
This well-equipped, centrally located aquatic and fitness centre has a 50m heated indoor swimming pool, a leisure pool with wave machine, hydrotherapy pools, basketball courts and a good gym, with physiotherapy also available. It hosts various classes and team sports; the aqua aerobics classes are especially popular. At the time of writing, it was undergoing major waterproofing refurbishment.

Ian Thorpe Aquatic Centre

458 Harris Street, Ultimo (9518 7220/www.itac.org.au). CityRail Central/LightRail Convention/Monorail Convention. **Open** 6am-9pm Mon-Fri (gym till 10pm); 6am-8pm Sat, Sun. **Admission** *All facilities* $16; $8.50 reductions. *Pool only* $6; $3.70-$4.40 reductions; $15 family. **Credit** AmEx, MC, V. **Map** p328 D8.
This $40 million facility, which opened at the end of 2007, provides the residents of Ultimo with a fantastic sports centre. There are three indoor pools (one Olympic-sized), lots of Aquatic Education services, a spin and fitness studio with classes galore, and steam, sauna and spa. There's even parking on site. Oh, and it's all housed in a fabulous Harry Seidler-designer white wave-form building (*see p76* **When Harry met Sydney**).

Hang-gliding, skydiving & paragliding

For a bird's-eye view of the city and an adrenalin rush that'll last months, a tandem flight with **Sydney Hang Gliding Centre** (4294 4294, www.hanggliding.com.au) starts at $199, including in-flight photos.

Beginners can experience the thrill of skydiving in tandem with an instructor (along with a whole range of other hair-raising activities) through **Adrenalin Club** (1300 791 793, 8755 3100, www.adrenalin.com.au). It costs from $275-$325. **Sydney Skydiving Centre** (1800 805 997, 9791 9155, www.sydneyskydivers.com.au) also offers a pulse-racing accelerated free-fall (AFF) course. Prices start at $430, including gear hire, training and membership.

If jumping off a cliff with only a parachute and an instructor to save your bones sounds like fun, **Sydney Paragliding Centre** (4294 9065, www.sydneyparagliding.com) offers tandem adventures from $195, about an hour out of the city. Contact the **Australian Parachute Federation** (6281 6830, www.apf.asn.au) for further information, safety advice or just a bit of reassurance.

Horse riding

The only horse-riding point in central Sydney is the old Sydney Showgrounds in Centennial Park. The **Centennial Parklands Equestrian Centre** (114-120 Lang Road, next to Fox Studios, 9332 2809, www.centennialparklands.com.au) administers the site and offers lessons to novice or experienced riders of all ages. Prices start at $70, while simple rides in the park along the 3.6km (2.2 mile) bridleway cost $95 per hour.

Rollerblading (in-line skating)

You won't walk far along the promenades at Manly and Bondi Beaches without encountering a group of rollerbladers. Centennial Park, with its flat roads and moderate traffic, also attracts more than its fair share of multi-wheeled pedestrians, and **Centennial Park Cycles** (9398 5027, www.cyclehire.com.au) hires out blades plus safety gear for $18 an hour, $25 for two hours or $35 for four hours. Skates can also be hired from some surf shops at the beaches.

Sailing

Sailing, fishing, houseboats, sea tours, function boat hire – you name it, if it's of a nautical nature, the **Australian Charter Guide Directory** (9818 8640, www.charterguide.com.au) will provide you with information.

If you'd rather get your hands on the ropes than be a passenger, the **Pacific Sailing School** (9326 2399, www.pacificsailingschool.com.au) in Rushcutters Bay is one of the many schools in the Sydney Harbour, Middle Harbour and Port Hacking areas. **Eastsail** (9327 1166, www.eastsail.com.au), also based in Rushcutters Bay, offers courses in crewing and sailing: courses cost $645 each, with discounts for group bookings. The nationwide company **Ausail** (1300 135 632/9960 5451, www.ausail.com.au) also provides lessons, as well as luxury yacht charters.

For more information, including details of companies and locations, get in touch with **Yachting New South Wales** (8116 9800, www.nsw.yachting.org.au).

Scuba diving

The Great Barrier Reef may be a few thousand kilometres north, but the diving opportunities around Sydney are magnificent. As well as its own reefs, the city's coast offers gobsmacking marine life – including non-threatening sharks and the freakishly unique weedy seadragon – sponge gardens and wrecks.

One of the most experienced diving companies in Australia, **Pro Dive** (1800 820 820/9255 0300, www.prodive.com.au), has scuba centres throughout Sydney. It organises day trips and scuba holidays, and its PADI Open Water Certification (which will allow you to dive pretty much anywhere in the world) includes classroom theory, pool skills training and ocean dives, and costs $395 per person. The linked outfits **Dive Centre Manly** (10 Belgrave Street, 9977 4355, www.divesydney. com) and **Dive Centre Bondi** (192 Bondi Road, 9369 3855, www.divebondi.com.au) also offer a variety of courses for everyone, from beginners to advanced.

Surfing

Surfing is as integral a part of Sydney life as enjoying a drink in the sunshine. Manly, Dee Why and Freshwater have good waves for beginners, while Bondi, Bronte, Cronulla and any of the northern beaches tend to attract the more confident wave-riders. Most beaches have a surf lifesaving club to help you stay out of trouble and you can hire surfboards and body boards for around $15 an hour.

If you've never stood up on a board before, consider having some lessons. Matt Grainger at **Manly Surf School** (9977 6977, www.manly surfschool.com) has 25 years' experience of teaching novices. Beginner, intermediate and advanced courses cost $55 for a two-hour group session and $80 an hour for a one-to-one. **Let's Go Surfing** in Bondi (128 Ramsgate Avenue, 9365 1800, www.letsgosurfing.com.au), charges $85 per person for a group class, with three sessions for $195 or a one-to-one, 90-minute lesson for $160. **Long Reef Surf** in Collaroy (1012 Pittwater Road, 9982 4829, www.longreefsailboards.com.au), offers lessons too, while **Surfing Australia** (6674 9888, www.surfingaustralia.com) also arranges courses in conjunction with local shops all along the coast.

Girls are welcome at the **Manly Surf School**.

For the latest information about surfing conditions, go to www.coastalwatch.com or www.realsurf.com.

Swimming

THE SEA
Different sections of beaches are marked for swimming each day. These are considered safe and are patrolled by professional surf lifesavers, so always swim between the red and yellow flags. For more advice on safety and details of Sydney's best beaches, *see p134*.

OCEAN/HARBOUR POOLS
If you fancy sea water without the hostility of the waves, try one of Sydney's tidal swimming pools. **North Bondi** has two small paddling pools, while south Bondi has the lane-marked **Bondi Icebergs** pool, famous for the winter exploits of the Speedo-clad elderly men who have for years braved the freezing waters on Sunday mornings. **Wylie's Baths** in Coogee is the best-preserved of the seaside pools, and there are also women-only baths about 200 metres south of Wylie. You'll also find pools at Collaroy, Bronte, Cronulla, Palm Beach and Dee Why beaches, all of which get jammed in the summer. Some harbour beaches, including Clontarf, Balmoral, Nielsen Park and Double Bay, have enclosed swimming areas.

PUBLIC POOLS
One of the many grand sporting venues that graced Sydney for the 2000 Olympics is the **Sydney International Aquatic Centre** (*see p263*), a fantastic facility with wonderful play areas for kids, which is open to the public when there isn't a competition on.

In town, there are Olympic-sized pools at the **Ian Thorpe Aquatic Centre** (*see p258*) and **Cook & Phillip Park** (*see p258*), as well as at **Prince Alfred Park** (near Central Station, off Chalmers Street, 9310 3641) and at **Victoria Park** (near Sydney University, between City Road and Broadway, 9660 4181). Two splendidly sited outdoor pools are the **North Sydney Olympic Pool** (*see p112*), beneath the northern end of the Harbour Bridge at Milsons Point, and the **Andrew (Boy) Charlton Pool** (*see p73*) by the Botanic Gardens.

The **NSW Swimming Association** (9763 5833, www.nswswimming.com.au) has information about other pools.

Tennis

Public tennis courts are run by local councils and charge around $12-$30 an hour. Ever keen to promote the sport, **Tennis NSW** (9763 7644,

www.tennis.com.au) will happily advise on courts in your area. The website has a facility that allows you to search by area for a court, partner, coach or club.

If you're in town for a while and you take your tennis seriously and/or would like it to be part of your social life, it may be worth joining the **White City Tennis Club** (30 Alma Street, Paddington, 9360 4113, www.whitecitytennis. com), one of the best-known tennis clubs in central Sydney (and the former host of the Sydney International). It costs $1,056 per year and no longer has a joining fee.

Waterskiing

Adding a shot of adrenalin to the visual thrill of exploring Sydney's waterways, this somewhat intimidating sport benefits from the Aussie 'too easy' attitude. The **Wisemans Ferry Water Sports** (River Road, Wisemans Ferry, 4566 4544, www.skischool.com.au) operates out of the NSW Water Ski Federation Ski Grounds, and is located about an hour and 15 minutes' drive north of Sydney. Lessons cost $170 an hour, which includes coaching and the use of skis and wetsuits. There is also a ski gate charge of $3.50 per person per day to enter the ski grounds. If you want to make a night (or two) of it, accommodation is available in the ski grounds in cabins or camping at an extra cost.

Windsurfing

Opportunities for windsurfing – 'sailboarding' to watersports purists – are abundant in the waters around Sydney. The **Balmoral Sailing School** (9960 5344, www.sailingschool.com.au) at Balmoral Beach is one of the best places to learn. Courses range from introductory to advanced; a basic four-hour course costs $265. The school also hires out fully rigged windsurfers (as well as dinghies, Hobie Cats and kayaks) for $40 an hour, on a sliding scale for the next two hours ($15 for second and third hour) until the fourth hour is free.

Already know your stuff? In that case, for north-easterlies, the best spots are Pittwater at Palm Beach, Narrabeen Lake, Balmoral Beach, Rodd Point in the harbour and Botany Bay south of the airport. Silver Beach at Kurnell is good for westerlies, and southerlies favour the area around Captain Cook Bridge in Sutherland. Much of the enjoyment of windsurfing depends on weather and wind direction, so make sure you call the boating weather forecast (1 900 926 101 – which comes with a 77¢-a-minute call rate) before setting off.

Windsurfing NSW (www.windsurfing.org/ nsw.htm) has more information.

Spectator sports

Venues

Since 2000, Homebush Bay has been Sydney's centre of gravity for top-level spectator sport. There, **Sydney Olympic Park** (*see p263*) comprises a cluster of venues for both national and local sporting events. **ANZ Stadium** (formerly Telstra Stadium; *see below*), the focal point of the park, is its pride and joy. The authorities are keen to use its massive capacity to recoup some of the money that went into building it, so a number of big events have been moved from Moore Park's **Sydney Cricket Ground** and **Sydney Football Stadium** (for both, *see below*) to this spot 20 kilometres (12.5 miles) west, in Sydney's demographic centre, if not its heart.

The **Sydney Olympic Park Visitor Centre** (1 Showground Road, 9714 7888, www.sydneyolympicpark.com.au) has details of all the venues. Its website is a cyber-shrine to sport in Sydney, well worth checking out.

TICKETS

Ticketek (13 2849, www.ticketek.com) is the main outlet for most sporting events in Sydney, including those held at any of the Olympic venues at Homebush Bay, but **Ticketmaster** (13 6100, www.ticketmaster.com.au) also sells tickets for many fixtures. Both charge booking fees. You can sometimes buy tickets at the venue on the day, often for cash only.

ANZ Stadium

Olympic Boulevard, Sydney Olympic Park, Homebush Bay (8765 2000/guided tours 8765 2300/www.anz stadium.com.au). CityRail Olympic Park/RiverCat Sydney Olympic Park then bus 401.

The stadium's stands were moved closer together after the Olympics for visibility and atmosphere's sake, and in 2008 the former Telstra Stadium was renamed by its new sponsor ANZ bank. Crowds fill almost half of its 83,500 capacity at regular rugby league games, while it tends to be nearly full for exhibition events, and you'll struggle to get a ticket for rugby union tests or State of Origin rugby league games. For information on tours, *see p263* **Sydney Olympic Park**.

Sydney Cricket Ground (SCG) & Sydney Football Stadium (SFS)

Driver Avenue, Moore Park (1800 801 155/9360 6601/tours 1300 724737/www.sydneycricket ground.com.au). Bus 372, 373, 374. **Tours** 10am, 1pm Mon-Fri; 10am Sat. **Tickets** $25; $17 reductions; $65 family. **Map** p332 J/K11.

Book ahead for a one-and-half hour tour.

Sri Lanka's Sangakkara appeals against Australia's Gilchrist.

A whole new sphere

Twelve years ago, to associate the word 'football' with a round ball in Australia pretty much amounted to treason. But now the word officially refers to the hands-off game so revered in Europe, South America and Asia. It's the fastest-growing sport in the country, and with the Australian national team, the Socceroos, getting to the second round in the 2006 World Cup (for the first time in more than 30 years) bowing out to eventual Cup champions Italy in a tense match, the game's popularity is soaring.

In August 2005 the formation of the eight-team **Hyundai A-League** (www.a-league.com.au) cemented the way forward for Australian soccer. The signs are good: the football may not be of the highest standard – think second-tier level in the major European leagues – but it's improving steadily. After all, the crowds are healthy, the sponsorship pretty meaty and the winner goes into the Asian version of the Champions League. No wonder several of the game's household names in Britain are considering a move down under and international players are coming to Australia to test their skills.

The local side, **Sydney FC** (www.sydneyfc.com), started with a bang, winning the A-League's inaugural season and, in 2007, playing to capacity crowds in Sydney in a

friendly against LA Galaxy, which included a much-anticipated performance from David Beckham. Becks scored with a trademark bending free kick, but it was Sydney FC who won decisively, 5-3. Sydney plays most of its games at the **Sydney Football Stadium** (*see p261*) to a crowd of newly converted Aussies plus expats hitherto deprived of their footy fix and happy to support a different team away from home.

You'll struggle to find a pub in Sydney without a television screen, and there are some good options for football fans. In the CBD, you could try **Cheers Bar** (561 George Street, 9261 8313, www.cheersbar.com.au), **Jacksons** on George (176 George Street, 9247 2727, www.jacksonsongeorge.com.au) or long-standing fave **Scruffy Murphy's** (corner of Goulbourn and George Streets, 9211 2002, www.scruffymurphys.com.au). Bang on Bondi Beach, meanwhile, is expats' favourite **Hotel Bondi** (178 Campbell Parade, 9310 3271, www.hotelbondi.com.au).

And for really homesick footie fans, there are a number of local supporters' clubs for British Premier League teams, including Arsenal's **Ozarsenal** (www.ozarsenal.com), the **Manchester United Supporters Club of NSW** (www.manutdnsw.com) and **Ozspurs** (www.ozspurs.com).

Sydney International Aquatic Centre

Olympic Boulevard, Sydney Olympic Park, Homebush Bay (9752 3666/www.sydneyaquaticcentre.com.au). CityRail Olympic Park/RiverCat Sydney Olympic Park then bus 401. **Open** 5am-9pm Mon-Fri; 6am-8pm Sat, Sun. **Tours** on request only. **Admission** *Swim & spa* $6.40; $4.40-$5 reductions; $20 family. *Swim & gym* $13; $9.30 reductions. **Tours** $3 self-tour, phone for group guided tours. **Credit** MC, V.

Having hosted the pool events during the Olympics, this place is still home to high-quality international meets and rather less illustrious inter-school competitions. Great venue for serious lane-pounders, and impressive enough just to visit.

Sydney International Athletics Centre

Edwin Flack Avenue, Sydney Olympic Park, Homebush Bay (9752 3444/www.sydneyathletic centre.com.au). CityRail Olympic Park/RiverCat Sydney Olympic Park then bus 401. **Open** *Visits* 3-8pm Mon-Fri; 8am-1pm Sat; 9am-1pm Sun.

Sydney Olympic Park Sports Centre

Olympic Boulevard, Sydney Olympic Park, Homebush Bay (9763 0111/www.sports-centre.com.au). CityRail Olympic Park/RiverCat Sydney Olympic Park then bus 401. **Open** *Visits* 7.30am-10.30pm daily.

It hosted tae kwon do and table tennis during the 2000 Olympics and now is home to various indoor spectator sports including gymnastics, soccer, badminton, volleyball, hockey and martial arts.

Sydney Olympic Park Tennis Centre

Rod Laver Drive, Sydney Olympic Park, Homebush Bay (9764 1999/www.sydneyolympicpark.com.au). CityRail Olympic Park/RiverCat Sydney Olympic Park then bus 401.

Closed until late 2008 for the resurfacing of the courts with a flash new Plexicushion surface, the Tennis Centre is expected to open in time for the Medibank International (6-12 January 2009).

Athletics

Australians follow athletics with more of a passionate roar than a thoughtful stroke of the beard. The **Sydney International Athletics Centre** (*see above*) is home to various major events, including trials for Commonwealth and Olympic Games. Contact **Athletics Australia** (03 9820 3511, www.athletics.org.au) or, for competition within the state, **Athletics NSW** (9746 1122, www.nswathletics.org.au).

Aussie Rules

Forget its tooth-spitting image abroad – this hybrid of soccer, rugby and Gaelic football is a truly remarkable spectator sport, involving great athleticism, strength and tactical prowess. Sydneysiders used to have a lukewarm relationship with the sport, as it was traditionally played south of the state border: it was invented in Melbourne around 1858, and even the local team, the **Sydney Swans** (9339 9123, www.sydneyswans.com.au), were a South Melbourne team until they relocated in 1982.

For a long time, poor results meant that the Swans didn't catch on in their new home. However, slow but steady progress came to a climax when they won a historic Australian Football League premiership title in 2005. Many of Sydney's unconverted turned fanatical, and the team now regularly sells out the 42,000-seat **Sydney Cricket Ground**; even for its occasional matches at the city's huge **ANZ Stadium** (for both, *see p261*), Aussie Rules fans make enough of a dent for there to be a decent, family-based atmosphere.

The season is between March and September. If you're feeling perverse, go and support the Kangaroos of Melbourne – keen to make inroads into the Sydney market, they usually play about five 'home' games at the SCG.

Baseball

Baseball has a small but thriving scene in Sydney, with most areas having a team in the state's 'Major League'. The season runs from September to February, with games taking place on Wednesday and Thursday evenings and Sunday afternoons. Women's games are on Friday nights, and there is also a beginners' league and under-18s competition. **NSW Baseball League** (9675 6872, www.nsw. baseball.com.au) has information, or for more general information about the sport in Australia, visit www.baseball.com.au.

Basketball

Sydney's two teams in the National Basketball League (www.nbl.com.au) are the **Sydney Kings** and relative newcomers the **West Sydney Razorbacks**. The Kings (9281 1777, www.sydneykings.com.au) play at the **Sydney Entertainment Centre** (*see p249*), and the Razorbacks, aka the Pigs (4720 3880, www.razorbacks.com.au), at Homebush's **Olympic Park Sports Centre** (*see p263*). The **Sydney Uni Flames** (9351 4969, www.sydneyuniflames.com) is the city's women's NBL side. The season runs from September to February, and tickets are affordable, starting at around $10.

For more information about the sport, contact the **NSW Basketball Association** (8765 8555, www.nswbasketball.net.au).

Arts & Entertainment

Cricket

Yes, they still love it. And despite a beleagured team in 2007 Australia is still largely unbeatable. During the summer months, cricket – a national obsession for well over a century – enjoys a stranglehold on the sporting calendar, for both spectators and participants. If there's an international match on, a trip to the famous **Sydney Cricket Ground** (*see p261*) is a must for any visitor.

Matches involving Australia at the SCG are viewed – both live and on TV – with an almost religious obsession, and the highlight of the cricketing calender is the Sydney Test, played over five days against a touring side, usually in the first week of January. You can also expect a handful of one-dayers at the SCG in the afternoon and under lights in the evening. If you find drawn-out tests slow, the much faster one-day cricket, which always produces a winner, is the best option.

Getting tickets for the bigger matches can be difficult, but local games don't usually sell out. For information on matches, phone the SCG or visit www.baggygreen.com.au.

Hardcore fans craving the thwack of leather on willow when there are no internationals on can see the New South Wales cricket team, the NSW Blues, play around five matches at the SCG between October and March in the interstate Pura Cup competition. The early March final, should NSW reach it, always takes place in Sydney. The Blues also play other one-dayers at various locations around the city. Meanwhile, hundreds of fields around Sydney host cricket matches of all levels on summer Saturday afternoons. **Cricket NSW** (9339 0999, www.cricketnsw.com.au) has information on fixtures and venues.

Golf

Melbourne tends to get the bigger golf events, but Sydney's lusher, plusher courses usually get to host the odd match in the PGA Tour of Australasia, which pitches the best Australian players against a handful of overseas stars. Tickets can cost anything from $48 a day. You can see up-to-date match schedules at www.pgatour.com.au.

Greyhound racing

Wentworth Park Greyhound Track

Wentworth Park Road, Glebe (9552 1799/ www.wentworthparksport.com.au). LightRail Wentworth Park. **Open** 6-11pm Mon, Sat. **Admission** $6. **No credit cards. Map** p328 C8.

Ten races each Saturday and Monday night starting at around 7.30pm. The Sydney Roosters rugby league club also trains here.

Harness racing

Harold Park Paceway

Wigram Road, Glebe (9660 3688/www.haroldpark. com.au). LightRail Jubilee Park/bus 433. **Open** *Mar-Sept* 1-5.30pm Tue; 7-11pm Fri. *Oct-Feb* 7-11pm Fri. **Admission** $10. **No credit cards.**

'The trots' (think horse racing meets Ben Hur) are held most Friday nights and Tuesday afternoons.

Horse racing

There are race meetings in Sydney every Saturday as well as several midweek events. The **Australian Jockey Club** (9663 8400, www.ajc.org.au) runs meets at Royal Randwick, flanking Centennial Park at its southern edge, and in the southern suburbs at Warwick Farm. The **Sydney Turf Club** (9930 4000, www.theraces.com.au), meanwhile, organises programmes at Rosehill Gardens in Parramatta and in Canterbury Park to the south. Admission is from $7-$12 ($4 reductions) $20-$30 for major races, with under-18s going free.

Evening racing is a regular weekday fixture at Canterbury from October to the end of February and makes a fantastic night out.

Major milestones on the Sydney racing calendar include the Australian Jockey Club's four-day carnival every Easter, which includes the down-under versions of Doncaster Day and Derby Day, and features $10 million in prize money. Other huge events are the Golden Slipper at Rosehill, usually held a week before Derby Day, and the Spring Carnival at Randwick. Melbourne Cup Day, the country's leading horse-racing event, held on the first Tuesday in November, is also the biggest day in Sydney in terms of crowds drawn to the day's meets at the Royal Randwick. Many people take the afternoon off work, and there's a party atmosphere all over town. In 2007, the racing season was blighted with an outbreak of equine flu, which famously closed down race courses and caused much gnashing of teeth and loss of revenue.

Canterbury Park Racecourse *King Street, Canterbury (9930 4000). CityRail Canterbury then shuttle bus or bus 428.*
Rosehill Gardens Racecourse *Grand Avenue, Rosehill (9930 4000). CityRail Rosehill/RiverCat Parramatta then shuttle bus.*
Royal Randwick Racecourse *Alison Road, Randwick (9663 8400). Bus 372, 373, 374, 376, 377, 391, 392, 393, 394, 395, 396, 397, 398, 399.*
Warwick Farm Racecourse *Hume Highway, Warwick Farm (9602 6199). CityRail Warwick Farm then shuttle bus.*

Rugby league

In Sydney, rugby league is the biggest of all the permutations of 'football'. Australia's domestic league, run by the **National Rugby League** (9339 8500, www.nrl.com.au), starts in March and culminates in a four-week finals series at the **Sydney Football Stadium** and **ANZ Stadium** (for both, *see p261*) in October. The centenary of rugby league in Australia will be celebrated in 2008, with huge crowds expected. Adult tickets can cost well over $100 for a prime seat, but average at around $20.

The city's fixation with the sport won't waver any time soon, especially following Manly's defeat in the Grand Final of 2007. Russell Crowe's attempts to take over his favourite club, the fanatically supported and comically inept South Sydney Rabbitohs, also help keep the sport in the news.

Other big matches to look out for include the State of Origin series, when New South Wales takes on Queensland. To find out about the international doings of the Kangaroos, Australia's national team, contact the **Australian Rugby League** (9232 7566, www.australianrugbyleague.com.au).

Sydney teams

Bulldogs *9789 2922/www.bulldogs.com.au.*
Cronulla-Sutherland Sharks *9523 0222/ www.sharks.com.au.*
Manly-Warringah Sea Eagles *9970 3000/ www.mightyeagles.com.*
Parramatta Eels *8843 0300/ www.parraeels.com.au.*
Penrith Panthers *4720 5555/ http://penrith.panthers.com.au.*
St George Illawarra Dragons *9587 1966/ www.dragons.com.au.*
South Sydney Rabbitohs *8306 9900/ www.rabbitohs.com.au.*
Sydney Roosters *8063 3800/ www.sydneyroosters.com.au.*
Wests Tigers *8741 3300/ www.weststigers.com.au.*

Rugby union

It may still be bridesmaid to rugby league, but union has enjoyed a steady rise in popularity in Australia thanks to World Cup victories in 1991 and 1999 and the country's successful hosting of the World Cup itself in 2003.

The Super 14 competition pitches provincial teams from all across Australia, New Zealand and South Africa against each other. It runs from February to May, and involves a handful of home matches for the **NSW Waratahs** (www.waratahs.rugby.com.au) at the **Sydney Football Stadium** (*see p261*). The national side, the Wallabies, play occasional test or tri-nation matches at the Sydney Football Stadium or **ANZ Stadium** (*see p261*). More information is available from the **Australian Rugby Union** (8005 5555, www.rugby.com.au).

Surfing

Competitive surfing is a serious business in Sydney, and competitions take place at lots of the city's beaches every summer weekend, ranging from local inter-club meetings to junior tournaments to professional events involving the world's best surfers.

Contact the sport's governing body, **Surfing NSW** (6674 9888, www.surfingaustralia.com.au) for information on events and locations.

SURF LIFESAVING

More than a century after the country's first lifesaving club was founded at Bondi in 1906, there are now over 115,000 registered surf lifesavers in Australia. According to a recent study, they would cost the authorities around $1.5 billion a year in wages if they weren't volunteers. A series of competitions throughout the year helps develop and demonstrate the skills involved. For more information, contact **Surf Life Saving NSW** (9984 7188, www.surflifesaving.com.au). Its website has a comprehensive events calendar.

Swimming

Sydney is famously full of breathtaking places to have a dip, and swimming is also a massive spectator sport. Several World Cup swim meets take place in the city, and the **Sydney International Aquatic Centre** (*see p263*) in the Homebush Bay Olympic Park is the venue for most of the major local events.

A more alien spectacle to non-locals are the local beach swims, in which up to 500 local and international competitors embark on one- to three-kilometre swims in the ocean from different beaches around Sydney.

More details of all competitions are available from the **NSW Swimming Association** (9763 5833, www.nswswimming.com.au).

Tennis

The Sydney International, a warm-up event in January for the better-known Australian Open in Melbourne, is held at the **Sydney International Tennis Centre** (*see p263*) in Homebush Bay. It's a prime opportunity to see world-class tennis in Sydney.

For upcoming tournaments being held in the city, contact **Tennis NSW** (1800 153040, www.tennisnsw.com.au).

Arts & Entertainment

Theatre & Dance

Flipping the script.

There's been a rumble down under in Sydney's theatre community for several years now, but when the city's favourite daughter, Cate Blanchett, arrived to take the helm at the **Sydney Theatre Company** (*see p268 and p271* **The Cate factor**), that rumble became more of a roar. The energy is palpable and exciting to be around: Sydney has waited in the wings for such an explosion and it isn't just our Cate who's on a high. Neil Armfield at **Company B** (*see below*) is firing on all cylinders, and actors all over town – some of them theatre virgins – are lining up to take part in the thrill of live performance. Sure, not every production is a hit, but the groundswell is starting to grow.

Stoking the engine are a host of top visiting shows and performances. Theatrical luminaries such as Sir Ian McKellen, Brenda Blethyn and Philip Seymour Hoffman have all hit the boards, the latter as a director, and many more stars are on their way. For mainstream theatre, both the Sydney Theatre Company and the **Ensemble Theatre Company** (*see p267*) are highly reliable, while Company B and the **Griffin Theatre Company** (*see p267*) showcase new Australian writing. But if you fancy a cheaper and chancier artistic option, check out the **Old Fitzroy Theatre** (*see p269*), the **Darlinghurst Theatre** (*see p268*), Griffin Theatre's Stablemates programme and B Sharp, the fringe arm of Company B: it's rare to find artistic standards this high for ticket prices so low.

Dance in Sydney is awaiting its own cultural revolution, which it may well get with the shock departure of inspirational choreographer Graeme Murphy from the **Sydney Dance Company** (*see p272*) and the introduction of Cuban Yosvani Ramos to the **Australian Ballet** (*see p272*). Often the best dance comes from touring interstate and overseas groups, although **Bangarra Dance Theatre** (*see p272*) can be brilliant.

INFORMATION AND TICKETS

For detailed information about what's on where, when it starts and how much it costs, check the 'Theatre' section of *Time Out*'s weekly magazine, which is published on Wednesdays and sold in newsagents, or the 'Stage' pages of the Metro supplement in Friday's *Sydney Morning Herald*.

In general, tickets bought directly from theatre box offices offer the cheapest deal: you can view the seating plan and choose your price range. Alternatively, you can use a booking agency such as **Ticketek** (13 2849, www.ticketek.com.au), **Ticketmaster** (13 6100, www.ticketmaster.com.au) or **MCA Ticketing** (1300 306776, www.mca-tix.com), though all charge booking fees.

Theatre

Companies

Australian Theatre for Young People
9251 3900/www.atyp.com.au.
Australia's premier theatre for the 'young' (generously defined) still manages to make often wonderful and essential work by and for the young and young at heart. Under artistic director Timothy Jones, this long-established outfit has extended its reputation for worthwhile work, though there's still a whiff of star-factory fantasy about the company. It's based within the arts precinct at Walsh Bay and performances take place in venues all over Sydney – many at Fort Street Primary School in the Rocks. Nicole Kidman is its patron and film director Baz Luhrmann its ambassador – both trod the boards with the company as children.

Bell Shakespeare Company
8298 9000/www.bellshakespeare.com.au.
In 1970 actor-director John Bell founded the Nimrod company, widely regarded as spearheading the Australian theatre revival of that decade in Sydney. This company is his current venture, featuring a regular ensemble of some of Australia's most talented young and less-young actors. It focuses on innovative, utterly comprehensible and intelligent remountings of the canon, bearing the unofficial motto 'Shakespeare with an Australian accent'. Based in Sydney, with regular seasons at the Opera House, Bell also tours all over Australia. The 2008 season combines the directorial talents of local visionaries Bell, Marion Potts and Michael Gow. Catch some of Australia's rising stars here, such as Brendan Cowell.

Company B
9698 3344/www.belvoir.com.au.
The most creative and iconic mainstream theatre group in Sydney, Company B, under the inspirational artistic directorship of Neil Armfield, specialises in bold readings of the classics and new

'Some more tea, Vicar?' **Ensemble Theatre Company**.

Australian plays, with a strong history of exploring indigenous voices and the Aboriginal experience in contemporary Australia. Many of the country's best actors and directors have created their strongest work in collaboration with the company – think Geoffrey Rush, Cate Blanchett, Deborah Mailman and Richard Roxburgh. Its fringe arm, B Sharp, presents often cutting- and bleeding-edge work. The company's home is the newly poshed-up Belvoir Street Theatre (*see p268*).

Ensemble Theatre Company
9929 8877/www.ensemble.com.au.
Founded in 1958 by American Hayes Gordon, the Ensemble is the oldest surviving professional theatre company in NSW, and in 2008 celebrates its 50th anniversary with possibly its most exciting season to date: if you're in town in October don't miss Greta Scacchi playing Queen Elizabeth in Schiller's *Mary Stuart*. Sandra Bates is the artistic director, a role she's held for more than 20 years. The company manages without government funding, though it treads a fine line between cosseting and challenging the legion of loyal subscribers on whom it depends. Among its usual highlights is a combination of new plays and seasoned classics, with Arthur Miller the house speciality. It has its own theatre in Kirribilli (*see p268*) and also performs at the Opera House's Playhouse (*see p270*), the Theatre Royal (*see p268*) and the Seymour Centre (*see p270*).

Griffin Theatre Company
9332 1052/www.griffintheatre.com.au.
One of the essential engines of Sydney's theatre scene, Griffin is the city's only company solely dedicated to nurturing, developing and performing new Australian work. Founded in 1978, this not-for-profit venture produces four to six shows a year at the Stables Theatre (*see p270*) while touring and operating its respected Playwright's Residency programme. The annual Griffin Award for the best unproduced new Australian play is also an important event in the local calendar. Hit films *Lantana* and *The Boys* both started their lives as plays here.

New Theatre
9519 3403/www.ramin.com.au/online/newtheatre.
Established back in 1932 as a workers' theatre, the New – like Newtown, the once working-class inner-city suburb in which it resides – has changed substantially over the decades. Although it's still committed to political and socially enquiring work, the company has moved away from simplistic agit-prop and now has a wide remit ranging across classics, neglected Australian repertoire, contemporary European and American work, gay theatre and musicals performed on its stage in King Street (*see p269*). Technically amateur (the actors are all unpaid), the New is at its best when mounting large-cast classics that are no longer considered economically viable anywhere else.

PACT Youth Theatre

9550 2744/www.pact.net.au.
Sydney's perennially edgy youth theatre is where those aged 17 to 26 experiment with their own emerging identities, both theatrical and social; there are also workshops for kids as young as nine. It specialises in contemporary performance technique and group-devised shows at its Erskineville home (*see p269*).

Sydney Theatre Company (STC)

9250 1700/www.sydneytheatre.com.au.
Sydney's official state theatre company was directed by one of Australia's finest actors, Robyn Nevin, from 1999. In 2008 the actor/director team continues with Oscar-winning Cate Blanchett and her playwright husband Andrew Upton taking the helm (*see p271* **The Cate factor**). One of the more daring changes of the Blanchett/Upton collaboration is to take the theatre off the national grid, but the STC will continue to bring successful international productions over for Australian audiences, so expect the likes of David Hare and Tom Stoppard to pop up alongside works by local playwrights (including Upton). The STC performs in several venues – its home at the Wharf Theatres (*see p272*), the Drama Theatre at the Opera House (*see p270*), and the Sydney Theatre (*see p270*) – while the Actors Company is a resident ensemble formed in 2006 and still at the STC's beating heart.

Urban Theatre Projects

9707 2111/www.urbantheatre.com.au.
Urban Theatre Projects' mission is to work with Sydney's diverse cultures to make challenging and relevant contemporary theatre. Based in western Sydney (Bankstown), its work is produced through collaboration between artists and local residents, with a focus on storytelling, geographical identity and multimedia. UTP can be found performing in warehouses, railway stations, schools, shopping centres, town squares, private homes, buses and occasionally even theatres.

Venues

The plush, 1,200-seat **Theatre Royal** in the CBD (MLC Centre, King Street, 9224 8444) once hosted major productions on a regular basis, but, thanks to having Sydney's least-capacious foyer and the perennial rumble from nearby undergound trains, it's now rarely used. It does, however, see some brief action around Sydney Festival time. The **National Institute of Dramatic Art** (215 Anzac Parade, Kensington, 9697 7600, www.nida.edu.au), Australia's most eminent drama school – and the alma mater of Mel Gibson, Cate Blanchett and several thousand people you've never heard of – is also an occasional venue. Stand-up and some touring theatre shows put in an appearance at the **Enmore Theatre** in Newtown, though it's better known as a rock venue (*see p248*).

Belvoir Street Theatre

25 Belvoir Street, at Clisdell Street, Surry Hills (9699 3444/www.belvoir.com.au). CityRail/LightRail Central. **Box office** 9.30am-6pm Mon, Tue; 9.30am-7.30pm Wed-Sat; 2.30-6pm Sun. **Tickets** *Company B productions* $54; $25-$45 reductions. Production prices vary. **Credit** AmEx, MC, V. **Map** p329 F11.
This one-time tomato sauce factory, now owned by a non-profit consortium of performers, actors, writers and their supporters, is home to the innovative Company B (*see p266*), which has exclusive use of the brilliantly intimate 350-seat Upstairs Theatre. The even more personal 80-seat Downstairs space hosts Belvoir's B Sharp fringe season. Belvoir Street attracts Sydney's most discerning and loyal theatre-goers and recently enjoyed an $11.6 million redevelopment, which gave it a much-needed spruce and polish, with a bigger bar and much comfier seats.

Capitol Theatre

13 Campbell Street, between Pitt & George Streets, Haymarket (box office 1300 136166/admin 9320 5000/www.capitoltheatre.com.au). CityRail Central/ LightRail Capitol Square. **Box office** 9am-5pm Mon-Fri. **Tickets** $45-$112.90. Production prices vary. **Credit** AmEx, DC, MC, V. **Map** p329 E8.
Completed in 1893, the interior of the Capitol (originally known as the Hippodrome) was designed by an American theatre specialist to create the illusion of sitting outdoors under the stars. Like most illusions, it generally fails. Once reduced to being a too-big porn cinema and then nearly derelict for years, the Capitol was expensively and extensively restored just as the fashion for gargantuan long-running musicals peaked. It's deeply kitsch, and at the time of writing served as the perfect venue for worldwide hit *Billy Elliot The Musical.*

Darlinghurst Theatre

19 Greenknowe Avenue, at Baroda Street, Elizabeth Bay (8356 9987/www.darlinghursttheatre.com). CityRail Kings Cross/bus 311, 312. **Box office** 6pm on performance days. *Phone bookings* 9.30am-6pm Mon-Sat. **Tickets** $35; $30 reductions. **Credit** (phone bookings only) AmEx, MC, V. **Map** p330 J6.
The 111-seat Darlo is located on the edge of Kings Cross, and has comfortable, individually sponsored seats (with name-plates – which semi-famous actor will you sit on tonight?) and excellent sight lines. The theatre co-produces a variety of new work and updated classics in collaboration with a range of local and touring companies. One of Sydney's best-value theatres, with a happily eclectic programme.

Ensemble Theatre

78 McDougall Street, at Willoughby Street, Kirribilli (9929 0644/www.ensemble.com.au). CityRail Milsons Point/ferry Kirribilli. **Box office** 9.30am-4.30pm Mon; 9.30am-7.30pm Tue-Sat; 1.30-4.30pm Sun. **Tickets** $46-$62; from $22 reductions. **Credit** AmEx, DC, MC, V.
Hayes Gordon transformed an old boathouse into Sydney's first in-the-round space in the 1950s, but the theatre has since recovered from the fickle

No need for rotten tomatoes at the **Belvoir Street Theatre**.

whims of offshore trendiness. The company (*see p267*) is now consistently commendable and has reclaimed its inner pros arch. Beautifully run since 1986 by Sandra Bates, it has one of Sydney's best foyers and a house style of honest, no-nonsense work.

Lyric Theatre

Star City Casino, 80 Pyrmont Street, between Jones Bay Road & Union Street, Pyrmont (9777 9000/ bookings 1300 795267/www.starcity.com.au). LightRail Star City/ferry Darling Harbour/bus 443. **Box office** 9am-5pm Mon-Sat; 11am-5pm Sun; later on show days. **Tickets** prices vary. **Credit** AmEx, DC, MC, V. **Map** p326 C6.
Designed for Lloyd-Webber musicals and similar fare, the Lyric is a state-of-the-art theatre that, like the Capitol, is generally the home of big budget musicals. Sightlines are good and there are bars and restaurants aplenty in the complex – if the show's rubbish, as it sometimes is, you can even have a flutter at the gambling tables.

New Theatre

542 King Street, between Angel & Knight Streets, Newtown (9519 3403/bookings 1300 306776/ www.ramin.com.au/online/newtheatre). CityRail Newtown or St Peters/bus 308, 370, 422. **Box office** 10am-6pm Mon-Fri; & 1hr before show. **Tickets** $27; $22 reductions. **Credit** (phone bookings only) MC, V. **Map** p334.
An intimate 160-seater that's home to the New Theatre (*see p267*), Australia's most committed continuously producing company. Cheap as chips and far more nourishing, the New is usually one of Sydney's best, and best-value, aesthetic options.

Old Fitzroy Theatre

129 Dowling Street, at Cathedral Street, Woolloomooloo (9294 4296/bookings 1300 438849/ www.trstheatre.com.au). CityRail Kings Cross/ bus 200. **Box office** from 6.30pm on show days. **Tickets** $20-$28; $34 beer/laksa/show. **Credit** MC, V. **Map** p330 H7.
Founded in 1997 by a desperately hip yet talented collective of Sydney actors called the Tamarama Rock Surfers Theatre Company, and located under an old backpacker's pub, the Fitz programmes first-time playwrights, as well as contemporary takes on classics and whatever's currently hip, hot or happening. It hosts up to 12 main productions a year and also puts on the work of visiting companies. Book a 'beer, laksa and show' ticket and pick up the first two an hour before the third.

PACT Theatre

107 Railway Parade, at Sydney Street, Erskineville (9550 2744/www.pact.net.au). CityRail Erskineville. **Box office** 1hr before show. **Tickets** $20; $15 reductions. **No credit cards**. **Map** p334.
This old factory space (yeah, another one) is home to the oft-exciting PACT Youth Theatre (*see p268*) and occasionally hosts itinerant fringe companies of immensely varying quality.

Parramatta Riverside Theatres

Corner of Church & Market Streets, Parramatta (8839 3399/www.riversideparramatta.com.au). CityRail/RiverCat Parramatta. **Box office** 9am-5pm Mon-Fri; 9.30am-1pm Sat; & 1hr before show. **Tickets** $25-$55; $15-$35 reductions. Production prices vary. **Credit** AmEx, MC, V.

This Bicentennial project is a council-mandated but difficult multi-theatre complex, perched beside the pleasant, if brownish, Parramatta River. It gets shows touring from inner Sydney venues and other states and hosts the annual and excellent Big Laugh Comedy Festival (late March/early April).

Performance Space

245 Wilson Street, Eveleigh (8571 9111/bookings 1300 438849/www.performancespace.com.au). CityRail Redfern or Macdonaldtown. **Box office** 10am-6pm Mon-Fri; & 1hr before show. **Tickets** $20-$25; $15 reductions. **Credit** MC, V. **Map** p328 B12.

A former Greek-language cinema and dance hall with a surviving sprung floor, the Performance Space is contemporary, funky and has the only foyer in Sydney where banging on about 'post-performative practice' won't earn you instant derision. Inconsistent for all the best reasons, the P Space remains the finest escape from the stultification of the mainstream, and also hosts shows as part of the Mardi Gras Festival (*see p217 and p243* **Hoorah for the Mardi Gras!**).

Seymour Centre

Corner of City Road & Cleveland Street, Chippendale (box office 9351 7940/admin 9351 7944/www. seymour.usyd.edu.au). Bus 370, 422, 423, 426, 428. **Box office** 9am-6pm Mon-Fri; 11am-3pm Sat; & 2hrs before show. **Tickets** $15-$58; $10-$45 reductions. Production prices vary. **Credit** AmEx, MC, V. **Map** p328 C11.

The Seymour Centre showcases a grab-bag of productions that have usually failed to find a better venue elsewhere. The main stage, designed with Tyrone Guthrie's open-stage model in mind, can be a bit too open. Apart from university student work, it remains the place where, alas, all too often good art goes to die in Sydney. The outdoor bar area is great on a summer's night.

Stables Theatre

10 Nimrod Street, at Craigend Street, Kings Cross (9361 3817/bookings 1300 306776/www.griffin theatre.com.au). CityRail Kings Cross. **Box office** (in person) 1hr before show. **Tickets** *Griffin productions* $43; $25-$35 reductions. Production prices vary. **Credit** AmEx, DC, MC, V. **Map** p330 J8.

Seating a closely packed and usually sweaty audience of 120 (after three decades of performances, is functional air-con perhaps possible this millennium?), this former stables, complete with camp painted horses, is home to the Griffin Theatre Company (*see p267*). New Oz is the house style, and fine productions with excellent acting make it a local treasure.

Star Theatre

Star City Casino, 80 Pyrmont Street, between Jones Bay Road & Union Street, Pyrmont (9777 9000/ bookings 1300 795267/www.starcity.com.au). LightRail Star City/ferry Darling Harbour/bus 443. **Box office** 9am-5pm Mon-Sat; 11am-5pm Sun; later on show days. Production prices vary. **Credit** AmEx, DC, MC, V. **Map** p326 C6.

It's big, it's brassy but at least you get bar service during the entertainment. Star City's 950-seat, cabaret-style room manages to recreate some of the tackiness of Las Vegas. Often popular for jukebox musicals and stage versions of TV shows.

State Theatre

49 Market Street, between Pitt & George Streets, CBD (admin 9373 6852/bookings 13 6100/www. statetheatre.com.au). CityRail St James or Town Hall/Monorail City Centre. **Box office** (in person) 9am-5pm Mon-Fri; & until 8pm on show days. **Tickets** $50-$135. Production prices vary. **Credit** AmEx, DC, MC, V. **Map** p327 F6.

Designed at the dawn of talking pictures, the impossibly over-the-top State is Australia's only example of true rococo. All plaster and all fake, the State hosts rare theatre pieces too supersized to belong elsewhere. It's a good cinema and average sit-down music venue, but not great for live theatre.

Sydney Opera House

Bennelong Point, Circular Quay (box office 9250 7777/www.sydneyoperahouse.com). CityRail/ferry Circular Quay. **Box office** 9am-8.30pm Mon-Sat; & 2hrs before show Sun. **Tickets** *Opera Theatre* $70-$250; $70-$195 reductions. *Concert Hall* prices vary. *Drama Theatre & Playhouse* $35-$80; $30-$60 reductions. *Studio* $25-$50; $25-$40 reductions. **Credit** AmEx, DC, MC, V. **Map** p327 G3.

Danish architect Jørn Utzon's difficult child, the Opera House is a wonderful piece of sculpture masquerading as a functional arts venue. Despite the fact that it's best appreciated from the outside, experiencing the weirdness of Sydney's best-known built icon is probably essential. In addition to the Opera Theatre and the larger Concert Hall, it contains three theatre spaces: the Drama Theatre (oddly widescreen and distant), the smaller Playhouse (mid-sized) and the Studio (a late attempt to reclaim the funk). Regardless of the building's drawbacks, the work can be very good, with the STC (*see p268*), Ensemble (*see p267*) and Bell Shakespeare (*see p266*) all performing, plus some excellent touring shows. For music productions, *see p254*.

Sydney Theatre

22 Hickson Road, opposite Pier 6/7, Walsh Bay (9250 1999/www.sydneytheatre.org.au). CityRail/ ferry Circular Quay then 15min walk. **Box office** 9am-8.30pm Mon-Sat; 3-5.30pm Sun (show days only). **Tickets** $59-$79; $40-$67 reductions. Production prices vary. **Credit** AmEx, MC, V. **Map** p327 E3.

The well-designed, recently constructed Sydney represents the city's longstanding lust for a quality theatre space. Because it's programmed by the STC (*see p268*), the nigh-on-900-seater theatre doesn't depend on the whims of commercial producers. It often features good drama, and occasionally good dance, though its construction means you can't walk out before the interval without making a great deal of noticeable noise. Not that that stops anyone. Also on site is the Hickson Road Bistro, offering pre- and post-dining, drinks and coffee.

The Cate factor

Theatre has never been Sydney's thing. In Australia, Melbourne is traditionally home to the arts, and globally the antipodean theatre scene lags way behind Europe and New York. But the room was packed to bursting for the 2007 press conference announcing the imminent appointment of Cate Blanchett and her scriptwriter husband Andrew Upton for a three-year tenure as joint artistic directors of the Sydney Theatre Company (*see p268*).

Incumbent director and serious luvvie Robyn Nevin must have been bewildered to see so many turning out to meet the newcomers, but few could ignore the allure of an Oscar-winning Hollywood star. Following in the footsteps of Kevin Spacey, artistic director at London's Old Vic, Blanchett is giving back in a major way both to her hometown and to her first calling – the theatre. The response, however, was mixed: critics argue that Blanchett and Upton have no experience of running a major theatre company, and question how the actress could possibly devote enough time to the job while still appearing on the big screen (and that's before you consider the couple's newly expanded brood).

As the duo prepares to take over the STC helm, one thing is certain: their passion for the task has ignited a fire under the local theatre industry. There's talk of Blanchett using her star quality to pull in big names from overseas – which will in turn translate to more bums on seats. On top of that, she has already signed up designer Giorgio Armani as a patron: in October 2007 he made a donation described as 'one of the largest ever individual financial gifts to an Australian theatre company', with the promise of more in the future. There was also the suggestion that Armani may become involved in providing costumes for productions.

But it isn't all glitz and glamour: Cate is a serious actress, and at the close of 2007 she and Upton proudly announced a heavyweight first season including an eight-hour War of the Roses project, distilling Shakespeare's eight history plays spanning the period into a challenging cycle performed by the STC Actors Company – including Cate herself. How the new dream team fares in the hot seat remains to be seen, but there's never been so much excitement on Sydney's boards.

Wharf Theatres

Pier 4/5, Hickson Road, Walsh Bay (9250 1777/ www.sydneytheatre.com.au). CityRail/ferry Circular Quay then 15min walk. **Box office** 9am-7pm Mon; 9am-8.30pm Tue-Fri; 11am-8.30pm Sat; 2hrs before performance Sun. **Tickets** $48-$79; $42-$67 reductions (not Fri, Sat). Production prices vary. **Credit** AmEx, MC, V. **Map** p327 E2.

A converted wharf and warehouse on the western side of the Harbour Bridge, near the Sydney Theatre (*see p270*). Surrounded by ever more swanky residential redevelopment, it houses the STC's (*see p268*) artistic, managerial and production staff, rehearsal space and a lovely restaurant, as well as two theatres, Wharf 1 and Wharf 2. The Sydney Dance Company (*see below*), Australian Theatre for Young People (*see p266*) and Bangarra Dance Theatre (*see below*) also perform here. The complex also boasts Sydney's best foyer – on a summer's night, its G&T is well worth the view. Get off at Circular Quay, walk through the Rocks and under the Bridge, and even before the show you'll experience aesthetic magic.

Dance

Keep an eye out for Gideon Obazarnek's once-groovy **Chunky Move** (9645 5188, www. chunkymove.com). A Sydney-expat company based in Melbourne, the Chunksters usually visit Sydney once a year and are worth catching.

Australian Ballet

9669 2700/1300 369741/www.australianballet. com.au.

Australia's national classical ballet company is based in Melbourne and is a perfect example of why static European art traditions don't always translate to new climes. The company usually performs two seasons of very stock-standard ballet a year at the Sydney Opera House (*see p270*) – although the recent appointment of young Cuban Yosvani Ramos as Principal Artist may yet add some much needed spice to the company's work. Along with Opera Australia (*see p255*), this is the only taxpayer-propped company that isn't required to programme new Australian work.

Bangarra Dance Theatre

9251 5333/www.bangarra.com.au.

Australia's leading contemporary indigenous dance company, Bangarra has been artistically directed by Stephen Page since 1991. Its value is in its mix of contemporary style with ancient Aboriginal traditions of physicality, movement and bodily storytelling. Consistently popular, Bangarra regularly tours the world and remains one of Australia's only distinctive arts exports. A unique experience.

Sydney Dance Company

9221 4811/www.sydneydance.com.au.

At the end of 2007 the Sydney Dance Company lost the choreographic wind beneath its wings with the departure of artistic directors Graeme Murphy and Janet Vernon: Murphy especially is a colossus of Australian dance and a huge loss. How the company copes remains to be seen – in the meantime it has announced a series of international guest choreographers to host the 2008 season. Watch this space.

Bangarra Dance Theatre – Australia's leading contemporary indigenous dance company.

Trips Out of Town

Short Trips

Go wild in the country.

Escaping Sydney only takes a couple of hours' drive in any direction. Inland, to the west are the World Heritage-listed **Blue Mountains** (*see below*), with breathtaking views across deep valleys, sheer cliffs, waterfalls and bushland. To the north is **Hunter Valley** (*see p280*), famous for its wineries, while a trip south leads to the historic villages of the **Southern Highlands** (*see p286*) and **Canberra** (*see p288*), the federal capital. Beautiful beaches, rainforests and national parks can be found up and down the coast, with plenty to see along the way.

It's best to get around by car – *see p296* for hire companies – but we've also included details of local trains, buses and internal flights where possible. Journey times are from central Sydney.

INFORMATION

CountryLink (central reservations 13 2232, www.countrylink.info) operates trains and coaches in NSW, around Canberra, and in Queensland and Victoria. Visit its website for details of its good-value multi-day train and tour packages to destinations in NSW.

For general information on areas around Sydney, visit the **Sydney Visitor Centre** (*see p306*). **Tourism New South Wales** (9931 1111, www.tourism.nsw.gov.au) will direct you to a regional tourist office.

Heading West

Blue Mountains

A mere two hours west of the CBD, the Blue Mountains are one of Australia's most popular natural playgrounds and a must-visit for any tourist. This spectacular wilderness covers over 10,000 square kilometres (almost 4,000 square miles) of breathtakingly beautiful and rugged country: in 2000 the **Blue Mountains National Park**, which covers nearly 2,500 square kilometres (965 square miles), was grouped together with six other nearby national parks to form the **Greater Blue Mountains World Heritage Area**. Most of it is so isolated from Sydney's urban sprawl to the east that it could hide a species of tree, the Wollemi pine, that was thought to have been extinct for 150 million years.

The Blue Mountains – in reality a maze of plateaus and dramatic gorges – are part of the Great Dividing Range, which separates the eastern seaboard and its cities from Australia's rural and desert heart. They only look blue from a distance, due to sunlight refracting through the eucalyptus oil that evaporates from the bush's legion of gum trees.

For decades after the first settlers arrived in Sydney, the Blue Mountains were thought to be impassable – but the very future of the colony depended on breaking through the dense bush and bridging its gaping canyons. With no sheep tracks to follow and river paths ending in crashing waterfalls, it took until 1813 before its secrets were finally unlocked and farmers had access to the sprawling fertile land beyond. Today the area is easily traversed by rail and car (thanks to the efforts of a group of prisoners who were offered pardons if they could complete the first road in a matter of months – they did).

The administrative region called the City of the Blue Mountains is a narrow strip of townships and villages snaking its way along a high plateau between vast tracts of virginal bush. The townships are usually deliberately picturesque, full of twee 'Olde Wares' shops and pricey 'Devonshire' teas. Lavishly restored cottages nestle amid English cold-climate gardens, though some residents are radically embracing native flora, often to the discomfort of older locals who like their traditional conifers, rose beds and topiary hedges.

With nature the area's star attraction, the best way to explore is by taking one or several of the numerous well-signposted and maintained bushwalks. These range from hour-long quickies to camping treks of several days' duration. Good advice on walks can be found at the **Blue Mountains Information Centre** (*see p279*). More adventurous types can enjoy rock climbing, abseiling and the thrill of riding mountain bikes in actual mountains.

Almost all Sydney-based tour companies offer a one-day bus trip for a quick look around, but the better (and cheaper) option is to catch a CityRail train from Sydney's Central Station. Trains depart hourly every day, and take around two hours to reach the upper mountains.

While most townships have their own bush trails, the centre of the action lies in the

Blue Mountains.

Take a tour

Plenty of tour operators run interesting and entertaining day trips in and around the Blue Mountains. Some tours start in Sydney, while others leave from Katoomba. The following outfits are recommended:

Australian School of Mountaineering

4782 2014/www.asmguides.com.
Prices phone for details.
Based in Katoomba, ASM has provided outdoor training and guiding for more than two decades. It runs an impressive range of canyoning, rock climbing and abseiling trips.

Fantastic Aussie Tours

4782 1866/1300 300915/www.fantastic-aussie-tours.com.au. **Prices** from $70.
A day tour to Jenolan Caves from Katoomba, with cave entrance. Cheaper tickets are offered for bushwalkers who just want a bus service to the caves.

High 'n' Wild

4782 6224/www.high-n-wild.com.au.
Prices from $99.
This Katoomba-based adventure outfit runs canyoning expeditions involving swimming, wading and squeezing through tight spaces,

as well as other outdoor fun options including bushwalking, ice climbing, mountain biking and abseiling. It also offers snow- and ice-climbing courses.

Oz Trek Adventure Tours

9666 4262/www.oztrek.com.au. **Prices** $55.
A packed day trip from Sydney includes a visit to the Olympic site at Homebush, a tour of the major Blue Mountain sites and a one-to two-hour bushwalk.

Visitours

9499 5444/www.visitours.com.au.
Prices from $83.
The Blue Mountains tour from Sydney also includes a stop at Wentworth Falls and Scenic World, where you can ride the world's steepest railway. Learn about Aboriginal culture and rock engravings.

Wonderbus

9630 0529/1300 556357/www.wonderbus.com.au. **Prices** from $89.
A range of tours to the Blue Mountains, including a day trip from Sydney that involves three hours of bushwalking and covers most of the area's main sites, such as the Three Sisters and a local winery.

---

adjoining townships of **Katoomba** and **Leura**. One easy sightseeing option is the **Blue Mountains Explorer Bus** (4782 1866, 1300 300915, www.explorerbus.com.au). It's a double-decker (for some reason painted in the livery of a red London bus) departing just across from Katoomba train station 12 times a day between 9.45am and 4.15pm ($33, $28-$16.50 reductions, $82.50 family). It stops at 30 resorts, galleries, tea rooms and general scenic attractions around Katoomba and Leura. You can get off and on as often as you like, and tickets are valid for up to seven days. CityRail also offers a combined train-plus-Explorer-bus ticket.

Katoomba is the most popular township for visitors thanks to its proximity to attractions such as the **Three Sisters** rock formation near Echo Point and **Scenic World** (*see p277*), where a range of gravity-defying vehicles grant spectacular views as you travel over and into the Jamison Valley. If you've got some time, descend the precipitous 841-step **Giant Staircase** next to the Sisters (only the genuinely athletic or masochistic should attempt to climb up it), and then do the two-

and-a-half-hour easy walk through the Jamison Valley to the foot of the Scenic Railway for a sweat-free, mechanised ascent.

Katoomba is home to the Blue Mountains City Council, three pubs, a swathe of cafés and plenty of writers, artists and poets of steeply varying quality. Its chief built attractions are the 1880s **Carrington Hotel** (*see p277*), a popular wedding venue, and the intimate and terribly 'heritage' **Paragon Café** (65 Katoomba Street, 4782 2928). There are also some excellent second-hand bookshops. The three best for dusty bibliophiles are **Brian's Books** (44 Katoomba Street, 4782 5115), **Mr Pickwicks** (86 Katoomba Street, 4782 7598) and **Blue Mountains Books** (92 Katoomba Street, 4782 6700).

Linked to Katoomba by bus, train, a panoramic cliff drive or a half-hour walk is Leura, with its more upmarket guesthouses, vastly smarter shops and manicured gardens. In local parlance, if Katoomba is Mount Penrith, then Leura is Mount Paddington. One of the world's chintz capitals, Leura is a delight for all lovers of knick-knacks, baubles and ornamental flummery.

Further into the mountains beyond Katoomba, the **Hydro Majestic Hotel** (*see below*) in Medlow Bath is popular for pricey coffee with an expansive view. More down to earth is the village of **Mount Victoria**, the starting point for many more fine mountain hikes.

On the northern side of the mountains, off the Bells Line of Road above the Grose Valley, is the quintessentially transplanted English hamlet of **Mount Wilson**. This charming village is best visited in spring or autumn, when some house-proud locals open their gardens for your viewing pleasure and herbaceous envy. It's also notable for **Withycombe** (corner of the Avenue and Church Avenue), the house where the parents of Australia's only Nobel literature laureate, Patrick White, lived for a time. For more natural splendour, try the hushed and majestic remnant rainforest grandiloquently named the **Cathedral of Ferns**.

Also in the area are the magnificent **Mount Tomah Botanic Gardens** (4567 2154, www.rbgsyd.nsw.gov.au), which showcase cool-climate plants from around the world. A range of guided and self-guided tours – including bushwalks – is available, but bookings (call 4567 2154) are essential.

You'll need to travel to the south-western edge of the Blue Mountains to reach the other main attraction in the area: the **Jenolan Caves** (1300 763 311, www.jenolancaves.org.au). A tangled series of extraordinary underground limestone caverns, complete with stalagmites and stalactites, within a large and peaceful nature reserve, they're open 9am to 5pm daily. The caverns come in two flavours – easy guided tours with walkways and steps, and various adventure caves requiring helmets, overalls and climbing (from $60). If you're less adventurous, take a tour of the Lucas Cave ($23, $16 reductions, $59 family). There's also a hotel within the complex (*see below*).

Scenic World

Corner of Cliff & Violet Streets, Katoomba (4782 2699/www.scenicworld.com.au). **Open** 9am-5pm daily. **Tickets** *Skyway return trip* $16; $8 children; $40 family. *Cableway & Railway return trip* $19; $10 children; $48 family. **Credit** AmEx, DC, MC, V.
Views and vertigo are the main features of this collection of tourist transports. The Scenic Skyway – a cable-car system over the Jamison Valley – was renovated a few years ago. The new cars have glass floors, so now you can see it really is a long way down – 270m (890ft), in fact. The Scenic Railway features an old coal train reinvented as the world's steepest rail incline, which takes you down into the rainforested valley – as does the Scenic Cableway, another cable car ride. There's a 2km (1.25-mile) boardwalk between the lower Railway and Cableway stations, so you can go down on one and back on the other.

Where to stay & eat

Blue Mountains YHA

207 Katoomba Street, Katoomba (4782 1416/ www.yha.com.au). **Rates** $26-$29 dorm; $73-$82 double; $104-$116 family. **Credit** MC, V.
The Blue Mountains outpost of the YHA empire is an excellent modern hostel in a historic 1930s art deco building right in the centre of Katoomba.

Carrington Hotel

15-47 Katoomba Street, Katoomba (4782 1111/ www.thecarrington.com.au). **Rates** from $119 B&B. **Credit** AmEx, DC, MC, V.
A gorgeous, rambling, old-style resort hotel with lots of antiques and oodles of 19th-century charm. Cocktails on the balcony are a must.

Hydro Majestic Hotel

Great Western Highway, Medlow Bath (4788 1002/ www.hydromajestic.com.au). **Rates** from $210 midweek; $280 weekend. **Credit** AmEx, DC, MC, V.
An upmarket, beautifully restored historic hotel with astonishing views and a Victorian feel, once famous for its spa cures, hence the 'Hydro'. Worth a visit for tea and scones.

Jenolan Caves House

Jenolan Caves (1300 763311/www.jenolancaves resort.com.au). **Rates** B&B plus dinner per person from $85 midweek; $110 weekend. **Credit** AmEx, DC, MC, V.
Inside the caves complex, this dark, wood-panelled hotel with roaring fires has the feel of a grand English country house. Next door, the Gatehouse Jenolan offers four-bed dorms for $30 a head.

Lilianfels Blue Mountains

Lilianfels Avenue, Echo Point, Katoomba (4780 1200/www.lilianfels.com.au). **Rates** $389-$705 deluxe; $679-$995 executive suite. **Credit** AmEx, DC, MC, V.
This five-star pile perched just above Echo Point is the poshest accommodation in the mountains, with two famous restaurants (Darleys, serving Mod Oz cuisine, and Tre Sorelle, serving Italian) plus great views.

Getting there

By car

Springwood, Faulconbridge, Wentworth Falls, Leura, Katoomba & Mount Victoria
Take Great Western Highway (Route 32) and/or Western Motorway (Route 4). It's 109km (68 miles) from Sydney to Katoomba – about 2hrs.
Kurrajong & Mount Tomah Take Great Western Highway (Route 32) or Western Motorway (Route 4); turn off to Richmond via Blacktown; then Bells Line of Road (Route 40). Mount Wilson is 6km (3.75 miles) off Bells Line of Road.
Jenolan Caves Take Great Western Highway (Route 32) via Katoomba and Mount Victoria; then turn south at Hartley; it's another 46km (29 miles) to the caves.

enjoy the view

Explore the Blue Mountains by train and bus

 The **1 day Blue Mountains ExplorerLink** includes return same day CityRail travel to Katoomba Station with all day access to the 'hop-on-hop-off' Explorer Bus. Prices start from $48.80 for an adult and $19.70 for a child.

 The **3 day Blue Mountains ExplorerLink** includes return CityRail travel and access to the 'hop-on-hop-off' Explorer Bus over the three days. Prices start from $64.80 for an adult and $27.70 for a child.

Both ExplorerLink tickets can be purchased 7 days a week, from most stations. These tickets are unavailable to half fare concession holders and Pensioner fares are only available on the one day ticket. Prices correct at time of printing.

www.cityrail.info
Transport Infoline **131 500**
TTY **1800 637 500**
(Teletypewriter service for hearing and speech impaired customers only)

CR-P-239_TO_JB1334

By train

Trains depart hourly from Central Station. It's about 2hrs to Katoomba.

Tourist information

Also check out the websites www.katoomba-nsw.com and www.bluemts.com.au.

Blue Mountains Information Centre

Echo Point Road, Katoomba (1300 653408/www. visitbluemountains.com.au). **Open** 9am-5pm daily.

Heading North

If you've ever wondered what the west coast of Scotland would look like without the rain, mist and midges, head to the stunning Hawkesbury River. It's like Argyll with sunshine. Skirting the outer edges of Australia's biggest city for much of its length, the great greenish-brown giant licks over 1,000 kilometres (620 miles) of foreshore as it curls first north-east and then, from Wisemans Ferry, south-east towards the sea, emptying into an estuary at Broken Bay. The river's fjord-like saltwater creeks and inlets are ideal for exploring by boat, and houseboating holidays are popular.

The town of **Windsor** retains many of its original buildings, as well as its waterwheel and charm. Among the stalwarts is the oldest inn in Australia still being used for its original purpose (the Macquarie Arms, built in 1815),

Australia's oldest courthouse (1822), St Matthew's Anglican Church, built by convict labour from a design by convict architect Francis Greenway (also in 1822), and the oldest Catholic primary school still in use (1836). Also of note is John Tebbutt's house and observatory, with its outsized telescope.

It's worth taking a cruise with **Hawkesbury Valley Heritage Discovery Tours** (4577 6882), as you'll get the enthusiastic low-down on the area's history from a local guide.

Within easy reach of Windsor, there's more colonial architecture at **Richmond**, a tree-lined garden town whose railway station dates back to 1822, and **Ebenezer**, with Australia's oldest church (on Coromandel Road, built 1809).

The Hawkesbury's change of course is marked by an S-bend at **Wisemans Ferry**, another of the river's historic villages. It has Australia's oldest ferry service, which still runs 24 hours a day (and is one of the few remaining free rides in New South Wales). On the far side of the ferry is a section of the convict-built Great Northern Road, once 264 kilometres (164 miles) long, which shows just what sweat and toil really mean.

Up the road in the Macdonald River Valley, in the secluded hamlet of **St Albans**, is another colonial inn, the **Settlers Arms** (1 Wharf Street, 4568 2111). A couple of kilometres from here, in the Old Cemetery on Settlers Road, lies the grave of William Douglas, a First Fleeter who died in 1838. Rumours also suggest that St Albans was Windsor magistrates' preferred venue for illicit nooky over the years.

The lower reaches of the Hawkesbury are its most spectacular, with steep-sided forested banks and creeks branching off its wide sweep.

Hawkesbury River.

Near the end of **Berowra Creek** (west of the Pacific Highway), at the foot of two deep, bush-covered hills, is beautiful **Berowra Waters**. There's not much here apart from a small car ferry, a cluster of bobbing boats and a few restaurants offering fine cuisine (including Hawkesbury oysters). Much of the remainder of the river, as it makes its way to the sea, is equally tranquil – notably the slender fingers of water that make up **Cowan Creek** (east of the Pacific Highway). It's here, in the sweeping expanse of the **Ku-ring-gai Chase National Park**, that many people choose to cruise or moor for a spot of fishing.

If you haven't got time for houseboating, Australia's last **riverboat postman** may be the answer. The four-hour cruise from Brooklyn allows you to participate in the delivery of mail while taking in the scenery – an inside view that few see. The boat leaves Brooklyn Wharf at 9.30am weekdays, excluding public holidays; for details call 9985 7566.

Otherwise, you could hike from Berowra railway station down to Berowra Waters along a fascinating, well-marked bush track (part of the Great North Walk). A round trip takes about four hours.

Where to stay & eat

Able Hawkesbury Houseboats
3008 River Road, Wisemans Ferry (1800 024979/ 4566 4308/www.hawkesburyhouseboats.com.au). **Rates** from $530 (2 days, 1 night) midweek. **Credit** MC, V.
Choose from seven different sizes of boat, ranging from 26ft to 52ft in length. Facilities are wide ranging, and include shower, toilet, fridge, TV, barbecue, cutlery and crockery.

Berowra Waters Fish Café
199 Bay Road, Berowra Waters (9456 4665). **Open** 9am-8pm Mon-Sat; 8.30am-7pm Sun. **Main courses** $11-$17. **Credit** MC, V.
A great setting with views across the water. Serves fish and chips in various guises. BYO.

Court House Retreat
19 Upper Macdonald Road, St Albans (4568 2042/ www.courthousestalbans.com.au). **Rates** from $160. **Credit** MC, V.
B&B accommodation in a historic sandstone building that once housed a courtroom, police station and lock-up. Booking essential.

Retreat at Wisemans
5564 Old Northern Road, Wisemans Ferry (4566 4422/www.wisemans.com.au). **Rates** from $120. **Credit** AmEx, DC, MC, V.
Comfortable rooms with views of the golf course or river. The Riverbend Restaurant, serving Mod Oz food, is recommended (about $36 for two courses).

Ripples Houseboat Hire
87 Brooklyn Road, Brooklyn (9985 5534/www. ripples.com.au). **Rates** from $500 for 2 nights midweek. **Credit** MC, V.
Two kinds of boat, sleeping up to four or ten.

Getting there

By car
Richmond & Windsor It's 59km (37 miles) from Sydney to Windsor, and the journey takes 60-90mins. **Via Hornsby** Pacific Highway (Route 83) to Hornsby; Galston Road; then Pitt Town Road. **Via Pennant Hills** Epping Road (Route 2) to Pennant Hills; then Route 40. **Via Parramatta** Western Motorway (Route 4) to Parramatta; then Route 40.
Wisemans Ferry & St Albans Pacific Highway (Route 83) to Hornsby; Galston Road; then Old Northern Road.
Berowra Waters Pacific Highway (Route 83); 12km (7 miles) north of Hornsby, Berowra turn-off signed. The Brooklyn turn-off is 12km (7 miles) further north.

By train
Richmond & Windsor There's a regular train service to Windsor and the upper Hawkesbury River area on the Richmond line (via Blacktown) from Central Station. Journey time is around 1hr.
Berowra Waters The main Sydney-Newcastle line from Central Station goes to Berowra Waters (via Berowra Station) and Brooklyn (via Hawkesbury River Station). The trip takes about 40mins (not all trains stop at both stations).

By bus
For details of coach services to the Hawkesbury region, contact the local tourist office (*see below*) or CountryLink NSW (13 2232, www.countrylink.info).

Tourist information

Hawkesbury River Tourist Information Centre
5 Bridge Street, Brooklyn (9985 7064). **Open** 9am-5pm Mon-Fri; 9am-4pm Sat; 11am-3pm Sun.

Tourism Hawkesbury
Ham Common, Windsor Road, Clarendon (4578 0233/www.hawkesburytourism.com.au). **Open** 9am-5pm Mon-Fri; 9am-4pm Sat, Sun.

Hunter Valley

The second-most visited region in New South Wales after the Blue Mountains is the state's main wine-growing region – and that is the reason to visit. The area around the main town of **Pokolbin**, two hours north of Sydney, boasts more than 75 wineries (from the smallest boutiques to the big boys, such as Lindemans), which offer tastings and cellar-door sales of wine ranging from semillon and shiraz to buttery chardonnays. Mingled among the vineyards are award-winning restaurants and luxury hotels, but there are plenty of cheaper options too.

While such wine-based indulgence has put the Hunter firmly on the tourist map, the area's personality is, in contrast, also bound up with coal mining. The very waterway from which the region gets its name was originally known as the Coal River (it was renamed in 1797 after the then NSW governor, John Hunter), and the founder of the Hunter's wine-making industry, Scottish civil engineer James Busby, arrived in Australia in 1824 partly to oversee coal-mining activities in nearby Newcastle. But while the Hunter Valley once boasted the largest shaft mine in the southern hemisphere, which held the world record for coal production in an eight-hour shift (Richmond Main Colliery, now a museum and open irregularly), all but two of its mines have now closed.

The wine industry sprouted from humble beginnings in the 1830s, but has fared rather better. The original vines were cuttings taken from France and pre-dated the phylloxera disease that tainted European wine. Thus Australian grapes are now claimed to be more authentic than modern-day French wines, which use roots from American vines. Seeing out the tough 19th century, then the Depression of the 1930s and later fighting off competition from other antipodean wine regions, such as South Australia, the Hunter made it to the 1970s wine rush and ever since then it has done little but flourish.

Despite its small area – the main vineyard district north of the town of **Cessnock** is only a few kilometres square – the sheer number of wineries in the Lower Hunter Valley can present the wine tourist with a problem: where to start? Inevitably, familiarity leads many to the bigger, more established vineyards – which is a good way of gaining an insight into wine-growing traditions. Large family companies in Pokolbin, such as **Tyrrell's** (Broke Road, 4993 7000) and **Tulloch** (Glen Elgin Estate, DeBeyers Road, 4998 7580) have been producing wine in the area for more than a century, while at **Lindemans** (McDonalds Road, 4998 7684) – in existence for 150 years – there's a museum exhibiting old wine-making equipment. Other big wineries, such as **Wyndham Estate** (Hermitage Road, 4998 7412), on the banks of the Hunter River itself and Australia's oldest continually operating winery, and **McGuigan Simeon** (corner of Broke and McDonalds Roads, 4998 7402), offer full on-site facilities, including galleries, museums, restaurants and cafés.

But it would be a shame to miss out on the smaller enterprises. Places such as **Oakvale** (set against the Brokenback Range, Broke Road, 4998 7520) and Petersons (Mount View Road, 4990 1704) offer the time and space for a more individual tasting experience. Many of these boutique wineries are set within picturesque surroundings. **Hungerford Hill** (Broke Road, 4998 7666) – formerly housed in a beautiful tiny converted church, and recently moved into a new landmark designer building – has some of the best 'stickies' (dessert wines and rich ports) in the area. The grounds of **Pepper Tree Wines** (Halls Road, 4998 7539) incorporate a former convent – the area's swishest guesthouse (*see p283*) – which was moved lock, stock and barrel to the Hunter for the purpose. Further afield, in Lovedale, the **Wandin Valley Estate** (Wilderness Road, 4930 7317) offers accommodation in villas, and has its own cricket ground. Talking of which, have a look at **Brokenwood** (McDonalds Road, 4998 7559) to enjoy its always cracking Cricket Pitch and Graveyard wines. And yes, they do both come from vines grown on cricket pitches and graveyards.

Look out for vintages produced in 1988, 2000 and 2003: these were the best years in the Hunter Valley for decades.

Since the Hunter is reasonably flat and compact, and the wineries never far apart, it's a good place to ditch four-wheel transport. Bikes are available from some guesthouses for a small charge, while **Grapemobile** (4991 2339/0418 404 039) hires out bikes and also runs enjoyable day and overnight cycling and walking tours of the wineries from Cessnock. Finally, if you're not high enough already, see the regimented rows of vines from above with a sunrise balloon flight: try **Balloon Aloft** (*see p282* **Enjoy the ride**) – prices vary based on the number of people and the season.

BARRINGTON TOPS

Although it's less than an hour's drive north of the Hunter Valley, the Barrington Tops is as different from the wine-growing district as it's possible to be. A national park with a world heritage listing, its upper slopes are thick with subtropical rainforest containing thousand-year-old trees, clean mountain streams and abundant wildlife. With its swimming holes, camping and bushwalking, the Barrington Tops is a domain for outdoor enthusiasts. The area can also be explored with mechanical help: try eco-specialist **Bush Track Tours** (0419 650 600, www.bushtracktours.com). Further south are green hillocks and greener valleys, the sort of landscape that insists you jump out of bed straight on to the back of a horse or a

Trips Out of Town

Enjoy the ride

Perhaps it's people's reluctance to mix drinking wine and driving, but there are many unusual ways to take in – and get to – the Hunter Valley.

Rather than spend two hours in a car on the freeway, you can now fly up in an amphibious aircraft with **Sydney Seaplanes** (1300 732752/9388 1978, www.sydney seaplanes.com.au). Departing from Rose Bay, the seaplane takes off over Sydney Harbour and then traces the coast past the northern beaches and Central Coast, before landing at Cessnock Airport, where you can be met by a tour bus or hire a car.

Balloon Aloft (1800 028568/4938 1955, www.balloonaloft.com) offers hot-air balloon rides for people staying overnight; rendezvous are an hour before dawn, though, so best not to sample too much of the local drop

the night before. The relaxing flight takes in the spectacular landscape of vineyards, rivers, forests and the rolling hills of the valley, followed by a champagne reception back on land.

For a slower place, travel in style by horse and carriage. **Hunter Valley Wine & Dine Carriages** (0410 515358, www.huntervalley carriages.com.au) can pick you up from your hotel and tailor a tour of wineries and somewhere for lunch. Tours are also available in a chauffeur-driven Cadillac with **Hunter Valley Cadillac Tours** (4996 4059, www.cadillactours.com.au).

Or if you're feeling guilty about all the wine and cheese you've consumed, hire a bicycle and burn off a few calories. Contact **Hunter Valley Cycling** for hire or tours (0418 281480, www.huntervalleycycling.com.au).

---

mountain bike. If you have your own transport and three or four days to spare, you might consider visiting the triangle of attractions in this area – the Hunter Valley, Barrington Tops and Port Stephens. An excellent and unique place to base yourself is the award-winning **Eaglereach Wilderness Resort** (Summer Hill Road, Vacy, 4938 8233, www.eaglereach. com.au). Perched on a mountain top, you have vistas in all directions from your luxury log cabin (from $250 per night) set in 400 hectares (1,000 acres) of raw bushland. Despite the luxury, nature is on your doorstep – expect to see kangaroos at your window and giant lizards in the front yard.

Wine tours

While many vineyards offer tastings at the cellar door, the local cops rightly take exception to drink-driving, so the best idea may be to take an organised tour. You can travel in old-fashioned style in a horse-drawn carriage: **Pokolbin Horse Coaches** (4998 7189, 0408 161133) offer regular tours and can custom-design a tour (minimum four) to suit your needs. The **Hunter Valley Wine Country Visitor Centre** (*see p283*) has details of other outfits.

Activity Tours Australia

9904 5730/www.activitytours.com.au. **Rates** (with lunch) $100; $94 reductions.
Day trips from Sydney to the Hunter Valley, taking in five wineries, a tour to see how wine is made and a cheese factory. Maximum 19 people.

Hunter Vineyard Tours

4991 1659/www.huntervineyardtours.com.au. **Rates** from $55; $80 with lunch.
Full-day tour in 12- or 22-seat buses, taking in five wineries (lunch optional) in the Cessnock area. Pick-up from local hotels.

Trekabout Tours

4990 8277/www.hunterweb.com.au/trekabout. **Rates** $45 half day (Mon-Fri only); $55 full day.
Half- or full-day winery tours for up to six people. The shorter tour visits four to five wineries. Pick-up is from hotels in the Cessnock/Pokolbin area.

Where to stay & eat

Most Hunter Valley guesthouses won't take bookings for less than two nights, especially over weekends. Rates drop considerably midweek. There are more – and cheaper – hotels and motels in Cessnock.

Barringtons Country Retreat

1941 Chichester Dam Road, 15mins drive from Dungog, Barrington Tops (4995 9269/www. thebarringtons.com.au). **Rates** (minimum 2 nights) from $120. **Credit** MC, V.
If you like to flirt with rural surroundings safe in the knowledge that modern comforts are close at hand, try this place. Log cabins overlooking the valley, spa baths and imaginative cooking at moderate rates.

Casuarina Restaurant & Country Inn

Hermitage Road, Pokolbin, Hunter Valley (4998 7888/www.casuarinainn.com.au). **Rates (**suite) $185 weekdays; $310 weekend. **Credit** AmEx, DC, MC, V.

Over-the-top themed suites are the thing here: pick from the Moulin Rouge, Casablanca, the French Bordello, Susie Wong's, Italian Bordello, Out of Africa, Love Boat, Palais Royale and, finally, Casanova's Loft. Plus a pool, tennis court and a pretty good Mediterranean-style restaurant.

Peppers Convent Guest House

Grounds of Pepper Tree Wines, Halls Road, Pokolbin (4993 8999/www.peppers.com.au). **Rates** (double) from $328 Mon-Thur, Sun; from $792 Fri, Sat. **Credit** AmEx, DC, MC, V.
The ultimate indulgence, with lots of antiques and surrounding vineyards. One of the country's classiest restaurants, Robert's, is also here.

Tallawanta Lodge

Hunter Valley Gardens, next to McGuigan Winery, corner of Broke Road & McDonalds Road, Pokolbin (4998 4000/www.hvg.com.au). **Rates** (B&B) from $334 Mon-Thur, Sun; $848 weekend 2-night stay. **Credit** AmEx, DC, MC, V.
A pleasant place to lay your head, right in the heart of the wine area. The associated Harrigan's Irish Pub also has decent rooms from $251.

Wandin Valley Estate

Wilderness Road, Lovedale (4930 7317/www.wandin valley.com.au). **Rates** from $175. **Credit** AmEx, DC, MC, V.
Winery accommodation in six self-contained, well-appointed villas and studios just five minutes from Pokolbin. Great restaurant too.

Getting there

By car

Lower Hunter Valley Sydney-to-Newcastle Freeway (Route 1) to Freemans Interchange; then turn off to Cessnock (Route 82). Alternatively, leave Route 1 at Calga; head through Central Mangrove towards Wollombi; then turn off to Cessnock (Route 132). Journey time: 2hrs. The main wine-growing district around Pokolbin and Rothbury is about 12km (7 miles) north-west of Cessnock.
Barrington Tops The journey takes about 3hrs.
Direct route Sydney-to-Newcastle Freeway (F3/Route 1) to Maitland turn-off on New England Highway (Route 15); Paterson Road; then turn right for Dungog approx 5km (3 miles) beyond Paterson.
Via Hunter Valley Follow signs from Cessnock to Maitland (via Kurri Kurri), then as above.

By train

Dungog, just south of Barrington Tops, is served by a few daily trains from Sydney (journey time just over 3hrs) via Newcastle (90mins). Some guesthouses will pick up from Dungog.

By bus

Rover Coaches (4990 1699, www.rovercoaches.com.au) runs a daily service to the Hunter Valley from Sydney (departing at 8.30am, returning at 7.15pm), plus day and weekend tours of the region; call for departure points.

Tourist information

Gloucester Visitor Information Centre

27 Denison Street, Gloucester (6558 1408/www.gloucester.org.au). **Open** 8.30am-5pm Mon-Fri; 8.30am-3pm Sat, Sun.
For information on the Barrington Tops.

Hunter Valley Wine Country Visitor Centre

455 Wine Country Drive, Pokolbin (4990 0900/www.winecountry.com.au). **Open** 9am-5pm Mon-Fri; 9.30am-5pm Sat; 9.30am-3.30pm Sun.

Port Stephens

The third point in a triangle of northern attractions that includes the Hunter Valley and Barrington Tops, Port Stephens Bay is a beautiful stretch of water most famous for its whale and dolphin cruises. Two pods of dolphins – around 70 individuals – inhabit the bay, and your chances of getting up close to them are very high. Whales come into the calmer waters of the bay on their migration route from Antarctica.

The main town in the area is **Nelson Bay**, on the northern bank of the harbour, where you'll find hotels, restaurants and takeaways.

Several operators run good dolphin- and whale-watching tours. Highly recommended is a cruise on **Imagine** (5104 Nelson Bay Road, Nelson Bay, 4984 9000, www.imaginecruises.com.au; *photo p284*), a luxury catamaran operated out of Nelson Bay Marina by Frank Future and Yves Papin. All year except June and July they offer a daily two-hour dolphin trip departing at 10.30am ($22, $14-$20 reductions), and a range of longer cruises departing from d'Albora Marina. There's a boom net on board, which is lowered over the edge for thrill-seekers to lie in and get really close to the dolphins. They also operate humpback whale cruises from June to mid November. You can also go looking for dolphins in a kayak with **Ocean Planet** (4342 2222, www.kayaktours.com.au).

Another option for nature lovers is a visit to the **Tomaree National Park** (4984 8200, www.nationalparks.nsw.gov.au) on the southern shore of the inner harbour. Here, you can see low-flying pelicans skidding in to land on the water, and there's a large breeding colony of koalas at Lemon Tree Passage. And if you have access to a 4WD, you can't miss **Stockton Beach**, a 32-kilometre (19-mile) expanse of sand starting at Anna Bay, where you can drive through the waves or even take a shot at dune-bashing over the towering silica hills (providing you have someone to help tow you out when you get stuck – or overturn).

All aboard! Whale watching with **Imagine** off the coast of Port Stephens. *See p283.*

Also worth a visit is **Fighter World** (Medowie Road, Williamtown, 4965 1810, www.fighterworld.com.au, $7, $5 reductions, $20 family). An offshoot of the RAAF Williamtown airbase, it celebrates Australia's fighter-plane history with a wide variety of exhibits.

Where to stay & eat

Peppers Anchorage Port Stephens

Corlette Point Road, Corlette (4984 2555/www.peppers. com.au). **Rates** from $285 midweek; $368 weekends (minimum 2 nights). **Credit** AmEx, DC, MC, V.
Part of the Peppers chain, this is a top-class resort right on the water. Private balconies offer sweeping views across the bay.

Port Stephens Motor Lodge

44 Mangus Street, Nelson Bay (4981 3366). **Rates** $80-$155. **Credit** AmEx, DC, MC, V.
A motel-like place located a short stroll from the main township. There's also a swimming pool.

Salamander Shores

147 Soldiers Point Road, Soldiers Point (4982 7210/ www.salamandershores.com). **Rates** from $149 midweek. **Credit** AmEx, DC, MC, V.
A pleasant hotel featuring lovely rooms with sea views, a pretty garden and a good restaurant.

Getting there

By car

Take Sydney-to-Newcastle Freeway (F3/Route 1); it's a 2.5hr drive.

By train

CityRail trains run almost hourly from Central Station to Newcastle. Buses connect with the trains for transfers to Port Stephens.

By bus

Port Stephens Coaches (1800 045949, 4982 2940, www.pscoaches.com.au) runs a daily service to Nelson Bay, departing Eddy Avenue, Central Station, Sydney, at 2pm. It leaves Nelson Bay for the return trip daily at 9am. The journey takes 3.5hrs.

Tourist information

Port Stephens Visitor Information Centre

Victoria Parade, Nelson Bay (4980 6900/www. portstephens.org.au). **Open** 9am-5pm daily.

Heading South

South Coast

According to most of the people who live there, particularly residents of the Shoalhaven region (which stretches 160 kilometres/100 miles south of the town of Berry), this is the area of New South Wales that has it all: wilderness galore, including large tracts of national park and state forest; beaches so long and white they make Bondi look like a house party at a sewage dump; some of the cleanest, clearest water in Australia; a bay 82 times the size of Sydney

Harbour, with pods of crowd-pleasing dolphins; easy access to magnificent mountain vistas; heritage and antiques; 'surfing' kangaroos at Pebbly Beach, just to the south of Ulladulla; and the best fish and chips in the country at Bermagui (head for the marina and just follow the seagulls).

If you're driving from Sydney along the Princes Highway (Route 1), take a quick detour towards Stanwell Park and drive along Hargrave Road between Coalcliff and Clifton to marvel at the spectacular **Sea Cliff Bridge**, which twists and turns as it hugs the rocky coastline below and the ragged cliffs at your side. Back on the Princes Highway and beyond the Royal National Park, the first region you encounter is Illawarra, the administrative centre of which is the city of **Wollongong**. It's perhaps unfair to view Wollongong as one of the two ugly sisters on either side of Sydney (the other being Newcastle), but as you approach its smoking industrial surroundings it's hard not to.

The road then begins to slide prettily between the coast on one side and the beginnings of the Southern Highlands on the other (Illawarra comes from an Aboriginal word meaning 'between the high place and the sea'). The first seaside town worthy of a stop is **Kiama**. The town's main attraction is the **Blow Hole**, which spurts spray up to 60 metres (200 feet) into the air from a slatey, crenellated outcrop next to a comparatively tranquil harbour. Also by the harbour is a fresh fish market, while on the way into town there's a block of 1885 quarrymen's cottages that have been renovated and turned into restaurants and craft shops. On the way out, don't miss the wonderful sign 'Stan Crap – Funeral Director'.

Kiama is a good base for exploring the subtropical **Minnamurra Rainforest**, the **Carrington Falls** and nearby **Seven Mile Beach**, an undeniably impressive caramel arc, backed by a hinterland of fir trees.

An alternative base is the tree-lined inland town of **Berry**, a little further south. It's an entertaining hybrid of hick town and quaint yuppie heaven, where earthy locals mix with weekending Sydneysiders in search of antiques and fine dining. The former are catered for by a couple of daggy pubs, while many of the latter bed down at the **Bunyip Inn Guest House** (*see p286*).

JERVIS BAY
Undoubtedly the Shoalhaven region's greatest attraction, and the one that drives normally restrained commentators to reach for their superlatives, is Jervis Bay. A huge place, it encompasses the wonderful **Booderee**

National Park and 56 kilometres (34 miles) of shoreline. It also has a history of close shaves. First, in 1770, Captain Cook sailed straight past it on the way towards Botany Bay, recording it only as 'low-lying wetlands' and missing entirely its deep, wide natural harbour (which made it an ideal alternative to Sydney as fulcrum for the new colony). Later, this ecologically sensitive beauty spot was mooted as a possible port for Canberra and the ACT. And in 1975, Murrays Beach, at the tip of the national park, was chosen as a site for a nuclear reactor (a project thankfully defeated by public protest).

These narrow escapes and a fortuitous lack of population growth around Jervis Bay mean that this coastal area remains one of the most undisturbed and beautiful in Australia. Divers testify to the clarity of its waters; swimmers are sometimes literally dazzled by the whiteness of its sands (Hyams Beach is said to be the whitest in the world). It's not just popular with people: among its regularly visiting sea and bird life are fur seals, giant rays, whales (southern right, pilot and killer), sharks, sea eagles, penguins and many, many more.

A good way to get a feel for Jervis Bay and meet its resident bottlenose dolphins is to hook up with **Dolphin Watch Cruises** (50 Owen Street, Huskisson, 4441 6311, www.dolphin watch.com.au), which also runs whale cruises. **Huskisson**, the launching point for the cruises, is one of six villages on the shores of the bay. It's got a couple of accommodation options, a dive shop – **Deep6Diving** (64 Owen Street, 4441 5255, www.deep6divingjervisbay.com.au) – wonderful fish and chips, and a pub with a bistro, the **Husky Pub** (4441 5001) on Owen Street. Just south of Jervis Bay there is excellent sailing, snorkelling and swimming at St George's Basin, and fishing at **Sussex Inlet**.

You could stay in Huskisson, but it's well worth bringing a tent to get a proper feel for the Booderee National Park (admission $10 per vehicle per day), which is jointly managed by the local Aboriginal community. The best place to camp is at **Caves Beach**, where you wake up to the calls of birds and eastern grey kangaroos. **Green Patch** has more dirt than grass, but better facilities and can accommodate camper vans as well. The Christmas/New Year period sees a ballot for places. Book through the park's visitor centre (*see p286*).

ULLADULLA
Despite all the stunning scenery around Jervis Bay, it can be worth venturing further south to the sleepy fishing town of Ulladulla for somewhere to stay. Ulladulla's protected harbour may not quite recall Sicily, but the town has a sizeable Italian fishing community

(guaranteeing decent local pizzas and pasta), and the **Blessing of the Fleet** is an annual event on Easter Sunday. From here it's easy to access wilderness areas to the west and further south – **Budawang** and **Murramarang National Parks** – plus yet more expansive beaches, such as **Pebbly Beach** (which is actually sandy) with its resident kangaroos.

Where to stay & eat

Bunyip Inn Guest House

122 Queen Street, Berry (4464 2064). **Rates** from $120 midweek, $140 weekend. **Credit** AmEx, DC, MC, V.

A National Trust-classified former bank with 13 individually styled rooms, one with a four-poster bed. There's also a swimming pool.

Huskisson Beach Tourist Resort

Beach Street, Huskisson (4441 5142/www.huskisson beachtouristresort.com.au). **Rates** from $30 camping; from $85 cabin. **Credit** MC, V.

This resort offers various cabins (including self-catering ones) as well as plenty of camping spots right opposite the beach. There's a pool too.

Jervis Bay Guest House

1 Beach Street, Huskisson (4441 7658/www. jervisbayguesthouse.com.au). **Rates** from $145. **Credit** AmEx, DC, MC, V.

This four-and-a-half-star guesthouse opposite a beach has just four rooms, with balconies overlooking the sea and the sunrise, and is a short walk to the shops and restaurants in Huskisson. All this makes it very popular, so book well ahead.

Ulladulla Guest House

39 Burrill Street, Ulladulla (1800 700905/4455 1796/www.guesthouse.com.au). **Rates** from $248. **Credit** AmEx, DC, MC, V.

A popular five-star option with great service and ten lovely rooms. It also has self-catering units, a pretty saltwater pool, sauna, hot tub, small gym, art gallery and an excellent French restaurant. A variety of in-room massages is available.

Getting there

By car

Take Princes Highway (Route 1). Allow at least 2hrs to Jervis Bay, 3hrs to Ulladulla and slightly longer to Pebbly Beach.

By train

There are regular trains from Central Station to Wollongong, Kiama, Gerringong, Berry and Bomaderry (for Nowra and Ulladulla), via the South Coast line, changing trains at Dapto. It's 3hrs to Bomaderry; from there a limited coach service operated by Premier Bus Services (13 3410/4423 5233, www.premierms.com.au) continues on through Nowra as far as Ulladulla.

By bus

Interstate coaches travelling the Princes Highway between Sydney and Melbourne stop at many of the towns mentioned above. There are also local bus and coach services along the coast. Contact the local tourist offices for more details.

Tourist information

Booderee National Park Visitor Centre

Jervis Bay Road, Jervis Bay (4443 0977/www. environment.gov.au/parks/booderee). **Open** 9am-4pm daily.

Shoalhaven Tourist Centre

Corner of Princes Highway & Pleasant Way, Nowra (1300 662808/4421 0778/www.shoalhaven.nsw. gov.au/region). **Open** 9am-5pm daily.

Ulladulla Visitors Centre

Princes Highway, Civic Centre, Ulladulla (4455 1269). **Open** 10am-6pm Mon-Fri; 9am-5pm Sat, Sun.

Tourism Kiama

Blowhole Point, Kiama (1300 654262/4232 3322/ www.kiama.com.au). **Open** 9am-5pm daily.

Southern Highlands

The Southern Highlands, known by wealthy 19th-century Sydneysiders as the 'sanatorium of the south' for its cool climes and fresh air, has recently experienced something of a renaissance as a tourist destination. It's easy to see why – just a two-and-a-half-hour train ride from Sydney, the area has well-preserved villages such as Berrima (founded 1831), fading stately homes such as Ranelagh House in Robertson and a range of cosy accommodation, all set in a gently undulating landscape so easy on the eye that it evokes a different country (even before the area was first settled, Governor Macquarie said it reminded him of England).

There's some truth to the local saying that the Southern Highlands are mostly for 'the newly-weds and the nearly-deads', but there is something here for most tastes: the highlands encompass tropical and subtropical rainforest, the second-largest falls in NSW and the edge of Morton National Park.

Of the many pleasant approaches by car, two leading from the main coastal road (Princes Highway) stand out. The first is to take the Illawarra Highway (from Albion Park) through **Macquarie Pass National Park**; the second is to take the tourist drive from just beyond Berry. The route from Berry – rising, bending and finally dropping towards the **Kangaroo Valley** – is often romantically thick with mist, but on even a partly clear day it affords luscious views of the countryside.

Kangaroo Valley Village, despite its iron roofs and sandstone-pillared Hampden Bridge (built in 1897), is a little disappointing, but the walking and camping nearby are excellent, as are canoeing and kayaking on the **Kangaroo River** (contact Kangaroo Valley Tourist Park near the bridge, 1300 559977/4465 1310, www.holidayhaven.com.au/kangaroovalley).

Leaving Kangaroo Valley, the road rises and twists once more before leading to the **Fitzroy Falls**. A short saunter from the impressive **Fitzroy Falls Visitor Centre** (4887 7270, open 9am-5.30pm daily) and you are amid scenery that's as Australian as Paul Hogan. There are five falls in the vicinity, but Fitzroy is the nearest and biggest, plummeting 81 metres (266 feet) into Yarunga Valley. Take any of the walks around the falls and you could encounter 48 species of gum tree, lyre birds and possibly a wombat.

Another way of exploring the top end of underrated **Morton National Park** is to use the town of **Bundanoon** as a base for bushwalking and cycling. Bundanoon, which means 'a place of deep gullies', is as Scottish in flavour as its name sounds. Every year in the week after Easter the town transforms itself into Brigadoon for a highland gathering, featuring traditional games, Scottish dancing and street parades. Bundanoon was also once known as the honeymoon centre of the Southern Highlands – in its heyday it had 51 guesthouses – but these days the bedsprings rarely squeak, as it has largely fallen out of fashion.

Slightly north of the forgettable town of Moss Vale is **Berrima**, considered Australia's finest example of an 1830s village. This is the town the railways forgot, so many of its early buildings remain in pristine condition. A highlight is the 1838 neo-classical **Court House** (corner of Wilshire and Argyle Street, 4877 1505, www.berrimacourthouse.org.au) with its sandstone portico and curved wooden doorways. Don't miss the reconstruction of the 1843 trial of the adulterous Lucretia Dunkley and her lover: particularly good is the judge's sentencing of the pair for the murder of her dull husband. Other historic buildings include **Harper's Mansion** and Australia's oldest continually licensed hotel, the **Surveyor General Inn** (*see below*), both built in 1834.

An unexpected delight on the long road to **Bowral** is **Berkelouw's Book Barn** (Old Hume Highway, 4877 1370, open 9.30am-5pm daily), containing some 200,000 second-hand books. Bowral itself is attractive enough, especially during the spring Tulip Festival, but its biggest claim to fame is as the town that gave Australian cricket the late Donald Bradman. The great man is honoured in the **Bradman Museum** (St Jude Street, 4862 1247, www.bradman.org.au, open 10am-5pm daily, $8.50, $4-$7 reductions, $22 family) on the edge of the lush Bradman Oval, opposite the old Bradman home. If cricket doesn't captivate you, then take a trip up **Mount Gibraltar**, overlooking the surrounding countryside, and the view surely will.

About 60 kilometres (37 miles) west of the town of Mittagong (via part-dirt road), the mysterious and beautiful **Wombeyan Caves** feature a number of unique encrustations and deposits. You can take a guided tour, and there's on-site accommodation and camping: contact the **Wombeyan Caves Visitor Centre** (Wombeyan Caves Road, Taralga, 4843 5976, www.jenolancaves.org.au, open 8.30am-5.30pm daily) for details.

Destined to become the area's most famous village, and all because of a talking pig, is the sleepy hollow of **Robertson**, where the film Babe was shot. Almost the entire cast is on the breakfast menu at **Ranelagh House** (*see below*). On the way back to Sydney, be sure to take the road out of Robertson to the Princes Highway for some spectacular sea views as you twist and turn your way down the hillside.

Where to stay & eat

Briars Country Lodge & Inn
Moss Vale Road, Bowral (4868 3566/www. briars.com.au). **Rates** from $120 midweek; $190 weekend. **Credit** AmEx, DC, MC, V.
A country retreat with 30 garden suites set in beautiful parkland. Adjacent to the lodge is the Georgian Briars Inn (c.1845), which has a true country atmosphere, with cosy bars and bistro food. You can even take in a bit of fly fishing in the hotel area.

Bundanoon Hotel
Erith Street, Bundanoon (4883 6005/www. bundanoonhotel.com.au). **Rates** (per person) $65-$80. **Credit** AmEx, DC, MC, V.
This creaky old hotel boasts a wonderful billiards table and the occasional poetry reading.

Ranelagh House Guesthouse
Illawarra Highway, Robertson (4885 1111/www. ranelagh-house.com.au). **Rates** (per person) from $55 midweek; $70 weekend B&B. **Credit** AmEx, MC, V.
The best place in the area to take a leisurely cream tea. It also offers a 'country-style' lunch and has a good dinner menu.

Surveyor General Inn
Old Hume Highway, Berrima (4877 1226/www. highlandsnsw.com.au/surveyorgeneral). **Rates** from $60 midweek; $80 weekend. **Credit** AmEx, MC, V.
The rooms are simple, with brass beds and a shared bathroom, but the inn oozes historical charm.

Trips Out of Town

Getting there

By car

The inland route (120km/75 miles) via Hume Highway (Route 31) takes just under 2hrs. The coastal route is via Princes Highway (Route 60); then turn inland on Illawarra Highway (Route 48) by Albion Park. It's slightly longer (130km/80 miles) and slightly slower (just over 2hrs).

By train

Trains to the Southern Highlands depart from Sydney's Central Station every day. Most stop at Mittagong, Bowral, Moss Vale and Bundanoon. The journey takes about 2.5hrs.

By bus

Several bus companies serve the Southern Highlands area, among them Priors Scenic Express (1800 816234, 4472 4040) and Greyhound (13 2030, www.greyhound.com.au).

Tourist information

Tourism Southern Highlands

62-70 Main Street, Mittagong (1300 657559/ 4871 2888/www.southern-highlands.com.au). **Open** 9am-5pm Mon-Fri; 9am-4pm Sat, Sun.

Canberra

Canberra, sitting in its own Australian Capital Territory (ACT), was created in 1911 as the compromise choice of federal capital to end the squabbling between arch-rivals Sydney and Melbourne. It's always been dogged by bad press. It's the city that people from other Australian cities love to hate, the New Zealand of intra-Australian jokes ('a waste of a good sheep paddock'), regarded by detractors as a sterile, low-level metropolis full of also-(Canber)rans, a mundane mecca for politicians and bureaucrats. For those Australians who have visited the city, Canberra can also evoke some-less-than favourable memories of being escorted (by the ears if necessary) around endless exhibitions and galleries as a kid, or of getting lost in the car among the city's eccentric roundabouts.

There's some truth to those clichés. Yet Canberra is also loved with a passion by many of its residents, who point to its space, clean air, tranquillity and proximity to unspoilt bushland. There were few trees on the plains around Canberra when white settlers came; hundreds of thousands have been planted since. New householders were given two trees to plant in front of their homes in exchange for not building walls or fences – perhaps a factor in the dreadful bushfires around Christmas 2002, when some 200 houses burned to the ground.

Whether you side with Canberra's detractors or defenders is partly a matter of taste and partly a matter of perception. On a clear day, viewed from **Mount Ainslie**, the **Black Mountain Tower** (Black Mountain Drive, Acton, 1800 806718, 6219 6111) or the basket of a hot-air balloon (try Balloon Aloft, 7 Irving Street, Phillip, 6285 1540, www.canberra balloons.com.au), Canberra can appear stately, elegant and positively Washingtonesque. Back on the ground, the city may seem less disorienting from the saddle of a bicycle. In fact, compared with the murderous streets of Sydney, Canberra is a cyclist's heaven, with relatively flat terrain, plenty of cycle paths, negligible traffic (riding is permitted on pavements, anyway) and most of the sights within easy pedalling distance.

Doing a circuit of the central artificial **Lake Burley Griffin** (a two-hour ride) might even win you over to the vision of 'the city beautiful' that Canberra's architect, Walter Burley Griffin, originally had in mind. The **National Capital Exhibition** (Regatta Point, Commonwealth Park, 6257 1068, www.nationalcapital.gov.au/ visiting, open 9am-5pm daily, free) is on a knoll overlooking the lake. The exhibition provides further insights into Griffin's competition-winning design for Canberra, eloquently drawn by his wife Marion Mahoney. There is also a model of the city, which makes it a good starting point for a tour.

Whatever Canberra's faults, as federal capital it can claim to have many of Australia's most important national monuments, buildings and galleries, the most significant (and visited) being Parliament House, the Australian War Memorial, the National Gallery of Australia and the **National Museum of Australia** (Lawson Crescent, Acton Peninsula, 6208 5000, www.nma.gov.au, 9am-5pm daily, free). The latter, which opened in 2001, is the first official museum dedicated to the nation of Australia. It utilises state-of-the-art technology and hands-on exhibits to take visitors through Aboriginal and Torres Strait Islander cultures and histories, Australian society and its history since 1788, and the interaction of people with the Australian environment. It relies heavily on image and sound rather than actual objects, so might not be everyone's cup of tea.

Opened in 1988, **Parliament House** (6277 5399, www.aph.gov.au, 9am-5pm daily, free) might look like an oversized wigwam from afar – thanks to an 81-metre (265-foot) stainless-steel flagpole – but it's as imposing as it is humble, as human as it is functional. From its position on Capital Hill it dominates Canberra's landscape, yet its turfed roof allows people to stand above their elected representatives.

The foyer, the Great Hall and both chambers (Senate and House of Representatives) are airy and refreshingly bathed in natural light, and there are displays of Australian art and photos. Interesting free guided tours take place every 30 minutes from 9am to 4pm – try to join one early, before the coaches arrive. You can also view the goings-on in both chambers from the public galleries when parliament is in session.

Beneath this comparative baby of a building, but far from eclipsed by it, stands the **Old Parliament House** (King George Terrace, Parks, 6270 8222, www.oldparliamenthouse. gov.au, 9.30am-5pm daily, $2, $1 reductions, $5 family), Australia's seat of democracy from 1927 to 1988. Opposite the main entrance, somewhat incongruous among the manicured lawns and rose gardens, is the **Aboriginal Tent Embassy**, a haphazard collection of tents and wobbly-looking structures hung with flags and a campfire. It was established in 1972 in protest at the government's refusal to recognise Aboriginal land rights: the founders described the site as an embassy because of their sense of alienation from their own land. Since then, the Tent Embassy has been removed, rebuilt, demolished, threatened by fire and relocated – only to move back again. It was recognised by the Australian Heritage Commission in 1995, ensuring its future protection, though that has done nothing to reduce the controversy it provokes among both indigenous and non-indigenous people.

Old Parliament House is also home to the **National Portrait Gallery** (6270 8236, www. portrait.gov.au, 9am-5pm daily; *photo p290*) and the **National Archives of Australia** (Queen Victoria Terrace, Parkes, 6212 3600, www.naa.gov.au). With leather sofas and film noir-ish frosted windows embossed in gold lettering, the latter reeks of the machinations of Australia's political past. Just down the road, and reputedly once linked to Old Parliament House by a white line so that worse-for-wear politicians could find their way there at night, is the **Hotel Kurrajong** (6234 4444, www.hotel kurrajong.com.au). Once the Canberra home of prime ministers and other eminences, it's now a lovely boutique hotel and also home to the Australian International Hotel School.

Located nearby is Australia's foremost art institution, the **National Gallery of Australia** (Parkes Place, Parkes, 6240 6411, www.nga. gov.au, 10am-5pm daily, free), which houses good collections of international, Australian, Aboriginal and Torres Strait Islander art, as well as major exhibitions from overseas that often bypass Sydney. Next door is the innovative **Questacon National Science & Technology Centre** (King Edward Terrace,

Parkes, 6270 2800, www.questacon.edu.au, 9am-5pm daily, $18, $11.50-$13 reductions, $49 family), with hands-on exhibits and a fairly realistic earthquake simulation.

On the other side of the lake stands the **Australian War Memorial** (Treloar Crescent, top of Anzac Parade, Campbell, 6243 4211, www.awm.gov.au, 10am-5pm daily, free). Commemorating as it does the country's 102,000 war dead from 11 international military involvements since 1860, this is a poignant place – especially the Hall of Memory and the Tomb of the Unknown Soldier.

If you've ever wondered how Australia, with its relatively small population, is able to produce so many top-class athletes, a visit to the **Australian Institute of Sport** (Leverrier Crescent, Bruce, 6214 1111, www.ais.org.au) and its Sports Visitor Centre on the city's outskirts will shed some light. It's a university for the country's elite sportspeople, and a tour ($15, $10-$8 reductions), led by one of the sleek and toned resident athletes, will probably leave you guiltily pondering your fat content.

The name Canberra is derived from an Aboriginal word for 'meeting place': local tribes used to gather to feast on bogong moths, which can end up here in their millions after being blown off course (they migrate from the grassy plains further north to high spots along the Great Dividing Range where they hole up for the summer). While the range of Canberra's cuisine has obviously grown since then, it can still seem something of a gastronomic desert after Sydney. However, in the suburb of Manuka, near the Parliamentary Triangle, you'll find the city's café culture alongside a cluster of restaurants and clubs.

The capital rarely gets overcrowded, except during the annual **Celebrate Canberra Festival** (13 2281, www.celebratecanberra.com), held over ten days in March. This colourful event marks the city's founding in 1913 and includes hot-air balloons, exhibitions, theatre, music and dance. There's also **Floriade** (6205 0044, 1300 554114, wwwfloriadeaustralia.com), a big and cheery celebration of all things floral. It usually runs from mid September for a month.

Where to stay & eat

Canberra has one of the highest room-occupancy rates in Australia, so be sure to book well in advance of your intended stay.

Brassey Hotel

Belmore Gardens, Barton (6273 3766/www.brassey. net.au). **Rates** from $125. **Credit** AmEx, DC, MC, V. A historic boutique hotel within walking distance of most attractions.

National Portrait Gallery. *See p289.*

Canberra City YHA

7 Akuna Street, Canberra City (6248 9155/www.
yha.com.au). **Rates** from $25 dorm; $80 double/
twin. **Credit** MC, V.
Opened in 2006, Australia's newest YHA has its own
pub, café, pool, spa and sauna.

Chairman & Yip

108 Bunda Street, Canberra City (6248 7109).
Open 6-10.30pm Mon, Sat; noon-2.30pm, 6-10.30pm
Tue-Fri. **Main courses** $28-$35. **Credit** AmEx, DC,
MC, V.
Popular with political bigwigs, the Chairman serves
modern Asian food, with lots of fish.

Medina Classic Canberra

11 Giles Street, Kingston (6239 8100/www.
medinaapartments.com.au). **Rates** from $149.
Credit AmEx, DC, MC, V.
Just minutes from Parliament House in fashionable
Kingston, the Medina has comfy and very good-
value one-, two- and three-bedroom suites. There's
a heated pool, spa and gym too.

Mezzalira

Melbourne Building, 55 London Circuit, Canberra
City (6230 0025/www.mezzalira.com.au). **Open**
noon-2pm, 6-10pm Mon-Fri; 6-10pm Sat. **Main**
courses $33-$37. **Credit** AmEx, DC, MC, V.
Smart modern Italian food in a converted bank dating from 1921. If you're spoilt for choice, try the tasting menu ($80/$105 with local wines).

Olims Canberra Hotel

Corner of Ainslie & Limestone Avenues, Braddon
(6243 0000/www.olimshotel.com). **Rates** from $115.
Credit AmEx, DC, MC, V.
Set in manicured lawns and just a short walk from
the city, Olims has simple but comfortable enough
rooms, with a couple of pleasant dining options.

Republic

20 Allara Street, Civic (6247 1717). **Open** 7.30am-
4pm Mon-Fri. **Main courses** $13-$23. **Credit**
AmEx, DC, MC, V.
A top-class café with great dining and modern decor.

Rydges Lakeside Canberra

London Circuit, at Edinburgh Street, Canberra City
(9261 4929/www.rydges.com). **Rates** from $140.
Credit AmEx, DC, MC, V.
This is the prime city address at which to stay, next
to Lake Burley Griffin.

Tilley's Devine Café Gallery

Corner of Brigalow & Wattle Streets, Lyneham
(6247 7753/www.tilleys.com.au). **Open** 9am-10pm
Mon-Sat; 9am-5pm Sun. **Main courses** from $7.90.
Credit AmEx, MC, V.
A huge bar and pavement café, and a major venue
for touring music acts – it stays open later on
Fridays and Saturdays if there's a band playing.

Getting there

By air

Canberra has a small domestic airport about 15mins
drive from the city centre. Both Qantas (13 1313,
www.qantas.com.au) and Virgin Blue (13 6789,
www.virginblue.com.au) fly there several times
a day; the trip from Sydney takes 30-40mins.

By car

Canberra is 288km (179 miles) south of Sydney. Take
M5 motorway connecting with the Hume Highway
(Route 31); turn off to Canberra on Federal Highway
beyond Goulburn. Journey time: up to 3.5hrs.

By train

CountryLink's very handy Xplorer train service
(13 2232, www.countrylink.info) runs from Central
Station to Canberra and back again three times
a day. The trip takes just over 4hrs.

By bus

Most big firms run services to Canberra; try
Firefly Express (1300 730740/03-8318 0318,
www.fireflyexpress.com.au) or Greyhound
(13 2030, www.greyhound.com.au).

Tourist information

Canberra Visitor Centre

330 Northbourne Avenue, Dickson (1300 554114/
6205 0044/accommodation 1300 733 228/
www.canberratourism.com.au). **Open** 9am-5pm
Mon-Fri; 9am-4pm Sat, Sun.

Directory

Features

Bridge Climb. *See p61*.

Directory

Getting Around

By air

Sydney Airport (9667 9111, www.sydneyairport.com.au) is on the northern shoreline of Botany Bay, nine kilometres (six miles) south-east of the city centre. Opened in 1920, it's one of the oldest continuously operating airports in the world. Since a swanky upgrade for the 2000 Olympics and another upgrade of the domestic terminal in 2005, it's now among the world's best – and quite proud of it.

There are three terminals: **T1** is for all international flights on all airlines and for QF (Qantas) flights 001-399; **T2** is a domestic terminal for Virgin Blue, Regional Express, Jetstar, OzJet, Aeropelican, Air Link, Big Sky Express and QF flights 1600 and above; **T3** is the Qantas terminal for QF domestic flights 400-1599.

The international terminal is a great place to shop, with more than 120 outlets ranging from ordinary duty-free stores and international designer showcases to Aussie gear such as Done Art & Design, Between the Flags, Swim by Beach Culture and RM Williams, plus souvenir outlets selling Aboriginal artefacts and kitsch mementos.

GETTING TO AND FROM THE AIRPORT

Built for the Olympics, the **Airport Link** rail service (131 500, www. airportlink.com.au) between Sydney Airport and Central Station runs an efficient service every ten minutes from both international and domestic terminals. The line is a spur of the green CityRail line, so serves all the main inner-city interchanges. It takes

ten minutes to reach Central Station from the domestic terminals and 13 minutes from the international one. Trains run from 5.19am to 11.45pm Monday to Friday and from 5.06am to 11.43am Saturday and Sunday. A single fare from the international terminal to Central Station costs $13.80; $9.40 reductions daily. It's $13.40; $9.20 reductions, daily from the domestic terminals.

Bus-wise, the KST Sydney Airporter (9666 9988, www.kst. com.au) shuttle runs a door-to-door service to all hotels, major apartment blocks and backpacker joints in the city, Darling Harbour and Kings Cross. A single costs $12-$13. Look for the white buses with a blue and red logo outside 'The Meeting Point' outside T1 and at 'The Horseshoe' outside both T2 and T3. Book three hours in advance for hotel pick-ups and give yourself plenty of time to get to the airport, as the shuttle will take twice as long as a taxi.

Each terminal has its own sheltered taxi rank, with supervisors in peak hours to ensure a smooth and hassle-free flow of taxis. You never have to wait for long, even in the vast sheep-pen-style queuing system of the international terminal, where 190 vehicles are on call. If you have any special needs – wheelchair access, child seats or an extra-large vehicle – go to the front of the queue and tell the supervisor, who will call you a specially fitted taxi. It takes about 25 minutes to get into the city, depending on the traffic and time of day, and costs around $35.

The main car rental companies all have desks at the airport.

AIRLINES: INTERNATIONAL

Around 40 airlines operate regular flights into Sydney, including:
Air Canada 1300 655767/ www.aircanada.com
Air New Zealand 13 2476/ www.airnewzealand.com.au
British Airways 1300 767177/ www.britishairways.com
Cathay Pacific 13 1747/ www.cathaypacific.com
Emirates 1300 303777/ www.emirates.com
Garuda Indonesia 1300 365330/ www.garuda-indonesia.com
JAL (Japan Airlines) 9272 1111/ www.jal.co.jp

Malaysia Airlines 13 2627/ www.malaysiaairlines.com
Qantas 13 1313/ www.qantas.com.au
Singapore Airlines 13 1011/ www.singaporeair.com
Thai Airways 1300 651960/ www.thaiair.com
United Airlines 13 1777/ www.united.com
Virgin Atlantic 1300 727340/ www.virgin-atlantic.com

AIRLINES: DOMESTIC
Aeropelican 13 1313/ www.aeropelican.com.au
Jetstar 13 1538/ www.jetstar.com
OzJet 1300 737000/ www.ozjet.com.au
Qantas 13 1313/ www.qantas.com.au
Regional Express (Rex) 13 1713/ www.regionalexpress.com.au
Virgin Blue 13 6789/ www.virginblue.com.au

By bus

Lots of bus companies operate throughout Australia. Handily, they all use the **Sydney Coach Terminal** located in Central Station as their main pick-up and drop-off point. National carrier **Greyhound** (1300 473946, from abroad +61 2 9212 1500, www.greyhound. com.au), transports more than a million passengers a year.

By rail

The State Rail Authority's CountryLink (reservations 13 2232, www.countrylink.info) operates out of Central Station with extensive user-friendly services to all main NSW and interstate destinations.

By sea

International cruise liners, including the QE2, dock at the Overseas International

Passenger Terminal located on the west side of Circular Quay, or in Darling Harbour.

Public transport

To get around Sydney you'll probably use a combination of trains, ferries, buses and maybe the 'airborne' Monorail or the chic LightRail streetcars. As well as the Sydney Buses network (run by the State Transit Authority, STA), there are CityRail trains and Sydney Ferries. The other transport services are privately run and therefore generally more expensive. The centre of Sydney is so small that if you're in a large group, it's often cheaper to pool for a taxi.

Transport Infoline

13 1500/www.131500.info. **Phone enquiries** 6am-10pm daily.
A great, consumer-friendly phone line and website offering timetable, ticket and fare information for STA buses, Sydney Ferries and CityRail, plus timetabling (only) for cross-city private bus services.

Fares & tickets

There are several combination travel passes covering the government-run transit system, and they're worth buying if you plan extensive use of public transport.

TravelPass

Unlimited seven-day, quarterly or yearly travel throughout the zones for which it has been issued, on buses, trains and ferries. These passes are aimed at commuters, but can be useful if you're in Sydney for any length of time. To find the right TravelPass for you, check the STA website or ask at any train station or bus information kiosk (where you can also buy them). Newsagents displaying a Sydney Buses Ticket Stop sign, and ticket offices or vending machines at Circular Quay and Manly also sell passes.
Passes are also available for a combination of buses and ferries, or for travel solely by bus, ferry or train. TravelPasses cannot be used on the STA premium Sydney Explorer and Bondi Explorer bus services, Sydney Ferry harbour cruises, JetCats or private buses.

SydneyPass

This one is specifically aimed at tourists. Unlimited travel on selected CityRail trains, buses (including premium services such as the Explorer buses) and ferries (including premium services such as JetCats and cruises). Valid for any three, five or seven days within an eight-day period. A three-day pass costs $110 ($55 reductions, $275 family); for a five-day pass it's $145 ($70 reductions, $360 family); and $165 ($80 reductions, $410 family) for a seven-day pass.

DayTripper

Unlimited one-day travel on buses, ferries and CityRail trains until 4am – but not on the Explorer buses or JetCats. It costs $16 ($8 reductions) and is available on board buses, from STA offices and at Sydney Ferries ticket offices.

BusTripper

A pass offering unlimited all-day travel on buses only – except for the premium Explorer bus services. It costs $12.10 ($6 under-16s).

Buses

Buses are slow but fairly frequent, and offer a better way of seeing the city than the CityRail trains, which operate underground within the centre. Buses are the only option for transport to popular areas such as Bondi Beach, Coogee and the northern beaches (beyond Manly), which aren't served by either train or ferry. Sydney is divided into eight zones; the city centre is zone 1. The minimum adult fare is $1.80 (90c reductions), which covers two zones.

The bus driver will not stop unless you hold out your arm to request a ride. Pay the driver (avoid big notes) or validate your travel pass in the machine at the door.

The bus route numbers give you an idea of where they go. Buses **131-193** service Manly and the northern beaches; **200-296** the lower north shore (including Taronga Zoo) and the northern suburbs; **300-400** the eastern suburbs (including Bondi, Paddington, Darlinghurst and Sydney

Airport); **401-500** the inner south and inner west suburbs, including Balmain, Leichhardt, Newtown and Homebush; and **501-629** the north-west including Parramatta and Chatswood. In general, the 100s and 200s start near Wynyard Station and the 300s-600s can be found around Circular Quay.

Bus numbers starting with an 'X' are express services, which travel between the suburbs and major centres on the way into the city. Stops are marked 'Express'. Limited-stop or 'L' services operate on some of the longer routes to provide faster trips to and from the city (mainly for commuters).

Buses in the central and inner suburbs run pretty much all night, but services from central Sydney to the northern beaches stop around midnight. **Nightrider** buses operate hourly services to outer suburban train stations after the trains have stopped running until 5am.

STA also runs the tourist-oriented **Sydney Explorer** and **Bondi Explorer** bus services. For full details of both these, and private bus tours, *see p59.*

CityRail

CityRail (www.cityrail.info) is the passenger rail service covering the greater Sydney region (and the sister company to CountryLink, covering country and long-distance routes within NSW). The sleek, double-decker silver trains run underground on the central **City Circle** loop – Central, Town Hall, Wynyard, Circular Quay, St James and Museum stations – and overground to the suburbs (both Central and Town Hall stations provide connections to all the suburban lines). Although certainly quicker than the bus, trains are not as frequent as many would like and waits of 15 minutes, even in peak time, are not uncommon. For one of the best rides in Sydney, take the train from the city to the north shore – it passes over the Harbour Bridge and the views are spectacular.

CityRail tickets can be bought at ticket offices or vending machines at rail stations. Expect huge queues in rush hour. A single ticket anywhere on the City Circle costs $2.60 ($1.30 reductions); an off-peak return costs $3.60 ($2.60 under-16s).

For more details of CityRail services, call the **Transport Infoline** (*see p293*) or visit www.cityrail.info. For a map of the CityRail city network, *see p336*.

Ferries

No trip to Sydney would be complete without clambering aboard one of the picture-postcard green-and-yellow ferries that ply the harbour and are used daily by hundreds of commuters. All ferries depart from Circular Quay ferry terminal, where **Sydney Ferries** operates from wharves 2 to 5. These stately vessels are a great way to explore the harbour: there's plenty of room to take pictures from the outdoor decks or just to sit in the sun and enjoy the ride. JetCats – sleek, fast catamarans – operate a service to Manly, taking 15 minutes, as opposed to 30 minutes on an ordinary ferry.

Ticket prices vary, but a single from Circular Quay to destinations within the Inner Harbour costs $5.20 ($2.60 reductions). A single JetCat fare is $8.20. If you plan to use the ferries a lot, the FerryTen pass covers ten rides within the Inner Harbour and costs $33.50 ($16.70 reductions); and $48.10 ($24 reductions) to Manly (by ferry only, not the JetCat). A JetCatTen costs $67.80.

Tickets are sold at ticket offices and vending machines at Circular Quay and Manly. Tickets for Inner Harbour services can also be purchased from on-board cashiers. For a map of the ferry system, *see p335*. For **sightseeing cruises**, *see p60*.

Sydney Ferries Information Centre
Opposite Wharf 4, Circular Quay (13 1500/www.sydneyferries.info). CityRail/ferry Circular Quay. **Open** 6.45am-6.15pm Mon-Sat; 7.15am-6.15pm Sun. **Map** p327 F4.

Metro LightRail

In 1997 Sydney welcomed back its streetcars. Trams were abolished in the early '60s, but the privately run Metro LightRail, operated by Veolia Transport Sydney (which is also in charge of the Metro Monorail), now provides a slick 14-station service from Central Station via Darling Harbour, Pyrmont and Star City casino to the inner west. It's useful for visiting Darling Harbour, Paddy's Market, Sydney Fish Market, Glebe and the Powerhouse Museum.

Trams operate 24 hours a day, seven days a week, between Central and Star City stations, and from 6am to 11pm Monday to Thursday and Sunday, 6am to midnight Friday and Saturday, from Central all the way out to Lilyfield in the west. Trams run about every ten to 15 minutes from 6am to 11pm, and every 30 minutes outside these hours. The line is divided into two zones. Single tickets for zone 1 cost $3.20 ($2 reductions), and tickets for both zones cost $4.20 ($3.20 reductions). A Day Pass offers unlimited trips for $9 ($6.50 reductions). Tickets are available from Central Station or on board the train.

For more info, call 8584 5288 or visit www.metro lightrail.com.au.

Metro Monorail

Sydneysiders are not great fans of the noisy aerial monorail that runs anti-clockwise around the CBD at first-floor office level, but it's often the first thing tourists notice and does provide a fun, novelty ride between Darling Harbour, Chinatown and the city centre. It runs every three to five minutes, 7am to 10pm Monday to Thursday, 7am to midnight Friday and Saturday, 8am to 10pm Sunday.

The seven-station loop costs $4.80 (free under-5s) whether you go one stop or all the way. A Supervoucher Day Pass ($9.50) offers a full day of unlimited travel, plus some discounts on museum admissions. Tickets can be bought at station ticket offices or vending machines.

For more details, call 8584 5288 or visit www. metromonorail.com.au.

It's quite easy to flag down a taxi in Sydney and there are many taxi ranks in the city centre, including ones at Central, Wynyard and Circular Quay. Staff in a restaurant or bar will also call a taxi for you. A yellow light indicates the cab is free, and it's common to travel in the front passenger seat alongside the driver. Drivers will often ask which of two routes you want to follow, or if you mind if they take a longer route to avoid traffic. But there are swags who don't know where they're going and will stop to check the map; if this happens, make sure they turn off the meter. Tipping is not expected, but passengers sometimes round up the bill.

The standard fare is $1.79 per kilometre from 6am to 10pm (add an extra $1.20 per km from 10pm to 6am), plus a $3 hiring fee and, if relevant, a $1.60 telephone booking fee. If a cabby takes you across the Bridge, the $3 toll will be added to the fare, even if you travelled via the toll-free northbound route.

Taxi companies

Legion Cabs 13 1451/ www.legioncabs.com.au
Premier Cabs 13 1017/ www.premiercabs.com.au
RSL Cabs 9581 1111
St George Cabs 13 2166/ www.stgeorgecabs.com.au
Silver Service Taxis 13 3100/ www.silverservice.com.au Sydney's popular luxury taxi service; amazingly, the same price as a regular taxi, but often hard to book.
Taxis Combined Services 13 3300/www.taxiscombined.com.au
Zero200 Wheelchair Accessible Taxis Service 8332 0200/ www.zero200.com.au

Water taxis

Great fun, but expensive. The cost usually depends on the time of day and the number of passengers, but the fare for two from Circular Quay to Doyles fish restaurant at Watsons Bay, which takes ten to 12 minutes, is around $60. The outfits below accept all major credit cards, and can be chartered for harbour cruises.

Beach Hopper Water Taxis

0412 400990/1300 306676/www.watertaxi.net.au. If you want to be dropped off at a beach – literally on to the sand – call Sydney's only beach-landing water taxi service. It also operates a summer 'Beach Safari' service: for $35 per person per day, you can hop on and off at any number of harbour beaches on its run.

Water Taxis Combined

9555 8888/www.watertaxis.com.au. This company can pick you up from almost any wharf, jetty or pontoon provided there is enough water depth, and, in the case of private property, there is permission from the owner. The limousine taxis take up to 20 passengers.

Driving

Driving in Sydney can be hair-raising, not so much because of congestion (Sydneysiders may complain, but it's not at all bad for a major city), but primarily because of the fast and furious attitude of locals.

Under Australian law, most visitors can drive for as long as they like on their domestic driving licence without the need for any additional authorisation. A resident must apply for an Australian driving licence after three months, which involves a written test. You must always carry your driving licence and your passport when in charge of a vehicle; if the licence is not in English, you need to take an English translation as well as the original licence.

Driving is on the left. The general speed limit in cities and towns is 60kph (38mph), but many local and suburban roads have a 50kph (30mph) limit. The maximum speed on highways is 100kph (60mph), and 110kph (70mph) on motorways and freeways. Speed cameras are numerous and there are heavy penalties for speeding. The legal blood alcohol limit is 0.05 per cent for experienced drivers, zero for provisional or learner drivers. Seat belts are mandatory and baby capsules or child seats must be used for all children.

Fuel stations

Petrol stations are fairly plentiful, and easy to find on main roads, although you won't find so many in central Sydney. At the time of writing, the cost of petrol (regular unleaded) was $1.40 per litre.

Parking

In central Sydney parking is a pain and not recommended. In some suburbs, such as tree-lined Paddington, the quality of the road surface is poor, and narrow one-way streets with parking on both sides compound the problem. Note that you must park in the same direction as the traffic on your side of the road.

Rates at city-centre car parks range from $16 to $23 for one hour, with $20 to $62 the day rate. 'Early Bird' special rates often apply if you park before 9am and leave after 3.30pm. Look under 'Parking Stations' in the *Yellow Pages* for more car parks.

Secure Parking

60 Elizabeth Street, CBD (9233 2445/www.secureparking.com.au). **Open** 7am-10.30pm Mon-Thur; 7am-midnight Fri; 8am-midnight Sat; 8.30am-6pm Sun. Credit AmEx, DC, MC, V. **Map** p327 F6. **Other locations** 2 Market Street, CBD (9283 1383; 1 Martin Place, entrance on Pitt Street, CBD (9231 4933).

Wilson Parking – Cinema Centre

521 Kent Street, between Bathurst & Liverpool Streets, CBD (9264 5867/www.wilsonparking.com.au). **Open** 24hrs daily. **Credit** AmEx, DC, MC, V. **Map** p329 E7. **Other locations** CitiGroup Centre, 2 Park Street, CBD (9261 4710); St Martin's Tower, entrance on Clarence Street, CBD (9261 5568).

Tolls

The toll for the Harbour Bridge and Tunnel is currently $3 for cars heading south (free for northbound cars). The toll for the 'eastern distributor' is $4.50 for northbound cars travelling into the city, free for those heading out or south. The Cross-City Tunnel (www.crosscity.com.au) running west to east opened in 2005 to ease congestion in the CBD, but has proved much less popular than expected because of the toll fees – considered extortionate for a trip of just over two kilometres. The toll fee depends on the size of your vehicle, most pay $3.50 for the Eastbound Tunnel (Darling Harbour to Eastern Distributor Exit or Rushcutters Bay), $3.50 for the Westbound Tunnel (Rushcutters Bay to Darling Harbour) and $1.60 for Sir John Young Crescent Exit (from the

Directory

East). For vehicles with a height exceeding 2.8m, or length exceeding 12.5m, it's $7 (Eastbound and Westbound) and $3.20 for Sir John Young Crescent.

Vehicle hire

Most of the major car rental firms are situated on William Street in Kings Cross, and also have outlets at Sydney Airport. Rates vary almost hourly and all offer discounted deals. What's given below is the rate for the cheapest hire car available for a one-day period quoted on a given day. Rates drop if the car is hired for a longer period. More outfits are listed in the *Yellow Pages* under 'Car &/or Minibus Rental'. Those offering ultra-cheap deals should be approached with caution, though: always read the small print before you sign.

You will need to show a current driver's licence and probably your passport. Credit cards are the preferred method of payment and are nearly always asked for to cover insurance costs, even if you do eventually pay by cash or travellers' cheque. A few firms will rent to 18-year-olds, but usually you have to be over 21 and hold a full driving licence to rent a car in NSW. If you're under 25, you'll probably have to pay an extra daily surcharge, and insurance excesses will be higher.

Avis
200 William Street, at Dowling Street, Kings Cross (9357 2000/ www.avis.com.au). CityRail Kings Cross. **Open** 7.30am-6pm Mon-Thur, Sat, Sun; 7.30am-7pm Fri. **Rates** (unlimited km) from $48/day. **Credit** AmEx, DC, MC, V. **Map** p329 H7.
Other locations Central Reservations (13 6333/9353 9000); Sydney Airport (8374 2847).

Budget
93 William Street, at Crown Street, Kings Cross (8255 9600/www. budget.com.au). CityRail Kings Cross. **Open** 7.30am-6pm daily. **Rates**

(unlimited km) from $38/day. **Credit** AmEx, DC, MC, V. **Map** p329 G7.
Other locations Central Reservations (1300 362 848/9353 9399); Sydney Airport (9207 9165).

Hertz
Corner of William & Riley Streets, Kings Cross (9360 6621/www.hertz. com.au). CityRail Kings Cross. **Open** 7.30am-6pm daily. **Rates** (unlimited km) from $39/day. **Credit** AmEx, DC, MC, V. **Map** p329 G8.
Other locations Central Reservations (13 3039); Sydney Airport (9669 2444).

Red Spot
Hyde Park Plaza, 38 College Street, at Oxford Street, Sydney (1300 668810/9356 8333/www.redspot rentals.com.au). CityRail Museum. **Open** 8am-5pm Mon-Thur; 8am-6pm Fri; 8am-noon Sat, Sun. **Rates** (unlimited) $35/day. **Credit** AmEx, DC, MC, V. **Map** p329 G8.
Other locations Sydney Airport (9352 7466/9317 2233).

Thrifty
75 William Street, at Riley Street, Kings Cross (8374 6177/www.thrifty. com.au). CityRail Kings Cross. **Open** 7.30am-6pm daily. **Rates** (unlimited km) from $40.50/day. **Credit** AmEx, DC, MC, V. **Map** p329 G7.
Other locations Central Reservations (1300 367227); Sydney Airport (1300 367227).

Cycling

Sydney's steep hills, narrow streets and chaotic CBD make cycling a challenge, even for the most experienced of cycle couriers. However, Centennial Park and Manly both offer safe cycle tracks. Helmets are compulsory for all cyclists, including children carried as passengers. During the day a bicycle must have at least one working brake and a bell or horn. At night, you'll need a white light at the front and a red light at the rear, plus a red rear reflector. There are lots of other road rules, as cycles are considered to be vehicles: for full details, see www.rta.nsw. gov.au. You may get fined if you break the rules.

Cycle nuts are vocal in Sydney and are being heeded by the state-sponsored Bike Plan 2010, which promises the

creation of a series of arterial cycle networks across NSW, resulting in 200 kilometres (125 miles) of bikeways being constructed across the state each year until 2010. The RTA provides 'Cycleways' maps for the Sydney metropolitan area. View them online at www. rta.nsw.gov.au or phone 1800 060607 to get hard copies.

Centennial Park Cycles
50 Clovelly Road, between Avoca & Earls Streets, Randwick (9398 5027/ www.cyclehire.com.au). Bus 339, X39. **Open** 8.30am-5.30pm daily. **Rates** mountain bikes from $12/hr; children's bikes from $10/hr. **Credit** AmEx, MC, V. **Map** p333 N14.
Family-run, Sydney's largest cycle and in-line skate hire shop has been in operation for more than 30 years. They have everything here, from tandems to tricycles, pedal cars and scooters. They also provide a bicycle pick-up and delivery service. Credit card details and photo ID are required to hire equipment.

Manly Cycle Centre
36 Pittwater Road, at Denison Street, Manly (9977 1189). Ferry Manly. **Open** 9am-6pm Mon-Sat; 10am-5pm Sun. **Rates** $15/hr; $35/day. **Credit** AmEx, MC, V. **Map** p334.
Located a block from Manly Beach, this full-service bike shop hires out front-suspension mountain bikes, and even jogging pushchairs for ultra-fit mums and dads. Credit card details and photo ID are necessary.

Walking

Walking is often the most practical – and enjoyable – way of getting around central areas, though there can be long waits for pedestrian lights. There are a number of marked scenic walks that you can do: ask at the Sydney Visitor Centre (*see p307*) for details. Some harbour and beachside walks are detailed in the Sightseeing chapters. For central Sydney street maps, *see p326*. To buy street maps, travel guides and national park walking guides, visit Map World (*see p194*) or Dymocks (*see p193*) or most newsagents stock Sydney street guides and travel guides.

Resources A-Z

Addresses

Addresses begin with the apartment or unit number, if any, followed by the street number, followed by the street name. For example, Apartment 5, 50 Sun Street would be written as 5/50 Sun Street. This is followed by the locality and then by the state or territory and postcode – for instance, Paddington, NSW 2021. Postcodes cover a much larger area than their UK equivalents. Many residents and businesses have post office box numbers instead of personalised addresses.

Age restrictions

It is legal to buy and consume alcohol at 18. A learner's driving licence can be applied for at 16. A driving test can be taken at age 17, and if passed, drivers must then show a provisional 'P' plate (red P for one year, green P for two years), before being eligible for a full driving licence. Both gays and heterosexuals can have sex at 16 in NSW (though be warned, laws vary from state to state). It is illegal to sell cigarettes to anyone under 18, but there is no legal minimum age for smoking.

Business

Conventions & conferences

Sydney Convention & Exhibition Centre
Darling Harbour (9282 5000/ www.scec.com.au). Ferry Darling Harbour/Monorail/LightRail Convention. **Map** p328 D7.
This integrated convention and exhibition centre has 30 meeting rooms and six exhibition halls, plus two business centres, inhouse catering and audio-visual services, 24-hour security and parking for more than 900 cars.

Couriers & shippers

Australia Post (13 1318, www.auspost.com.au) has national and international courier services: **Messenger Post Courier** is the national service, while **Express Courier International (ECI)** dispatches to more than 180 countries. Other services you could try include **Allied Express** (13 1373, www.alliedexpress.com.au) and **DHL Worldwide Express** (13 1406, www.dhl.com.au).

Office hire & business services

The multinational **FedEx Kinko's** chain (www.kinkos.net.au) has several branches around Sydney, some of which are open round the clock for internet access, self-service computers, photocopying and printing. The company also offers commercial shipping.

Servcorp
Level 17, BNP Centre, 60 Castlereagh Street, between King Street & Martin Place, CBD (9231 7500/www.servcorp. com.au). CityRail Martin Place. **Open** 8.30am-5.30pm Mon-Fri. **Credit** AmEx, DC, MC, V. **Map** p327 F6.
Servcorp offers office space in CBD and North Sydney for one- to 15-person companies with full business services (minimum lease one month) – and it claims to be cheaper than a secretary. Geared to foreign clients, with a multilingual support team. It also provides 'virtual' receptionists and business addresses.

Secretarial services

AW Secretarial Services
Suite 3, Level 5, 32 York Street, between King & Market Streets, CBD (9262 6812). CityRail Town Hall. **Open** 8.30am-5pm Mon-Fri. **Credit** MC, V. **Map** p327 E6.
For word processing, CVs and spreadsheets.

Translators & interpreters

Commercial Translation Centre
Level 20, 99 Walker Street, North Sydney (9954 4376/www.ctc4.com). CityRail North Sydney. **Open** 9am-5pm Mon-Fri. **Credit** MC, V.
The worldwide CTC has 80 linguistic staff with languages that include Japanese, Mandarin, Korean, Thai, Malay, French, German, Spanish, Dutch and Swedish.

Useful organisations

Australian Stock Exchange
20 Bridge Street, CBD (13 1279/ 9338 0000/www.asx.com.au). CityRail Wynyard or Circular Quay. **Open** 10am-4.30pm Mon-Fri. **Map** p327 F4.

Australian Taxation Office
100 Market Street, CBD (13 2861/ www.ato.gov.au). CityRail St James. **Open** 8.30am-4.45pm Mon-Fri. **Map** p327 F6.

State Chamber of Commerce
Level 12, 83 Clarence Street, CBD (1300 137 153/www.the chamber.com.au). CityRail Wynyard. **Open** 9am-5pm Mon-Fri. **Map** p327 E6.

Consumer

The excellent and practical website of the **NSW Office of Fair Trading** (*see p298*) offers advice for consumers on how to avoid 'shady characters, scams and rip-offs' and for businesses on how to do the right thing by their customers. The excellent **Traveller Consumer Helpline** (1300 552001) provides a rapid response (including access to translators) for travellers who experience unfair employment schemes, problems with accommodation or car rental, faulty goods or overcharging.

NSW Office of Fair Trading

1 Fitzwilliam Street, Parramatta (13 3220/www.fairtrading.nsw.gov.au). Ferry/CityRail Parramatta. **Open** 8.30am-5pm Mon-Fri.

Customs

Before landing on Australian soil you will be given an immigration form to fill out, as well as customs and agriculture declaration forms. You will pass through either the Green (nothing to declare) channel or the Red (something to declare) channel. Your baggage may be examined by Customs, regardless of which channel you use.

Anyone aged 18 years or over can bring in $900 worth of duty-free goods ($450 for under-18s), 2.25 litres of alcohol and 250 cigarettes or 250 grams of other tobacco products. You must declare amounts of $10,000 or more. Visitors can bring items such as computers into Australia duty-free, provided Customs is satisfied that these items are intended to be taken away again on departure.

UK Customs & Excise (www.hmce.gov.uk) allows travellers aged 18 and over returning from outside the EU to bring home £145 worth of gifts and goods, 200 cigarettes or 250 grams of tobacco, one litre of spirits or two litres of fortified wine, 60ml perfume and 250ml toilet water. USCustoms (www.customs.ustreas.gov) allows Americans to return from trips to Australia with goods valued up to US$800.

Quarantine

You must declare all food, plant cuttings, seeds, nuts or anything made from wood, plant or animal material that you bring into Australia. This includes many souvenirs and airline food. If you don't, you could face an on-the-spot fine of $220, or prosecution and fines of $60,000. Sniffer dogs will hunt out the tiniest morsel as they roam the airport with their handlers.

Quarantine officers use high-tech X-ray machines to check your luggage. Quarantine bins are provided at the airport for you to ditch any food and plants you may have about you before you reach immigration. Check the website of the **Australian Quarantine & Inspection Service** (www.daffa.gov.au) for details.

Australia also has quite strict laws prohibiting and restricting the export of native animals and plants, and items deemed 'moveable cultural heritage'. These include birds and their eggs, fish, reptiles, insects, plants, seeds, fossils and rock art. Products made from protected wildlife, such as hard corals and giant clam shells, are not allowed to be taken out of the country. If in doubt, check with the **Department of the Environment & Heritage** (6274 1111, www.deh.gov.au).

If you need to carry medicine for yourself in or out of the country, it is advisable to have a prescription or doctor's letter. Penalties for carrying illicit drugs in Australia are severe and could result in a jail term. Check the **Customs National Information Line** (1300 363263, www.customs.gov.au).

Disabled

It was not until 1992 that building regulations required that provisions be made for disabled people, so some older venues do not have disabled access. Restaurants tend to fare better, as most of them have ramps.

New transport standards will require that people with disabilities have access to most public transport within 20 years. For the time being, many Sydney streets are far from wheelchair-friendly. Constant construction upheavals and the city's hills aside, the standard of pavement surfaces in the inner suburbs leaves a lot to be desired. Poor street lighting compounds the problem.

For more information, check out the excellent website of the **Disability Information Resource** (www.accessibility.com.au), which provides details on wheelchair access throughout the city, from music venues and restaurants to museums and public toilets. Or contact the following:

Information on Disability & Education Awareness Services (IDEAS)

Suite 208, 35 Buckingham Street, Surry Hills (1800 029904/9657 1796/www.ideas.org.au). **Open** 8.30am-4.30pm Mon-Fri. **Map** 329 F10.
Provides information and referral on all disabilities for the whole of NSW and has a great, up-to-date database on eastern suburbs services.

Spinal Cord Injuries Australia

9661 8855/www.scia.org.au. This organisation provides consumer-based support and rehabilitation services to help people with physical disabilities participate fully in society. Phone/internet enquiries only.

State Library of NSW Disability Information

State Library of NSW, corner of Macquarie Street & Cahill Expressway, CBD (9273 1583/ www.sl.nsw.gov.au/access). **Open** Phone enquiries 9am-5pm Mon-Fri. **Map** p327 G5.
Helpful info line that offers a great starting point for disabled visitors.

Drugs

Cannabis and harder drugs are illegal in Australia, but that hasn't prevented a huge drug culture – and problem – from developing. High-volume imports from Asia ensure cheap and dangerously pure strains of heroin on the streets, while cannabis, ecstasy, cocaine and ice (crystal meth) are the chosen poisons of the city's youth.

Kings Cross is the epicentre of drug dealing in Sydney and has been the target of a clean-up campaign by the local government. The future of the 'shooting gallery' safe injection room in the area hangs in the balance, as nay-sayers and project supporters argue over its success rates. Still, come nightfall it's not uncommon for addicts to shoot up on the streets, in the parks and even on beaches. Needle disposal bins are everywhere. *See also p301* **Helplines**.

Electricity

The Australian domestic electricity supply is 230-240V, 50Hz AC. UK appliances work with just a basic plug adaptor, but US 110V appliances will need a more elaborate form of transformer as well.

Embassies & consulates

Canada
Level 5, Quay West Building, 111 Harrington Street, at Essex Street, CBD (9364 3000/visa information 9364 3050/www.canada.org.au). CityRail/ferry Circular Quay. **Open** 8.30am-4.30pm Mon-Fri. **Map** p327 E4.

Ireland
Level 26, 1 Market Street, CBD (9264 9635/www.dfa.ie). CityRail Town Hall. **Open** 10am-1pm, 2.30-4pm Mon-Fri. **Map** p327 E6.

New Zealand
Level 10, 55 Hunter Street, at Castlereagh Street, CBD (8256 2000/pm). CityRail Martin Place or Wynyard. **Open** 9am-12.30pm, 1.30-5pm Mon-Fri. **Map** p327 F5.

South Africa
Rhodes Place, State Circle, Canberra (6272 7300/www.sahc.org.au). **Open** 8.30am-1pm, 1.45pm-5pm Mon-Fri.

United Kingdom
Level 16, The Gateway, 1 Macquarie Place, at Bridge Street, CBD (9247 7521/www.britaus.net). CityRail/ferry Circular Quay. **Open** *Phone* 9am-5pm Mon-Fri. *Counter* 10am-12.30pm, 1.30pm-4pm Mon-Fri. **Map** p327 F4.

USA
Level 59, MLC Centre 19-29 Martin Place, CBD (9373 9200/http://sydney.usconsulate.gov/sydney). CityRail Martin Place. **Open** *Phone* 8am-5pm Mon-Fri. *Counter* 8am-11.30am Mon-Fri. **Map** p327 F5.

Emergencies

For the fire brigade, police or ambulance, dial **000**. It's a free call from any phone.

For hospitals, *see below* **Health**. For other emergency numbers, *see p301* **Helplines**. You can contact the **Poisons Information Centre** (open 24 hours daily) at 13 1126.

Gay & lesbian

The quickest way to find gay-related information is via weekly newspapers *Sydney Star Observer* (www.ssonet.com.au), the boysy *SX* (www.evolution publishing.com.au/sxnews), or, for women, the excellent monthly mag *Lesbians on the Loose* (www.lotl.com). All are available free from newsagents, clubs and bars all over town.

Help & information

For information on STDs, HIV & AIDS, *see p300*.

Gay & Lesbian Counselling Service of NSW
8594 9596. **Open** 5.30pm-10.30pm daily.
Information and phone counselling.

Gay & Lesbian Tourism Australia
0414 446401/ www.galta.com.au.
A non-profit organisation dedicated to the welfare of gay and lesbian travellers in Australia.

Health

The universal government healthcare system, Medicare Australia, has a reciprocal agreement with Finland, Italy, Malta, the Netherlands, New Zealand, Norway, Republic of Ireland, Sweden and the UK, entitling residents of those countries to get necessary medical and hospital treatment for free. This agreement does not cover all eventualities (for example, ambulance fees or dental costs), and only applies to public hospitals and casualty departments.

If you have travel insurance, check the small print to see whether you need to register with Medicare before making a claim; if not, or if you don't have insurance, you can claim a Medicare rebate by taking your passport and visa, together with the medical bill, to any Medicare centre.

For more information, phone or write to the information service below. *See also p300* **Doctors** *and p300* **Prescriptions**.

Medicare Information Service
Postal address: PO Box 9822, Sydney, NSW 2001 (13 2011/ www.medicareaustralia.gov.au). **Open** *Phone enquiries* 9am-4.30pm Mon-Fri.

Accident & emergency

In an emergency, call **000** for an ambulance.

Prince of Wales Hospital
Barker Street, Randwick (9382 2222). Bus 373, 374.

Royal North Shore Hospital
Pacific Highway, St Leonards (9926 7111). CityRail St Leonards.

Royal Prince Alfred Hospital
Missenden Road, Camperdown (9515 6111). Bus 412.

St Vincent's Public Hospital

Corner of Burton & Victoria Streets, Darlinghurst (8382 1111). CityRail Kings Cross/bus 333, 378, 380.

Complementary medicine

Australians are very open to complementary medicine and treatments; indeed, many conventional doctors take a holistic approach and combine mainstream treatments with complementary care. Look in the *Yellow Pages* under 'Alternative Health Services' for hundreds of practitioners.

Australian Natural Therapists Association

1800 817577/www.anta.com.au.

Australian Traditional-Medicine Society

Postal address: PO Box 1027, Meadowbank, NSW 2114 (9809 6800/www.atms.com.au).

Contraception & abortion

FPA Health (Family Planning Association)

Clinics and advice: 1300 658886/www.fpahealth.org.au. **Open** 9am-5.30pm Mon-Fri.

Marie Stopes International

1800 003707/www.mariestopes.com.au. **Open** 8am-9pm Mon-Fri; 9am-2pm Sat.

Dentists

Dental treatment is not covered by Medicare, and therefore not by the reciprocal agreement (*see p299* **Health**). In the absence of medical insurance be prepared for hefty fees. Check the *Yellow Pages* for listings, though it's a good idea to ask locals to recommend a dentist they know and trust.

Doctors

For listings of doctors, see the *Yellow Pages* under 'Medical Practitioners'. If your home country is covered under the reciprocal Medicare agreement, and your visit is for immediately necessary treatment, you can claim a refund from Medicare. Try to get to one of the increasingly rare 'bulk billing' medical practices, where your trip will be free. Otherwise you will only get back a proportion of the fee, which must be claimed in person.

Hospitals

Hospitals are listed in the *White Pages* at the front of the phone book in the 'Emergency, Health & Help' section, with a location map. For hospitals with 24-hour A&E, *see p299* **Accident & emergency**.

Opticians

See p210.

Pharmacies

Standard opening times for chemists are 9am to 5.30pm Monday to Friday, and usually 9am to 5.30pm Saturday, 10am to 5pm Sunday (though weekend opening times depend on the area). Many convenience stores and supermarkets stock over-the-counter drugs. *See also p211.*

Prescriptions

In Australia, prescription costs vary depending on the drugs being prescribed. On the Pharmaceutical Benefits Scheme (PBS) you shouldn't have to pay too much – but to get the price you must have a Medicare card or temporary Medicare card, available to visitors from nations with a reciprocal health care agreement from any Medicare office, with your passport and visa.

STDs, HIV & AIDS

AIDS Council of NSW (ACON)

9 Commonwealth Street, Surry Hills (1800 063060/9206 2000/www.acon.org.au). CityRail Museum. **Open** 10am-6pm Mon-Fri. **Map** p329 F9. Information, advice and support.

HIV/AIDS Information

9332 9600/www.sesahs. nsw.gov.au/albionstcentre. **Open** 8am-7pm Mon-Fri; 10am-6pm Sat. Statewide information service.

Sydney Sexual Health Centre

Sydney Hospital, 8 Macquarie Street, opposite Martin Place, CBD (1800 451624/9382 7440). CityRail Martin Place. **Open** *Phone enquiries* 9.30am-6pm Mon-Fri. *Clinic* 10am-6pm Mon, Tue, Thur, Fri; 2-6pm Wed. **Map** p327 G5/6. Government-funded clinic aimed at young people at risk, gay men and sex workers.

Travel advice

For up-to-date information on travel to a specific country – including the latest news on safety and security, health issues, local laws and customs – contact your home country government's department of foreign affairs. Most have websites packed with useful advice for would-be travellers.

Australia
www.smartraveller.gov.au
Canada www.voyage.gc.ca
New Zealand
www.safetravel.govt.nz
Republic of Ireland
www.foreignaffairs.gov.ie
UK www.fco.gov.uk/travel
USA www.travel.state.gov

Helplines

Alcohol & Drug Information Service *1800 422599/9361 8000.* **Open** 24hrs daily.
Crisis counselling, information, assessment and referrals.

Alcoholics Anonymous *9387 7788/www.alcoholicsanonymous.org. au.* **Open** 24hrs daily.
Manned by volunteers who are recovering alcoholics.

Child Abuse Line *13 2111/www.community.nsw.gov.au.* **Open** 24hrs daily.
For immediate help, advice and action involving children at risk.

Domestic Violence Line *1800 200526.* **Open** 24hrs daily.
Call 000 if in immediate danger, otherwise this service offers expert counselling and advice.

Gamblers Counselling Service *9951 5566/G-Line 1800 633635/www.wesleymission.org.au.* **Open** 9am-5pm Mon-Fri. *G-Line* 24hrs daily.
A face-to-face counselling service plus 24-hour telephone helpline.

Kids Helpline *1800 551800/www.kidshelp.com.au.* **Open** 24hrs daily.
Confidential support for children and young people aged five to 18. Counsellors available by email or for real-time web counselling.

Law Access *1300 888529/www.lawaccess.nsw.gov.au.* **Open** 9am-5pm Mon-Fri.
Advice and information on all on legal issues.

Lifeline *13 1114.* **Open** 24hrs daily.
Help for people in crisis.

Rape Crisis Centre *1800 424017/9819 7357.* **Open** 24hrs daily.
Rape counselling over the phone.

Salvation Army Salvo Care Line *1300 363622.* **Open** 24hrs daily.
Help for anyone in crisis or contemplating suicide.

Insurance

Getting some travel insurance is advisable, especially if you're aiming to stay in backpacker hostels, where thefts are common. Australia has reciprocal health care agreements with many countries; *see p299* **Health**.

Internet

Cybercafés are everywhere in Sydney. Most backpacker hotels have internet links, and most libraries will provide access.

Language

Despite the country's history, contemporary vernacular Australian owes more to US English than the UK variety, so you may read about a 'color program', and 'pissed' means annoyed not drunk. Words that have a peculiarly Australian flavour include: *arvo* (afternoon); *bludger* (scrounger, as in 'dole bludger'); *daggy* (nerdy or goofy); *daks* (trousers); *doona* (duvet); *dunny* (lavatory/loo/ toilet); *Manchester* (household linen); and *thongs* (flip-flops, not G-strings). Take special care when talking about your roots (root means shag/bonk/ sexual encounter or just plain knacker – anything but your ancestry or blonde streaks in your hair).

You will probably hear 'G'day, mate' and 'Fair dinkum', but often said with a knowing wink.

Left luggage

There are left-luggage lockers for hire in the international terminal of **Sydney Airport** (call 9667 0926 for information). They cost $11 per bag for up to 24 hours.

Legal help

For embassies and consulates, *see p299*. For information on the Law Access service, *see above* **Helplines**.

Lost property

For belongings lost on State Transit public transport, try phoning the main STA switchboard on 9245 5777, or 9379 341 for CityRail and CountryLink. For the Monorail and LightRail, phone 9285 5600. If you've left something behind in a cab, phone the relevant taxi company. For property lost on the street, contact the police on 9281 0000. For items lost at the airport, phone 9667 9583 or contact the airline.

Media

Magazines

Time Out magazine has a fantastic food and drink section plus full entertainment listings and local features. It launched in 2007 and is going strong. It comes out every Wednesday and is sold in all major newsagents. Check out the website as well at www.timeoutsydney.com.au.

Newspapers

DAILIES

Sydney has two local papers, the broadsheet *Sydney Morning Herald* (www.smh. com.au, owned by Fairfax) and the tabloid *Daily Telegraph* (http://dailytelegraph.news. com.au, News International, owned by Rupert Murdoch). The *SMH* is an institution with an ego to match. Local stories prevail, with solid coverage of politics and events, but beware the comment columns. It is accompanied by *the (sydney) magazine*, a self indulgent monthly freebie, filled with Versace and Porsche ads.

The *Daily Telegraph* puts out two editions, morning and afternoon, giving it the edge over the *SMH* for scoops. In true tabloid style, it also carries plenty of bitchy celebrity news in its 'Sydney Confidential' spread.

News International also produces a freebie newspaper, *MX* (www.mxnet.com.au), handed out at CityRail stations Monday to Friday.

The two national newspapers, the *Australian*

Directory

(www.theaustralian.news.com.au, Murdoch) and the *Australian Financial Review* (http://afr.com, Fairfax), are both based in Sydney, and both have that bias in their coverage. The *Australian* has been trying to shake out its starchiness, but the result has been a rather bizarre mish-mash of armchair trendiness and what could be called a kind of 'gentle conservatism'. The *Review* offers excellent news coverage, plus business and politics.

WEEKEND

The weekend *Sydney Morning Herald* is a vast publication, mainly due to a surfeit of classified advertisements. The *Saturday Telegraph* is not as thick, but still has its fair share of supplements. The *Australian* aspires to stylish minimalism, with a slick, svelte weekend broadsheet on Saturday, accompanied by a print-heavy magazine. On Sundays there is Fairfax's tabloid *Sun-Herald*, designed to compete with the popular *Sunday Telegraph*.

Radio

AM stations

NewsRadio (ABC) 630 AM
Rolling news service with strong international content and daytime coverage of parliament.
Radio National (ABC) 576 AM
Intelligent, provocative talk shows, arts and current affairs.
Radio 2GB 873 AM
Veteran talk show radio station that feeds off local whingeing, humorous tirades and chatty hosts.
SBS Radio 1107 AM
Ethnic, multilingual programmes for Sydney's diverse communities.
2BL (ABC) 702 AM
The Australian Broadcasting Corporation's popular talk station features non-commercial, non-ranting, reasonably intelligent banter.
2CH 1170 AM
Easy, yawn, listening.
2KY 1017 AM
Racing, racing and more racing.
2UE 954 AM
The place for controversial talkback shows.

FM stations

ABC Classic FM 92.9 FM
Classical music for non-purists, and some cool jazz.
MIX 106.5 FM
Celine Dion, Phil Collins, the Spice Girls – oh, and is that Lionel Ritchie?
FBi 94.5 FM
Take a side-step from the mainstream and discover the groovin' underground.
Nova 96.9 FM
This relative newcomer is young, brash and cheeky.
SBS Radio 97.7 FM
Special-interest ethnic programming.
Triple J 105.7 FM
Well respected as the station most devoted to the discovery and spread of new music.
2DAY 104.1 FM
Made its name by taking women seriously. And the listeners flocked. Funny, that.
2000FM 98.5 FM
Ethnic specialist with community-driven shows.
2MMM (Triple M) 104.9 FM
Rock, ads and then more rock.
Vega 95.3 FM
Sydney's newest radio station, launched in 2005, targeting the baby-boomers with talk and music.
WSFM 101.7 FM
Classic hits from the 1960s to '80s, every one a singalong.

Television

The government-funded TV and radio networks are **ABC** (Australian Broadcasting Corporation) and **SBS** (Special Broadcasting Service). ABC has strong links with the BBC and tends to get first dibs on new BBC series. It also has a lot of homemade shows and is good for documentaries and current affairs. SBS has a remit to support multicultural programming and is woefully underfunded. It features foreign films (subtitled), has good world news at 6.30pm every night and is renowned for its documentaries, many commissioned from independent Australian producers. It's also where you'll find comprehensive European football coverage.

The other three networks – **Seven**, **Nine** and **Ten** – are commercial and, for the most part, populist, featuring a large dose of US TV, heaps of local lifestyle shows and ads seemingly every five minutes. Pay TV (satellite and digital) is growing, with (Murdoch-owned) **Foxtel** dominating the market so far.

Money

In 1966 Australia relinquished the old country's pounds, shillings and pence for the Australian dollar ($) and cent (c). Paper money comes in $100, $50, $20, $10 and $5 denominations. Coins come in bronze $2 and $1 pieces, and silver 50c, 20c, 10c and 5c pieces. At the time of writing, the tourist exchange rate was approximately $2.25 to £1, $1.15 to US$1 and $1.65 to €1.

ATMs

There are 24-hour ATMs all over town – outside banks, and increasingly in pubs, bottle shops and convenience stores.

Most banks will accept each other's cards, but will often charge a fee for doing so. Some ATMs accept credit cards – check the card logos displayed. Be aware that withdrawing money on your credit card usually incurs a hefty rate of interest straight away. Most ATMs also accept debit cards linked to international networks such as Cirrus, Connect and Barclays.

Banks

The banks below have branches throughout the city. All are open 9.30am to 4pm Monday to Thursday, and 9.30am to 5pm Friday.

ANZ
97 Castlereagh Street, CBD (13 1314/www.anz.com). CityRail St James. **Map** p327 F6.

Commonwealth Bank of Australia
48 Martin Place, CBD (13 2221/ www.commbank.com.au). CityRail Martin Place. **Map** p327 F5.

Creature discomforts

Australia's array of mini-creatures is legendary. And Sydney, being temperate and humid, is the perfect breeding ground for all things cold-blooded or with six or more legs. Most bugs, arachnids and reptiles are completely harmless, and most tend to bother residents rather than visitors in built-up areas, but there are a few nasties to look out for. The following are the critters you should be aware of.

SPIDERS

While many different types of spider tend to congregate in Sydney, there are two with a potentially fatal bite – the **funnel web** and the **redback**. The funnel web is a nasty, aggressive creature native to the Sydney bush. Reddish-brown and hairy, it lives in holes in the ground. If bitten, apply pressure and immobilise the wounded area, using a splint if possible, and get to a hospital (or dial 000) immediately. The redback, which is smaller and black with a red stripe on its body, lives mainly outside. Apply ice if bitten and seek immediate medical help.

SNAKES

Five of the ten most dangerous snakes in the world are said to live in Australia, with names like **king brown**, **taipan** and **tiger**. Most are more scared of you than you are of them, but a couple can be more aggressive – so it is sensible to play it safe: always wear boots when hiking through the bush, don't put your hands in any holes or crevices, and watch where you're walking. If someone with you is bitten, assume that the snake is venomous. Wrap the limb tightly, attach a splint and keep the victim still and calm, then seek immediate medical attention. Snake bites will not cause immediate death and antivenin is usually available from medical services.

COCKROACHES

They say the cockie would be the only thing to survive a nuclear holocaust – whether or not this is true, Sydneysiders will try anything short of napalm to wipe them out. Despite being nasty, the cockroaches (which seem to grow to the size of frogs during summer – perhaps a response to the chemical warfare being waged against them) are harmless.

FLIES AND MOSQUITOES

Flies and mozzies are a fact of Aussie life, but besides imparting an itchy bump (mozzies) and an irritable disposition (flies), they're not dangerous. There are also a couple of flies that bite, such as the **march fly** – but their bite is not poisonous, just a tad painful. Some people can experience nasty allergic reactions to bites – if this is you, try prescribed or over-the-counter antihistamines (ask the pharmacist for advice). Personal repellents, such as Aeroguard or Rid, tend to be fairly effective, or you can buy coils to burn outdoors, or repelling candles. Mosquito nets and screens are a good idea in summer.

BUSHLAND BRUTES

If you plan to fit in a little bushwalking anywhere on Australia's east coast, there are a couple of creatures you need to watch out for besides snakes.

Ticks are very dangerous, if not removed immediately, as they excrete a toxin that can cause paralysis or, in extreme cases, even death. So each day after bushwalking check your body for lumps and bumps – they tend to like hairy areas, skin creases and ears – and slowly pull or twist any ticks out with sharp-pointed tweezers. **Leeches** are common bushland suckers – literally. However, they aren't dangerous and can easily be persuaded to let go by applying salt or heat.

National Australia Bank

75 Elizabeth Street, CBD (13 2265/ www.national.com.au). CityRail Martin Place. **Map** p327 F6. **Other locations** throughout the city.

Westpac

60 Martin Place, CBD (13 2032/ www.westpac.com.au). CityRail Martin Place. **Map** p327 F/G5. **Other locations** throughout the city.

Bureaux de change

American Express

105 Pitt Street, between Martin Place & Hunter Street, CBD (1300 139060/www.americanexpress.com/ australia). CityRail Wynyard. **Open** 9am-5pm Mon-Fri. **Map** p327 F5. **Other locations** throughout the city.

Travelex

Queen Victoria Building, 455 George Street, between Market & Druitt Streets, CBD (9264 1267/www. travelex.com). CityRail Town Hall. **Open** 9am-6pm Mon-Fri; 10am-3pm Sat. **Map** p327 E6. **Other locations** throughout the city.

Credit cards

MasterCard (MC), Visa (V), Diners Club (DC) and American Express (AmEx) are widely accepted. You can also

Directory

use credit cards to get cash from any bank (take your passport), and some ATMs. To report lost or stolen cards, call (free) these 24-hour numbers: **American Express** 1300 132639 **Diners Club** 1300 360060 **MasterCard** 1800 120113 **Visa** 1300 651089

Tax & tax refunds

A ten per cent **GST** (Goods & Services Tax) is charged on some goods, food and services, including accommodation, and is included in the display price. Tourists can reclaim it on selected goods when they leave the country using the **Tourist Refund Scheme** (TRS). This scheme applies only to goods you carry as hand luggage or wear onto the aircraft or ship when you leave.

The refund can be claimed on goods costing a total of $300 or above (including GST) bought from one shop no more than 30 days before you leave. You can buy several lower-priced items from the same shop, either in one go or at different times, provided you've spent at least $300 total within the 30-day period. And you can reclaim tax for items bought from any number of shops, as long as you've spent at least $300 in each one.

To claim a refund, you must get a tax invoice from the shop or shops in question. You then claim your refund at a TRS booth, after passport control. Here you'll need to show the goods, the tax invoices, your passport and international boarding pass. Refunds are paid by cheque or credit to an Australian bank account, or to a credit card. Customs aims to post cheque refunds within 15 business days, while bank and credit card refunds are issued within five business days.

Full details are on the Australian Customs website, www.customs.gov.au – click on 'travellers'.

Natural hazards

With a dangerously thin ozone layer, the sun is Sydney's biggest natural hazard. The best way to avoid it is to 'slip, slap, slop' – slip on a T-shirt, slap on a hat, and slop on some sun-cream, preferably SPF 30.

For information about Sydney's wildlife hazards, *see p302* **Creature discomforts**.

Opening hours

Shops are usually open from 8.30am or 9am to 5pm or 6pm Monday to Saturday, and from 10am or 11am to 4pm or 5pm Sunday. Thursday is late-night opening (usually until 9pm). Some shops close at noon on Saturdays. Banks are usually open from 9.30am to 4pm Monday to Thursday, until 5pm on Friday, and closed at the weekend.

Police stations

To report an emergency, dial **000**. If it is not an emergency, call the police at **13 1444**. The **City Central Police Station** is at 192 Day Street, CBD (9265 6499). More info at www.police.nsw.gov.au.

Postal services

Australia Post (13 1318, www.auspost.com.au) says about 90 per cent of letters within the metropolitan area arrive the next business day. Post is delivered once a day Monday to Friday, with no delivery on Saturdays or Sundays. Post to Europe takes four to ten days. Stamps for postcards to Europe and the USA cost $1.10; for letters it's $1.85 (up to 50 grams), and international aerogrammes cost 95c. Letters within Australia cost from 50c to $2.45.

Most post office branches open from 9am to 5pm Monday

to Friday, but the GPO Martin Place branch is also open on Saturdays. Stamps can also be bought at some newsagents and general stores. Suburban post offices will receive post for you; otherwise have it sent Poste Restante (general delivery) to GPO Sydney, NSW 2000 – and collect it from the address below. Most post offices also rent out PO boxes, but only on an annual basis.

General Post Office
1 Martin Place, CBD (9244 3713). CityRail Martin Place or Wynyard. **Open** 8.15am-5.30pm Mon-Fri; 10am-2pm Sat. **Map** p327 F5/6.

Poste Restante
Level 2, Hunter Connection Building, 310 George Street, CBD (13 1318). CityRail Martin Place or Wynyard. **Open** 9am-5pm Mon-Fri. **Map** p327 F5.

Religion

Have a look in the *Yellow Pages* under 'Churches, Mosques and Temples' for places of worship.

Safety & security

Sydney is a fairly safe city, although car theft, vandalism and burglary are on the increase. That said, you will frequently read about drug-related shootings, and racial tension has heightened since the Bali bombings and the riots on Cronulla Beach in 2005. And while the stereotype of hot-blooded Aussie males ending an alcohol-fuelled evening with a pub brawl is not the norm, it's not entirely unknown either – so steer clear of drunk rednecks at closing time.

In an emergency, dial **000**.

Smoking

Smoking is banned on public transport and in cafés, restaurants and a wide range of enclosed spaces, such as theatres, shopping malls and community centres. Smoking in pubs and clubs is now completely banned. There are fines for tossing cigarette butts out of car windows.

Study

Anyone can apply to study in Australia, but you must obtain a student visa before starting a course. For more details, visit the Department of Immigration's website at www.immi.gov.au. You'll be granted a student visa only for a full-time registered course.

Universities

University of NSW

Postal address: University of NSW, Sydney, NSW 2052 (9385 1000/ www.unsw.edu.au). Location: Anzac Parade, Kensington. Bus 302, 303, 391, 392, 393, 394, 395, 396, 397, 399, 400, 410, 890, L94.
The UNSW is one of the leading teaching and research universities in Australia. Almost 9,000 of its 40,000 students are foreign.

University of Sydney

Postal address: University of Sydney, NSW 2006 (9351 2222/www. usyd.edu.au). Location: City Road, Darlington, & Parramatta Road, Camperdown. City Road entrance: bus 422, 423, 426, 428/Parramatta Road entrance: bus 412, 413, 435, 436, 437, 438, 440, 461, 480.
Australia's first uni has around 46,000 students, of whom nearly 9,000 are international.

Macquarie University

Postal address: Macquarie University, NSW 2109 (9850 7111/www.mq.edu.au). Location: Balaclava Road, North Ryde. Bus 288, 292.
Macquarie has more than 30,000 students, around 9,000 of them from overseas. The university is set in bushland north of Sydney, offering a rural alternative to city universities.

Telephones

Dialling & codes

The country code for Australia is **61**; the area code for NSW, including Sydney, is **02**. You never need to dial the 02 from within the state. Numbers beginning 1800 are free when dialled within Australia; numbers beginning 13 or 1300 are charged at a 25c flat fee.

Making a call

To make an international call from Sydney, dial an international access code – either **0011** or **0018** (*see below*) – followed by the country code, area code (omitting the initial 0 if there is one), and then the number.

The different international access codes have different pricing systems. Telstra, the dominant Australian phone company, offers a choice of 0011 Minutes or 0018 Half Hours. The 0011 calls are for shorter chats, charged per second. The 0018 calls are for a long chat and you'll know exactly how much your call will cost up front. Warning beeps tell you when your half-hour is almost up.

The country code for the UK is **44**, for New Zealand **64**, for the United States 1, for the Republic of Ireland **353** and for South Africa **27**.

Standard local calls are untimed flat-fee calls between standard fixed telephone services within a local service area. To check if local call charges apply, call 13 2200.

STD calls (national long-distance calls) are charged according to their distance, time and day, plus a fee. Each call starts with five pip tones.

Public phones

There are public phones dotted around the city, as well as in bars, cafés, railway stations and post offices. You can also make long-distance and international calls at many internet cafés. Most public phones accept coins ($1, 50c, 20c, 10c). Some also accept major credit cards. Cheap international phonecards are available from newsagents.

Directory enquiries

Dial **1223** to find a number within Australia, and **1225** for international directory enquiries.

Operator services

For operator-assisted national or international calls, phone **1234**.

Mobile phones

Australia's mobile phone network operates on dual-band 900/1800 MHz (megahertz). This means that if you're coming from the UK you should be able to use your own mobile phone – but that's not as simple as it sounds.

If you keep your UK SIM card in the phone, when you arrive your phone will register itself with a local network with which your UK service provider has an agreement. If you want to use this facility, check with your service provider before you go, as you may need to set your phone up to work abroad. This is the easiest method, but potentially very expensive: calling numbers in Australia will cost the same as calling back to the UK – a lot – and you'll have to pay to receive calls as well as to make them.

Another simple option is to to buy or rent a phone. Plenty of Sydney companies offer competitive mobile phone rentals with local networks, for a minimum of three days, billed to your credit card. Or you could just buy or rent a SIM card for an Australian network and put it in your UK phone (and top it up as required). However, your phone may have been 'locked' so that it works only with your UK service provider's SIM card. You're entitled to get the phone unlocked, and the service provider has to give you an unlocking code – for free – if you ask for it. Once you've unlocked your phone you can put any SIM card in it. In practice, service providers tend not to make this easy, and the process can be fraught with difficulties. Alternatively, any mobile phone repair shop will do it, for about $40.

If you're in Sydney for a year or more, you could get a phone or SIM card on a billed package. To get this kind of plan – usually 12 months minimum – you'll need an Australian credit rating, and it takes six months to get one.

To investigate further, look under 'Mobile Telephones & Accessories' in the *Yellow Pages* or try these places:

Paddington Phones

241 Commonwealth Street, at Foveaux Street, Surry Hills (9281 8044/www.paddingtonphones.com. au). CityRail Central. **Open** 9am-5.30pm Mon-Fri. **Map** p329 F9. Rentals, pre-paid and fixed-term deals are all available.

Vodafone Rentals

Arrivals Hall, T1 International Terminal, Sydney Airport (9700 8086/www.vodafone.com.au). **Open** 6.30am-9pm daily. Rent or buy a phone or SIM card as soon as you arrive. **Other locations** 333 George Street (8753 3324); Westfield Bondi Junction (8753 3302).

Tickets

You can book tickets for all major venues (music, theatre, dance and so on) through agencies **Ticketek** (13 2849, www.ticketek.com.au) and **Ticketmaster** (13 6100, www.ticketmaster.com.au). Also try **MCA Ticketing** (1300 306776, www.mca-tix.com) or **Moshtix** (1300 438849, www.moshtix.com.au). All charge booking fees.

Time

New South Wales operates on **Eastern Standard Time** (GMT plus 10 hours). Between October and March, Daylight Saving Time comes into operation, and the clocks go forward one hour. Australia has three time zones – the others are Western Standard Time (GMT plus 8 hours) and Central Standard Time (GMT plus 9.5 hours). Confusingly, Queensland doesn't recognise Daylight Saving Time.

Tipping

Tipping is appreciated but not usually expected in restaurants and cafés, where ten per cent is the norm. Locals never tip in taxis.

Toilets

There are plenty of free, well-maintained public lavatories in Sydney – in department stores, shopping centres, rail stations, beaches and parks. It is frowned upon to use the toilet in a bar if you're not also buying a drink. And a note for women: Sydney's sewage pipes are a lot narrower and so more prone to blockage than most of those elsewhere, tampons and sanitary towels being the main culprits. It's not something anyone tells you until you've got the plumber there and a hefty bill – use a bin instead!

Tourist information

As well as the visitor centres below, the City of Sydney's website – www.cityofsydney. nsw.gov.au – and Tourism NSW's site – www.visitnsw. com.au – have lots of useful information. If you're planning to travel elsewhere in the country, Australia's official website – www.australia.com – is packed with helpful ideas and information.

Sydney Visitor Centre

Level 2, corner of Argyle & Playfair Road, The Rocks (9240 8788/1800 067676/www.sydneyvisitorcentre. com). *CityRail/ferry Circular Quay.* **Open** 9.30am-5.30pm daily. **Map** p327 F3.

Other locations 33 Wheat Road, Darling Harbour (9240 8788). *Ferry Darling Harbour/City Rail Town Hall/Monorail Darling Park.* **Open** 9.30am-5.30pm daily. **Map** p328 D7.
This is the main official information resource, with two city-centre locations – in the Rocks and in Darling Harbour.

Cadman's Cottage/ Sydney Harbour National Park Information Centre

110 George Street, between Argyle Street & Mill Lane, The Rocks (9247 5033/www.nationalparks.nsw.gov.au). CityRail/ferry Circular Quay. **Open** 9.30am-4.30pm Mon-Fri; 10am-4.30pm Sat, Sun. **Map** p327 F3.

Manly Visitor & Information Centre

Manly Wharf, Manly (9976 1430/ www.manlytourism.com). Ferry Manly. **Open** 9am-5pm Mon-Fri; 10am-4pm Sat, Sun (5pm summer). **Map** p334.

Parramatta Heritage & Visitor Information Centre

346A Church Street, next to Lennox Bridge, Parramatta (8839 3311/ www.parracity.nsw.gov.au). CityRail/ ferry Parramatta then 10mins walk. **Open** 9am-5pm daily.

Visas & immigration

All travellers, including children – except for Australian and New Zealand citizens – must have a visa or an **ETA** (Electronic Travel Authority) to enter Australia. An ETA is sufficient for tourists from EC countries – including the UK and Ireland, except holders of GBN (British National Overseas) passports – the USA, Canada and Japan (but not South Africa), who are intending to stay for up to three months.

ETAs, available for straightforward tourist and business trips, are the simplest to arrange: your travel agent or airline or a commercial visa service can arrange one on the spot if you give them details or a copy/fax of your passport (no

Average climate

Month	Temperature (°C/°F)	Rainfall mm/in
January	19-26/66-79	89/3.5
February	19-26/66-79	102/4
March	17-25/63-76	127/5
April	15-22/58-72	135/5.3
May	11-19/52-67	127/5
June	9-17/49-61	117/4.6
July	8-16/49-61	117/4.6
August	9-18/49-63	76/3
September	11-20/52-66	74/2.9
October	13-22/56-72	71/2.8
November	16-24/61-75	74/2.9
December	17-25/63-77	74/2.9

photo or ticket is required). You don't need a stamp in your passport: ETAs are confirmed electronically at your port of entry. Alternatively, you can apply for an ETA online via www.eta.immi.gov.au. The service costs $20, and you can be approved for entry in less than 30 seconds.

If your entry requirements are more complex or you want to stay longer than three months, you will probably need a non-ETA visa, which you apply for by post or in person to the relevant office in advance of your trip. For up-to-date information and details of the nearest overseas office where visa applications can be made, check www.immi.gov. au. For details on working visas, *see below* Working in Sydney.

Weights & measures

Australia uses the metric system.

When to go

Sydney has a moderate climate, with warm to hot summers, cool winters and rainfall all year round.

Spring brings blossoming flowers and clear blue skies,

with temperatures warm enough to shed the woollies, especially when the sun shines. In summer, Sydneysiders live in shorts. In January and February the sun bakes the city, and temperatures can top 30°C (90°F) – and even go over 40°C (104°F). In autumn, the city is swept by strong winds, while winter mornings and nights mean low temperatures that can – but rarely do – dip down to 6°C (43°F). Winter daily maximums tend to hover between 14°C (57°F) and 18°C (64°F), and on occasion snow falls in the Blue Mountains.

NSW public holidays

New Year's Day (1 January); **Australia Day** (26 January); **Good Friday**; **Easter Monday**; **Anzac Day** (25 April); the **Queen's Birthday** (2nd Monday in June); **August Bank Holiday** (1st Monday in August); **Labour Day** (1st Monday in October); **Christmas Day** (25 December); and **Boxing Day** (26 December).

Women

Chauvinism may still be alive even in Sydney, but Australian women more than hold their own. The nation was the second country to give women the vote (in 1894 in South Australia). In real terms Australian women still do not earn the same as their male

counterparts, and in many industries they're a long way off breaking the glass ceiling. Sydney is pretty safe for women, but take care when leaving the hub of the city at night; you don't have to go far for it to feel remote.

Feminist Bookshop

Orange Grove Plaza, Balmain Road, Lilyfield (9810 2666/www.feminist bookshop.com). Bus 440, 445, 470. **Open** 10.30am-6pm Mon-Fri; 10.30am-4pm Sat. **Credit** AmEx, MC, V.
Books, journals and mags.

Working in Sydney

If you want to work while in Sydney, you'll need to have a visa that allows this. The **Working Holiday Program** provides opportunities for people aged 18 to 30 from some countries (including Belgium, Canada, Republic of Cyprus, Denmark, Estonia, Finland, France, Germany, Hong Kong, Republic of Ireland, Italy, Japan, Republic of Korea, Malta, Netherlands, Norway, Sweden, Taiwan and the UK) to holiday in Australia and supplement their funds through incidental employment. The visa allows a stay of up to 12 months from the date of first entry to Australia, regardless of whether or not you spend the whole time in Australia. You are allowed to do any kind of work of a temporary or casual nature, but you cannot work for more than three months with any one employer.

Working holiday visas can be obtained by making an application on the internet at www.immi.gov.au, or by lodging a written application at an overseas visa office.

If you do not fit the working visa mould, you may still be able to work if you are sponsored by a company or if you apply for residency. Be warned though, the latter option is complex, expensive and takes a great deal of time.

Directory

Further Reference

Books

Non-fiction

Clark, Manning *A History of Australia*
Six-volume history, with sympathy for the underdog.
Dalton, Robin *Aunts Up the Cross*
Dalton's affectionate memoir of life in Sydney's most raffish locale, Kings Cross.
Drewe, Philip *Sydney Opera House*
An incisive and intellectual examination of Utzon's building.
Dupain, Max & Rex *Inside Sydney*
Max Dupain's 1920s and '30s photographs reflected Sydney's emergence as a modern city.
Evans, Matthew & Thomson, Simon (eds) *The Sydney Morning Herald Good Food Guide*
The *SMH*'s annual round-up of the best restaurants, cafés and bars in Sydney and beyond.
Facey, Albert *A Fortunate Life*
Successful autobiography tracing Facey's life from Outback orphanage to Gallipoli, the Depression and beyond.
Foster, David & others *Crossing the Blue Mountains*
Accounts of journeys into the interior from Sydney, including that of Darwin in 1836.
Gill, Alan *Orphans of the Storm*
Shocking true story of the thousands of people who came to Australia in the 20th century as child migrants.
Gregory's *Sydney Compact Street Directory*
A bit of a brick, but the best guide to Sydney's streets you'll find.
Halliday, James *Australia Wine Companion*
Good to take on a tour of vineyards.
Hooke, Huon & Kyte-Powell, Ralph *The Penguin Good Australian Wine Guide*
This long-running annual guide to the Australian wine industry is aimed mostly at enthusiasts, but accessible to beginners as well.
Hughes, Robert *The Fatal Shore*
Epic tale of brutal early convict life; made into a TV series.

Hughes Turnbull, Lucy *Sydney, Biography of a City*
Authoritative tome from way back to now. Good reference material.
James, Clive *Unreliable Memoirs*
Ironic memoir of a Sydney childhood by Britain's favourite Aussie.
Keneally, Thomas *The Commonwealth of Thieves*
History of the colony in the time of the first three fleets.
Ker Conway, Jill *The Road from Coorain*
Moving account of growing up on a remote NSW sheep farm, made into a compelling TV series starring Juliet Stevenson. Girlhood solitude, despair during an eight-year drought and dreams of a new destiny make for gripping reading.
Moorhouse, Geoffrey *Sydney*
A fresh look at the city's history by a distinguished travel writer.
Morgan, Sally *My Place*
Bestselling autobiography of an Aboriginal woman from Western Australia.
O'Brien, Siobhan *A Life By Design: The art and lives of Florence Broadhurst*
The mysterious death and extraordinary life of Sydney socialite and wallpaper queen Florence Broadhurst.
Pilger, John *A Secret Country*
Passionately critical account of Australia by the expat journalist.
Walsh, Kate *The Changing Face of Australia*
A pictorial chronology of a century of immigration, underlining the shift towards a multiculture.
Wheatley, Nadia *The Life and Myth of Charmian Clift*
Well-crafted biography of one of Australia's best writers.

Fiction

Carey, Peter *Bliss, Illywhacker, Oscar and Lucinda, The True History of the Kelly Gang, Theft*
Booker Prize-winning novelist.
Courtenay, Bryce *Brother Fish, Whitethorn*
Australia's bestselling writer, though he doesn't always stick to Oz-related subject matter.

Franklin, Miles *My Brilliant Career*
Famous 1901 novel about a rural woman who refuses to conform.
Gibbs, May *Snugglepot and Cuddlepie*
Most famous of Gibbs's children's books about the gumnut babies.
Keneally, Thomas *Bring Larks and Heroes; The Chant of Jimmy Blacksmith*
Two novels about oppression – of convicts in the former, Aboriginal people in the latter.
Lawson, Henry *Joe Wilson and His Mates*
Collection of short stories about mateship and larrikinism by the first Australian writer to be given a state funeral (in 1922).
Lindsay, Norman *The Magic Pudding*
Splendidly roguish children's tale – as Australian as a book can get. Made into a so-so movie.
Park, Ruth *The Harp in the South; Poor Man's Orange*
Tales of inner-city struggle, written in the 1940s. Park also wrote the wonderful children's book The Muddle-Headed Wombat.
Slessor, Kenneth *Selected Poems*
The quintessential Sydney poet.
Winton, Tim *Cloudstreet; That Eye, the Sky*
The best novels from a twice winner of the Miles Franklin literary award.

Travel

Bryson, Bill *Down Under*
Amusing travel writer Bryson dissects the Aussie character and explores the brown land.
Carey, Peter *30 Days in Sydney*
Having lived in New York for ten years Peter Carey returns to Sydney and rediscovers the city with his usual wit and fortitude.
Dale, David *The 100 Things Everyone Needs to Know About Australia*
Essential background reading: covers everything from Vegemite to Malcolm Fraser's trousers.
Jacobson, Howard *In the Land of Oz*
Parodic account of Jacobson's travels down under.

Film

The Adventures of Priscilla, Queen of the Desert
(Stephan Elliott, 1994)
Terence Stamp joins Guy Pearce and Hugo Weaving in high heels for this gritty high camp tale of Sydney drag queens on tour.
Australia (Baz Luhrmann, 2008)
Nicole Kidman and Hugh Jackman star in this local epic about an English aristo who inherits a ranch in rural Australia.
Candy (Neil Armfield, 2006)
Heath Ledger is mesmerising as the cocky heroin addict also in love with the beautiful Candy (Abbie Cornish). Set in Sydney and Melbourne it's a depressing and deeply affecting tale, made even more poignant in the light of Ledger's death in 2008.
The Home Song Stories
(Tony Ayres, 2007)
Based on tales from his own family's life, Ayres' film about a Hong Kong nightclub singer who marries an Australian sailor and migrates to Melbourne offers a glimpse of multicultural Australia.
Lantana (Ray Lawrence, 2001)
AFI award-winning thriller about marriage and relationships, set in Sydney. Stars Aussie actors Geoffrey Rush, Kerry Armstrong and Anthony LaPaglia.
Little Fish (Rowan Woods, 2005)
A telling look at Sydney's murky underworld of drug dealing and addicts in Cabramatta starring Cate Blanchett.
Looking for Alibrandi
(Kate Woods, 2000)
An Italian-Australian battles with her identity in Sydney's western suburbs. Pia Miranda excels.
Moulin Rouge! (Baz Luhrmann, 2001)
OTT love story from local boy Baz Luhrmann, filmed at Sydney's Fox Studios.
Newsfront (Phillip Noyce, 1978)
Rival news teams in 1950s Sydney battle to shoot the best newsreel.
Rabbit-Proof Fence
(Phillip Noyce, 2002)
The 'stolen generations' seen through the true 1930s story of three Aboriginal children's struggle to get back to their mother.
Romulus My Father
(Richard Roxburgh, 2007)
Eric Bana proves he's more than just the Hulk in this poignant film.

The Sum of Us (Geoff Burton & Kevin Dowling, 1994)
A youthful Russell Crowe plays a gay plumber looking for love in Sydney.
Ten Canoes (Rolf de Heer, 2006)
Set in Arnhem Land this is a gripping tale of family disputes within an Aboriginal community.
Two Hands (Gregor Jordan, 1999)
Bryan Brown plays an underworld Sydney crime boss, with Heath Ledger as the hapless lad who's entangled in his world.
Wolf Creek (Greg McLean, 2005)
Three backpackers get stuck in the Outback, meet a helpful local, unpleasantness follows.

Music

AC/DC Formed in Sydney in 1973. Angus Young's schoolboy attire has become one of rock's oddest brands. Most recent album was *Stiff Upper Lip*, released in 2000.
INXS Sydney's ultimate rock star, Michael Hutchence, headed this international rock band of the 1980s and '90s until his death in a Double Bay hotel room in 1997.
Cave, Nick Enigmatic, brooding vocalist from the Bad Seeds.
Goodrem, Delta Latest popsicle from *Neighbours*. Writes her own stuff, plays the piano and sang at the opening of the 2006 Commonwealth Games.
Hirschfelder, David One of Australia's most successful modern composers.
Imbruglia, Natalie After leaving soap *Neighbours*, Imbruglia moved to London and launched a smash music career helped by her winsome voice. Her debut single *Torn* (1997) was a huge worldwide hit.
Lee, Ben Released his solo debut *Grandpaw Would* in 1995 aged just 16, for which he was dubbed 'the greatest Australian songwriter of all time'. Won four Australian Recording Industry Association (ARIA) awards in 2005 after releasing album *Awake Is the New Sleep*.
Midnight Oil The band, known for 'Beds are Burning' effectively split in 2002 when singer Peter Garrett decided to concentrate on politics – he's now a NSW Labor MP.

Rogue Traders Another *Neighbours* offshoot, as they're fronted by Natalie Bassingthwaighte.
Silverchair Fronted by Daniel Johns (Mr Natalie Imbruglia), the three-piece first performed in Europe in 1995. Now back in Sydney, they have a huge following. *Diorama* (2002) was another huge hit and won them six ARIA awards, but Daniel Johns's struggle with arthritis that year stopped them touring.
The Whitlams After years of crap venues and no money, frontman Tim Freedman begged, borrowed and finally scraped the funds for a last-ditch CD. Its single *No Aphrodisiac* became the ARIA award-winning monster hit of 1998. Double album *Little Cloud* was released in 2006.
The Veronicas Identical twin sisters who rule the local pop world. Actually born in Brisbane, but regulars in Sydney. Their debut album *The Secret Life Of...* went four times platinum. The girls' second album *Hook Me Up* was released at the end of 2007 to much applause.
Wolf Mother The Grammy Award winning Aussie hard rock band hail from Erskineville. Their debut album *Wolfmother* was released in 2005 but fans eagerly await the next one promised to be on release in late 2008 or early 2009.

Websites

Backpackers Ultimate Guide
www.bugaustralia.com/sydney
Useful site for those travelling in Sydney on a budget.
Bureau of Meteorology
www.bom.gov.au
Get the latest weather forecast.
City of Sydney
www.cityofsydney.nsw.gov.au
Weekly update of events.
De Groots Best Restaurants of Australia
www.bestrestaurants.com.au
Fulsome restaurant listings, with photos and menus.
Eatability
www.eatability.com.au
More restaurant information, plus pubs, cafés and bars.
Time Out
www.timeoutsydney.com.au
Updated weekly from the local *Time Out* magazine.

Directory

Street Index

Advertisers' Index

Please refer to the relevant pages for contact details

Area name	PADDINGTON
Major sight or landmark	▮
Park	▢
Hospital/university	▢
CityRail station	⇆
Monorail station	○
LightRail station	▢
Steps	▬

Maps

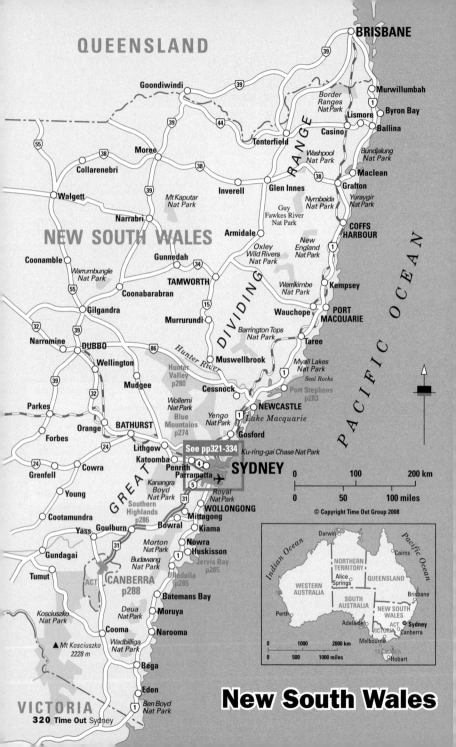

New South Wales

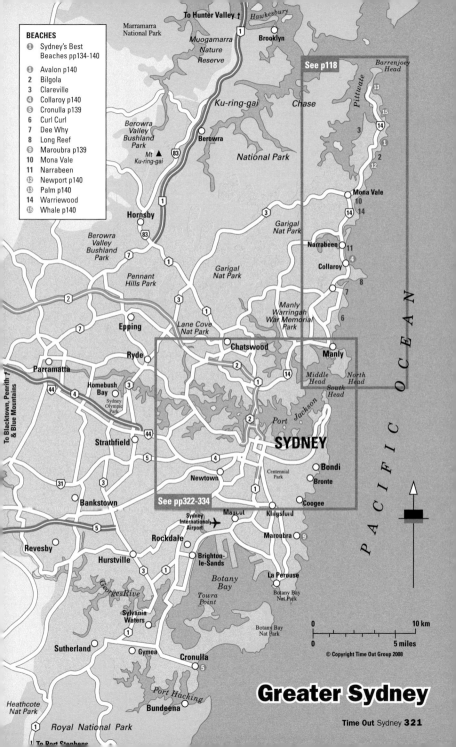

BEACHES

1. Sydney's Best Beaches pp134-140

1. Avalon p140
2. Bilgola
3. Clareville
4. Collaroy p140
5. Cronulla p139
6. Curl Curl
7. Dee Why
8. Long Reef
9. Maroubra p139
10. Mona Vale
11. Narrabeen
12. Newport p140
13. Palm p140
14. Warriewood
15. Whale p140

See p118

See pp322-334

Greater Sydney

© Copyright Time Out Group 2008

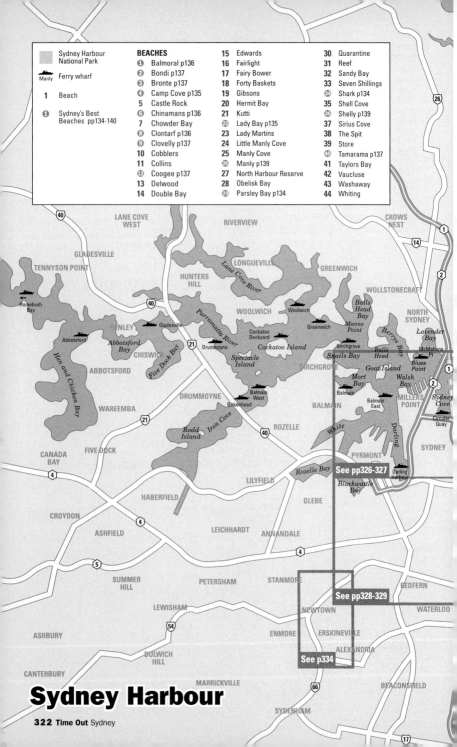

BEACHES

❶ Balmoral p136	15 Edwards	30 Quarantine
❷ Bondi p137	16 Fairlight	31 Reef
❸ Bronte p137	17 Fairy Bower	32 Sandy Bay
❹ Camp Cove p135	18 Forty Baskets	33 Seven Shillings
5 Castle Rock	19 Gibsons	❸❹ Shark p134
❻ Chinamans p136	20 Hermit Bay	35 Shell Cove
7 Chowder Bay	21 Kutti	❸❻ Shelly p139
❽ Clontarf p136	㉒ Lady Bay p135	37 Sirius Cove
❾ Clovelly p137	23 Lady Martins	38 The Spit
10 Cobblers	24 Little Manly Cove	39 Store
11 Collins	25 Manly Cove	❹⓪ Tamarama p137
⑫ Coogee p137	㉖ Manly p139	41 Taylors Bay
13 Delwood	27 North Harbour Reserve	42 Vaucluse
14 Double Bay	28 Obelisk Bay	43 Washaway
15 Edwards	㉙ Parsley Bay p134	44 Whiting

Sydney Harbour

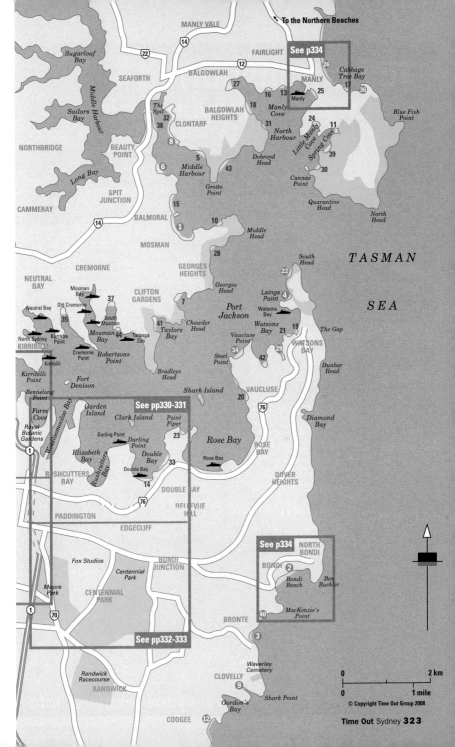

To the Northern Beaches

MANLY VALE

FAIRLIGHT

See p334

MANLY

Sugarloaf Bay

SEAFORTH

BALGOWLAH

26

Cabbage Tree Bay

36

27

16 13

25

17

Middle Harbour

The Spit

32

38

CLONTARF

BALGOWLAH HEIGHTS

18

Manly Cove

Manly

Blue Fish Point

Sailors Bay

31

North Harbour

24

11

Spring Cove

Little Manly Cove

NORTHBRIDGE

BEAUTY POINT

8

5

Dobroyd Head

39

6

Middle Harbour

43

30

Cannae Point

Long Bay

SPIT JUNCTION

Grotto Point

Quarantine Head

CAMMERAY

15

North Head

1

10

BALMORAL

Middle Head

MOSMAN

TASMAN

CREMORNE

28

GEORGES HEIGHTS

South Head

NEUTRAL BAY

Mosman Bay

37

CLIFTON GARDENS

Georges Head

22

SEA

Old Cremorne

Laings Point

4

Neutral Bay

35

South Mosman

7

Port Jackson

Watsons Bay

North Sydney

Kurraba Point

Mosman Bay

44

Taronga Zoo

41

Taylors Bay

Chowder Head

Watsons Bay

21

19

The Gap

KIRRIBILLI

Cremorne Point

Robertsons Point

Vaucluse Point

34

42

WATSONS BAY

Kirribilli

Bradleys Head

29

Dunbar Head

Kirribilli Point

Fort Denison

Shark Island

VAUCLUSE

Bennelong Point

20

Farm Cove

Woolloomooloo Bay

Garden Island

See pp330-331

76

Royal Botanic Gardens

1

Clark Island

Point Piper

Diamond Bay

Darling Point

23

Rose Bay

Elizabeth Bay

Darling Point

Double Bay

33

ROSE BAY

RUSHCUTTERS BAY

Rushcutters Bay

Double Bay

Rose Bay

14

DOVER HEIGHTS

PADDINGTON

DOUBLE BAY

76

RELIEVIIE HILL

EDGECLIFF

See p334

NORTH BONDI

Fox Studios

BONDI JUNCTION

BONDI

2

Moore Park

Centennial Park

Bondi Beach

Ben Buckler

1

70

CENTENNIAL PARK

MacKenzie's Point

40

BRONTE

See pp332-333

3

Randwick Racecourse

Waverley Cemetery

RANDWICK

CLOVELLY

9

Shark Point

Gordon's Bay

COOGEE

12

0   2 km
0   1 mile

© Copyright Time Out Group 2008

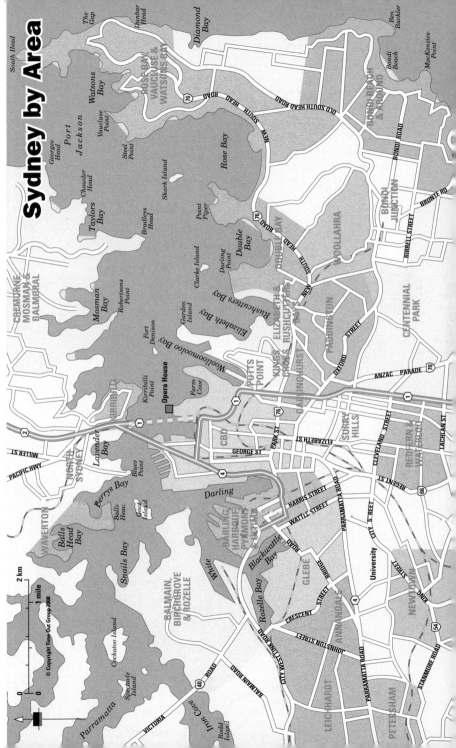

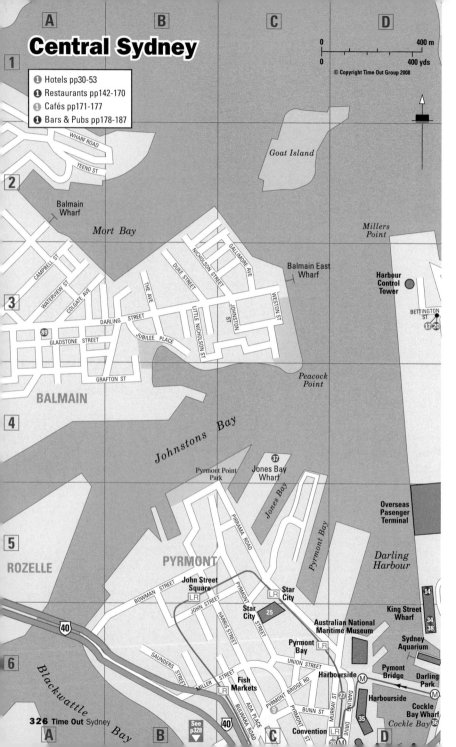

Central Sydney

A   **B**   **C**   **D**

1

- ❶ Hotels pp30-53
- ❶ Restaurants pp142-170
- ❶ Cafés pp171-177
- ❶ Bars & Pubs pp178-187

0   400 m
0   400 yds

© Copyright Time Out Group 2008

2

WHARF ROAD

YEEND ST

Goat Island

Balmain
Wharf

Mort Bay

Millers Point

CAMPBELL ST

NICHOLSON STREET

GALLIMORE AVE

Balmain East
Wharf

Harbour
Control
Tower

3

WATERVIEW ST

COLGATE AVE

THE AVE

DUKE STREET

JOHNSTON ST

WESTON ST

BETTINGTON ST

DARLING   STREET

LITTLE NICHOLSON ST

89

JUBILEE PLACE

17 20

GLADSTONE STREET

GRAFTON ST

Peacock Point

4

BALMAIN

Johnstons Bay

37

Pyrmont Point
Park

Jones Bay
Wharf

Jones Bay

Pyrmont Bay

Overseas
Pasenger
Terminal

5

ROZELLE

PYRMONT

PIRRAMA ROAD

*Darling
Harbour*

BOWMAN STREET

John Street
Square

LR

JOHN STREET

PYRMONT STREET

LR

Star
City

King Street
Wharf

14

40

HARRIS STREET

Star City

25

Australian National
Maritime Museum

34
38

Sydney
Aquarium

6

SAUNDERS STREET

MILLER STREET

Pyrmont
Bay

LR

UNION STREET

Harbourside

M

Pyrmont
Bridge

Darling
Park

*Blackwattle
Bay*

See
p328
▼

40

Fish
Markets

LR

9

PYRMONT BRIDGE RD

ADA PLACE

BULWARA ROAD

PYRMONT ST

BUNN ST

MURRAY ST

DARLING DRIVE

27
26

Convention

LR

M

35

Harbourside

Cockle
Bay Wharf

Cockle Bay

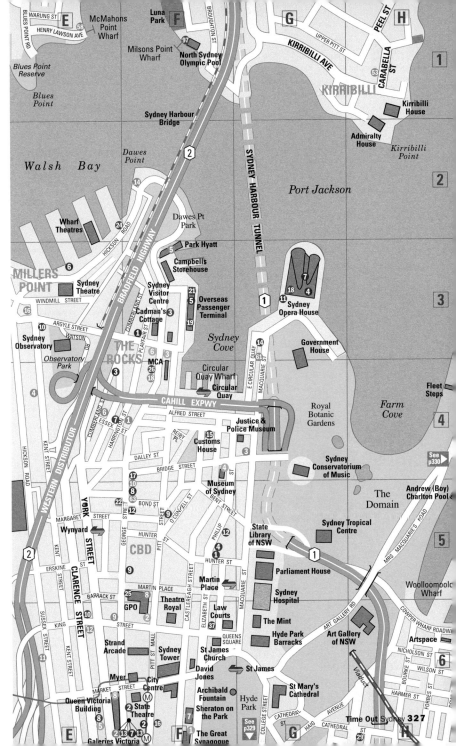

WARUNG ST
HENRY LAWSON AVE
BLUES POINT RD
E 58

McMahons
Point
Wharf

Luna
Park
F 97

BROUGHTON ST

G

UPPER PITT RD

PEEL ST
KIRRIBILLI AVE

CARABELLA ST
H 1
53

Milsons Point
Wharf
North Sydney
Olympic Pool

KIRRIBILLI

Kirribilli
House

Blues Point
Reserve

Blues
Point

Sydney Harbour
Bridge

Admiralty
House

Kirribilli
Point

Walsh   Bay

Dawes
Point

2

SYDNEY HARBOUR TUNNEL

Port Jackson

2

14

Wharf
Theatres

HICKSON ROAD
24

BRADFIELD HIGHWAY

Dawes Pt
Park

Park Hyatt
5

7

3

MILLERS
POINT
6
16

Sydney
Theatre

WINDMILL STREET

Sydney
Observatory
10

CUMBERLAND ST

Sydney
Visitor
Centre
21
5

Campbells
Storehouse

Cadman's
Cottage
3

18
4

11
Sydney
Opera House

Overseas
Passenger
Terminal
19

Government
House

Farm
Cove

Fleet
Steps

ARGYLE STREET

WATSON

Observatory
Park
4

THE
ROCKS
3

6

MCA
26
18

Sydney
Cove

Circular
Quay Wharf

E CIRCULAR QUAY
14

MACQUARIE ST

Royal
Botanic
Gardens

3

4

See
p330

HICKSON ROAD

KENT STREET

WESTERN DISTRIBUTOR

CAHILL EXPWY

ALFRED STREET

Circular
Quay

Justice &
Police Museum
15
Customs
House
3

Andrew (Boy)
Charlton Pool

ESSEX ST
HARRINGTON ST
7
1

REIBY PL

DALLEY ST

BRIDGE STREET
17
10
8
6

4
Museum
of Sydney

Sydney
Conservatorium
of Music

The
Domain

5

CUMBERLAND ST

BOND ST
22
12

O'CONNELL ST
9

BENT STREET

PHILLIP

12

State
Library
of NSW

Sydney Tropical
Centre

1

MRS MACQUARIE'S ROAD

Wynyard

GEORGE STREET

HUNTER ST

PITT ST

HUNTER ST
1

Phillip

Parliament House

Woolloomooloo
Wharf

2

KENT STREET
ERSKINE STREET

CLARENCE STREET

YORK STREET

CBD

MARTIN PLACE
25
8

Martin
Place

MACQUARIE ST
Sydney
Hospital

ART GALLERY RD
Art Gallery
of NSW

COWPER WHARF ROADWAY

Artspace

SUSSEX STREET
KENT STREET
KING STREET

Theatre
Royal

GPO
2

9
STREET
12

CASTLEREAGH STREET

ELIZABETH ST

Law
Courts
37

The Mint

Hyde Park
Barracks

NICHOLSON ST
WILSON ST

6

BARRACK ST
10

9

BARRACK ST

QUEENS
SQUARE

BOURKE ST

Strand
Arcade

Sydney
Tower

PITT ST MALL

St James
Church

St James

St Mary's
Cathedral

Viaduct

HARMER ST

FORBES ST

Myer

City
Centre
M

David
Jones

Hyde
Park

CATHEDRAL ST
HAIG AVE

Time Out Sydney 327

Queen Victoria
Building
8
5

MARKET STREET
2
State
Theatre
2
16
13
M

Archibald
Fountain
Sheraton on
the Park
7

COLLEGE STREET

See
p329

G

CATHEDRAL ST
29

H

Galeries Victoria

F
The Great
Synagogue

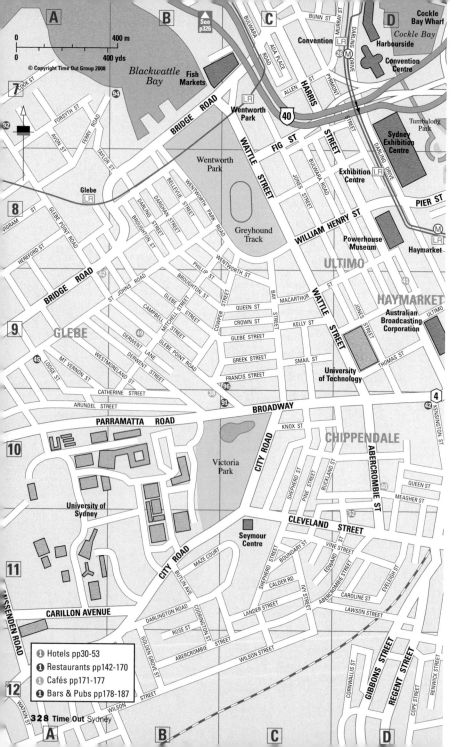

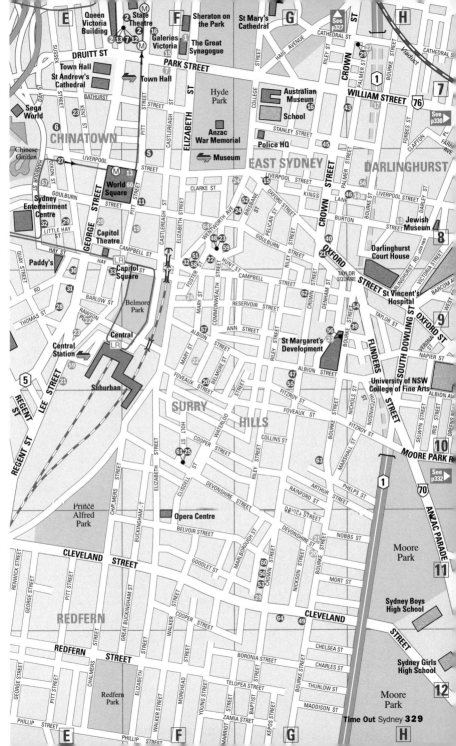

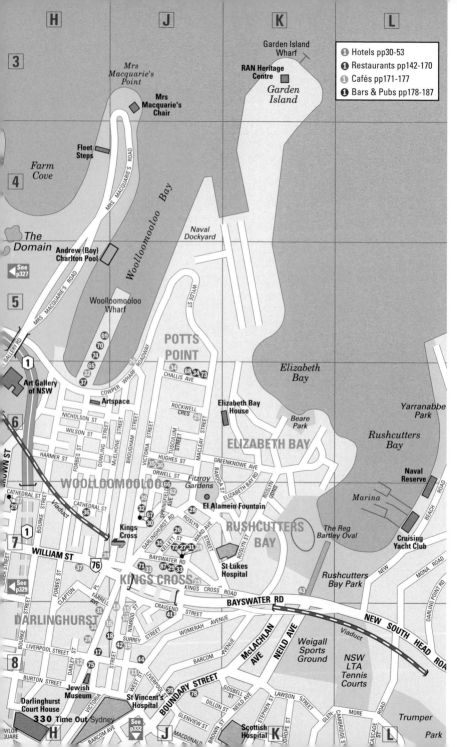

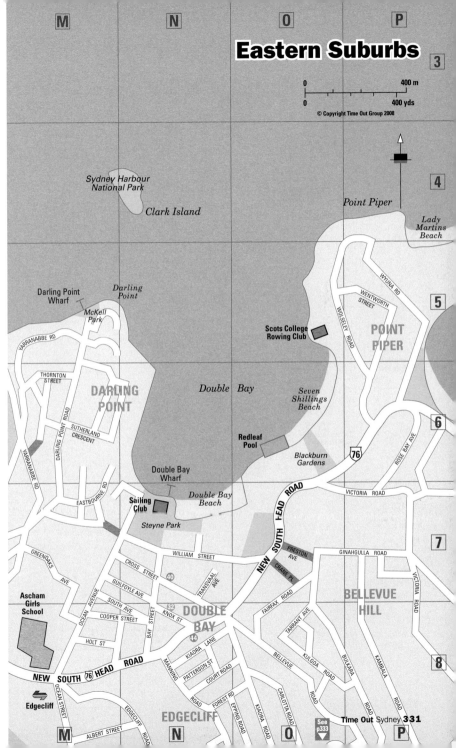

M   N   O   P

3

0   400 m
0   400 yds
© Copyright Time Out Group 2008

4

Sydney Harbour
National Park

Clark Island

Point Piper

*Lady
Martins
Beach*

Darling Point
Wharf

*Darling
Point*

*McKell
Park*

Scots College
Rowing Club

**POINT
PIPER**

5

YARRANABBE RD

THORNTON
STREET

**DARLING
POINT**

Double Bay

*Seven
Shillings
Beach*

WYUNA RD

WENTWORTH
STREET

WOLSELEY ROAD

DARLING POINT ROAD

SUTHERLAND
CRESCENT

Redleaf
Pool

*Blackburn
Gardens*

76

ROSE BAY AVE

6

YARRANABBE RD

Double Bay
Wharf

*Double Bay
Beach*

NEW SOUTH HEAD ROAD

VICTORIA ROAD

EASTBOURNE RD

Sailing
Club

Steyne Park

WILLIAM STREET

PRESTON
AVE

GINAHGULLA ROAD

7

VICTORIA ROAD

GREENOAKS AVE

CROSS STREET

40

GUILFOYLE AVE

TRANSVAAL AVE

CRANE PL

FAIRFAX ROAD

**BELLEVUE
HILL**

**Ascham
Girls
School**

OCEAN AVENUE

SOUTH AVE

32

KNOX ST

**DOUBLE
BAY**

TARRANT AVE

BELLEVUE

KULGOA ROAD

BULKARA ROAD

KAMBALA ROAD

COOPER STREET

BAY STREET

HOLT ST

44

KIAORA LANE

PATTERSON ST

COURT ROAD

FOREST RD

KIAORA ROAD

CARLOTTA ROAD

8

NEW SOUTH 76 HEAD ROAD

MANNING ROAD

EPPING ROAD

⇐
Edgecliff

OCEAN STREET

EDGECLIFF ROAD

EDGECLIFF

ALBERT STREET

See
p333
▽▽▽

M   N   O   P

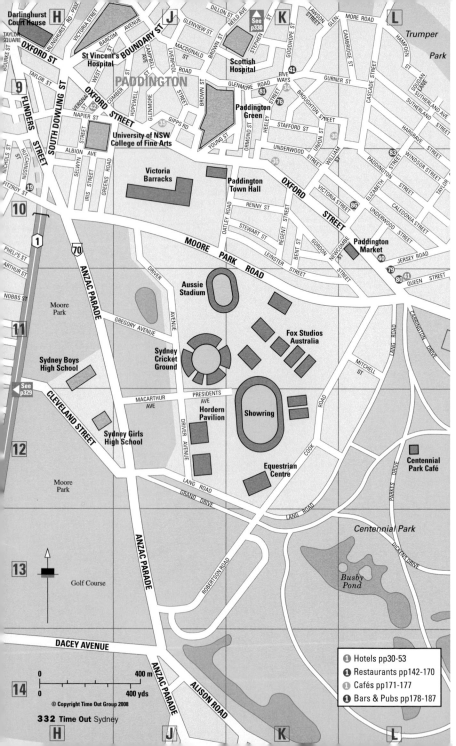

© Copyright Time Out Group 2008

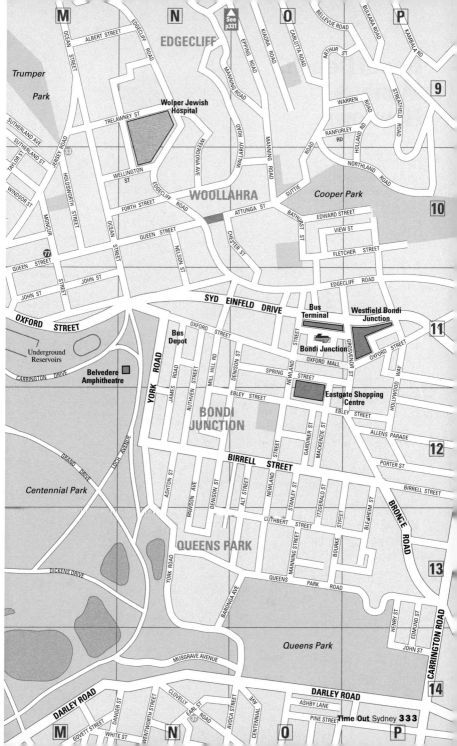

Bondi Beach, Manly & Newtown

- ❶ Hotels pp30-53
- ❶ Restaurants pp142-170
- ❶ Cafés pp171-177
- ❶ Bars & Pubs pp178-187

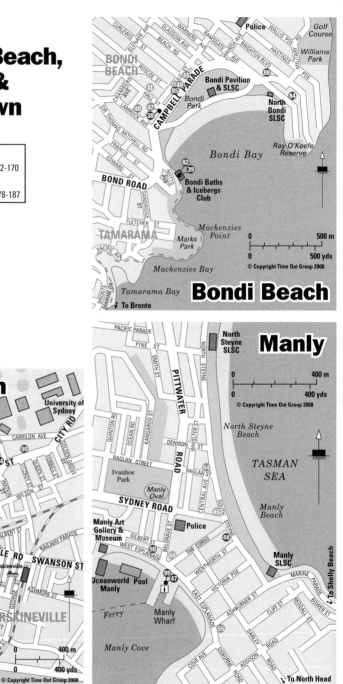

Bondi Beach

CURLEWIS ST · GLENAYR AVE · GLASGOW AVE · WARNERS AVE · RAMSGATE AVE · WALLIS PDE
Police · Golf Course · Williams Park
BONDI BEACH · ROSCOE ST · BEACH RD · WAIROA AVE · BRIGHTON BLVD · HASTINGS PDE · MILITARY PDE
88
CHAMBERS AVE · HALL ST · 31 · 85 · CAMPBELL PARADE
84
Bondi Pavilion & SLSC
Bondi Park · North Bondi SLSC
LAMROCK AVE · 47 · 48 · 38
SIR THOMAS MITCHELL RD
Ray O'Keefe Reserve
FRANCIS ST · Bondi Bay
EDWARD ST
82 · 39
BOND ROAD · SANDRIDGE ST · NOTTS AVE
Bondi Baths & Icebergs Club
FLETCHER ST
TAMARAMA · Mackenzies Point · Marks Park
0 · 500 m
0 · 500 yds
© Copyright Time Out Group 2008
PACIFIC AVE
Mackenzies Bay
BRONTE MARINE DR
Tamarama Bay
↓ To Bronte

Newtown

Camperdown Park · University of Sydney
MISSENDEN RD · CITY RD
AUSTRALIA ST · CHURCH ST · CARRILON AVE · GOLDEN GROVE
PROBERT ST · O'CONNELL ST · 38 · ST · 90 · FORBES ST
44 · 95 · QUEEN ST · WATKIN ST
EGAN ST · FITZROY ST · WILSON ST · RAILWAY PARADE
NEWTOWN · 51 · KING · ST
43 · LENNOX ST · 43
Town Hall · 33 · KING ST · ERSKINEVILLE RD · ALBERT ST
46 · Newtown · SWANSON ST
ENMORE RD · Erskineville · ASHMORE ST
Enmore Theatre
ENMORE · ANGEL ST · UNION ST · GEORGE ST
CAMDEN ST · 50 · KING ST
ALICE ST · KNIGHT ST · ERSKINEVILLE
JOHN ST · CONCORD ST
DARLEY ST · St Peters · LORD ST
0 · 400 m
0 · 400 yds
© Copyright Time Out Group 2008

Manly

PACIFIC PARADE
PINE ST · NORTH STEYNE
North Steyne SLSC
SMITH ST · PITTWATER
0 · 400 m
0 · 400 yds
© Copyright Time Out Group 2008
QUINTON RD · OCEAN RD · KANGAROO ST · DENISON ST · WHISTLER ST
North Steyne Beach
RAGLAN STREET · ROAD · RAGLAN ST
Ivanhoe Park · CENTRAL AVE
TASMAN SEA
Manly Oval
SYDNEY ROAD · BELGRAVE ST
Manly Beach
Manly Art Gallery & Museum · GILBERT ST · Police
WEST ESPLANADE · 93 · 44 · THE CORSO · 48
WENTWORTH ST · Manly SLSC
Oceanworld Pool Manly · 99 · 47 · VICTORIA PDE · MARINE PARADE
EAST ESPLANADE · ASHBURNER ST · CLIFF ST · REDDALL ST · BOWER ST
Ferry · Manly Wharf
55 · DARLEY ROAD
COVE AVE · OSBORNE ROAD · ADDISON ROAD
Manly Cove
↓ To North Head
To Shelly Beach

Sydney Ferries

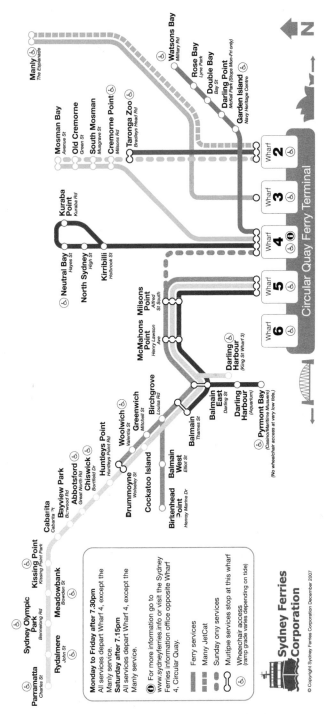

N

Manly *The Esplanade* ♿

Watsons Bay *Military Rd* ♿

Rose Bay *Lyne Park*

Double Bay *Bay St*

Darling Point *McKell Park (Stops Mon–Fri only)*

Garden Island *Navy Heritage Centre* ♿

Mosman Bay *Avenue St*

Old Cremorne *Green St*

South Mosman *Musgrave St*

Cremorne Point *Milsons Rd* ♿

Taronga Zoo *Bradleys Head Rd* ♿

Kuraba Point *Kuraba Rd*

Neutral Bay *Hayes St* ♿

North Sydney *High St*

Kirribilli *Holbrook St*

McMahons Point *Henry Lawson Ave*

Milsons Point *Alfred St South*

Darling Harbour *(King St Wharf 3)* ♿

Balmain East *Darling St*

Darling Harbour *(Aquarium)*

Pyrmont Bay *(Casino/Maritime Museum)* ♿
(No wheelchair access at very low tide)

Balmain *Thames St*

Balmain West *Elliot St*

Birchgrove *Louisa Rd*

Greenwich *Mitchell St*

Woolwich *Valentia St* ♿

Huntleys Point *Huntleys Point Rd*

Drummoyne *Wolseley St*

Cockatoo Island

Birkenhead Point *Henry Marina Dr*

Chiswick *Bortfield Dr* ♿

Abbotsford *Great North Rd* ♿

Bayview Park *Burwood Rd* ♿

Cabarita *Cabarita Pk*

Kissing Point *Kissing Point Park* ♿

Meadowbank *Bowden St*

Sydney Olympic Park *Bennelong Rd* ♿

Rydalmere *John St*

Parramatta *Charles St* ♿

Wharf **2** ♿

Wharf **3** ♿

Wharf **4** ℹ ♿ ♿

Wharf **5** ♿

Wharf **6** ♿

Circular Quay Ferry Terminal

Monday to Friday after 7.30pm
All services depart Wharf 4, except the Manly service.

Saturday after 7.15pm
All services depart Wharf 4, except the Manly service.

ℹ For more information go to www.sydneyferries.info or visit the Sydney Ferries information office opposite Wharf 4, Circular Quay.

Ferry services

Manly JetCat

Sunday only services

Multiple services stop at this wharf

♿ Wheelchair access
(ramp grade varies depending on tide)

Sydney Ferries Corporation

© Copyright Sydney Ferries Corporation December 2007

CityRail's Sydney suburban network

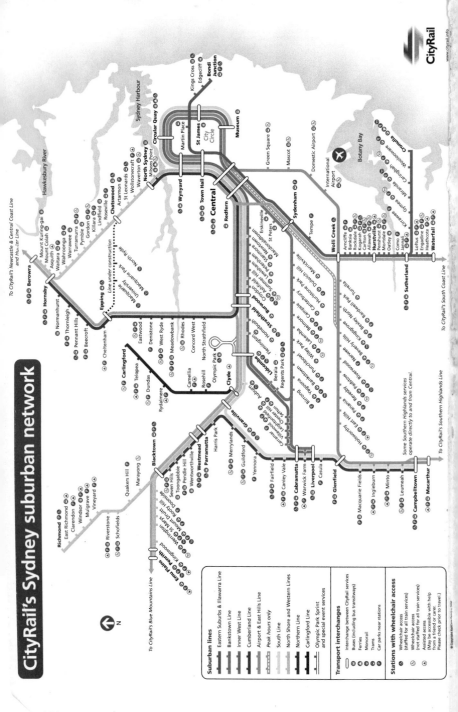

Suburban lines

- Eastern Suburbs & Illawarra Line
- Bankstown Line
- Inner West Line
- Cumberland Line
- Airport & East Hills Line
- South Line
- North Shore and Western Lines
- Northern Line
- Carlingford Line
- Olympic Park Sprint and special event services

Transport interchanges

- Interchange between CityRail services
- Buses (including bus transitways)
- Ferries
- Monorail
- Trams
- Car parks near stations

Stations with wheelchair access

- Wheelchair access (staffed for all train services)
- Wheelchair access (not staffed for all train services)
- Assisted access (May be accessible with help from a friend or carer. Please check prior to travel.)